Immigration

The International Library of Essays in Law and Society
Series Editor: Austin Sarat

Titles in the Series:

Law and Religion
Gad Barzilai

Police and Policing Law
Jeannine Bell

Law and Society Approaches to Cyberspace
Paul Schiff Berman

Law and Families
Susan B. Boyd and Helen Rhoades

Rhetoric of Law
Marianne Constable and Felipe Gutterriez

Law in Social Theory
Roger Cotterrell

Ethnography and Law
Eve Darian-Smith

International Law and Society
Laura Dickinson

Legal Lives of Private Organizations
Lauren Edelman and Mark C. Suchman

Courts and Judges
Lee Epstein

Consciousness and Ideology
Patricia Ewick

Prosecutors and Prosecution
Lisa Frohmann

Intellectual Property
William T. Gallagher

Human Rights, Law and Society
Lisa Hajjar

Race, Law and Society
Ian Haney Lopéz

The Jury System
Valerie P. Hans

Crime and Criminal Justice
William T. Lyons, Jr.

Regulation and Regulatory Processes
Robert Kagan and Cary Coglianese

Law and Social Movements
Michael McCann

Colonial and Post-Colonial Law
Sally Merry

Social Science in Law
Elizabeth Mertz

Sexuality and Identity
Leslie J. Moran

Law and Poverty
Frank Munger

Rights
Laura Beth Nielsen

Governing Risks
Pat O'Malley

Lawyers and the Legal Profession, Volumes I and II
Tanina Rostain

Capital Punishment, Volumes I and II
Austin Sarat

Legality and Democracy
Stuart A. Scheingold

The Law and Society Canon
Carroll Seron

Popular Culture and Law
Richard K. Sherwin

Law and Science
Susan Silbey

Immigration
Susan Sterett

Gender and Feminist Theory in Law and Society
Madhavi Sunder

Procedural Justice, Volumes I and II
Tom R. Tyler

Trials
Martha Merrill Umphrey

Immigration

Edited by

Susan Sterett

University of Denver, USA

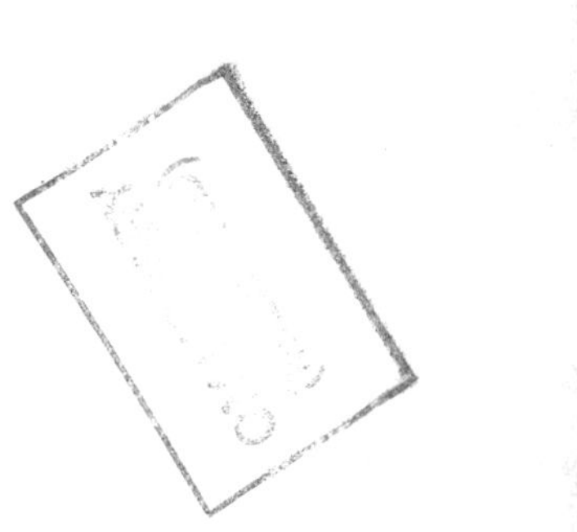

ASHGATE

Published by
Ashgate Publishing Limited
Gower House
Croft Road
Aldershot
Hampshire GU11 3HR
England

Ashgate Publishing Company
Suite 420
101 Cherry Street
Burlington, VT 05401-4405
USA

Ashgate website: http://www.ashgate.com

British Library Cataloguing in Publication Data
Immigration. – (The international library of
essays in law and society)
1. Emigration and immigration 2. Aliens 3. Refugees –
Legal status, laws, etc.
I. Sterett, Susan Marie,
342'.082

Library of Congress Cataloging-in-Publication Data
Immigration / edited by Susan Sterett
p. cm. – (The international library of essays in law and society)
Includes bibliographical references.
1. Emigration and immigration law–Social aspects. 2. Aliens–Legal status, laws, etc.–Social aspects. 3. Asylum, Right of–Social aspects. 4. Aliens–Government policy. I. Sterett, Susan Marie. II. Series.

K3275.1475 2005
342.08'2–dc22

2005053065

ISBN 0 7546 2474 9
ISBN 978-0-7546-2474-5

Printed in Great Britain by TJ International Ltd, Padstow, Cornwall

Contents

PART III FAMILY AND IDENTITY

PART IV REFUGEES AND ASYLUM-SEEKERS

Acknowledgements

The editor and publishers wish to thank the following for permission to use copyright material.

Blackwell Publishing for the essays: R. Amy Elman (2000), 'The Limits of Citizenship: Migration, Sex Discrimination and Same-Sex Partners in EU Law', *Journal of Common Market Studies*, **38**, pp. 729–49. Copyright © 2000 Blackwell Publishers Ltd; Kitty Calavita (1998), 'Immigration, Law, and Marginalization in a Global Economy: Notes from Spain', *Law and Society Review*, **32**, pp. 529–66. Copyright © 1998 Law and Society Association; Janet A. Gilboy (1997), 'Implications of "Third Party" Involvement in Enforcement: The INS, Illegal Travelers, and International Airlines', *Law and Society Review*, **31**, pp. 505–29. Copyright © 1997 Law and Society Association; Claudia Fonseca (2002), 'Inequality Near and Far: Adoption as Seen from the Brazilian Favelas', *Law and Society Review*, **36**, pp. 397–431. Copyright © 2002 Law and Society Association; Barbara Yngvesson (2002), 'Placing the "Gift Child" in Transnational Adoption', *Law and Society Review*, **36**, pp. 227–56. Copyright © 2002 Law and Society Association; Kamal Sadiq (2005), 'When States Prefer Non-Citizens Over Citizens: Conflict Over Illegal Immigration into Malaysia', *International Studies Quarterly*, **49**, pp. 101–22. Copyright © 2005 International Studies Association.

Linda S. Bosniak (1996), 'Opposing Prop. 187: Undocumented Immigrants and the National Imagination', *Connecticut Law Review*, **28**, pp. 555–619. Copyright © 1996 Linda S. Bosniak.

Brill for the essay: Jacqueline Bhabha (2001), 'Minors or Aliens? Inconsistent State Intervention and Separated Child Asylum-Seekers', *European Journal of Migration and Law*, **3**, pp. 283–314. Copyright © 2001 Kluwer Law International.

Elsevier for the essay: Kathleen M. Moore (2000), 'U.S. Immigration Reform and the Meaning of Responsibility', *Studies in Law, Politics, and Society*, **20**, pp. 125–55. Copyright © 2000 Elsevier.

Michigan Journal of Race and Law for the essay: T. Alexander Aleinikoff (1999), 'Between National and Post-National: Membership in the United States', *Michigan Journal of Race and Law*, **4**, pp. 241–62.

Oxford University Press for the essay: Cécile Rousseau, François Crépeau, Patricia Foxen and France Houle (2002), 'The Complexity of Determining Refugeehood: A Multidisciplinary Analysis of the Decision-Making Process of the Canadian Immigration and Refugee Board', *Journal of Refugee Studies*, **15**, pp. 43–70. Copyright © 2002 Oxford University Press.

Taylor and Francis Ltd for the essays: Virginie Guiraudon (2003), 'The Constitution of a European Immigration Policy Domain: A Political Sociology Approach', *Journal of European Public Policy*, **10**, pp. 263–82. Copyright © 2003 Taylor and Francis Ltd; Robert Manne (2002), 'Reflections on the *Tampa* "Crisis"', *Postcolonial Studies*, **5**, pp. 29–36. Copyright © 2002 Institute of Postcolonial Studies.

American Anthropological Association and University of California Press for the essay: Susan Bibler Coutin (2003), 'Cultural Logics of Belonging and Movement: Transnationalism, Naturalization, and U.S. Immigration Politics', *American Ethnologist*, **30**, pp. 508–26.

University of Chicago Press for the essay: Margot Canaday (2003), '"Who is a Homosexual?": The Consolidation of Sexual Identities in Mid-Twentieth-Century American Immigration Law', *Law and Social Inquiry*, **28**, pp. 351–86. Copyright © 2003 American Bar Foundation; Todd Stevens (2002), 'Tender Ties: Husbands' Rights and Racial Exclusion in Chinese Marriage Cases, 1882–1924', *Law and Social Inquiry*, **27**, pp. 271–305.

University of Illinois Press for the essay: Mae M. Ngai (2003), 'The Strange Career of the Illegal Alien: Immigration Restriction and Deportation Policy in the United States, 1921–1965', *Law and History Review*, **21**, pp. 69–107. Copyright © 2003 Board of Trustees of the University of Illinois.

Every effort has been made to trace all the copyright holders, but if any have been inadvertently overlooked the publishers will be pleased to make the necessary arrangement at the first opportunity.

Series Preface

The International Library of Essays in Law and Society is designed to provide a broad overview of this important field of interdisciplinary inquiry. Titles in the series will provide access to the best existing scholarship on a wide variety of subjects integral to the understanding of how legal institutions work in and through social arrangements. They collect and synthesize research published in the leading journals of the law and society field. Taken together, these volumes show the richness and complexity of inquiry into law's social life.

Each volume is edited by a recognized expert who has selected a range of scholarship designed to illustrate the most important questions, theoretical approaches, and methods in her/his area of expertise. Each has written an introductory essay which both outlines those questions, approaches, and methods and provides a distinctive analysis of the scholarship presented in the book. Each was asked to identify approximately 20 pieces of work for inclusion in their volume. This has necessitated hard choices since law and society inquiry is vibrant and flourishing.

The International Library of Essays in Law and Society brings together scholars representing different disciplinary traditions and working in different cultural contexts. Since law and society is itself an international field of inquiry it is appropriate that the editors of the volumes in this series come from many different nations and academic contexts. The work of the editors both charts a tradition and opens up new questions. It is my hope that this work will provide a valuable resource for longtime practitioners of law and society scholarship and newcomers to the field.

AUSTIN SARAT
William Nelson Cromwell Professor of Jurisprudence and Political Science
Amherst College

Introduction

Throughout the West immigration is widely denounced; nationals claim that there is no more room, no more jobs, and no welcome for transformations in culture that people from new places bring. States still receive people who settle, whether as asylum-seekers or refugees, family members of those already settled or sometimes as labor migrants. Many who move violate the immigration rules either in coming to a country or in staying past a time limit; the problems illegality entails for migrants shapes much of the law and society scholarship on migration. The border and its enforcement have spread and the officials in charge of enforcing it have expanded as state officials enlist non-state actors to exclude or enforce, and transnational agreements state guidance and establish structures but do not state clearly enforceable rules. In immigration, the state and the border are everywhere, with its enforcement officials including reluctant or uninterested employers, airlines and vindictive neighbors as well as police, immigration officers and schools (Calavita, 1990; Constable, 1993; Gilboy, 1991, 1992, 1997; Sterett, 1997a). While the focus of discussion in recent years has been on control and exclusion in Western postindustrial states, in earlier years it was not, or not for all people. New people could be strategically useful for state officials, and still are in some poorer countries (Sadiq, 2005), or simply not a matter of concern (Gutierrez, 1999).

Documentation has been crucial to the work of both exclusion and inclusion in the bureaucratic state. One is what one can document. Therefore, Susan Coutin writes of Salvadoran immigrants in Los Angeles who accumulate papers – drivers' licenses, work permits, social security numbers – in the generally mistaken belief that accumulation will make them legal (Coutin, 2000, pp. 49–78). In a mirror image of regulation in the West, Kamal Sadiq explains in this volume that in Malaysia, which does not have regular registration of births and citizens, undocumented migrants can become legal by buying false papers, entitling them to vote when their unregistered citizen neighbor cannot (Sadiq, 2005, p. 105). What one can document is what is real, however much documentation is disconnected from other reality. As Sadiq argues, the ability to buy papers so readily in poorer countries ought to raise real concerns for states about security.

Immigration law has made nations; who states have chosen to exclude has often demonstrated who they think can culturally belong. For many years Australia and Canada had 'white' policies (Curthoys, 2003; Jupp, 2002; Markus, 2003; Razack, 1999). The United States excluded the Chinese first, decided that Asians were ineligible for citizenship, then excluded people in a way that favored northern Europe and Canada from the 1920s until 1965 (see e.g., Daniels, 2002). In Europe, migration once was from former colonies, or under a formal guestworker program as in Germany; Britain had free movement immediately after the Second World War for all from its Commonwealth (Layton-Henry, 1992). As people who flee countries now are racialized as others within Western states, national states have debated what it means to maintain a nation and include multiple cultures (see e.g., Jayasuriya, 2003). Australia, for example, has rapidly become more closely tied to Asia, not least because of a demand for labor not met by migration from Europe, in addition to the movement of refugees (Jayasuriya and Pookong, 1999; Jones, 2003; Jupp, 1995, 2002).

Simultaneous to trying to exclude migrants and put 'bogus asylum seekers' on a 'fast track' out of the country (on South Africa, see Handmaker, 2002), Western receiving states have also insisted that they welcome genuine refugees, and have policies that allow in family members of those legally settled. How did states begin this categorization of the legal and the illegal? Mae Ngai explores this question for the United States in her article reprinted here discussing the practices of systematic exclusion between 1921 and 1965 (2003). When states have enforced immigration laws against people already settled, they have sometimes found themselves criticized for violating non-discrimination policies, or for excluding people who have contributed. Case-by-case, these claims get settled by administrative officials or in courts, allowing some flexibility in exclusion without ever challenging the principles of exclusion themselves. In individual cases, deportation as a remedy for violating immigration laws can seem tremendously unfair, whether to an official charged with enforcing the law or, sometimes, to a political advocacy group. Deportation evokes implicit moral understandings of what the law should be: as Kathleen Moore argues here with regard to the United States in this volume, advocates will argue that officials should not deport people who have been responsible, working and contributing in the country in which they live (Moore, 2000; Razack, 1999).

Credible immigration regulation requires deportation. Otherwise, once people are in the country to which they wish to migrate, they become members. The ability to settle legally would depend wholly on one's ability to get to the intended country and to stay there, hardly a criterion that we usually see as either rational or ethically justifiable. The marginal status of immigrants has allowed countries to limit the remedies available for deportation, whether in the United States through limits on habeas corpus (Neuman, 2001) or in Europe through coordination of exclusion, discussed below. Advocates for immigrants criticize deportation and argue that enforcement of domestic labor standards would eliminate the competitive advantage in hiring undocumented people. Few defend eliminating immigration controls, as Linda Bosniak explains in her discussion of how those who are critical of limits on benefits frame their criticism, reprinted in this volume (Bosniak, 1996). She explains that we cannot mean to defend access to jobs and benefits only for those who by happenstance or persistence were able to stay here. Defending those who have made it to the United States (or, by extension, any receiving country) would logically require that we defend our sense of obligation to all around the world, not only to those within our national state. Few take that position. More common is the belief that if one works hard and pays taxes, sends one's children to school and otherwise contributes to a society, one must be able to earn the right to settle (Duvell and Jordan, 2003; Coutin, 2000, pp. 61–2). While migrants might have that belief, it is only sometimes enacted in the law (Coutin, 2000; Thorpe, 2005). Deportation separates families and sometimes brings on violent, forceful official enforcement (see e.g., Young, 1996, pp. 67–76) and the pain that creates for individuals (not for some generalized 'immigrants') sometimes garners favorable press (see e.g. Bernstein, 2005); campaigns against deportation in Western Europe depend on the strategy of portraying individual pain and hard work.

If people have an implicit moral sense of what should count in the law, it can be hard to respect a law that only occasionally and rather unpredictably recognizes that sense. Legal rules draw lines. That means officials treat one person as legal, though he might not attend to his children or work hard at his job, simply because he followed an annoying set of procedures to enter a country, or was ahead of a numerical cut-off. Officials treat another person as illegal because she did not follow those procedures but has indeed worked, sent children to school, and been kind to her neighbors (Coutin, 2000; Ngai, 2003). As Kitty Calavita has argued with regard to Italy and in this volume Spain, legal status is one immigrants can slip in and out of as rules change or decisions take so long that one's visa expires; complying with the law for those working in Europe at the margins and with no access to legal benefits can be impossible and seem morally irrelevant (Calavita, 1994, 1998, 2005; Garcia-Jourdan, 2004). In their article on South Africa reprinted in this volume, Jonathan Klaaren and Jaya Ramji (2004) argue that a similar political dynamic operates there. If the law does not respect the work that immigrants do, immigrants and their advocates may find that they have little reason to respect the law. The ordinary moral sense that one ought to be able to 'earn' legal status is not wholly written out of the law; people have gained legal status when states grant amnesties, or when states provide for discretionary suspensions of deportation (DeGenova, 2002, p. 420; Sadiq, 2005, p. 111; Schuck, 1992). The discretion and an amnesty's cut-off date add a layer of arbitrariness from the point of view of those being regulated. Suspensions of deportation and amnesties provide the leeway in a system of rules that remains uneven; discretion alongside legal rules makes unworkable programs at least somewhat manageable (Scott, 1998). When one reasons from the point of view of legal subjects, however, the law looks crazy (DeGenova, 2002).

Illegality is an additional dimension in which people have lived alongside their documented neighbors (Coutin, 2005; Gutierrez, 1999). Many non-governmental officials are responsible for enforcing immigration law: employers, airlines, rail carriers in an earlier day, making every activity potentially legally risky. One is illegal when one drives or works. People denounce their neighbors to immigration officials or a husband may threaten a wife with divorce, making her subject to deportation (Sterett, 1997b). Indeed, in Britain, officials get more denunciations than they can follow (Duvell and Jordan, 2003; on denunciations in early US regulation, see Ngai, 2003, p. 94). Migration officials are actors in the power plays within families and among neighbors, actors with the force to deport. The reliance upon businesses to enforce immigration law can create complicated webs of dependence between business and officials. Janet Gilboy studied exclusion in the United States both by border officials and by airlines; in her article reprinted in this volume she explores the implications for the state of reliance on airlines (1997).

Refugees and Asylum-Seekers: Transnational Governance in the European Union

Some of those who may slip into illegality or otherwise be subject to policing are fleeing persecution in their home state. Since 1951, the United Nations High Commissioner for Refugees (UNHCR) has identified a refugee as someone who has a well-founded fear of persecution based in race, national origin, religion or membership in a specific social group (UNHCR, 1996). National states interpret who is a refugee and as Colin Harvey argues in the article reprinted in this volume, states make different choices concerning how to interpret all of these terms (Harvey, 2000). In their in-depth study of decision making in Canada reprinted here, Cécile Rousseau, François Crépeau, Patricia Foxen and France Houle make clear the differences in standards, the difficulty of interpreting facts, and the political and organizational pressures in deciding who counts as a refugee (2002). Advocates for refugees and asylum-seekers argue that the conditions under which people must flee their home countries for fear of persecution far exceed what the UNHCR recognizes. The UNHCR was designed for the problems from the Second World War, not for the civil wars and massive displacement of peoples that have occurred over the last thirty years. Because the agent persecuting must be a state, for example, the Convention would not seem to recognize those fleeing civil wars.

The documentation required in a bureaucratic state has policed sexuality as well (Coutin, 2000, p. 30; DeGenova, 2002, p. 427), including with regard to refugee status. Today, persecution on the basis of sexual orientation is the basis for a claim to refugee status in some states, requiring demonstrating evidence of homosexuality; one must produce a sexual partner. The secrecy that the physical danger of persecution requires can make it difficult for the law to recognize persecution (McGhee, 2001).

State decisions also raise questions concerning what is political activity that the UNHCR protects against. Jacqueline Bhabha, a prominent human rights and immigration lawyer who has practiced in Britain, explains in her article in this volume that throughout the western world, children seek asylum apart from their families, often as a family strategy. She also argues that the numbers of separated children seemed to increase during the late 1990s. States do not always recognize children's political activity, such as stone-throwing (Bhabha, 2001), as a basis for granting refugee status. Some national officials are skeptical that children might actually be subject to forced military service, and will deny refugee status on that basis. Similarly, women's political activity can be invisible to officials, just as officials can dismiss women's persecution at home as not state violence and therefore not a matter for a legitimate claim to asylum. Choices people make concerning who in a family should flee intersect with states' choices about persecution to put children particularly at risk.

While states still differ in what they recognize for a claim to asylum, transnational networks of state actors coordinate governance in immigration. The coordination is often through informal agreements and other forms of soft law. In Europe, the Schengen Agreement and the Dublin Convention coordinate the regulation of migration among the signatory states. The goal of Schengen is to lower internal borders; that of the Dublin convention to share asylum-seekers among signatory countries, in part by ensuring that people could not forum-shop (Neuman, 1993). Asylum-seekers must have their case determined in the first safe country in which they land. These agreements look as though they enact a uniform policy for all of Europe. Nicola Scuteri, in her exploration of the implementation of the Dublin Convention reprinted here, argues that it does not. For example, Germany does not recognize non-state persecution. Further, to return a person to the country in which s/he first landed requires documenting travel, which can be difficult to do (Scuteri, 2002). Many national states would rather exclude before anyone can enter into the appeal system. Such exclusion is on occasion a matter of scandal in receiving states, as Robert Manne discusses with regard to Australia in the article reprinted in this volume (Manne, 2002).

The assumption in the Dublin agreement is that people do forum-shop; while a favorable forum partly makes Germany look better than Italy, people most often settle because their family members and compatriots have settled. That explains most of the migration into Britain as well; the fears articulated in politics across party divides concern the inability of the British to accommodate people from very different cultures. (On fears of foreignness in Britain, particularly connected with ascension to the EU, see Darian-Smith, 1999). Despite the national concern that 'too many' people from South Asia or Afghanistan will transform

Britain, the overwhelming majority of migrants to the United Kingdom are those from Ireland, the Old Commonwealth (Australia and New Zealand) and the EU (Duvell and Jordan, 2003, p. 311).

Virginie Guiraudon in her pathbreaking work reprinted in this volume has argued that European states moved toward soft law and informal agreements from the 1980s onward precisely because advocates for immigrants had been so successful in getting courts, both domestic and supranational, to interpret the statutes and rules in a way that would protect immigrants (2003, p. 268; on efforts to 'fast track' claims in South Africa, see Handmaker, 1999). Government officials hoped that there would be less to work with if there was less law to appeal to courts and more cooperation across national boundaries. Organizations adapt to their environments, and in response non-governmental organizations began to cooperate transnationally as well (Guiraudon, 2003); a network of attorneys with a range of experience and level of political commitments work administrative appeals systems and courts for asylum seekers (Appelqvist, 2000; Sterett, 1997a). For example, advocates in Britain called counterparts in other countries to find how claimants were treated at the border or when in detention. They could find enough evidence to counter presumptions that European countries were safe and that therefore immigrants could not forum-shop (see e.g., Harvey, 2000, pp. 381–2). In response, the British state closed off such litigation through legislation. These disaggregated networks of 'experts and enthusiasts' (Slaughter, 2004, p. 9, quoting Martin Shapiro), including courts, make law that often does not go through any general deliberative process.

Immigration, perhaps more than other policy issues, is one that many policy makers would like to address outside the glare of public debate, or sometimes address it via individual cases that make the spotlight, so that unprincipled but pragmatically satisfying results are possible. This policy domain, more than others, might be particularly amenable to being addressed bit by bit by courts and less visible administrative officials. Those less visible officials include immigration inspectors who understand that they have no public support for excluding some people and therefore do not, despite the formal law. (Gilboy, 1992, pp. 300–308; Guiraudon, 2003; Sterett, 1997a). (On the power to keep immigration from the United States to Canada out of public debate during the Vietnam War in the United States, see Hagan, 2000). Increasing restriction and empowering case-level officials and non-state actors to exclude people can couple with the occasional suspension of deportation in a sympathetic case or grants of refugee status to those who do make it into the system, to provide exclusion with something that publicly looks like mercy, with the arbitrariness that mercy implies.

Legal Regulation, Family, and Transnationality

Immigration law has governed partly through the family. Family law might have seemed thoroughly domestic, not in the slightest concerned with the politics of sovereignty, which immigration implicates. However, immigration law has deeply concerned itself with who might appropriately be considered a family. The Council of Europe's European Convention on Human Rights includes a right to family life, and under that provision people a state tries to deport have litigated their deportation, arguing that a state's decision deprives them of their family. Other regulations concerning family are simply part of the ordinary politics of statutory interpretation.

Since immigration law has allowed one to bring in a wife but not a friend, a daughter but not a friend's child, decision makers in immigration law must make relationships fixed. Practices that might in other circumstances have been fluid or part of an informal structure of caretaking–watching a neighbor's child, cohabiting and raising children together – must be legible, to use James Scott's term, or comprehensible within legal categories (Scott, 1998). One is or is not married, is or is not a parent; such a simple categorization requires a formal system of marriage and birth registration. In poorer countries, the lack of a formal system of birth registration makes documentation only irregularly connected to citizenship status (Sadiq, 2005). In Europe, as Amy Elman argues in her article reprinted here, that legal definition of family in the European Union (including in the European Court of Justice and the European Court of Human Rights) has been one that privileges the heterosexual family. As states have provided benefits for citizens–an ability to move, access to survivors' benefits for family members–they have provided incentives to become included in a legal definition of family. If one wants to move, one will find that states provide money to live comfortably in Brussels for the husband of a Eurocrat but not for another's same-sex domestic partner (Elman, 2000).

Because people can treat legal rules as instructions concerning how to accommodate them, legal regulations partly produce families as well: if having a child together will persuade officials that a marriage is genuine, new spouses will produce children (Sterett, 1999). Children document the genuineness of a marriage in some national states, leading to rapid birth of a child in a marriage involving immigration. Legal officials also erase relations; in recognizing those who were born in a country and those who have legal status, but not those who are undocumented, state practices produce what Susan Coutin has called 'legal aconsagnuity' (Coutin, 2000, p. 32). That is, some relatives are not relatives for the purposes of the law, or a relationship has no legal effect.

Determining who was kin plagued the immigration officials responsible for regulating the immigration of the Chinese in early twentieth-century United States. For example, within the Chinese community in the United States, it was perfectly acceptable for men to maintain a household in China and a secondary household and wife in the United States, an understanding of kinship that did not match that of the American immigration officials (McKeown, 1999, pp. 98–9). Since a legally settled person could bring in his own children, officials and applicants engaged in an ornate interplay of coaching to pass immigration inspection exclusion by suspicious officials, and appeal to the courts (Salyer, 1995).

Contests over what counts as enough evidence of persecution – the credibility issue – continue to be central to the regime of regulating refugees, including questions of sexual identity as outlined above. While now to become included one must produce some substantial evidence, when states were excluding rather thin evidence could allow inferences concerning sexuality. Margaret Canaday has searched the case law of the mid-twentieth-century United States governing deportation on the grounds of homosexuality. Her article reprinted in this volume argues that the legal officials in the throes of hunting out people they saw as having the fixed identity of homosexual could produce very little evidence of minor violations of the law (loitering in a public restroom) as evidence of homosexuality and therefore grounds for deportation (Canaday, 2003, pp. 360–262). (The mismatch between the rigid categories of the law and the malleability of people's lives also allowed strategizing and led to dilemmas for officials who enforced the Chinese Exclusion Act in the United States (Calavita, 1999).

Susan Coutin is an anthropologist who has long studied the legal experiences of Salvadorans in Los Angeles. In her article reprinted in this volume, she argues that becoming a citizen can as much be a way of ensuring that one can live transnationally as it is the choice of the United States that the immigration service celebrate (2003). Transnationality in family life disrupts the classical image in political theory of citizenship as an expression of singular and deep ties to one national state (Brubaker, 1997). Migrants both wealthy and not often experience migration as creating transnational families and ties, not a life fixed in one place to which one has moved (Coutin, 2003; Ong, 2001). Yet immigration is policed via national boundaries and national rules, or supranational boundaries and rules within Europe, making for odd mismatches between images of citizenship as sacred and exclusive, enacted in naturalization, and experiences of life as transnational.

Ties between here and there meant that Chinese families were routinely criticized in the early twentieth-century United States for being sojourners: people would stay for awhile, then return to China to establish a family, then return to the United States to work again. They experienced family as transnational. Although they were singled out for criticism as not truly American, their practices were little different from those of other immigrants who would also return to the land from which they migrated to see family members, or who would send money to families left in Sicily. Legal status allowed Chinese-Americans to have families in China (McKeown, 1999); it also allowed for arranged marriages, or bringing a wife to the United States (Ling, 2000, p. 52). Because the state granted marriage legal significance, citizenship in the United States allowed men to have Chinese wives in the United States, women who were otherwise deportable (McKeown, 1999; Stevens, 2002). If one is a citizen of the United States but with ties elsewhere, one can freely move between Los Angeles and El Salvador to visit relatives and celebrate holidays (Coutin, 2003; on similar travel between Malaysia and the Philippines, see Sadiq, 2005, p. 108; on Cuba, see Eckstein and Barberia, 2002). Such travel is dangerous if one is undocumented. By the late twentieth-century in Europe, legal status allowed one to bring in a spouse from a country of origin, and to travel freely with a spouse within the boundaries of the European Union. Alexander Aleinikoff argues that classical ideas of citizenship do not capture the American regulatory system very effectively, but membership is not now wholly post-national either (Aleinikoff, 1999); denizenship more accurately captures emergent regulation of belonging both in the United States, Aleinikoff's focus, and Europe. Legal citizenship facilitates transnationality, since it more readily allows family ties across borders.

The regulation of transnationality in families has included presumptions concerning gender. In the early twentieth-century United States, officials were more likely to believe that wives and daughters were genuinely relatives than men who claimed to be sons of those legally settled, so would question them less aggressively (McKeown, 1999, p. 85). In Britain, until the European Court of Human Rights declared Britain's policy to be against the Convention in 1985, the British state would allow men to bring in wives with little evidence required but not provide the same privilege to women (Sterett, 1997a). Even today, the European Court of Justice (ECJ) has applied the European Convention on Human Rights right to a family life in just the same way: to deport a woman would interfere with *her husband's* right to family life; she could not claim a right to family life before the ECJ since she was not a European national (Groussot, 2003, p. 190). Despite the declining rates of marriage throughout the Western countries, in Europe and the United States the rights attendant upon marriage still matter, particularly for immigrants (Elman, 2000; Ong, 2000).

Drawing national borders creates transnationality, including transnational families. Since the nineteenth century's redrawing of the lines between Mexico and the United States, many ethnically Mexican people (born in the United States or in Mexico) have experienced the American southwest as a 'third space,' to use David Gutierrez's term: neither Mexico nor the United States (Gutierrez, 1999). Before the restrictive immigration laws of the 1920s, United States immigration officials ratified this sense by not seeing movement from Mexico into the United States as anything within its jurisdiction (Ngai, 2003, p. 82). The third space that Gutierrez describes is a physical borderland; the ties of migration to family, empire and refugee flows have created something like these borderlands throughout Europe.

Children are also the grounds for regulating family and migration, not only through marriage, asylum-seeking and deportation but through intercountry adoption. Intercountry adoption also inscribes global regulation through family. About 30,000 children move annually from sending countries to receiving countries, and states have signed onto the Hague Convention on Intercountry Adoption to regulatemovement (Selman, 2000). People have always made provision for someone else to care for a child they cannot raise, but the adoptive family was long a family that lived nearby. Adoption may or may not have meant complete loss of a birth family; it usually did not mean a change in nationality until the mid-twentieth century (Fonseca, 2002; Johnson, 2002). Even after that, kin adoptions across national boundaries made some adoptive family formation little different from the formation of other transnational families (Lovelock, 2000). Stranger adoptions after the mid-twentieth century were ones from war-torn countries–first Europe, then Korea, then Vietnam, inscribing the history of war in the twentieth century into transnational family formation. The later burst in intercountry adoption from the 1990s onwards has come from poor countries, in particular China and Russia. Adoption across national boundaries usually cuts ties between a child and the birth family; when adoptive families try to recognize transnationality, they do so by substituting nation for family, as Barbara Yngvesson has argued (Yngvesson, 2002, pp. 236–48). Regulation of intercountry adoption has shadowed and intersected with immigration policy, domestic race relations policy and domestic adoption policy (Lovelock, 2000).

Conclusion

The processes of the legal regulation of movement produce identities, families and statuses. Law and society scholars have done superb work of documenting not only the legislative politics of immigration regulation, but the much lower-profile use of airline carriers, employers, border guards, courts and administrative agencies.

References

Appelqvist, Maria (2000), 'Refugee Law and Cause Lawyering: A Swedish Study of the Legal Profession', *International Journal of Refugee Law*, **12**, pp. 71–85.

Bernstein, Nina (2005), 'Caught Between Parents and the Law', *New York Times*, (February 17), p. A24.

Brubaker, Rogers (1997), *Citizenship in France and Germany*, Cambridge, MA: Harvard University Press.

Calavita, Kitty (1990), 'Employer Sanctions Violations: Toward a Dialectical Model of White Collar Crime', *Law and Society Review*, **24**, pp. 1041–70.

Calavita, Kitty (1994), 'Italy and the New Immigration', in Wayne A. Cornelius, Philip L. Martin and James F. Hollifield (eds), *Controlling Immigration*, Palo Alto, CA: Stanford University Press, pp. 303–26.

Calavita, Kitty (1999), 'The Paradoxes of Race, Class, Identity, and "Passing": Enforcing the Chinese Exclusion Acts, 1882–1910', *Law and Social Inquiry*, **24**, pp. 1–40.

Calavita, Kitty (2005), *Immigrants at the Margins: Law, Race and Exclusion in Southern Europe*, New York: Cambridge University Press.

Constable, Marianne (1993), 'Sovereignty and Governmentality in Modern American Immigration Law', *Studies in Law, Politics and Society*, **13**, pp. 249–71.

Coutin, Susan (2000), *Legalizing Moves: Salvadoran Immigrants' Struggle for US Residency*', Ann Arbor: University of Michigan Press.

Coutin, Susan (2005), 'Being en Route', *American Anthropologist*, **107**, pp. 195–207.

Curthoys, Ann (2003), 'Liberalism and Exclusionism: A Prehistory of the White Australia Policy', in Laksiri Jayasuriya, David Walker and Jan Gothard (eds), *Legacies of White Australia: Race, Culture and Nation*, Crawley, Western Australia: University of Western Australia Press.

Daniels, Roger (2002), *Coming to America: a History of Immigration and Ethnicity in American Life*, New York: Perennial.

Darian-Smith, Eve (1999), *Bridging Divides: The Channel Tunnel and English Legal Identity in the New Europe*, Berkeley: University of California Press.

Davidson, Alastair (2003), 'The Politics of Exclusion in an Era of Globalisation', in Laksiri Jayasuriya, David Walker and Jan Gothard (eds), *Legacies of White Australia: Race, Culture and Nation*, Crawley, Western Australia: University of Western Australia Press, pp. 129–44.

DeGenova, Nicholas (2002), 'Migrant "Illegality" and Deportability in Everyday Life', *Annual Review of Anthropology*, **31**, pp. 419–47.

Duvell, Franck and Bill Jordan (2003), 'Immigration Control and the Management of Economic Migration in the United Kingdom: Organisational Culture, Implementation, Enforcement and Identity Processes in Public Services', *Journal of Ethnic and Migration Studies*, **29**, pp. 299–336.

Eckstein, Susan and Barberia, Lorena (2002), 'Grounding Immigrant Generations in History: Cuban Americans and their Transnational Ties', *International Migration Review*, **36**, pp. 799–838.

Ewick, Patricia and Silbey, Susan (1998), *The Common Place of Law: Stories from Everyday Life*, Chicago: University of Chicago Press.

Garcia-Jourdan, Sophie (2004), 'L'Union Européenne Face à l'Immigration', in *Notes of the Foundation*, Paris: Robert Schuman Foundation.

Gilboy, Janet A. (1991), 'Deciding Who Gets In: Decisionmaking by Immigration Inspectors', *Law and Society Review*, **25**, pp. 571–600.

Gilboy, Janet A. (1992), 'Penetrability of Administrative Systems: Political "Casework" and Immigration Inspections', *Law and Society Review*, **26**, pp. 273–314.

Groussot, Xavier (2003), 'UK Immigration Law under Attack and the Direct Application of Article 8 ECHR by the ECJ', *Non-State Actors and International Law*, **3**, pp. 187–200.

Gutierrez, David G. (1999), 'Migration, Emergent Ethnicity, and the "Third Space": The Shifting Politics of Nationalism in Greater Mexico', *Journal of American History*, **86**, pp. 481–517.

Guiraudon, Virginie (1998), 'Third Country Nationals and European Law: Obstacles to Rights' expansion', *Journal of Ethnic and Migration Studies*, **24**, pp. 657–74.

Hagan, John (2000), 'Narrowing the Gap by Widening the Conflict: Power Politics, Symbols of Sovereignty, and the American Vietnam War Resisters' Migration to Canada', *Law and Society Review*, **34**, pp. 607–51.

Handmaker, Jeff (1999), 'Who Determines Policy? Promoting the Right of Asylum in South Africa', *International Journal of Refugee Law*, **11**, pp. 290–309.

Handmaker, Jeff and Parsley, Jennifer (2002), 'Migration, Refugees and Racism in South Africa', *Refuge*, **20**, pp. 40–51.

Jayasuriya, Laksiri (2003), '*Fin de Siècle* Musings', in Laksiri Jayasuriya, David Walker and Jan Gothard (eds), *Legacies of White Australia: Race, Culture and Nation*, Crawley, Western Australia: University of Western Australia Press, pp. 190–98.

Jayasuriya, Laksiri and Kee Pookong (1999), *The Asiainisation of Australia? Some facts about the Myths*, Carlton South, Victoria: Melbourne University Press.

Johnson, Kay (2002), 'Politics of International and Domestic Adoption in China', *Law and Society Review*, **36**, pp. 379–96.

Jones, Gavin W. (2003), 'White Australia, National Identity and Population Change', in Laksiri Jayasuriya, David Walker and Jan Gothard (eds), *Legacies of White Australia: Race, Culture and Nation*, Crawley, Western Australia: University of Western Australia Press, pp. 110–28.

Jupp, James (1995), 'From "White Australia" to "Part of Asia": Recent Shifts in Australian Immigration Policy Towards the Region', *International Migration Review*, **29**, pp. 207–29.

Jupp, James (2002), *From White Australia to Woomera: The Story of Australian Immigration*, Cambridge: Cambridge University Press.

Kibreab, Gaim (2003), 'Citizenship Rights and Repatriation of Refugees', *International Migration Review*, **37**, pp. 24–73.

Layton-Henry, Zig (1992), *The Politics of Immigration : Immigration, Race and Race Relations in Post-War Britain*, Cambridge, MA: Blackwell Publishers.

Ling, Huping (1999), 'Family and Marriage of Late-Nineteenth and Early-Twentieth Century Chinese Immigrant Women', *Journal of American Ethnic History*, **19**, pp. 43–63.

Lovelock, Kirsten (2000), 'Intercountry Adoption as a Migratory Practice: A Comparative Analysis of Intercountry Adoption and Immigration Policy and Practice in the United States, Canada and New Zealand in the Post WWII Period', *International Migration Review*, **34**, pp. 907–53.

Markus, Andrew (2003), 'Of Continuities and Discontinuities: Reflections on a Century of Australian Immigration Control', in Laksiri Jayasuriya, David Walker and Jan Gothard (eds), *Legacies of White Australia: Race, Culture and Nation*, Crawley, Western Australia: University of Western Australia Press, pp. 175–89.

McGhee, Derek (2001), 'Persecution and Social Group Status: Homosexual Refugees in the 1990s', *Journal of Refugee Studies*, **14**, pp. 20–42.

McKeown, Adam (1999), 'Transnational Chinese Families and Chinese Exclusion, 1875–1943.' *Journal of American Ethnic History* **18**(2), pp. 73–110.

McKeown, Adam (2003), 'Ritualization of Regulation: The Enforcement of Chinese Exclusion in the United States and China' *American Historical Review*, June, pp. 377–403.

Neuman, Gerald L. (1993), 'Buffer Zones Against Refugees: Dublin, Schengen and the German Asylum Amendment', *Virginia Journal of International Law*, **33**, pp. 503–26.

Neuman, Gerald L. (2001), 'The Assault on Habeas Corpus in Immigration Law', *Human Rights*, Winter, pp. 16–17.

Ngai, Mae M. (2004), *Impossible Subjects: Illegal Aliens and the Making of Modern America*, Princeton: Princeton University Press.

Ong, Aihwa (2001), *Flexible Citizenship*, Durham, North Carolina: Duke University Press.

Razack, Sherene H. (1999), 'Making Canada White: Law and the Policing of Bodies of Color in the 1990s', *Canadian Journal of Law and Society*, **14**, pp. 159–84.

Salyer, Lucy (1995), *Laws Harsh as Tigers: Chinese Immigrants and the Shaping of Modern Immigration Law*, Chapel Hill: University of North Carolina Press.

Schuck, Peter H. (1992), 'The Politics of Rapid Legal Change: Immigration Policy in the 1980s', *Studies in American Political Development*, **6**, pp. 37–92.

Scott, James C. (1998), *Seeing Like a State: How Certain Schemes to Improve the Human Condition Have Failed*, New Haven, CT: Yale University Press.

Selman, Peter (2000), 'The Demographic History of Intercountry Adoption' in Peter Selman (ed.), *Intercountry Adoption: Developments, Trends and Perspectives*. London: British Agencies for Adoption and Fostering, pp. 15–39.

Slaughter, Anne-Marie (2004), *A New World Order*, Princeton: Princeton University Press.

Sterett, Susan (1997a) *Creating Constitutionalism?*, Ann Arbor, MI: University of Michigan Press.

Sterett, Susan (1997b), 'Domestic Violence and Immigration in Britain', *PoLAR: Political and Legal Anthropology Review*, **20**, pp. 63–9.

Sterett, Susan (1999), 'Intercultural Citizenship: Statutory Interpretation and Belonging in Britain', in Sally J. Kenney, William M. Reisinger and John C. Reitz (eds), *Constitutional Dialogues in Comparative Perspective*, London: Macmillan Press, pp. 119–42.

Thorpe, Helen (2005), 'Head of the Class', *Westword*, (December 2–8), pp. 27–30.

United Nations High Commissioner for Refugees (1996), *Convention and Protocol*, http://www.unhcr.ch/cgi-bin/texis/vtx/basics

Young, Alison (1996), *Imagining Crime*, London, Thousand Oaks and New Deli: Sage Publications.

Part I
Illegality, Mercy and the Language of Deservingness

[1]

OPPOSING PROP. 187: UNDOCUMENTED IMMIGRANTS AND THE NATIONAL IMAGINATION

Linda S. Bosniak[*]

"Political imagination is, almost always, national imagination."[1]

I. Introduction

Among the many bruising battles engendered by the recent immigration wars in this country, the battle over California's Proposition 187 has touched an exceptionally deep nerve. Approved by the state's voters in 1994, this "anti-illegal alien initiative" will—if the courts uphold it—deny health care, education and other public services to undocumented immigrants and require social service providers to report any

* Associate Professor of Law, Rutgers Law School-Camden. B.A., 1980, Wesleyan University; M.A., 1988, University of California-Berkeley; J.D., 1988, Stanford Law School. For their very helpful critical readings of earlier drafts, I want to thank Alex Aleinikoff, Perry Dane, Richard Delgado, Karen Engle, David Frankford, Hiroshi Motomura, Judy Rabinovitz, Jamie Raskin, Peter Spiro, Allan Stein and members of the Faculty Workshop at New York University Law School. Thanks are also due to Lina Avidan and Robert Rubin for extremely useful conversations about Prop. 187 and its associated campaigns, and to Josh Byrne and Gueneviere Van Best for excellent research assistance. I was supported during the writing of this article by a summer research grant from Rutgers Law School.

1. Richard Rorty, Unger, Castoriadis, and the Romance of A National Future, 82 Nw. U. L. Rev. 335, 343 (1988).

service user they suspect of undocumented status to law enforcement authorities.[2] Support for Prop. 187—and now for its progeny in other states[3]—has been wide and deep; in fact, these measures have served

2. The initiative's provisions are codified at CAL. EDUC. CODE § 48215(a) (West Supp. 1995); CAL. HEALTH & SAFETY CODE § 130(a) (West Supp. 1995); CAL. WELF. & INST. CODE § 10001.5 (West Supp. 1995).

On the day following its approval in the Nov. 8, 1994 election, opponents filed several lawsuits in both state and federal courts seeking to enjoin the initiative's implementation; these were consolidated into three actions and quickly produced temporary restraining orders. In one of these cases, U.S. District Court Judge Mariana Pfaelzer of the Central District of California subsequently invalidated those provisions of the initiative which would require state school and welfare officials to demand proof of legal immigration status and to report "suspected" undocumented immigrants to federal and state authorities, on grounds that the federal government is exclusively empowered to regulate immigration. See Gregorio T. v. Wilson, No. 94-7652 (MRP) (C.D. Cal. Nov. 20, 1995) (partial summary judgment). On the same grounds, the court held that the state may not deny undocumented immigrants any public services that are fully or partly funded by the federal government. Id. Finally, the court also invalidated those provisions which would deny K-12 education to undocumented children, on grounds that they conflict with the Supreme Court's 1982 ruling in Plyler v. Doe, 457 U.S. 202 (1982). Id. The State has indicated it will appeal these rulings, and the remaining issues are expected to go to trial. *See* Ken McLaughlin, *Judge Guts Core of Prop. 187*, SAN JOSE MERCURY NEWS, Nov. 21, 1995, at 1A; Laura McCoy, *Prop. 187 Backers Hope to Win Appeal*, S.F. EXAM., Nov. 24, 1995, at A27.

3. In Florida, anti-immigration activists are currently collecting signatures in an effort to place "Florida-187" on the 1996 November ballot in that state. *See* Angelica Quiroga, *Copycat Feber: Proposal To Ban Social Services For Illegal Immigrants*, 8 HISPANIC 18 (April, 1995) ("Since [Prop. 187's] passage by the citizens of California, several states, such as Arizona, Washington, Oregon and Florida have begun to consider similar measures."); Sergio R. Bustos, *Immigration Debate Organizing: Opposing S. Florida Groups Fight For, Against State Ballot on Services*, SUN SENTINEL, Aug. 5, 1995, at 1B. *See also* Patrick McDonnell, *Despite Legal Snags, Prop. 187 Reverberates*, L.A. TIMES, Nov. 8, 1995 ("Proposition 187-type initiative drives have sprouted in other states, notably Florida and Arizona, and related movements have even gained momentum in Oregon and ostensibly liberal Massachusetts."); Maria Puente, *States Setting Stage For Their Own Prop. 187's*, USA TODAY, Nov. 18, 1994, at 3A (discussing efforts to enact similar laws in Arizona, Florida, New York, and Texas).

In addition, some members of Congress have sought to amend federal law to ensure that access to all federally funded programs other than emergency medical care is denied to undocumented immigrants. For a limited sampling, see 104 H.R. 1377 (1995) (bill to amend the Immigration and Nationality Act to authorize States to deny public education benefits to aliens not lawfully present in the United States); 104 H.R. 341 (1995) (bill to prohibit direct federal financial benefits and unemployment benefits for illegal aliens); 104 H.R. 438 (1995) (bill to amend the Internal Revenue Code of 1986 to deny the earned income credit to illegal aliens); 104 H.R. 484 (1985) (bill to prohibit public welfare assistance to aliens not lawfully in the United States); 104 H.R. 560, § 301 (1995) (provisions of proposed immigration reform package that would prohibit direct federal financial benefits and unemployment benefits to aliens who are not lawful permanent residents); 104 H.R. 637 (1995) (bill to limit alien eligibility for public welfare assistance to aliens residing permanently and lawfully in the United States); 104 S. 999 (1995) (bill denying aliens not lawfully in the United States any direct Federal financial benefit or social insurance benefit, unemployment benefit and housing benefit). *See also* Faye Fiore, *Congressman's Proposal Mirrors Prop. 187*, Los Angeles Times July 19, 1995, at 3.

to mobilize reserves of mass disaffection with immigration the likes of which have not been seen for nearly eighty years.[4] Despite the substantial popularity of such measures, however, political liberals and progressives have almost uniformly opposed them, finding them wrongheaded as a matter of policy, and often offensive as well. Prop. 187 has become, for its critics, a symbol of the excesses of the current wave of anti-immigrant anxiety in this country, and the shorthand for a dangerous politics of ressentiment.[5]

Much has been said elsewhere about the nature of the Prop 187 enterprise, including the nature of the support it has received.[6] My concern in this article is, instead, with its critics. The question I want to examine, in general terms, is this: What is the basis for the deeply-felt antipathy toward Prop. 187 and similar restrictionist efforts among the initiative's opponents? What, precisely, do the critics understand to be wrong with Prop. 187? And how far does their aversion to such

---

The electoral success of Prop. 187 has also created political momentum for more dramatic reform. Some of the original promoters of Prop. 187 have drafted an advisory ballot measure for the 1996 elections in California which calls for an amendment to the federal Constitution to eliminate automatic birthright citizenship for the U.S.-born children of undocumented immigrants. (The measure's acronym, SOS II, is a shorthand for "Save Our Sovereignty.") *See* Patrick J. McDonnell, *Despite Legal Snags, Prop. 187 Reverberates*, L.A. TIMES, Nov. 8, 1995, at A1. Similar efforts are now pending in Congress. See e.g. 104 HJR 93 (1995) (joint resolution proposing an amendment to the Constitution of the United States to provide that no person born in the United States will be a U.S. citizen unless one parent is a U.S. citizen or possesses lawful immigration status at the time of birth). For a useful critical analysis of recent efforts to abolish birthright citizenship for the children of undocumented aliens, see Note, *The Birthright Citizenship Amendment: A Threat to Equality*, 107 HARV. L. REV. 1026 (1994).

4. For accounts of the anti-immigrant movements of the early part of this century and their effects, see THOMAS J. CURRAN, XENOPHOBIA AND IMMIGRATION 109-44 (1975); JOHN HIGHAM, STRANGERS IN THE LAND (2d ed. 1984); LUCY E. SALYER, LAWS HARSH AS TIGERS: CHINESE IMMIGRANTS AND THE SHAPING OF MODERN IMMIGRATION LAW (1995).

5. "The term 'ressentiment,' derived from Nietzche, . . . connotes impotent hatred, envy, repressed feelings of revenge, the inability to act out antagonistic impulses in open conflict." Lewis A. Coser, *Max Scheler, An Introduction*, in MAX SCHELER, RESSENTIMENT 21 (1961). *See* F. NIETZCHE, GENEOLOGY OF MORALS, 34-38 (1964). The concept has been invoked by contemporary historians of nationalism to characterize certain defensive aspects of the development of national consciousness and national identity. *See, e.g.*, LIAH GREENFELD, NATIONALISM: FIVE ROADS TO MODERNITY 15-17 (1992).

6. *See, e.g.*, Ann Davis, *The Return of the Nativists*, NAT'L L.J., June 19, 1995, at A1; Marc Cooper, *Prop. 187's True Colors: After the Vote, Will Californians Ever Get Along?*, VILLAGE VOICE, Dec. 6, 1994, at 13; Elizabeth Kadetsky, *Bashing Illegals In California*, THE NATION, Oct. 17, 1994, at 416; Stanley Mailman, *California's Proposition 187 and Its Lessons*, N.Y.L.J., Jan. 3, 1995, at 3; Peter Schuck, *The Message of 187*, AM. PROSPECT, No. 21, Spring 1995, at 85, 89-91; *Tough Proposition*, NAT'L REV., Nov. 21, 1994, at 20; Mike Davis, The Social Origins of the Referendum, NACLA Report on the Americas, vo. XXIX, No. 3, Nov/Dec 1995, at 24.

measures extend?

During the course of the "No On 187" campaign, activists set forth a variety of compelling objections to the proposed initiative. Sometimes the organizations that worked against it disagreed over how to articulate the arguments; their divisions were often divisions over strategy, though at times they diverged over principle as well. In the end, however, there was a striking uniformity in what most critics said, and correspondingly, in what they did not say, when opposing the initiative. In particular, while opponents advanced critical arguments on empirical, consequentialist and normative grounds, arguments invoking the injustice of the measure for the actual *objects* of the initiative's provisions—the undocumented immigrants themselves—were rarely heard. Whatever was wrong with Prop. 187, in other words, the problem was apparently *not* that it treats undocumented immigrants unfairly.

My purpose in this article is to examine the complex political and intellectual challenges faced by critics in opposing Prop. 187 and similar initiatives. I first outline the shape of the opposing arguments that activists set out during the course of the campaign in California and some of the tensions that surrounded their making. I then turn to the question of why the "unfairness" argument was heard so rarely and reflect upon the meaning of its omission. I understand this omission, in significant part, as a pragmatic response to the recent wave of anti-immigrant anxiety that has recently swept this country. In a hostile political climate, emphasizing the initiative's negative consequences for Americans' own self-interest is more effective and less risky than representing undocumented immigrants (who are, after all, the apparent source of the public's anxiety) as legitimate subjects of concern and interest.

Yet I also understand the significance of the omission to extend beyond the realm of pragmatic politics. I suggest that the question of whether measures like Prop. 187 treat undocumented immigrants unjustly—and the question of how to articulate the nature of that injustice, if so—are often extremely problematic for these measures' critics in both normative and analytical terms. To be sure, the question of the measure's justice may be perceived as largely irrelevant by some of the initiative's more mainstream opponents, who understand the unauthorized presence of these immigrants to place them outside the scope of common normative concern by legal definition. But I suggest that for many progressives, including progressive scholars, who instinctively oppose Prop. 187, the matter of the measures' injustice in principle is far more troubling. For, on the one hand, progressives are fundamentally committed to challenging the systematic exclusion and subordination of classes of people in our society, and by this measure, Prop. 187 and its progeny plainly must be condemned as unjust. At the same time, however, most progressives tend to think about justice in distinctly national terms; they tend to collectively possess what I call a "national political imagination," one which regards the national community as the predominant community of normative concern and presumes the legitimacy, and perhaps the necessity, of maintaining boundaries around it. This nationally informed vision of social life, I argue, stands in tension with progressives' broader commitments against social marginalization, and it gets in the way of our ability to robustly articulate the interests of undocumented immigrants in this society.

I should make clear at the outset (if it is not clear already) that I am a staunch opponent of Prop. 187 and similar anti-immigrant measures. Yet I also count myself among those who have struggled to articulate the basis for that opposition—not merely in strategic terms but also as a matter of principle. Addressing the status of undocumented immigrants requires progressives—activists and scholars alike—to confront important tensions within our own commitments (diverse and multiple though they are) concerning the normative significance of national boundaries. The recent wave of immigration-related anxiety in this country presents this question in very stark terms and provides us with an opportunity for critical self-reflection on this difficult subject. The following reading of opponents' rhetorical efforts to combat measures like Prop. 187, and the various questions I pose in response, are offered in the interests of contributing to such a project.

II.

In order to convince California voters to reject the Prop. 187 ballot initiative, it was up to opponents to provide them with reasons to vote "no." Articulating these reasons, it turned out, was a delicate task, since the art of political campaigns requires fashioning a message that simultaneously reaches as many and offends as few people as possible—and the possibilities for offense on the subject of immigration are, unquestionably, immense. A variety of opposition groups worked throughout the state to defeat the measure, and they often differed amongst themselves as to how best to frame the arguments. But in the end, the opposition's message was fairly consistent in outline, and was comprised of three principal claims.[7]

The first claim was that Prop. 187 is objectionable because it is racist or xenophobic. In its most trenchant form, the racism argument charged that supporters of Prop. 187 are motivated by animus against the growing population of Latinos in California, Mexicans in particular; it also charged that the initiative's "reporting requirements" will allow for a widespread campaign of racial harassment against people of color in the state.[8] A "softer" version of the argument emphasized that ethnic minorities in the state will be affected disproportionately by the measure, since social service providers will often wrongly assume that people of color are undocumented;[9] it further stressed that the initiative's terms will create the perception, if not the reality, of racial scapegoating, thereby fanning flames of ethnic strife in the state.[10] Either by

7. I should emphasize that my characterization of the campaign and the arguments it proffered in Parts I and II of this essay represent not so much reportage as an interpretive reading of the dynamics of argument and omission that characterized the "No On 187" campaign. While grounded in the particulars of the campaign as it unfolded, my purpose here is to highlight silences and tensions, both covert and expressed, characterizing the campaign, as well as the parties' public postures. Various players involved in opposition to the initiative may well disagree with aspects of my reading—although some of them have provided me with information and views which have formed the basis of my own thoughts here.

8. For example, Taxpayers Against 187, one of the two principal opposition organizations, repeatedly emphasized that "the people behind 187 (namely, the Federation For American Immigration Reform, or FAIR) have close ties to a White Supremacist Group," called the Pioneer Fund, which Taxpayers characterized as "a secretive group that believes in the genetic superiority of the white race." *See generally* Taxpayers Against 187, Memo to Opponents of Proposition 187 RE: Press Coverage of Prop. 187 Promoters, Campaign Literature (on file with the author).

For post-mortem analysis of the initiative which stresses its racial motivation, see, e.g., Duane Campbell & Eric Vega, *Immigrants' Rights After NAFTA: The Struggle Against Prop. 187*, DEM. LEFT, Jan-Feb 1995, at 18 ("Make no mistake about it. This was an anti-Mexican, anti-Latino campaign. While the Governor [Republican Pete Wilson] said he welcomed legal immigrants, the photos, the references, and the scapegoating were clear. Governor Wilson and the Republican party gave over $400,000 to the Yes campaign, and he used most of his commercials to promote stereotypes and prejudice.").

9. *See, e.g.*, Mexican American Legal Defense and Education Fund, (MALDEF), Information on Proposition 187 (undated campaign literature, on file with the author) ("Prop. 187 creates a police state mentality. It would force public officials to deny vital services and report anyone they 'suspect' might not be a legal resident, but Prop. 187 does not define the basis for suspicion. This increases the probability of discrimination. Will the suspicion be based on the way you speak? The sound of your last name? The color of your skin?") *See also Don't Panic*, NEW REPUBLIC, Nov. 21, 1994, at 7 ("If Proposition 187 passes, no one doubts that a Hernandez would be more suspect than a Smith"); Isaac Guzman, *Students At UCLA Protest*, L.A. TIMES, Oct. 7, 1994, at B1 ("More than 200 boisterous UCLA students and civil rights activists marched through the Westwood campus Thursday, some saying that Proposition 187 would subject them to unwarranted racial stereotypes. At a rally after the march, Miya Iwataki of Californians United Against Prop. 187 decried what she saw as the creation of 'an environment ripe for racism' by 'save our state' proponents.").

10. For example, in a statement deploring the passage of Prop. 187, the National Conference

design or inadvertence, therefore, Prop. 187's measures will make California a less hospitable place for its minority population.

The racism critique is clearly a powerful and indispensable critique of the initiative; there is simply no way to address Prop. 187 without recognizing its deep imbrication in a politics of racial anxiety in this country—and many Californians no doubt recognized as much. But despite its importance, this argument only goes so far. For as it turned out, African-Americans and Asians ended up voting for Prop. 187 in surprisingly large numbers, and the Hispanic vote in favor was substantial as well.[11] The likely reason for such broad-based minority support (despite the initiative's clear racial overtones) is that it formally targets only one relatively small segment of the immigrant population—that is, immigrants without legal immigration papers, or the undocumented.[12] Most voters in the state, including minority voters, apparently saw the initiative less as a referendum on ethnic relations than as a response to the illegal immigration status of one specific group of newcomers and voted accordingly.[13]

The "illegality" issue, of course, lay at the heart of the pro-187 message. Supporters promoted the initiative, in instrumental terms, as a sure-fire method of controlling undocumented immigration; the claim was that undocumented immigrants come to this country in order to obtain social benefits, so that making those benefits unavailable will deter people from coming in the first place—or will induce those who are here to go home.[14] They also promoted the initiative as a much-

---

of Catholic Bishops stated that the initiative "established an intimidating tone that could foster 'harassment of persons who may look or sound "undocumented."'" David Gonzalez, *Bishops Assail An Initiative About Aliens*, N.Y. TIMES, Nov. 18, 1994, at A1.

11. Fifty-six percent of African-Americans voters and fifty-seven percent of Asian-American voters reportedly supported the proposition, as did thirty-one percent of the state's Hispanic voters. *After Prop. 187: Heading North*, ECONOMIST, Nov. 19, 1994, at 29.

12. Broadly speaking, undocumented or "illegal" immigrants are people who either entered this country without formal permission, or who entered legally but subsequently violated the terms of their visas. The undocumented are estimated to represent approximately 13% of the total number of foreign-born persons (including naturalized citizens) currently residing in the United States. MICHAEL FIX & JEFFREY R. PASSEL, IMMIGRATION AND IMMIGRANTS: SETTING THE RECORD STRAIGHT 21-25 (1994). On the other hand, approximately 43% of the country's undocumented reside in California. Elizabeth Kadetsky, *Bashing Illegals in California*, NATION, Oct. 17, 1994, at 416-17.

13. *See, e.g.*, Evelyn C. White, *Immigration A Tough Call For Blacks: Proposition 187 Debate Has Stirred Deep Feelings*, S.F. CHRON., Oct. 10, 1994, at A1.

14. As Alan C. Nelson, former Commissioner of the Immigration and Naturalization Service and one of the initiative's key sponsors, stated: "Proposition 187 contains several components aimed at stopping illegal immigration [and will] prompt[ ] many illegal aliens to return to their

needed method for preventing an outlaw population from brazenly robbing Californians of their hard-earned tax-dollars. As the initiative's sponsoring organization, "Save Our State" (or S.O.S.) put it, "it's time to stop rewarding illegals for successfully breaking our laws."[15] Given the resonance of these arguments for many people in the state, opponents of Prop. 187 had to go beyond a critique of the initiative on grounds of racism to address the specific anxiety over illegal immigration promoted by the "Yes" campaign.

Opponents, therefore, set out two additional arguments against the initiative, each of which addressed the illegal immigration issue directly.[16] First, opponents sought to refute supporters' instrumental claim that denial of social benefits to the undocumented will serve as an effective method of immigration control. Opponents produced data showing that undocumented immigrants come to this country not to avail themselves of public medical services and public education but to work and to join their families.[17] According to this "no deterrence"

---

home countries. Proposition 187 provides the only comprehensive vehicle to accomplish this goal." Alan C. Nelson, *Proposition 187: An Important Approach to Prevent Illegal Immigration*, 2 HUMAN RIGHTS BRIEF 8 (Winter 1995).

Notably, emphasis by Prop. 187's supporters on the immigration-control objectives of the initiative serves to undermine the position of the state of California in pending federal litigation against the initiative. Plaintiffs have charged, with substantial success so far, that to the extent California is engaged in "immigration regulation," the measure is preempted by federal law. For a general discussion of the preemption question in the immigration context, with special attention to Prop. 187, *see* Peter J. Spiro, *The States and Immigration in an Era of Demi-Sovereignties*, 35 VA. J. INT'L L. 121 (1994); Linda S. Bosniak, *Immigrants, Preemption and Equality*, 35 VA. J. INT'L L. 179 (1994); Hiroshi Motomura, *Immigration and Alienage, Federalism and Proposition 187*, 35 VA. J. INT'L L. 201 (1994); Michael A. Olivas, *Preempting Preemption: Foreign Affairs, State Rights, and Alienage Classifications*, 35 VA. J. INT'L L. 217 (1994). *See also* Gregorio T. v. Wilson, No. 94-7652 (MRP) (C.D. Cal. Nov. 20, 1995) (partial summary judgment).

15. S.O.S., Save Our State, California's Illegal Immigration Control Initiative (undated promotional flyer) (on file with the author); Anna Cekol et al., *Backers of Anti-Illegal Immigrant Petition Deliver Signatures*, L.A. TIMES, May 17, 1994, at A3 ("'We've allowed California to be a welfare state for illegals too long,' said one of the Initiative's key sponsors.").

16. Many opponents nevertheless characterized the "illegality" question as a mask for hostile racial attitudes. *See, e.g.*, John Roemer & Marta Sanchez-Beswick, *Can SOS Be Stopped?*, S.F. WEEKLY, Aug. 24, 1994, at 13 ("Backers of Prop. 187 want to "Save Our State" from a supposed flood of undocumented immigrants. But defiant Latino activists say the real emergency is the rising tide of bigotry and racial scapegoating.").

17. *See, e.g.*, Mexican American Legal Defense and Educational Fund, Preliminary Section-by-Section Analysis of Proposition 187, June 30, 1994, at 3 (on file with the author) ("[T]he underlying premise of the initiative is that immigrants come to the U.S. to receive public benefits and services. In fact, immigrants come for jobs, for family reunification and to flee persecution . . . . If anything, public benefits are the last thing immigrants want from this country . . . . [U]ndocumented immigrants tend to avoid any institution that even resembles gov-

argument, Prop. 187 won't work on its own terms; it won't do what it is ostensibly meant to do, which, once again, is to control unauthorized immigration.

Second, opponents of Prop. 187 made the consequentialist argument that, far from solving the state's social problems, the initiative would lead to frightening social pathologies for the people of California. They contended, for example, that to impose illiteracy on a class of children in the state will only undermine both the economy and the democratic fabric of society.[18] Similarly, they pointed out, people afraid to go to the doctor will simply create the conditions for a public health catastrophe and will end up costing the state more money later on.[19]

---

ernment or official authority.") Opponents pointed out, in addition, that under the law as it existed prior to Prop. 187's passage, undocumented immigrants were already excluded from access to all public services other than education, emergency medical care and school lunch programs in any event; thus, the charge that access to social services motivates them to come to this country is simply nonsensical. *Id.*, at 2-3.

18. Angelica Quiroga, *Copycat Fever: Proposal To Ban Social Services For Illegal Aliens*, 8 HISPANIC No. 3, at 18 (1995) ("Opponents of Proposition 187 . . . contend that the social damage created by an increase in juvenile delinquency and illiteracy are far too costly"). Justice Brennan made this same argument in *Plyler v. Doe*. "It is difficult," he wrote, "to understand precisely what the State hopes to achieve by promoting the creation and perpetuation of a subclass of illiterates within our boundaries, surely adding to the problems and costs of unemployment, welfare and crime" already faced by the nation. Plyler v. Doe, 457 U.S. 202, 230 (1982).

19. *See, e.g.*, Paul Feldman, *Proposition 187: Measure's Foes Try to shift Focus From Walkouts To Issues*, L.A. TIMES, Nov. 4, 1994, at A3 ("At a Los Angeles news conference, top Los Angeles health officials said passage of 187 would have drastic health repercussions for the public. 'If we do not immunize undocumented children, we will increase the incidence of measles, whooping cough, mumps, rubella, diphtheria and hepatitis B in all children, not just the undocumented,' said Dr. Brian D. Johnston, secretary of the Los Angeles County Medical Association . . . . [He said, furthermore, that] '[e]very dollar spent on prenatal care saves between $3 and $10 later on in caring for babies who are born with medical problems that could have been prevented . . . . . . Every dollar spent on immunization saves between $10 and $14 in future disease and disability costs.'").

In addition, critics argued that Prop. 187 would serve to substantially undermine efforts to fight crime. *See, e.g.*, Californians United Against Prop. 187 (San Jose), Statement of Opposition to Proposition 187 (undated) (on file with the author) ("By requiring law enforcement agencies to report to the Immigration and Naturalization Service (INS) any individuals they suspect to be undocumented, criminals would prey upon the entire community because many witnesses and victims would fear coming forward because of the possibility of being reported to the INS. This provision would severely undermine efforts in many cities to implement community policing and other effective models of police-community cooperation.").

Opponents also objected to the initiative's requirements that teachers and health care workers and other social service providers verify the legal status of students and service users on grounds that it would turn providers into tools of a "big brother state," with serious civil liberties concerns for everyone. *See* Californians United Against Proposition 187, No On 187 (undated campaign material, on file with the author) (Prop. 187 will "create a 'big brother' police state as people are forced to turn in one another as suspected of being undocumented.").

Each of these latter arguments against Prop. 187 was important to make because each appears to be correct as a matter of fact. Research on the causes of undocumented immigration indicates that these immigrants come to this country primarily for employment and family reunification purposes, so that denial of social benefits will poorly serve restrictionist objectives.[20] Likewise, both common sense and expert opinion suggest that exclusionary measures such as these will, in fact, produce frightening social pathologies.[21]

In addition to the consequentialist arguments noted here and in the text, opponents also argued that passage of Prop. 187 would cost the state billions of dollars in federal funding annually. Federal law prohibits release of information about publicly funded schools and universities, *see* Family Educational Rights and Privacy Act (FERPA), 20 U.S.C. § 1232 et seq., and Prop. 187 opponents argued that the initiative's reporting requirements would stand in direct contravention of these provisions, thereby jeopardizing millions in federal education funding to California. *See* Beth Shuster, *Prop. 187 To Cost L.A. Schools Put At $450 Million*, L.A. TIMES, Sept. 21, 1994, at B1.

20. *See, e.g.*, Wayne A. Cornelius et al., *Introduction: The Ambivalent Quest for Immigration Control*, in CONTROLLING IMMIGRATION: A GLOBAL PERSPECTIVE, 3, 37 (Wayne A. Cornelius et al. eds, 1994) ("[T]here is little empirical evidence for the proposition that availability of social services or entitlements is a powerful magnet for would-be illegal entrants, as compared to other demand-pull factors.").

Professor Cornelius has argued elsewhere as follows:

> Having spent the past 20 years studying Mexican migrants to California, most of whom entered illegally, I have yet to encounter a single one for whom getting access to some tax-supported service was the principle reason for coming here.
>
> In my own studies, as well as those of dozens of other researchers, only 2% to 5% of would-be migrants or those interviewed on U.S. soil mentioned social services as even a secondary or contributing factor in their decisions to migrate. In all extant studies, the availability of higher-paying jobs and family ties with immigrants already living in this country were the overwhelming incentives . . . .[Furthermore], [i]t is inconceivable that an immigrant family, in many cases containing at least some members who are here legally, a family that is already permanently settled in California, with at least one member of the household regularly employed, would pack up and return to a place where they have no viable economic options and no possibility of attaining anything remotely resembling even a modest U.S. standard of living . . . .If serious research is any guide, the vast majority of undocumented immigrants and their children who have been living continuously in California for five years or more will stay here, whether or not [restrictive social measures] are approved.

Wayne A. Cornelius, *Don't Vote for a Fix That Won't Work*, L.A. TIMES, Oct. 28, 1994, at A11.

21. Professionals in many fields have predicted that the enforcement of Prop. 187 will substantially undermine the health and well-being of American society.

Law enforcement officials, for instance, have argued that Prop. 187 could exacerbate crime by rendering immigrants afraid to cooperate in community policing efforts. *See You May Be Surprised At Who's Against Prop. 187; Conservative, Business, Police Leaders See Measure as Grave Mistake*, L.A. TIMES, Nov. 6, 1994, at B2. The public health threats posed by measures like Prop. 187 are also severe. Dr. Bernard Lo, a medical ethics expert from the University of California, has argued that requiring medical personnel to report patients' immigration status may

Compelling as these arguments are, however, it is worth noting that their precise formulation was sometimes the source of substantial disagreement among different groups of Prop. 187 opponents. With respect to the "no-deterrence" argument, some opposition groups—including the mainstream Taxpayers Against 187—bent over backwards to assure the public that they shared its concern over illegal immigration, and agreed it has to be controlled; they simply contended that Prop. 187 is not the most effective method for achieving that goal.[22] As an alternative, they and their allies affirmatively called for sending the National Guard to the U.S.-Mexican border and toughening enforcement of employer sanctions laws.[23] Other opposition groups, like the more progressive Californians United Against Prop. 187, made efforts to avoid such inflammatory restrictionist rhetoric; they commonly charged that Prop. 187 supporters were engaged in "immigrant bashing,"[24] and if pressed on the

well give rise to increased spreading of tuberculosis, among other epidemic diseases. He writes: "Proposition 187 supporters argue that those who are ill will return to their native countries for medical care. It is equally plausible that people will deny illness, try home remedies, obtain medications from friends or delay seeking care, thereby worsening their medical conditions and potentially threatening public health." Tal Ann Ziv & Bernard Lo, 332 NEW ENG. J. MED. 1095, 1096-97, Apr. 20, 1995. (In fact, although most provisions of Prop. 187 have yet to be enforced, many undocumented immigrants have already been deterred from seeking needed medical care, sometimes with fatal consequences. *See, e.g.*, Lee Romney & Julie Marquis, *Calif. Measure Contributed To Boy's Death, Activists Say*, PHIL. INQUIRER, Nov. 24, 1994, at A4; P. Burdman, *Woman Who Feared Prop. 187 Deportation Dies at S.F. General*, S.F. CHRON., Nov. 26, 1994, at A14.) Lo has argued, in addition, that the initiative's reporting requirements would "harm[ ] medical professionalism" because it would require "the potentially unlimited disclosure of medical information and will undermine medical confidentiality." Ziv and Lo, *supra*, at 1095. For these and other reasons, the California Medical Association and the California Association of Hospitals and Health Systems opposed the measure. *Id.*

22. "Illegal immigration IS a problem, but 187 won't fix it. 187 will only make a bad situation worse . . . It does absolutely nothing to beef-up enforcement at the border or crack down on employers who break the law and knowingly hire illegal immigrants." Taxpayers Against 187, "Memorandum To Opponents of Proposition 187," (undated), at 2 (on file with author).

23. *Id.* Additionally, California Senator Barbara Boxer (Dem.), an opponent of Prop. 187, supported supplementing border patrol agents with "'well-trained, well-equipped' military personnel as an innovative solution to that state's illegal immigration problem." *Senator's Plan To Fight Illegal Immigration Shunned By Pentagon*, Los Angeles Times, August 7, 1994, at A19. Along with California Senator Diane Feinstein (Dem.), who is also a Prop. 187 opponent, Boxer has also "suggested that a peso loan be linked to Mexico stopping illegal immigrants from crossing the border." Susan Ferriss, *Tougher Weapons Against Illegals*, S.F. CHRON., Feb. 24, 1995, at A2. And Kathleen Brown, the unsuccessful Democratic candidate for the governorship in 1994, and likewise a Prop. 187 opponent, "favors using military troops at the border and wants to issue tamper-resistant Social Security cards to make it harder for illegal workers to get jobs." Maria Puente, *Illegal Immigration: An Ignitable Issue*, USA TODAY, Apr. 4, 1994, at A8.

24. *See generally* Elizabeth Kadetsky, *'Save Our State Initiative': Bashing Illegals In California*, NATION, Oct. 17, 1994, at 416; *A New Initiative For Immigrant-Bashing* (Editorial), S.F.

border control issue, they tended to argue that the most effective way to deter undocumented immigration is to enforce the nation's wage and hour laws.[25]

There were also differences amongst opposition groups over how to frame the consequentialist "Prop. 187 will be bad for Californians" argument. In particular, Taxpayers Against 187 commonly campaigned against the initiative by warning that its passage would result in an increase in truancy and gang violence in the state—on the theory that kids who are kept out of school are likely take to the streets.[26] Taxpayers also warned of the health threats posed by the initiative by declaring that passage of Prop. 187 would result in immigrants "spreading disease throughout the state."[27] Many progressive opponents, on the other hand, strongly objected to what they regarded to be the not-so-veiled appeals to racist and classically nativist anxieties in these formulations.[28]

CHRON., June 13, 1994, at A22.

Additionally, opponents sometimes argued that the generalized hostility toward undocumented immigrants embodied in measures like Prop. 187 serves to mask the fact that they contribute more to the overall economy than they derive from it in the form of tax-supported services. *See, e.g.*, Mexican American Legal Defense and Educational Fund, Preliminary Section-by-Section Analysis of Proposition 187, June 30, 1994, at 1-2 (on file with the author) (While "Proposition 187 claims that the people of the state are suffering economic hardship caused by the presence of undocumented immigrants . . . .[e]very reputable study which has been undertaken to date shows that immigrants—both documented and undocumented—contribute far more in tax revenues and to the economy than they utilize in government services.").

25. Conversation with Lina Avidan, Californians United Against Prop. 187 (Feb. 11, 1995). *See also* Robert Scheer, *The Dirty Secret Behind Proposition 187: If Wilson Was Serious About Illegal Immigration, He'd Put Muscle Behind the Labor Laws*, L.A. TIMES, Sept. 29, 1994, at B7.

26. "187 is opposed by law enforcement because it will mean MORE crime, not less. It will kick an estimated 300,000 kids out of school and onto OUR streets, with no supervision." Taxpayers Against 187, Memorandum, *supra* note 8, at 2.

27. Patrick J. McDonnell, *Foes of Prop. 187, Toeing A Difficult Line*, L.A. TIMES, Sept. 26, 1994, at A16. *See also* Marc Cooper, *The War Against Illegal Immigrants Heats Up*, VILLAGE VOICE, Oct. 4, 1994, at 28 (quoting an Orange County Democratic candidate for state assembly, who opposed Prop. 187, as follows: "'Do you really want people cooking your food, cleaning your babies and taking care of your old folks when they have no access to health care?'").

28. *See, e.g.*, Lisa Duran et al., *Prop. 187: Where do We Go From Here?* FORWARD MOTION, Jan. 1995, at 11, 13-14:

> In the name of 'realism,' some coalitions focused their appeal on the relatively large bloc of moderate-to-conservative Reagan democrats . . . By appealing to the self-interest of this admittedly racist and anti-immigrant voter bloc, they may have jeopardized the long-term struggle for immigrant rights . . . Let us be clear. The groups desperately trying to defeat Prop. 187 were up against daunting electoral realities. But while a debate about electoral tactics is appropriate, we oppose any public documents that reduce the humanity of immigrants or reinforce the ideology of racism and xenophobia.

III.

Despite these and other differences in style and approach among members of the opposition, however,[29] what is striking in retrospect is the relatively narrow range of arguments that were made against Prop. 187 by opponents overall, and the corresponding absence of certain sorts of arguments almost entirely. Especially notable was the near-complete omission from the public debate of one particular opposing argument which might have seemed, in theory, an obvious one to make: this is the argument that Prop. 187 should be rejected on grounds that its treatment of undocumented immigrants is unjust.[30] I say that this argument might seem an obvious one to make given the express terms of the initiative itself. Prop. 187 is, after all, a law that specifically targets undocumented immigrants for social exile from the most basic institutions of our society; to say that it imposes on them a comprehensive form of legal apartheid is hardly mere hyperbole. One might think

See also Kadetsky, *supra* note 6, at 421 (Taxpayers Against Prop. 187, "an effort of the Republican-leaning P.R. firm Woodward & McDowell, has spent so much energy nodding its head about the presumed 'problem' of illegal immigration that individuals like Maria Erana from the American Friends Service Committee in San Diego have been left with the feeling that 'even if Prop. 187 is defeated, the use of these kind of arguments will be detrimental to all of us afterwards.'").

29. Perhaps the issue that most divided opponents of Prop. 187 concerned the demonstrations by Los Angeles students—including thousands of high school students who had walked out of classes—against the initiative in the days before the November balloting. The demonstrations' most controversial aspect was that many of the students carried Mexican and Salvadoran flags; and images of the flag-waving students were widely disseminated by the media during the days before the election. Dick Woodward of the consulting firm Woodward & McDowell, which managed the "No" campaign for Taxpayers Against 187, declared after the election that the marchers had "'polarized the issue.'" "'We cringed every time we saw [images of flag-waving students.] We didn't want them to march, because we knew exactly what would happen, and we have the polling data to show that's exactly what did happen.'" Patrick J. McDonnell, *State's Diversity Doesn't Reach Voting Booth*, L.A. TIMES, Nov. 10, 1994, at A1; *see also* Robert Suro, *California Teenagers Rise Up; Latino Marches Add Unpredictable Element as Proposition 187 Vote Nears*, WASH. POST, Nov. 5, 1994. Some members of Californians' United Against Prop. 187 also expressed concern about the marches on tactical grounds. Conversation with Lina Avidan (Feb. 11, 1995).

30. When I speak of the absence of justice arguments in the debate, I refer to the formal positions put out by the principle organizations opposing the initiative. Many people, of course, regarded the initiative as unfair to the immigrants and said so amongst themselves, but such sentiments were rarely expressed in general public fora. Journalist Ruben Martinez has recently made the same observation; *see* Ruben Martinez, *Fighting 187: The Different Opposition Strategies*, NACLA: Report On The Americas, Vol. XXIX, No. 3, Nov/Dec 1995, at 32 ("Absent from the discourse of most mainstream institutions (and elected officials) [was] word on the fate of the undocumented, who are, at least ostensibly, the direct target of 187.").

that the damaging effect of these measures on their designated objects would be an excellent—and indispensable—ground for political criticism.

Yet during the debate over Prop. 187, such arguments were rarely heard—with only two consistent exceptions. First, church-based organizations often objected to the initiative on grounds that it represented an affront to the immigrants' "human dignity."[31] Second, claims that the initiative treated its designated objects unjustly were heard sometimes on behalf of undocumented children—"innocent children," as they invariably were described, who should not be made to suffer for the sins of their parents.[32] Otherwise,[33] what the public mainly heard—in

31. Cardinal Roger Mahoney, Archbishop of Los Angeles, criticized Prop. 187 "within the biblical perspective that sees every human person as created in the image of God and therefore endowed with an innate dignity and worth. It is a society's duty, the Cardinal concludes, to protect this dignity, not to undermine it, as Proposition 187 would do." *The Territorial Imperative, California Style* (Editorial), AMERICA, Nov. 5, 1994, at 3. Archbishop John R. Quinn of the San Francisco Archdiocese also denounced Prop. 187 as "a great wound to humanity." *See* Coalition For Immigrants Rights and Services, 187 Update, No. 2, Dec. 8, 1994, at 3. *See also* Bee News Services, *Wilson Links Prop. 187, Mandatory ID Cards*, FRESNO BEE, Oct. 26, 1994, at A1 (At an event in Sacramento, local religious leaders called the measure an 'affront to humanity' that particularly targets innocent children . . . .[According to Bishop William Weigand,] "'we have to be concerned about the human dignity and the sacredness of all of our people, including those who happen to be illegal immigrants.'").

32. Of course, defending the interests of the "innocent child" assigns culpability to the adult undocumented immigrant by implication. Justice Brennan set out the contrast between innocent child and culpable adult in its fullest form in Plyler v. Doe, 457 U.S. 202 (1982), a case in which the Supreme Court struck down a state law effectively barring undocumented immigrant children from the public schools. The "innocent" undocumented immigrant children, he wrote, "'can affect neither their parents' conduct nor their own status.' Even if the State found it expedient to control the conduct of adults by acting against their children, legislation directing the onus of a parent's misconduct against his children does not comport with fundamental conceptions of justice." *Id.* at 220, (quoting Trimble v. Gordon, 430 U.S. 762, 770 (1977)). For further discussion of the culpable adult/innocent child distinction in the *Plyler* opinion, see Linda S. Bosniak, *Membership, Equality and The Difference That Alienage Makes*, 69 N.Y.U. Law Rev. 1047, 1121-23 (1994); *see also* T. ALEXANDER ALEINIKOFF, GOOD ALIENS, BAD ALIENS AND THE SUPREME COURT, IN DEFENSE OF THE ALIEN, 46, 48 (1986); Peter H. Schuck, *The Transformation of Immigration Law*, 84 COLUM. L. REV. 1, 55 (1988).

33. In addition to the exceptions indicated in the text, I should note that many individuals stepped forward to make their moral opposition known. For just one example, see Ernie McCray, *A School Principal Speaks Out Against 187* (Editorial), SAN DIEGO TRIBUNE, Nov. 4, 1995 *(reprinted in)* NACLA: Report on the Americas, Vol. XXIX, No. 3, Nov/Dec 1995:

> Despite the passage of Proposition 187, my disposition remains the same. I will not, in any way, play a role in willfully hurting another person.
>
> I have sat at the back of the bus. I've had someone tell me to get my 'black ass' out of a hotel when there were plenty of rooms available. I've skated at the rink on special 'Negro' days.
>
> I know the hurt and humiliation that come with being mistreated. So, needless

addition to charges of racism—were empirically-based predictions that the proposed policy provisions would fail to achieve their stated goal, and arguments highlighting the deleterious effects of the law on Americans (or Californians). The former arguments, of course, are not, by their terms, concerned with matters of justice at all, and although the latter arguments address human interests by addressing the law's social consequences, their concern is the law's effect on *American* well-being, and *American* interests. Even the racism argument, which is fundamentally an argument about justice, most often characterized the problem as one in which United States citizens or lawful permanent residents of color would be either maliciously or mistakenly ensnared by the initiative's provisions. The actual referent in the justice-based race argument, in other words, was generally not the undocumented immigrants themselves but a class of nationals and perhaps lawful permanent residents of color who would be (collaterally or directly) harmed by, or in the process of, efforts to crack down on those immigrants.[34]

The obvious question, therefore, is how we can account for the omission of the undocumented immigrant as an explicit subject of concern in most opponents' critiques of the initiative. If the initiative is meant to harm, and will in fact harm, a class of people residing and working in the state, why shouldn't the fact of this harm, both intended and actual, serve as grounds for political criticism?

In the case of many of Prop. 187's mainstream opponents, the reason for the omission is probably straightforward: they presume the moral interests of undocumented immigrants to be largely irrelevant. While these critics are concerned with the initiative's human costs, the costs they worry about are those borne by persons presumed to be members of the American national community. Undocumented immigrants—whose presence in this country, as these critics themselves often emphasized, is in violation of national law[35]—are understood to stand outside that community; and as a result, their interests (beyond those, presumably, in being afforded a minimum of fair procedural treatment) simply don't matter.

> to say, there is no way on God's green earth that I could ever treat fellow human beings with such disrespect that I would ask them to prove to me their right to be in this corner of the world.

Id.

34. *See, e.g.*, Guzman, *supra* note 9 ("'The general public can't tell the difference between an illegal immigrant and any other person of color,' said English major Ryan Masaaki Yokota. 'I personally stand to lose a lot if this passes.'")

35. *See supra* notes 22 and 23.

For other opponents, however, excising the undocumented and their experience from the "No On 187" message was, I think, more troubling. These latter critics—I will call them the "progressive" critics here—at times wished to make more affirmative arguments on behalf of the undocumented, but they also recognized that an apparently pro-immigrant message would backfire given the current hostile anti-immigrant mood in this country.[36] Indeed, since the pro-187 forces had characterized the presence of undocumented immigrants as precisely the problem the initiative would serve to redress, critics considered it good strategy to deflect the debate away from the undocumented, and focus on exposing the flaws in the proponents' own reasoning and methodology. For pragmatic reasons, in other words, they narrowed their arguments.[37]

On the other hand, the reluctance most progressive critics felt to argue affirmatively on behalf of undocumented immigrants (at least on behalf of undocumented adults) cannot be attributed entirely to the intense wave of anti-immigrant anxiety currently sweeping this country. For, in fact, advocates for immigrants have always had a difficult time figuring out how to frame affirmative arguments on behalf of the undocumented.[38] The reason is that advocates invariably find themselves

36. Conversation with Lina Avidan, Californians United Against Prop. 187, (Feb. 11, 1995).

37. Antonia Hernandez, President and General Counsel of the Mexican-American Legal Defense and Education Fund published an unusually candid statement about the pragmatic considerations involved in shaping the "No On 187" message. According to Hernandez:

> When Proposition 187 came around, we knew we had to strategize. We had to look into the mind of the person who would vote for Proposition 187. The coalition opposed to Proposition 187 hired the best political consultants. For this fight, they had to be Republicans. They also had to have won an initiative that dealt with controversial issues. We hired them, and they were good. They told me not to talk about compassion, so I did not. They said, "You cannot be out in the forefront . . . speaking on this issue. We will put you in the closet. We have got to find the League of Women Voters, people who look like they came from Nebraska, and Orange County types. We are going to get them to speak on the issue." They told me we would talk about self-interest and economics. I said, "Well, I want to win. Let's do it."

Antonia Hernandez, *The Shading of America: Keynote Address Before the 1995 National Conference of Law Reviews*, 26 ST. MARY'S L.J. 927 (1995).

38. This difficulty has existed, I should say, so long as undocumented immigrants have existed as such. Gerald Neuman suggests that the category undocumented immigrant, or "illegal alien," was not a meaningful category in American thought until at least 1875. *See* Gerald Neuman, *The Lost Century of American Immigration Law (1776-1875)*, 93 COLUM. L. REV. 1833, 1898-99 (1993).

On the other hand, formulating arguments on behalf of undocumented immigrants may have been somewhat easier a decade ago when advocates could more easily point to government inaction on the issue—and argue that penalizing the immigrants for the sins and omissions of

constrained by the near-sacred commitment in conventional political discourse to one of the cardinal norms of the system of state sovereignty — that countries have the rightful authority to control both the entry of foreigners into the national territory and (within certain limits) the terms of their membership once present. Advocates have long struggled to formulate a defense of immigrants' rights and interests without appearing to disregard the sovereignty imperative; in practical terms, they have sought to frame their advocacy in such a way as to avoid the (not uncommon) accusation that they favor "open borders"—a charge which, if it sticks, effectively writes them out of the political debate altogether.[39] Because undocumented immigrants appear to embody a violation

---

others is simply unfair. Today such arguments are less convincing—and are less often heard—given the enactment of employer sanctions legislation in 1986 and other concerted government efforts to crack down on undocumented immigration.

39. According to Pro-187 forces: "The defeat of Prop. 187 would be a declaration of open borders. Millions of new illegals will flood into California, swelling the hundreds of thousands who already come here every year." Save Our State (S.O.S.), Proposition 187, The "Save Our State" Initiative: The Fiction and the Facts, Undated Campaign Literature (on file with the author).

Notably, not all immigrants rights advocates are concerned that they will be charged with supporting "open borders;" some affirmatively embrace the notion. For example, the Raza Rights Coalition and the San Diego chapter of the National Chicano Moratorium Committee are sponsoring "a National March/Protest and counter-convention" to be held during the Republican National Convention in San Diego, California Saturday August 10, 1996. According to the organizations, the "demands of the march" will include the following:

Rescind Prop. 187
[. . .]
Abolish the I.N.S. and the Border Patrol
Tear down the false border between Mexico & the U.S.
Annul NAFTA
Impeach Pete Wilson

Electronic Mail Message from Raza Rights Coalition to subscribers of "187resist" mailing list, Aug. 29, 1995 (message on file with the author). *See also* Martinez, *supra* note 30, at 29, 30, 31 (describing "post-nationalist" anti-187 activists who "decry the line between San Diego and Tijuana. The new thinking—reflected in the popular slogan, 'We didn't cross the border, the border crossed us,'—re-imagines the old Mexico that governed the Southwest before the Mexican American War.").

On the other hand, many progressive advocates have publicly acknowledged the need for immigration control (humanely executed) precisely to avoid being dismissed from the debate (although they also point out that such control efforts are bound to be only marginally effective given the massive global forces, economic and social, which give rise to unauthorized immigration in the first place; *see* discussion accompanying notes 141-145, *infra.*) . Yet the advocates' willingness to state that border control is politically legitimate (within limits) has its own costs: it tends to reinforce the perception that the presence of these immigrants in this country is itself illegitimate, thus apparently undermining the force of their claims to just treatment (i.e., how can people whose presence here is in violation of law make claims upon the government for the benefits of membership?) Advocates often respond to this problem by pointing out that most

of state sovereignty by definition,[40] any direct defense of their interests can easily be read as an assault on the very legitimacy of state borders. Under the circumstances, advocates have often found it preferable to frame their message in other terms.

Still, the public outrage over undocumented immigration that is currently convulsing parts of this country has made the invocation of any argument that might possibly be construed as "pro-illegal" that much less attractive to the immigrants' advocates.[41] If ever there were a time

---

undocumented immigrants come here because there is a persistent demand for their labor, and that demand, in turn, is facilitated by government failure to enforce the wage and hour laws (making undocumented immigrants especially desirable to employers). According to this argument, the immigrants should not be penalized for the sins and omissions of others. This response, though powerful, creates its own difficulties since it suggests that undocumented immigrants undersell domestic labor—a point that advocates are often at pains to deny. For further discussion of the effect of undocumented workers on domestic labor, *see* text accompanying notes 114-115, *infra.*

40. *See generally* Linda S. Bosniak, *Human Rights, State Sovereignty and the Protection of Undocumented Migrants Under the International Migrant Workers Convention*, 25 INT'L MIGR. REV. 737 (1991).

41. The fact that the subject of illegal immigration is so highly charged and so politically treacherous arguably accounts for the strategy many immigrants' rights and ethnic rights groups have recently pursued in response to the immigration reform measures now pending in Congress. As of this writing, both the House and the Senate are considering legislation that would not only enhance control of undocumented immigration via greater border patrol and workplace enforcement expenditures, but would also substantially curtail legal immigration to this country. *See* S. 1394, S. 269, H.R. 2202. In response, many organizations have pursued a "splitting" strategy, urging that legal and illegal immigration be treated as separate and distinct issues. As the major national immigrants' rights coalition put it, joining the issues "unfairly and unwisely punishes legal immigrants and refugees as an overreaction to public concerns about illegal immigration. Moving a sweeping bill that blurs the distinction between illegal immigration and legal immigration will punish those who have played by the rules and waited in line to enter the U.S. legally." National Immigration Forum, H.R. 2202 Alert, Oct. 5, 1995 at 2 (on file with the author). *See also* Statement of Raul Yzaguirre, President, National Council of La Raza, House Judiciary Committee, June 29, 1995 ("The NCLR takes the position that the U. S. has a right and a duty to control its borders. We are in agreement with the overall goal of the current policy debate; indeed, the critical question is not, "Should the U.S. control its borders?" but rather, "How, do we achieve this goal?" . . . [But] NCLR is concerned that the legislation before this Subcommittee goes well beyond the question of preventing illegal entry, including sweeping and dramatic provisions to revise the legal immigration system as well. We believe such changes are unwarranted and unjustified; grappling with legal immigration in the same legislation as immigration control is likely to confuse the issues, and result in approaches which are inadequate on both fronts.").

This splitting strategy was the cornerstone of the Clinton Administration's immigration policy during the first part of his term. *See* Tom Morgenthau, *America: Still A Melting Pot?* NEWSWEEK, Aug. 9, 1993 ("Bill Clinton's goal, like that of most defenders of continued large-scale immigration, is to drive home the distinction between legal immigration (good) and illegal immigration (very, very bad)."). In fact, for the administration, demonstrating a willingness to crack down on undocumented immigration was understood as crucial precisely in order to safe-

that a "compassion" message might seem counterproductive, this is it.

IV.

Yet if fashioning affirmative arguments on behalf of undocumented immigrants represents a political tightrope act for anti-187 activists, it is also true that the difficulties faced by the initiative's progressive critics are not merely those of practical politics. Their dilemma goes deeper; it is also a dilemma of theory and of principle—and as such, it poses a fundamental intellectual challenge for the left overall. For strategy aside, there remains the question whether, in fact, we should regard Prop. 187's treatment of undocumented immigrants as unjust, and in what respects, if so. Although the injustice of the initiative's measures usually is regarded as axiomatic by immigrants' rights advocates, the question of the measure's justice turns out to be a far more difficult and more profound question for most progressives—including progressive legal scholars—than one might initially suppose.

At the heart of the difficulty is the question of how far progressives' articulated commitment to the pursuit of social justice can be understood to extend. Despite the enormous variety of substantive and methodological concerns that characterize contemporary progressive legal and political thought,[42] one of its consistent normative themes

---

guard the legal immigration system from the draconian cuts that some Republicans were threatening; the imperative was "to close the back door so as to keep the front door open," in the conventional formulation. Significantly, however, in 1995, the Congressionally-created U.S. Commission on Immigration Reform—headed by the late Democrat Barbara Jordan—concluded that *legal* immigration should likewise be curtailed, *see* U.S. COMMISSION ON IMMIGRATION REFORM, *Legal Immigration: Setting Priorities: A Report To Congress, Executive Summary*, 1995, and the Administration quickly embraced its conclusions. *See* Janet Hook, *Immigration Cutback Urged By U.S. Panel*, L.A. TIMES, June 8, 1995, at A1.

42. As I use the term here, "progressive thought" is concerned very broadly with advancing social criticism of various institutionalized relationships of subordination and exclusion. The term "progressive" can be construed in more affirmative and aspirational terms than these. (For one such understanding, see Robin West, *Constitutional Skepticism*, 72 B.U. L. REV. 765, 774 (1992) (characterizing the "progressive" vision as concerned with promoting "autonomy," "rewarding work, education and culture," and "life affirming connections with intimates and co-citizens" that are "free from the disabling fears of poverty, violence and coercion.")) But for my purposes here, I am concerned with progressive thought in its critical modes. There are many different scholarly enterprises that will qualify as "progressive" under this understanding, including (but not necessarily limited to) feminist theory, critical legal studies, critical race theory, and some strands of pragmatism, civic republicanism, and law and society scholarship (though not all work in these traditions will qualify all of the time). Once again, what links these projects most consistently for my purposes, are their normative commitments against vari-

has been a commitment to challenging the systematic exclusion and subordination of various classes of people in our society.[43] Progressives vari-

---

ous forms of social subordination and exclusion of classes of people in our society. On the other hand, substantial differences in approach among and between these projects certainly exist; for further discussion, *see* note 43, *infra.*

I should note that while I include various forms of "critical scholarship" in my list of progressive intellectual enterprises, not all self-described "critical theorists" will agree that their enterprise is a normative one. While one critical scholar descibes critical theory as entailing "an emancipatory interest" on the part of its practitioners, see IRIS MARION YOUNG, JUSTICE AND THE POLITICS OF DIFFERENCE 5 (1990), some post-modern critical theorists have criticized the what they have called the "emancipatory metanarratives" characterizing "modern" progressive thought, *e.g.*, JEAN-FRANCOIS LYOTARD, THE POSTMODERN CONDITION: A REPORT ON KNOWLEDGE (1984), and reject normative legal and political theory almost entirely. *E.g.*, Pierre Schlag, *Normative and Nowhere to Go*, 43 STAN. L. REV. 167 (1990); Pierre Schlag, *Normativity and the Politics of Form*, 139, U. PENN. L. REV. 801 (1991); Steven Winter, *For What It's Worth*, 26 LAW & SOC. REV. 789, 801-07 (1992). Others have argued, in response, that a left critique of normativity is itself incoherent. *See* Mark Tushnet, *The Left Critique of Normativity: A Comment*, 90 MICH. L. REV. 2325 (1992), and that there is no inherent contradicition between "a continuing loyalty to a postmodern perspective and the practical implementation of a radical political agenda." Allan C. Hutchinson, *Doing The Right Thing? Toward A Postmodern Politics*, 26 LAW & SOC. REV. 773, 774 (1992). Others still have criticized the post-modern critique of normativity on normative grounds. *See* Martha Minow, *Partial Justice: Law and Minorities, in* THE FATE OF LAW 15, 62-63 (Austin Sarat & Thomas R. Kearns eds., 1991):

> Unlike the postmodernists, whose politics often remain hidden or diffuse, the scholars from the margin [who advocate on behalf of women and people of color] feel the urgency of political action and the need for aspiration, direction and change . . . [P]ost modernists may respond, with some force, that I have fallen into the old trap of consoling myths of reason, and have made the particular mistake of treating identities and experiences as essential and grounded rather than shifting and containing their opposites . . . [But any] theory that seems to produce quiescence and a sense of helplessness is not good enough.

See also Martha Minow, *Incomplete Correspondence: An Unsent Letter To Mary Joe Frug*, 105 HARV. L. REV. 1096, 1101, n.19 (1992); *see also* Handler, *Postmodernism*, *supra.*

43. I make no claim that the literature I characterize as "progressive" is internally uniform and coherent in all respects. In fact, the various strands of work that maintain an "emancipatory" normative commitment, see note 42 *supra*, diverge over extremely important matters. In the first place, concerns with marginalization and exclusion, on the one hand, and subordination and domination, on the other, are not necessarily identical concerns nor are they necessarily expressed by the same authors—although they may be. Furthermore, within progressive literature, scholars often disagree amongst themselves about the ontological status of the various groups of people whose domination and/or exclusion is being protested. While some scholars emphasize the core and distinctive experience and "voice" of members of various subordinated and excluded groups—employing what Sandra Harding has called "standpoint epistemology," *see* SANDRA HARDING, THE SCIENCE QUESTION IN FEMINISM 26-29 (1986)—other scholars have criticized the "essentialism" of such formulations. One critique of essentialism protests the tendency in some progressive thought to treat the experience of membership in such groups as monolithic, thereby excluding diverse voices and perspectives *within* the group. *See, e.g.*, Kimberlé Crenshaw, *Mapping the Margins: Intersectionality, Identity Politics, and Violence Against Women of Color*, 43 STAN. L. REV. 1241, 1242 (1991) ("The problem with identity politics is . . . that it frequently conflates or ignores intragroup difference."); Angela P. Harris, *Race and Essentialisim in Femi-*

ously have championed breaking down boundaries against "outsiders,"[44] dismantling hierarchy and subordination,[45] "unmasking" and criticizing the exercise of power,[46] and attending to social "domination

---

nist Legal Theory, 42 STAN. L. REV. 581 (1990). A second critique of essentialism rejects treatments of identities per se as natural and essential, and emphasizes the contingency and social constructedness of these identity categories even as it pursues progressive critique. *See, e.g.*, AFTER IDENTITY: A READER IN LAW & CULTURE (Dan Danielsen & Karen Engle, eds., 1995) (a collection of essays which criticize the "essentialism" of much left "identity politics," but whose authors are, nevertheless, "committed to social struggle." Danielsen and Engle, Introduction, in *id.*, at xix). *See also* Cornell West, *The New Cultural Politics of Difference*, *in* THE CULTURAL STUDIES READER, 212, 213 (Simon During ed., 1993) (critiquing "essentialist rhetoric[ ]" of some African-American social criticism, but nevertheless embracing "demystificatory criticism" or "'prophetic criticism' . . . which makes explicit its moral and political aims. It is partisan, partial, engaged . . . yet always keeps open a sceptical eye to avoid dogmatic traps, premature closures, formulaic formulations, or rigid conclusions.").

While it is worth keeping these distinctions in mind, they are largely immaterial for my purposes here. To the extent they do bear upon the argument, I will make that clear.

44. *See, e.g.*, Martha Minow, Partial Justice, *supra* note 42, at 54 (approvingly describing "the 'outsiders' story" about recent developments in legal and political theory. "This is a story of exclusion and resistance. It is about the theories and experiences of people made marginal by the [insiders story]—women, children, members of racial and religious minorities, and disabled persons."); Mari Matsuda, *When the First Quail Calls: Mutiple Consciousness as Jurisprudential Method*, 11 WOMEN'S RIGHTS L. REP. 7, 9 (1988) (urging attention to "communities of outsiders struggling around their immediate needs—for jobs, for education, for personal safety."); Margaret Jane Radin, *The Pragmatist and the Feminist*, 63 S. CAL. L. REV. 1699, 1724 (1990) (urging importance in pragmatist thought of hearing "the outsiders who have been silent and are now trying to speak").

45. *See, e.g.*, CATHARINE A. MACKINNON, FEMINISM UNMODIFIED: DISCOURSES ON LIFE AND LAW (1987) (seeking to understand and undo "the subordination of women to men"); Duncan Kennedy, *Political Power and Cultural Subordination: A Case For Affirmative Action in Legal Academia*, *in* Danielson & Engle, *supra* note 43, at 84 (arguing that "we should structure the competition of racial and ethnic communities and social classes in markets and bureacracies, and the political system, in such a way that no community or class is systematically subordinated"); Ruth Colker, *Anti-Subordination Above All: Sex, Race and Equal Protection*, 61 N.Y.U. L. REV. 1003, 1007 (1986) ("[T]he anti-subordination perspective . . . seeks to eliminate the power disparities between men and women, and between whites and non-whites, through the development of laws and policies that directly redress those disparities."); Boaventura de Sousa Santos, *Three Metaphors for a New Conception of Law: The Frontier, The Baroque, and the South*, 29 LAW & SOC. REV. 569, 579 (1995) (urging critique of "all forms of subordination brought about by the capitalist world system: exploitation, expropriation, suppression, silencing, unequal differentiation, and so on.").

46. Mari J. Matsuda, *Voices of America: Accent, Antidiscrimination Law, and a Jurisprudence For The Last Reconstruction*, 100 YALE L.J. 1329, 1394 (1991) ("The work of feminists, critical legal scholars, critical race theorists, and other progressive scholars has been the work of unmasking: unmasking a grab for power disguised as science, unmasking a justification for tyranny disguised as history, unmasking an assault on the poor disguised as law."); MARTHA MINOW, MAKING ALL THE DIFFERENCE: INCLUSION, EXCLUSION AND AMERICAN LAW 112 (1990) (arguing that "attributions of difference should be sustained only if they do not express or confirm the distribution of power in ways that harm the less powerful and benefit the more powerful.").

and oppression"[47] as integral parts of the struggle for social justice. In so doing, they have urged greater attention to those on the losing end of such processes: to the silent, the marginalized, and those located (in one scholar's evocative phrase) "at the bottom."[48]

Undocumented immigrants would appear, at first glance, to constitute precisely the sort of class that progressives are usually most concerned about. These are people who routinely do much of our society's least desirable work—as dishwashers and janitors and sweatshop operatives and farm laborers and nannies and lawn care workers.[49] While

47. YOUNG, *supra* note 42, at 3. *See also* Catharine Frances Lee Ansley, *Stirring the Ashes: Race, Class and The Future of Civil Rights Scholarship*, 74 CORNELL L. REV. 993, 1024 n.129, 1073 (1989) (urging the importance of overcoming "relations of white dominance and nonwhite subordination," which she calls "white supremacy"); John Calmore, *Critical Race Theory, Archie Shepp, and Fire Music: Securing An Authentic Intellectual Life In a Multicultural World*, 65 S. CAL. L. REV. 2129, 2228 (1992) (arguing that "critical race scholarship provides an oppositional expression that challenges oppression"); Frances Olsen, *Statutory Rape: A Feminist Critique of Rights Analysis*, 63 TEX. L. REV. 387, 430 (1984) ("The conditions that make 'rights' seem necessary must be changed, and these conditions cannot be changed as long as women are oppressed."); Mary Joe Frug, *A Post-Modern Feminist Legal Manifesto (an Unfinished Draft)*, 105 HARV. L. REV. 1045, 1067 (1992) (endorsing "using law to oppose the oppression of women."); Richard Delgado, *Storytelling For Oppositionists and Others: A Plea For Narrative*, 87 MICH. L. REV. 2411, 2437 (1989) (urging process of storytelling because "stories about oppression, about victimization, about one's own brutalization—far from deepening the despair of the oppressed, lead to healing, liberation, mental health."); Martha A. Mahoney, *Whiteness and Women, In Practice and Theory: A Reply to Catherine MacKinnon*, 5 YALE J. L. & FEM. 217, 250 (1993) ("I agree with the many feminists who assert the necessity of feminist struggle against all oppression.").

48. Mari Matsuda, *Looking To The Bottom: Critical Legal Studies and Reparations*, 22 HARV. C.R.-C.L. L. REV. 323, (1987). *See generally* Margaret Jane Radin, *The Pragmatist and the Feminist*, 63 S. CAL. L. REV. 1699, 1720, 1724 (1990) (urging importance in pragmatist thought of "accepting the significance of the perspective of the oppressed" and hearing "the outsiders who have been silent and are now trying to speak"); Patricia Williams, *The Obliging Shell*, *in* PATRICIA WILLIAMS, THE ALCHEMY OF RACE AND RIGHTS 98, 121 (1991) ("Blacks and women are the objects of a constitutional omission that has been incorporated into a theory of neutrality . . . .It is thus that affirmative action is an affirmation; the affirmative act of hiring—or hearing—blacks is a recognition of individuality that includes blacks as a social presence"); Frank Michelman, *Law's Republic*, 97 YALE L.J. 1493, 1529 (1988) ("[T]he pursuit of political freedom through law depends on 'our' constant reach for inclusion of the other, of the hitherto excluded—which in practice means bringing to legal-doctrinal presence the hitherto absent voices of emergently self-conscious social groups."); Minow, *Making All The Difference*, *supra* note 46, at 16 (urging "taking the perspective of the traditionally excluded or marginal group" as a means of "remak[ing] the meaning of difference.").

49. Undocumented immigrant workers in this country are largely concentrated in the service sector (especially domestic and janitorial services and in restaurants); in the low-wage manufacturing sector (especially garment, electronics and footwear), in construction, and in agriculture (as farm-workers). *See* Jeffrey Passel, *Undocumented Immigration*, in IMMIGRATION AND AMERICAN PUBLIC POLICY, 487 ANNALS OF THE AMERICAN ACADEMY OF POLITICAL AND SOCIAL SCIENCE (1986), at 181, 192-94; SASKIA SASSEN, THE MOBILITY OF LABOR AND CAPITAL 79-82

they formally are afforded the minimum rights of personhood under the law, they lie entirely outside the law's protections for many purposes,[50] and they live subject to the fear of deportation at virtually all times.[51] It would be hard to find a group of people who live further at the margins, or closer to "the bottom," than the undocumented.

As a practical matter, however, undocumented immigrants have rarely been treated as the explicit subjects of progressives' concern. Outside the relatively small field of immigration law, undocumented immigrants—and noncitizens in general—have been largely absent in the work of progressive legal theorists.[52] Indeed, in the various theoretical literatures on exclusion and subordination, there is little indication that the subject of alienage—or of exclusion on account of alienage—is even on the radar screen; most progressives simply seem to ignore

---

(1988); Saskia Sassen, *Why Migration?* 26 Report on the Americas (NACLA) 14, 17-18 (1992). Their wages, while not routinely below minimum-wage, are low relative to U.S. workers. BARRY R. CHISWICK, ILLEGAL ALIENS: THEIR EMPLOYMENT AND THEIR EMPLOYERS 145 (1988). For discussion of the economic effects of undocumented immigrants, *see* notes 114-115, *infra*.

50. *See generally* Linda S. Bosniak, *Exclusion and Membership: The Dual Identity of the Undocumented Worker Under United States Law*, 1988 WIS. L. REV. 955 1988. In particular, undocumented immigrants are ineligible for virtually all forms federally-funded public benefits. *See* Passel & Fix, *supra* note 12, at 62. They are effectively denied the right to obtain drivers licences in many states, *see, e.g.*, Jerry Gilliam, *DMV, INS to Check New License Applicants*, L.A. TIMES, June 22, 1994, at B3 (California); Marcy C. Fitzgerald, *Bills Would Make Illegal Aliens Illegal Drivers*, TRENTON TIMES, July 25, 1992, at A1 (New Jersey); virtually all states deny them unemployment compensation insurance, *see, e.g.*, CALIFORNIA UNEMP. INS. CODE § 1264(a) (1995) (limiting unemployment benefits to aliens who were lawfully present at time qualifying employment was performed); TEXAS LAB. CODE § 207.043(a) (1996) (same); FLA. STAT. § 443.101(7) (1995) (same); and some states deny them, or substantially limit their access to, worker's compensation and wrongful death benefits. *See, e.g.*, Collins v. New York City Health and Hospital Corporation, 206 N.Y.L.J. 27 (1991) (holding undocumented immigrant cannot receive wrongful death benefits for lost wages at U.S. rates); Iver Peterson, *Senate Votes To Toughen Stance on Illegal Aliens*, N.Y. TIMES, Oct. 20, 1995 at BG (describing New Jersey State Senate proposal to deny workers compensation payments to undocumented aliens). Furthermore, even when they are formally protected under the law, they are often ineligible for any remedy associated with the law's violation. *See, e.g.*, Bosniak, *Exclusion and Membership*, *supra*, at 985, 1022-35 (describing lack of availability of remedies for undocumented immigrants who are victims of labor and employment law violations); Maria Ontiveros, *To Help Those Most in Need: Undocumented Workers' Rights and Remedies Under Title VII*, 20 N.Y.U. REV. L. & SOC. CHANGE 607 (1993-94) (same in employment discrimination context).

51. *See generally* Bosniak, *Exclusion and Membership*, *supra* note 50. *See also* text accompanying notes 88-90, *infra*.

52. For examples of scholarship associated with the field of immigration law which examine and critique the status of undocumented immigrants in the United States, see Bosniak, *Exclusion and Membership*, *supra* note 50, Kevin Johnson, *Los Olvidados: Images of the Immigrant, Political Power of Noncitizens, and Immigration Law Enforcement*, 1993 B.Y.U. L. REV. 1139 (1993); Gerald Lopez, *Undocumented Mexican Migration: In Search of a Just Immigration Law and Policy*, 28 U.C.L.A. L. REV. 615 (1981); Ontiveros, *supra* note 50.

the issue of immigration status altogether.[53] One measure of this inattention can be found in the routine inventories of oppressed or excluded groups that progressive theorists often set out in their work. Martha Minow, for example, writes of progressives' concern in recent years with the exclusion of "women, children, disabled people and members of religious, racial and linguistic minorities," and of "other disfavored groups includ[ing] incarcerated felons, prostitutes, drug addicts, alcoholics, persons with terminal illnesses, and persons with contagious diseases."[54] When the inventories get as specific as this, the omission of noncitizens from the list is striking.

The lack of attention paid to alienage, and to illegal alienage in particular, as a category of exclusion and domination in much of the progressive literature no doubt can be accounted for in a variety of ways. Some critics, first of all, may assume that undocumented immigrants are, in fact, present in the critical discourse by way of the attention progressives pay to the exclusion of racial, cultural and linguistic minorities in this country. Necessary as such attention is, however, subsuming alienage-based exclusion into analyses of racial and cultural marginalization is problematic, not merely because not all undocumented immigrants belong to ethnic and racial minority groups,[55] but also because it fails to capture what is specific about the exclusion experienced by undocumented immigrants, which is constituted, in substantial

---

53. One partial exception is the examination by Kimberlé Crenshaw of the way in which the irregular legal status of undocumented immigrants works in tandem with racism and gender oppression to produce the specific form of powerlessness experienced by battered immigrant women of color. *See* Kimberlé Crenshaw, *Mapping the Margins*, *supra* note 43, at 1246-50. Yet Crenshaw's analysis only goes part of the way, for although she *shows* that immigration status structures the experience of these women, she does not *theorize* it: rather, she characterizes the problem as one that arises "[w]here systems of race, gender and class domination converge." *Id.* at 1246. The issue of alienage, *per se*, in other words, is obscured.

54. *See, e.g.*, Minow, *Partial Justice*, *supra* note 42, at 36, 36 n.20. Elsewhere Minow adds "age, height, weight, family membership [and] sexual orientation" to the list.). Minow, *Making All The Difference*, *supra*, note 46, at 112. In this latter list, Minow also mentions "nationality" as a category of exclusion. *Id.* By including nationality, she acknowledges that foreign origin or citizenship can give rise to exclusionary attitudes and practices. However, the word "nationality" is most often associated with "the status of belonging to a particular nation," AMERICAN HERITAGE DICTIONARY OF THE ENGLISH LANGUAGE 874 (1992); and references to exclusion on account of nationality tend to suggest exclusion based on dislike for the particular nation from which a person hails (i.e., national origin). Alienage, in contrast, denotes the lack of full formal membership (i.e., citizenship) in the state, irrespective of national origin.

55. Although the great majority of undocumented immigrants are from Latin America or Asia, at least 13 % of the undocumented population is of European and Canadian descent. FIX & PASSEL, *supra* note 12, at 24.

part, by their irregular status under the country's immigration laws.[56] Another possible reason for the absence of attention to alienage in most progressive scholarship is that noncitizens—especially undocumented noncitizens—have mobilized politically *qua* noncitizens only rarely,[57] and they are quite unlikely to affirmatively assert their lack of citizenship as an identity to be proclaimed and revalued; in other words, there has been no self-conscious mass social movement based specifically on alienage—and on illegal alienage especially—to spur Americans to sit up and take notice. At the same time, public policy debate regarding the general status of noncitizens—undocumented noncitizens especially—has been relatively limited until quite recently.

Today, however, the subjects of alienage and citizenship are squarely on the political agenda in this country.[58] It therefore seems reason-

---

56. *See* text accompanying notes 88-90, *infra*.

57. Various immigrant-based organizations have been actively lobbying against restrictionist immigration reform and anti-immigration welfare reform legislation now pending in Congress. However, these organizations are usually identified with particular ethnic groups or nationalities, and their members are mostly citizens. *See, e.g.*, Testimony of Raul Yzaguirre, President, National Council of La Raza, before the House Judiciary Committee (June 29, 1995) (in testimony on pending immigration legislation, stating that two-thirds of the national Hispanic organization's members are "not immigrants"). Also politically active on immigration issues are resettlment service organizations, immigrants rights groups, and church-based organizations, but the work of these groups is undertaken largely by Americans on behalf of the immigrant and refugee communities, and not by the immigrants themselves.

58. I refer not merely to the campaign over Prop. 187 in California, and its likely analogues in other states, *see* text accompanying notes 1-5, *infra*, but also the debates in Congress about whether noncitizens, including lawful permanent resident aliens, should be precluded from receiving virtually all public benefits, *see, e.g.*, Personal Responsibility and Work Opportunity Act of 1995, 104 H.R. 4 (1995) (Act that would deny most legal immigrants SSI and Food Stamps, and would permit states to deny such aliens other social benefits, including AFDC and non-emergency Medicaid) (vetoed by Pres. Clinton, January 9, 1996); *see also* sources cited *supra* note 3. I refer, in addition, to federal and state efforts to amend the federal Constitution to deny birthright citizenship to children born in the United States of undocumented parents. *See* Citizenship Amendment Introduced, United Press International (Lexis), May 25, 1995 (Twenty House members introduced measure that would amend the Constitution's guarantee of U.S. citizenship to any child born on U.S. soil by requiring that at least one parent have lawful status under federal immigration laws); Michael Winters, *Prop. 187 Sequel Would Narrow Door To Citizenship*, S.F. EXAM., Oct. 16, 1995, at A4 (describing planned California ballot initiative which would register state's support to amend the federal constitution so to deny birthright citizenship to children born in this country of undocumented alien parents.) *See also supra* note 3. I should note that debates over all of these measures are taking place alongside ongoing public controversy over the future of the country's immigration policy. Congress is currently considering legislation that will substantially limit the numbers and categories of immigrants admitted, and will further enhance border patrol efforts and employer sanctions regulations. *See generally* S. 1394, S. 269, H.R. 2202. For an overview of the pending immigration reform legislation, see *Senate Subcommittee Approves Legal Immigration Reform Measure*, 72 INTERPRETER RELEASES 1605 (1995).

able to assume that the issue will increasingly capture the attention of progressive scholars as well. But even if progressives become more attuned in the coming years to alienage as a category of exclusion and subordination, it is nonetheless hardly clear that undocumented immigrants can simply and unproblematically be added to "the list." The reason, I want to suggest, is that the particular form of marginalization that undocumented immigrants experience, which derives from their legal status as outsiders to the national society, is a marginalization which, at least in part, is presupposed, and possibly even required, by the terms of much progressive thought itself.

Here is the problem: Despite progressives' commitment to challenging systemic forms of subordination and marginalization, the political and legal landscape they are concerned with is most often a national landscape, and the boundaries they seek to dismantle are, most often, political and legal boundaries that exist within the already bounded community of the nation-state. Although there are exceptions,[59] most progressive legal scholarship produced in this country devotes nearly exclusive attention to relationships among people who are already presumed to be national community members, and in this work, the nation's boundaries provide the frame for analysis.[60] Sometimes, this

59. The principal exceptions are in the field of progressive international legal scholarship. See text accompanying notes 121-124, infra.

60. To the extent that the subject of progressive legal scholars's attention is American law, they are naturally apt to concern themselves with the community in which that law is effective and relevant—i.e., the United States. Much progressive legal scholarship falls into this category. For example, progressive constitutional scholarship in this country is fundamentally concerned with the significance of the American constitutional document and its readings to those to whom the Constitution is addressed: "We The People." *See, e.g.*, Robin West, *Constitutional Scepticism*, 72 B.U. L. REV. 765 (1992) (urging attention to the question "whether our Constitution is *desirable* . . . [whether it] further[s] the 'good life' for the individuals, communities, and subcommunities it governs"); MARK TUSHNET, RED, WHITE AND BLUE: A CRITICAL ANALYSIS OF CONSTITUTIONAL LAW (1988); Frank Michelman, *Law's Republic*, 97 YALE L.J. 1493, 1499-1500 (1988) (analyzing "American constitutionalism.") Likewise, most critical race theory is concerned with the subordination and exclusion of people of color in the American legal context, *see* Kimberlé Crenshaw, *Race, Reform and Retrenchment: Transformation and Legitimation in Antidiscrimination Law*, 101 HARV. L. REV. 1331, 1336 (1988) (describing her work as a "consideration of race in the American legal context"). And so forth.

At the same time, methodological approaches in progressive legal theory which emphasize interpretive readings of law also often lead to national preoccupations. To the extent, for example, that progressive scholars understand law as "a communal language"—one through which "individuals and groups make meaning" collectively, *see* Martha Minow, *Interpreting Rights: An Essay for Robert Cover*, 96 YALE L.J. 1860, 1861, 1862 (1987), they are going to be naturally inclined to attend to the community of those who collectively speak that language and make those meanings—which very often will be a community constituted in national terms. *E.g.*, *Id.*, at 1911 ("Rights can be understood as a kind of communal discourse that reconfirms the diffi-

frame is made explicit, as when scholars directly invoke the United States or "America"[61] or the constitutional Republic[62] as their community of normative concern. More often, it is entirely unspoken;[63] the fact that the normative world which preoccupies progressives is a national world is apparently so obvious, so much a given, as to require no specific assertion at all.[64] In either case, progressives tend to pos-

cult commitment to live together even while engaging in conflicts and struggles.").

61. As I indicated in note 60, supra, many progressive legal scholars make clear that they are concerned in their work with social and legal relations which prevail within the bounds of the United States; their work expressly addresses American law and American society. *See, e.g.*, Radin & Michelman, *Pragmatist and Post Structuralist Critical Legal Practice*, 139 U. PENN. L. REV. 1019, 1048 (1991) (arguing that "hierarchies of race and sex remain cruelly entrenched, economically socially and culturally, in American life," and urging attention to "the informal, ebedded, transinstitutional oppressions of life in America.")

Sometimes, however, the United States appears not merely as the presumed backdrop for the analysis, but as an affirmative normative presence or value. Thus, Mari Matsuda professes a belief in "a collective national soul," Matsuda, *Voices of America*, *supra* note 46, at 129, and she likewise writes: "I can say that as an American, I am choosing as my heritage the 200 years of struggle by poor and working people, by Native Americans, by women, by people of color, for dignified lives in this nation." Matsuda, *When The First Quail Calls*, *supra* note 44, at 10. *See also* Calmore, *supra* note 47, at 2228, 2230 (urging a struggle "to bring oppressed peoples into the national community as American citizens or members of society who are viably integrated within the nation's structures of opportunity, power and privilege" and concluding the article with the query: "Can we save the children so that they will have their chance to save the nation?").

For further discussion of affirmative invocations of the concept of national community in progressive thought, *see* text accompanying notes 109-111, *infra*.

62. In their work, progressive civic republicans likewise invoke a normative community—the "political community," or the Republic— which is more-or-less explicitly depicted as the community of the nation-state. *See, e.g.*, Frank Michelman, *Conceptions of Democracy: The Case of Voting Rights*, 41 FLA. L. REV. 441, 445 (1989) ("The special mark of republican constitutional thought is affirmation of . . . a common interest existent and determinable . . . at the encompassing level of the sovereign or law-making state."); Stephen M. Feldman, *Republican Revival/Interpretive Turn*, 1992 WIS. L. REV. 679, 717 (using terms "political community" and "state" interchangably.). Notably, members of the Republic are usually referred to in this literature as "citizens." *See, e.g.*, Michelman, *Law's Republic*, *supra* note 48, at 1503, 1531 (defining "citizenship" as "participation as an equal in public affairs, in pursuit of the common good," whether directly through the state or through various arenas in (national) civil society.).

63. However, even if the national character of the social world that concerns them is not specifically acknowledged, the idea is often conveyed by other means. Use of the terms "society" and "culture" commonly serve as proxies. *See, e.g.*, Ruth Colker, *Anti-Subordination Above All: Sex, Race, and Equal Protection*, 61 N.Y.U. L. REV. 1003, 1007 (1986) ("Under the anti-subordination perspective, it is inappropriate for certain groups in society to have subordinated status because of their lack of power in society as a whole."); Elizabeth Schneider, *The Dialectics of Rights and Politics: Perspectives from the Women's Movement*, *in* AT THE BOUNDARIES OF LAW: FEMINISM AND LEGAL THEORY 302 (Martha Albertson Fineman & Nancy Sweet Thomadsen eds., 1991) ("The idea that legal rights have some intrinsic value is widespread in our culture.").

64. *See* R.B.J. Walker, *State Sovereignty, Global Civilization and the Rearticulation of Po-*

sess what we might call a "national imagination,"[65] according to which political life is understood to take place in the territorial nation-state, among members of that state.[66] But if the presumptive normative uni-

---

litical Space, Princeton University, Center For International Studies, 1988, at 3, 22 ("Most political ideologies and political aspirations now take statist forms of political community as given . . . .[For] those concerned with justice, freedom, community and progress within states . . . sovereignty has become normalized.").

65. The phrase is Richard Rorty's. *See* Rorty, *supra* note 1. (Note, however, that although Rorty asserts that "[p]olitical imagination is, almost always, national imagination," *id.*, he nevertheless believes that the political imagination of the American academic left is insufficiently national in character. *See* Richard Rorty, *The Unpatriotic Academy*, N.Y. TIMES (op-ed), Feb. 13, 1994, at E15 (critiquing academic left on grounds that "it is unpatriotic. In the name of 'the politics of difference,' it refuses to rejoice in the country it inhabits. It repudiates the idea of national identity, and the emotion of national pride."))

For diverse critical analyses of the "national" or "statist" imagination and its construction, see BENEDICT ANDERSON, IMAGINED COMMUNITIES: REFLECTIONS ON THE ORIGIN AND SPREAD OF NATIONALISM (1983); R.B.J. WALKER, INSIDE/OUTSIDE; INTERNATIONAL RELATIONS AS POLITICAL THEORY (1993); Martha Nussbaum, *Patriotism and Cosmopolitanism*, XIX BOSTON REVIEW No. 5, at 3 (1994).

66. A word about terminology is in order here. When I use the phrase "national imagination," I refer to a habit of thought which presumes that political community is constituted by ties amongst members of the nation-state, and that the boundaries of the nation-state represent the horizons of political community. Later in the text, I similarly refer to what I call the "nationalist premise," or the "normative nationalism" imbedded in much progressive thought; by these phrases, I refer to the habit (conscious or not) of granting normative priority to nation-state members over perceived outsiders to the nation-state.

Yet use of the words "national" and "nationalist" in this context may lead to some confusion. I should make clear that I do *not* use the words to specifically refer to the distinctive ethnic or cultural identity of a people, as many analyts do. *See, e.g.*, ERNEST GELLNER, NATIONS AND NATIONALISM 125 (1983) (defining nationalism as "the principle of homogenous cultural units as the foundations of political life"). Rather, in this context, I use the adjectives "national" and "nationalist" to refer to the nation-state and its attributes. In this usage, it does not matter whether any particular nation-state defines itself largely in ethno-cultural terms, in civic-political terms or otherwise; the word "national" simply serves as an adjectival shorthand for the nation-state, however constituted. This understanding of the term is conventional in much political thought: For example, we commonly speak of "international" rather than "interstate" relations or society, and members of a state are commonly referred to as its "nationals." In such usage, "nation" refers to the (currently predominant) unit of human political organization which is understood to possesses sovereignty; i.e., the nation-state. This usage of the term is widespread not merely in popular discourse but among academics as well.

In fact, this latter, state-linked understanding of the word "national" is the sense in which Rorty (whose phrase "national imagination" I have borrowed) uses the term; when he speaks of a "national imagination," he speaks of the imagination associated with people's ties to particular nation-state communities, without any presumption that these ties are specifically cultural or ethnic in character. The example he gives is Roberto Unger's (asserted) imaginitive ties to Brazil, *see* Rorty, *supra* note 1, a country which, as it happens, is a decidedly multicultural and multiethnic state.

In any event, because I use the terms "national" and "nationalist" to refer to attributes of nation-states, I sometimes substitute the terms "statist" or "statism" to describe the habits of mind I am concerned with. Some have critiqued the conflation of state and nation in contem-

verse in the work of most progressive American scholars is the American national community, then undocumented immigrants, who are nonmembers of the American state by legal definition, present what can only be described as an awkward case.

I do not mean to suggest that progressives' predominantly national vision of social life leaves them unequipped or unprepared in all circumstances to treat undocumented immigrants as subjects of their normative concern. On the contrary, progressives can issue powerful criticism of measures like Prop. 187 from within a national idiom. They can insist, for example, that—notwithstanding the circumstances of their entry—those undocumented immigrants who live and work among us are entitled to the basic rights of (national) membership by virtue of their contributions to our society, and that to treat them as outsiders and deny them such rights is both a formalist lie and a means of ensuring their continued subordination in the workplace and elsewhere.[67] They also can protest the social exclusion, by law, of undocumented immigrants on grounds that this country's own articulated political ideals cannot permit it; a democratic and egalitarian political community, they can insist, cannot abide the sort of entrenched caste structure which such exclusion produces.[68]

But compelling as these arguments are, they only go so far. The problem is that the presence of undocumented immigrants does not merely implicate social relations within the national society (undocumented immigrants are not merely "inside-outsiders," to borrow a phrase[69]), nor do they simply spring up here by magic. Rather, they come, from the outside, as part of a global process of formally unau-

---

porary political discourse, *see, e.g.*, Walker Connor, *A Nation Is a Nation, Is A State, Is an Ethnic Group, Is A . . .*, *in* NATIONALISM 36, 38 (John Hutchinson & Anthony D. Smith eds., 1994) (criticizing "the propensity to employ the term nation as a substitute for that territorial juridical unit, the state"); *see also* WALKER, INSIDE/OUTSIDE, *supra* note 65, at 164 (critiquing the common "presumption that sovereignty, state, and nation are more or less interchangeable terms."). On the other hand, it has also been suggested that the fact that such substitutions are as common as they are "indicat[es] profound theoretical controversy" about the relationship between the terms. WALKER, *supra* note 65, at 186, n.4.

67. This argument has been made by immigration scholars. *See, e.g.*, Johnson, *Los Olvidados*, *supra* note 52; Bosniak, *Exclusion and Membership*, *supra* note 50.

68. *See, e.g.*, KENNETH L. KARST, BELONGING TO AMERICA: EQUAL CITIZENSHIP AND THE CONSTITUTION 142-43 (1989); Bosniak, *Immigrants, Preemption and Equality*, *supra* note 14, at 379.

69. Lea Brilmayer, *Carolene, Conflicts, and the Fate of the 'Inside-Outsider,'* 134 U. PENN. L. REV. 1291 (1986). According to Brilmayer, "[t]he individual who does not participate in political processes, but who is nevertheless subject to the results of those processes, is the 'inside-outsider.' Such persons are inside from the perspective of who can be bound but outside from the perspective of who can participate." *Id.* at 1316.

thorized movements of people across national borders. And sooner or later, progressives must face the question not merely of how undocumented immigrants should be treated once they are here, but also of how to approach the fact of their arrival in the first place. Progressives must, in other words, determine their position on enforcement of national borders against undocumented immigrants.

Yet on this question—the question of the legitimacy of enforcement of the nation's borders, it turns out that progressive scholars are far less equipped or inclined (or both) to offer critique.[70] Such disinclination or incapacity might at first glance seem unlikely, since progressives are committed, as we have seen, to challenging officially-sponsored social exclusions of classes of people; and enforcement of the border against aspiring entrants, which entails a literal, physical exclusion backed by force, could reasonably be described as the ultimate form of social exclusion. When the provenance of the great majority of these aspiring immigrants is taken into account—they are most often from less developed countries with a history of economic and cultural subordination to the United States;[71] they are most often people of color; and they are very often from the laboring classes in their home societies[72]—their

70. Usually, progressive scholars tend to avoid or otherwise deflect the question because it is so difficult and discomfitting—and this is something for which they have been criticized. *See Statement of David Martin*, 1994 ASIL PROCEEDINGS 461-462 (1994) (inquiring, in response to panel critical of exclusionary immigration rhetoric and policy: "Is there legitimacy for some restriction? What would the panel propose as a base for immigration control, even if it is only a minimalist system?").

71. For discussions of the way in which many current countries of immigration are historically linked to the United States through histories of colonialism or other forms of economic subordination, *see, e.g.*, ALEJANDRO PORTES & RUBEN G. RUMBAUT, IMMIGRANT AMERICA: A PORTRAIT 225 (1990) ("The countries supplying these large contingents of [Hispanic] immigrants were, each in its time, subjects of an expansionist pattern through which successive U.S. governments sought to remold [this] country's immediate periphery. This pattern of intervention undermined the framework of social and economic life constructed under Spanish colonial rule and reoriented it toward North American institutions and culture. The restructuring process preceded, not followed, the onset of massive labor migrations that gave rise to today's major Hispanic communities."); Philip L. Martin, The United States: Benign Neglect Toward Immigration, in *Controlling Immigration, supra* note 20, at 89 ("[M]ost of today's migration streams have their origins in the colonial or labor recruitment policies of industrial countries."); SASKIA SASSEN, THE MOBILITY OF LABOR AND CAPITAL 9 (1988) (arguing that "U.S. business, military, or diplomatic activities were a strong presence in countries that have significant migration to the U.S.").

72. Analysts estimate that the great majority of undocumented immigrants in the United States are from developing countries in the Third World. According to a recent Immigration and Naturalization Service study, 62% of the undocumented population residing in the United States in 1992 were from Central America and the Caribbean (with only one half of these, or 31% overall, from Mexico), 11% from Asia, 6% from South America, 4% from Africa and 13%

exclusion can seem more problematic still.

Yet as it turns out, progressive thought, more often than not, tends to normatively embrace the very national boundary which serves to effect, and justify, the immigrants' exclusion. This embrace takes both explicit and implicit forms. Explicitly, the left has a long history of national protectionist commitments in economic matters, among which immigration protectionism has figured prominently. To this day, much of the American labor movement is committed to restricting unauthorized immigration—even though many unions support a generous legal immigration policy and labor rights for those who are here.[73] Many environmental organizations express even more restrictive views,[74] and

---

from Europe and Canada. Robert Warren, *Estimates of the Resident Illegal Alien Population: October 1992*, Immigration and Naturalization Service (Aug. 1993).

Furthermore, while many analysts have emphasized that undocumented immigrants are not the very poorest and least educated members of their home societies, *see, e.g.*, Passel, *supra* note 49, at 194, some have suggested that they are nevertheless "unskilled not only relative to the native U.S. population, but also relative to [their home] population." *See* GEORGE J. BORJAS, FRIENDS OR STRANGERS: THE IMPACT OF IMMIGRANTS ON THE U.S. ECONOMY 69 (1990).

73. For samples of organized labor's positions on immigration regulation today, see, e.g., Statement by Rudy Oswald, Director of Economic Research, AFL-CIO, to the Senate Judiciary Subcommittee on Immigration, Sept. 13, 1995 (on file with the author) ("We believe that United States workers should have a first claim on jobs in the U.S.A. Wages and working conditions in the United States should not be undermined by workers from other lands."); Statement By Markley Roberts, Assistant Director of Economic Research, AFL-CIO, To The House Committee on the Judiciary, Subcommittee on Immigration, Federal News Service, May 17, 1995 (supporting "employer sanctions as the most effective way to deter employers from hiring illegal aliens."). *See also* Complaints of Immigrants Come From All Colors, Morning Edition, National Public Radio, July 26, 1993 (reporting that William Lucey, President of the Coalition of Black Trade Unionists, is "among a number of black, Hispanic and Korean leaders who signed on to a petition sent to President Clinton last month urging an immediate moratorium on immigration.").

Nevertheless, as I note in the text, many unions have come to embrace the view that undocumented immigrants who are present and working should be organized—on the grounds that not doing so ultimately serves to undermine unions' power. *See, e.g.*, United Electrical, Radio and Machineworkers of America, Worker Unity: Organizing and Representing Undocumented Workers, Nov. 1987; David Bacon, *Unions Take New Look At Immigrants*, PAC. NEWS SERV., Apr. 20-24, 1992; Peter Rachleff, *Seeds of A Labor Resurgency: A Page From History?* NATION, Feb. 21, 1994. Many also support more vigorous enforcement of employment-protective laws as a means of deterring employers from seeking out undocumented immigrants as employees. *See* Statement of John J. Sweeney International President Service Employees International Union, [now-President of the AFL-CIO], Sept. 19, 1995, Before The House Judiciary Committee (Full Committee Markup, Immigration Overhaul) (urging a "focus on raising labor standards and improving enforcement in order to reduce the attractiveness of undocumented workers to employers."); Statement by Markley Roberts, *supra*. For further discussion of the increasing receptivity of some unions to organizing undocumented workers, *see* Bosniak, *Exclusion and Membership*, *supra* note 52, at 995-96.

74. *See, e.g.*, *NPG Says 'Yes' To Simpson Immigration Control Bill*, PR NEWSWIRE, Mar. 14,

some racial and ethnic rights organizations have supported restrictionist policies as well.[75] The core impulse fueling left protectionism is the de-

---

1995 ("The national population and environmental organization Negative Population Growth, or NPG, Inc. today announced that it is moving aggressively into the immigration policy front in an effort to advance immigration reduction legislation in the 104th Congress.") Sierra Club Books recently published a volume which calls for drastic reductions in legal immigration and "serious efforts" to "put an end to clandestine immigration." LEON BOUVIER & LINDSEY GRANT, HOW MANY AMERICANS? POPULATION, IMMIGRATION AND THE ENVIRONMENT 115 (1994). Nationally, the Sierra Club has been wracked by an internal struggle during the past two years about the policy it will adopt on immigration matters. Edward Epstein et al., *Campaign Watch*, S.F. CHRON., Oct. 7, 1994, at A12; Barbara Ruben, *Coming to America: Immigrants and the Environment*, 26 ENVIRON. ACTION MAG. 23, June 22, 1994. (The organization nevertheless came out against California's Prop. 187 in 1994. *See* Epstein et al., *supra).* The National Audubon Society has likewise been divided on the issue of immigration. *See* Ruben, *supra*.

Other national environmental organizations that have made immigration restriction a priority include Population-Environmental Balance and Carrying Capacity Network. *See* Population-Environment Balance, Letter to Concerned Citizen (undated, received November 13, 1995) (on file with the author) ("For the 263 million residents of the United States, both native-and foreign-born, *America's current immigration policy is a disaster*") (original italics); Carrying Capacity Network Clearinghouse Bulletin (various issues). The major national restrictionist organization, the Federation For Immigration Immigration Reform, or FAIR, describes itself as a "'pro-limits population organization'" and has its roots in the population control and environmental movements. *See* Merrick Carey, *Too Many Americans?* WASH. TIMES, Sept. 6, 1995, at A19.

By contrast, some environmental organizations have affirmatively refused to adopt immigration control as a policy goal. According to a spokesperson for the Natural Resources Defense Council, "[i]t is improper, impractical and immoral for developed countries to try to have stability within their own countries without working to improve conditions for other nations." (quoted in Ruben, *supra*) For further critique, *see* Cathi Tactaquin, *Finding Common Ground: Population and Consumption*, 26 ENVIRON. ACTION 24 (June 22, 1994).

75. *See, e.g.*, Jack Miles, *Blacks vs. Browns*, ATLANTIC MONTHLY, Oct. 1992, at 41, 58 ("In July 1992, the Black Leadership Forum, a coalition headed by Coretta Scott King and Walter E. Fauntroy, wrote to Senator Orrin Hatch urging him not to repeal the sanctions imposed on employers of illegal aliens under the Immigration Reform and Control Act of 1986. 'We are concerned, Senator Hatch,' the group wrote, 'that your proposed remedy to the employer sanctions-based discrimination, namely, the elimination of employer sanctions, will cause another problem—the revivial of the pre-1986 discrimination against black and brown U.S. and documented workers, in favor of cheap labor—the undocumented workers.'") *See also* Howard Jordan, *African-American Doubts About Immigration*, NACLA Report on the Americas, Vol. XXIV, No. 3 (Nov./Dec. 1994) at 36:

> The immigration issue [has] divided the African-American community, with one part of the leadership clearly suspicious of the merits of promoting immigrant rights. Sensitive about high unemployment among African Americans, these leaders see Latino immigrants as unwelcome competition for scarce jobs. [For example], when a 1990 Congressional Accounting Office Study found 'a pattern of widespread discrimination against Latino and Asian Immigrants' in the wake of the Immigration Reform and control Act of 1986, the National Association for the Advancement of Colored People (NAACP) refused to join the calls of Latino civil rights orgnaizations for repeal of the law.

On the other hand, African-American civil rights organizations are not alone in expressing concern about undocumented immigration; Hispanic-American and Asian-American civil rights orga-

sire to enforce what might be described as an enabling boundary around the nation-state: in this view, the nation's borders must be enforced—the boundary between inside and outside must be sustained—so that social justice can be pursued within.[76]

But even if progressives do not advocate immigration protectionism per se (and in progressive legal and political theory, few, if any, do),[77] many still endorse the national border in a subtler fashion. As I argued earlier, most American progressives approach the United States as the fundamental normative universe in their political lives. They tend to view it as the site in which struggles for justice (or inclusion or equality or freedom) take place, and also as a normative community—the community of people among whom such struggles unfold and among

---

nizations have done so as well. *See, e.g.*, Testimony of Raul Yzaguirre, President, National Council of La Raza, before the House Judiciary Committee, June 29, 1995 (stating in hearings on pending immigration reform legislation that the "NCLR takes the position that the U. S. has a right and a duty to control its borders. We are in agreement with the overall goal of the current policy debate; indeed, the critical question is not, "Should the U.S. control its borders?" but rather, 'How do we achieve this goal?'")

For other arguments that immigration hurts domestic minorities, especially African-Americans, in economic terms, *see* Vernon M. Briggs, Jr., *Immigration Policy Sends Blacks To the South*, 5 CONTRACT 270, 271 (1995) ("For much of the nation's urban black population outside the South, immigration policy is but a revised instrument of institutionalized racism. It provides a way to bypass the national imperative to address the employment, job preparation and housing needs of much of the urban black population."); Nicolaus Mills, *Affirmative Action, Immigration Clash*, NEWSDAY, May 29, 1994, at A42 ("[I]mmigrants don't simply take the low-paying, difficult work that nobody else wants. They take a variety of jobs . . . and in recent years they have not only been challenging native-born minorities for entry-level jobs. They have been challenging them for affirmative-action slots . . . . Immigration undermines [the] link between past and present when, as is now the case, a newly arrived immigrant who is also a minority-group member is as eligible for affirmative action as an African-American whose roots go back to the 17th Century."). *See also* Toni Morrison, *On The Backs of Blacks*, TIME, Dec., 1993, at 57 (arguing that the process of incorporation of new immigrants ordinarily entails a symbolic reenactment of blacks' national denigration and marginalization: "Whatever the lived experience of immigrants with African Americans—pleasant, beneficial, or bruising—the rhetorical experience renders blacks as noncitizens, already discredited outlaws . . . .It does not matter anymore what shade the newcomer's skin is. A hostile posture toward resident blacks must be struck at the Americanizing door before it will open.").

76. As one progressive commentator recently put it, however compelling the needs of immigrants can often seem, "[t]here is no credible way to talk about compassion for those living beyond our borders when we have so little regard for the needs of our own poor." Nicolaus Mills, *Lifeboat Ethics and Immigration Fears*, *Dissent*, 37, 44 (Winter, 1996). For similar arguments, see MICHAEL LIND, THE NEXT AMERICAN NATION: THE NEW NATIONALISM AND THE FOURTH AMERICAN REVOLUTION 319-322 (1995) (articulating a "pro-worker rationale for immigration restriction.").

77. The principle, and influential, exception is MICHAEL WALZER, SPHERES OF JUSTICE: A DEFENSE OF PLURALISM AND EQUALITY 31-52 (1983).

whom they matter.[78] This is often an unspoken commitment, although again, for some writers, it is made more affirmative or explicit.[79]

But the idea of the nation-state, or the United States in particular, as a community is, by its nature, both exclusivist and exclusionary. The concept of "national community" not only entails the notion of group identity grounded in nation-state membership; it also, and correspondingly, presumes the existence of a category of "others" or outsiders to the community, who are non-members of the nation-state.[80] Progressives' conception of the United States as a normative community, in other words, implicitly entails an assumption of the naturalness—and perhaps the legitimacy as well—of its outer boundaries.[81] Indeed, the very idea that the national society is a community may even require the sense of boundedness and closure that borders provide: in this view, it is the border dividing insiders and outsiders that helps to construct the experience of community for those on the inside in the first place.[82]

Of course, the fact that progressives assume the existence of a

---

78. *See supra* notes 60-66 and accompanying text.

79. *See supra* notes 61-63 and accompanying text.

80. The concept of the "nation" "is crucial to the way a state is linked to its subjects, distinguishing them from the subjects of other states, and to the state's larger environment." Katherine Verdery, *Wither Nation and Nationalism?* 122 DAEDALUS 37, 38 (Summer, 1993).

81. As Michael Walzer has written, "[t]he idea of distributive justice presupposes a bounded world within which distributions take place among a group of people committed to dividing, exchanging, and sharing social goods, first of all among themselves. That world . . . is the political community, whose members distribute power to one another and avoid, if they possibly can, sharing it with anybody else." *See* Walzer, SPHERES OF JUSTICE, *supra* note 77, at 31. *See also* Sanford Levinson, *Constituting Communities Through Words That Bind: Reflections on Loyalty Oaths*, 84 MICH. L. REV. 1440, 1446 (1986) ("A 'community' truly open to all comers is almost a contradiction in terms . . . . A community without boundaries is without shape and identity; if pursued with single-minded determination, tolerance is incompatible with the very possibility of community.'").

82. *See* Chantal Mouffe, Democratic Citizenship and the Political Community, *in* DIMENSIONS OF RADICAL DEMOCRACY: PLURALISM, CITIZENSHIP, COMMUNITY 225, 234-35 (Chantal Mouffe, ed., 1992):

> Political life concerns collective, public action; it aims at the construction of a 'we' in a context of diverstiy and conflict. But to construct a 'we,' it must be distinguished from the 'them' and that means establishing a frontier, defining an 'enemy.' Therefore, while politics aims at constructing a political community and creating a unity, a fully inclusive political community and a final unity can never be realized since there will permanently be a 'constitutive outside,' an exterior to the community that makes its existence possible.

See also Jamin Raskin, *Legal Aliens, Local Citizens: The Historical, Constitutional and Theoretical Meanings of Alien Suffrage*, 141 U. PENN. L. REV. 1391, 1446 (1993) (suggesting that "the community's sense of 'social solidarism' today depends precisely on the exclusion of those who are not citizens.").

boundary between nationals and nonnational others does not, by itself, require that they endorse the precise ways these boundaries are drawn nor the precise manner of their enforcement. Indeed, some progressives have offered devastating criticisms of both.[83] Yet assuming as given the existence of national boundaries (as the nation-centered orientation of most progressive thought does) means assuming that those boundaries can legitimately be enforced against outsiders under at least some circumstances—for otherwise, how can any boundaries be said to exist at all?[84] A community's boundaries serve to separate those on the inside from those without, and to the extent their existence is understood as an inevitable fact of life, the basis for normative critique is substantially limited.

This is not to say, once again, that progressives' nation-centered worldview leaves them no room at all for critique of border enforcement. They still may advance procedural critiques and critiques of the magnitude or scope of border exclusion.[85] They also may respond to immigration restrictionism with the empirical claim that exclusionary measures at the border will inevitably fail to stanch the flow, and that undocumented immigrants will continue to come despite the government's best efforts;[86] by this last argumentative move, they are able to shift the normative debate back to the easier question of how undocumented immigrants who are already here should be treated. But the practice of national border control, per se, is not so easily criti-

83. Progressive critics of the country's immigration policy and practice often argue for greater openness to immigrants who seek to come to the United States for purposes of family reunification, employment and safe-haven, and for rights of those noncitizens who are here against many forms of discrimination. They also consistently criticize the procedures pursuant to which the federal government enforces the immigration laws. Among other things, they have challenged what they allege to be increasing violence by federal agents at the national border, overly restrictive detention policies, and insufficient due process in administrative deportation and exclusion proceedings. There are a great variety of fora in which such critiques are advanced. Advocacy organizations publish newsletters which set forth these views; examples include *Immigration Newsletter* (Published by the National Immigration Project of the National Lawyers Guild, Boston, MA); *Immigration Policy Matters* (Published by the National Immigration Forum, Washington, D.C.); *Torch For the Immigrant-Services and Resettlement Community* (Published by the New York Association For New Americans, Inc., New York, NY); *Eye On Immigration Policy* (Published by the Coalition for Immigrant and Refugee Rights and Services, San Francisco, CA). Some American immigration law scholarship advances such critiques as well.

84. A boundary, after all, is "[s]omething that indicates a border or a limit." AMERICAN HERITAGE DICTIONARY OF THE ENGLISH LANGUAGE (1992).

85. *See supra* note 83.

86. Bosniak, *Exclusion and Membership*, *supra* note 50, at 1012-19; Johnson, *supra*, note 52, at 1221. *See also infra* note 144.

cized—and it rarely is. Instead, the position of most progressives on the border can best be described as one of basic acquiescence.

Of course, it is precisely this acquiesence to borders which makes undocumented immigrants such a troubling case for progressive thought. For while their social exclusion usually appears to be deeply objectionable to progressives, their territorial exclusion (at least some of the time) seems somehow inevitable—as a precondition for achieving social justice within the community, and, perhaps, as a necessary condition of the political community's existence altogether. Yet because progressives are surely loathe to say anything that might appear to reinforce the current epidemic of anti-immigrant feeling in this country, they are unlikely to air their confusion (assuming they think about it at all). In fact, they are most apt to avoid the subject of border control altogether.

V.

While progressives can therefore offer apparently powerful criticism of measures like Prop. 187 which mandate the social exclusion of those undocumented immigrants who are already here, they cannot so easily criticize efforts to keep undocumented immigrants out of the national territory in the first place—and they may sometimes even endorse such efforts. A breach exists, in other words, between their potentially robust denunciations of government exclusion of undocumented immigrants in the interior and their acquiescence—whether active or passive—in these same immigrants' exclusion at the border. This breach, as we have seen, produces substantial confusion for progressives about when, and even whether, to regard undocumented immigrants as the subjects of their normative concern.

But the breach raises further difficulties as well. For although some analysts would view these contrasting approaches to border and interior as entirely compatible and even mutually required as a matter of justice,[87] the two positions, in fact, stand in substantial tension with one another. In the first place, progressives' acquiescence to border exclu-

87. Political theorist Michael Walzer, in particular, has made a strong affirmative case for simultaneous commitments to external boundedness and internal inclusion. *See* Walzer, SPHERES OF JUSTICE, *supra* note 77, at 63 (an adequate "theory of distributive justice . . . must vindicate at one and the same time the (limited) right of closure, without which there could be no communities at all, and the political inclusiveness of the existing communities."). For a detailed analysis of Walzer's dual commitment to external closure and internal inclusiveness, see Bosniak, *The Difference That Alienage Makes*, *supra* note 32, at 1068-87.

sion ultimately serves to undermine any efforts they might wish to make on behalf of undocumented immigrants who are already here, including any efforts against measures like Prop. 187. At the same time, acquiescence to borders more generally undermines their articulated concern with the construction and subordination of outsiders.

Progressives' general presumption of the legitimacy of national borders serves to thwart any efforts they might make on behalf of undocumented immigrants who are already here because, simply stated, it is precisely enforcement of these borders which produces the immigrants' powerlessness here in the first place. The problem is that the sharp divide that progressive thought tends to presume between the national state's border and its interior is more fiction than reality, especially where undocumented immigrants are concerned. National border enforcement does not take place merely at the physical border, and it is not concerned merely with stopping people at the moment of territorial entry. Instead, enforcement of the border occurs wherever government immigration authorities have jurisdiction to enforce the immigration laws—which in this country is virtually everywhere.[88] And such enforcement is as concerned with removing from the territory those people who lack legal permission to remain as it is with preventing their entry in the first place.[89]

---

88. *See* Bosniak, *Exclusion and Membership*, *supra* note 50, at 987-88: ("The INS [Immigration and Naturalization Service] has deployed the major part of its resources at the border and the largest number of apprehensions occur there. However, much of the agency's enforcement effort has been focused in the interior. Although the INS's interior enforcement powers have been somewhat restrained by the judiciary, agents still detain, question, and arrest people on the street, in their homes, in their cars, in bars, and even on souplines. In recent years, however, the single most significant site of INS law enforcement, after the immediate border area itself, has been the workplace.") (citations omitted).

For a report of recent interior enforcement efforts, *see* Ronald Smothers, *New Tactic Is Tested on Illegal Immigrants*, N.Y. TIMES, Sept. 26, 1995, at A19 (describing "major sweep of illegal workers in non-border states" called "Operation South P.A.W. (Protecting American Workers)," in which undocumented workers at restaurants, manufacturing plants, food processing operations, and construction sites in the southeast were arrested, and employers fined).

89. The Immigration and Nationality Act designates a great many grounds of deportation for aliens who are present in the United States. Immigration and Nationality Act, 8 U.S.C. §§ 1101 *et seq.* (1952 and Supp. 1996). Among those most relevant to the undocumented are the provisions which designate "entry without inspection" a deportable offense, I.N.A. § 241(a)(1)(B), 8 U.S.C. § 1251 (1952 and Supp. 1996), and which render deportable aliens who violated the terms of their initial visas. *See* I.N.A. § 241(a)(1)(C), 8 U.S.C. § 1251 (1952 and Supp. 1996). Recently the Clinton Administration has signalled its intent to substantially upgrade its interior enforcement efforts. *See* Smothers, *supra* note 88; Robert Pear, *Clinton Will Seek Spending To Curb Aliens, Aids Say*, N.Y. TIMES, Jan. 22, 1995, at A1 (describing Administration efforts to obtain increased funding to deport criminal aliens).

This means that undocumented immigrants residing in this country are potentially subject to government border enforcement in the form of deportation during virtually every moment of their lives. And as a consequence, they are usually reluctant to avail themselves of any rights they do have for fear of coming to the attention of the immigration authorities.[90] The result is that even if undocumented immigrants are not specifically denied access to education and healthcare and other social services, as Prop. 187 and similar measures would require, and even if they are not penalized for seeking to avail themselves of these services, the constant threat of deportation will continue to structure their lives in this country, and will ensure their continued marginalization and domination. To the extent that the left's acquiescence to national border enforcement allows this, any critique they may advance of Prop. 187 and other such initiatives is, quite plainly, ineffectual at best.[91]

One response to this difficulty is for progressives to argue, as some have done, that by virtue of their participation in and contribution to our society, undocumented immigrants deserve full recognition as members by law; in practical terms, undocumented immigrants would be provided *with documentation*, or legal status.[92] The legalization argument represents a far stronger and more affirmative case for undocumented immigrants than simple opposition to measures like Prop. 187 does precisely because it would eliminate much of the effect that internal border enforcement has on these immigrants; it would ensure that they would no longer be subject to the constant specter of deportation which so defines their lives here. Yet this argument raises important

90. *See* Bosniak, *Exclusion and Membership*, *supra* note 50, at 986 ("[E]ven where formal rights exist, the ability of the undocumented to exercise these rights in practice is limited. Undocumented aliens often fear exposing themselves to the exclusionary powers of the state and will often forego the exercise of membership rights in order to avoid such an eventuality. Undocumented immigrants commonly decline to report private or official abuse and are frequently unwilling to pursue civil claims in court or to step forward to receive benefits to which they are entitled.") (citations omitted).

91. I do not mean to suggest that efforts to protect the rights of undocumented immigrants which fall short of demands for their legalization are meaningless or otherwise lacking in value—far from it. My point is simply that without legalization, the undocumented will continue to suffer social exclusion and marginalization notwithstanding any other rights or protections they might be afforded.

92. I should note that this argument is radical by today's political standards, and is virtually never heard in the current immigration debates. However, it was sometimes heard a decade ago during the debates leading to the Immigration Reform and Control Act of 1986, Pub. L. No. 99-603 (1986), which ultimately included provisions for legalizing a portion of the then-existing undocumented population.

questions in its own right, among them: Would legalization apply only to those undocumented who arrived before a date certain, or would its effect extend forward in time, so that the very category "undocumented alien" would be effectively eliminated in the law?[93] If the former—if legalization were a one-time reform—then there is no doubt that a new class of undocumented immigrants would spring up in short order, and would suffer the same sorts of domination and marginalization as those who came before.[94] But if legalization were ongoing—if the mere fact of making it into the territory of the United States were automatic grounds for acquiring legal status here—then progressives' attachment to national borders would seem to be substantially undermined, since the incentive to come (for those who are otherwise interested) would surely be overwhelming, and this, in turn, would render control of the borders far more difficult.

The point is that progressives' acquiescence to national border enforcement works at cross-purposes with their commitment to defending the interests of the undocumented. For to the extent they retain the attachment, or acquiesence, to borders, they ensure that the immigrants will continue to be marginalized; but conversely, to the extent they effectively attack the marginalization the immigrants suffer, they necessarily must challenge the enforcement of borders as well. The two commitments (against marginalization of persons and for borders around the community) are mutually incompatible, at least where the status of undocumented immigrants are concerned.

But progressives' acquiescence to national border enforcement also undermines their efforts on behalf of the immigrants in another way as well — and here we see that this acquiescence more generally stands in tension with progressives' commitments against social exclusion and subordination. Notice the structure of their argument when they critique Prop. 187's provisions or otherwise advocate on behalf of the undocumented: they are demanding, in effect, that the national community recognize certain rights of membership for a class of people who, they

93. To be exact, "undocumented alien" is not a legal category per se. The term is used colloquially to refer to people who entered in violation of immigration law or have violated the terms of their visas once here. People less sympathetic to this group of immigrants tend to use the phrase "illegal alien," although this is as much a term of art as is "undocumented alien."

94. The legalization provisions included in the 1986 Immigration Reform and Control Act (IRCA) more than bear this out. The number of undocumented today (approximately 3.2 million) is virtually identical to the number that existed a decade ago, despite IRCA's provision of legalization to 2.8 million. *See* MICHAEL FIX & JEFFREY S. PASSEL, IMMIGRATION AND IMMIGRANTS: SETTING THE RECORD STRAIGHT 21-22, 24 (Urban Institute, 1994).

have also allowed, might legitimately have been barred from access to the territory—and thereby from access to any membership rights altogether—had they been stopped at the physical border.[95] The critics, in other words, divide the world between those people who have managed to enter or remain in the territory, whose interests they defend, and those who have not managed to enter or remain, whose interests they generally ignore (and whose continued exclusion they sometimes endorse). The territorial bias this position entails may be reasonable from the perspective of the national society (it is a bias American law itself maintains),[96] but it is far more problematic to the extent that progressives claim to be concerned with the interests and experience of the immigrants themselves. For from the immigrants' point of view, their success at crossing into the national territory and/or remaining here undetected is usually an enormously fortuitous affair, and most undocumented immigrants who are currently here have family members and friends who were not so lucky as they.[97] Additionally, the composition of the class of undocumented immigrants is changing constantly; among some segments of the undocumented population, people leave the territory, and people return, with relative frequency.[98]

95. I should emphasize here that in legal terms, "the border" is constituted not merely by the physical boundary at the territory's perimeter, but also by those entry points into the territory which are, in fact, often located inside the country's territorial perimeters; airports, for example, are instances of "the border" in the sense I am using the term here (and in the terms of American law as well). *See, e.g.*, Almeida-Sanchez v. United States, 413 U.S. 266, 272-73 (1973) (treating airport as "functional equivalent of the border . . . ."). It is important to keep this in mind, because although Americans tend to imagine that undocumented immigrants enter surreptitiously at the physical border (usually at the U.S.-Mexican border), more than half of the undocumented population enters at airports after formal government inspection; they later fall into undocumented status by failure to depart when their visas expire or by otherwise violating the terms of their visas. *See also* Fix & Passel, *supra* note 94, at 25 ("Only 4 out of 10 undocumented aliens cross the border illegally or enter without inspection. Six out of ten undocumented immigrants enter legally—as visitors, students, or temporary employees—and become illegal by failing to leave when their visas expire.").

96. *See generally* Yick Wo v. Hopkins, 118 U.S. 356, 369 (1886) (the provisions of the fourteenth amendment "are universal in their application, to all persons within the territorial jurisdiction"); Plyler v. Doe, 457 U.S. 202, 210 (1982) (same); U.S. v. Verdugo-Urquidez, 110 S.Ct. 1056, 1063-66 (1990) (both fifth and fourth amendments apply only to aliens who are territorially present).

97. For diverse accounts of the general challenges faced by undocumented immigrants who seek to cross the border into the United States and the various fortuities involved, see generally SARAH J. MAHLER, AMERICAN DREAMING: IMMIGRANT LIFE ON THE MARGINS (1995) (especially Chapter 3: "The Trip As Personal Transformation"); TED CONOVER, COYOTES: A JOURNEY THOUGH THE SECRET WORLD OF AMERICA'S ILLEGAL ALIENS (1987).

98. *Id. See also* Borjas, *supra* note 72, at 62-63 (describing "the transient nature of the immigration for many" undocumented immigrants); ALEJANDRO PORTES & ROBERT L. BACH,

Membership in the class of people who happen to be in undocumented status in the United States at any given time, in other words, is both adventitious and mutable. But this being the case, it becomes clear how arbitrary it is for progressives to champion only those immigrants who are territorially present. Why shouldn't progressives be concerned as well with the status and well-being of people who lived and worked here in the past, or with those less lucky at the border, or with those aspiring to come for the first time—all of whom often possess the same desire to work, to rejoin family, to flee their countries, to construct a new life, as those who are already here possess?[99] By treating the

---

LATIN JOURNEY: CUBAN AND MEXICAN IMMIGRANTS IN THE UNITED STATES 80 (1985) (Mexican immigration has been characterized by a strong return orientation and a cyclical pattern, in which periods of work in the United States alternate with periods of residence in Mexico."); Carlos Monsivais, *Dreaming of Utopia*, NACLA: Report on the Americas, vol. XXIX, No. 3, Nov/Dec. 1995, at 39, 41 ("Mexico has evolved from being a sedentary country to a nomadic one. Villages and towns in the states of Michoacan, Guerrero, Oaxaca, Morelos, Hidalgo, San Luis Potosi and Chiapas empty out every six months . . . .The hundreds of thousands of migrant workers who go to the United States and who return every year reconsruct and diversify their country of origin."); Richard Walker, *California Rages Against the Dying of the Light*, 209 NEW LEFT REV. 42, 64 (1995) ("The whole concept of legal and illegal migration is dubious to Mexicans who move in a continuous circuit back and forth across the border, wherein workers return to their villages for holidays, weddings, health reasons, between jobs, and after building a nest egg of repatriated wages to buy a little land. Half of those crossing the border 'illegally' already have jobs in the U.S. to which they are returning."). On the other hand, analysts have suggested that in recent years, the rate of permanent settlement of undocumented immigrants in this country is on the rise. *See, e.g.*, Wayne Cornelius, *Impacts of the 1986 U.S. Immigration Law on Emigration From Rural Mexican Sending Communities*, in UNDOCUMENTED MIGRATION TO THE UNITED STATES: IRCA AND THE EXPERIENCE OF THE 1980S at 227, 238 (Frank D. Bean et al. eds., 1990) ("The long-term trend toward a higher an incidence of permanent settlement by Mexican immigrants in the United States appears to have been reinforced by IRCA.")

For further discussion of the continued links many communites of undocumented immigrants in this country maintain with their home communities, *see* text accompanying note 146, *infra*.

99. Some scholars have argued that the interests of immigrants, including undocumented immigrants, should be of increasing concern to Americans as the immigrants' "stake" in this country increases. By "stake" they mean particular attachments and commitments and expectations that develop over time through relationship. *See generally* David Martin, *Due Process and Membership In The National Community: Political Asylum and Beyond*, 44 U. PITT. L. REV. 165 (1983). Territorial presence, in this view, would be one indicia, although possibly quite a minimal one, of stake; on this theory, therefore, privileging the interests of those who are territorially present over those who are not might make some kind of sense. (*But see* U.S. v. Verdugo-Urquidez, 110 S. Ct. 1056, 1064-65 (1990), holding that *involuntary* physical presence in the national territory does not entail sufficient "connections with this country" to place a person "among 'the people' of the United States" for purposes of applying fourth amendment protections.).

One might respond, however, that there are many people not territorially present who also have substantial stake in this country, either by virtue of prior residence and labor here, or

mere fact of national territorial presence as morally significant (by defending the interests of the territorially present and not others), progressives overlook the interests of many people whose claim on their concern might otherwise be equally compelling. And to the extent that they grant moral significance to territorial presence, progressives end up privileging with their concern a particular class of outsiders—those who happen to be inside national borders—while leaving the rest precisely where they were.

VI.

I have argued so far that progressive critics of restrictionist immigration policy, including measures like Prop. 187, are hampered and constrained in the arguments they can make on undocumented immigrants' behalf not merely by the pragmatic demands of current political life (although these are substantial), but also by what I have characterized as their own predominantly "national imaginations." The national imagination, as I have described it, treats the national society—in this case, American national society—as the predominant community of normative concern, and presumes the legitimacy, if not the inevitability, of its boundaries. This vision of social life, I have suggested, serves to limit the reach and efficacy of the arguments that progressives can make on undocumented immigrants' behalf, for the social marginalization and domination these immigrants suffer is produced in large part by the enforcement, or threatened enforcement, of the same national borders whose legitimacy progressives tend to presume. While progressives may forcefully argue, therefore, that subjecting a class of people who live and work among us to exclusion from basic human services—as Prop. 187 and its progeny do—is morally

because of the close family connections they maintain with people who currently reside here. Furthermore, some sort of stake in this country might also be said to exist in the case of people who have, for example, been displaced from their land in their home country by a U.S.-owned agribusiness company, or who have been injured by an oppressive government regime armed and supported by the United States; in this latter case, their stake might be said to be the result of "the injury we have done them." *See* Walzer, SPHERES OF JUSTICE, *supra* note 77, at 48.

Yet however broadly or narrowly we might construe it, the "stake" theory assumes the premise that I am seeking to interrogate here: that national borders are morally significant, and that the "we" constituted by national community membership (however broadly construed) deserves normative priority over non-national others.

intolerable, they cannot so easily condemn efforts to keep these immigrants out in the first place, nor can they easily advocate for an end to enforcement of the border against these immigrants altogether. In this respect, undocumented immigrants represent a terribly confounding case for progressives: for these immigrants suffer the kind of social exclusion progressives routinely deplore, yet at the same time, their exclusion from territory and membership quite often seems a necessary, if unfortunate, condition of political life as we have both known and imagined it.

All of that said, however, it may reasonably be argued that the tensions produced by progressives' particularist national commitments are all-but inevitable; for in a world in which "[b]oundaries and categories of some form are inevitable,"[100] what possible alternative to national boundaries is there? The principal alternative in conventional political thought is some version of liberal cosmopolitanism, according to which the concerns of justice should lie with "people in general rather than people living within some particular political jurisdiction."[101] Strictly speaking, liberal cosmopolitanism is morally indifferent to national boundaries, and therefore should endorse a policy of open borders; in its view, freedom of movement is "an important liberty in itself and a prerequisite for other freedoms" as well.[102]

Yet it is easy enough to point to this model's limitations. First of all, while liberal cosmopolitanism, in the form of human rights theory, has recently lent real rhetorical, and sometimes practical, support to various movements against subordination around the world,[103] and

100. Minow, *Making All The Difference*, *supra* note 46, at 390.

101. Robert E. Goodin, *If People Were Money . . .* , *in* FREE MOVEMENT: ETHICAL ISSUES IN THE TRANSNATIONAL MIGRATION OF PEOPLE AND MONEY 6, 7 (Brian Barry & Robert E. Goodin, eds., 1992).

102. Joseph Carens, *Migration and Morality: A Liberal Egalitarian Perspective*, *in* Barry & Goodin eds., *supra* note 101, at 25. Most liberals have nevertheless declined to embrace the open borders position absolutely, arguing that where borders are necessary to "protect the ongoing process of liberal conversation," they will support them. *See* BRUCE ACKERMAN, SOCIAL JUSTICE IN THE LIBERAL STATE 95 (1980). *See also* Carens, *supra* at 25 (restrictions on movement "may sometimes be justified because they will promote liberty and equality in the long run or because they are necessary to preserve a distinct culture or way of life.").

103. *See, e.g.*, Robert A. Williams Jr., *Encounters on the Frontiers of International Human Rights Law: Redefining the Terms of Indigenous Peoples' Survival in the World*, 1990 DUKE L.J. 660, 701 ("In the context of the contemporary indigenous struggle for survival and international legal protection, rights discourse has functioned effectively in generating a shared, empowering vocabulary and syntax for indigenous peoples. The discourse of international human rights has enabled indigenous peoples to understand and express their oppression in terms that are meaningful to them and their oppressors."). Richard Delgado & Jean Stefancic, *Cosmopoli-*

while it has helped to loosen the borders around many nation-states by way of the international refugee protection regime,[104] many progressive and critical theorists have themselves importantly challenged it,[105] arguing, among other things, that its universalist and individualist premises are implausibly abstract and ignore the concrete particularity of commitments which actually give shape and meaning to human life.[106] Many contemporary scholars, in fact, have made the affirmative case that particularity of attachments in the form of community represents an important normative good in itself,[107] with political community per-

---

tanism Inside Out: International Norms and The Struggle For Civil Rights and Local Justice, 27 CONN. L. REV. 723 (1995) ("On a number of fronts, progressive people working on behalf of historically disenfranchised groups have been turning, ever hopeful, to international human rights law as a source of aid.").

104. The United Nations Convention Relating To The Status of Refugees, 189 U.N.T.S. 137 (1951), as amended by the U.N. Protocol Relating To the Status of Refugees, 606 U.N.T.S. 267 (1967), provides, among other things, that state parties may not return persons fearing persecution on account of race, religion, nationality, membership of a particular social group or political opinion to the country of persecution. (Convention, Articles 1 and 33). For arguments that refugee protection should be approached as an international human rights issue, see James C. Hathaway, *Reconceiving Refugee Law as Human Rights Protection*, 4 J. REFUGEE STUD. 113 (1991); LOUIS HENKIN, THE AGE OF RIGHTS 48-50 (1990).

105. In addition to the critique presented in the text, progressive critics have also challenged the human rights model on practical and political grounds, arguing, among other things, that the international human rights regime associated with the United Nations is embedded in a "womb of hegemonial and statist logic" and is seriously constrained by lack of enforcement mechanisms due to continued international commitments to state sovereignty. RICHARD FALK, HUMAN RIGHTS AND STATE SOVEREIGNTY 47 (1981).

Additionally, some postmodern theorists have advanced an epistemological challenge to the notion of human rights, described by one analyst as follows:

> [P]ostmodern theorists ask how we can understand the narrative of human rights when we no longer believe that its claims are true or that metanarratives are even possible. Instead of searching for first principles and metanorms, postmodernists analyze the discursive form of the notion of rights and read this form as a part of the historically limited Enlightenment project that today has lost its relevance.

Renata Salecl, *Law and the Postmodern Mind, Rights in Psychoanalytic and Feminist Perspective*, 16 CARDOZO L. REV. 1121 (1995).

106. *See, e.g.*, Michael Walzer, *The Communitarian Critique of Liberalism*, 18 POL. THEORY 6 (1990) ; Mark Tushnet, *Rights: An Essay in Informal Political Theory*, 17 POL. AND SOCIETY 403, 409-12 (1989); RICHARD RORTY, CONTINGENCY, IRONY, SOLIDARITY 59 (1989) (arguing that morality derives from "ourselves as members of a community, speakers of a common language," and rejecting the notion that "there is something which stands to my community as my community stands to me, some larger community called 'humanity' which has an intrinsic nature."). Among the classic texts which have elaborated the critique of liberal premises in such terms are ALASDAIR MACINTYRE, AFTER VIRTUE: A STUDY IN MORAL THEORY (1981); MICHAEL SANDEL, LIBERALISM AND THE LIMITS OF JUSTICE (1982); CHARLES TAYLOR, HEGEL AND MODERN SOCIETY (1979).

107. *E.g.*, ROBERTO UNGER, KNOWLEDGE AND POLITICS (1975); BENJAMIN BARBER, STRONG DEMOCRACY (1984); Sandel, supra note 106. *But see* YOUNG, *supra* note 42, at 226-36 (arguing

haps the greatest expression of that good.[108] The nation-state, for better or worse, is the paramount political community of the age and is likely to remain so in the coming years.[109] Some progressive theorists

---

that "the ideal of community denies, devalues, or represses the ontological difference of subjects, and seeks to dissolve social inexhaustibility into the comfort of a self-enclosed whole.").

108. *See, e.g.*, Walzer, SPHERES OF JUSTICE, *supra* note 77, at 29 (the political "community is itself a good—conceivably the most important good—that gets distributed."); Charles Taylor, *Cross-Purposes: The Liberal-Communitarian Debate, in* LIBERALISM AND THE MORAL LIFE, (Nancy L. Rosenblum, ed. 1989) at 159, 165-66 ("in order to have a free society [one must have] a willing identification with the polis on the part of the citizens, a sense that the political institutions in which they live are an expression of themselves . . . [P]atriotism is based on an identification with others in a particular common enterprise. I am not dedicated to defending the liberty of just anyone, but I feel the bond of solidarity with my compatriots in our common enterprise, the common expression of our respective dignity."). *See also* Frank Michelman, *Law's Republic*, 97 YALE L.J. 1493 (1988).

For progressive arguments that the communitarian (or the related civic republican) vision possesses "authoritarian" tendencies, see Adeno Addis, *Individualism, Communitarianism and the Rights of Ethnic Minorities*, 67 NOTRE DAME L. REV. 615, 645-48 (1991). *See also* Derrick Bell & Preeta Bansal, *The Republican Revival and Racial Politics*, 97 YALE L.J. 1609 (1988); YOUNG, *supra* note 42, at 227 ("The ideal of community . . . expresses a desire for the fusion of subjects with one another which in practice operates to exclude those with whom the group does not identify. The ideal of community denies and represses social difference."); Steven Winter, *For What It's Worth*, 26 LAW & SOC. REV. 789, 795 (1992) ("In post-modernity, all is diversity and heterogeneity; any discourse of 'community' is suspect as a discourse of oppression.").

109. This is Richard Rorty's point in the passage from which this article's epigraph is drawn:

> Political imagination is, almost always, national imagination. To imagine great things is to imagine a great future for a particular community, a community one knows well, identifies with, can make plausible predictions about. In the modern world, this usually means one's nation. Political romance is, therefore, for the foreseeable future, going to consist of psalms of *national* future rather than of the future of 'mankind.'

Rorty, *supra* note 1, at 343: *See also* RICHARD RORTY, IRONY, CONTINGENCY, SOLIDARITY 189-99 (1989) (arguing that by nature, we experience solidarity with our compatriots far more readily than with humanity in general); Jean Bethke Elshtain *Sovereignty, Identity, Sacrifice*, 20 Millennium 395, 401 (1991) (arguing that nationalism is inevitable "in some form or another, for we must all locate ourselves in a particular place."); Yael Tamir, LIBERAL NATIONALISM 6 (1993) (arguing that nationalism appropriately acknowledges "the importance of belonging, membership, and cultural affiliations, as well as the particular moral commitments that follow from them.").

On the other hand, as Sanford Levinson has noted, many communitarians invoke the ideal of "community" with no express reference to the community of the nation. "One does not know if this is an explicit rejection of nationalist claims or, instead, a retreat to euphemism lest one be tarred with the negative associations linked to nationalism (that are presumably absent in regard to family, etc.)." Sanford Levinson, *Is Liberal Nationalism an Oxymoron? An Essay For Judith Shklar*, 105 ETHICS 626, 629-30, n.9 (1995) (citing WILL KYMLICKA, LIBERALISM, COMMUNITY AND CULTURE (1989) and Michael Sandel, *Political Liberalism*, 107 HARV. L. REV. 1765 (1994). Others embrace political community as an affirmative value while denying that such communities must take the nation-state form. *See, e.g.*, Guyora Binder, *The Case For Self Determination*, 29 STAN. J. INT'L LAW 223, 262-70 (1993).

have even suggested that the American nation-state should be actively valued and defended as a community—despite the distaste they might feel for the chauvinistic forms such valuation can take,[110] and despite their critique of the relations of power and subordination that often prevails among community members.[111] It follows, for at least some theorists, that in order for the nation-state (or the United States in particular) to remain a community, it must be free to establish certain boundaries around itself: As Michael Walzer has argued, the "distinctiveness" of national community life "depends upon closure;" and the community's members must therefore have the right to preserve their distinctiveness by "mak[ing their] own admissions policy, to control and sometimes restrain the flow of immigrants."[112]

Furthermore, even if we dislike the particular sort of normative statist thinking embodied in much communitarian thought, and even if we find the idea of open borders attractive in the abstract, it still may be that at least some degree of national protectionism in the immigration context is a practical necessity under current conditions. For if borders were simply dismantled or otherwise ignored, it seems quite likely that the numbers of people who would choose to come to this country to live and work would be great enough that their arrival would serve to compound the powerlessness of those already residing here "at the bottom."[113] A great influx of immigrants, for example,

---

110. Sanford Levinson, for example, writes "I suspect that at least some readers of this essay, especially those (like myself) who are fearful of the 'new patriotism' that suffuses much modern political rhetoric, are uncomfortable with the [expression of] intense patriotism . . . . But can one imagine a political community without love of country and commitment to what one would hope to be its highest ideals?" Sanford Levinson, *Constituting Communities Through Words That Bind: Reflections on Loyalty Oaths*, 84 MICH. L. REV. 1440, 1441 (1986). (Levinson concludes, however, that he is "much more certain about [his] inchoate feelings of membership in the American community than [he is] about [his] ability to confess to any peculiarly 'American' set of faith propositions . . . ." *Id.* at 1444).

111. The embrace by some scholars of the concept of national community is intimately linked with a critique of relations of domination and exclusion within that community. *See, e.g.*, KENNETH L. KARST, BELONGING TO AMERICA: EQUAL CITIZENSHIP AND THE CONSTITUTION 173 (1989) ("The American civic culture . . . offers the individual a community of meaning, and thus an identity, that overarches his assortment of group identifications. More specifically, effectuation of the Fourteenth Amendment's guarantee of equal citizenship reinforces the civic culture's value of nationalism, nourishing both a national identity and the sense of national community."); Mari Matsuda, *Voices of America*, *supra* note 46, at 1396 (urging the embrace of an American "nationalism" grounded not in "uniformity [or] pride in America singularly defined," but based on "a living, moving interactive culture, imaginable as expanding circles of sameness and difference.") *See also id.* at 1405 ("I still believe we can wash the blood off the [American] flag and wave it proudly.")

112. Walzer, SPHERES OF JUSTICE, *supra* note at 39.

113. Of course, the conventional projections about how all the world would come to the Unit-

almost certainly would drive down wages in some sectors to a rate that only the immigrants themselves could afford to accept—if even they could;[114] and under such conditions, it seems likely that those suffer-

---

ed States in the absence of border control are surely exaggerated; Americans like to think of their country as intoxicatingly, irresistibly, desirable—and everyone outside our borders as desperate to have us. Despite the regressive ideological uses to which this kind of argument has usually been put, however, there is clearly some truth in it: the United States is highly attractive to many people around the world for an array of economic, political and cultural reasons (for a vivid characterization of the idealized images of this country maintained by many prospective immigrants, *see* MAHLER, *supra* note 97, at 83-104), and there is no denying that in the absence of border controls, the incentive to enter would be great.

114. *See, e.g.*, Joseph H. Carens, *Immigration and the Welfare State*, *in* DEMOCRACY AND THE WELFARE STATE 207, 212 (Amy Gutmann ed., 1988) ("With open borders, no immigrants would be legally vulnerable in the way that current illegal immigrants are. But intense economic competition among unskilled workers would make welfare-state regulations governing work even more difficult to enforce, and enforcement would only further increase the large and increasing pool of the unemployed. Here is a potential reserve army of unemployed greater than anything Marx could have imagined.").

I should note that some advocates of immigration restrictionism argue that undocumented immigrant workers *already* displace domestic workers both because they add to the overall supply of low-wage workers (thus exercising a depressive effect on wages), and because they will work for wages lower than, or endure conditions less favorable than, those which domestic workers can or will accept. *See, e.g.*, VERNON BRIGGS, MASS IMMIGRATION AND THE NATIONAL INTEREST (1992); VERNON M. BRIGGS, JR., IMMIGRATION POLICY AND THE AMERICAN LABOR FORCE 158-66 (1984); Donald Huddle, *Immigration and Jobs: The Process of Displacement*, NPG FORUM, May 1992, at 6. Other analysts, however, have refuted the displacement argument with data that shows precisely the contrary. *See, e.g.*, GEORGE BORJAS, FRIENDS OR STRANGERS: THE IMPACT OF IMMIGRANTS ON THE U.S. ECONOMY 91 (1990) (arguing that "the weight of the empirical evidence . . . indicates that immigration has practically no impact on the earnings and employment opportunities of natives."); Frank Bean et al., *Undocumented Mexican Immigrants and the Earnings of Other Workers in the United States*, 25 DEMOGRAPHY 35, 45-46 (1988) (in study of the labor market effects of undocumented immigrants in five southwestern states, authors conclude that "[t]he concern that undocumented immigration may be depressing the earnings of native-born workers is not borne out"). Moreover, many analysts have argued that access to the relatively lower-wage labor undocumented immigrants provide has enabled some economic sectors (including the garments, automotive parts and electronics industries) to continue to produce in the United States rather than relocate abroad, thereby benefitting the national economy (including the labor market) overall. *E.g.*, Peter Dawkins et al., *The Microeconomic Analysis of Immigration In Australia and The United States*, *in* NATIONS OF IMMIGRANTS: AUSTRALIA, THE UNITED STATES AND INTERNATIONAL MIGRATION 111, 121 (Gary Freeman & James Jupp eds., 1992). Finally, a sizable percentage of legal immigrants are self-employed, and their businesses provide jobs for undocumented immigrants in what are commonly described as ethnic "enclave communities." *Id.* at 119-20. This and other evidence suggests that in the aggregate, the labor market effect of undocumented immigrants with regard to both employment and wages is not deleterious to low-wage domestic workers and may even be positive.

The debate about the labor market impact of undocumented immigrants has yet to be resolved—among other reasons, because no one can "answer the counterfactual question of what would . . . happen[ ] to technology or employer efforts to recruit and train underclass American workers if immigrants [were] not . . . available." Philip L. Martin, *supra* note 71, at 97, n.8. In my view, the critics have the better argument, at least under current conditions. Nevertheless, it

ing most would be Americans of color.[115] These are prospects progressives would understandably wish to avoid.

The limitations of liberal universalism, the attractions (for some) of

---

seems reasonable to assume that in the (admittedly unlikely) event that national border controls were substantially relaxed or abandoned, some sort of job displacement and wage depression effect would occur, at least in the short-run. Such an outcome seems especially likely if the relaxation or removal of barriers to movement were to take place without simultaneous attention to the massive economic inequalities that exist between the United States and most undocumented immigrants' countries of origin. Simply put, immigrants' incentive to move here would be far weaker to the extent that relatively comparable jobs were available at home. Of course, there are dozens of additional, hard-to-predict factors that would presumably bear on the displacement effect, including the nature of the labor and employment protection laws in place and the vigor with which they were enforced; the nature and availability of a social safety net for unemployed workers; and the state of the economy overall. My point for the moment is simply to suggest that opening up or substantially relaxing national borders to population movements would quite possibly serve to threaten the economic interests of the least well-off domestic workers, at least in the short term.

In addition to the effects that relatively free movement of people might have on the labor market, this country would also surely be faced with pressing questions about the fiscal ability of the state and federal governments to provide basic social services for the newly augmented population. Some analysts contend that undocumented immigrants *already* cost the government far more than it can afford. *See* Donald Huddle, *The Cost of Immigration*, Carrying Capacity Network, Washington, D.C., Revised July 1993; *see also* Gary Freeman, *Migration and the Political Economy of the Welfare State*, 487 ANNALS AAPSS 51 (1986). Other analysts dispute these claims, arguing, that undocumented immigrants contribute in taxes more than they receive in tax-funded benefits on a net national level. FIX & PASSEL, *supra* note 12, at 57-67; JULIAN SIMON, THE ECONOMIC CONSEQUENCES OF IMMIGRATION 293-94 (1989). Once again, I think the critics have the better view on this question as things currently stand. But if borders to movement were substantially relaxed or dismantled, it seems indisputable that public resources would be significantly strained, at least in the short term, and that those who rely most on public services—i.e., the least well-off—would likely be most affected.

115. Americans of color are disproportionately represented in the low-skilled and low-wage economic sectors in which undocumented immigrants tend to work, *see* Briggs, *Immigration Policy and the American Labor Force*, *supra* note 114, at 160 (suggesting that in the event of a substantial relaxation of border controls, minority workers would likely feel the competitive effects of an expanded labor pool most strongly.)

Notably, some analysts argue that under the *current* immigration regime, minority workers disproportionately bear the economic brunt of the presence of undocumented immigrants, *see, e.g.*, Briggs, *Mass Immigration and the National Interest*, *supra* note 114, at 211-15. This position, however, is far from universally accepted. For a sample of studies which conclude otherwise, *see* Frank Bean, Lindsay Lowell & Lowell J. Taylor, *Undocumented Mexican Immigrants and the Earnings of Other Workers in the United States*, 25 Demography 35, 46 (1988) (concluding that "the effects of increases in supply of [undocumented workers] are negligible on native-born Mexican-Americans, the group that a priori might be expected to be most affected, both because of the geographic concentration of Mexican Americans in local labor markets receiving the greatest numbers of undocumented Mexicans and because the labor forces of both groups tend to be concentrated in unskilled and semiskilled occupational positions."); George Borjas, *Immigrants, Minorities and Labor Market Competition*, 40 INDUST. & LABOR REL. REV. 382, 391-92 (1987) (concluding in study of nation-wide Census data that "black native-born men have, if anything, gained slightly from increases in the immigrant supply.")

communitarian thought, and a pragmatic assessment, in progressive terms, of the alternatives might therefore appear to lead us, however reluctantly, to accept our own acquiescence in the enforcement of national borders—despite its dissonance at times with other values that we embrace. Such an acceptance would require us to live with the tensions and ambiguities that surround progressive efforts to advocate on behalf of undocumented immigrants. It would require us, as well, to acknowledge that when it comes to undocumented immigration, the line between injustice and necessity is exceptionally, and uniquely, hard to place.

Yet before we bow to the weight of the seemingly inevitable, I would like to suggest that we pause briefly and turn a critical eye upon our own conventional ways of viewing the world. In particular, we might consider the injunction of those critical scholars who have urged us to challenge aspects of our social and political lives which have long appeared to us as both necessary and ineluctable. These theorists have criticized the widespread tendency we all sometimes possess to "assum[e] as given institutional structures that ought to be brought under normative evaluation;"[116] they have also encouraged close attention to the exercise of power in taken-for-granted arrangements and practices in our society.[117] They have urged, above all, that we exercise our imaginations to envision the possibility of alternative social arrangements: As Iris Marion Young has written, "[i]magination is the faculty of transforming the experience of what is into a projection of what could be, the faculty that frees thought to form ideals and norms."[118]

---

116. YOUNG, *supra* note 42, at 3. *See also* Radin & Michelman, *supra* note 61, at 1048 ("[S]ometimes it is the habitually most taken-for-granted cultural landscape features that most cry out for redescription"); ROBERT W. GORDON, NEW DEVELOPMENTS IN LEGAL THEORY, THE POLITICS OF LAW 420 (David Kairys ed.) (revised ed. 1990) (arguing that critical legal scholars are concerned to "use the ordinary rational tools of intellectual inquiry to expose belief structures that claim that things as they are must necessarily be the way they are. There are many varieties of this sort of critical exercise, whose point is to unfreeze the world as it appears to common sense as a bunch of more or less objectively determined social relations and to make it appear as (we believe) it really is: people acting, imagining, rationalizing, justifying.").

117. *See* Martha Minow, *Foreward: Justice Engendered*, 101 HARV. L. REV. 10, 68 (1987) ("Power is at its peak when it is least visible, when it shapes preferences, arranges agendas, and excludes serious challenges from discussion or even imagination. Daily social practices that reinforce existing arrangements stand in the way of efforts to expose unstated assumptions about the power behind attributions of difference. It becomes hard, in the face of such daily practices, to regard glimpses of dominant conceptions as contestable assumptions.")

118. YOUNG, *supra* note 42, at 6; Boaventura de Sousa Santos, *Three Metaphors For a New Conception of Law: The Frontier, the Baroque and the South*, 29 LAW & SOC. REV. 569, 573 (1995) (urging a utopian scholarly enterprise in which "the imagination [is used] to explore

It seems worth inquiring what implications this injunction might have for us here. Could we, on this advice, begin to consider that our predominantly statist approach to questions of justice might be subject to interrogation and revision beyond what we had thought either necessary or possible? Can we imagine thinking about questions of justice in terms that transcend national borders without resorting to the abstractions of liberal universalism? And what implications might such efforts have for our normative approach to exclusion at the nation's borders?

These are extremely difficult questions, and the task of responding to them is an exceptionally tall order. While some scholars have begun to take some of them on,[119] fuller development is a project that, I sus-

new modes of human possibility and styles of will and to oppose the necessity of what exists on behalf of something radically better that is worth fighting for, and to which humanity is fully entitled."); ROBERTO UNGER, SOCIAL THEORY: IT'S SITUATION AND ITS TASK 36 (1987) (emphasizing importance of "the role of the imagination of associative possibility in awakening people to the belief that there are uncreated social worlds worth fighting for.") *See also* Rorty, *supra* note 1 ("[I]f there is social hope it lies in the imagination—in people describing a future in terms which the past did not use.") (Note, however, that this is the same article in which Rorty declared that "political imagination is, almost always, national imagination," *see* text accompanying note 1, *supra,* a statement which does not, itself, reveal much acknowledgement of imaginitive possibility.

119. *See* R.B.J. Walker & Saul H. Mendlovitz, *Interrogating State Sovereignty* in CONTENDIN. G SOVEREIGNTIES: REDEFINING POLITICAL COMMUNITY 7-8 (R.B.J. Walker & Saul H. Mendlovitz, eds., 1990):

> "[Q]uestions about the nature of political life and the contours of political community [are] matters that have long been of concern to students of political theory. Yet . . . [u]nderstandably preoccupied with reproblematizing the character of political life within states, political theorists have rarely broached with much confidence the transformative implications of interdependence or world politics . . . . [Among some scholars, however, the] increasingly global reach of the processes that affect people's lives is increasingly understood to require sustained rethinking of who 'we' are and of how 'we' might relate to each other. [Some are beginning to] explore the ways that accounts of political community formalized in the principle of state sovereignty are being rearticulated in response to profound structural transformations on a global scale. [They] seek to explore the multiplicity of possible communities that might emerge from contemporary transformations . . . [This work] acknowledges the extent to which contemporary political discourse has been shaped by the presumption that state sovereignty provides the only plausible account of who we are as political beings."

For a brief selection of diverse recent efforts in various disciplines to critically interrogate the presumptive normative statism which undergirds much contemporary political and social thought, see, e.g., David Held, *Democracy, The Nation-State and the Global System, in* POLITICAL THEORY TODAY (David Held ed., 1991); Charles Beitz, *Sovereignty and Morality in International Affairs, in* POLITICAL THEORY TODAY, *supra*; WILLIAM E. CONNOLLY, IDENTITY/DIFFERENCE; DEMOCRATIC NEGOTIATIONS OF POLITICAL PARADOX 198-222 (1991); E.J. HOBSBAWM, NATIONS AND NATIONALISM SINCE 1780 (1990); YASEMIN SOYSAL, LIMITS OF CITIZENSHIP: MIGRANTS AND POSTNATIONAL MEMBERSHIP IN EUROPE (1994); ANDREW LINKLATER, MEN AND CITIZENS

pect, will be undertaken by many people over many years. For now, I will simply set out a few tentative thoughts and raise some additional questions in the hopes of prompting further discussion.

To begin with, it is important to recognize that despite the pervasiveness of what I have called normative nationalism in much contemporary progressive legal thought,[120] some progressives have, in fact, been developing alternatives to both nationalist and liberal individualist approaches to questions of social justice. At the level of theory, much progressive scholarship in the field of international law has been devoted in recent years to interrogating and critiquing statist constructions of social and political life. Although this work is exceedingly diverse in methodological and substantive terms, one of its recurrent themes has been to challenge the ways in which statist thinking serves to exclude or occlude or subordinate classes of people whose collective identities or interests transcend or otherwise resist conventional state boundaries.[121] Some analysts, for example, have criticized the denial of legal recognition, self-determination and territory to trans- and sub-national indiginous communities under the prevailing state system.[122] Others have challenged the ways in which the legal norm of state sov-

---

IN INTERNATIONAL RELATIONS (1982); ETIENNE BALIBAR & IMMANUEL WALLERSTEIN, RACE, NATION, CLASS: AMBIGUOUS IDENTITIES (1991); R.B.J. WALKER, INSIDE/OUTSIDE: INTERNATIONAL RELATIONS AS POLITICAL THEORY (1993); BASCH, GLICK- SCHILLER, & SZANTON-BLANC, NATIONS UNBOUND: TRANSNATIONAL PROJECTS, POSTCOLONIAL PREDICAMENTS & DETERRITORIALIZED NATION-STATES (1994); Craig Calhoun, Foreward, *in* MICHELINE ISHAY, INTERNATIONALISM AND ITS BETRAYAL (1994); Katherine Verdery, *Whither 'Nation' and 'Nationalism,'* 122 DAEDALUS 37 (1993); Michael J. Shapiro, *Moral Geographies and the Ethics of Post-Sovereignty*, 6 PUBLIC CULTURE 479 (1994). *See also* text accompanying notes 121-124, *infra*.

120. *See* note 66, *supra* for a clarification of my use of the term "normative nationalism" here.

121. I cannot even begin to do justice to this vast and varied literature here. My point is simply to acknowledge that despite the predominance of normative nationalism in progressive scholarly thought, there are some progressive scholars who imagine the social world in ways that are not entirely circumscribed by national borders. In the text and notes following, I give just a few examples of the kind of work I am referring to. For a bibiolography of "alternative approaches to international law" which contains references to a broad range of critical and progressive international law scholarship, *see* David Kennedy & Chris Tennant, *New Approaches To International Law: A Bibliography*, 35 HARV. INT'L. L.J. 417 (1994).

122. *See, e.g.*, Patrick Macklem, *Distributing Sovereignty: Indian Nations and Equality of Peoples*, 45 STAN. L. REV. 1311 (1993); Robert A. Williams, Jr., *Encounters On the Frontiers of Interantional Human Rights Law: Redefining the Terms of Indigenous Peoples Survival in the World*, 1990 Duke L. J. 660. *See also* Maivan Clech Lam, *Making Room For Peoples at the United Nations: Thoughts Provoked by Indigenous Claims to Self-Determination*, 25 CORNELL INT'L L.J. 603 (1992); Chris Tennant, *Indigenous Peoples, International Institutions, and the International Legal Literature From 1945-1993*, 16 HUMAN RIGHTS Q. 1 (1994); Gerald Torres & Kathryn Milun, *Translating Yonnondio By Precent and Evidence*, 1990 DUKE L.J. 625 (1990).

ereignty serves to obscure and insulate the oppression of women in the so-called "private" realms from critique and institutional redress.[123] These and other critiques, which challenge the exclusionary power of the sovereignty principle and which address the status of communities of people whose interests and identities are distinctly nonconvergent—and are often antagonistic—with those of the nation-state,[124] provide an instructive contrast to the explicit or implicit statism of much contemporary progressive thought.

---

123. This critique, part of a broader developing effort to "describ[e] the silences and fundamentally skewed nature of international law" as it relates to women, *see* Hilary Charlesworth et al., *Feminist Approaches to International Law*, 85 A.J.I.L. 613, 615 (1991), has been articulated in a variety of ways, and has been subject to much internal debate (particularly regarding the coherence of the distinction between private and public in the first place). Among the core arguments is the claim that

> "[m]uch of the abuse [suffered by] women can be seen as immunized from international scrutiny by two levels of public/private distinction . . . On the first level, international law involves national states' dealings with other national states; on a second level, international law may become involved to limit particularly brutal treatment of individuals, but only if that brutal treatment is afforded by a nation state. Thus, until the development of human rights law, the abuse of women was not seen as an international matter because women were not national states. Even after the development of human rights law, the abuse of women continued often not to be seen as an international matter because the *abusers* of women were not national states. Insofar as the chief abusers of women are not state actors as such, human rights law may offer inadequate protection to most women.

Frances E. Olsen, *International Law: Feminist Critiques of the Public/Private Distinction*, *in* RECONCEIVING REALITY: WOMEN AND INTERNATIONAL LAW (Dorinda B. Dallmeyer ed., 1993), *supra*, at 157, 159. For an introduction to the critique and its associated debates, *see* Charlesworth et al., *supra*; Rebecca J. Cook, *Accountability In International Law for Violations of Women's Rights By Non-State Actors*, *in* RECONCEIVING REALITY, *supra*, at 93; Karen Engel, *After The Collapse of the Public/Private Distinction: Strategizing Women's Rights*, *in* RECONCEIVING REALITY, *supra*, at 143; Karen Knop, *Re/Statements: Feminism and State Sovereignty in International Law*, 3 J. TRANSNATIONAL L. & CONTEMP. PROBLEMS 293 (1993); Olsen, *supra*; Shelley Wright, *Economic Rights, Social Justice and the State: A Feminist Reappraisal*, *in* RECONCEIVING REALITY, *supra*, at 117.

124. For additional work along these lines, see, e.g., Ruth Buchanan, *NAFTA, Regulatory Restructuring and the Politics of Place*, 2 GLOBAL LEGAL STUDIES J. 371, 379, 374 (1995) (arguing that "the changing nature of borders in the global economy has posed a direct challenge to the old concept of sovereignty" because borders now represent not merely boundaries or dividing lines between states but also "geographical and cultural zone[s] and space[s]" where "populations that live on both sides of the border may find they have more in common with their counterparts 'across the line' than with their national governments."); Perry Dane, *Maps of Sovereignty*, 12 CARDOZO L. REV. 959, 964-65 (1991) (endorsing legal scholarship that "refuses to limit the domain of law to the state" and that "challenge[s] the rigid identification of sovereignty with the state."); Binder, *supra* note 109, at 262-263 (arguing that sovereignty "is just any legally enforceable disposition over the powers of others," and that sovereignty characterizes not merely statehood but also "bounded communit[ies]" of any kind which are dedicated to "the serious pursuit of any moral end.")

At the same time, efforts to forge an alternative path to both nationalism and liberal cosmopolitianism can be found at the level of progressive political practice. Activists in the peace and disarmament, feminist, labor, environmental and solidarity movements, among others, have in recent years begun to organize across borders to achieve their political ends, in a process one analyst has called "globalization from below."[125] The recent effort waged by activists against the North Amer-

125. Richard Falk, *The Making of Global Citizenship*, *in* JEREMY BRECHER ET AL., GLOBAL VISIONS: BEYOND THE NEW WORLD ORDER 39 (1993), at 47-48. The phenomenon of "globalism from below" has been the subject of increasing commentary in recent years. Describing the process in general terms, Richard Falk writes:

> [T]ransnational activism started to become very important for social movements during the 1980's. With respect to the environmental, human rights and women's movements, activism on a transnational basis became prominent for the first time in history. This meant that the real arena of politics was no longer understood as acting in opposition within a particular state, nor the relation of society and the state, but that it consisted more and more of acting to promote a certain kind of political consciousness transnationally that could radiate influence in a variety of directions, including bouncing back to the point of origin. Amnesty International and Greenpeace are emblematic of this transnational militancy with an identity, . . . that can't really be tied very specifically to any one country or even any region but may also be intensely local in its activist concerns . . . .These networks of transnational activity, conceived both as a project and as a preliminary reality, are producing a new orientation toward political identity and community. Cumulatively, they can be described as rudimentary, generally unacknowledged forms of participation in a new phenomenon, global civil society.

Falk, *supra*, at 39. *See also* Catherine L. Thorup, *Citizen Diplomacy and Cross-Border Networks and Coalitions in North America: New Organizational Patterns in the Immigration Arena*, RAND, March 1993 (describing "transnationalization of civil society.").

For further treatments of "globalization from below," *see* RICHARD J. BARNET & JOHN CAVANAUGH, GLOBAL DREAMS: IMPERIAL CORPORATIONS AND THE NEW WORLD ORDER (1994) ("Local citizens movements and alternative institutions are springing up all over the world to meet basic economic needs, to preserve local traditions, religious life, cultural life, biological species. .and to struggle for human dignity . . . More and more people who are bypassed by the new world order are crafting their own strategies for survival and development, and in the process are spinning their own transnational webs to embrace and connect people across the world."); Michael Peter Smith, *Can You Imagine? Transnational Migration and the Globalization of Grassroots Politics*, 39 SOCIAL TEXT 15 (1994) (describing "new transnational forms of political organization, mobilization and practice" which he terms "transnational grassroots politics); JEREMY BRECHER & TIM COSTELLO, GLOBAL VILLAGE OR GLOBAL PILLAGE: ECONOMIC RECONSTRUCTION FROM THE BOTTOM UP 78-117 (1994); Mary McGinn & Kim Moody, *Labor Goes Global*, PROGRESSIVE, March, 1993; Peter J. Spiro, *New Global Communities: Nongovernmental Organizations in International Decision-Making Institutions*, 18 WASH. Q. 45 (1994) ("Dramatically multiplied transnational contacts at all levels of society have not only resulted in a greater awareness of the global context, but have also created new commonalities of identity that cut across national borders and challenge governments at the level of individual loyalties."). Thalia Kidder & Mary McGinn, *In the Wake of NAFTA: Transnational Workers Networks*, 25 SOCIAL POLICY 14 (1995). *See also* note 127, *infra*.

ican Free Trade Agreement (NAFTA) provides one recent example of such organizing: during the campaign, many grassroots opponents from the United States, Mexico and Canada saw themselves as engaged in what might best be called a transborder communitarian practice,[126] a form of opposition produced and constituted by cross-border alliances of workers, environmentalists and consumers working commonly against the agreement.[127] To be sure, opposition to NAFTA overall was dominated by national protectionist thinking, and protectionist views were commonly espoused in this country by traditional liberals as well as by the likes of Ross Perot.[128] But parts of the opposition movement also

---

126. A similar phrase is used by Warren Magnusson. *See* Warren Magnusson, *The Reification of Political Community*, in WALKER & MENDLOVITZ, *supra*, note 119, at 45, 50 (describing "emergent transnational communities, such as those of feminists, environmentalists or pacifists.").

127. *See generally* Jeremy Brecher, *Global Village or Global Pillage*, NATION, Dec. 6, 1993, at 685:

> [T]he struggle against NAFTA generated new transnational networks based on . . . common interests. A North American Worker-to-Worker Network links grass-roots labor activists in Mexico, the United States and Canada via conferences, tours, solidarity support and a newsletter. Mujer a Mujer similarly links women's groups. The Highlander Center, Southerners for Economic Justice, the Tennessee Industrial Renewal Network and a number of unions have organized meetings and tours to bring together Mexican and U.S. workers . . . .These new networks are developing transnational programs to counter the effects of global restructuring. Representatives from environmental, labor, religious, consumer and farm groups from Mexico, the United States and Canada [have also worked together.]

See also Thorup, *supra* note 125 at 3 (describing "the networking and coaltion-building among a variety of heretofore disconnected individuals and domestic interest groups in the United States, Mexico, and Canada" working against the agreement); John Cavanagh and John Gershman, Free *Trade Fiasco*, PROGRESSIVE, Feb. 1992, at 33 ("Unwittingly, Bush has offered the citizens' movements of the Western Hemisphere a tremendous opportunity. Already, groups in Canada, the United States, and Mexico have formed to oppose the free-trade pact, and they are working together to propose alternative trade and development models."); William Greider, *A 2,000-Mile Love Canal: People On Both Sides Lose With the Free Trade Agreement*, UTNE READER, Jan.-Feb. 1993 (environmental activists are doing "what they were never able to do before--organize citizens on both sides of the border and form alliances for a new kind of cross-border politics."). For a useful historical overview of the development of the tri-national anti-NAFTA coalitions, *see* Allen Hunter, *Globalization From Below? Promises and Perils of the New Internationalism*, 25 SOCIAL POLICY 6 (1995).

128. ROSS PEROT, SAVE YOUR JOB, SAVE OUR COUNTRY: WHY NAFTA MUST BE STOPPED NOW (1993). For a characterization of much of the American anti-NAFTA environmental movement as protectionist, see Ileana M. Porras, Trading Places: Greening World Trade or Trading In the Environment? 88 A.S.I.L. PROC. 540, 544 (1994):

> [I]n the context of NAFTA, many U.S. environmental advocates appeared to have become inward-gazing: gone was the generosity of outlook, gone the concern with neighbors, gone the belief in globalism, gone the promise of interdependence. The dominant rhetoric was one of parochialism. Anti-NAFTA sentiment and activism were incited by images of the effect on *our* jobs, *our* communities, *our* standard of living,

contained the seeds of something else: a new breed of "internationalism," perhaps,[129] characterized by joint action and felt affinity among similarly situated groups in the three affected countries.[130]

> *our* environmental standards, *our* environmental health. Confronted with the possibility of eliminating boundaries, the reaction was (original emphasis) to ensure their continuance.

See also Brecher, *supra* note 127 (describing "nationalistic protectionism of some in the labor movement" during campaign against NAFTA.); Hunter, *supra* note 127, at 10 (describing how "the sovereignty 'card' was played by participants in the campaigns against NAFTA and GATT.").

129. The concept of "internationalism," of course, is nothing new for the left. Internationalism is a key aspirational tenet of socialist thought, and during some periods, the idea was a significant feature of socialist politics. *See* Alejandro Colas, *Putting Cosmopolitanism Into Practice: The Case of Socialist Internationalism*, 23 MILLENNIUM 513 (1994) for a useful historical review. However, both the recent decline of socialism as a viable political alternative in the contemporary world and the widespread intellectual critiques of enlightenment ideologies have together made the notion of international proletarian solidarity seem quaint and outdated even to most progressives. On the other hand, contemporary progressives could be said to be embracing new "internationalisms" in the form of new cross-boundary social movements, including the environmental, feminist, and peace movements. For a discussion of progressive internationalism, old and new, *see* Peter Waterman, *Internationalism is Dead! Long Live Global Solidarity? in* BRECHER ET AL, *supra* note 125, at 257. For an analysis of the challenges faced by grassroots activists in maintaining an internationalist vision during the anti-NAFTA campaign, *see* Hunter, *supra* note 128.

Beyond the domain of progressive activism, the concept of "internationalism" has recently begun to receive increased attention at the level of social and cultural theory. For a useful recent overview, *see* Bruce Robbins, *Some Versions of U.S. Internationalism*, 45 SOCIAL TEXT 97 (1995).

130. Several political colations representing hundreds of grass roots organizations from the United States, Mexico and Canada drafted a proposed alternative to NAFTA during the anti-NAFTA campaign in a position paper called *A Just And Sustainable Trade and Development Initiative For North America.* This alternative program would, among other things, guarantee enhanced labor rights for workers in all three countries, tie wage increases to productivity, guarantee the right to toxic-free communities and workplaces, institutionalize democratic accountability of corporate and governemnt decisionmakers, and promote income transfers to the poorer and less developed regions. *See* Alliance For Responsible Trade, Citizens Trade Campaign and The Mexican Action Network on Free Trade, *A Just and Sustainable Trade and Development Initiative For North America*, December 9, 1994, (available from the Institute For Policy Studies, Washington, D.C.). *See also* Cameron Duncan, *Trade and Environmental Policy, Greenpeace*, Testimony before the Committee On Foreign Relations, United States Senate on The North American Free Trade Agreement and the Environmental Side Accord, Oct. 27, 1993 ("Greenpeace has participated in a transnational citizens' effort to develop an alternative vision of continental economic integration. This vision is based on the principles of respect for human rights, the promotion of democracy, citizen participation in decisionmaking, environmental sustainability, and the reduction of economic inequalities among and within countries."); *Four Coalitions of NAFTA Opponents Offer An Alternative To Free Trade Pact*, BUREAU OF NATIONAL AFFAIRS LABOR REPORT, Sept. 29, 1993; Brecher, *supra* note 127, at 685 ("Rather than advocate protectionism—keeping foreign products out—many NAFTA opponents urged policies that would raise environmental, labor and social standards in Mexico, so that those standards would not drag down those in the United States and Mexico. This approach implied that people in

It is no doubt premature to characterize this tri-national, grassroots effort against NAFTA as one that entirely transcended the conventional national political imagination. For while forging cross-border alliances entailed in this case a recognition that national borders cannot constrain finance capital and jobs and toxic emissions, and the conviction that the increasingly transnational character of these phenomena must therefore be directly confronted in popular struggles for social justice,[131] the ultimate objective of these alliances still remained that of compelling individual nation-state governments to better protect the interests of nation-state members from the damaging effects of corporate-driven economic globalization. In this respect, the transnational activism that emerged during the anti-NAFTA campaign was likely perceived by a majority of its participants as much as a necessary strategy for pursuing greater justice within the individual states involved than as an intrinsic value in and of itself. Still, what is notable about this and other cross-national political efforts is that their frame of normative reference extends beyond the nation-state and its boundaries; interests and identities other than those defined by national membership, in other words, structure normative political discourse.[132]

But what of immigration? Even though it is important to recognize the emerging signs of transnational imagination in some progressive theory and practice, does such imagination necessarily entail normative opposition to the enforcement of national borders against transnational population movements? The answer, it seems, is not necessarily. The critique of statism in international legal scholarship so far has yielded little in the way of a sustained and systematic critique of borders to movement, except, perhaps, in the area of refugee protection.[133] And

different countries have common interests in raising the conditions of those at the bottom.").

131. *See, A Just And Sustainable Trade and Development Initiative For North America*, *supra* note 130.

132. As Cathryn Thorup writes of the developing cross-national political linkages between American and Mexican activists,

> Increasingly, instead of nationally-rooted cleavages with U.S. actors on one side of an issue and Mexican actors on the opposing side, there is now a new configuration with U.S. and Mexican actors on one side of an issue and an opposing constellation of U.S. and Mexican actors on the other side. As the domestic/foreign policy interface blurs, conflict in the bilateral relationship has the potential to become less nationally-grounded and more closely linked to class, issue-based and sectoral interests.

See Thorup, *supra* note 125, at 5.

133. I do not mean to suggest that the migration/immigration issue has been entirely ignored. A recent panel at the Annual Meeting of the American Society of International Law, for instance, took some steps in the direction of developing such a critique. *See Panel: Immigration Politics and Sovereignty: National Responses To 'Bad Aliens,'* 88 A.S.I.L. PROC. 439 (1994).

even if some progressive activists are beginning to approach certain political questions in transnational terms—even if they have begun to organize with their counterparts in other countries, and to envision themselves as part of communities that extend beyond their national borders—there is little indication that they will easily endorse the unobstructed transnational movement of people. Indeed, although immigration was not itself on the table during the NAFTA debates,[134] one of the central substantive messages that progressive opponents of NAFTA sought to drive home is that simply removing the constraints of national borders without addressing the relationship between the societies those borders divided and the social conditions prevailing within each of them will end up redounding against those who are already the most powerless on either side of the line.[135] While NAFTA seeks to dis-

---

But the issue remains distinctly underdeveloped in the literature overall. And although there *does* exist a developing critical immigration law scholarship (for a few relevant sources, *see supra* note 52; *see also* IMMIGRANTS OUT! THE NEW NATIVISM AND THE ANTI-IMMIGRANT IMPULSE IN THE UNITED STATES, Juan F. Perea, ed. 1996) (forthcoming)), its focus is largely domestic, and there has so far been only limited cross-fertilization between the immigration literature and the work of progressive international scholars.

As suggested in the text, progressive international legal scholars have to date devoted more attention to critiquing the international refugee protection regime and state exclusion of refugees under various circumstances. *See, e.g.*, Isabel Gunning, *Expanding the International Definition of Refugee: A Multicultural View*, 13 FORDHAM INT'L L.J. 35 (1989-90); Isabelle R. Gunning, *Modernizing Customary International Law: The Challenge of Human Rights*, 31 VA. J. INT'L L. 211 (1991); Harold Koh, *Refugees, The Courts and the New World Order*, 1994 UTAH L. REV. 999; Louis Henkin, *An Agenda For The Next Century: The Myth and Mantra of State Sovereignty*, 35 VIR. J. INT'L L. 115 (1994).

134. The transnational movement of labor was kept off the agenda almost entirely by the United States during negotiations, *see* Cornelius, et al., *supra* note 20, at 33; Buchanan, *supra* note 124, at 386-387, and with the exception of a few provisions facilitating the transnational movement of corporate employees, neither the main agreement nor the side agreements address the subject of immigration at all. *Id.* On the other hand, there was a great deal of debate in this country about the immigration consequences of the agreement, with supporters usually claiming that NAFTA would serve to curtail rates of undocumented immigration, and many opponents arguing that it would increase the flows. *See* Buchanan, *supra* note 124, at 387.

135. *See e.g.*, Cameron Duncan, *Greeenpeace*, Testimony before the Committee On Foreign Relations, United States Senate on The North American Free Trade Agreement and the Environmental Side Accord, Oct. 27, 1993 ("[Greenpeace has] concluded that the Agreement promotes a brand of economic integration that benefits a small sector in each country at the cost of rising inequalities and continued degredation of the ecosystems on which we and future generations depend."); Elaine Bernard, *What's the Matter With NAFTA?* 25 RADICAL AMERICA 19, 19-21 (1994) ("What is termed 'free trade' in the context of the . . . NAFTA agreement is actually deregulating international commerce . . . . There are and will continue to be rules of trade, regardless of what happens with NAFTA. But, NAFTA locks in, on a continental scale, the re-regulation of these rules in a very adverse way for most workers and citizens in all three countries. NAFTA increases the influence and safeguards the interests of multinational corporations in this essentially free investment pact."). *See also* Melvin Burke, *The Human Costs of NAFTA*,

mantle most national barriers to the movement of capital, many critics have argued that it does so in a way that ignores gross inequalities among the parties and their populations and also undermines government social protections from the market for everyone (other than the transnational corporations themselves).[136] It is, of course, precisely a lack of social protections and the existence of inequalities across borders that often have proved compelling to the corporations and that have prompted them to do business across national boundaries in the first place.[137] If progressives were to endorse the free movement of people, therefore, they would likely do so only as part of a broader program of transnational integration entailing redistributions of wealth and improvements in social status and social protections both within and across boundaries.[138]

HUMANIST, Sept./Oct. 1993, at 3.

136. For general critiques of NAFTA along these lines, *see e.g.*, Bernard, *supra* note 135, at 19; Burke, *supra* note 135, at 3; Brecher, note 127, at 685.

Many of NAFTA's progressive opponents contrasted the agreement's socially regressive "free trade" vision with an alternative vision they called "fair trade." A "fair trade" agreement would, among other things, provide assistance for development of the less developed parties to the agreement, provide compensatory financing for all parties suffering temporary dislocations and increased financial pressures from integration, and upwardly harmonize labor, environmental and consumer protection regulations. The major tri-national grassroots coalition opposing NAFTA, for example, (see text accompanying notes 126-132, *supra*) stated its support for

> "the initiation of new negotiations to craft rules that encourage mutually beneficial trade, investment, and development activities. Our countries *can* reduce trade barriers and remove some obstacles to investment, as long as we embrace a new framework of initiatives for our hemisphere and for the world that steer trade and investment to promote fair paying jobs, democratic and self-reliant communities, and a healthy environment."

The Alliance For Responsible Trade, et al., *A Just and Sustainable Trade and Development Initiative For the Western Hemisphere*, December 9, 1994, at 1 (original emphasis). For further discussions contrasting the free trade and fair trade visions, *see generally* George E. Brown, et al., *Making Trade Fair: A Social and Environmental Charter For North America*, 9 WORLD POLICY JOURNAL 326 (1992); Jorge G. Castaneda and Carlos Heredia, *Another NAFTA: What A Good Agreement Should Offer*, *in* THE CASE AGAINST FREE TRADE: GATT, NAFTA, AND THE GLOBALIZATION OF CORPORATE POWER 78 (1993); *Free Trade: The Ifs, Ands & Buts*, RESOURCE CENTER BULLETIN, Nos. 31/32, Spring 1993 ("Economic integration and expanding trade can be made to serve a broader agenda embracing social values. The goal is to construct a framework for integration that protects human beings, their communities, and the environment, not just the trade and investment decisions of transnational corporations"). *See also* Raul Hinojosa-Ojeda, *The North American Development Bank: Forging New Directions In Regional Integration Policy*, 60 J. AM. PLAN. ASS'N 301 (1994) (endorsing a "NAFTA-Plus" scenario, a "substantially enhaced NAFTA, which establishes specific institutional mechanisms" for ensuring that "the economic benefit of trade liberalization . . . serve[s] the explicit goals of upgrading the environment and improving communities on both sides of the border.").

137. *See e.g.*, BARRY BLUESTONE & BENNETT HARRISON, THE DEINDUSTRIALIZATION OF AMERICA 170-178 (1982).

138. As I stated in note 136, *supra*, many of NAFTA's progressive opponents called for an

This sort of transnational integrationist vision, I think, represents a compelling imaginative alternative to the nation-centered vision of social life which has traditionally informed American progressive thought.[139]

integration program which makes the reduction of economic inequalities between countries and regions a priority. On the other hand, few opponents addressed the immigration question directly. Some anti-NAFTA activists and researchers sought to rectify this ommission at a conference following NAFTA's passage, arguing that that "a fair trade positition consistent with global equity has to support immigrant rights and concern itself with the mobility of people as well as capital and products," Conference Report, *Beyond NAFTA: Toward Equity and Sustainability,* Havens Center, University of Wisonsin, 1994) (Madison Conference)), at 23. The conference called, specifically, for "a solution to the migration problem from an economic and labor vision that recognizes the asymmetries among our countries. Said recognition should consider the creation of compensatory funds for sustainable development which, if administred democratically with broad social participation, can contribute to the generation of social and productive infrastructures that promote jobs and well-being in our communities." *Id.*, at 39-40. Note, however, that this statement is hardly a call for free labor mobility among the NAFTA states; in fact, it could be read to suggest that sustainable development is desirable because it would serve to curtail the incentives for labor migration in the first place. Some supporters of immigration restriction have made just this point; *see* Philip Martin, *supra* note 71, at 89 (describing efforts of international and multilateral organizations to "relieve[e] the supply-push factors that encourage migrants to leave their countries" through "accelerating growth in emigration nations," and promoting "'stay-at-home' development.").

139. This vision also clearly bears some resemblance to the process of economic and political integration currently ongoing within the European Union. The Maastricht Treaty and other accords provide for free movement for European Union citizens within the territory of the member countries, and guarantee important political rights for those EU nationals who reside in other EU countries. At the same time, Maastricht provides for substantial development aid to the less developed countries in the Union, and the European Community Charter of Fundamental Social Rights of Workers and other instruments guarantee enforcement of certain community-wide workplace and environmental standards, thereby constraining the possibility of a corporate-driven "race to the bottom." These provisions were enacted as part of a broader process of European political and economic integration whose future scope and character remain uncertain. For a comprehensive overview of the European integration process as it pertains to social, environmental and development policy, *see e.g.*, SIMON BRONNITT, FIONA BURNS & DAVID KINLEY, PRINCIPLES OF EUROPEAN COMMUNITY LAW 431-442, 527-566 (1995). For an overview of the provisions pertaining to free movement and political rights of EU citizens, *see* David O'Keefe, *Union Citizenship, in* LEGAL ISSUES OF THE MAASTRICHT TREATY (David O'Keefe and Patrick M. Twomey, eds. 1994).

It is important to note, however, that in conjunction with a regime of increasingly free movement for European Union citizens within EU territory, the external boundaries of the Union have become increasingly tightened against non-EU citizens, and their status in Europe is expected to suffer. *See generally* Mehmet Ugur, *Freedom of Movement vs. Exclusion: A Reinterpretation of the 'Insider'-'Outsider' Divide In The European Union,* 29 INT'L MIGRATION REV. 964 (1995); Andrew Convey & Merek Kupiszewski, *Keeping Up With Schengen: Migration and Policy In The European Union,* 29 INT'L MIGRATION REV. 939 (1995); Tony Bunyan, *Borders Go Down, Walls Go Up,* GUARDIAN, Feb. 15, 1995, at 20. For a critical analysis of the reinscription of exclusionary boundaries at the European level through European Community law, *see* Joseph H. Weiler, *Thou Shalt Not Oppress A Stranger: On the Judicial Protection of the Human Rights of Non-EC Nationals—A Critique,* 3 EUR. J. INT'L L. 65 (1992).

Yet seeking its realization for the United States and its neighbors is a long-term project, to be pursued over decades, if it is ever pursued at all.[140] In the meantime, we are faced with different conditions entirely: Formally unauthorized transnational movements of people take place outside the context of any system of formal transnational integration, under conditions of substantial inequality, and with few social protections for most parties involved. Where does this leave progressives on the subject of unauthorized immigration today? Can we begin to imagine alternatives to our fundamentally nation-centered approach to the subject of exclusion at the borders under current conditions as well?

One could well argue that we *must* imagine such alternatives. For the fact is that there are powerful forces at work that bring the immigrants here, including a persistent demand for their labor,[141] job scarcity and comparatively poor living standards in their home countries,[142] and the immigrants' close ties to family and other community members that have come before.[143] It is clear that government border

---

140. The challenges involved in pursuing such an agenda in the North American context are substantial. For, in the words of one analyst,

> [d]evelopment disparities are much wider between North American countries than between any other group of countries that have attempted to integrate their economies. Countries within the European Union and the European Free Trade Association started wtih far smaller differences in per capita (and total) GDP than what exists between Mexico and the United States. [Furthermore], [i]ncome distribution disparities within the United States and Mexico are also much wider than those within member countries of the European Union.

Hinojosa-Ojeda, *supra* note 136, at 301.

141. *See e.g.* Cornelius et al, supra note 20, at 34 (describing the "persistence [in the United States and other] industrialized economies, of employer demand for low-cost flexible labor - a *structural* demand that has become decoupled from the business cycle.").

142. Note, however, that despite the common conception that it is the poorest and least educated people who come as immigrants to this country, analysts have concluded that "[t]he very poor and the unemployed seldom migrate . . . and unauthorized immigrants tend to have above-average levels of education and occupational skills in comparison with their homeland populations." PORTES & RUMBAUT, *supra* note 71, at 10-11.

143. Analysts have concluded that one of the most significant—and often overlooked—determinants of undocumented immigration to the United States are "immigrant networks"—ties of family and community that link immigrants in this country with compatriots remaining in the home country. *See, e.g.*, PORTES & RUMBAUT, *supra* note 71, at 230-32, 234:

> Contrary to the assumption that international labor migration is basically an outcome of individual decisions governed by the law of supply and demand, we argue that the phenomenon is primarily socially embedded. Networks developed by the movment of people back and forth in space are at the core of the microstructures that sustain migration over time . . . .[For example], [m]ost recent arrivals from Mexico, including the undocumented, are reported to find jobs within a few days thanks to the assistance of family and friends. The same social networks serve as financial safety nets and as sources of cultural and political information . . . . Although [employer

control measures (even assuming their legitimacy) can, at best, slow, but not stop, this process.[144] Mustn't progressives develop a normative politics of the border that takes these ineluctable facts into account?[145]

Arguably, the need to develop an alternative border politics is especially urgent given the stated commitment by some progressives to interrogate conventional structures of thought and social organization in light of the experience of the marginalized. The experiences of the marginalized in this case—the immigrants themselves—quite often do not conform with conventional modes of nation-centered thinking at all. Because although undocumented immigrants do live constantly subject to the legal authority of the United States' national border, they also reside in social worlds that simply are not confined by national territorial boundaries. In fact, anthropologists and other social scientists have shown that many undocumented immigrants have constructed lives that traverse political, geographic, cultural and political borders altogether. These immigrants maintain "multiple relationships—familial, economic, social, organizational, religious and political—in both home and host societies . . . .[They] take actions, make decisions, and develop subjectivities and identities embedded in networks of relationships that connect them simultaneously to two or more nation-states."[146] These

> demand] is likely to activate the potential for migration in the first place, it is the consolidation of social networks that gives the process its self-sustaining and cumulative character.

For more on immigrant networks, *see e.g.*, Douglas Massey, *The Social and Economic Origins of Immigration, Annals*, 510, AAPSS at 60, 68-70 (1990).

144. *See* Cornelius, et al., *supra* note 141, at 36 ("It is easy to be deceived by the apparent short-term efficacy of some of the sweeping changes in the rules of the immigration game now being implemented or considered. There is still no basis for claiming that these drastic remedies have 'worked' where they have been tried, at least in the terms specified by their advocates. Nor are there, necessarily, grounds for believing that with the passage of more time, with more 'fine-tuning,' more public education, etc., such measures will sharply and durably modify patterns of migration and employer behavior in the anticipated way. There are many routes to failure and frustration."). Elsewhere, Professor Cornelius has written (about Mexican undocumented immigration): "Short of a full-scale militarization of the border, no policy will prevent a continued influx into this country of Mexican migrants who cannot meet the stringent criteria for admission as permanent residents, usually because they lack immediate relatives who are U.S. citizens. These people will come legally if they have a legal-entry option, illegally if they do not." Wayne A. Cornelius, *Simpson-Mazzoli vs. The Realities of Mexican Immigration, in* AMERICA'S NEW IMMIGRATION LAW: ORIGINS, RATIONALES, AND POTENTIAL CONSEQUENCES 141 (Wayne A. Cornelius and Ricardo Yanzaldua Montoya, eds., 1983).

145. One might argue, moreover, that doing so is particularly necessary in light of the historical relations of domination and subordination between the United States and many of the migrant-sending countries that have contributed to the process of unauthorized immigration in the first place. *See* text accompanying notes 71-72, *supra*.

146. BASCH ET AL., *supra* note 119, at 7. *See also* Robert Smith, Transnational Localities:

experiences of multiple memberships and deterritorialized identities begin to suggest the increasing inadequacy of conventional normative approaches to the national border.

I would like to think that progressives' substantive normative commitments against subordination and exclusion, and their methodological commitments against regarding the given as necessary, make imagining (and constructing) convincing alternatives to the prevailing system of territorial exclusion possible. Yet I am also less than certain that such alternatives will be easily forthcoming. Progressive or critical political thought is engaged, as political philosopher Iris Young has put it, in articulating "normative possibilities unrealized but felt in a particular given social reality."[147] Political imagination, in other words, develops in response not to abstract conceptions of the right and the just, but to "unrealized possibilities" latent in the imaginer's political culture.[148] But one wonders to what degree our own political culture now contains the unrealized normative possibility of a politics of inclusion at the border. Normative nationalism remains "the most universally legitimate value in the political life of our time."[149] Even for most progressives,

---

Community, Technology and the Politics of Membership Within the Context of Mexico-U.S. Migration (paper presented to the American Sociological Association Meetings, August 1995) (on file with the author), at 28 (advancing analysis which acknowledges "the simultaneous memberships of migrants and their children, and which can describe the processes of diasporization, the creation of transnational civil society, or transnational community formation."); Rosemary Coombe, *The Cultural Life of Things: Anthropological Approaches to Law and Society in Conditions of Globalization,* 10 AM. U. J. INT'L L. & POL'Y 791, 795 (1995) (Anthropologists argue that their discipline must address "identities forged in transnational communities by peoples engaged in ongoing 'migratory circuits' that traverse national borders and boundaries;" it must pose "interpretive questions about the tactics and cultural practices of peoples who simultaneously inhabit multiple cultural frames of reference."); Douglas S. Massey, Luin Goldring & Jorge Durand, *Continuities In Transnational Migration: An Analysis of Nineteen Mexican Communities,* 99 AM. J. SOC. 1492, 1500 (1994): ("Over time, migrant communities become culturally 'transnationalized' incorporating ideologies, practices, expectations and political claims from both societies to create a 'culture of migration' that is distinct from the culture of both the sending and receiving nation.").

147. YOUNG, *supra* note 42, at 6. *See also* UNGER, *supra* note 118, at 204 ("The imagination works by a principle of sympathy with the suppressed and subversive elements in experience. It sees the residues, memories, and reports of past or far away social worlds and neglected or obscure perceptions as the main stuff with which we remake our contexts."); MICHAEL WALZER, INTERPRETATION AND SOCIAL CRITICISM 33-66 (1987).

148. YOUNG, *supra* note 42, at 6.

149. Anderson, *supra* note 65, at 12. *See also* JOHN DUNN, WESTERN POLITICAL THEORY IN THE FACE OF THE FUTURE 57, 66 (1979, 1993) ("Nationalism is . . . the very tissue of modern political sentiment, the most widespread, the most unthinking and the most immediate political disposition of all . . . Even at its most ideologically pretentious, the species has not yet *conceived* a practical form in which to transcend the nation-state); WALKER, *supra* note __, at 179 ("[S]tates

the boundaries of the national state still represent "the conventional limits of our understanding of what political life can be."[150] The ideals and norms that critics articulate "arise from the yearning that is an expression of freedom: it does not have to be this way, it could be otherwise."[151] But can it really be otherwise, at least in the short-term, with respect to enforcement of this country's borders against undocumented immigrants? It is not yet clear that our collective political imaginations can or will extend this far.

VII. CONCLUSION

Opposing Prop. 187 and its progeny is a more complex undertaking than it might initially appear to be. This is not to say that the question of whether to oppose such measures is open to any serious question. In fact, Prop. 187 and similar measures provide relatively easy targets of criticism: They are fundamentally xenophobic measures, as their critics have charged, which will poorly serve their own stated objectives of deterring unauthorized immigration and saving taxpayers' money; and to the extent they are enforced, they will produce a broad range of social pathologies in this country besides. Arguing this much is simple enough, though critics have differed among themselves about precisely how to frame each of these arguments for public consumption.

More difficult for the critics, however, is the prospect of arguing that these measures are wrong because they are unfair to their intended objects—the undocumented immigrants themselves. However intuitive the injustice argument might be, it is often a difficult argument for opponents to make, because defending the interests of these accused border violators is commonly viewed as an assault on the integrity of sovereign statehood itself. In political debate, therefore, the critics have tended to stick with more instrumental arguments, and to keep their concerns for the undocumented to themselves.

Yet the difficulty involved in characterizing measures like Prop. 187 as unjust is not merely one of practical politics. I have argued that

---

have become (second) nature and come to seem inevitable. We have inhereited . . . Hobbes' sense that there can be no solution to the difficulties and contingencies of modern life without the eternal presence of the sovereign state."); Charles Beitz, *Cosmopolitan Ideals and National Sentiment*, 80 J. PHIL. 591, 592 (1983) (arguing that the "national ideal is still dominant in common-sense moral thought.").

150. Walker & Mendlovitz, *supra* note 119, at 3.

151. Young, *supra* note 42, at 6. *See also* Unger, *supra* note 118.

even beyond the immediate pressures of public political discourse, the question of how to articulate what is wrong with these measures poses an important intellectual challenge for progressive thought. Certainly, progressives can, and do, criticize policies which mandate the wholesale social exclusion of a class of people who reside and work here as normatively intolerable. But the problem is that undocumented immigrants are not entirely like other classes of subordinated people whose condition progressives have addressed and whose inclusion they have championed. These immigrants are not merely "inside-outsiders"[152] (although they are this as well); instead, they come to this country from the outside and without formal permission, and the full story of their subordination lies not merely in the social exclusion they face after their arrival, but also in the efforts by government to keep them from coming in the first place and to remove them once they are here. Yet progressives' normative nationalism—whether tacit or explicit—makes them far less able and less likely to criticize the immigrants' exclusion from territory in the first place. The result is a gap—between a politics of inclusion within the national society, and a politics of exclusion, or acquiescence to exclusion, at the society's boundaries. And the trouble with this gap, among other things, is that it renders progressives unable to fully address the distinct reality of the undocumented, whose lives are shaped by compound forms of exclusion, including exclusion at and in relation to the border.

Whether there is any way of bridging this gap is a question I hope progressives will begin to address more directly. Yet posing the question is not entirely easy, not merely because our conventional political imaginations tend to make the issues involved difficult for us to see, but also because doing anything other than criticizing the nasty anti-immigrant mood currently sweeping this country might seem to run the risk of fanning its flames. But it is precisely the recent resurgence of anti-immigrant hostility, including the promulgation of exclusionary measures like Prop. 187, that makes the development of progressive thought on these matters particularly urgent.

Beyond the specific subject of immigration, however, posing these questions is also important for the development of progressive or critical thought more broadly. As we have seen, progressive scholarship defines itself, in part, as an oppositional project concerned with the construction and subordination of outsiders. Undocumented immigration

152. *See* text accompanying note 69, *supra*.

presents progressive thought with an especially "hard case," for while these immigrants are often understood as quintessential outsiders, their exclusion from the national society can also seem a necessary condition for political life as we have come to know and imagine it. The subject of undocumented immigration represents for progressives a kind of political crucible: it provides both a site in which to examine just how far our commitments against exclusion and subordination extend, and an occasion to explore the possible reaches of progressive political imagination.

[2]

Immigration, Law, and Marginalization in a Global Economy: Notes from Spain

Kitty Calavita

This case study of immigration law in Spain examines the contradiction between the rhetoric of immigration politics stressing immigrant integration and the reality of immigrant exclusion and marginalization. Drawing from a variety of secondary sources, government documents, and interviews, I show how Spanish policies regularly "irregularize" Third World immigrants. Further, I argue that this legal construction of illegality consigns these immigrants to the margins of the economy where they provide what policymakers appreciatively call "flexibility" to the post-Fordist Spanish economy. Finally, I discuss the ways in which racial "otherness," exclusion, and economic function are mutually constituted, and the role of law in that process.

Scholars of immigration and globalization often argue that a paradox exists between the contemporary forces of globalization and the dismantling of economic borders on one hand, and the increasingly restrictionist stance of Western capitalist democracies regarding immigration on the other (Aman 1994; Cesarani & Fulbrook 1996; de Lucas 1996; Hollifield 1992; Lusignan 1994; Scanlan 1994; Zolberg 1994). One example of this presumed paradox is the increasing ease with which capital and goods move in and out of Western Europe, while at the same time the "European Fortress" steps up control of its external borders (de Lucas 1996; Colectivo Virico 1994; Pugliese 1995; den Boer 1995:95). Perhaps even more conspicuous is the contrast between the North American Free Trade Agreement (NAFTA), which allows for the free movement of investments and goods between Mexico and the United States, and U.S. immigration policies that appear to be increasingly restrictionist.

Another theme that runs through much of the academic literature on immigration is the recurring gap between the declared intent of immigration laws and their outcomes. It is noted, for example, that despite concerted efforts to control immigra-

Address correspondence to Professor Kitty Calavita, Criminology, Law and Society, University of California, Irvine, School of Social Ecology, Irvine, CA 92697-7080 (email kccalavi@uci.edu).

tion from developing countries, in most advanced capitalist democracies these efforts have been glaringly unsuccessful in controlling either the size of the flow or its composition, and in some cases have had a series of apparently unintended and counterproductive consequences (see Cornelius, Martin, & Hollifield 1994).

The study of Spanish immigration law on which this article is based was undertaken as a way to explore such apparent contradictions. As a country that has undergone enormous political and economic transformation in the last two decades—almost overnight joining the roster of Western capitalist democracies—and that arguably experiences the contradictions of advanced capitalist development in an intensified fashion, Spain provides an interesting case study for such analysis. One of the preeminent scholars of Spanish immigration law has said, "The immigration of workers and their families from the 'third world' is . . . the social-demographic phenomenon that most clearly reveals the contradictions, internal and international, of Spanish society in the last years of the twentieth century" (Izquierdo 1996:133). As we will see, this recent immigration to Spain and the laws that purportedly attempt to control it can shed light not only on the contradictions of Spanish society, as Izquierdo notes, but also on the broader contradictions of immigration and immigration control in the new global economy.

As I began this study of immigration laws in Spain, I was soon struck by the marked contrast between the integrationist rhetoric accompanying these laws (for example, the Preamble to the first comprehensive law in 1985 proclaims that its purpose is to guarantee immigrants' rights and assure their integration in the host society) and their actual content, which systematically marginalizes immigrants and circumscribes their rights. I argue here that as Spain's economy took off in the 1980s and it joined the emerging European Community, the economic importance of Third World immigrants increased at the same moment that Spain was pressured by its European neighbors to control its borders, which had become the southern gate to the new Fortress Europe. The consequence was a series of contradictory policies that say one thing and do another. While the dual rationale of the 1985 law and its successors has been to control the borders while ensuring immigrants' rights, they do neither. Indeed, rather than controlling the number of immigrants entering Spain, these laws focus primarily on defining levels of social and economic inclusion/exclusion. I further argue that these policies are crafted in such a way that the predictable consequence is to marginalize Third World immigrants and consign them to the extensive underground economy.

A central component of this marginalization concerns legal status. Not only do illegal immigrants "work scared and hard," as the former Secretary of Labor (Marshall 1978:169) once said of undocumented immigrants in the United States, but they are excluded from most of the benefits of Spain's welfare state such as universal health care and social security, thus compounding their vulnerability and the urgency of their dependence on whatever work they can find. I will show here that the significant number of illegal immigrants (or "irregulars," as they are called) in Spain—and thus the high degree of marginalization of much of the country's immigrant stock—is the direct consequence of Spanish immigration law.

It has often been noted that law, at some fundamental level, creates illegality, in that without the boundaries of law, there are no "outlaws." But my argument here goes beyond this labeling theory insight. For Spanish immigration law actively and regularly "irregularizes" people, by making it all but impossible to retain legal status over time. Indeed, it makes little sense to draw distinctions between legal and illegal immigrants, as if they were different populations, because the law ensures that legal status is temporary and subject to continuous disruptions. In other words, not only does the law actively create "outlaws," but the boundaries between legal and illegal populations are porous and in constant flux, as people routinely move in and out of legal status. With lapses into illegality built into the system, Spanish immigration policy not only continually reproduces an extensive illegal population but also ensures the precariousness of its (temporarily) legal immigrants as well.

Young (1996) and Simon (1993) have eloquently discussed the "outlaw as other." Young depicts the exclusion of these "others" as a counterproductive effort at community building. Simon argues that in the postindustrial society of the late 20th century, we have returned once again to the concept of the "dangerous classes" and the criminalization of the unemployed underclasses. In the case discussed here, the point instead will be that the immigrant "other" is constructed as an outlaw (not vice versa), and that it is precisely immigrants' particular status as *workers* (not economic castoffs) that prompts this marginalization.

I hope that this analysis can make contributions at a number of levels. First, this research may help make sense of the apparent paradoxes outlined above. Not only has Spain only recently established its first immigration laws, as it experiences in fast motion and with considerable force the "internal and international contradictions" of advanced capitalist development, but these laws also offer a striking example of the intent/outcome discrepancy. My analysis addresses that discrepancy and in so doing begins to unpack the presumed paradox of heightened immigration restrictionism just as the forces of globalization increase. Indeed, I argue not only that there is no real paradox here but also that the current globalization and these particular forms of restrictionism go hand in hand.

Second, I hope to contribute to our understanding of the concepts of marginalization and social exclusion. Much of the discussion of immigrant marginalization and racism in European mass media and policy circles presumes that the dynamics of exclusion take place primarily at the level of culture (highlighting, for example, cultural differences between Muslim immigrants and the Western, Christian traditions of the host society, and calling for increased mutual respect and the undoing of stereotypes) (see, e.g., Consejo de Ministros 1995; Stolcke 1993, 1994; Cantero 1994; Touraine 1995; del Campo 1992; Santamaría 1993; Manco 1996). But my analysis demonstrates that marginalization and social and economic exclusion are not only—or even primarily—cultural issues but are systematically produced by law and the structural and economic imperatives it secures.

Finally, this case study of the legal construction of marginality may contribute to the ongoing discussion of the constitution of the marginalized "other" in late capitalist societies and the role of law in that process (Goldberg 1993; Simon 1993; Young 1996). Several bodies of literature in law and society, most notably critical race theory and feminist jurisprudence, have focused on the complicity of law in marginalizing people of color and women (Omi & Winant 1986; Tonkin, McDonald, & Chapman 1989; Danielsen & Engle 1995; Crenshaw 1990; Pateman 1988; Rhode 1989; Hoff 1991). Others have exposed the marginalizing impact of U.S. immigration law on undocumented immigrants and refugees (Cockcroft 1986; Calavita 1992; Coutin 1994). This case study of Spanish immigration law offers another striking example of such marginalizing effects of law and highlights the economic function of that marginalization.

The data for this piece were gathered during six months of study and fieldwork in Spain from January to July 1997. It was not always an easy task to locate reliable information on certain basic aspects of Spanish immigration policy. The social science literature is more oriented toward qualitative analysis and less number-driven than in the United States. While government reports often provide useful statistics on the number of legal residents and the distribution of work permits, other statistics on such basic issues as the number of annual deportations are remarkably hard to obtain.[1] A second difficulty compounded my efforts. While there are voluminous and numerous works documenting the letter of Spanish immigration law (often, for exam-

[1] Deportations are carried out by the police under the auspices of the Department of Justice, while most other functions relating to immigration (such as the issuing of work permits) are primarily the responsibility of the Department of Labor. In part because deportations are conceived of as a police and security function, these statistics are not made public.

ple, focusing on the conflicts between the law and the Spanish Constitution), little analytical work has been done—and little systematic information is available—on the actual workings of the law (the difficulty of locating data on deportations being one indication). As a result, the process of data collection often felt like a scavenger hunt, in which some seemingly straightforward and basic pieces of information remained stubbornly elusive until the very end.

This search eventually produced an eclectic body of data from a wide variety of sources. It includes information culled from an exhaustive survey of secondary sources—academic and journalistic—government reports, parliamentary discussions, official statistics, public opinion surveys, and interviews with academics and union officials. I have also made use of several excellent qualitative studies of the immigrant experience in Spain—including substantial, unedited interviews with a variety of legal and illegal immigrant workers and their families. There are inevitably gaps in the data—particularly pertaining to the actual practice of immigration policy in a highly decentralized state made up of relatively autonomous regions and municipalities. Nonetheless, the diversity of these data sources and their internal consistency contribute to my confidence in the findings reported here.

The next section presents a brief descriptive overview of post-Franco Spain, with a focus on its economic development, the emergence of its welfare state, and the concomitant improvement in the standard of living for most Spaniards, as well as an introduction to the concepts of "globalization" and "post-Fordism" as they establish the context for our understanding of Spanish immigration law. Following that, I provide a general picture of the volume and distribution of immigrants in Spain and their role in the economy. Then, I sketch in broad strokes the foundations of Spanish immigration law, beginning with the Organic Law on the Rights and Liberties of Foreigners in Spain of 1985 and tracing its subsequent elaborations and interpretations. Finally, the more analytical sections focus on the ways law constructs the social reality of illegality and marginalization and the relationship between that marginalization and the role of immigrants in Spain's economy.

Economic Growth, the Welfare State, and Labor "Rigidity"

The industrialization of modern Spain began in the 1950s and escalated in the 1960s, but this industrialization process took place within the confines of a dictatorial regime and relatively scant public investment in infrastructure.[2] Since Franco's death in 1975, the economy has grown by spurts, undergoing unprecedented levels of expansion between 1986 and 1990. This growth is perhaps best reflected in the GNP, which in 1960 stood at about 56% of the European average but which had increased to 76% by 1996 (Economist 1996:4). During the high-growth period of 1986-90, over two million new jobs were created in Spain, more than in any other European country (Maxwell & Spiegel 1994:89).

While Spain's GNP per capita was still lower than the European average by the 1990s, the structure of employment had changed dramatically—even more than that of its European neighbors—and wages and the standard of living had improved markedly. Between 1960 and 1985, the percentage of the population employed in agriculture fell more than 20 points, from 38.7% to 18% (Jimeno & Toharia 1994:7). During the same period, average real wages more than doubled and the official minimum wage skyrocketed more than 25-fold (Maté García 1994:18, 27).

Massive internal migrations helped fuel this growth, with poorer, more rural populations from the southern regions of Andalusia and Extremadura, and Galicia in the west, pouring into Madrid and Barcelona and other more prosperous areas during the 1950s and 1960s. By 1970, 38% of the population of Catalonia (the region of which Barcelona is the capital) was born elsewhere—with 16% coming from Andalusia—and in Barcelona itself the figure was 47% (Woolard 1986:57). Much as south-north migration was central to Italy's industrialization in this period, the massive influx of cheap labor from other regions of Spain into its industrial centers was pivotal to its economic development in the 1950s and 1960s.[3]

Large regional differences still characterize the Spanish economy. The Spanish Constitution of 1978 divides the country into 17 regions, each with its own president, local parliament, and courts and with a high degree of autonomy. This political decentralization is paralleled by pronounced cultural and economic distinctions. For example, the poorer regions of Andalusia and Extremadura have per capita incomes that are about 70% of the national average, while the richest regions of Navarre, the Balearic Islands, and Madrid boast per capita incomes that are more than 121% of the average, with GNP numbers showing comparable gaps (Maxwell & Spiegel 1994:78–79).

[2] Investment in the public sector in Spain in 1972 reached just 21% of its GNP, while the comparable figures were 50% for the United Kingdom, and between 34% and 38% for the United States, Germany, and Italy (Elgar 1993:401).

[3] A number of Spanish social scientists have addressed this internal movement, which at the time was conceptualized as immigration. Thus, when sociologist Carlota Solé wrote in 1982 of the importance of "immigrants" in Catalan society, it was these internal migrants who were her focus (see also Jutglar 1977).

The Spanish economy is cross-cut by sharp structural divisions as well. Again like its Italian counterpart, the economy in Spain is bifurcated into a technologically advanced primary sector which is highly unionized and state-regulated, and an extensive underground. This underground—traditionally concentrated among homeworkers, agriculture, and the self-employed—expanded dramatically in the economic restructuring of the 1970s and 1980s (to be discussed below as part of the ongoing "post-Fordism") and now includes sectors that are integral parts of Spain's industrial economy. One author notes of this expansion, "The news in recent years is that 'irregular' work has become 'organized,'" that is, it has moved beyond the confines of a relatively chaotic and small-scale, secondary economy to become a central component of Spain's industrial strategy (Miguélez Lobo 1989:118). In 1985, one official survey concluded that 22% of all work in Spain was underground, with the figures for agriculture at 31%, services at 23%, and industry at 16% (cited in ibid., p. 116). A recent study concludes that there has been a "spectacular" increase in the underground economy since 1986, and that by 1997 it contributed some 14% to the gross national product in Spain (cited in El País 1998:55). Some specific industries rely primarily on underground labor. It is estimated, for example, that 80% of the vast shoe industry in Valencia operates in the underground economy (Miguélez Lobo 1989:118).

A second duality permeates the contemporary economy in Spain, as a result of the proliferation of part-time and temporary work. While long-term contracts are highly regulated in Spain both by the federal government and by unions, contracts for less than three months are subject to far fewer restrictions. According to one study, 75% of work contracts in 1996 were for three months or less, with 50% lasting only one month (Mazuelos 1997:17). As a result of this trend, the labor force is increasingly split between older, long-term workers whose job security is ensured by government regulations and union contracts, working side by side with contingent employees with fixed-term contracts.

Unemployment in Spain is the highest in Western Europe, hitting a peak of over 24% in 1994 before settling at about 22% in 1996 (Boletín Mensual de Estadística 1997:297; Anuario El País 1997:434).[4] The figures are worse for certain regions and segments of the population. In Extremadura and Andalusia, for example, it is estimated that unemployment reaches as high as 33%, and among those under 25, the national unemployment rate is more than 40% (Economist 1996:6).

---

[4] The rate of *registered* unemployed was about 15% in 1996 (Economist 1996:6). The higher figures reported here are derived from official labor market surveys and are generally considered to be more accurate, although it is often pointed out that the extensive underground economy may absorb some of these "unemployed" workers (ibid., p. 7; Maxwell & Spiegel 1994:89).

It has become popular to attribute this high unemployment rate to the "rigidities" of the Spanish labor market (ibid.; Elgar 1993; Maxwell & Spiegel 1994; El País 1997; for further discussion, see Navarro 1997:13). Some observers, for example, point to the fact that people no longer seem willing to move to seek work (Economist 1996:7). Indeed, internal migrations away from the poorer regions of Spain have come to an abrupt halt; in recent years, Andalusia, Extremadura, and Galicia have even registered net increases in migration into their regions, as former migrants out of the area return home for their retirement (Ministerio de Asuntos Sociales, Direccion de Migraciones 1995a:197–98). Others (Maxwell & Spiegel 1994:89–90; Maté García 1994:26) point to the "inflexibility" of government regulations and collective bargaining—which now covers 75% of the country's private workforce—overseen by the two major union confederations in Spain (the socialist UGT and the communist CC.OO). Counterintuitive as it may seem, it is argued that Spain's high unemployment rate is due to the laws and union contracts that make it expensive and legally complex to lay off workers (and hence, the argument goes, discourage new hiring).[5] So widespread is this notion that the rigidity of the Spanish labor market is to blame for high unemployment that one commentator has referred to it as the "new dogma in Spain" (Navarro 1997:13).[6]

A relatively generous welfare state cushions the worst impacts of this unemployment. Between 1980 and 1993, Spain registered one of the highest rates of growth on social spending in the EC, together with Italy and Greece (Consejo Economico y Social 1995:491). While the bulk of this spending goes to old-age pensions and the national health care system, Spain ranks first in the European Community in the proportion of social spending on unemployment compensation (ibid., p. 493). This compensation, which applies only to those who have been previously employed and has a maximum duration of two years, is less generous than that of some of its European neighbors. Nonetheless, it is indicative of Spain's commitment to at least minimum income-maintenance policies. In part as a result of the country's economic growth and in part because of these social welfare policies,

[5] The latest response to this perception of labor market rigidity is a labor-management accord struck in the spring of 1997 between the largest employer associations and the union confederations. This highly acclaimed and increasingly controversial pact makes it easier and cheaper for employers to lay off workers and provides for a certain percentage of subcontract wages for entry-level apprentices. In exchange, employers have promised to limit the amount of part-time, fixed-term contracts (Noanin 1997:17; Zaguirre 1997:64).

[6] That analyst counters this dogma with the observation that Spanish employers are intransigent in their labor relations, seemingly trying to reproduce the conditions that existed before the legalization of independent labor unions in 1977. He points out, "As much talk as there is about labor rigidity, there is little discussion of the great rigidity of employers" (Navarro 1997:14).

the poverty rate in Spain has fallen substantially since 1980, no matter which indices are used to define poverty (Ruíz-Huerta & Martinez 1994:47–49).

Roughly coinciding with the end of the Franco period in 1975 and the acceleration of Spain's economic development in the 1980s are two other developments shared by most advanced capitalist economies. First is what has been loosely called "globalization." The term has been used in countless ways, for myriad purposes, and with much slippage.[7] Henk Overbeck (1995) suggests that the term "globalization," as it applies to increased integration of the world economy, is misleading. He argues that instead of more economic integration of the world economy, the contemporary period is undergoing a capital *"contraction,"* with economic activity increasingly centered in three principal regions—North America, Western Europe, and East Asia—and with the Third World (particularly Africa) heavily marginalized in this restructuring. He notes that in 1967, 31% of foreign direct investment was located in the Third World; by 1989, that figure had plummeted to 19%.

Overbeck's insight is important here. The argument is that the late 20th-century world economy has crystallized around a few decisionmaking capitals in the First World (whose economies are increasingly integrated and interdependent), some low-wage manufacturing in select Third World countries, and the majority of the world's population marginalized from this "global" process. Thus, I use the term *globalization* guardedly to refer to this process of the stepped-up integration of First World economies, their increased dominance of world economic processes, and their increasing reliance on Third World labor in select countries, even while many countries of the world are heavily marginalized from this process.

The second development of importance here is the phenomenon known as "post-Fordism." A substantial literature since the early 1980s has noted the "crisis of Fordism" in late capitalist economies (Harvey 1982; Lipietz 1987; Piore & Sabel 1984; Sayer & Walker 1992). As this literature explains, these economies had operated since World War II on the "Fordist" principles of mass production of standardized products, mass consumption, internal job ladders, relative employment security, and a government system of social security and income maintenance.[8] Beginning in the mid-1970s, the argument goes, line-balancing problems (with gluts and shortages in production inputs and inventories), labor

[7] For an excellent discussion of various "globalization narratives," see Silbey 1997.

[8] This was referred to as "Fordism" because of the recognition by Henry Ford early in the century that widespread consumption—and thus increased profits—depended on a workforce with expendable income and that worker productivity was enhanced by worker loyalty to the company, as well as by the dictates of scientific management. Gramsci (1971) was the first to subject what he called American Fordism, and its effects on class-consciousness, to critical analysis.

resistance, low-wage competition from less developed countries, and a generally rigid production structure, jeopardized profitability, and the system started to unravel to varying degrees in all late capitalist economies. Whatever its precise causes, Fordist principles of mass production, internal job ladders, relative job security, and welfare state protections have increasingly given way to an emphasis on "just-in-time" production inputs, labor cost reductions, flexibility in hiring and firing, an increase in contingent or part-time jobs, and gradual retrenchments of the welfare state. This constellation of economic and policy changes comprises the ongoing "post-Fordism." In Spain, its symptoms are most clearly evident in the rapid proliferation of part-time and contingent work and in the increasing importance of the underground and secondary economies, side by side with persistent complaints by employers and state officials about the "rigidities" of the labor market.

It was within this context that Spain crafted its first immigration laws. Despite the restrictionist rhetoric accompanying immigration politics, the value of immigration was fully recognized in some circles. The former Director-General of Migration put it bluntly in 1991, noting that immigration helped offset the "rigidities and strangulation of the labor market" (quoted in Izquierdo 1996:162). To preview the argument I make here, Spain's immigration laws—which systematically marginalize Third World immigrants but do not stem their immigration—provide the Spanish economy with precisely the type of vulnerable workers required to impose post-Fordist discipline on at least a substantial segment of the workforce. Further, this "immigrant control" is by no means antithetical to the current globalization, as I have defined it; indeed, the increasing polarization of the world economy and the integration of rich countries that characterizes this globalization finds its domestic counterpart in the sorting of people through immigration laws into categories of "otherness" according to their positions in this global economic order. Thus, as we will see, while foreigners from other First World countries are easily integrated into Spanish social and economic life, Third World immigrants from countries on the margins of the current globalization find their marginal status—and economic function—reinforced from within by Spain's immigration policies.

Overview of Spanish Immigration

It has become a commonplace to observe that Spain has gone from being a country of emigration to a country of immigration over the past two decades (Casey 1997:9; Cornelius 1994; Izquierdo 1996:38–39; Solé 1995:20). Massive labor migrations are by no means a new phenomenon in Spain; as we saw above, they have been an integral part of the country's industrialization process. What is new is the unprecedented level of *external* immigration. In fact, since the mid-1980s Spain has experienced substantial net immigration into the country for the first time in modern history (Ministerio de Asuntos Sociales, Direccion General de Migraciones 1995). This migration into Spain includes large numbers of returning Spaniards who had sought work in northern Europe and the Americas after World War II (ibid., pp. 73–80). More pertinent here, beginning in the 1980s rapidly increasing numbers of Third World immigrants entered Spain seeking work.

One observer has called this the "tercermundializacion" (or "Third Worldization") of immigration to Spain (Casey 1997:12). While in 1980, about 66% of foreign residents in Spain were from Western Europe and North America, and tended to be retirees and others seeking the pleasures of the Mediterranean climate and lifestyle, by the 1990s this percentage had shrunk to a little more than 50% (Comisíon Interministerial de Extranjería 1995:138; Ministerio de Asuntos Sociales 1994, 1995a, 1995a; Casey 1997:12–13).

A terminological curiosity reveals the disproportionate weight of Third World immigration in the public discourse. The official term for all foreign residents in Spain—regardless of how long they intend to stay—is *extranjero* ("foreigner"). There is no official category of "immigrant," probably in part because as we will see later, until 1996 there was virtually no permanent legal status for foreign residents and thus no "immigrants" in the sense that the term is used in the United States.[9] But in popular parlance a distinction is made between *extranjeros* on one hand and *inmigrantes* on the other, with the latter category reserved for those who come from the Third World seeking work. Thus, when the "immigration problem" is discussed in government circles, in the media, among academics, or in public opinion surveys, it invariably refers to Third World immigration, leading one commentator to refer to First World immigrants as "authentic *desaparecidos*" (Izquierdo 1996:71).[10]

The absence of an official category of "immigrants" in Spain, and the popular use of the term "immigrant" to refer exclusively to Third World residents (regardless of the length of their sojourn) presents an awkward terminological dilemma. For the

9 People are classified officially as legal immigrants in the United States largely on the basis of having secured a "green card," which qualifies them for permanent legal status. Foreign students, temporary workers on short-term visas, and others who are admitted for fixed periods are not considered immigrants.

10 So pronounced and taken for granted is this distinction that an acquaintance of mine—an expatriot of the United States who has lived in Spain for 25 years as a freelance writer—reports that he is regularly corrected if he refers to himself (playfully, because he too knows the distinction) as an *inmigrante.* He is politely but firmly told he is an *extranjero—los inmigrantes* are those who toil in the fields and factories, even if, unlike my American friend, they remain for only a few months and have no intention of "immigrating."

sake of simplicity, I will use the generic terms "foreigners" and "legal (or illegal) residents" when referring to the whole population of foreign residents, consistent with Spanish law and official documents, and "immigrants" when referring to those from less developed countries, as is the convention in Spain. It is this latter group that is the focus of this article. While I recognize the risk of reinforcing stereotypes by using this separate terminology, nonetheless "immigrants" are in fact socially constructed as different and it is this social construction that is of interest here.

As shown by Table 1, the number of legally resident foreigners in Spain increased from just over 183,000 in 1980 to almost 500,000 in 1995. Estimates of the number of foreigners living in Spain without valid residence permits range from 60,000 to 600,000 (Casey 1997:14; Colectivo Ioe 1992; Solé 1995:25; the Red Cross, cited in ibid., p. 25).[11] It is difficult to arrive at good estimates of these *irregulares,* in part because the undocumented often leave no paper trail, but also because these are not distinct populations: Not only do legal residents lose their status when their work permits expire, as we will see, but periodic regularization campaigns temporarily reduce the number of illegal residents, sometimes rather dramatically. Nonetheless, the more reliable independent sources estimate that the combined number of legal and illegal residents is close to one million (see, e.g., Solé 1995: 25).

Table 1. Foreigners Living in Spain with Valid Residence Permits, 1980–1995

Year	Legal Residents	Year	Legal Residents
1980	183,264	1988	380,032
1981	197,870	1989	249,559
1982	200,743	1990	278,796
1983	210,177	1991	360,655
1984	226,289	1992	393,100
1985	241,971	1993	430,422
1986	293,208	1994	461,364
1987	334,933	1995	499,773

SOURCE: Comisíon Interministerial de Extranjería 1995:24; Izquierdo 1996:21.

Roughly 51% of these legal foreign residents come from other countries in Europe, who by virtue of being citizens of the EC are extended the same rights of Spaniards to reside and work in Spain, and may even vote in local elections (Comisíon Interministerial de Extranjería 1995:24, 22). Indicative of their special status among foreigners, the rights of EC members in Spain

[11] One scholar points out that the wide divergence in estimates may have to do with the political agendas of those who use these numbers. For example, the low estimate of 60,000 comes from the communist union confederation CC.OO, an advocate for immigrants' rights in Spain, which is concerned for what the confederation sees as the sensationalizing of the immigration issue; the high estimate of over 600,000 comes from the Red Cross, which is a principal source of social services for immigrants in Spain and which, this observer notes, may have an interest in highlighting the problem so as to enhance funding (interview with John Casey, Universidad Autonoma de Barcelona).

are dealt with primarily through the regulations and treaties of the EU, rather than through immigration law.

The single largest source country of foreign residents is Morocco, with about 75,000 legal residents. Africa as a whole provides 19% of Spain's legal foreign residents, the Americas 22%, and Asia 8% (ibid.). It must be remembered that these numbers and percentages refer only to those with legal status. Were legal and illegal residents considered together, the proportions would shift substantially, since the legal status of citizens of Third World countries is dependent on elusive visas and residence and work permits (discussed below). One immigration scholar estimates that about 40% of all foreign residents in Spain—legal and illegal—are from the developed world, with 60% coming from the Third World (interview with John Casey, Universidad Autonoma de Barcelona).

Most Third World immigrants work in agriculture, construction, or services. Statistics gathered during the 1993 regularization process reveal that of the more than 110,000 legalized immigrants that year, most worked in domestic service (where the vast majority of women are concentrated), followed by construction, agriculture, and hotels and restaurants (Table 2).

Table 2. Economic Activities of Regularized Immigrants, 1993, by Sector

Sector	%
Domestic service	21.2
Construction	15.2
Agriculture	14.3
Hotels and restaurants	12.2
Retail	7.9
Other	29.2

Source: Ministerio de Asuntos Sociales, elaborated in Izquierdo 1996:114.

Many of these immigrants work in the underground economy. One study of Moroccans, Central Africans, and Filipinas in 1987 found that 80% of the immigrants interviewed had obtained their first job in the underground economy and had remained there for three or four years (Solé 1995:28). Qualitative studies of Moroccan communities in Madrid (Gonzalez-Anleo 1993; Pumares 1996), African farmworkers in Catalonia (Jabardo 1995) and Andalusia (Roquero 1996), Africans and Latin Americans in Barcelona (Valls, Estrada, & Ferret 1995), and other Third World immigrants (Ramirez Goicoechea 1996) consistently come to the same conclusion. These immigrants—sometimes with legal status and sometimes not—work at the most arduous and low-paying jobs and experience rapid turnover, not infrequently working up to seven jobs in one year (Pumares 1996:88).

Wages vary widely, depending on the sector of the economy and the region of the country. Women from Morocco who do live-in domestic service work in and around Madrid reportedly make between 70,000 and 80,000 pesetas per month, or roughly $550 (Pumares 1996:75). Another study reports that Moroccan domestics sometimes make as little as 40,000 pesetas (Ramirez Goicoechea 1996:29). Moroccan men in construction, working as day laborers in the underground economy, can make as much as 8,000 to 9,000 pesetas a day, or about $60, while their counterparts in agriculture make less than half that (Pumares 1996:81; Roquero 1996:19). Those who distribute propane gas tanks bring in only about 8,000 pesetas per *week*, depending on tips to make it through the month (Pumares 1996:85).

Despite this variation, one thing remains constant: Immigrant wages are beneath those paid to Spanish workers in every sector. One study carried out by the Catalan government found that remuneration per hour paid to immigrant workers was 21% less than that paid to indigenous workers for similar work in agriculture, 18% less in construction, 40% less in industry, and 50% less in the service sector where most immigrants are concentrated (Generalitat de Catalunya 1995:63). The former Director-General of Migration once estimated that 25% of the immigrants in Spain receive less than minimum wage (cited in Malgesini 1994:16–17). Studies done for Caritas, a Catholic immigrant-advocate group, estimate that 78% of immigrants in Spain have a monthly income of less that 50,000 pesetas (about $360) (cited in de Lucas 1996:34).

Spanish Immigration Law: Rhetoric and Reality

The Legal Framework

Prior to 1985, Spain had no explicit immigration policy or any comprehensive legislation regarding the treatment of foreigners within its territory. The Spanish Constitution of 1978 had specified only, "Foreigners in Spain will enjoy the rights and liberties put forth here, according to the terms set by international treaties and the law," with the qualification that foreigners did not have the same rights as Spaniards to vote and to serve as elected officials (Spanish Constitution, arts. 13 and 23, reproduced in Ministerio del Interior 1996:210, 214). A Constitutional Court decision in 1984 was similarly vague: "There exist rights that are equal between Spaniards and foreigners . . . [but] there exist other rights that do not by any means apply to foreigners (e.g., those recognized in Article 23 of the Constitution . . .); and, there exist others that apply to foreigners or not according to various treaties and laws" (quoted in Santos 1993:94).

This absence of legal specificity created a kind of legal limbo for immigrants "who carried out their work and social lives without any great anxiety and without a consciousness of being illegal" (Izquierdo 1996:142). One study of Moroccan immigrants prior to 1985 found that they were better integrated in the social fabric than later cohorts, were more likely to be self-employed, and often had their families with them (ibid.).

In June 1985, Spain joined the European Community, and that same month five EC member countries (Belgium, France, Germany, Luxembourg, and the Netherlands) signed the Schengen Agreement, designed to dismantle their internal borders. While the primary purpose of Schengen was to unify further the EC, security and external border controls were central themes. In this broader European context, the Spanish Representative Assembly passed the Ley Organica sobre Derechos y Libertades de los Extranjeros en Espana (Organic Law on the Rights and Liberties of Foreigners in Spain). The Senate quickly followed suit,[12] and the law became effective on 1 July 1985, just days after Spain signed the treaty for entry into the European Community (Boletín Oficial del Estado 1985:20824–29).

Evidence suggests that the law was in part the result of negotiations surrounding Spain's entrance into the EC (Casey 1997:24). Indeed, many observers have noted that the evolution of Spain's immigration laws goes hand in hand with the process of European integration (Borrás 1995a:21; Casey 1997:24). It is important to note here that while the EC has increasingly attempted to coordinate its border control policies, each country retains exclusive jurisdiction over immigration matters, with coordination being confined largely to statements of intent and principals.[13]

According to its Preamble, the Organic Law on the Rights and Liberties of Foreigners in Spain (LOE) had the dual purpose of guaranteeing foreigners' rights and controlling illegal immigration (Congreso de los Diputados 1985). The law has been called "vague and imprecise" (Sagarra & Aresté 1995:169) and "ambiguous and incoherent" (Aresté 1995b:192), in part because of its generality and absence of detail. Together with its regulations, which were finally published in May 1986, the LOE had six main foci. First, they made sharp distinctions between types of foreigners and their corresponding rights, with a dichotomy being drawn between the Regimen Comunitario (which applied to

12 The bill, which was introduced by the Socialist government, was uncontroversial in both the House and Senate and elicited little public debate prior to its passage. In the House, 274 representatives voted in favor, with 3 against and 3 abstentions. In the Senate, there were no negative votes, with 136 in favor and 34 abstentions.

13 The third major step in European unification—the Maastricht Treaty, which officially created European citizens—was signed by EC members in February 1992, to be effective in November 1993. Title VI of this agreement dealt with asylum, border controls, immigration, drugs, and establishing a European policing system (Europol). It also formed a committee to advise the Council of Ministers of Interior and Justice of the member countries. While Schengen and Maastricht have attempted to move toward a coordinated European policy on immigration and asylum, as one high official put it, there remain "teething problems" (quoted in Benyon 1996:365).

EC members) and the Regimen General (which applied to all non-EC members), with EC members being granted all the rights of free circulation, residence, and work in Spain. Second, the new policies required for the first time that most non-EC entrants have visas (LOE art. 12). Third, in addition to these entrance visas, those who intended to stay in Spain longer than 90 days were required to obtain residence and work permits (LOE arts. 13 and 15). As a result, "The great majority [of immigrants] became illegals" (Sagarra & Aresté 1995:165). Fourth, the law provided that legal residents would have certain rights of assembly, public education, and unionization, with the proviso that these rights were operative only insofar as they did not conflict with the "national interest, security, public order, health, morality, or rights and liberties of Spaniards" (LOE arts. 7–10, LOE, in Boletín Oficial del Estado 1985:20825). Fifth, the law made sharp distinctions between legal and illegal aliens and explicitly excluded the latter (which as a result of the law made up the bulk of non-EC foreigners) from any of the rights spelled out above (LOE arts. 7–10). In recognition of the vast numbers thus excluded from any legal rights, a "regularization" program was established through which foreign residents could apply for legal status within a brief window of opportunity.[14] Finally, the LOE spelled out the grounds for deportation, including lack of proper residence and/or work permits, being involved in activities that are "contrary to the public order or internal security," being convicted of a felony, and being without sufficient funds (LOE art. 26).[15]

A privileged status was created for foreigners from Latin America, Portugal, the Philippines, Equatorial Guinea, and for Sephardic Jews, Andorrans, and natives of Gibraltar, who were not required to hold entrance visas and were given preference in obtaining residence and work permits; in addition, natives of the Maghreb countries (Morocco, Tunisia, and Algeria) were exempt from the visa requirement—a privilege that was soon to be revoked, as we will see (LOE art. 23).

The LOE, still the only comprehensive law on the books relating to immigration matters and the rights of foreigners in Spain, took up barely five pages in the Federal Bulletin (Boletín del Estado 1985:20825–29), leaving not just the details but vast terrains of uncharted policy to be worked out through adminis-

[14] There were only 44,000 applicants to this program, which was widely criticized for its lack of publicity and coordination and which was launched at a time of widespread fear and confusion among immigrants who had become illegal overnight as a consequence of the new visa and permit requirements. Of these applicants, only 23,000 were able to fulfill the program requirements relating to ongoing, legitimate work contracts or other means of support in the formal economy (Colectivo Ioe 1992; Izquierdo 1992).

[15] A provision that would have allowed administrative authorities to conduct deportations without judicial input was declared unconstitutional in 1987 (Tribunal Constitucional, Sentencia Num. 115/1987).

trative regulation. Subsequent policy has been hammered out almost entirely by administrative policies and official decrees, leading one constitutional law expert (Santos 1993:113) to call it "à la carte" immigration policy. The most substantive of these administrative actions was the Council of Ministers Agreement on Regularizing Foreign Workers of 7 June 1991. This regularization program specified that illegal aliens who could verify that they were already in the country by 15 May 1991, and either had ongoing work contracts, were self-employed in a lucrative, legitimate enterprise, or had previously had a valid residence and work permit could apply for legalization (reproduced in Boix 1991). This legal status was valid for only one year; renewal was possible, but was contingent on the above conditions persisting.

A government decree in May 1991 imposed visa requirements for the first time on entrants from the Maghreb countries and from Peru and the Dominican Republic. The new controls followed reports that these countries were the source of large numbers of illegal residents, together with stepped-up pressure from the EC as Spain joined the Schengen Agreement in June 1991.

On 26 May 1993, a Council of Ministers Agreement established annual quotas for foreign workers in three sectors where there were reported to be insufficient local workers: agriculture (10,000 workers), unskilled construction work (1,100 workers), and various services (5,000 for domestic service and 3,500 for other services) (Aresté 1995b:191). Of the 20,600 slots provided, only 5,220 were filled, primarily due to the requirement that employers make requests for workers 40 days before specific jobs were to begin, and other such administrative hurdles in sectors of the economy known for their informality and unpredictability (Casey 1997:27). The following year, the administrative restrictions associated with requesting these quota workers were loosened, and while the numbers vary slightly from year to year, the program remains an integral part of Spain's immigration policy.

Finally, a government decree in February 1996 (Real Decreto 155/1996, reproduced in Ministerio del Interior 1996) launched Spain's third regularization program, stipulating this time that it applied only to those who had once had residence and work permits but who for a variety of reasons had been unable to renew them. This decree also created a permanent residence and work permit for those who could show they had remained in an uninterrupted legal status for at least six years, that is, successfully renewing their temporary permits with no lapses.[16]

[16] Throughout this period, Spain's refugee and asylum procedures were increasingly restrictive, as were those of other EC countries at this time. By 1993, 96% of applicants for refugee status in Spain were denied, with only 1,287 admitted (Izquierdo 1996:104). By 1996, there were only about 5,500 refugees living in Spain, mostly from the former Yugoslavia, China, and central Africa (Casey 1997:28; Comisíon Interministerial de Extranjería 1995).

While the Constitutional authority for immigration issues ultimately rests with the federal government,[17] the actual operation of the system is decentralized in the regions, provinces, and municipal localities (Casey 1997:22). The 17 regional governments into which the country is divided in effect have their own set of immigration policies. These are technically administrative blueprints for the execution of federal policy, but in part because the latter is so ambiguous, the regions enjoy "an ample margin of discretion" (Santos 1993:113).[18] As we will see later, this radical decentralization plays an important part in the uncertainty and ambiguity that plagues immigrants who are attempting to secure legal residence, work permits, and social services, and thereby contributes to their marginalization.

Between these autonomous regions and the local municipalities lie the Provincial governments, which exercise substantial authority as well. In fact, they are among the most influential players in the renewal of work permits and in operating the periodic regularization programs. A federal government decree in 1991 established local Offices of Immigration (Oficinas Unicas de Extranjeros) within each province (Boletín Oficial del Estado 1991), and among other tasks, they—together with the Provincial Directors of Labor—were responsible for implementing the Regularization Program of 1991 (Aresté 1995a:186).

Control and Integration as Rhetorical Themes

Throughout this legal evolution, the justification for policy choices was the need to control illegal immigration and integrate legal residents. The Preamble to the LOE, still the most powerful symbolic statement of Spain's stance toward foreigners, proclaimed its dual intentions of preserving their rights and—many argue, primarily for the EC audience—controlling its borders. The Preamble declared nobly that its purpose was "to extend to foreign residents the maximum level of rights and liberties" and "to facilitate the integration of aliens into Spanish society" (Congreso de los Diputados 1985:29–30), while its text concentrated on restricting immigrants' rights. One commentator has remarked, "If you were an immigrant and read the Preamble to the LOE, you would think you had arrived in a legal paradise, where words like 'rights,' 'guarantees,' 'maximum rights and liberties' abound," only to find that the content of the law was actually repressive (Mariel 1994:131).

[17] The office of Director-General of Immigration, after several moves, is currently located in the Department of Labor and Social Security.

[18] Noting the absence of legislative detail in developing immigration policy, one legislator in 1991 told his colleagues in the House of Representatives that they shouldn't "give a blank check to the executive branch" (Cortes Generales 1991:4889).

Similarly, a 1991 Congressional Resolution cited as its dual concerns the fight against illegal immigration and "the social integration of immigrants" into Spanish society (reproduced in Ministerio del Interior 1996:248–49). The Council of Ministers launched the legalization program of 1991, urging, "It is necessary . . . to ensure the social integration of the regularized immigrants and facilitate the maintenance of their legal status" (quoted in Aresté 1995a:184). In 1992, the Minister of the Interior told the House of Representatives (Cortes Generales 1992:17465), "[T]he objective of all our immigration policies is the successful and harmonious integration between the local population and the immigrants who come to live and work among us." He continued, "[In this] there are two key concepts: control [of illegal immigration] and openness [to facilitate integration]."

In 1994, the Council of Ministers brought to the House of Representatives a Plan for the Social Integration of Immigrants. The stated goals of this plan were to "eliminate all types of unjustified discrimination," "promote peaceful coexistence and tolerant attitudes," "guarantee immigrants a legal situation and social stability . . . so as to end their marginalization," "combat the barriers to integration," "eradicate all signs of exploitation," and "mobilize the whole society to fight racism and xenophobia" (Ministerio de Asuntos Sociales 1995b:9–10). The plan proposed 26 measures to accomplish these ends, although virtually no funds were set aside or administrative machinery established for their implementation.

Murray Edelman (1977) once observed that political rhetoric serves an important symbolic purpose, in that "it induces a feeling of well-being: the resolution of tension" (p. 38). Quoting Kenneth Burke, Edelman calls "political rhetoric . . . 'secular prayer' whose purpose is 'to sharpen up the pointless and blunt the too sharply pointed'" (p. 33). In fact, says Edelman, there is often a contradiction between the rhetoric and the reality it is meant to "blunt": "It is not uncommon to give the rhetoric to one side and the decision to the other" (p. 39).

As we will see, the integrationist discourse within Spain's immigration policies clashes head-on with the actual substance of those policies. A number of observers have noted that there is a striking contrast between "the generosity of the Preamble of the [LOE] and the restrictiveness of its text" (Sagarra & Aresté 1995:170).[19] This contrast permeates immigration politics in Spain, with the official rhetoric extolling the importance of immigrant integration and the actual policies ensuring their marginalization. The remainder of this article explores the spe-

[19] Edelman (1977:27) points out, "Typically, a preamble (which does not pretend to be more than symbolic, even in legal theory) includes strong assurances . . . [of] fairness, balance, or equity."

cifics of this marginalization, in particular the role of law in constructing immigrant precariousness and vulnerability through the construction of their illegality.

Constructing Immigrant Marginalization

Mercedes Jabardo (1995:86–87), an anthropologist studying African farm labor in Catalonia, observed of the 1985 immigration law, "The new legislation [LOE] . . . generates irregularity among the vast majority of the immigrant community. . . . In other words, the Law creates the legal category of immigrant and . . . generates the category of the 'illegal.'" This is true in the obvious sense that before the LOE there was no comprehensive immigration policy in Spain, and thus no illegal immigrants.[20] Similarly, the 1991 visa requirement for Moroccans, Peruvians, and Dominican Republicans *ipso facto* produced large numbers of illegal immigrants.

But the law produces "irregularity" in a more subtle way as well, for lapses into illegality are *built into* Spanish immigration law. This construction of illegality through law is the product of a variety of overlapping factors, the most important of which are the temporary and contingent nature of legal status, and a series of bureaucratic catch-22s.

The temporary nature of legal resident status is a central component of Spain's policies toward foreigners. Spain grants nationality primarily according to the principle of *jus sanguinis* and not *jus soli*. This means that unless one has Spanish "blood," it is very difficult to obtain the full rights of Spanish citizenship. Thus, for example, children born of noncitizen parents on Spanish soil are not automatically conferred citizenship and indeed may from time to time be illegal, depending on their parents' status.[21] Foreigners who marry Spanish citizens fare no better; as of 1996, illegal aliens who marry Spanish citizens must wait three years before they acquire even legal resident status.[22]

20 There were of course immigrants who were working illegally in the underground economy, but they were under no threat of deportation and were reportedly better integrated in the community than later cohorts (Izquierdo 1996).

21 There are a limited number of ways for those without blood ties to Spain to acquire citizenship (leading some observers to note that the Spanish nationality system is a hybrid of *jus sanguinis* and *jus soli;* Casey 1997:21; Santos 1993:122). For example, if a foreigner has lived for 10 years legally in Spain, s/he can apply for naturalization, but this is relatively rare in part because of the difficulties of maintaining continuous legal status (arts. 17 and 22, Civil Code; see also Boletín del Estado 1990). Somewhat shorter waiting periods are required of refugees and asylees, nationals of countries with historical-cultural ties to Spain, and those with particular ties to Spaniards (marriage, for example).

22 Union official and immigrant advocate Miguel Pajares explains that these spouses "remain in a strange kind of limbo" in which they are not technically legal (and therefore have no right to work) during the three-year wait, but they cannot be deported (El Periódico 1997).

There are few other routes to permanent legal status besides citizenship. Prior to 1996, it generally took 10 years of continuous legal status before one could apply for permanent residence. Since the regulatory reform of 1996 (Real Decreto 155/1996, reproduced in Ministerio del Interior 1996), the waiting period has been reduced to 6 years. Nonetheless, very few applications for this permanent residence category have been received, largely because of the near impossibility of piecing together 6 years of uninterrupted work and residence permits (interview with Miguel Pajares, Director of Immigrant Services, CC.OO [Communist Union Confederation], Barcelona).

The temporary nature of legal status is underscored by the instability inherent in the very program purportedly designed to facilitate integration—the much-touted "regularization" of illegal aliens. The first of these regularizations was launched by the LOE in 1985–86. This was followed by the larger program of 1991 and a smaller one in 1996. While not technically "regularization" programs, the quota worker system established in 1993 for agriculture, construction, and domestic service has also become an avenue of regularization for those already residing in Spain.

All these legalization programs are specifically and exclusively for foreign *workers* (and under some limited conditions, their families)[23] and are contingent on either having a legitimate work contract or having had one in the recent past. The difficulties of illegal immigrants meeting this standard, given their concentration in the underground economy, are legion. Not only are underground employers often unwilling to formalize work contracts, but some clearly *prefer* the undocumented status of their workers and the vulnerability that status ensures. According to qualitative studies based on in-depth interviews with Latin American and African immigrants in and around Barcelona and Madrid, a number of immigrants have been fired for pursuing the possibility of legalization with their bosses (Valls et al. 1995;

[23] When the LOE was passed in 1985, it made no mention of the possibility of, or procedures for, family unification, a "conspicuous omission," according to one expert (Martinez 1995:196). Subsequent regulations spelled out "preferential treatment" for visas and work and residence permits for those seeking family unification, and required that the family member with whom unification in Spain was sought be well established and have the economic means to support the applicant. Two years later, the policy was abruptly changed by an administrative decree from the Minister of Labor, who set extensive new restrictions on family unification, e.g., adding to the requirements the condition that the family member with whom unification was sought had to have lived legally in Spain for at least three years (ibid., p. 198). The only exceptions were for citizens of the EC, Latin America, Canada, the United States, Australia, Equatorial Guinea, Israel, Japan, and New Zealand (citizens of the Philippines and the Maghreb countries were noticeably absent from the list of exceptions). In 1992, Spanish consulates received "instructions" to place a moratorium on *all* family unification visas, effectively freezing the program until the ban was lifted by administrative fiat in 1994 (p. 199). By the mid-1990s, family unification had become so restrictive that it was only a realistic possibility for a few foreigners in "preferred" categories and for a small number of refugees (Martinez 1995). This despite the fact that in 1993, a panel of EC officials signed a resolution that "all states recognize the right of family unification" (ibid., p. 196).

Pumares 1996).[24] An Equatorial Guinean who lost his job when he asked his boss to help him with legalization put it this way, "Here when they hire an immigrant, they prefer that he work in conditions that are not legitimate, and preferably illegal, that way they can pay what they want and under conditions convenient to them." A Gambian immigrant explained, "If you work in the fields, and you go to your boss and ask for a contract, that's the day you lose your job" (quoted in Valls et al. 1995:125, 127).

Those who do manage to get regularized find it difficult to retain their legal status. In fact, Spain's legalization programs *build in* a loss of legal status unless one can demonstrate on an annual basis that the original conditions persist (most important and most daunting, a formal work contract).[25] Some immigrants do not qualify for renewal because the work contracts on which their regularization had been based have ended; in other cases, the original contract commitments were never fulfilled by employers. For example, among Moroccans it was not uncommon for "pre-contracts" to evaporate when the employer refused to pay social security or satisfy other formalities, leaving the newly legalized immigrants to work without a contract, and making it impossible for them to renew their regularization at the end of the year (Pumares 1996:87–89; Izquierdo 1996:73).

Izquierdo (1996:125) points out that a large percentage of the women who secured domestic service positions through the 1993 and 1994 quota systems "have been reclaimed by the underground economy." As he explains (p. 73), "[It is] difficult for the regularized to maintain legal status, for they tend to work in precarious and unstable jobs in sectors (such as construction, textiles, agriculture and personal services) where irregular contracts and the underground economy are the norm."

Statistics on immigrants who have not successfully renewed their regularization attest to this reality. Of the original 128,000 applicants for regularization in 1991, only 64% of them were legal after two years (ibid., pp. 150–51). The regularization program of 1985, which had drawn only 44,000 applicants, saw an even higher drop-off rate, with only one-third still legal after three years (Pumares 1996:59). Izquierdo (1996:149) surveys the outcome of Spain's regularization programs and concludes ruefully, "A regularization program that maintains immigrants in il-

[24] These studies included, respectively, interviews with 75 Latin American and African immigrants in the Barcelona region and 50 Moroccan families in Madrid.

[25] Beginning in 1996, regularized immigrants may secure a two-year permit after their original one-year legalization, to be followed by a three-year permit, and eventually (if they fulfil the rigorous requirement of five years of *uninterrupted* legal status) permanent legal status. Although government statistics have not yet been published on the granting of this permanent status, my informants—including the director of one of the largest immigrant-advocacy groups in Barcelona—know of no instances in which such status has been achieved.

legality or sends a significant portion of the immigrant community back to that status, isn't worth much."

The work permit system operates in conjunction with, and parallel to, these regularization programs. Foreign residents who have been legalized must secure a preliminary work contract with an employer, with which they then apply for a work permit. Seven kinds of work permits were provided for in the LOE regulations: Type A was for work of no longer than nine months; Type B lasted a maximum of one year, was only valid for one particular occupational activity and geographic area, and was renewable for one year; Type C lasted for five years and was valid for any occupation or region (preference was given to Latin Americans, Portuguese, Andorrans, Filipinos, Sephardic Jews, and Equatorial Guineans for this highly coveted type); Type D was for the self-employed, lasted one year and was geographically limited; Type E lasted five years, with no geographical or occupational limitations. Type F was for EC members who resided in their own country and came into Spain only to work. As Santos (1993:120) has put it, "[T]he result [of these multiple types of permits] is a system that keeps the alien in a constant state of uncertainty about the immediate future and necessitates engaging in frequent and trying bureaucratic proceedings." Further, all these work permits are temporary, with the vast majority (Types A and B) lasting one year or less. As with regularization, securing a work permit—and renewing it when it expires—is contingent on maintaining a legitimate work contract, an insurmountable barrier for most Third World immigrants.

Hurdles built into the legal requirements and Byzantine bureaucratic procedures compound these difficulties. For example, while Type A permits last only 9 months, in order to renew them the applicant must wait 12 months from the date it was issued, *structuring in 3 months of illegal status*. Even those who secure permits that last one year inevitably experience periods of illegality. It is well known, for example, that in renewing these permits immigrants confront delays of up to 6 or 8 months (Mariel 1994:134; interview with Miguel Pajares, Director of Immigrant Services, CC.OO, Barcelona). In some cases, it takes so long that the permit has almost expired by the time the immigrant receives it; there are even cases in which the permit has passed its expiration date by the time it is issued (Casey 1997:25, 41).[26] As Casey (p. 25) describes it, "The attitude of the administration seems to be to erect as many obstacles as possible to getting permits. . . . The consequence is to maintain immigrants in a position of continual supplication and permanent precariousness." Borrás and Gonzalez (1995:213) concur. "Delays in the granting and re-

26 One immigrant worker who had lived in Catalonia for 12 years addressed these delays with resignation and dry humor: "The problem is always the same . . . well, the [Spanish bureaucracy] makes an art out of not-doing" (quoted in Valls et al. 1995:37).

newing of permits and the excessive presence of short-term permits, place a large part of the immigrant population in a position of uncertainty and absolute precariousness."

A catch-22 in the permit process also contributes to what one Spanish immigration law scholar calls the "institutionalized irregularity" of the system (Santos 1993:111). In order to secure legal status, foreigners must (1) secure a work contract commitment from an employer; (2) take this pre-contract to the provincial Labor Department to apply for a work permit; (3) take this provisional work permit and other documents to the Department of Interior and the police for a residence permit; (4) finally, secure a work/residence permit which authorizes them to live and work in Spain (again, usually expiring after one year). The catch-22 in this already complex circuit is that the labor contract, the work permit, and the residence permit are in effect mutually dependent on each other, a fact that one observer has called "the vicious circle in which clandestine immigrants are trapped" (de Lucas 1994:92).

One Mexican worker living in Catalonia for three years described his experience, "The work permit was very difficult to get because [first] you need to present a work contract . . . but to get a work contract you need a permit, no? So, which comes first the chicken or the egg?" (quoted in Valls et al. 1995:39). On some occasions, "there have been situations so absurd as immigrants losing their residence permit or work permit because one of them expired while waiting for the other to be issued" (ibid., p. 40). A Gambian worker tells this story:

> My boss signed a year's pre-contract with me, but my work permit kept being delayed. . . . I went every two months to Barcelona to get the official stamp . . . well, after a year, still no work permit. One day, my boss says to me, "Well, the year is up already!"
>
> I say, "Yes, I know, but tomorrow I'm going to Barcelona again to see if I can get my papers." So, I go to the provincial authorities in the Interior, and they say, "Your papers are at the Labor Department," and I go to the Labor Department and they say, "Your papers are with Interior." When I go back to Interior, I tell them my name, they finally give me my papers, but then they say, "Oh, but your residence permit has expired . . ."

Metaphors abound in describing these bureaucratic tangles. As one indignant member of the House of Representatives (Cortes Generales 1991:4889) told his colleagues, "It is the famous fish that ate his tail: you can't get residence if you don't have a work permit and you can't get a work permit if you don't have residence."

Political decentralization and administrative discretion exacerbate the difficulties. As a member of the Immigrant Collective of Catalonia put it,

> [One] fact that characterizes Spanish immigration law is the frequent ambiguity of the concepts employed in its text, which results in very different interpretations in differing provinces and regions. That is what happened with the regularization of 1991, which gave rise to a veritable Tower of Babel between civil servants and applicants. (Kingolo 1994:157)

It is not just that discretion was maximized but that in the process, "a veritable bureaucratic labyrinth came into being, in which the government institutions contradict each other" (Valls et al. 1995:37). So contradictory and ambiguous are government policies that even the experts are divided on what it all means, with some declaring, for example, that all immigrants have a right to public education and health care and others citing government Decrees, "Instructions," "Circulars," and Constitutional mandates that seem to affirm just the opposite (see Santos 1995; Sagarra & Aresté 1995; Borrás & Gonzalez 1995). More important here, the lack of clarity heightens immigrants' insecurity and "can translate into an instrument for maintaining foreign workers in a clandestine status" (Santos 1993:117).

Given the difficulties of securing permits, it is not surprising that most Third World immigrants work without them, illegally. In 1996, with an immigrant worker population of about 300,000,[27] fewer than 90,000 work permits—including renewals—were issued (Ministerio de Trabajo y Asuntos Sociales 1997:201). Independent census studies of Third World immigrant communities find a preponderance of "irregulars." According to Izquierdo's calculations (1996:24), "Among Moroccan and Algerian immigrants, irregularity is the norm, not the exception." Among African farm workers in Catalonia, it is estimated that four out of five workers are illegal (Jabardo 1995).

The Social Reality of Exclusion and Marginalization

Public opinion polls show Spaniards to be among the least anti-immigrant populations in Europe. The two most prestigious public opinion surveys in Spain, conducted by the Centro de Investigaciónes sobre la Realidad Española (CIRES 1995) and the Centro de Investigaciónes Sociológicos (CIS 1996), consistently report relatively low scores of racism and xenophobia, with the number of Spaniards who believe immigration to be a major problem remaining fairly low, even as the number of immigrants

27 EC citizens are authorized to work through a separate system. This estimate of the non-EC worker population is derived from estimates of the number of non-EC immigrants in Spain, nonrenewed work permits, etc. (Casey 1997).

increases.[28] Acts of violence against immigrants are by no means unknown, and there is some evidence that they are increasing, as documented by SOS Racismo (1995, 1996); nonetheless, their rates are low compared with other European countries.

Some have linked these limited expressions of xenophobia and anti-immigrant violence to the fact that Spain receives fewer immigrants than other developed countries (CIRES 1995). Others have pointed out that stereotypes, prejudices, and cultural exclusion—particularly directed against the Arab population—are indeed rampant in Spain, but that surveys are unlikely to tap these politically incorrect sentiments (de Lucas 1992, 1996; Santamaría 1993; Buisef 1994). Whatever its causes and contested sincerity, this laissez faire stance toward immigrants, relative to other EC countries, contrasts markedly with the high degree of socioeconomic exclusion and marginalization actually experienced by the immigrant population in Spain.[29] Extensive documentary evidence confirms what de Lucas (19985) sums up as "the existence of pockets of work, frequently clandestine, such that Moroccans, Guineans, and others, live in conditions of housing . . . health and wages that approach those of slavery."

The Centro de Investigaciones Sociologicos (Ramirez Goicoechea 1996) voluminous qualitative study of the life experiences of immigrants in Spain attests to the limited access of Third World immigrants to social services, such as health clinics, as well as other life necessities. The inadequate housing of much of the immigrant population was dramatized in October 1994, when a large shanty-town outside Madrid that housed a significant portion of the city's Moroccan population burned to the ground, leaving thousands homeless (Izquierdo 1996). Recent studies and government reports confirm the more mundane realities of crowding, lack of sanitation, and the ghettoization of Third World immigrants (Ramirez Goicoechea 1996; Valls et al. 1995;

[28] In the CIS study done in June 1996 on a random sample of 2,500 Spaniards, only a small minority expressed any hostility toward immigrants. According to the index of xenophobia constructed in a 1995 CIRES study, 60% of Spaniards are "not at all" xenophobic, with about 7% being "quite" or "very" xenophobic. Further, 95% responded that all people should have the freedom to live and work in whatever country they choose. Sixteen percent said they would object to having Moroccans as neighbors (either "a lot," "pretty much," or "a little"); 15% would object to having central Africans as neighbors, and 10% would object to Latin Americans as neighbors. Asked to rank 10 ethnic and immigrant groups, Spaniards consistently place "Arabs" and "gypsies," respectively, at the bottom (CIS 1996; CIRES 1995; SOS Racismo 1996:183).

[29] Touraine (1995:12) points out that there are at least three dimensions to the concept of inclusion in a national community. One is nationality, which includes the political rights of citizenship; another is what he calls "integration," which refers to socioeconomic equality; and the final dimension is assimilation, or the acquisition by immigrants of the dominant group's cultural codes. Touraine argues that true integration is not possible if assimilation takes place, since the latter extinguishes an immigrant group's cultural identity, thereby negating their equality. The point here is somewhat different, although I too am arguing for not conflating different levels of inclusion.

Pumares 1996; Comissionat de l'Alcaldia per a la Defensa dels Drets Civils 1995).

More important here, Third World immigrants experience substantial marginalization in the labor market. As we saw above, they are concentrated in the underground economy and receive wages significantly below those of native workers. In study after study, they speak for themselves: Gambian gardeners paid 20,000 pesetas (roughly $150) for a six-day week; Senegalese garment shop workers paid 28,000 pesetas a week working from eight at night to ten in the morning; a waiter who works for three weeks, is terminated, and not paid (Valls et al. 1995:136; Pumares 1996:86). Jamal, a Moroccan immigrant, sums it up, "It is marginalized work . . . cleaning who knows what. . . . I go in a factory and, well, I do the worst jobs: clean, gather, load, unload, do this, do that, whatever no one else can (sic) do" (quoted in Valls et al. 1995:131).

Turnover is high in these jobs, both because the workers cannot subsist long under these conditions and because employment is unsteady and haphazard. As the Gambian gardener cited above said, "The problem is, one week they give you work and the next week they don't. You can't live like this" (quoted in ibid., p. 137). Pumares (1996) found it not uncommon for these workers to have seven or eight different jobs in a year, some of which overlapped with each other, in an effort to make ends meet.

Sociologist Cesar Manzanos (1994:169), addressing the double marginality of incarcerated immigrants, writes, "The situations of marginalization which the current socioeconomic system produces are not residual categories, but necessary for its reproduction." The marginalization described here is similarly not "residual" but is the predictable consequence of immigration policies that ensure immigrant vulnerability. The immigrants themselves explain their vulnerability this way: "I don't like being illegal. Because being illegally in a country means being without words; you can't speak, because if you open your mouth, [they say] 'Where are your papers?' So, when I want to speak, I tell myself, 'I am here illegally'" (quoted in Valls et al. 1995:35). A Peruvian says, "They don't pay me much because, well, because I'm irregular; if I was legal maybe they would pay me more, no?" (quoted in ibid., p. 137). An Equatorial Guinean speaks of the low wages he received in one job and says, "I kept my mouth shut, because I wasn't going to complain. If I complained, they'd show me the door" (ibid.).

Spanish law requires that to file a labor complaint, a worker must have a work permit, thus freeing employers of illegal workers from abiding by prevailing labor standards. A grower who employs African farm workers explains the advantages of this system from his perspective, "I try them out and if I see they don't work hard, I fire them" (quoted in Jabardo 1995:88).

The subjective side of this vulnerability and marginalization is intense fear. Deportation is relatively rare in Spain,[30] but the threat of detection is all too real for many immigrants. A provision in the LOE allows for administrative authorities to detain those they suspect are deportable for up to 40 days in immigrant detention centers (LOE art. 26). While statistics on the number thus detained are not available, extensive anecdotal evidence gathered annually by SOS Racismo attests to the relative routineness of this practice and to the disruptions it wreaks on immigrants' lives (SOS Racismo 1995, 1996). One woman described her fear, "I swear, sometimes I wet myself, I'm so scared. I don't have legal residence and when I see the police, I'm terrified" (quoted in Valls et al. 1995:50). An Algerian said, "Our life is a continual flight from the police because we don't have papers. We live with permanent anxiety. It seems like we have a sign on our foreheads 'I am illegal'" (quoted in Dahiri & Acosta 1994:119). This fear of the police and vulnerability to detection has very tangible consequences. A Moroccan woman working as a domestic servant described turning down a better-paying job when her employer threatened to report her to the police if she left (Pumares 1996:76).

Clearly, the production and reproduction of illegality through law enhances the precariousness and marginalization of those who are thereby illegalized. This marginalization is not limited to the illegal population, however, but affects those who are (temporarily) legal as well. Indeed, in this system, there are few real distinctions between the two, since legal status is always a fragile state and almost inevitably gives way to periods of illegality. As Miguel Pajares, director of one of the largest union immigrant advocate groups in Barcelona, told me, "Immigrants in Spain always have to pass through periods of illegality."

Valls, Estrada, and Ferret (1995:35) follow this logic through, "If this [marginalization] is true for immigrants all over the world, it is especially true in Spain, where it is so easy to go from a situation of legality to illegality. . . . The notion that there is a dichotomy of legal and illegal immigrants as if they were two intrinsically distinct categories, is false."[31]

Just as there is not a dichotomy between the illegal and the temporarily legal populations, so there is often little change in an

[30] The number of deportations officially ordered each year hovers around 15,000, but most of these fall through the cracks in a system that relies primarily on voluntary compliance with deportation orders. In 1996, 4,837 deportations were actually completed (personal correspondence, Direccion General de la Policia, 1997).

[31] Legislators and the media continually reinforce this perception that there are two very distinct types of immigrants—legal and illegal—despite the reality that they are generally alternating states (Boletín del Estado 1985; Cortes Generales 1990:2115, 2118; Vanguardia 1997:12).

immigrant's life as s/he goes from one to the other. Pumares (1996:81), who studied Moroccan families in Madrid, described their disillusionment over this discovery: "There was a period, just after the regularization [of 1991], when Moroccans, hopeful over their new permits, tried to use them to get legal work, which many times turned out to be impossible."

There is widespread recognition of this marginalization of immigrants in Spain. Not only immigrant advocates and academics, but politicians and the mass media decry the creation of immigrant "ghettos," even "apartheid," within Spanish society (Cortes Generales 1990:2112). And as we have seen, public policy is almost without exception rhetorically framed in terms of the need for integration and cultural tolerance. In marked contrast with this rhetoric, Spanish law systematically reproduces illegality, marginality, and precariousness. The social and economic exclusion and marginalization of Spain's immigrants is neither unpredictable nor incidental; rather, it is the most significant achievement of Spanish immigration law.

Immigrants and "Others" in a Post-Fordist Economy

Of course, there is no smoking gun of intent here. A comprehensive search of parliamentary proceedings turned up surprisingly little real discussion on immigration policy, in large part because in Spain the debates accompanying parliamentary hearings take place off the record. The bulk of the published record consists of eloquent, formal statements extolling the dual virtues of controlling illegal immigration and integrating legal immigrants (reinforcing the misperception that illegal and legal immigrants are two distinct populations).

There may be no smoking gun, but there is nonetheless a lot of smoke in the air. For the marginalization that is systematically constructed by Spain's immigrant policies is eminently compatible with the economic flexibility that policymakers and employers repeatedly cite as the sole contribution of immigrants to Spanish society. An employer summed up the advantages of immigrant labor:

> Moroccans and Moors are better workers than the people around here: they are tougher [*sufridores*, or tolerate suffering]; and to work here you have to have the capacity to suffer. [Other] workers won't put up with what they put up with. They [other workers] come one week, but they don't last longer than that. These [immigrants] stay. (Quoted in Jabardo 1995:85)

One observer of the role of African immigrants in Catalan agriculture describes their economic contribution this way:

> The competitive success of coastal agriculture is based on . . . a workforce that includes segmentation and hierarchy of tasks. It is a matter of being able to attract new farmworkers who oc-

> cupy the lowest levels of the labor market. . . . It is not a coincidence that the development of this intensive agriculture is linked to the phenomenon of illegal immigration. . . .
>
> It is precisely their urgency and dependence that make the immigrant workers more economical for employers, even than Andalusian day laborers who . . . are not inclined to agree to the conditions that have been gradually getting more precarious. (Jabardo 1995:81, 84)

Surveying the contribution of Third World immigrants to agriculture and construction, Izquierdo (1996:22) argues there is a "structural dependence" on this pliable labor source.

There is nothing new in immigrants occupying the lowest rungs of the occupational hierarchy and enduring the worst working conditions and wage scales. An extensive immigration literature has for years documented the historical role of cheap immigrant labor (Bustamante 1978; Calavita 1984, 1992; Cornelius 1989; Marshall 1978; Castles & Kozack 1973). There are indications, however, that the contemporary situation is distinctive, particularly as it is unfolding in Spain. First, while in the past immigration to industrializing countries ebbed and flowed with the business cycles, decreasing and sometimes reversing direction during periods of high unemployment, today in Spain as in the rest of Western Europe and the United States, immigration flows are relatively unaffected by unemployment rates. This suggests that it is no longer simply an expanding economy that requires additional labor power, but a particular kind of labor power that is called for.

More specifically, the new immigration to Spain and other Western capitalist economies is occurring at a time of substantial post-Fordist restructuring. In Spain, as we saw earlier, this entails an expansion of the underground economy, rapid increases in the number of contingent and fixed-term contracts, and an emphasis on labor market flexibility. Pugliese (1995:61–62) describes these new conditions:

> The crisis of the Fordist model of production has serious consequences for labour demand and consequently on the occupational structure. . . . Very important for the occupational location of immigrants is a decrease in the amount of regular, steady, year-round employment. . . . Precarious employment tends to characterise many of the new jobs in industry and, above all, the service sector. Casualisation of the labour force is one of the most powerful trends in the labour market. . . . This explains why immigrants are located [even] . . . in regions where unemployment rates are high.

Spanish politicians regularly and unself-consciously proclaim the dependence of the Spanish economy on Third World labor, not simply as a way to supplement the labor supply (with a 23% unemployment rate, this would be a difficult argument to make), but to offset rigidity and enhance competitiveness in a post-

Fordist global economy. Third World immigrants whose desperation and vulnerability have been reinforced by law are ideal for these purposes. The former Director-General of Migration has pointed out that a high unemployment rate and the need for immigrant workers are not mutually contradictory, noting that the Spanish labor market "contains certain rigidities" which Third World labor helps counteract (quoted in Mercado 1992:27). The 1993 law that established a guestworker system was accompanied by a government document addressing "the rigidities in the labor market" and a large "informal" sector that required an infusion of Third World workers (quoted in Izquierdo 1996:163). The same year, the Director-General of Domestic Policy announced that the government would not close the door to immigration, since "there are sectors of the labor market that are not occupied by Spaniards" (quoted in Vanguardia 1993). The 1994 Consejo de Ministro Plan for the Social Integration of Immigrants (1995:29) concluded that "rigidities in the labor market, resistance [of native populations] to move with employment opportunities, and high levels of social protection" necessitated importing foreign workers, despite high levels of unemployment among the native population.

Third World immigrants who are excluded by law from the civil, political, and social rights that make up membership in Western democratic societies (Marshall 1950) are the perfect antidote to the "high levels of social protection" accorded to members of the modern welfare state and corresponding labor "rigidities."

Conclusion

Thränhardt and Miles (1995:5) comment on the effects of the current globalization, "There will be one single organized club of rich countries," with citizens of poor countries consigned to the margins. Furthermore, they argue, "Underlying and shaping the practice of exclusion are . . . racist conceptions of 'otherness'" (p. 3).

Immigrants are in some ways the quintessential "other," having crossed physical borders to relocate in a community other than their own. Sociologist Georg Simmel (1950) long ago discussed the notion of the immigrant as "stranger"—physically present in a community but not part of it. More recently, Bourdieu (1991:9) has described the immigrant as "'atopos,' without place, displaced," a "bastard" between citizen and real outsider. And Rogers Brubaker (1992:47) talks about "the modern figure of the foreigner—not only as a legal category but as a political epithet . . . condensing around itself pure outsiderhood."

But in this new economic and social order, it is more complicated than the dichotomies of immigrant/citizen or stranger/member imply. Legally, politically, and ideologically, the community has extended beyond the nation-state to include—in the case of Spain—the rest of Western Europe, or the European Community. Thus, not all foreigners come from "outside the community" and not all foreigners are "strangers" or "other."[32] Increasingly, the determinant of who is truly an outsider to be restricted and controlled is based on the person's location in the global economy, not on his or her technical status as an immigrant.

Race, of course, plays a part in this exclusion, but is not the definitive criterion, nor could it be since race itself is socially constructed. Just as Italian and Spanish workers in Germany, France, and Switzerland in the 1950s and 1960s were considered racially and culturally inferior, only to become "Caucasians" and members of the European Community 30 years later, so it is with the marginalized workers of the Maghreb and certain South American countries in Spain that race, exclusion, and economic function are of one piece. The law plays a central role in this alchemy. For migrants who have crossed geographic borders, the law sorts and ranks and, for some, symbolically reconstitutes those borders. No longer physically out*siders*, they are now out*laws*.

The visa requirements imposed in 1991 for nationals of Peru and the Dominican Republic serve as a powerful example of the mutually constitutive effects of race, exclusion, and economics. For while in the past the preferences for Latin American countries were justified on the grounds of shared cultural traditions and heritage, these criteria are now trumped by development status. Thus, despite their cultural, religious, and linguistic ties to Spain, those from Peru and the Dominican Republic have fallen from their "preferred" status and are now defined as racially distinct outsiders. In the Spanish context, the "racist conception of 'otherness'" to which Thränhardt and Miles (1995:3) refer is itself a product of marginal economic status and corresponding legal categories. In other words, the perception of certain immigrants as racially "other" is the consequence of their social, economic, and legal marginalization, rather than its cause.

The presumed paradox with which we began has thus unraveled. For in this era of globalization, immigration restriction largely entails the marginalization of people according to their location in this new economic order. As we have seen in Spain, despite the rhetoric of control and integration, immigration laws and policies have one conspicuous effect: Instead of controlling immigration, they control the immigrant. Indeed, Spain's immi-

---

[32] Non-EC foreigners are evocatively called *extracomunitarios*, or community outsiders.

gration policies are more accurately policies that define the parameters of foreigners' inclusion or exclusion in the national community and the corresponding limitations on their rights and freedoms.

This emphasis on denying immigrants' rights and marginalizing them from the national community is by no means unique to Spain. There are strong parallels between this control of the immigrant in Spain in lieu of entry controls and recent "immigration reforms" in the United States that focus almost exclusively on barring immigrants from welfare and social services (see Calavita 1996). And as summarized by Cornelius et al (1994:10), most other Western European countries have increasingly "whittled away at . . . the rights and protections previously accorded immigrants" (see also den Boer 1995).

We can take this one step further. Not only are globalization and immigration restriction of this sort not inconsistent, they are natural companions. For, as Spain's politicians are fond of pointing out, post-Fordist economies with an emphasis on flexibility derive substantial benefits from marginalized Third World immigrants. As we have seen, law is a pivotal factor in shoring up this marginalization and the economic flexibility that is its welcome byproduct. Not only does immigration law sort people according to their inclusion/exclusion in the global economy, but—for Third World peoples who cross geographic borders into developed countries—it recreates and perpetuates from within their outsider status.

References

Aman, Alfred C., Jr. (1994) "Introduction: Migration and Globalization," 2 *Indiana J. of Global Legal Studies* 1–4.

Anuario El País (1997) *Anuario El País.* Madrid: Ediciones El País.

Aresté, Pedro (1995a) "Regularizaciones," in Borrás, ed. 1995b

——— (1995b) "Los Cupos de Trabajadores en 1993 y 1994," in Borrás, ed. 1995b.

Benyon, John (1996) "The "Politics of Police Co-operation in the European Union," 24 *International J. of the Sociology of Law* 353–79.

Boix, Vicente Font (1991) *El Trabajador Extranjero y la Regularizacion de 1991.* Barcelona: Itinera Cuadernos.

Boletín Mensual de Estadística (1997) *Boletín Mensual de Estadística,* vol. 64, April. Madrid: Instituto Nacional de Estadística.

Boletín Oficial del Estado (1985) *Boletín Oficial del Estado,* 3 July 1985, No. 158.

——— (1991) *Boletín Oficial del Estado,* 26 Oct. 1991, No. 257.

Borrás, Alegría (1995a) "La Influencia de la Evolución en el Medio Internacional sobre el Derecho Español de Extranjería en el Período 1985–1995," in Borrás, ed. 1995b.

———, ed. (1995b) *Diez Años de la Ley de Extranjería: Balance y Perspectivas.* Barcelona: Fondación Paulino Torras Doménech.

Borrás, Alegría, & Cristina González (1995) "Aspetos Generales de la Integracíon," in A. Borrás, ed., *Diez Anos de la Ley de Extranjería: Balance y Perspectivas.* Barcelona: Fondación Paulino Torras Doménech.

Bourdieu, Pierre (1991) "Preface," in Sayad Abdelmalek, *L'immigration: Ou les Paradoxes de l'Altérité.* Brussels: De Boeck-Wesmael.

Brubaker, Rogers (1992) *Citizenship and Nationhood in France and Germany*. Cambridge: Harvard Univ. Press.

Buisef, Dris (1994) "Medios de Comunicación y Visiones del Magreb," 6 *Voces y Culturas* 11–21.

Bustamante, Jorge (1978) "Commodity-Migrants: Structural Analysis of Mexican Immigration to the U.S.," in S. Ross, ed., *Views across the Border*. Albuquerque: Univ. of New Mexico Press.

Calavita, Kitty (1984) *U.S. Immigration Law and the Control of Labor: 1820–1924*. London: Academic Press.

——— (1992) *Inside the State: The Bracero Program, Immigration, and the INS*. New York: Routledge.

——— (1996) "The New Politics of Immigration: 'Balanced-Budget Conservatism' and the Symbolism of Proposition 187," 43 *Social Problems* 284–305.

Cantero, Josep Maria Navarro (1994) "Requisitos para el Desarrollo de una Cultura de Respeto a la Diversidad," in el Colectivo Virico, eds., *Extranjeros en el Paraíso.* Barcelona: VIRUS.

Casey, John (1997) "La Admisión e Integración de los Inmgrantes Extranjeros," in J. Subirats & R. Goma, eds., *Las Políticas Públicas en España*. Madrid: Ariel.

Castles, Steven, & Godula Kozack (1973) *Immigrant Workers and Class Structure in Western Europe*. New York: Oxford Univ. Press.

Centro de Investigaciones sobre la Realidad Española (CIRES) (1995) *Informe CIRES: Actitudes hacia los Inmigrantes,* October 1995. Madrid: BBK.

Centro de Investigaciones Sociológicos (CIS) (1996) *Actitudes ante la Inmigración,* June 1996. Madrid: CIS.

Cesarani, David, & Mary Fulbrook, eds. (1996) *Citizenship, Nationality and Migration in Europe*. New York: Routledge.

Cockcroft, James D. (1986) *Outlaws in the Promised Land: Mexican Immigrant Workers and America's Future.* New York: Grove Press.

Colectivo IOE (1992) "Los Trabajadores Extranjeros en España: Informe para el Instituto Sindical de Estudios." Madrid: Colectivo IOE.

Colectivo Virico, eds. (1994) *Extranjeros en el Paraíso*. Barcelona: VIRUS.

Comisión Interministerial de Extranjería (1995) *Anuario Estadístico de Extranjería*. Madrid: Secretaría General Técnica, Ministerio de Justicia e Interior.

Comissionat de l'Alcaldia per a la Defensa dels Drets Civils (1995) *Alguns Textos sobre la Integración dels Treballadors Estrangers i llurs Families*. Barcelona: Ajuntament de Barcelona.

Congreso de los Diputados (1985) *Boletín Oficial de las Cortes Generales*, 8 May, No. 132.

Consejo de Ministros (1995) *Plan para la Integración Social de los Inmigrantes*. Madrid: Ministerio de Asuntos Sociales.

Consejo Economico y Social (CES) (1995) *Economia, Trabajo y Seguridad: Memorias sobre la Situación Socioeconomica y Laboral, España*. Madrid: Consejo Economico y Social.

Cornelius, Wayne A. (1989) "The U.S. Demand for Mexican Labor," in W. A. Cornelius & J. A. Bustamante, eds., *Mexican Migration to the United States: Origins, Consequences, and Policy Options*. La Jolla: Center for U.S. Mexican Studies, Univ. of California, San Diego.

——— (1994) "Spain: The Uneasy Transition from Labor Exporter to Labor Importer," in Cornelius, Martin, & Hollifield, eds. 1994.

Cornelius, Wayne A., Philip L. Martin, & James F. Hollifield, eds. (1994) *Controlling Immigration: A Global Perspective*. Stanford, CA: Stanford Univ. Press.

Cortes Generales (1990) *Diario de Sesiones del Congreso de los Diputados.* 13 June 1990, No. 44.

——— (1991) *Diario de Sesiones del Congreso de los Diputados.* 9 April 1991, No. 100.

——— (1992) *Diario de Sesiones del Congreso de los Diputados.* 9 Dec. 1992, No. 580.

Coutin, Susan (1994) "Enacting Law through Social Practice: Sanctuary as a Form of Resistance," in M. Lazarus-Black & S. Hirsch, eds., *Contested States: Law, Hegemony and Resistance.* New York: Routledge.

Crenshaw, Kimberle (1990) "A Black Feminist Critique of Antidiscrimination Law and Politics," in D. Kairys, ed., *The Politics of Law: A Progressive Critique.* New York: Pantheon Books.

Danielsen, Dan, & Karen Engle (1995) *After Identity: A Reader in Law and Culture.* New York: Routledge.

Dahiri, Mohamed, & Diamantino García Acosta (1994) "La Inmigración en España," in Colectivo Virico, eds. 1994.

de Lucas, Javier (1994) *Europa: ¿Convivir con la Diferencia? Racismo, Nacionalismo y Derechos de las Minorias.* Madrid: Editorial Tecnos.

——— (1996) *Puertas que se Cierran: Europa como Fortaleza.* Barcelona: Icaria.

del Campo, Salustiano (1992) "Sobre el Racismo y la Xenofobia," 73–74 *Cuenta y Razon del Pensamiento Actual* 10-14.

den Boer, Monica (1995) "Moving between Bogus and Bona Fide: The Policing of Inclusion and Exclusion in Europe," in Miles & Thränhardt, eds. 1995.

Economist (1996) "A Survey of Spain," *Economist,* 14 Dec. 1996, pp. 3–18.

Edelman, Murray (1977) *The Symbolic Uses of Politics.* Urbana: Univ. of Illinois Press.

El País (1997) "La OCDE Recomienda a España que Siga la Política de Liberalización y Abarate el Despido," *El País,* 27 May 1997, p. 55.

——— (1998) "La Economia Sumergida Supone 11 Billones, Según un Estudio," *El País,* 9 July 1998, p. 55.

El Periódico (1997) "Boda 'Ilegal' para Denunciar los Obstáculos a los Matrimonios Interétnicos," *El Periódico,* 26 March 1997, p. 26.

Elgar, Edward (1993) "Spain: Shaping Factors," in A. Jacquemin & D. Wright, eds., *The European Challenges, Post-1992: Shaping Factors, Shaping Actors.* Brookfield, VT: E. Elgar Pub.

Generalitat de Catalunya (1995) *Entre el Sud i el Nord: Els Treballadors Immigrants Estrangers a Catalunya.* Barcelona: Generalitat de Catalunya.

Goldberg, David Theo (1993) *Racist Culture: Philosophy and the Politics of Meaning.* Cambridge, MA: Blackwell Publishers.

Gonzalez-Anleo, J. (1993) "El Poblado Marroquí de Manuel Garrido: Una Aproximación Sociológica," 1 *Sociedad y Utopia: Revista de Ciencias Sociales* 171–92.

Gramsci, Antonio (1971) *Selections from the Prison Notebooks of Antonio Gramsci.* London: Laurence & Wishart.

Harvey, David (1982) *The Limits to Capital.* Oxford: Basil Blackwell.

Hoff, Joan (1991) *Law, Gender and Justice: A Legal History of U.S. Women.* New York: New York Univ. Press.

Hollifield, James F. (1992) *Immigrants, Markets, and States: The Political Economy of Postwar Europe.* Cambridge: Harvard Univ. Press.

Izquierdo, Antonio (1992) *La Inmigración en España: 1980–1990.* Madrid: Ministerio de Trabajo y de la Seguridad Social.

——— (1996) *La Inmigración Inesperada.* Madrid: Editorial Trotta.

Jabardo, Mercedes (1995) "Etnicidad y Mercado de Trabajo: Inmigración Africana en la Agricultura Catalana," 36 *Perspectiva Social* 81–95.

Jimeno, Juan, & Luis Toharia (1994) *Unemployment and Labor Market Flexibility: Spain.* Geneva: International Labour Office.

Jutglar, Antonio, ed. (1977) *La Inmigración en Cataluña.* Barcelona: Edima.

Kingolo, Saoka (1994) "El Antirracismo desde la Perspectiva de los Colectivos de Inmigrantes," in Colectivo Virico, eds. 1994.

Lipietz, Alain (1987) *Mirages and Miracles: The Crisis of Global Fordism.* London: Verso.

Lusignan, Guy de (1994) "Global Migration and European Integration," 2 *Indiana J. of Global Legal Studies* 179–90.

Malgesini, Gabriela (1994) "Dilemas de la Movilidad: Inmigración y Refugiados en España y la CE," in Colectivo Virico, eds. 1994.

Manco, Altay A. (1996) "Social Development at the Local Level and Developing Public Services," 11 *International Sociology* 79–90.

Manzanos, César (1994) "Contribucíon de la Política Carcelaria Estatal a la Marginación Racial," in Colectivo Virico, eds. 1994.

Mariel (1994) "El Reto Legal ante la Extranjería," in Colectivo Virico, eds. 1994.

Marshall, F. Ray (1978) "Economic Factors Influencing the International Migration of Workers," in S. Ross, ed., *Views across the Border.* Albuquerque: Univ. of New Mexico Press.

Marshall, T. H. (1950) *Citizenship and Social Class and Other Essays.* New York: Cambridge Univ. Press.

Martínez, Antonio (1995) "La Reagrupación Familiar," in Borrás, ed. 1995b.

Maté García, Jorge J. (1994) *Demanda, Oferta y Ajustes Salariales en el Mercado de Trabajo Español.* Valladolid: Secretariado de Publicaciones, Univ. de Valladolid.

Maxwell, Kenneth, & Steven Spiegel (1994) *The New Spain: From Isolation to Influence.* New York: Council on Foreign Relations Press.

Mazuelos, Almudena (1997) "Tres de cada Cuatro Contratos Firmados en el 96 Duraron Menos de Tres Meses," *Ya,* 24 Jan. 1997, p. 17.

Mercado (1992) "Miedo a lo Desconocido," *Mercado,* 24 Feb. 1992, p. 27.

Miguélez Lobo, Faustino (1989) "El Trabajo Sumergido en España en la Perspectiva del Acta Única Europea," 32 *Papers: Revista de Sociologia, Universitat Autonoma de Barcelona* 115–25.

Miles, Robert, & Dietrich Thränhardt, eds. (1995) *Migration and European Integration: The Dynamics of Inclusion and Exclusion.* London: Pinter Publishers.

Ministerio de Asuntos Sociales, Direccion General de Migraciones (1994) *Anuario de Migraciones.* Madrid: Secretaría General Técnica, Ministerio de Asuntos Sociales.

——— (1995a) *Anuario de Migraciones.* Madrid: Ministerio de Asuntos Sociales, Secretaría General Técnica.

——— (1995b) *Plan para la Integración Social de los Inmigrantes.* Madrid: Ministerio de Asuntos Sociales.

Ministerio del Interior (1996) *Normativa Básica de Extranjería.* Madrid: Secretaría General Técnica, Ministerio del Interior.

Ministerio de Trabajo y Asuntos Sociales (1997) *Boletín de Estadísticas Laborales,* April, No. 143. Madrid: Secretaría General Técnica, Ministerio de Trabajo y Asuntos Sociales.

Navarro, Vicenc (1997) "Un Nuevo Dogma en España," *El País,* 5 May 1997, pp. 13–14.

Noanin, Idoya (1997) "La Crítica de la Mayoría de IU al Papel Sindical en el Pacto Laboral Hace Aflorar Contradicciones Internas," *El País,* 20 April 1997, p. 17.

Omi, Michael, & Howard Winant (1986) *Racial Formation in the United States: From the 1960s to the 1980s.* New York: Routledge & Kegan Paul.

Overbeck, Henk (1995) "Towards a New International Migration Regime: Globalization, Migration and the Internationalization of the State," in Miles & Thränhardt, eds. 1995.

Pateman, Carole (1988) *The Sexual Contract.* Stanford, CA: Stanford Univ. Press.

Piore, Michael, & Charles Sabel (1984) *The Second Industrial Divide.* New York: Basic Books.

Pugliese, Enrico (1995) "New International Migrations and the 'European Fortress,'" in C. Hadjimichalis & D. Sadler, eds., *Europe at the Margins: New Mosaics of Inequality*. New York: John Wiley & Sons.

Pumares, Pablo (1996) *La Integración de los Inmigrantes Marroquíes: Familias Marroquíes en la Comunidad de Madrid*. Barcelona: Fundación "la Caixa."

Ramírez Goicoechea, Eugenia (1996) *Inmigrantes en España: Vidas y Experiencias*. Madrid: Centro de Investigaciónes Sociológicas.

Rhode, Deborah L. (1989) *Justice and Gender*. Cambridge: Harvard Univ. Press.

Rivista Española de Derecho Internacional (1996) "El Nuevo Reglamento de la Ley de Extranjería de 2 de Febrero de 1996," 48 *Rivista Española de Derecho Internacional* 466–71.

Roquero, Esperanza (1996) "Asalariados Africanos Trabajando Bajo Plástico," 28 *Sociología del Trabajo* 3–23.

Ruiz-Huerta, Jesus, & Rosa Martínez (1994) "La Pobreza en España: Que Nos Muestran las EPF?" 96 *Documentación Social* 15–109.

Sagarra, Eduard, & Pedro Aresté (1995) "Evolución en la Administración desde 1985 en el Tratamiento de la Extranjería," in Borrás, ed. 1995b.

Santamaría, Enrique (1993) "(Re)presentación de una Presencia: La 'Inmigración' en y a Través de la Prensa Diaria," 12 *Archipielago: Cuadernos de Crítica de la Cultura* 65–72.

Santos, Lidia (1993) "Elementos Jurídicos de la Integración de los Extranjeros," in G. Tapinos, ed., *Inmigración e Integración en Europa*. Barcelona: Itinera Libros.

Sayer, Andrew, & Richard Walker (1992) *The New Social Economy: Reworking the Division of Labor*. Cambridge, MA: Blackwell.

Scanlan, John A. (1994) "A View from the United States—Social, Economic, and Legal Change, the Persistence of the State, and Immigration Policy in the Coming Century," 2 *Indiana J. of Global Legal Studies* 79–141.

Silbey, Susan (1997) "'Let Them Eat Cake': Globalization, Postmodern Colonialism, and the Possibilities of Justice," 31 *Law & Society Rev.* 207–35.

Simmel, Georg (1950) *The Sociology of Georg Simmel*. Trans. & ed. by Kurt H. Wolff. New York: Free Press.

Simon, Jonathan (1993) *Poor Discipline: Parole and the Social Control of the Underclass, 1890–1990*. Chicago: Univ. of Chicago Press.

Solé, Carlota (1982) *Los Inmigrantes en la Sociedad y en la Cultura Catalanas*. Barcelona: Ediciones Península.

——— (1995) *Discriminación Racial en el Mercado de Trabajo*. Madrid: Consejo Económico y Social.

SOS Racismo (1995) *Informe Anual Sobre el Racismo en el Estado Español*. Barcelona: SOS Racismo.

——— (1996) *Informe Anual Sobre el Racismo en el Estado Español*. Barcelona: SOS Racismo.

Stolcke, Verena (1993) "El 'Problema' de la Inmigración en Europa: El Fundamentalismo Cultural Como Nueva Retórica de Exclusión," 55 *Mientras Tanto* 73–90.

——— (1994) "Europa: Nuevas Fronteras, Nuevas Retóricas de Exclusión," in Colectivo Virico, eds. 1994.

Thränhardt, Dietrich, & Robert Miles (1995) "Introduction," in Miles & Thränhardt, eds. 1995.

Tonkin, Elizabeth, Maryon McDonald, & Malcolm Chapman (1989) *History and Ethnicity*. New York: Routledge.

Touraine, Alain (1995) "Minorías, Pluriculturalismo e Integración," *El País*, 12 Jan. 1995, p. 12.

Valls, Andreu Domingo, Jaume Clapés Estrada, & Maria Prats Ferret (1995) *Condicions de Vida de la Població d'origen Africà i Llatinoamericà a la Regió Metropolitana de Barcelona: Una Aproximació Qualitativa*. Barcelona: Diputació de Barcelona.

Vanguardia (1993) "El Síndic de Grueges Pide una Actitud más Integradora hacia los Inmigrantes," *Vanguardia,* 8 Oct. 1993, p. 10.
——— (1997) "Inmigrantes en Cataluña," *Vanguardia,* 29 March 1997, p. 12.
Woolard, Kathryn A. (1986) "The 'Crisis in the Concept of Identity' in Contemporary Catalonia, 1976–1982," in G. W. McDonogh, ed., *Conflict in Catalonia: Images of an Urban Society.* Gainesville: Univ. of Florida Press.
Young, Alison (1996) *Imagining Crime: Textual Outlaws and Criminal Conversations.* London: Sage Publications.
Zaguirre, Manuel (1997) "Un Acuerdo Histórico," *El País,* 9 May 1997, p. 64.
Zolberg, Aristide R. (1994) "Changing Sovereignty Games and Internation Migration," 2 *Indiana J. of Global Legal Studies* 153–70.

[3]

Implications of "Third-Party" Involvement in Enforcement: The INS, Illegal Travelers, and International Airlines

Janet A. Gilboy

This article is part of a larger study about the factors shaping the exercise of discretion by Immigration and Naturalization Service (INS) inspectors. It focuses on an infrequently examined topic: how agency behavior is affected when government depends on private enterprise to help enforce legal requirements. My examination of the INS's relationship with international airlines reveals that airlines are part of a third-party liability system. Airlines are mandated by law to screen foreign travelers prior to transporting them to the United States, in order to ensure foreign travelers' admissibility to the country, as well as required to remove all inadmissible travelers at airline cost. The study shows how third-party liability requirements generate a complex system of exchange relations and dependence between the INS and international airlines, a system that affects in important ways how the INS handles the cases of suspected inadmissible travelers.

Law enforcers cannot be everywhere policing activity. It is often more cost efficient and effective for government agencies to deter misconduct by enlisting the assistance of private entities. I here explore one such situation—the Immigration and Naturalization Service's (INS) use of international airlines in enforcement.

Today in a wide variety of contexts we use private parties as de facto "cops on the beat" (Kraakman 1986:53; Gilboy 1996). The Internal Revenue Service, for instance, requires lawyers, accountants, real estate brokers, and boat and car dealers to report large cash transactions possibly indicative of money laundering

This article is drawn from a larger study of immigration inspection work supported by the National Science Foundation (SES-8911263) and the American Bar Foundation. The study would not have been possible without the extensive assistance of the Immigration and Naturalization Service. I am deeply indebted to the Immigration Service District Director, whose personal interest and considerable efforts made this scholarly study possible. I also thank the Port Director, supervisors, and inspectors who generously gave of their time to help answer my numerous questions. Helpful comments on earlier drafts were received from anonymous reviewers and from John Braithwaite, William L. F. Felstiner, Gary T. Marx, John R. Schmidt, and Susan Shapiro. A very special word of appreciation goes to Robert M. Emerson whose many suggestions and valuable insights I have drawn on in preparing this article. Address correspondence to Janet A. Gilboy, American Bar Foundation, 750 N. Lake Shore Dr., Chicago, IL 60611 (e-mail: j-gilboy@nwu.edu).

(Holmes 1990; Glaberson 1990). Physicians, social workers, and school principals are mandated by law to report suspected child abuse to government child protective agencies (Zellman 1990). Still other laws require businesses to make payroll deductions to ensure that workers pay court-ordered child support or outstanding debts (Chambers 1979:ch. 11; Shellenbarger 1992). Typically, government imposes civil or criminal sanctions on private parties to compel their assistance in detecting deviance or ensuring compliance with legal requirements.

These private entities or third parties whose help the government enlists are neither the principal authors nor beneficiaries of the illegal conduct they police (Kraakman 1986). Their assistance, however, can be invaluable in supplementing government efforts at direct deterrence of wrongdoers. Particularly when illegal behavior cannot be detected except at great public cost, private parties can assist in enforcement by disclosing private information or by withholding support or services essential to wrongdoers' activities (ibid.).

Most theoretical[1] and empirical discussions of third-party liability systems focus on the behavior of the *third parties* themselves. Their actions are of scholarly and practical interest because, unlike some third-party enforcers who stand to benefit from compliance (e.g., consumer complainants, workers concerned with health and safety violations),[2] private entities in liability systems often are compelled to assist without benefit or compensation. Their behavior is thought to vary with the costs imposed by the scope of legal requirements and possible penalties (Kraakman 1986:75, 94). Both compliant behaviors (Kagan & Skolnick 1993) as well as forms of noncompliance are reported, including complacency in policing (Calavita 1990; Rolph & Robyn 1990:45), avoidance of legal responsibilities (Shellenbarger 1992; Whitford 1979:1050), and withholding of cooperation (Levi 1991:112).

This literature, however, does not exhaust examination of behavior in third-party liability systems. The meeting of the worlds of third parties and government enforcers raises a seldom explored issue. Government agencies seeking to augment their enforcement powers are not just the bearers of liability or merely watchdogs of private sector performance of imposed obligations. They are also potentially affected by the encounter.

This article shifts our attention to the effects of third-party liability systems on *government agencies*. How are agency officials' enforcement practices and decisionmaking affected by reliance on private enterprise to help enforce legal requirements?

[1] This literature is predominantly normative in nature and includes legal and economic analyses. Among the most thorough discussions is Kraakman's (1986) analysis and framework for assessing the advantages and limitations of third-party liability regimes; see also Lorne (1978) and Lowenfels (1974).

[2] See generally Bardach & Kagan 1982; Hawkins 1984a:381.

This situation is examined through a case study of the INS. Immigration has one of the earliest third-party liability systems. During the 20th century, laws have required transportation carriers (initially steamships and now also airlines) to screen travelers prior to transporting them to the United States in order to ensure their admissibility to the country, as well as to remove all inadmissible travelers they transport.

This study focused on INS inspectors whose principal task at international airports is to question suspected inadmissible travelers in order to determine their eligibility to enter the country. Inspectors operate in a situation where the last step of enforcement—the removal from the country of an inadmissible traveler—is not performed or paid for by the agency but by the international airline that transported the traveler.

The article describes the ways in which third-party liability requirements generate a complex system of exchange relations and dependence between the INS and international airlines, a system that affects in important ways how the INS handles the cases of suspected inadmissible travelers.

Although several explanations exist for why officials come to cooperate with private enterprise, the study suggests that officials' behavior is shaped not by direct pressures from the industry but more indirectly by specific agency constraints that establish practical work concerns and conditions that increase the *dependence* of inspectors on the cooperation and goodwill of airline personnel.[3] In devising solutions for the problems they confront, agency officials become enmeshed in exchange relations[4] with airline personnel in which both come to expect quid pro quo exchanges (within limits) through which each acknowledges and acts to further certain special interests and concerns of the other.

This phenomenon is not unique to immigration. Levi (1991) describes a similar situation of dependence and cooperative relations between government enforcers and British banks. To deter money laundering, banks are legally required to inform enforcers of suspicious conduct by bank clients. Levi makes clear that although banks operate under disclosure laws, enforcement officers desire assistance not legally required—such as freezing client assets, interpretation of records, and prompt information (ibid., pp. 114–15). Enforcers have comparatively little leverage in the relationship (p. 115) but are able to promote cooperation by extending various courtesies as well as by threatening leaks to the media about bank uncooperativeness (p. 121).

[3] On an earlier draft Robert M. Emerson provided valuable comments about dependency relationships that I have drawn on in preparing this and other sections.

[4] These working relations were based on exchanges of "privileges and courtesies," not unlike those reported in other settings, that facilitate each party's interests (Blumberg 1976:261).

This work highlights the place of government officials' dependence on private enterprise in promoting cooperative relations. The nature of officials' "dependence" on private enterprise, however, varies with important implications for their behavior. When officials depend on private entities for assistance required by legal rules, their dependence exists only in a weak sense as no special obligation to the private entity is incurred because they are required to perform these functions. Officials' dependence, however, does exist in a stronger, exchange sense when they seek to get the private entity to do something it does not have to do—and does not want to do. Development of cooperative relations is especially critical in those instances when the third party has discretion to act in its own interest in matters officials depend on for effective enforcement.

Although studies have focused on how various features of an agency's task environment may influence officials' behavior, few have focused on the aspect described here—the situation in which agency officials may be particularly dependent on private enterprise to accomplish government goals. Given the potential problems of such dependencies, it is useful to explore more fully their origins as well as how officials respond in such situations.

I. Research Setting and Data Collection

This study of immigration inspection work took place at a large international airport in the United States. Annually, thousands of travelers fly into this airport and seek to be admitted to the country. Decisions as to their admissibility are made by the INS.

First, all arriving foreign nationals and U.S. citizens receive a *primary inspection* in which their entry documents (passports, visas, visa waiver forms, etc.) are examined. Most travelers (98%) are admitted at this stage.

If there are questions regarding a person's admissibility, they receive a *secondary inspection*. Most are admitted after this further inquiry. Relatively few (6%) are thought to be inadmissible (e.g., they appear to have fraudulent documents or to be intending to work illegally).

This article focuses on discretionary decisionmaking at the secondary inspection stage. Observations and interviews for the larger study took place during 102 days (about 700 hours). Secondary inspections were observed during 73 of these days, and each of the 18 inspectors assigned to this work were observed and interviewed several times.

Like other types of law enforcers, secondary inspectors have considerable discretion in carrying out their work. This arises from broad delegations of legal power as well as from features of exclusion processing. There are nine categories for the exclusion of foreign nationals (including criminal, security and health reasons).[5] Broad discretionary power lies in the fact-finding process for establishing these grounds: what type of evidence and how much is necessary to establish inadmissibility. For example, how much information is enough to conclude the individual is coming to work illegally? What type of information will be gathered: Will handbags and luggage be checked? Other choices of action or inaction (Davis 1969:4) are largely left to the discretion of the inspector, such as whether to expand the inquiry by questioning family or friends in the airport arrival area or by making calls to the employer or school to which the individual is going.

Moreover, given the nature of exclusion processing, inspectors have considerable scope in which to exercise their discretion.[6] They interview travelers in a personal interview. Decisions to admit travelers to the country after an inspector's interview are not normally reviewed by supervisors. Findings of inadmissibility by inspectors seldom are reviewed by an immigration judge. Most travelers found inadmissible (90%) are removed from the airport without further legal processing.[7] Hence, secondary inspection often is the final stage of case processing.

As discussed earlier, removing an inadmissible traveler is the responsibility of the transporting airline. This airline duty is part of a liability system dating back to early in the century.[8] In its contemporary form the system seeks to compel the assistance of airlines in the screening of foreign travelers through the levying of *fines* ($3,000 per passenger) for failure to determine a passenger had improper documentation to enter the United States; the imposition of *detention costs and custody responsibilities* in certain situations; and the imposition of a *duty to transport* all inadmissible travelers brought to the United States (Immigration Act of 1990:1227).

---

5 See Immigration Act of 1990. See generally *Interpreter Releases* 1991a, 1991b, 1991c.

6 Secondary inspectors' discretion is not unlimited, however. In cases where an inspector concludes that the traveler is inadmissible, the case is briefly reviewed by a supervisor at the airport. There is a tendency for the review to be the most thorough in cases for which the supervisor anticipates receiving complaints (Gilboy 1992) or when the case will be reviewed by an immigration judge.

7 The remainder receive an exclusion hearing before an immigration judge on the issue of whether they can be admitted. This major characteristic of immigration enforcement is in part related to the fact that often individuals eligible for an exclusion hearing waive their right to it and agree to depart voluntarily. It is also related to the fact that some travelers seeking to enter the United States have no right to a hearing upon a finding by inspectors of their inadmissibility. In recent years travelers from many nations have been allowed to use "visa waivers" (rather than having to obtain a visa) to enter the United States. When using a visa waiver, they give up a formal immigration hearing if they are found upon inspection to be inadmissible.

8 For a description of the concerns behind this system see Mayock's statement in U.S. Congress (1951:184). On early attempts to regulate, see Proper (1900). Recently, carrier liability legislation has been introduced in most countries in the European Union (Cruz 1994).

This article focuses on secondary inspection work and airline removal of inadmissible travelers. With the focus on this aspect of inspectors' work, readers may tend to visualize relatively infrequent situations, such as the removal of inadmissible travelers under the work conditions discussed here, as if they were common, everyday phenomena. In this research setting, such was not the situation. At the port of entry studied, about 1,600 foreign nationals were inspected daily of which about 35 to 40 received secondary inspection and only 1 or 2 were found inadmissible and returned. Moreover, the practical work problems of inspectors discussed here did not arise in each of these cases. Nevertheless, although the public-private relationship described here is not built on or tested in daily case encounters, inspectors developed, maintained, and nourished that relationship in anticipation of both routine enforcement needs and the unusual situations where they needed special airline cooperation.

II. Removing Inadmissible Travelers

A. Priority of Avoiding Detention

A high priority of inspectors and supervisors is avoiding the overnight detention of inadmissible travelers. Removal of these travelers on the day they arrive at the airport is pursued as a means to deal with several problems.

First, inspectors view overnight detentions as creating undesired contingencies to removal. Like other kinds of decisionmakers, inspectors routinely consider the "downstream consequences" or implications of their decisions (Emerson & Paley 1992; see also Lundman 1980; Schuck 1972). One concern is that a successfully completed case—one where an inadmissible traveler has agreed to return home voluntarily—can evaporate with overnight detention if the detainee changes his mind and demands an exclusion hearing.

Inspectors consider hearings to be a costly, ineffective, and inefficient way of enforcing exclusion laws. With hearings, the INS district office has to spend monies to detain and process the person through multistage proceedings in which there are many opportunities for delay. Moreover, hearings are seen as producing uncertainty in outcomes. At the time of the research, the INS Port Director believed that inadmissible travelers might not be found excludable at a hearing because his secondary inspectors were relatively inexperienced. Inspectors also are familiar with past cases in which, even if the foreign national was found inadmissible at a hearing, the immigration judge did not enter an exclusion order (with its tougher provisions for reentry to the United States) but instead allowed the individual to return voluntarily after withdrawing his application to enter. This disposition was one that inspectors thought could have been achieved "in the first place," and more efficiently, by immediate removal from the airport.

Second, inspectors also believe overnight detentions invite outside political interference in case handling. With detainees, calls sometimes come to the INS Port Director, the District Director, or the Commissioner's office in Washington from individuals pressuring the agency to admit the person. These contacts—typically from the "casework" of federal legislators or local politicians—if handled insensitively could jeopardize the program support the agency relies on (Gilboy 1992, 1995). The problem is illustrated in the case of a young man who had withdrawn his application to enter the country.

> INSPECTOR 20: His brother was in this country and called his father who was in Saudi Arabia, who then called someone in Washington. [The supervisor] was on the phone all day and night. Finally he was let in. . . . They fought it, but eventually they let him in for a short stay. But he was in custody for a day or so. . . .
>
> QUESTION: So things can change if they're held?
>
> INSPECTOR: Yeah, you want to get them out as soon as possible [using his hands to indicate a plane zooming off]. (Feb. 1989)

The strategy of same-day removal helps to insulate enforcement decisionmaking. From the practical viewpoint of inspectors, it is difficult for outsiders successfully to pressure the INS for reversal of a decision when the person is midair on the way home.

Third, at times during the research, detention funds were limited. Superiors directed inspectors to use detention only for extremely serious violators (e.g., individuals excludable because of past criminal activity). Others had to be removed on the day of their arrival or released and told to return the next day for removal. Since inspectors consider their reappearance at the airport the next day very unlikely, achieving same-day removals was important.

Finally, in some cases, in varying degrees, inspectors saw overnight detention as undesirable (e.g., for juveniles or for young women arriving to work as au pairs, technical mixups when company workers arrive with inappropriate visas). These concerns are illustrated in an inspector's comments about a case he was processing.

> We don't want to detain him. First, the detention is too severe for this man. His intentions were not to deceive us. The feeling in the office is it's too severe. You have to take them to whatever jail they have and put him in that. That doesn't always work out to be a good jail. Second, we have to pay for the detention, and then, too, it's more manpower and paperwork. (Inspector 6; Dec. 1988)

Inspectors see same-day removals, then, as increasing their ability to enforce the law. They can avoid the particularly difficult situation of deciding what to do with a person who is legally inadmissible but for whom overnight detention seems "too severe" a punishment given characteristics of the individual or case.

B. Airline Cooperation and Avoidance of Detention

Same-day removal of inadmissible travelers takes on considerable importance for inspectors given the problems they perceive with holding returnees overnight. These removals, however, take place within the special enforcement context they confront.

On the one hand, the law is clear that every airline is obligated to remove any inadmissible passengers it transports. The returnee is to be removed on the airline's "next available flight," in the place of a reservation passenger if necessary, at airline expense if there is no return ticket (54 *Fed. Reg.* 100; 53 *Fed. Reg.* 1791).

On the other hand, in some cases, airline "cooperation" is needed to avoid detention. Two sorts of cooperation are essential. First, although airlines are obligated to return their inadmissible passengers on the "next available flight," what constitutes the next available flight is affected by airline cooperation in arranging transportation removal. Inspectors encounter such acts of covert resistance by airlines in performing this legally mandated duty as "stalling" to avoid bumping a paying passenger in favor of seating the nonpaying returnee.[9] As one inspector explained:

> [Airline personnel] try to stall around if their flight is full, but we don't want [the inadmissible travelers] detained overnight. (Inspector 8; March 1990)

Probably the most important area of airline cooperation is in "rerouting" returnees on flights of other airlines. This is critical when the legally responsible airline no longer has flights departing to the returnees' point of origin that day, but another airline does. What the INS does in this situation depends in part on whether the returnee has a paid return-trip ticket. When none exists, inspectors do not seek airline cooperation in rerouting. But when a paid fare exists, inspectors prefer that the transporting airline turn over the return-trip ticket to an airline with a flight departing that day.

Rerouting arrangements are not legally mandated and are considered "favors" if done. Inspectors understand that requests for rerouting are viewed by some airlines, particularly smaller ones, as creating undesired financial losses and risks.

[9] Moreover, even when a returnee has a ticket, an airline with a full flight may prefer to put the returnee on a flight with empty seats the next day.

> If we have to deal with small international carriers, they don't care if the person is detained until tomorrow . . . in order that they get the $500 ticket. Other large carriers . . . are more likely to do what's in an individual's best interests, just book them and get them a ticket on another flight going out that day whether it's their carrier or not. (Inspector 4; Dec. 1988)

Inspectors also depend on the willingness of airlines to accept these tickets—particularly when "risky" or "problem" returnees are involved. They cannot assume that one airline will agree to transport another airline's passenger to the point of embarkation. Such help may require the airline to unseat a reservation passenger if the flight is full, or it may require ignoring wait-listed passengers to seat the returnee. It also may create other "problems." An inspector described these airline concerns:

> A lot has to do with who they're carrying back, such as Nigerians. They may abscond and they don't want to say they'll take them. If they feel it's a passenger who will become a problem, they want to stay out of it. But for an 18- or 19-year-old girl, they don't view that as a problem case. (Inspector 11; Feb. 1990)

Moreover, if an airline helps the INS, passengers may be offended by having to sit near an "unseemly character" (smelly or physically restrained during travel). In addition, the returnee might abscond or end up being costly to the airline (hotel, guards, etc.) if the airline cannot get him to his point of embarkation promptly. Hence, while inspectors report that airlines often will cooperate in rerouting, obtaining the assistance of some airlines may be difficult, and obtaining the assistance of any airline under certain circumstances can be unreliable.

III. Inspectors' Behavior and Airline Characteristics

The priority of avoiding overnight detentions imposes a set of constraints on inspectors. To avoid detentions, inspectors must work within the practical contingencies of return flights and flight schedules. As a result, in some instances case processing and dispositions reflect inspectors' adaptations of their work to airline schedules as well as crucial judgments about the moral character of travelers during this processing.

A. Accelerating Inspections to Make Departing Flights

As in other organizational settings, uncertainties critical to an organization's functioning are dealt with by more tightly coordinating activities with relevant entities (Pfeffer & Salancik 1978:285). At the airport, this phenomenon can be seen in the practice of accelerating inspections to parallel flight departure times, thus minimizing the likelihood of overnight detentions.

Two acceleration strategies are used. In some instances, inspectors take a short cut and eliminate the primary inspection. This most frequently occurs with "turnaround" flights, that is, international flights that have only brief stopovers at the airport before returning to their point of origin. Inspectors distinguish these turnaround flights from others because of the particular problems they present for their work—namely, timely inspections and removals (on work concerns and categorization, see Emerson 1988). In order to coordinate their inspections with departures, inspectors walk through the primary lines looking for travelers whose appearance suggests they may be one of the profiled "high-risk" travelers (Gilboy 1991). As one inspector explained: "Hunting for passengers saves 15 minutes, and with KLM and their tight schedule, this is important." Profiled travelers are taken out of the primary line to the secondary waiting area and their passports examined. Depending on the results, they are either admitted or called into the office for questioning and a possible removal.

Accelerating secondary questioning is the other way to avoid detentions. In paralleling questioning with flight departures, information gathering can be very hurried, and interviews dotted with questions and comments to airline representatives and to each other: "When is the airline leaving?" "Will they hold the plane?" So frantic can the removal processing become that deviations can occur, such as knowingly using another traveler's plane ticket for the returnee's removal. For example:

> Inspector 6 remarked to Inspector 7, "This is a passport of [a "high-risk" Asian nation], a real bad one. We're going to try to get him out today." Speaking to the airline representative, "What time does the flight leave, twenty after four?" [It did.] Inspector 7 speaking to the foreign national for the first time informed him: "We're going to send you back. Your government gave you a bad passport." The case became very rushed. The flight was leaving in just minutes. The officers hurried to get the paperwork done. The ticket they had did not contain the traveler's name. Somehow in the secondary office his ticket had gotten mixed up with another passenger's ticket. The officers pushed ahead. One officer sat doing the paperwork rapidly. No statement was taken from the foreign national. The foreign national signed the withdrawal of the application to enter the United States. Inspector 7 began to explain to me in front of the returnee, "He had all kinds of alterations on his passport." As the returnee began to protest this statement, Inspector 7 informed him of all the changes on the document. Inspectors 6 and 7 rushed off with the foreign national and boarded him on the plane using the ticket that belonged to another traveler. Airline representatives were aware of the irregularity. Later a supervisor told Inspector 6 the airline called about the "ticket mixup" and needed paperwork to explain the situation. (April 1988)

Making decisions in a time frame to fit flight schedules fosters abbreviated inspections. Perceptions that problems exist with accelerated processing, however, are for the most part muted. Shortcuts, policy deviations, and irregularities in case handling are tolerated and defended by inspectors as making no difference to the accuracy of case dispositions.

As illustrated below, with hurried inquiry, critical questions can be left unanswered. Despite the realization *after* the traveler was taken to the plane that basic information was missing, the case was viewed as a "clear-cut" instance of inadmissibility. Shared understandings between inspectors working on a case together reinforce the notions that one ordinarily expects returnees to "deny" wrongdoing and that an immigration judge's decision would be the same as an inspector's disposition. The following illustration reveals the pressured, incomplete nature of some inspections and the views of inspectors that underlie this case processing.

> Inspectors 8 and 16 study a passport [of a "high-risk" Asian national]. The airline representative informs them that the plane is leaving very shortly. Inspector 8 rushes to the passenger area and brings the individual in for an interview. Speaking in simple shorthand phrases to make himself understood he advises the foreign national:
>
> 4:15 P.M.: "You know, no good. Read this." [He pushes toward the traveler materials in English explaining the right to withdraw an application to enter the U.S.] He continues: "Do you chose to go home or go before an immigration judge? Passport no good. Changed. I don't know if this is you or not. This visa, writing is all altered. I will not admit you to the U.S. You can go home today on Alitalia or go to an immigration judge." The traveler responds, "I want to go." The officer goes to do the paperwork, saying the plane leaves in 5 minutes.
>
> 4:20 P.M.: The airline representative gets the traveler's bags off the carousel.
>
> 4:21 P.M.: It is explained to the man he is going to Rome to make his connection.
>
> 4:24 P.M.: They leave for the plane.
>
> Later Inspector 16 says to 8 that he didn't see him do the paperwork. Inspector 8 responds, "I didn't till I took him out to the plane." Inspector 16, "Did he deny it?" Inspector 8, "They always do." Later when Inspector 8 is working on the paperwork, he notices that the traveler had two passports (an old one and new one with a current visa) and that the pictures looked different, "Usually when you see two it's a dead give away." Looking more closely he observes, however, that the handwriting on the two pictures looks alike. He remarks, "If I had seen that, I'd have asked him to sign his name again." He concludes, however, "Maybe [both passports] were his and he

> just changed the visa. This is a 'clear-cut' case. If it went to a judge he'd deport him." (June 1990)

As illustrated, the tendency to parallel inspection work with departures affects the climate in which foreign nationals exercise their right to a hearing. Like other kinds of law enforcers, inspectors prefer a quick, informal "cooperative" plea-bargain type disposition, to a more costly, delayed formal adjudication (Blumberg 1976; Feeley 1979). In dealing with suspected inadmissible travelers who have the right to an exclusion hearing, inspectors routinely urge individuals to withdraw their application to enter the country. In accelerating inspections, encounters between inspectors and foreign nationals can involve extremely rushed advisements of rights and pressures on foreign nationals to decide "right now" whether to withdraw their applications to enter or request a hearing.

In addition, the not-so-subtle threat of lengthy detention pending a hearing and of the adverse consequences of an exclusion order by an immigration judge—without the benefit of full advisements regarding the positive features of a hearing[10]—further functions to rapidly dispose of cases by discouraging foreign nationals from exercising their right to a hearing. For example:

> Inspector 11 has in his secondary office a 25-year-old Ghanaian male who arrived at the airport with $300, no credit cards, and plans for a two-week stay with a "taxicab driver friend" who was to meet him in the passenger arrival area. Inspector 11 asks a senior inspector to check the validity of the passport but first gives his own impression that "He's probably okay." Inspector 11 heads to the passenger area to find the traveler's friend. After a look outside, he concludes the friend is not there—a black man standing near the information desk was not approached since the inspector thought he "wasn't dressed like a taxicab driver." A little later inspectors 6 and 10 make another check of the passenger area, this time more thoroughly, calling out the cab driver's name; no one answers (the man by the information desk is no longer there). The case was discussed with a supervisor who also concluded the man had insufficient money to enter the country. KLM airlines is now boarding. An airline representative runs to get the paperwork for reboarding. Inspector 10 is quickly typing a form for removal. In this pressured situation, Inspector 6 advises the traveler of his rights:
>
> Q: You have two options. You can go before an immigration judge and plead your case and you will be in jail for a few days or you can go home. We can't find your friend. We cannot verify your story and you do not have enough money.
>
> A: My friend . . .
>
> Q: You have two options.

[10] For a similar problem in deportation cases, see *Orantes-Hernandez v. Smith* (1982).

A: I cannot go to Denmark [where his wife is living]. I don't see why I have to go to jail.

Q: You're not admitted to the United States. You do not have enough money. We're not able to verify your story. You have no guarantee that you're going to a judge tomorrow. This is Thursday. You may see him Monday or Tuesday so you may be in jail for 3 or 4 days. You can go home now and have no record of it, or you can go to a judge. If he thinks the same thing, you'll get a record of deportation. You must decide right now. What are you going to do?

A: I don't understand the reason why.

Q: I just explained. You're not admissible. Your visa means you can apply for admission and the decision is made here and now, and we've made the decision that you're not admissible to the United States. [The Ghanaian says that he'll stay less time.] You have already established your intent. You want to go back?

A: Yes.

Q: If you want to go back, you must sign this here.

Inspectors 6 and 10 drive him to the plane. Fifteen minutes have passed since the plane began to board, and the returnee is removed. All of this was extremely rushed. At one point Inspector 10 calls to Inspector 6 and says "Are they [the airlines] going to wait for us?" Inspector 6 says, "No, you've got to hurry." Inspector 10 informs me that they are trying to get him on this plane because they will have "a detained problem. . . . If we detain them, then they think, okay, I'll go to a judge." Inspector 9 adds that they will eventually be removed from the country, but after more time and money. (Dec. 1988)

In sum, inspection work in some instances comes to be geared to getting those determined to be inadmissible on turnaround or other shortly departing flights. This requires inspectors to act with great speed, in doing so giving short shrift to foreign nationals' rights, and truncating their own inspections. Importantly, airline flight contingencies (daily flights and departure times) did *not* need to be a critical factor in shaping inspectors' case processing but became one because of inspectors' priority of avoiding overnight detentions.

B. Flight Contingencies, Moral Judgments, and Case Dispositions

Usually inspectors' efforts result in avoiding overnight detention. Occasionally, though, instances arise where detention is imminent due to flight schedules. The particular outcomes of these cases are fluid. As in many regulatory settings, final outcomes depend on enforcers' decisions about how strictly to enforce the law based on judgments about a violator's moral character and the severity of the offense committed (Hawkins 1984b:ch 8; Hutter 1988:105–20; Bardach & Kagan 1982:ch. 5.; Kagan 1994:387).

Inspectors distinguish two basic types of individuals. The foreign national may be a *decent* or honest person but misinformed, misled, or naive about what he or she could do on entering the United States. For example, a young woman may try to enter the United States on a tourist visa to become a mother's helper for low wages and room and board. Such persons are usually viewed as decent persons who either did not realize it is wrong to enter the United States to work without a work visa or did not realize the gravity of their attempted illegal entry. A foreign national, however, may be perceived as a *bad* person—scheming, underhanded, and well aware of the implications of his or her actions in attempting to enter the country. Those using stolen and altered entry documents (e.g., passports reconstructed with new pages or containing substitutions of photos) usually fall into this category. For inspectors, the judgments about moral character both explain the attempted illegal entry and shape their response to possible detention pending removal (see generally Emerson 1969:91).

There is little reaction, for instance, to detaining travelers perceived as morally "bad." On the other hand, in varying degrees, those falling in the "decent" category are viewed as inappropriate for overnight detention. The differing concerns are illustrated as follows:

> The Port Director noted that if individuals were not removed from the airport but held overnight, INS would try to put the women in a hotel and the men in a jail near the airport (if possible in a room away from other types of detainees). He emphasized, however, other considerations: "If you have an altered document case, someone like that, I don't care about that [detaining them]. But if it's someone with the wrong visa or something like that, not so bad, I don't like to do it. That's why I like to get them out."

The organizational relevance of categorization is most notable with respect to the "decent" category. Problems arise when travelers may be bona fide visitors (e.g., they appear to have legitimate arrangements to work) but enter with an inappropriate visa. Detention seems too harsh a sanction. The following illustrates the fluid nature of outcomes in such a situation, as well as suggesting how contingencies (departing flights, looming detention, and incomplete information) shape decisionmaking. Again, the character of the travelers is a recurring theme.

> Two supervisors spoke to three Englishmen in secondary inspection. One supervisor told them he hated to deport them because it was not their fault they were here on the wrong visas. "The kind of work you're coming to do you would have to have a different kind of visa [not the B-1 business visa]. . . . They [the company] only gave you one day to fly to the U.S. [not enough time to get an appropriate visa]. . . . I'd hate to detain you overnight. You don't deserve it. Like the supervisor said, you're

> not criminals. If you miss the flight you have to be detained overnight. When you signed the [visa waiver] form, you have no rights [gave up the right to an exclusion hearing]."
>
> The men reiterated the legitimate nature of their visit. They suggested calling England, but it was late in the day and presumably past work hours in England. They had no U.S. business number to call.
>
> The three Englishmen pointed out that 12 other workers had already entered and were here until Christmas and that the U.S. company they were joining was purchased by a British company. The supervisors speculated that an argument could be made that the three men were not being paid in the U.S. but from overseas. [T]he workers themselves, however, were unsure who was paying them.
>
> One supervisor thought further then reacted, "They are here already. . . . It's kind of a hard step to send three back when you're only here three weeks. It's important to get an appropriate visa [suggesting a specific type of visa]." The men were admitted.
>
> Later an officer discussed the case with me: "It doesn't serve any purpose to send the people back. I think you can build a case that the B-1 [business visa] is not bad here. Both are the same company, the one here and in England. But if it were over a prolonged period of time, they should get an E-1 treaty trader [visa]. So . . . under the circumstances I think it's rotten to send them back. The guys are awfully honest." (Nov. 1988)

In this case the inspectors were unable because of the international time differences to resolve several questions. Facing no remaining return flights that day and the detention of the three workers pending clarification of the facts, inspectors chose to focus on factors that would merit admission—indicators of the decent nature of the individuals or legitimate circumstances underlying their visit. As various supervisors commented, they were "awfully honest," "not criminals," "don't deserve" detention.

Inspectors also take a pragmatic approach to case dispositions when faced with overnight detention of a person committing a relatively minor offense. In the following case involving a suspected nanny, as soon as the inspector learned of the departure of the airline's last flight that day, the inspection was abruptly terminated.

> A young Swiss female was queried by Inspector 6. Her responses fit the port's "nanny" profile. Inspector 6 and I went out to the passenger arrival area and located the family the girl was visiting—a man, two children, and a woman very pregnant with a third child. After brief questioning the inspector remarked to me, "They're not good liars. They were not rehearsed. They didn't know that this was going to happen!" The inspector examined letters in the woman's luggage. One letter from a friend cautioned, "Good luck with customs." The in-

spector laughed,"We know what that means!" Learning from the airline representative that the last flight left at 4:20 P.M. and it is now 6:00 P.M., Inspector 6 informed the representative the individual would be admitted. (Feb. 1990)

In some cases, then, flight contingencies and inspectors' evaluations of the moral character of travelers shape how cases are disposed. Only one flight a day will mean that travelers assessed as "decent" will benefit from this practically constrained processing by being admitted, although doing so is not technically justified; travelers initially assessed as "bad" or "deliberately deceptive" will be processed for return. Another flight that day gives inspectors more time for the case—more time for extensive inquiry sometimes leading to more "punitive" outcomes (i.e., uncovering indications of "suspicion" of initially assessed "decent" travelers), and sometimes to more "lenient" outcomes (i.e., uncovering indicators of "decency" or "legality" etc. for previously judged "bad" cases).

IV. Immigration Service and Airline Relations

Although to avoid overnight detentions inspectors orient their work to airline flights and timetables, they also realize that in some instances they are dependent on special airline cooperation to achieve this priority.

Generally speaking, inspectors are dependent on airlines in several ways. Inspectors depend or rely on airlines for returning rejected foreign nationals. But such dependence incurs no special debt to airlines because the airlines are legally obligated to perform this service. Inspectors' dependence does exist in a stronger sense when they seek to induce airline cooperation in matters where the airline is not legally required to act and where it may not be in the airline's interest to provide assistance. Inspectors become indebted to airlines in several specific situations (see Table 1) in which airlines have latitude to act in their own interests, such as by refusing to reroute an inadmissible traveler on another airline's flight (not giving up a fare), declining to transport another airline's returnee (not assuming financial risk), and "stalling" in making return arrangements (not bumping a paying client).

Pressure to develop and maintain working relations with airline personnel grow out of these situations in which inspectors would like cooperation but the airline has discretion to act otherwise.

A. Airlines

It is useful to ask why airlines would bother to cooperate with the INS. After all, in many instances there is no legal obligation to do so. Several factors promote at least partial dependence of airline personnel on inspectors and thus facilitate a situation of mutual dependence and cooperation.

Table 1. Types of Airline Cooperation

Types of Cooperation	Examples
Skills and goods	Language interpretation for another airline's passenger; occasional office supplies
Revenues	Turning over inadmissible passengers' fares to other airlines for rerouting purposes
Equipment	Transporting other airlines' inadmissible passengers
Personnel services	Obtaining information from relatives of passengers sent to secondary inspection; locating luggage; "quickly" making removal arrangements

First, in a job with a high degree of emphasis on "passenger facilitation" or smoothing the way for passengers to reach their destination, access to special inspection services is useful to airline personnel. In the case of infirm or ill passengers, each airline would like special inspection handling (such as not requiring their client to wait in the primary inspection lines or having an inspector conduct the inspection on the plane).

Second, airlines particularly recognize the value of good working relations with inspectors with respect to passenger facilitation in situations in which the INS has greater latitude to ignore airline requests. For instance, an airline administrator may be coming into the United States and local airport personnel may want inspectors to provide VIP treatment to make them "look good" to their boss. Or an airline manager's family, or friends of an airline representative, or important travelers (e.g., Dr. Suzuki of the famed Suzuki School of Music or company CEOs) may be arriving, and an anticipated extended wait for primary inspection may lead an airline to want inspectors to give expedited processing to the individual.

As one representative of a large European airline described their working relations with the INS.

> It happens in a blue moon. . . . It is not much money [to reroute their passenger on another airline]. . . . We are all working in this area and if our boss comes from [European city] or there is a sick passenger, we ask the inspectors to help us.

Third, another factor promoting cooperation is that airlines cannot afford to isolate themselves from the issue of overnight detention of their passengers because airlines get calls of concern and complaints from detainees' relatives and risk possible negative publicity from any untoward event that may occur.

Finally, personnel from certain airlines prefer that returnees pay for their tickets home. If the returnee did not arrive with a return-trip ticket, they want an inspector to search the individual for any concealed money the individual might have to pay for the ticket.

Airline personnel consequently have an interest in helping inspectors and extend their cooperation in several ways besides helping with rerouting of returnees. Airlines provide interpreter services to the INS. The INS does not have interpreters at the airport, and among inspectors relatively few different foreign languages are spoken. Although having airline personnel interpret for their own passengers serves an airline interest in passenger facilitation, inspectors become indebted to airline personnel when they agree to interpret for *passengers other than their own.* Cooperating can be inconvenient. It reduces the number of airline staff members available to meet flights or may require reservation desk or office staff to be pulled away from their normal work.

Airline personnel also serve inspectors' interests by filling out passengers' entry documents, locating luggage of passengers sent to secondary inspection as well as soliciting information for the agency from family and friends in the airport arrival area, and quickly making removal arrangements for inadmissible travelers. These are important services for inspectors—lightening their workload, facilitating questioning, reducing complaints to the agency (from citizens or legislators) about inspection delays, and avoiding overnight detentions. These, too, also serve an airline interest in passenger facilitation. But airline personnel have discretion to be more or less energetic in assisting inspectors.

Thus, while providing resources can prove inconvenient, costly, time-consuming, and even at times risky to airlines, these resources are recognized as commodities of value to inspectors and knowingly extended by airlines with the expectation of some future benefit to themselves.

B. Immigration Service

Inspectors provide two types of favors to encourage airline cooperation.[11] First, there are "professional courtesies." These courtesies are largely in the form of expedited inspections. The

11 When one imagines an exchange relationship that is highly fine-tuned to airline interests, one can envision other possible kinds of favors by inspectors. This study does not preclude their existence, but they were not revealed during the study. For example, is immigration reporting of airline violations (such as transporting a person who has an expired visa, a violation that subjects the airline to a possible fine) affected by the larger mutual exchange of favors and services in the setting? Because of the difficulty of researching this and other sensitive subjects, some questions remain unanswered.

well-understood quid pro quo nature of these inspections is illustrated in a supervisor's comments:

> [W]e can give certain people VIP treatment. There was a station manager whose boss was coming in, and we gave him the VIP treatment. That made him look good. Or the person's wife and children are coming in and it's very crowded and there are long waits, he would come to us and ask if we could do a special inspection, and we did. I call it professional courtesy. . . . I will call him up and say to him that they need to take a passenger that's missed a flight. (Feb. 1990)
>
> [Talking about an airline that had provided interpreters for another airline's passengers] If the [airline's] manager comes in and there is a long line, I am going to give him preferential inspection here because they helped us . . . a lot of times when they shouldn't. . . . You have to cooperate with each other. The Service is not an entity by itself. (March 1990)

The officer further illustrated his point by mentioning the time they ran out of copy paper and an airline brought them a supply.

The exchanges generally are not manifested in the immediate swapping of privileges in particular cases. Instead, favors and services extended are either repaying help given in the past or building a treasure chest of goodwill to be drawn on later; and benefits or services accepted are understood as obligating the party to later return the favor.

During the research, the acceptable boundaries of these favors were still being tested, challenged, and freshly articulated. Requests for services sometimes were viewed as unreasonable or illegitimate. From an INS perspective, some airline requests are unreasonable because they potentially open the floodgates to other demands. For instance, a supervisor denied a request for expedited processing of an *entire flight* when passengers had been delayed in leaving Europe and needed to make connecting flights. The agency, he said, had not created the delay and such visible preferential treatment could mean that they would "have to do that for everyone."

Inspectors also learn about the limits of airline goodwill. In one case, a major airline was "burned" when transporting another airline's returnee—the returnee missed his connecting flight in Europe and the airline had to pay for housing, food, and guard service for several days. The airline's station manager advised an inspector that such requests probably were outside the limits of what the airline would be willing to do in the future.

Inspectors' favors are given with the expectation that they will be repaid by airline personnel. Occasionally inspectors face uncooperative behavior. In the following instance, an inspector encountered an airline representative who was reluctant to turn over the returnee's round-trip fare to another airline. This led the inspector to threatened to expose the airline representative for failure to cooperate.

> "This is a female. We don't like her in detention. It could fall back in your lap." The airline representative asked what he meant. The inspector responded, "If there's an inquiry or congressional, it will fall back in your lap if TWA or another airline was willing to take her today." Later to me he added the following: "If we get a congressional and it turns out there was another airline that could have taken her, I'm going to tell them. I'm not going to take the blame for this. [The airline] wants the revenue." (Dec. 1988)

This threat is like those reported elsewhere when an organization with meager resources to exchange for needed services extracts another organization's cooperation in exchange for "the decision not to carry through on the threat" (Emerson 1969:75).

A second favor inspectors can provide airlines is the employment of state power for private interests. Inspectors' exchange relations with airlines occasionally subject them to pressures by airlines to detain, interrogate, and search arriving foreign nationals—a special power sometimes of considerable value in protecting an airline's financial interests.

Airlines seek inspectors' powers to search in several circumstances, including searches for a returnee's "hidden" or "underreported" money that could used for return-trip fare. For example:

> Inspector 9 asked the Iranian male to "take everything out of your pockets." Perusing the items the officer exclaimed, "All the money you have is $43? Gee willikers. You have a one-way ticket." To the airline representative he remarked, "Another one." The foreign national was told he could not enter (his passport was altered). He agreed to return home. A few minutes later I noticed Inspector 12 walking the returnee off to another room. Joining him was the airline representative who, catching my eye, said: We're going to pat him down, see if he has any money. How else are we going to get money for the ticket?" (April 1988)

Occasionally airlines ask the INS to use its coercive powers in other situations. For instance, an airline informed the INS at the airport that two U.S. citizens traveling to the United States had purchased their tickets with a credit card not belonging to them. The airline asked the INS to detain the travelers because the airline had accepted the tickets and boarded the Americans, putting the matter outside the jurisdiction of the state police. But the INS viewed the demand as "unreasonable." As one supervisor said, "Can you imagine that? That's the kind of thing they want. They're there to make money."

Such use of state coercive powers for private interests was not condoned by the Port Director or supervisors. As one supervisor explained:

> This is not appropriate. It would exceed the authority of inspectors. We can search for social security cards or something like that. We're not here to search for the airlines. I wouldn't do it. Recently we had a case where the alien mentioned they had $700 and then said they said they had only $300. The representative said, "Where's the $400?" and they said to us to search, and we said no. (Feb. 1990)

As in other settings, strategies to nurture or cultivate relations with other institutions in the environment are not problem-free (Emerson 1969:29; Pfeffer & Salancik 1978:282). Although searches for airlines were not condoned by inspectors' superiors, they were nevertheless a commodity in the exchange relationship. Such services, though, were not by any means guaranteed to an airline; they required the cooperation or acquiescence of a willing inspector. Some, but not all, inspectors were willing to do this, and thus not all requests (or hints) for a search lead to one taking place.

Because of the relatively small number of searches observed (and the sensitivity of the subject), there is insufficient data to explain variations among inspectors. Behavior was affected to some extent by staff training and supervision. The agency was staffed by some less experienced inspectors, and the "slippage" between supervisors' views and inspectors' actions was a product of inadequate communication or training (Lipsky 1980:16). A few inspectors, however, were aware of higher-ups' views but did not share them. Their behavior was invisible to supervisors; they conducted the "pat down" behind closed doors and quickly to avoid detection.

V. Cooperative Relations in Context

This study of a third-party liability system provided an opportunity to explore a feature of the environment of government agencies that has not been dealt with extensively in the literature—situations in which the government is particularly dependent on private enterprise to accomplish governmental goals.

The research suggests that government's use of private enterprise in enforcement at times can have unintended and undesired consequences for the agency. Rather than simply an enforcement strategy being introduced into a setting, third-party liability systems can become entwined with the organizational circumstances of officials and become occasions for mutual dependencies and exchange between public and private entities that affect in important ways government's handling of cases.

The case study raises an important question. Do such relations exist in other settings where the government relies on private enterprise to assist in public enforcement? Data suggest that contexts differ widely in the existence and scope of such exchange behavior.

To understand why variations exist, consider the differing work concerns, risks, and opportunities that parties confront. First, in some enforcement contexts *practical work concerns and conditions* lead the government to depend on third-party enforcers for special favors. The immigration context is such a setting. Inspectors' high priority of avoiding detentions increased their dependence on the goodwill of airlines for removal assistance the airlines were not obligated to provide. Importantly, much opportunity existed in the context for developing working relations. Day in and day out, inspectors and airline personnel worked in tandem, and the routine work demands of both (processing sick or elderly passengers, returnees, etc.) meant that there was a *high probability of future needs and continuing interaction.* Levi (1991:115) presents a somewhat similar picture in the context of bank deterrence of money laundering. Enforcers viewed banks as "repeat players" that they had an "interest in cultivating" because good relations were essential to current and prospective special needs.

In contrast, to take an extreme case, the likelihood of the development of mutually dependent relations is negligible where businesses enforce no-smoking rules. Kagan & Skolnick (1993) describe this third-party enforcement area as one in which there is considerable public support for restrictions—customers and workers themselves will even seek to deal with violators. There was no evidence that municipal health inspectors were in regular contact with the regulated entities (there were few complaints a year requiring enforcement action) or that they were dependent on businesses for assistance beyond that which restaurants and firms were legally obligated to provide. Likewise, we might expect exchange relations to be minimal or nonexistent where private enterprise is long accustomed to performing enforcement duties in contexts where there is little reason for regular contact with enforcers (e.g., employer withholding of wages for taxes).

Second, the more *visible, resource consuming, or otherwise risky the request,* the less likely it seems that one party can rely on the other's cooperation. Levi's (1991:115) study suggests that banks were particularly reluctant to help enforcers with freezing client accounts, an action that was highly visible to a client and legally risky compared with other types of cooperation. In the immigration setting, cooperative exchanges also took place within limits. Inspectors refused to conduct VIP processing for an entire flight because it opened the door to similar requests by other airlines which made it their business to know how inspectors exercised their powers. Likewise, airlines held inspectors' requests in check—threatening not to accept rerouted passengers if doing so exposed them to significant out-of-pocket expenses difficult to justify to superiors. Exceptions highlight the general observation.

Unauthorized but relatively difficult to detect searches of returnees were conducted by some inspectors for airlines.

Finally, in some law enforcement contexts, government officials' preferences are relatively compatible with third-party enforcers, and thus opportunities for cooperative relationships are more likely. In the inspection setting, for instance, there is probably a greater *community of interest* between the INS and airlines in moving and disposing of cases than exists in some other third-party liability contexts. Compare, for example, the situation in which a securities underwriter is desperate to conclude a public offering of a corporate security while the Securities and Exchange Commission is not—having a far greater interest in reviewing the offering and ensuring that a fraudulent deal is not in the works. Cooperation also may be relatively lower in the area of regulation of money laundering. Money launderers are "good business" for banks, providing needed resources for liquidity and overhead. Banks have much incentive to drag their feet when it comes to more discretionary activity, such as how thoroughly potential customers are questioned, particularly since it is thought by banks that "critical inquisition . . . will simply displace them to rival financial institutions" (Levi 1991:112).

Compelled third-party participation in enforcement is a growing phenomenon but one for which there is relatively little empirical research about it effects on government behavior. By continuing to explore the conditions shaping the emergence of public-private exchange relations and dependence, our full understanding of the environment of enforcement will be enhanced, in all of its facets and dimensions.

References

Bardach, Eugene, & Robert A. Kagan (1982) *Going by the Book: The Problem of Regulatory Unreasonableness.* Philadelphia: Temple Univ. Press.

Blumberg, Abraham S. (1976) "The Practice of Law as a Confidence Game: Organization Cooptation of a Profession," in G. F. Cole, ed. *Criminal Justice: Law and Politics.* 2d ed. North Scituate, MA: Duxbury Press.

Calavita, Kitty (1990) "Employer Sanctions Violations: Toward a Dialectical Model of White-Collar Crime," 24 *Law & Society Rev.* 1041–69.

Chambers, David L. (1979) *Making Fathers Pay: The Enforcement of Child Support.* Chicago: Univ. of Chicago Press.

Cruz, Antonio (1994) *Carriers Liability in the Member States of the European Union.* Brussels, Belgium: Churches Commission for Migrants in Europe.

Davis, Kenneth Culp (1969) *Discretionary Justice: A Preliminary Inquiry.* Baton Rouge: Louisiana State Univ. Press.

Emerson, Robert M. (1969) *Judging Delinquents: Context and Process in Juvenile Court.* Chicago: Aldine Publishing Co.

——— (1988) "Discrepant Models of Categorization in Social Control Decision-making." Unpublished, Dept. of Sociology, UCLA.

Emerson, Robert M., & Blair Paley (1992) "Organizational Horizons and Complaint-Filing," in K. Hawkins, ed., *The Uses of Discretion.* New York: Oxford Univ. Press, Clarendon Press.

Feeley, Malcolm M. (1979) *The Process Is the Punishment: Handling Cases in a Lower Criminal Court.* New York: Russell Sage Foundation.

Gilboy, Janet A. (1991) "Deciding Who Gets In: Decisionmaking by Immigration Inspectors," 25 *Law & Society Rev.* 571–99.

——— (1992) "Penetrability of Administrative Systems: Political 'Casework' and Immigration Inspections," 26 *Law & Society Rev.* 273–314.

——— (1995) "Regulatory and Administrative Agency Behavior: Accommodation, Amplification, and Assimilation," 17 *Law & Policy* 3–22.

——— (1996) "Social Regulation and Business Responsibility." Presented at Law & Society Association Annual Meeting, Glasgow, Scotland (July).

Glaberson, William (1990) "I.R.S. Pursuit of Lawyers' Cash Clients Faces Tests," *New York Times,* 9 Mar., sec. A, p. 1, cols. 2–4.

Hawkins, Keith (1984a) "Creating Cases in a Regulatory Agency," 12 *Urban Life* 371–95.

——— (1984b) *Environment and Enforcement: Regulation and the Social Definition of Pollution.* New York: Oxford Univ. Press, Clarendon Press.

Holmes, Steven A. (1990) "A Drug Dealer Finds Many Eager to Launder His Drug Money," *New York Times,* 24 Jan., sec. A, p. 1, cols. 5–6.

Hutter, Bridget M. (1988) *The Reasonable Arm of the Law? The Law Enforcement Procedures of Environmental Health Officers.* New York: Oxford Univ. Press, Clarendon Press.

Interpreter Releases (1991a) "The Immigration Act of 1990 Analyzed: Part 12—Exclusion and Deportation," 68 *Interpreter Releases,* pp. 265–73 (March 11).

——— (1991b) "The Immigration Act of 1990 Analyzed: Part 13—Exclusion and Deportation Grounds Continued," 68 *Interpreter Releases,* pp. 305–19 (March 18).

——— (1991c) "State Dept. Implements Revised Exclusion Grounds," 68 *Interpreter Releases,* pp. 677–81 (June 3).

Kagan, Robert A. (1994) "Regulatory Enforcement," in D. H. Rosenbloom & R. D. Schwartz, eds., *Handbook of Regulation and Administrative Law.* New York: Marcel Dekker, Inc.

Kagan, Robert A., & Jerome H. Skolnick (1993) "Banning Smoking: Compliance without Enforcement," in R. L. Rabin & S. D. Sugarman, eds., *Smoking Policy: Law, Politics, and Culture.* New York: Oxford Univ. Press.

Kraakman, Reinier H. (1986) "Gatekeepers: The Anatomy of a Third-Party Enforcement Strategy," 2 *J. of Law, Economics, & Organization* 53–104.

Levi, Michael (1991) "Regulating Money Laundering: The Death of Bank Secrecy in the UK," 31 *British J. of Criminology* 109–25.

Lipsky, Michael (1980) *Street-Level Bureaucracy: Dilemmas of the Individual in Public Services.* New York: Russell Sage Foundation.

Lorne, Simon M. (1978) "The Corporate and Securities Adviser, the Public Interest, and Professional Ethics," 76 *Michigan Law Rev.* 423–96.

Lowenfels, Lewis D. (1974) "Expanding Public Responsibilities of Securities Lawyers: An Analysis of the New Trend in Standard of Care and Priorities of Duties," 74 *Columbia Law Rev.* 412–38.

Lundman, Richard J. (1980) "Routine Police Arrest Practices: A Commonweal Perspective," in R. J. Lundman, ed., *Police Behavior: A Sociological Perspective.* New York: Oxford Univ. Press.

Pfeffer, Jeffrey, & Gerald R. Salancik (1978) *The External Control of Organizations: A Resource Dependence Perspective.* New York: Harper & Row.

Proper, Emberson Edward (1900) *Colonial Immigration Laws: A Study of the Regulation of Immigration by the English Colonies in America.* New York: Columbia Univ. Press.

Rolph, Elizabeth, & Abby Robyn (1990) *A Window on Immigration Reform: Implementing the Immigration Reform and Control Act in Los Angeles.* Santa Monica, CA: RAND Corporation.

Schuck, Peter (1972) "The Curious Case of the Indicted Meat Inspectors: Lambs to Slaughter," 245 *Harper's Mag.*, pp. 81–88 (Sept.)
Shellenbarger, Sue (1992) "Work and Family: Child-Support Rules Shake Parents, Firms," *Wall Street J.*, 20 Jan., sec B, p. 1, col. 1.
U.S. Congress (1951) *Revision of the Immigration, Naturalization, and Nationality Laws.* Joint Hearings before the Subcommittees of the Committees on the Judiciary, 82d Cong., 1st Sess. Washington: U.S. GPO.
Whitford, William C. (1979) "A Critique of the Consumer Credit Collection System," 1979 *Wisconsin Law Rev.* 1047–1143.
Zellman, Gail L. (1990) "Child Abuse Reporting and Failure to Report among Mandated Reporters," 5 *J. of Interpersonal Violence* 3–22.

Case

Orantes-Hernandez v. Smith, 541 F. Supp. 351 (C.D. Cal. 1982).

Statutes & Regulations

Immigration Act of 1990, Pub. L. No. 101-649, 104 Stat. 5067, 8 *U.S.C.* 1182.
53 *Fed. Reg.* 1791 (22 Jan. 1988) (Proposed rule).
54 *Fed. Reg.* 100 (4 Jan. 1989) (Final rule).

[4]

Inside Illegality: Migration Policing in South Africa after Apartheid

Jonathan Klaaren and Jaya Ramji

South Africa's migration policing policy has not changed substantially since the demise of apartheid. Tactics used by the police in recent operations are dramatically similar to apartheid policing practices. While some amendments to the legislative regime have aimed to protect human rights, the structures introduced have failed to make any impact. The discretion allowed to police has contributed to the institutional and symbolic entrenchment of the lack of legal status for undocumented migrants. At the level of implementation, the police and the army have played major roles in migration policing with no more than administrative oversight from the Department of Home Affairs. The policing strategy pursued has been one of border control backed up with intrusive and extensive internal military-style policing. Corruption is an institutional feature of both the arrest and detention of undocumented migrants. Numerous human rights abuses occur in the arrest and detention of undocumented migrants as well as of refugees. Despite the embarrassing attention of domestic and foreign human rights organizations exposing certain instances of abuse, the principal features of this policing strategy have remained intact and human rights abuses have continued through to the present.

South Africa's migration policing policy has not changed substantially since the demise of apartheid. While some amendments to the legislative regime have been made that have aimed to protect human rights, the amendments were minor and the structures introduced have failed to make any significant impact. Indeed, the fundamental contribution made by the legislative framework has remained the entrenchment of the lack of legal status of undocumented migrants. At the level of implementation the police and, to a lesser extent, the army, have played larger roles in migration policing.

Despite the formation of a national coordination initiative, migration policing has been a disjointed effort. The cumulative effect has been numerous human rights violations and ethical abuses in the arrest and detention of undocumented migrants as well as refugees. These rights violations have led to the embarrassing attention of domestic and foreign human rights organizations. Moreover, corruption is an institutional feature of both the arrest and detention of undocumented migrants. This paper argues that the principal features of this policing strategy are likely to remain intact and that human rights abuses are likely to continue in terms of the government's policy initiatives presently under discussion.

Operation Crackdown

Operation Crackdown was the name given to a crime blitz begun in March 2000 and planned to last for three years. The Operation provides a stark example of the similarities between South Africa's current migration policing policy and the policing of the apartheid state. The policing policy operative from 1994 to 1999 has created an underclass of individuals whose basic human rights could be abused by the police with impunity. Operation Crackdown focused on areas predominantly populated by black immigrants, and on whether individuals in these areas had the proper "passes" or immigration papers. Police reportedly also operated in a manner to "make immigrants illegal" through the destruction of valid documents and other similar illegal tactics. Arrested individuals were sent to the Lindela Detention and Repatriation Centre (operated by a private body on behalf of the Department of Home Affairs) for deportation, often without a chance to provide evidence of their legitimate immigration status. Little distinction was made between refugees and asylum-seekers and other immigrants. All of this took place against a background whereby the Department of Home Affairs and other government bodies repeatedly and publicly characterized undocumented immigrants as "criminals."

During March 2000, the South Africa Police Services (SAPS) arrested a reported 7,068 "illegal immigrants" in the Hillbrow and Berea areas of Johannesburg (Cilliers 2000). According to widespread reports, the SAPS refused to allow these arrested persons the opportunity to go home to collect their valid immigration documents. Members of SAPS ripped up the valid documents of others. It appeared to many that orders to destroy documents had come from above, as the practice was systematic. Further, immigrants reported that SAPS officers assaulted many individuals prior to and during arrest. Lengthy delays in processing at the Braamfontein Office of the Department of Home Affairs also meant that many immigrants were unable to retain their legal status despite their best efforts (*Sapa* 2000a). The police detained some persons arrested temporarily in police stations and then sent them to the Lindela Detention and Repatriation Centre to be deported. The majority of the over 7,000 detained were sent to Lindela despite the fact that the facility was only designed to hold approximately 4,500 persons at maximum capacity. At least 400 of these individuals were then released as they possessed valid documentation. Many others were deported (*Dispatch* 2000).

Speaking for the South African Human Rights Commission (SAHRC), Chairperson Barney Pityana criticized the unwarranted nature of many of the arrests as well as the violent tactics used by the police (*Sapa* 2000b). Further, the SAHRC spoke out against the arbitrary nature of arrests, which generally depended on the physiognomy rather than the criminal record of the individual concerned (*WOZA/Sapa* 2000). According to Pityana, the speedy expulsion of immigrants prevented individuals from establishing their lawful status and violated their rights to due process of law.

The South African government took great umbrage at this criticism of the abuse of migrants and asylum-seekers. In an extraordinary statement, the cabinet criticized the SAHRC for undermining the government's efforts to control crime in South Africa and for "creating the impression of being sympathetic" to undocumented immigrants (*Business Day* 2000). Police Commissioner Jackie Selebi likewise stated that "There is no issue of human rights" in Operation Crackdown. Gauteng Premier Shilowa applauded the police for "sending a strong message to criminals" (*Sapa* 2000b). A SAPS spokesperson revealed the dubious assumptions informing the operation and its implementation, stating that "offenders of less serious crimes were arrested in an attempt to deter them from turning to more serious crime" (*Sapa* 2000c). Thus, immigrants were viewed as criminals per se, and arrested as a prophylactic measure. To further ensure that these "criminals" would be eliminated from South African society, Steve Tshwete, Minister of Safety and Security, stated that border controls would be strengthened so that deported migrants could not return (*Sapa* 2000d). Tshwete also asked civilians to "assist in the war against crime," thus encouraging vigilante justice and exacerbating xenophobia (*Sapa* 2000e).

Operation Crackdown exemplifies the process of criminalization of being black and foreign, just as apartheid criminalized blackness. As has happened before (Human Rights Watch 1998), migrants and asylum-seekers have been treated without regard to domestic and international human rights standards. Caught in a Kafka-esque web of bureaucracy, such persons are often prevented from maintaining their lawful status and they are consequently imprisoned and deported. Operation Crackdown exemplifies some of the major features of migration policing from 1994 to 1999 explored in the remainder of this article.

The Aliens Control Act and its Amendments

The major piece of legislation governing migration policing is the aptly named Aliens Control Act. Enacted in 1991, this Act consolidated into one piece of legislation a number of provisions regulating entry and residence (Peberdy and Crush 1998:33). The only significant attention given to the Act since the formal 1994 transition from apartheid occurred in 1995 with amending legislation. The substantive changes introduced at that time eliminated one or two of the most blatant violations of rights—such as the elimination of a clause purporting to oust judicial review—but did little beyond that. The Aliens Control Act is a piece of legislation that is riddled with unconstitutional provisions (Klaaren 1998). It remains essentially as it was at the time of transition. Overall, the 1995 amendment legislation was not presented in Parliament as having the primary purpose of effecting a constitutional audit. Instead, the primary purpose was the tightening up of control (Buthelezi 1996:6).

One innovation introduced in the 1995 amending legislation was a mechanism designed to protect the rights of persons in detention with a view toward deportation. According to Section 55(5) of the Act as revised, persons in detention beyond thirty days needed to have their cases reviewed (although not necessarily in person) in a court of law. This procedure was introduced at the specific request of the Parliamentary Portfolio Committee on Home Affairs and was intended to safeguard the rights of detainees. However well intentioned, this legislative policy has had practically no effect at the level of state administration. More than a year and a half after the commencement of this section, most courts reported that they had had no matters referred to them for review. Indeed, it has been the rare exception where this legislative directive has been observed (Human Rights Watch 1998:98–102).

On 4 December 1997, a research visit to the Lindela Repatriation Centre in Krugersdorp revealed that all twenty-seven persons there had been detained beyond the thirty-day limit and had not been afforded the opportunity of review. On two other occasions, representatives of the Law Clinic at the School of Law at the University of the Witwatersrand also found groups of detainees held at Lindela beyond the thirty-day limit required by Section 55(5). This pattern of neglect and maladministration led the South African Human Rights Commission to successfully bring a lawsuit against the Minister of Home Affairs.[1]

The Aliens Control Act has conferred extensive discretion upon the Department of Home Affairs and upon other implementing state bodies such as the police and the army. The extensive discretionary element to the Act has been noted by many commentators (Peberdy and Crush 1998; Klaaren 1998). The extensive use of discretion within the immigration bureaucracy does not derive solely from the content of the legislative policy contained in the Aliens Control Act. Indeed, this discretion is buttressed by the policy's essentially unchanged status from preapartheid days, and the weakness of most oversight institutions such as the Parliamentary Committees, the Public Protector, and even the South African Human Rights Commission.

The experience of those caught within the bureaucracy focuses on this extensive official discretion (Johnston and Simbine 1998). As Sheena Duncan once stated, "It is not easy to write an article about the application of the Aliens Control Act. Its administration is haphazard, ad hoc, arbitrary, and by no means transparent" (Duncan 1998). This discretion has also been the subject of a recent and far-reaching Constitutional Court decision sharply critical of such discretion. The Constitutional Court decision attacked the rights-infringing use of discretion by Department of Home Affairs officials and struck down one provision in the Act. However, the Court ordered that its declaration of invalidity be suspended for two years in order to allow the legislature the opportunity to remedy the constitutional violation (Constitutional Court 2000).

There is a second principal effect of the legislative policy that goes beyond the granting of enormous and unaccountable discretion to the state bodies charged with enforcing the Aliens Control Act. This is the institutional and symbolic effect of the Act, which can be seen in part through a comparison of South African immigration policy with that of Spain. In a recent article, Kitty Calavita has argued that Spanish immigration laws are constructed in a way to marginalize third world immigrants, to regularize the notion of the "irregulars." In her study, she shows how Spanish immigration law actively and regularly irregularizes people. This is done by making it all but impossible to retain legal status over time (Calavita 1998: 531). There are several mechanisms for this institutionalized illegality. They include a long wait for citizenship, the temporary and contingent nature of legal status, as well as various Catch-22s where a residence permit is needed for a work permit which is needed for an accommodation permit which is needed for a residence permit and so on (Calavita 1998:548).

The institutionalized mechanisms of "illegality" in South Africa are somewhat different from those in Spain, although they operate to much the same effect. The South African mechanisms include the following: (a) South African citizenship is difficult to obtain, leading to a large number of persons who are present in the country without any formal citizenship rights; (b) regularization programs are hampered by bureaucratic inefficiency and lack of political support (Crush and Williams 1999; Handmaker, Johnston, and Schneider 2000); (c) the lack of resources and the inefficiency of Home Affairs contributes to the production of illegality (through late, incorrect, or invalid delivery of citizenship and/or residence services); further, the narrow focus of the Department of Home Affairs on residence services and its failure to take the lead in the coordination of government departments in delivering other services such as health or housing often means that such services are unavailable to non–South Africans; and (d) the essential continuation of the "two-gates" system for temporary labor in South Africa (Crush and Tshitereke, in this issue).

The symbolic effect of the Aliens Control Act in the construction of illegality may be even greater than the institutionalized mechanisms of the Spanish case. Unlike the Spanish example, there is simply no rhetoric of integration in the South African legislation. The themes of control and illegality run rampant. Certainly in this symbolic sense, the South African immigration legislation *produces* the "illegal immigrant." In South Africa, the illegal immigrant is not merely illegal in the sense of being unregulated or beyond legal institutions (although that too is often true). The illegal immigrant is illegal in the sense of being contrary to law, of being prohibited. The illegal immigrant is not merely *beyond* law but is instead *against* law.

The most pure example of this is the concept of the "prohibited person." The Aliens Control Act is built around this legal category. This concept has its origins in South Africa's first national immigration legislation and the discretion allowed to immigration officials at ports of entry to declare prospective permanent residents to be undesirable (Peberdy and Crush 1998:20). Since its inception, the concept has expanded from its original purpose of applying a set of criteria to prospective permanent residents and has instead become an operative assumption for all government officials implementing migration control legislation. The assumption is that persons who are in violation of any provision of the Aliens Control Act (especially Section 39) are prohibited persons. As understood, the concept of prohibited persons means that such persons are without legal standing as persons. Many of the operative legislative provisions involved with apprehension, detention, and deportation either declare persons to be prohibited persons or allow government officials to deal with persons as prohibited persons.[2]

Indeed, the legal route of illegality was one that until very recently had to be taken by asylum applicants. In order to potentially take advantage of the refugee status determination procedure, persons would need to become prohibited persons, be issued with a section forty-one permit to prohibited persons, and only then be eligible to be determined as a refugee (de la Hunt 1998:132). This led to considerable insecurity of legal tenure for refugee applicants. Ironically, with the recognition of the legitimacy of refugee applicants within the migration policing apparatus, there has been a sharp reinforcement of the illegality of persons (such as undocumented migrants) who fall outside the category of asylum-seekers (Grobler 2000). Refugees are fine; illegals are not.

The total number of persons removed from South Africa has been increasing fairly steadily. In 1994, the removal figure for "illegal aliens" was 90,692. In 1995, it jumped sharply to 157,084. In 1996, the figure increased significantly again to 180,713. Over the next three years, it has essentially remained at this level, inching upward each year but the first. In 1997, the figure was 176,351. In 1998, 181,286 persons were removed and in 1999, 186,861 (Department of Home Affairs 1994–1999). However, basic statistics regarding what proportion of persons are apprehended by which government body are not available (Klaaren 1997). Nor are there statistics on the number of repeat deportations of the same person and therefore repeated infringements of basic rights.

There are four principal bodies engaged in migration policing: the South African National Defense Force (SANDF), the South African Police Service (SAPS), the SAPS Border Policing component, and the Department of Home Affairs. The police play an extremely significant role in enforcing the ACA. For instance, a 1995 bilateral between Home Affairs officials of South Africa and Zimbabwe resolved to convene a joint technical committee involving the police services of both countries to discuss deportation procedures. It confirmed that a representative of SAPS would attend all future meetings of the bilateral (Klaaren 1997). By 1996–1997, SAPS was represented on five bi- or trilateral forums as well as on regional and international border control structures (SAPS 1996–1997). A large number of police officers have been appointed by the Minister as immigration officers with the capacity to exercise the removal powers given under that Act (Klaaren 1997).

Institutionally, a separate component of the police dealing with border control was set up in July 1995 following several years of pushing for such a step within the police. The core function of this component is "to address the illegal crossborder movement of persons and goods into South Africa as well as the internal tracing of undocumented migrants/illegal aliens and illegal goods within the Republic" (SAPS 1997). One part of this component consists of specialized units—Internal Tracing Units of the Border Police—which operate both in the major urban areas and in border areas with high concentrations of undocumented migrants. Additionally, a national Aliens Investigation Unit concentrates on national level immigrant-smuggling and other criminal organizations closely involved with international migration (SAPS 1997; Human Rights Watch 1998:44).

The SANDF also has a large role to play in migration policing (Klaaren 1997). In general, neither Home Affairs nor SAPS police the borders, leaving that task to the SANDF.[3] The SANDF uses roadblocks both within short distances of the border and within the central economic region of Gauteng to detect and arrest suspected undocumented migrants. Additionally, the SANDF operates and patrols the electrified fence that is set up along part of the border between South Africa and Mozambique. While more than one hundred persons were killed by the lethal operation of this fence before 1990, since that time it has operated at a nonlethal voltage.[4] Nonetheless, there are reports of persons injured by the fence's operation (Human Rights Watch 1998:46–47).

The coordination among these migration policing agencies has been minimal. For instance, SAPS internal tracing units have not had access to Home Affairs computerized information after-hours. This has led some SAPS officers from Johannesburg to drive out to Johannesburg International Airport to use the Home Affairs information system available there after-hours. Such a disjointed approach led members of the migration policing agencies to acknowledge that there was no effective border control (Grobler 2000). The Border Police led the way in attempting to address the fragmentation and lack of coordination in migration policing (SAPS 1997). Approved by Cabinet, the primary national initiative to coordinate migration policing has been the National Inter-Departmental Structure on Border Control (NIDS). This initiative has involved the Department of Home Affairs, SAPS, and the South African Revenue Services (SARS) (Operational Working Team on Border Control 1997). Since its establishment in 1997, NIDS has had a focus broader than the migration policing covered here, focusing additionally on customs regulation and enforcement. Nonetheless, the

africa TODAY | 41 | JONATHAN KLAAREN AND JAYA RAMJI

lack of coordination essentially remains. After several years of operation, informed observers discount the effectiveness of the NIDS structures (Cilliers 2000). Instead of coordination, the border control system exhibits a situation of systemic crisis and is unlikely to sort itself out, at least within the foreseeable future.

Operation Crackdown is but one of numerous examples of police and security force abuses in migration control.[5] South African police forces, in coalition with the DHA and the SANDF, operate in a manner that make people illegal. Arrests of undocumented migrants are then used to boost police arrest statistics and to line the pockets of police forces. Indeed, the economic aspects of the migration policing regime (e.g., individual and institutional corruption) need to be highlighted as much as the more conventional human rights violations. Ironically, many victims of police brutality and corruption are documented migrants and South African citizens.

In one form of abuse, police forces use irrational standards to determine whether individuals are "illegal immigrants," including skin color and location of vaccination marks (SAHRC 1999:48–54; Crush 1996; Minnaar and Hough 1996). Individuals who do not have money to bribe the police forces are arrested, regardless of their true immigration status. According to one study, ten percent of detainees at the Lindela Detention and Repatriation Centre were released after arrest but prior to intake because they had lawful status in South Africa. Fourteen percent of those detained were released after intake because they were South African citizens or lawful residents (Human Rights Watch 1998:52–54). While the sample size was small, these numbers suggest the police force's failure to properly investigate individuals' status prior to arrest.

One instance of the application of irrational standards by the police and its consequences for an ordinary citizen was detailed by the South African Human Rights Commission:

> Nelsa was apprehended in Bara, Soweto about noon on 7 April 1998, where she was selling goods. A police officer approached her and asked her for her ID. She produced her ID, and the officer then asked her where she was born. She said that she was born in South Africa, and then the officer said that she was not born in S.A. She replied that he should phone her grandmother to check. The police officer asked her to show him her hands, which she did. He saw the inoculation mark on her left forearm and said that she is born in Mozambique. She started to explain to the police officer how she got the mark (a product of mixed South African and Mozambican family who moved back and forth between the countries over several generations). He told her that she lied and that she should accompany him to the police station. She gave him her ID and did not accompany him. The police officer took her ID to Dube Police Station and Nelsa phoned her grandmother and explained the

situation. Eventually, Nelsa went with her uncle, who had been at the place with Nelsa's grandmother in Orlando, to the Dube police station to retrieve her identification document. Upon arrival at the station, Nelsa identified the officer who had taken her ID to her uncle. The police officer spoke to her and said that nobody could take her. Nelsa believed that he was happy to see her as she had previously said that she wouldn't go to the police station. The officer spoke to her uncle . . . Her uncle told the officer that he was from Orlando East, and in reply to how he knows her, Nelsa's uncle said that he married her aunt (father's sister). The police officer then said that Nelsa was from Mozambique, and the uncle said that she was born in South Africa. The officer asked Nelsa to give Zulu words for various body parts—and she replied correctly. Police officer then still said that she was lying and must go back to Mozambique. The officer did not want to return her ID to her, instead he took her to a small room. After she started crying and told the officer that he was abusing her, he repeated the statement that she must return to Mozambique. The officer then told her uncle that he would take her to New Canada [a Department of Home Affairs district office] to check her ID and would return her. But he took her to Lindela instead. At Lindela, she was not told nor was she allowed to make one free phone call. (SAHRC 1997:17)

In certain instances, DHA officials not only apply irrational standards but actively "make people illegal" through refusal of access to buildings, endless lines, and failure to provide proper documentation. Police commonly destroy or confiscate the documents of individuals whom they have arrested (Human Rights Watch 1998:54–55). Further, police do not allow immigrants or citizens access to their homes to retrieve their documents establishing their legal status (SAHRC 1999: 51–57). The police frequently do not provide reasons for their arrest of individuals, and people therefore are unaware that the production of valid immigration documents could terminate their arrest and detention (SAHRC 1999:57–59):

I was marketing in D.F. Malan street. The police came from the back and stopped their truck. They asked me where I come from. I told them that I am from Kagiso. They asked me for my ID. I produced it and handed it to Mageza (a Venda police officer). He took it and put it in his pocket and told me that I am a "Kalanga" (illegal). They told me to get inside the truck but I demanded my ID. They refused and told me that they want to check it in the computer. I got into the van. We moved for about 3 hours going around. From there they took me to Newlands police station. They took our fingerprints and

> put us in cells. I asked about my ID and they told me that it was in the car (truck). They took me from the police station to Lindela. At the police they put that I am from Zimbabwe in my file. At Lindela they asked me about my ID and I told them that it is with the police who apprehended me. They told me that I can phone my wife and tell her to bring some sort of proof that I am South African. I could not because her work telephone numbers are in my ID. I don't know how I am going to get out from here and how am I going to get my ID. (SAHRC 1999:57–59)

Some aspects of the production of illegality are also a feature of the inefficient and dignity-destroying operating procedures at the Department of Home Affairs. As an example, the Refugee Reception Office in Braamfontein, Johannesburg, only accepts approximately twenty individuals per day. Asylum-seekers line up outside the office as early as three a.m. in order to obtain access to the building (*Sowetan* 2000). The majority of those individuals are denied access and are at risk of arrest and detention by police who wait outside the DHA office specifically to arrest such individuals.

Once individuals have been arrested and detained, further mechanisms ensure their "illegality." Police commonly do not allow undocumented migrants in Lindela to apply for refugee status, in violation of domestic and international law (SAHRC 1999:69–72). As pointed out above, migrants are frequently held in unlawful detention for over a month, contrary to the law, which states that any detention longer than thirty days must be reviewed by a High Court judge (SAHRC 1999:74–84). During detention, some immigrants' legal status will expire while they are unable to renew their documentation. The DHA then releases these individuals from Lindela with "must leave" papers, allowing them fourteen days to leave the country.

These sources of the condition of illegality lead to further abuse. During the arrest and detention process, undocumented migrants are subject to physical abuse and at the mercy of corrupt officials. Police commonly assault migrants and steal their money and other goods during arrest (SAHRC 1999:59–66). Corruption and bribery are widespread; immigrants must pay to be released from detention or even to access the telephone (SAHRC 1999:88–95). Once the individuals are in detention, they are subject to routine abuse at the hands of the police and the army, including physical assault and degrading language (SAHRC 1999:99–103, 107–109). Deaths of undocumented immigrants have occurred in police custody (Human Rights Watch 1998:55–64, 121).

At the end of the day, police turn arrests of undocumented migrants to their own advantage. Police use arrest statistics for "illegal immigrants" to increase their overall crime fighting figures. The SANDF also engages in this statistical enterprise. The police encourage South African citizens to join in the anti-immigrant game by participating in vigilante justice.

The DHA has even established a toll-free number and offers reward money to those who report undocumented migrants (Human Rights Watch 1998: 47). The business of migration control has proved to be a lucrative one for employees of the SAPS, the SANDF, and the DHA, providing bribe money, increased statistics, and a convenient scapegoat to direct the general public's attention away from the high crime rates in South Africa.

Conclusion

In versions of the new Draft Immigration Bill released in July 2000, increased discretion is given to agencies of the government implementing international migration legislation. Further, the Bill arguably increases the control aspects of the present legislation by shifting the focus of migration policing from one directed exclusively at border control and heartland policing to incorporate community policing. This Bill has not been received favorably by the Minister's colleagues in Cabinet and unqualified approval of the draft legislation by Parliament appears extremely unlikely. In addition, the Portfolio Committee in Parliament charged with oversight of the Department of Home Affairs pronounced negatively on the White Paper on International Migration upon which the Minister's Draft Immigration Bill is purportedly based. While it is unclear where this fractured policy process will lead, it is relatively clear that for the foreseeable future migration policing will continue to be governed by the ACA, characterized by discretion and by both institutional and symbolic illegality with continuing human rights and good government violations as results. There is no guarantee that things will be any different if the Draft Immigration Bill becomes law.

NOTES

1. This litigation is ongoing at the time of writing.
2. The Draft Immigration Bill in the version made public by the Minister of Home Affairs in July 2000 not only carries over the concept of a "prohibited person" used in the previous Aliens Control Act, but also adds two new concepts, that of an "illegal foreigner" and that of "undesirable persons." In this Bill, the term "illegal foreigner" does the work of the "prohibited person" term in the Aliens Control Act.
3. Of the total number of persons apprehended in 1995, 164,971, Home Affairs arrested 49,098. 28,541 were apprehended by the SANDF. SAPS arrested 83,079: 29,544 by Border Control and the rest, 53,535, by ordinary station commanders. A final 4,253 were "received from other offices" (Klaaren 1997).
4. The SANDF reported that four persons were killed in the course of their enforcement of the Aliens Control Act during 1995, three by shooting and one by shock (Klaaren 1997).
5. As detailed in the main text, allegations of abuse at the hands of immigration officers are common. However, there is apparently no institutionalized law enforcement complaints

investigation mechanism within the Department. According to Home Affairs: "Written complaints may be forwarded to Head Office or to any office of the Regional Director of Home Affairs, in whose region the alleged abuse occurred. Such complaints will be investigated and, where necessary, acted upon" (Klaaren 1997).

REFERENCES CITED

Business Day. 2000. HRC under Fire from Government over Police, 30 March.

Buthelezi, Mangosuthu. 1996. Introductory Speech. Speech given at Policy Debate, National Assembly, 4 June.

Calavita, Kitty. 1998. Immigration, Law, and Marginalization in a Global Economy: Notes from Spain. *Law and Society Review* 32:529–566.

Cilliers, Jakkie. 2000. Speech given at Regulating Migration in the Twenty-First Century: A South African Perspective Conference, Cape Town.

Constitutional Court of South Africa. 2000. *Dawood and Another v. Minister of Home Affairs and Others: Constitutional Court CCT 35/99* (7 June).

Crush, Jonathan. 1996. Migrancy: The Colour Of Alien-ation. *Democracy in Action* 10:6.

Crush, Jonathan and Vincent Williams, eds. 1999. *The New South Africans? Immigration Amnesties and their Aftermath*. Cape Town: Idasa.

de la Hunt, Lee Anne. 1998. Refugees and Immigration Law in South Africa. In *Beyond Control: Immigration and Human Rights in a Democratic South Africa* edited by Jonathan Crush. Cape Town and Kingston: Idasa and Southern African Migration Project.

Department of Home Affairs. 1994–1999. *Annual Reports*. Pretoria: Government Printer.

Dispatch. 2000. Aliens Languish in Dire State in Lindela Camp, 23 March.

Grobler, Piet. 2000. A Collective Approach to Border Control: Policing and Refugees. Unpublished paper.

Handmaker, Jeff, Nicola Johnston and James Schneider. 2000. The Status Regularisation Programme for Former Mozambican Refugees in South Africa. Unpublished paper, Wits Rural Facility.

Human Rights Watch. 1998. *Prohibited Persons: Abuse of Undocumented Migrants, Asylum-seekers, and Refugees in South Africa*. New York: Human Rights Watch.

Klaaren, Jonathan. 1997. Institutional Reform and Immigrant Management. In *Transforming South African Migration and Immigration Policy*, edited by J. Crush and F. Veriava. Cape Town and Kingston: Southern African Migration Project.

———. 1998. Immigration and the South African Constitution. In *Beyond Control: Immigration and Human Rights in a Democratic South Africa*, edited by Jonathan Crush. Cape Town and Kingston: Idasa and Southern African Migration Project.

Minnaar, Anthony and Mike Hough. 1996. *Who Goes There? Perspectives on Clandestine Migration and Illegal Aliens in Southern Africa*. Pretoria: Human Science Research Council.

Operational Working Team on Border Control. 1997. *Border Control Collective Approach: Implementation Plan*. Pretoria: Heads of the National Inter-Departmental Structure on Border Control.

Peberdy, Sally and Jonathan Crush. 1998. Rooted in Racism: The Origins of the Aliens Control Act. In *Beyond Control: Immigration and Human Rights in a Democratic South Africa*, edited by Jonathan Crush. Cape Town and Kingston: Idasa and Southern African Migration Project.

Sapa. 2000a. SAHRC Concerned about Police Search and Seizure Procedures, 20 March.

———. 2000b. Selebi, Tshwete Say Aliens Not Assaulted in Swoop, 20 March.

———. 2000c. Over 1,000 Arrested in First Two Days of Operation Crackdown, 30 March.

———. 2000d. SA Police in Position to Eliminate Crime: Tshwete, 20 March

———. 2000e. Sunnyside Residents Encouraged to Expose Criminals, 4 May.

South African Human Rights Commission. 1999. *Illegal? Report on the Arrest and Detention of Persons in Terms of the Aliens Control Act.* Braamfontein: SAHRC (http://www.lhr.org.za/refugee/hrcreport.htm).

South African Police Services. 1997. *Annual Report 1996/1997.* Pretoria: Government Printer.

Sowetan. 2000. Asylum Seekers Walk the Tightrope. 11 May.

WOZA/Sapa. 2000. Humanitarian Organizations to Visit Lindela Detention Centre, 21 March.

[5]

U.S. IMMIGRATION REFORM AND THE MEANING OF RESPONSIBILITY

Kathleen M. Moore

America is not just a nation of immigrants. It is a nation of immigrants committed to personal responsibility and the rule of law.

—Rep. Lamar Smith (R-Tx.) (Speaking in favor of H.R. 2202, the Illegal Immigration Reform and Immigrant Responsibility Act 1996)[1]

The American public is ambivalent about immigration. On the one hand, the Statue of Liberty, along with the famous words of Emma Lazarus inscribed on its pedestal ("Give me your tired, your poor, your huddled masses . . ."), attests to the nation's immigrant heritage and is a cultural icon as revered as the American flag. Advocates of immigration argue that newcomers confer benefits on the nation, such as scientific knowledge, artistic talents, the entrepreneurial spirit, and a rich cultural diversity as well as labor power at critical junctures in the expansion of the nation's economy and the American frontier (Reich 1991). On the other hand, periodically throughout American history immigrants have been reviled as agents of disease, violence, illicit drug trafficking, moral degradation, socialism, anarchism, labor unrest, illiberal traditions, and economic dependency.[2] Increases in immigration in the last three decades have stimulated substantial debate about immigration to the United States and have generated policy proposals at the federal and state levels to cut immigration, tighten border restrictions, require national identification cards and employer verification systems, limit provision of public services to legal and illegal immigrants, and deny birthright citizenship to children of undocumented aliens.[3] This ambivalence about immigration rests in part on the economy, which at various times has alternately needed and shunned immigrant labor. Yet at a semiotic level, this ambivalence also has significance for Americans' self-definition because it problematizes the symbolic ordering of the nation that designates the people as *e pluribus unum* and one-nation-under-god. If we hold what Representative Lamar Smith says in the epigraph of this paper to be true, that America is *not* simply a nation of immigrants, but rather is descended from a particular *type* of immigrant—those who are dedicated to responsibility and the rule of law—then the discursive ideal of "America" as an inclusive/unified community is being contested. Smith's rhetorical modification of the principle of universal membership, by tying it to a particular vision of what "America" should be like, negotiates an *exclusion* that paradoxically is premised on, exists in tension with, and reinstates, the inclusive/ universal norms of liberal democracy.

Smith's statement suggests the continual slippage in meaning, specifically, in the cultural signification of symbols where meaning becomes fluid and unstable. Presumably in Smith's view there exists a marginal area of American society, occupied by those "others" in the republic who remain *uncommitted* to personal responsibility and the rule of law.[4] This essay tries to show how making this distinction (i.e., mapping the margins of the nation) is an attempt to distance the threat of disorder and cultural difference. Why are debates over immigration to the United States being framed in terms of responsibility (and its antithesis, dependency)? While official discourses can be linked to structural foundations (e.g., the economy),[5] in this paper I argue that there is something more than anxieties over taxes, jobs, housing, or the continued supply of government services that is tacit in the enactment of the 1996 immigration law. While economic motives are a large part of the explanation, they alone are not sufficient to explain the persistence of the culturally and racially disparate impact of immigration reform.[6] Some forms of exclusion are "irrational" in that they are neither economically efficient nor salient as a means of achieving the ostensible goals of state policy (e.g., balancing the federal budget). The task I want to pose most centrally here is to explore the raced and gendered (rather than economic) character to the dominant discourses on citizenship and entitlement in late modernity (Brown 1995).[7] In order to understand more fully the impact of immigration reform on the definition of the nation, the racial and gender subtexts of this discourse need to be disclosed. Specifically here I interrogate the linkage between responsibility and "culture." Like the work ethic, responsibility becomes not only a *marker* or *index* of a superior "culture" (e.g., identified with Protestantism). It also becomes a vehicle for the conventions of power and privilege constitutive of the late modern regulatory state, through which certain individuals and groups are cast as marginal by virtue of what they lack (responsibility), while the powerful are normalized.[8] Consequently, laws mandating "responsibility" are understood not simply as an expression of authority; they reward certain forms of social organization (for instance, the nuclear family[9]) and have a differential impact, along color and gender lines, on members of the dominant versus minority subgroups in society.

In what follows I examine how responsibility and blame are located discursively *through* law, in the reinforcement of a national identity and, specifically, in the way recent reform of U.S. immigration law holds certain groups to blame for the social problems of the nation. I try to offer an approach to thinking about the contested nature of American identity, and how in contemporary political debates the word "responsibility" discursively feminizes doubly by rendering the subordinated legal subject (e.g., the immigrant) dependent and submissive, and by inscribing her as voiceless, lacking representation and subjectivity in official discourses. In the first part of the paper I provide a brief overview of what the immigration reform law provides, and major changes made in the rules governing the eligibility of legal immigrants for government assistance and benefits. Then, in the second section, my argument situates the rhetoric of responsibility, encompassed in congressional debates about immigration reform in 1996, within a broader discourse on economic recovery.[10] By charting the role played by public discourses in reproducing a particular national identity that is contingent on the "tax burden" hypothesis,[11] I excavate some of the tacit assumptions and connotations of the current usage of the word responsibility. I attempt to highlight the various ways the word is deployed to communicate concerns about federalism, criminality and welfare dependency. In the third section, I suggest that changes in Congress in 1994, "a year in which the issue of immigration grew in prominence" (Citrin et al. 1997, p. 859)[12] contributed to the ways in which the current immigration "crisis" is being handled by leaders in Congress and is especially potent in shaping the future of immigrants' (and potential immigrants') lives. These changes in the committee structure in Congress have altered the legislation that Congress produces and, in terms of welfare and immigration reform, express largely elite understandings of who is deserving and responsible. The tightening of immigration criteria has happened in spite of what I argue is a noticeable degree of moderation on the part of the American public with regard to immigration questions.[13]

In the section that immediately follows, I discuss what the 1996 law entails and the congressional debates that preceded its enactment.

THE ILLEGAL IMMIGRATION REFORM AND IMMIGRANT RESPONSIBILITY ACT: FEDERAL LEGISLATION IN THE 104TH CONGRESS

The last decade of the twentieth century has seen extraordinary change in the legislative and regulatory arenas affecting immigration. On September 30, 1996,

President Clinton signed the new immigration law, cumbersomely entitled the Illegal Immigration Reform and Immigrant Responsibility Act (hereinafter IIRIRA, Pub. L. No. 104-208, 110 Stat. 3009). The IIRIRA is a sweeping reform that tightens U.S. immigration, promising to restrict the influx of immigrants and the availability of employment for immigrants.[14] The new law focuses on illegal immigration, and contains "some of the toughest measures ever taken against illegal immigration" (Fragomen 1997, p. 438), although the law was originally conceived of by its sponsors in Congress as a means to reduce immigration to the United States from all sources, whether lawful or not.

"Responsibility" appears prominently in the title of this statute, and is a word used repeatedly in congressional debates over this legislation and in welfare reform legislation of the same year to mean employed, productive, and law-abiding workers. Congress' desire to increase "immigrant responsibility" is manifest in provisions of the 1996 immigration law that are designed to screen out those who demonstrate a "criminal propensity"[15] and those who may become public charges.[16] Some provisions preclude the entry of new arrivals with criminal records and accelerate the deportation of those residents who have committed crimes in the United States.[17] Others establish a "fiscal test," requiring that sponsors of new arrivals demonstrate their financial wherewithal to support the new immigrant by documenting an annual income equal to at least 125 percent of the federal poverty level. For instance, a permanent resident who wants to bring her brother, sister-in-law, and two nephews to the United States in 1997, who also has her own family of four to support, would have to earn at least $33,662.50 to meet 125 percent of the 1997 federal poverty income level (to support a family of eight).[18] This provision also makes the immigrant ineligible for means-tested programs (e.g., supplemental security income or Medicaid) for the first five years of her or his residence, and thereafter raises the eligibility standard by "deeming," or attributing a sponsor's income to the immigrant in order to determine whether the immigrant is eligible for means-tested benefits once the five-year residency requirement has been met.[19] The immigration law also requires that sponsors' affidavits of support be legally binding, creating new, legally enforceable responsibilities for immigrants' sponsors.[20] The expansiveness of these provisions, and especially the deeming requirement, show how sweeping Congress intended the restrictions on immigration to be, and reinforces an economic valuation to admissions standards that few members of Congress opposed.[21] While federal immigration law, since its inception in 1882, has barred the entry of immigrants likely to become "public charges," these new provisions mark a dramatic change because they deny legal immigrants access to federal means-tested public benefits that had previously been available to them.[22] The law "imposes new standards of financial self-sufficiency for sponsored, legal immigrants" (Espenshade and Huber 1998, p. 36). These provisions of the law suggest that immigrants (who are perceived as poor and/or criminal) are potential bearers of disorderliness, economic dependency, and crime. Moreover, and perhaps more surprisingly, they also suggest that the law can be an effective means for precluding irresponsible (i.e., nonproductive) riffraff from our midst.[23]

Congressional Debate

The concerns addressed by the IIRIRA certainly are not new in American immigration politics. To a large degree the debates over this act in Congress reflect the competing traditions of nativism and accommodationism that have run throughout American history regarding immigration and citizenship (see Smith 1997; Feagin 1997). The legislation was proposed in the House (H.R. 2202)[24] and Senate (S.1664) as an amendment of the Immigration and Nationality Act of 1990 (INA), a law that substantially liberalized immigration quotas during the Bush Administration but received little attention at that time from the media or the public. The IIRIRA was proposed to:

> amend the Immigration and Nationality Act to improve the deterrence of illegal immigration to the United States by increasing border patrol and investigative personnel, by increasing penalties for alien smuggling and for document fraud, by reforming exclusion and deportation law and procedures, by improving the verification system for eligibility for employment, and through other measures, to reform the legal immigration system and facilitate legal entries into the United States, and for other purposes.

Among its several provisions, the bill proposed to apply stiff criminal penalties for fraud and misrepresentation in the visa application and admission process, hire more law enforcement personnel to investigate and prevent visa overstays and illegal border crossings, fund the construction of additional fences along the U.S.-Mexican border, impose a life prison sentence for smuggling of undocumented aliens, and authorize U.S immigration inspectors with broad powers (known as expedited exclusion) to deny entry to foreign nationals whom they believe are either misrepresenting their purpose in traveling in the United States (i.e., they intend to work instead of play on their tourist visa) or are intending to violate the terms of their non-immigrant visa status. Persons who are refused entry by an immigration inspector under this provision of the law would be barred from returning to the United States for five years. Additionally, provisions of the proposed legislation strengthen requirements that prospective immigrants demonstrate that they are not about to go on welfare (the "public charge" provision) and sponsors are no longer able to disclaim responsibility for the immigrant(s) they brought into the United States (i.e., the affidavits of support would be legally binding).[25] The original versions of the bill in Congress proposed that sponsors demonstrate a minimum household income of 200 percent of the federal poverty income level, to allay concerns that immigrants come to the United States primarily to get public assistance. This was negotiated in Congress and between Congress and the President, however, so that that minimum income level was reduced first to 140 percent and ultimately, in negotiations with the White House, to 125 percent. Other provisions of the bill proposed drastic cuts in legal immigration, reducing the rate of legal immigration by as much as 30 to 40 percent over the next 5 years. Certain categories of immigration, especially the family-sponsored category, would be hit the hardest.[26]

As it wended its way through Congress the passage of the immigration reform bill was accompanied by a stormy debate about whether there is a connection between legal and illegal sources of immigration. The Democratic side of the House generally drew a sharp distinction between legal and illegal sources of immigration, while Republicans did not (Rep. Dick Armey, R-TX, is a notable exception). Representative Lamar Smith (R- TX) asserted upon introducing the bill that there *is* a causal connection between legal and illegal sources of immigration, and that the former contributes substantially to the latter. Smith stated that it is obvious that the immigration system is broken and that "drives the crisis in illegal immigration. Over 40 percent of all illegal aliens arrived as legal immigrants but overstayed their temporary visas" (*Cong Rec.-House*, Dec. 6, 1995). By cutting the levels of legal immigration, the government would be reducing the illegal immigration rate and lessening the "problems" (i.e., costs) associated with immigration.

Senator Richard Shelby (R-AL), speaking in support of the Senate version of this immigration bill (sponsored by Alan Simpson, R-WY), made a similar claim. He said, "One-half of all illegal immigrants enter the country legally and overstay their visa[s] . . . The only way, I believe, to effectively prevent illegal immigration is to reform our legal immigration system. Thus, I believe there is a clear link between legal and illegal immigration" (*Cong. Rec.- Senate*, April 25, 1996). Senator Shelby insisted in the Senate floor debate that we "bring the number of legal immigrants into line with our national interests" (*Cong. Rec. –Senate*, April 25, 1996, p. S4127). He conceded that immigration should continue, but at a reduced rate. The real issue he felt Congress must face is "what criteria should be used to determine those who will be admitted" (p. S4127). He felt the existing criteria were flawed because they admitted too many immigrants. "Three-fourths of the immigrants [to the United States] are legal immigrants. That's three times our level of illegal immigration" (p. S4128). No other country admits as many immigrants, he averred, and legal immigration overburdens the "taxpayer" as much as illegal immigration does. Legal immigration is linked to illegal immigration, he argued, because it has many of the same impacts. Both "involve large numbers of additional people, with legal in fact accounting for nearly three times more new U.S. residents every year than illegal immigration" (p. S4130). While many Congressional opponents of the bill argue that *illegal* immigrants take jobs away from "native" citizens, commit crimes, and cost taxpayers millions of dollars in public services, Senator Shelby argued that legal immigration is just as bad for the country.

Shelby characterized the problems associated with immigration as fiscal ones. He enumerated the problems as:

1. "Excessive numbers of legal immigrants puts a crippling strain on the American education system" (p. S4130). Because of the large numbers of non-English speakers, he says, the costs in education are astronomical.
2. "Immigrants also put a strain on our criminal justice system" (p. S4130). Twenty-five percent of federal prison inmates are foreign-born, he asserts.[27]
3. "Immigrants are 47 percent more likely to receive welfare than native-born citizens" (p. S4130; see also p. S4132). Here he makes a scarcity claim with respect to welfare and employment. He states: "At a time when we have severe budget shortfalls at all levels of government, our Federal immigration law continues to allow aliens to consume the limited public assistance that our citizens need. Moreover, high levels of immigration cost Americans their jobs at a time when we have millions of unemployed and underemployed citizens, and millions more who will be needing jobs as they are weaned off of welfare" (p. S4128).
4. Family-sponsored immigration must be stopped because of the effects of chain migration. In other words, he is concerned that "relatives predominate immigration . . . Immigrants should be allowed to bring in their nuclear family—that is their spouse and minor children—but not an extended chain of distant relatives . . . Each time we admit a new immigrant to this country under our present system, we are creating an entitlement for a whole new set of extended relatives" (p. S4128-9).

In the House of Representatives Independent Congressman Anthony Beilenson (Ind.-CA) also argued in favor of restricting immigration. He voiced opposition to H.R. 2202 primarily because in its final form the provisions requiring an employer verification system was taken out. Perhaps for reasons that differ from Senator Shelby's, Beilenson, too, wanted to reduce the number of *legal* immigrants who come into the United States. He said,

> [I]f the fundamental problem we are concerned with . . . is the impact of too many people arriving too quickly into this country, the sheer numbers dictate that we cannot ignore the role that legal immigration plays . . . It is the 800,000, more or less, legal immigrants, more so than the estimated 300,000 illegal ones, who determine how fierce the competition for jobs is, how overcrowded our schools are, and how large and densely populated our urban areas are becoming. More importantly, the number of foreigners we allow to settle in the United States now will determine how crowded this country will become during the next century. (*Cong. Rec. – House*, September 25, 1996, p. H11073).

Ultimately the provisions that would reduce levels of legal immigration were taken out of the immigration bill, separating some of the provisions affecting legal immigration from illegal, through the Abraham-Kennedy Amendment in the Senate Judiciary Committee, and the Chrysler-Berman-Brownback Amendment in the House floor debates. Beilenson pinned the blame for stripping the bill of its legal immigration restrictions on "intensive lobbying by business interests and by proimmigration organizations with the Clinton administration's blessing" (p. H11073).[28] He lamented that the failure to cut back on legal immigration will not auger well, that it:

> will only be to our Nation's great detriment. The rapid population growth that will result from immigration will make it that much more difficult to solve our most pervasive and environment [*sic*] problems such as air and water pollution, trash and sewage disposal, loss of agriculture lands, and many others, just to name some of the major ones . . . [H]owever we look at it, failing to reduce the current rate of immigration, legal and illegal, clearly means that our children and our grandchildren cannot possibly have the quality of life that we ourselves have been fortunate to have enjoyed (p. H11073).

Other representatives were less focused on the issue of legal immigration. For instance, Congressman David Dreier (R-CA) argued that:

> illegal immigration is a problem in its own right, but is also a factor that contributes to other problems. It undermines job creation by taxing local resources, it threatens wage gains by supplying undocumented labor, it has been a major factor in public school overcrowding, forcing nearly $2 billion in [California] State and local resources to be spend each year educating illegal immigrants rather than California's own children (*Cong. Rec. – House*, September 25, 1996, p. H11071).

Although the thrust of his comments are similar to Shelby's and Beilenson's, Dreier is not suggesting that the solution is to restrict immigration altogether. Instead he argues for improvements in border enforcement, penalties for document fraud, and faster and more effective deportation processes (p. H11071).

Upon reporting to the Senate on his late-night negotiations with the White House to insure passage of the immigration bill, Senator Alan Simpson said that the proposed legislation:

> is about new Border Patrol agents, 5,000. It is about new penalties for those who use or alter fraudulent documents . . .There are heavy penalties to those who misuse and abuse documents, and 300 INS investigators will be hired here to check on those who overstay their visas . . . There is a newly rewritten and streamlined removal process, combining exclusion and deportation into a single legal process. We also got rid of layers of people who love to bring class actions and disrupt the normal course of the INS' work. We make the sponsor's affidavit of support, finally, a legally enforceable document which should provide some relief to the U.S. taxpayer (*Cong. Rec. –Senate*, September 28, 1996, p. S11711).

Part of the "get tough" tone of this law placed financial responsibility squarely in the hands of the immigrant's sponsor. Senator Simpson lamented to the Senate that "we lost" the provision that would have required the sponsor to show evidence of at least 200 percent of the federal poverty income level; instead Congress and the White House agreed to a fiscal test of 125 percent of the federal poverty income level. Simpson insisted that it would be absurd to allow a person who is near poverty to bring in another person in poverty (p. S11711), thereby suggesting immigrants are poor persons and that chain migration will swell the welfare roll.

Some Democrats in Congress, although a distinct minority, have countered the argument that immigrants represent a net loss, economically speaking, by arguing that immigrants contribute significantly. They have argued, for example, that "[l]egal immigrants have provided the United States with a rich return on its investment. Legal immigrants and foreign-born citizens work hard and contribute to the economy well beyond the cost of services they consume" (Ed Pastor, D-AZ, *Cong. Rec. – Extension*, March 29, 1996, p. E506). "Immigrants do not come to America to hop on the public dole. In fact, according to the Urban Institute, immigrants generate an estimated $25 billion in surplus revenues over what they receive in social services (Major Owens, D-NY, *Cong. Rec.* . . .). "Only 3.9 percent of immigrants who come to the United States to join their families or to work, rely on public assistance, compared with 4.2 percent of native-born citizens. Yet, the myth persists that welfare benefits are the primary purpose for immigration to the U.S" (Jose Serrano, D-NY, *Cong Rec. –House*, March 20, 1996, p. H2567). They place an economic valuation on the worth of immigration and suggest that immigrants are self-reliant.

The framework these debates provide, over whether we can distinguish between the effects of legal versus illegal sources of immigration in any meaningful way, allows us the vantagepoint from which to view how the debate has been constructed around the demarcating line of the law. The language that describes immigrants on either side of the defining criteria of the law (in other words, as "lawful" vs. "undocumented") is used either to champion or to demean them. Thus regardless of how a senator or representative felt about legal immigration, a strong consensus formed against *illegal* immigration. *Undocumented* aliens, by virtue of their very presence in the United States, are "lawbreakers" and become the signifier of criminality. While on the campaign trail in California, Republican candidate for Congress Sonny Bono succinctly framed the matter as a commonsense assumption: "What are we talking about? It's illegal!" (cited in Gimpel 1999, p. 4). Representative Hayworth (R-AZ) made the distinction between illegal and legal sources when he said that Congress needed to take steps to end illegal immigration, but lawful immigrants are "willing to work hard and play by the rules" (*Cong. Rec. – House*, September 25, 1996, p. H11077). Further he says, "End an illegal act [i.e., breaking immigration laws] and instill responsibility" (p. H11077). Senator Bob Graham (D-FL) said "I underscore the difference between those persons who are here because they follow the rules and those persons who are in the country because they broke the rules" (*Cong. Rec. – Senate*, September 27, 1996, p. S11514).

The notion that undocumented aliens are "criminal" because they have broken the law through their means of coming to the United States is sufficient for many lawmakers to mark these immigrants for deportation or exclusion. But the legislative debates are explicit that this criterion is not broad enough for some legislators. There are people counted among the *lawful* population of immigrants that are also unacceptable because, it is argued, they place a burden on social services, compete for scarce jobs and welfare entitlements, and commit crimes. Within this framework members of Congress debate the relative attributes of lawful immigrants and whether the "costs" associated with immigration outweigh the benefits. These matters turn on the question of responsibility, and reduce persons to those outwardly observable characteristics that can be accounted for in postivistic definitions of identity.

In a cogent analysis of present-day restrictionist politics, Kitty Calavita has written recently about the passage of California's Proposition 187 in November 1994, a measure potentially restricting undocumented aliens' access to public services.[29] She notes that Proposition 187 "signals a renewed nativism" that, in terms of content, is in some ways similar to, but in other ways quite unlike earlier periods of nativistic sentiment (1996, p. 300). She examines the historically specific content of the nativism Proposition 187 seems to exemplify and links the current wave of nativism to prevailing economic conditions. While nativism at the turn of the last century characterized immigrants first as "strike breakers" (1880s-1890s) and then as "socialists, anarchists, and labor agitators" (1900 to World War I), Calavita notes the nativistic arguments of today portray immigrants primarily as *tax burdens* (see also Fix and Passel 1994). Immigrants have often been scapegoats for the social and economic problems endemic to American capitalism (see also Barrett and Roediger 1997; Citrin et al. 1997; and Feagin 1997). Yet each successive wave of nativism has had its own particular cultural and racist explanations that help the dominant racial/ethnic groups in American society position themselves favorably vis-à-vis the "new" immigrant who is constituted as culturally and racially inferior.

Calavita asserts that in contemporary times, public attention has been diverted from focusing on capital flight from the U.S. economy as its main source of social and economic malaise in the late-1980s to mid-1990s. Although the economic dislocations of capitalists' investment decisions are the primary cause of stagnant and declining wages, she argues, much criticism has been leveled instead at the welfare state and profligate government spending as the "true" cause of the declining American standard of living.

Symptoms of this "balanced-budget conservatism" include "disdain for government spending, taxpayer revolts, and hostility toward the poor who are perceived to be undeserving parasites on hard-working taxpayers, and toward the government, which is seen as fiscally irresponsible" (1997, p. 300). Animus is aimed both at Big Government and at those who are identified as economically dependent. Immigrants, like poor, are scapegoated for America's declining standard of living because allegedly they overburden government services and contribute to the federal deficit. Immigrants' use of public benefits is portrayed as a large part of what fuels runaway entitlement spending (see also Gimpel 1997, pp. 244-253). In the discourses of this current round of nativism and immigration reform, citizens are referred to almost exclusively as hard-working taxpayers and non-citizens exemplify profligacy by "wasting" the taxpayer's dollars. Certain kinds of public space—for example, the workplace, the state—and statuses—for example, worker, taxpayer—are privileged as fundamental building blocks of the nation.

Not one but *three* major pieces of federal legislation in 1996 dealt with immigration and immigrants and used the word "responsibility" fairly liberally. Like the IIRIRA, the legislation of welfare reform in 1996, called the Personal Responsibility and Work Opportunity Reconciliation Act, attempted to eliminate economic dependency and other structural costs of capitalism (e.g., unemployment, crime). *All* immigrants, but especially undocumented aliens—considered the "least deserving of the poor"—were a special target of this legislation. Initially the welfare reform law severely restricted legal immigrants' access to public assistance. However, this provision proved to be unpopular and subsequent negotiations between the Clinton Administration and Congress over the balanced budget agreement in the 105th Congress (1997) managed to restore many of these public benefits for legal immigrants. The Republican-led Congress attempted to go even further in the IIRIRA by promising to deport any permanent resident who used federal assistance (such as Pell Grants, a form of student loan) for an aggregate of twelve months over a seven-year period. However, also due to pressure from the White House, this measure was removed from the bill in the eleventh hour.

The third piece of related legislation, the Anti-Terrorism and Effective Death Penalty Act (AEDPA), also adopted in 1996, was designed ostensibly to accomplish at least two disparate purposes. First, the law combats lawlessness by removing aliens and fining permanent residents and citizens who financially support or are affiliated with groups named by the State Department as terrorist organizations. Second, the law attempts to preserve *minimal* due process guarantees for aliens who are subject to deportation hearings and may be deported even if they have not committed a crime. However, in the immigration bill, the IIRIRA, Congress severely restricted the rights of immigration judges to grant waivers and of federal courts to review immigration judges' decisions.

Elsewhere (Moore 1999) I have written about the ways in which the anti-terrorism law (AEDPA) advances particular definitions of citizenship and "alienness" and defines major status relationships constituting our society. Although the Anti-Terrorism and Effective Death Penalty Act of 1996 is ostensibly about terrorism, it should not be viewed in isolation from the enactment of the companion laws about immigration and welfare reform. All three are intertwined and together they are changing current immigration practices by creating new removal courts that allow secret procedures to be used to remove suspected alien terrorists;[30] by shifting the authority to make "expedited removals" to immigration inspectors at ports of entry; and by setting unprecedented limits on judicial review of immigration decisions. A provision of the IIRIRA, the constitutionality of which has already been affirmed by the Supreme Court in *Reno v. American-Arab Anti-Dis-*

crimination Committee (525 U.S. 471 1999), strips the federal courts of jurisdiction to hear legal challenges to the deportation process, and institutes a more restrictive regime that deprives the lower courts of jurisdiction over resident aliens' claims of selective enforcement of immigration laws against aliens who belong to groups characterized by the State Department as terrorist or communist organizations.

The implications of the IIRIRA in general and the Court's interpretation of the law in *Reno v. ADC* more specifically, raise a host of questions. In my earlier essay, I asked, How does this law attempt to distinguish between "insiders" and "outsiders" in morally defensible ways? Does it attempt to secure or to undermine a sense of full membership in the social and political life of society for all individuals in that society? In considering such questions it is important to recognize that historical context matters, and to understand the answers in light of the social conditions that gave rise to indicators of public unease with immigration, such as California Proposition 187, the Official English movement, and the proposed constitutional amendment to deny birthright citizenship to children of undocumented aliens. Thus although we may recognize the debates in Congress over the adoption of the IIRIRA as familiar ones, echoing earlier periods in history when public policy about immigration was most restrictive, we still need to ask about what precipitated such an extraordinary change in the law at this moment.

It is important to note that at the same time, through this law Congress proposed to reduce legal immigration to the United States for the first time since 1924 (Gimpel 1999, p. 3). In a liberalizing reform in 1965, Congress passed legislation repealing the immigration quotas system enacted in 1924, a change that "set the country on a new population trajectory" (Gimpel 1999, p. 21) and would significantly alter the racial/ethnic composition of the nation. Legal immigrants became increasingly Hispanic and Asian. "By the 1980s, only 12.5 percent of legal immigrants came from Europe or Canada, whereas 84.4 percent were from Asian or Latin American countries" (Bean et al. 1997, p. 251). As immigrants became more diverse in terms of appearance, language, and religions than earlier generations, U.S. immigration policy became an increasingly important and divisive issue in American politics. When the recent immigration reform bill was introduced in the House, it proposed to cut substantially the family-sponsored category of immigration by reducing preferences to include (conditionally) only the spouses and minor children of U.S. citizens and permanent residents and the parents of U.S. citizens, and exclude the siblings, adult children, and other relatives of citizens and permanent residents. Further, a yearly ceiling of 330,000 was proposed on the family-sponsored category. These provisions reflected the consternation of the bill's sponsors over the continued chain migration of family members of the most recent arrivals, who generally are immigrants from Asian and Latin American countries. The reduction can also be seen as a reaction against the changing demographics of the United States, and specifically, against the "browning" and "yellowing" of America.

Immigration is entwined with welfare in central ways. Welfare was a high priority in the Republicans' "Contract with America," and immigration quickly became a associated with welfare as a parallel cost burden on the public. However, public attitudes today are not as sharply opposed to immigration as some members of Congress may suggest—the California initiative Proposition 187 notwithstanding.[31] Opinion polls show that attitudes on immigration have moderated in the 1990s (Moore and Pelletier 1999), and while a majority may favor *some* cutbacks, most people do not wish to see major changes to immigration rates (Feagin 1997, p. 38; Citrin et al. 1997, p. 862).[32] Popular attitudes still strongly oppose illegal immigration, but most people differentiate between legal and illegal sources of immigration.[33] Joe Feagin writes,

> Immigrant myths and fictions are frequently created in the speeches of prominent politicians, the writing of establishment pundits, and the journalistic commentaries of the mass media. In particular, anti-immigrant advocates and nativist leaders often suggest that native-born Americans are strongly opposed to immigration and want it to be curtailed sharply or ended (1997, p. 38).

Yet the frequency with which politicians frame the debate about immigration in economic terms begs the question whether there is a relationship between the nation's economic health and Americans' tolerance of immigration. In the interest of addressing the meaning of responsibility, I raise (but do not necessarily answer) in the remainder of this essay the following questions. How is it that strict reform measures were proposed and, in many cases, adopted when the majority of the American public is ambivalent about, if not content with current immigration levels? What drives immigration reform in the U.S. Congress such that proposed restrictions on immigration play themselves out in congressional debates in a period of relative peace and prosperity?

RESPONSIBILITY: A WELFARE STATE

> *We need to remember that immigration is not an entitlement, it is a privilege . .*
> —Rep. Lamar Smith, R-TX., Congressional Record, 3/21/96, H2590).

By using the word "entitlement" in floor debates in the House of Representatives, Rep. Smith invoked a vocabulary that has a particular resonance with the recent discourse on welfare. Welfare-related meanings of entitlement carry unspoken assumptions and connotations that can influence the discourses of which they become a component—"in part by constituting a body of *doxa*, or taken-for-granted commonsense belief that escapes critical scrutiny" (Fraser and Gordon 1994, p. 310, citing Pierre Bourdieu). When immigration is spoken of in terms of "entitlement," the discursive logic makes it a correlate of welfare, even when Smith asserts emphatically that the immigrant *has* no legitimate claim to entitlement, because his denial of entitlement status implies that Smith is responding within a framework of welfare benefits. As Linda Gordon argues, the grounds for entitlement are constructed by various streams of political strategy and thinking about welfare (1996). Entitlement is an ideological term which carries a powerful pejorative charge. In the public mind it refers solely to public assistance, as opposed to other forms of middle class 'entitlement' such as social security insurance, and is associated most commonly with the condition of poor women "who maintain their families with neither a male breadwinner nor an adequate wage" (Fraser and Gordon 1994, p. 311). Thus, aligned with entitlements and welfare in policy conflicts, immigration becomes highly stigmatized and *gendered*, and the negative associations of poverty, dependency, lack of motivation, and so on, are strengthened.

Responsibility has become a key word in the 1990s and has multiple meanings. Foremost in congressional debates on the IIRIRA, responsibility is linked to difference; "race," "culture," "community," "work ethic," and "family values" all become markers of immigrant identity, and differentiate the new immigrant from the rest. Relatedly, the lack of responsibility (i.e., nonproductiveness) is continually described in terms that make it the anti-essence, or as Derrida would have it, the "constitutive outside" of the popular discourse of economic recovery. Ridding the nation of criminals is no small part of this discourse.

Personal Responsibility

Apart from the connotations discussed above, personal responsibility becomes defined in the immigration legislation as a characteristic demanded of immigrants' sponsors. The new law requires that an immigrant's sponsor sign a legally-binding affidavit of support that can be executed as a contract.[34] Through this document the sponsor commits to maintaining the sponsored immigrant at 125 percent of the federal poverty level, until the immigrant becomes a U.S. citizen or has worked in the United States for ten years (Fragomen 1997, p. 441). The affidavit is then legally enforceable against the sponsor by the sponsored immigrant, the federal and state governments, and by any entity that provides a means-tested public benefit to the sponsored immigrant. In floor debates on this provision of the bill, Rep. Lamar Smith addresses the financial responsibility of the sponsor of the immigrant, saying, "Just as we require *deadbeat dads* to provide for the children they bring into the world, we should require deadbeat sponsors to provide for the immigrants they bring into the country" (*Cong. Rec. – House*, September 25, 1996, p. H11080, emphasis added). Significantly, sponsors are positioned as parental authorities with respect to the immigrant, and are expected to provide financial support. They are spoken of—as deadbeat dads—in terms generated by social services and welfare debates. Critics of welfare *dependency* blame deadbeat dads for creating their counterpart, the "welfare mother," who is often depicted as single and young, usually black, unskilled and unmotivated to get off the welfare rolls. The power of this image of "deadbeat dads" equates the problems of immigrants with the problems of welfare mothers, and makes immigration (and welfare) not only the crux of the nation's fiscal crisis, but also the moral equivalent of welfare dependency.

Institutional Responsibility

At another level in the congressional debates, the word responsibility becomes charged with claims about new federalism, devolution, and unfunded mandates on the states. When the Federal government denies public benefits to immigrants and shifts the burden to the states, the argument goes, is it acting responsibly? The governors of several states (for instance, Lawton Chiles of Florida) have sued the federal government for reimbursement of the costs of providing public services to immigrants. Yet while the states *could* have stopped providing public services for immigrants under the new federal laws on immigration and welfare, most chose to continue to provide some welfare benefits. Nearly all states continued to provide federal cash, in the form of Temporary Assistance to Needy Families (TANF, which replaces AFDC), and health (Medicaid) benefits to legal immigrants present in the United States on August 22, 1996 (when the welfare law was enacted) who had completed five years of residence. Those arriving after the cut-off date are ineligible for assistance. Additionally, about one-third of the states, including the states where most immigrants live, used state funds to provide parallel benefits to some new immigrants who had not yet been in residence for five years (a period in which federal benefits are denied to new immigrants). The major expense to the states has been in restoring food stamp benefits to poor legal immigrants. Some of the benefits cut off at the federal level have been restored in subsequent years; for instance, in 1998 federal legislation restored the food stamp eligibility of the elderly, the disabled, and children of poor immigrants. President Clinton's proposed budget for 2000 included the restoration of further benefits to other immigrants who did not benefit from restorations enacted by the 105th Congress.[35]

In Senate debates about immigration reform, Senator Bob Graham (D-FL) picked up on the metaphor used by Rep. Lamar Smith of a "deadbeat dad" to imply that the Federal Government, and not the immigrant's sponsor, is irresponsible. Objecting to a provision that requires the immigrant's sponsor to pay for emergency medical services in the event the immigrant is injured or becomes ill, Senator Graham pointed out that because the sponsor may not be able to pay the bill, this would ultimately become an unreimbursed medical expense for public hospitals. This, he added, would amount to the Federal Government becoming a "deadbeat dad" by sticking the hospitals with the full cost, without Federal sharing or participation in providing emergency medical services (*Cong. Rec. – Senate*, September 27, 1996, p. S11514).[36]

Graham extended the argument to become one about federalism and the shift of costs associated with immigration to the state and local governments that amounts to an "unfunded mandate." In Senate debates it was proposed that the IIRIRA require all Federal, state, and local means-tested programs for social services, as well as State drivers' licenses and other state licensing departments, to first determine whether the individual applying for the public means-tested program or the license is an eligible immigrant. The verification data system would be something the state and local governments would have to provide at their own expense. The final version of the bill included a watered down rendition of this proposal that authorized three pilot programs to implement this verification task. Being from the state of Florida, Graham mentioned the fact that the then-Governor of Florida, Lawton Chiles, had brought suit in Federal courts to demand Federal compensation for the unreimbursed State money spent on providing public services for legal and illegal immigrants. The lawsuit also named Attorney General Janet Reno as a defendant for her failure to perform her duties imposed by immigration laws to prevent illegal immigration. The Circuit Court of Appeals (11th Circuit) ruled in 1995 that immigration is an area "committed to agency discretion by law" and the question of whether the Attorney General is adequately guarding the borders is not reviewable by the courts. Thus, the appellate court decision reads, "We conclude that whether the level of illegal immigration is an 'invasion' of Florida and whether this level violates the guarantee of a republican form of government presents nonjusticiable political questions" (*Chiles v the United States*, 69 F.3d 1094, 11th Cir, 1995).

Senator Graham referred to this decision as a judicial barrier to legal mobilization. He said the court decision channels him (and others seeking relief) to "seek justice in the political arm of the Federal Government, the Congress of the United States" (*Cong. Rec. – Senate*, September 27, 1996, p. S11514). He argued that the proposed IIRIRA does not remedy the unfunded mandates problem and furthers the imbalance of the cost shift to states and local authorities, which makes the Federal government a "deadbeat," irresponsible parent.

The point simply is that the debates about immigrants and welfare sparked a conflagration over the devolution of fiscal responsibility for resettlement of immigrants to the states, and in that policy conflict the meaning and locus of responsibility were contested. Critics of the investment of responsibility at the state and local levels argued in floor debates that the federal government was evading responsibility by reassigning it through the adoption of this law. In an effort to represent itself as decentralizing itself under the popular mandate of "new federalism," the federal government quite simply has foregone its responsibility and, with it, "much of its power in order to become 'kinder, gentler'" (Brown 1995, p. 194). Yet, as Wendy Brown points out, there is a paradox in this, because the federal government's role in setting immigration criteria and in constituting the subject who is *produced* by the effects of immigration and resettlement policies, is not diminished in the apparent shift of responsibility. Rather, the government's "power and privilege operate increasingly through disavowal of potency, repudiation of responsibility, and diffusion of sites and operations of control" (p. 194)

Employer Responsibility

At yet another level the concept of responsibility is used in the debates in Congress to support the idea of employer sanctions, apportioning blame for the current immigration "crisis" to U.S. employers who continue to exploit the labor of undocumented aliens. Although recommended by the Jordan Commission (appointed in 1993 to study the problems of immigration control) and supported by a fairly broad base of Republicans and Democrats, employer sanctions were watered down by the time the law was enacted. An intense lobbying effort by the business community and pro-immigrant groups kept employer sanctions minimal and effectively blocked the reduction in the level of legal immigration (Fragomen 1997, pp. 442-443).[37]

Cultural Responsibility

To turn for a moment to the question of demagoguery in electoral politics, let me turn our attention to the question of "culture." To explain the construction of the American immigration debates around "culture," Francis Fukuyama has pointed out a jeremiad of Patrick Buchanan's. At the Republican National Convention in Houston in 1992, when Patrick Buchanan challenged President George Bush for the Republican nomination, Buchanan strongly voiced his concern with unassimilable immigrants of color and his opposition to cultural diversity. He said:

> Our Judeo-Christian values are going to be preserved and our Western heritage is going to be handed down to future generations and not dumped on some landfill called multiculturalism (Feagin 1997, p. 36).

Furthe—and this is what concerns Fukuyama—Buchanan announced the advent of a block-by-block war to "take back our culture" from the rising tide of new immigrants of color. Fukuyama comments:

> Buchanan is right that a culture war is upon us, and that this fight will be a central American preoccupation now that the Cold War is over. What he understands less well, however, is that the vast majority of the non-European immigrants who have come into this country in the past couple of decades are not the enemy. Indeed, many of them are potentially on his side (Fukuyama 1994, p. 151).

Fukuyama continues by asserting that while the symptoms of "cultural decay" are all around us, recent immigrants are not to blame. Immigration, he writes, does not really threaten the core values upon which economic prosperity depends—the work ethic, family values, community—because while these values may have arisen from a specifically Christian, Anglo-Saxon culture they are not bound to that particular group. He argues that:

> Some groups, like [*sic*] Jews and Asians, might come to possess these values in abundance, while WASPs themselves might lose them and decay. The question thus becomes: which ethnic groups in today's America are threatening, and which groups are promoting, these core cultural values? (Fukuyama 1994, p. 156).

Yet in his own version of the "culture wars," Fukuyama still finds responsibility to be a cultural "fact" tied to particular origins. He valorizes the traditional values of so-called "Third World" immigrants, finding them to consist of hard work and family cohesion based on patriarchal authority and financial accountability for members of the extended family. Just as essentialist as Fukuyama's argument, many nativistic arguments link the immigrant biologically or culturally to negative stereotypes and point to particular characteristics that threaten the American value system. New immigrants are seen as being more prone to criminality, less committed to democratic values, and a strain on public education and the environment. "There are those for whom immigration poses a paramount threat to liberal democracy, economic progress [and] public safety" (Neiman and Fernandez 1998, p. 7) and many of these concerns are reflected in the debates in Congress as law makers struggle to locate and essentialize the elusive and desired "cultural" traits they look for in an acceptable immigrant, traits which the law now labels as responsibility.

Arguments about "culture" and "cultural traits" (including criminality or the work ethic), which surface in the debates leading up to the enactment of the IIRIRA, tend to conceal the racial and class-based objections to immigration implicit in these debates. Today the public expression of racism, nativism, and intolerance is often more complex than in the past, because it occurs in places where tolerance of diversity is the socially recognized (and legally sanctioned) norm. Yet unreflective uses of essentializing cultural arguments may be just as chilling as any other essentialist argument (e.g., race-based arguments), because they may "serve to enshrine certain interpretations of social life as authoritative and to delegitimate or obscure others, generally to the advantage of dominant groups in society and to the disadvantage of subordinate ones" (Fraser and Gordon 1994, p. 311). Holding the model of the male-breadwinning, nuclear family as the universal standard of social organization, while linking high birth rates to Hispanic Catholicism, or illicit drug use and addiction to an inner-city "underclass," raises a set of issues about, and creates causal connections with, so-called "cultural" traits while eliding the structural causes of poverty and dependency. In fairly subtle and indirect ways in debates on immigration, politicians speak of "cultural traits" in ways that dominate/subordinate the subjects produced through such regulatory discourses—subjects such as illegal aliens, criminal aliens, refugees, or permanent residents. Arguments about "culture/cultural traits" underscore the authority of institutional practices[38] that regulate immigration by obscuring the perhaps more inchoate race- and class-based motives for opposition that many people are reluctant or unable to acknowledge, given the dominant norms (and laws) that prohibit race and wealth discrimination. These institutional practices, and the actions individuals take with regard to them, are mediated through law. The procedural structure of immigration regulations—for example, rules governing deportation courts, regulations for granting visas—together with the language (i.e., the statutory scheme) that manifests that structure, indicate the ways in which the text and talk of politicians is privileged in the reproduction of a particular American identity through practices of exclusion and restriction of access to social resources.

The dramatic increase in the number of impoverished, female-headed households over the last two decades in the United States, and the concomitant regulatory discourses that erroneously cast African American women as virtually the sole recipients of public assistance, offer an interesting parallel to those discourses identifying the immigrant also as financially dependent. Dependence is the term "chosen by neoconservatives to indict the growth of the welfare state for producing a 'welfare-dependent' population" and is designed to highlight the contrast between welfare recipients and the supposedly "independent condition" of wage workers (Brown 1995, p. 171, note 10; see also Watkins 1998). Research has shown that such indictments of the welfare system "work" to the extent that they correlate with (and mobilize) presumptions commonly held among whites that the "welfare-dependent" population is non-white (Gilens 1995; Peffley, Hurwitz, and Sniderman 1997).[39] Prejudices and stereotypes about African-Americans as "lazy" and lacking the requisite commitment to the work ethic are still widespread and have a profound impact on whites' political thinking, no doubt about welfare but also about crime. Others have noted,

> Welfare and crime have become the 'hot button' issues of the political landscape because many see them as violative of the sacred values of the work ethic and lawfulness. Although neither issue is explicitly racial in the same fashion as affirmative action or busing, both become linked to race, inasmuch as white Americans (inaccurately) tend to see the typical welfare recipient and criminal as being African-American (Peffley, Hurwitz, and Sniderman 1997, pp. 30-31).

As a correlate to these meanings, the racial coding of immigrants as a significant fiscal burden on the state and the source of the criminalization of American society signals an uneasy tension with the changing composition of the immigrant population, now largely Asian and Latin American.

CHANGES INTRODUCED BY THE 104TH CONGRESS

Many of us came to Congress on a promise to do something about the failed welfare state. We want to end dependency, we want to encourage personal responsibility, we want to honor work so that welfare does not become a way of life.

—(rep. Lamar Smith, R-Tx., Congressional Record-House, July 31, 1996, p. H9383).

The Republican sweep of Congress in the November 1994 elections and Newt Gingrich's "Contract with America" placed fiscal conservatism squarely into the mainstream. Although reform of the nation's immigration laws was not a high priority in the Contract with America, it was important in particular regions of the nation, especially those states with the highest numbers of recent arrivals, such as California, Texas, New York, New Jersey, Illinois, and Florida. California voters passed Proposition 187 in the same election, and "throughout the 104th Congress, the California delegation pressured the GOP leadership to move ahead with immigration legislation" (Gimpel 1999, p. 213). In immigration and welfare reform, Republicans pushed for the exclusion of legal immigrants from federally funded entitlements as a matter of cost savings.

The Republican sweep also affected institutional arrangements within Congress. Changing party control put new leaders in charge of the House and Senate Judiciary Committees, the bodies charged with responsibility for immigration law. In the House, Rep. Henry Hyde (R-IL) replaced the previous chair of the Judiciary Committee, Jack Brooks (D-TX). Neither Hyde nor Brooks took much interest in immigration (p. 213), but the House Subcommittee on Immigration and Claims, a subcommittee of the Judiciary Committee, was turned over to Representative Lamar Smith, a congressman known for his strong restrictionist position. As chair of the immigration subcommittee in the House, Rep. Smith began sponsoring bills for immigration reform in 1994.

In the Senate, Orrin Hatch (R-UT) became the chair of the Judiciary Committee. Alan Simpson (R-WY), considered the Senate's leading expert on immigration (sponsor of the IRCA of 1986), replaced Sen. Ted Kennedy (D-MA) as the chair of the Senate's immigration subcommittee. Several interest groups and business associations on either side of the immigration debate (e.g., U.S. Chamber of Commerce, the National Council of La Raza, the Farm Bureau), who were concerned about the potential impact of new restrictions, were mobilized by Smith's and Simpson's elevation to chair of their respective subcommittees (Gimpel 1999, p. 215).

The most significant development in the 1994 party change in the House of Representatives created new channels that allowed more restrictionist proposals to make their way into the immigration reform bill. Parallel to the traditional committee system, the new House Speaker Newt Gingrich (R-GA) set up a number of task forces to address "lower-tier" issues and to make recommendations to House leaders, at times drafting the language of proposed legislation. Among these task forces was the Congressional Task Force on Immigration Reform, chaired by California Representative Elton Gallegly (R-CA), who represented a Southern California district that had voted overwhelmingly in favor of Proposition 187. The 54 members of Gallegly's task force focused on creating means to curb *illegal* immigration—by improving border enforcement, workplace enforcement, deportation procedures, and by limiting illegal immigrants' access to public benefits (Gimpel 1999, p. 216). The task force also pronounced efforts to impose restrictions on *legal* immigration, including the proposal to ban welfare benefits for permanent residents. Several of the task force's proposals were included in the reform bill that eventually was adopted.

These changes in committee structure, by the addition of parallel task forces, have produced significant change in the legislation coming out of Congress. In terms of welfare and immigration reform, just the small change introduced by the creation of the immigration reform task force, headed by Rep. Gallegly, produced fairly conspicuous changes in immigration policy and social services. After provisions of the welfare reform went into effect in August, 1996, and of the IIRIRA in April, 1997, Rep. Gallegly requested that the U.S. General Accounting Office (GAO) provide his task force with data concerning the number of naturalizations, and the number of recently naturalized citizens receiving public assistance, since the adoption of the welfare and immigration reform laws. Gallegly's concern was that, since the adoption of these reform laws, the ratio of recently naturalized to native-born citizens receiving means-tested benefits from public assistance programs had increased. In June 1999 the GAO provided Gallegly with the information he had requested. "In fiscal year 1996 alone, more than 1 million immigrants became naturalized—an all-time high" (*GAO Report* 1999).[40] Moreover, the proportion of recently naturalized citizens receiving benefits from four public assistance programs (TANF, SSI, Medicaid, and Food Stamps) during fiscal years 1996 and 1997 was higher than that of native born citizens. The GAO had gathered data from the five states that together account for nearly three-quarters of the recently naturalized citizens, from California, Florida, Illinois, New York, and Texas.[41] The findings showed that the rates varied across states for the major public assistance programs; for instance, the largest difference in the two populations' use of benefits was in California, where 23.7 percent of the recently naturalized citizens received Medicaid, compared to 8.2 percent of the population. In contrast, Texas showed a much smaller difference, with 9.6 percent of the recently naturalized population receiving Medicaid benefits compared to 6.1 percent of the native-born population.

The point for Gallegly's task force is that recently naturalized citizens represent a financial burden on federal and state governments by placing higher demands on public assistance programs. For Gallegly, who had introduced a provision (which failed) in the House version of the immigration reform bill to deny public assistance benefits to naturalized citizens, the GAO findings justify his continuing effort to put in place a two-tiered system of public benefits and prerogatives. Although the GAO report acknowledges that several factors may have contributed to the increased rates of naturalization in the 1990s, Gallegly infers from the statistics that the United States remains a "welfare magnet," which encourages the immigration of the least desirable (i.e., irresponsible) persons to the United States.

The power of welfare to attract immigrants to the United States is the source of the problem for many in Congress, and is tied into the idiom of responsibility as self-reliance. Testifying on immigration and welfare reform before the House Subcommittee on Immigration and Claims, Robert Rector, Senior Policy Analyst at the Heritage Foundation, a conservative think tank, summed up what many in Congress have argued, even if in an exaggerated way:

> The United States welfare system is rapidly becoming a deluxe retirement home for the elderly of other countries. This is because many individuals are now immigrating to the United States in order to obtain generous welfare that far exceeds programs available in their country [*sic*] of origin. Non-citizens today are among the fastest growing groups of welfare dependents. ("Immigration and Welfare Reform," 6/29/95).

Concerns that welfare has become a "way of life" for immigrants and that family-sponsored immigration accounts for the arrival of elderly parents of foreign-born citizens and permanent residents animates discussions about national prosperity and personal responsibility. They also express the modern emphasis on rugged individualism and independence, reflected in the fruits of hard work. Rep. Lamar Smith (R-TX), stated:

> Since the beginning of this century, immigrants have been admitted to the United States on the promise that they will not use public benefits. Yet every year the number of noncitizens applying for certain welfare programs increases an astonishing 50 percent. America should continue to welcome those who want to work and produce and contribute, but we should discourage those who come to live off the taxpayer. America should keep out the welcome mat but not become a doormat (*Cong. Rec. – House*, September 25, 1996, p. H11080).

At this point Rep. Smith then used the metaphor of the "deadbeat dad" to support the provision of the immigration reform bill that requires a contractual commitment from the immigrant's sponsor to financially support the immigrant. The sponsor is disciplined through the law not to become like a "deadbeat dad."[42]

CONCLUSION

> *[The IIRIRA] encourages legal immigrants to be self-reliant and discourages them from becoming a burden on the American taxpayer.*
>
> —(Rep. Smith, R-TX, Cong. Rec. – House, Dec. 6, 1995, p. H14029).

The intersection of these arguments about Responsibility—whether the immigrant is criminal, welfare-dependent, and the bearer of less than desirable "cultural traits"—have dominated the development of immigration reform. The place the immigrant takes in the legal imagination shapes the provisions contained in the IIRIRA that raise the bar of admissions standards and streamline the twin processes of deportation and exclusion. What legislators are looking for as responsible behavior dovetails with the language of welfare reform and entitlements. Finally, the law itself is viewed as an inducement to responsible behavior, capable of neutralizing or normalizing "every potentially subversive rejection of culturally enforced norms" (Brown 1995, p. 66) of personal responsibility.

Moreover, the meaning of Responsibility is provisional. In some places in the legislative debates it refers to immigrants' behavior as law-abiding, following the rules. Immigrants who break the rules threaten the social order and overburden the taxpayer, that other icon that persistently surfaces in stark contrast to "the huddled masses" of immigrants in these debates. Immigrants and taxpayers alike are reduced to certain social and behavioral attributes that can be defined empirically, rather than as social and discursive constructs. As Wendy Brown puts it, "these positivist definitions of persons as their attributes and practices [e.g., responsible, law-abiding, or taxpaying] are written into law, ensuring that persons describable according to them will now become regulated through them" (1995, p. 66). Immigrants become individually "responsible" through the disciplinary effects of the law when (and if) they no longer burden the taxpayer.

At other moments responsibility means the sponsors' financial responsibility, and casts the immigrant in a child-like, dependent and subordinate role. In turn, sponsors are cautioned not to become "deadbeat dads." At still other moments responsibility is turned around to accuse the Federal government of not making good on its promises, of failing to enforce existing laws that are meant to prevent illegal immigration, and of shifting the costs associated with immigration to the state and local entities. The locus of responsibility bobs and weaves. The twin targets of the public sector (government spending) and immigrants (who overburden entitlement programs and inflate government spending) are perceived as blameworthy.

The framework of the welfare regime, within which the 1996 immigration reform law was discussed, stresses the universal dominance of the male breadwinner family model. It subscribes to the idea of a male breadwinner (the "deadbeat dad" is the absence or failure of the male in that role), and the strength of the idea correlates with the ways in which immigrants have been treated in the social services system, and with the condescending idiom of childhood and dependence on the state.

Is the new immigration law, concerned with immigrant "responsibility," a symbolic statement of cultural dominance? The kind of analysis offered here, of the symbolic and coded language mobilized in the legislation of major reform of immigration law, may direct our attention to the lexical terms that are used in public debates today to reinforce the effects of institutional power, create a tiered system of entitlement and prerogative, and privilege a narrow vision of membership in American society. I hope that this has laid the groundwork for examining the connections between what Congress has signaled—an ideological shift toward greater restrictions—and what the administration of immigration laws (the INS and the Department of State) will be doing as it is charged with the implementation of this broad and complicated reform measure. Future research is needed to examine how the encouragement of the influx of direct foreign investment and labor is inextricably linked to Congress' project of construing responsibility in particular ways. Although the discourse on immigrant responsibility on the one hand, and the discourse of investment politics on the other, advance two seemingly distinct projects, strands within the two weave around images of the nation that are especially sensitive to the perception of the world as dangerous yet full of opportunity. In producing these images, the immigrant enables each discourse to serve as a dimension of the other.

What role does responsibility play in the signification of a national identity in the 1990s, during a period of economic recovery and shifting global power relations? What are we arguing against when we reinforce the imperative to be responsible (e.g., productive)? Anxieties about the constant undermining of the nation's borders by the transnational movement of people and capital are brought to the surface in these debates about economic dependency, recovery, and regulation, and these anxieties force competing notions of national identity to resignify.

NOTES

1. For a discussion of the symbolism of the Statue of Liberty, see Perea (1997).

2. See Evan Watkins' discussion of former California Governor Pete Wilson's 1994 reelection campaign, in which Wilson identified the influx of illegal aliens as posing the most serious threat to the well-being of his constituents (*Everyday Exchanges: Marketwork and Capitalist Common Sense*, 1998, p. 50ff). See also Watkins' analysis of how conservative politics in the 1990s has shaped the meaning of immigrant, and especially the illegal alien, as a danger to the nation.

3. At the national level, many of these proposals were endorsed by the bi-partisan U.S. Commission on Immigration Reform, chaired by Barbara Jordan (former Congressperson from Texas) beginning in 1993. See CIR Report: Reports of the U.S. Commission on Immigration Reform (1995). At the level of the states, see commentary on passage of California's Proposition 187 in the general elections of November 1994, in Calavita 1996.

4. Smith's statement implies that immigrants are "normalizable" through the disciplinary effects of law, and can be made to be responsible members of the community by means of immigration reform.

5. Joe Feagin stresses that nativism "remains an important perspective that many native-born Americans use to construct and interpret hard economic times" (1997, p. 37).

6. In fact, Citrin et al. (1997) find in studying public opinion data collected in 1992 and 1994 that "generalized feelings about Hispanics and Asians," the major immigrant groups, are a more significant determinant of restrictionist sentiment that personal economic circumstances are.

7. Race has been a powerful determinant of admissions standards and naturalization criteria from the beginning of American history. As Linda Gordon points out, during the Progressive Era, wel-

fare reformers concentrated on immigrants, whom they considered to be racially different. Many perceived immigrant cultures to be inferior and believed that "Americanization" was for their benefit. See Gordon 1995, p. 292f.). For an analysis of the racial impact of immigration and citizenship laws, see Smith 1997 and Haney-Lopez 1996. While the *means* through which official discourses become raced and gendered are increasingly concentrated in the state—for instance, through its welfare function—the overt masculinism in state powers becomes less and less discernible, and the raced and gendered character I am talking about has become more evasive. Feminist theorists of the welfare state, such as Wendy Brown, have argued that the masculinism of the state in late modernity has "become more diffuse and subtle even as it becomes more potent and pervasive in women's lives...[T]he central paradox of the late modern state...[lies in the fact that] its power and privilege operate increasingly through disavowal of potency, repudiation of responsibility, and diffusion of sites and operations of control" (Brown 1995, pp. 193-194). My argument simply is that recent legislative reforms of federal welfare and immigration laws have put in place changing (and more rigid) eligibility criteria for admission and residence in the United States. As a result the determination of whether an immigrant is economically "viable" and law abiding has intensified regulation of immigration by the state on an individualized level, even as the state eliminates certain immigrants from the welfare roles.

8. Wendy Brown makes a similar point with regard to the masculinist underpinnings of the late modern regulatory state. Brown critiques the elements of the contemporary liberal, capitalist, bureaucratic state that at one and the same time privilege a gendered and racialized order of dominance and carry with them the techniques of marginalization and subordination (1995, especially Chapter Seven).

9. For a discussion of how classical and contemporary liberal discourse casts the family as "natural" or divinely given, prepolitical, and constitutive of the private sphere, whereas in contrast the state and civil society (the economy) comprise the public sphere where rights and responsibilities are conferred and exercised, see Wendy Brown 1995, chap. 7).

10. The annual increase in the GDP was 3.1 percent in 1993 and 4.1 percent in 1994, compared to -.6 percent in 1991 and 2.3 percent in 1992. Continued growth was a central theme in the congressional election campaigns of 1994.

11. The tax burden hypothesis argues that social resources including public benefits are under severe pressure because of an influx of "foreigners." See Kitty Calavita's discussion of Sidney Plotkin and William Scheuerman's critique of balanced-budget conservatism in her essay, "The New Politics of Immigration: 'Balanced-Budget Conservatism' and the Symbolism of Proposition 197" (1996, pp. 17-47, and my discussion of this below).

12. Citrin et al. note that "a count of stories in *The New York Times* under the general heading of "Immigration and Emigration" shows that there were 192 such stories in 1993 and 195 in 1994, as compared to 76 in 1991 and 75 in 1992" (1997, p. 859, n. 2).

13. See Moore and Pelletier 1999 where we show that although polls taken since the 1960s have indicated an increasing anti-immigrant sentiment, in our 1998 national survey (n = 800) only slightly more than one-third of the population (37%) held that the level of immigration should be decreased. However these results are contradicted in the periodical literature on public attitudes toward immigration. See for instance, Citrin et al. (1997), where the authors argue that between 1992 and 1994 the proportion of the public favoring a reduced level of immigration increased from 49 percent to 66 percent. I am not sure of the reasons for the significant drop from the 1994 level of 66 percent to 37 percent in 1998. However other researchers suggest that public opinion on immigration has oscillated frequently in recent years. See National Research Council (1997, p. 389).

14. Illegal Immigration Reform and Immigrant Responsibility Act, Pub. L. 104-208, 110 Stat. 3009 (September 30, 1996). The press has been critical of many provisions of this law. In an editorial the New York times wrote, "The IIRIRA of 1996 is a morass of technical complexity that has yet to be fully explicated by the law's drafters or the immigration officers who are supposed to carry it out" ("Flaws in Immigration Laws," Section A, p. 18, September 29, 1997). The San Francisco Chronicle editorialized that changed to the immigration law introduced by the IIRIRA "could mean the mass

deportation for up to 300,000 refugees from Nicaragua, El Salvador, and Guatemala...because a Justice Department appeals board has interpreted the law as being retroactive," changing US residency requirements from 7 to 10 years before refugees can apply to stay permanently in the United States ("thousands of Refugees Face Unfair Deportation," p. A20, September 7, 1997). See also "Immigration Law Confusion," the Atlanta Journal and Constitution, P. 1B, april 19, 1997; "Pall Over Immigrants' American Dream," the Washington Post, p. A01, March 27, 1997; and "Reforms Limit Immigrants' Legal Options," the Chicago Sun-Times, p. 13, January 19, 1997.

15. A "criminal propensity" is demonstrated by an arrest record prior to arrival in the United States, and by conviction for a crime before or after arriving in the United States, The grounds of inadmissibility and deportation in the 1996 law include the showing of a "conviction" or a minimum "term of imprisonment." In this language a "conviction" exists if there is a formal judgment of guilt and, if adjudication has been withheld, in the case that a judge has ordered some form of punishment or penalty. The "term of imprisonment" includes any period of confinement including detention in jail prior to a trial proceeding. For details see Fragomen (1997), and Little (1998).

16. The law specifically bars those who may require public assistance for more than 12 months during the seven years following admission into the United States. The "deeming" requirement of the law, which means that the income of the immigrant's sponsor is counted as the immigrant's income, combined with the sponsor's "fiscal test" discussed below, is designed to prevent new immigrants from qualifying for public assistance.

17. As of this writing an estimated 15,000 immigrants with criminal histories remained jailed pending deportation by the INS, even though at least 12 federal courts have ruled against the INS policy of detaining *all* immigrants with criminal records regardless how serious the crimes were. Since the passage of these laws in 1996, several personal stories have been related through the media of individuals being jailed awaiting deportation for relatively minor crime (e.g., shoplifting) for which they had been convicted years ago. People can be deported for crimes ranging from murder to drunken driving, and it is difficult to estimate how many persons being deported are serious felons. The INS says that nearly one-half of the criminal immigrants deported in 1998 (total = 55,869) were convicted of drug offenses. About 5,500 deportees were legal residents of the United States. See Pan (1999).

18. The INS argues that the nationals hardest hit by this provision are Mexicans and Salvadorians, but many prospective immigrants across the globe are adversely affected by the pressures this puts on family-based immigration to the United States. A study done by the Urban Institute, based on 1993 Census Bureau data, indicated that forty percent of immigrant families and twenty-five percent of Americans born in the United States would not earn enough money to meet these requirements (Mailman and Yale-Loehr 1997, p. 3).

19. Deeming will cease once an immigrant becomes a naturalized U.S. citizen or has worked forty "qualifying quarters," a term used by Social Security to mean the equivalent of ten years of lawful employment for which FICA taxes have been withheld.

20. While affidavits of support are not new, the 1996 law has made then enforceable through contract law. The sponsors' affidavits are legally enforceable against the sponsor by the sponsored immigrant, the federal government, any state or by any other entity that provides a means-tested benefit program. See Fragomen (1997, p. 44).

21. For over one hundred years prospective immigrants to the United States have been required by law to show that they are not likely to become "public charges." However, critics of contemporary immigration policy have said that the INS standards of evaluation have been too flexible and have admitted too many immigrants who have ended up needing public assistance. Although some members of Congress objected to the fiscal test of 200 percent of the federal poverty income level that was initially proposed in the bill, they agreed to the lower figure of 125 percent. Few objected to the premise of a fiscal test.

22. Prior to 1996 any legal immigrant in the United States were generally eligible for public benefits on the same basis as U.S. citizens. Under the Welfare Reform of 1996, most future immigrants will not be allowed to apply for benefits under federal means-tested programs during their first five

years in the United States, and current legal residents as well as future immigrants admitted for permanent residence are permanently barred from receiving SSI (Social Security Income)—which provides cash aid to needy persons who are aged, blind, or disabled—and Food Stamps. Lawful permanent residents who were receiving SSI at the time the welfare law went into effect (August 22, 1996) were screened for one year to determine if they meet the new eligibility requirements Federal public benefits from which legal immigrants have been excluded under the welfare reform and immigration reform laws include any grant, contract, loan, professional license, or commercial license provided by a federal agency or by appropriated U.S. funds; any retirement, welfare, health, or disability benefits; public or assisted housing; postsecondary education; food assistance or unemployment benefit; or any similar benefit for which payments are provide by a U.S. agency or appropriated U.S. funds (e.g., block grants to the states). However some immigrants may be eligible to receive Temporary Assistance to Needy Families (TANF), social services and Medicaid, which are programs funded in part with U.S. funds and administered by the states, *after* the initial five-year residency requirement imposed by federal law. What is exempt from the five-year bar and is available to legal immigrants are for following public benefits: emergency services, including disaster relief and medical assistance; foster care and adoption assistance; school lunch and school nutrition programs; education assistance, such as Head Start and Pell Grants; and certain community services necessary for life and safety, as defined by the Attorney General. See Vialet 1998; and Fragomen 1997.

23. The very idea that the law can be successful in screening out undesired immigrants is a premise that continues to be questioned by members of Congress. In fact the failures of earlier legislation (esp. IRCA 1986) to end illegal immigration, and to enforce public-charge standards of inadmissibility (see Immigration and Nationality Act @212(a)(4), 8 USC @1182(1)(4), on inadmissibility) were precisely the reason this reform bill was introduced in Congress.

24. Rep. Lamar Smith (R-TX) originally introduced the bill as H.R. 1915, the Immigration in the National Interest Act, on June 22, 1995. He reintroduced the bill, after mark-up by his subcommittee, on August 4, 1995, as H.R. 2202.

25. Under @@531 and 551 of the IIRIRA, anyone who petitions to bring a relative for permanent residence in the United States must also make an affidavit of support, even if the prospective immigrant is financially well off. Unlike prior law, this law makes the affidavit of support legally binding, and the sponsor must meet minimum income requirements. The sponsor must agree that, if it becomes necessary, she will provide the support needed to maintain the immigrant at a level of at least 125 percent of the federal poverty line. If the immigrant is injured or becomes ill, the sponsor is responsible for reimbursing the emergency medical costs. These requirements are applied retroactively, to cover permanent residents who have arrived during the five years prior to enactment of the IIRIRA.

26. There are three general categories of immigration: family-based, employment-based, and humanitarian (e.g., refugees).

27. I want to issue a disclaimer here. I do not endorse, nor do I claim the accuracy of, any of the figures given in the *Congressional Record.*

28. See also Gimpel's account of the Senate Judiciary Committee action, especially regarding what he sees as the influence of the business and pro-immigrant coalition (1997, pp. 243-246.) It seems clear that the business community was especially keen on keeping a low-cost supply of labor that includes a significant proportion of immigrants. See Fragomen's (1997) account, where he writes that an intensive lobbying effort by the business community both softened the employer sanctions that were included in the final version of the bill, and succeeded in getting most provisions relating to legal immigration (at least those provisions having to do with numbers of visas) omitted from the final bill.

29. The electorate approved the initiative 59 percent to 41 percent, but Proposition 187 was challenged in court after the election. A federal district court judge ruled that provisions of the initiative were unconstitutional. The state of California appealed the ruling, but on July 29, 1999, the U.S. 9th Circuit Court of appeals accepted a mediated settlement: the State dropped it appeal of the district court ruling, and opponents of Proposition 187 agreed to permit its provisions that made it a state crime to manufacture and distribute false documents to go into effect. The mediation brought together

representatives of California's Governor Gray Davis (who replaced Pete wilson in 1998, and personally opposed the initiative), and such opponents of the initiative as the American Civil Liberties Union and the Mexican American Legal Defense and Education Fund. Governor Davis said that while he personally opposed the initiative, he wanted to respect the will of the electorate; further, he said that the "spirit of Proposition 187" is already incorporated in federal laws approved in 1996, so that most of the provisions are unnecessary. He said that the mediated settlement technically struck down Proposition 187, but "it is supplanted by federal legislation that is faithful to the will o the voters who passed 187 and [the federal laws] will require the state to deny virtually all of the benefits that would be denied under the terms of 187." See McDonnell (1999).

30. The AEDPA allows the INS to use secret evidence against suspected terrorists without providing the suspects or their lawyers an opportunity to view the evidence against them. Such evidence and witnesses may be presented to judges in private sessions held in judges' chambers without the defendants or their lawyers present. Immigration officials justify this procedure by saying that some evidence is sensitive intelligence that may endanger their sources of information and compromise national security. To date two dozen suspected terrorists, all Arabs, are being detained by the INS on the basis of secret evidence. See Rohde (1999).

31. Teun A. van Dijk suggests the following:

> Officially (i.e., according to democratic theory and norms), politicians are supposed to base their opinions on popular reactions to immigration and ethnic affairs, for instance, during election campaigns, hearings, or speeches they give for party members and others. However, their access to truly popular opinion is marginal or at best indirect; politicians talk mostly to other elites, and what they read is written by elites, even when such discourses claim to express the concerns of the population at large. Popular resentment against immigration...is filtered through the constructions or interpretations of popular reactions by journalists or other professionals. This means that both the media and the politicians are able to construct popular resentment as meaning what they please, for instance, as a 'democratic' majority legitimation for the restriction of immigration or civil rights (1997, p. 34).

32. Feagin cites a 1994 National Opinion Research Center poll, and Citrin et al. analyze results from a 1992 American National Election Study (ANES) poll. In response to the question, "should the current level of immigration be increased, kept the same, or decreased," Citrin et al. found that 26 percent of the sample (n = 2,428) favored reducing immigration levels "a little," and 23 percent wanted immigration decreased "a lot" (1997, p. 862). This constitutes a near-majority of 49 percent, a proportion that increased to 66 percent by 1994 (n = 1,719). The respondents were asked about *legal* immigration only.

33. A June 1999 L.*A. Times* poll showed that 60 percent believed that illegal immigrants should not receive public benefits (McDonnell 1999).

34. This represents a change in the requirements of the sponsor. Before the 1996 reform, sponsors were required to provide affidavits of support that were not legally enforceable.

35. For information on the states' burden under the welfare and immigration reform laws of 1996 (see Smothers 1998; Belanger 1999; and the website of the Urban Institute newfederalism.urban.org).

36. The final version of the bill that was signed into law provided that costs for emergency medical services for legal immigrants would be reimbursed by the federal government (see Vialet 1998).

37. Title IV of the IIRIRA provides for the establishment of three pilot programs to test electronic verification of employment eligibility through government databases.

38. In other words, the rules, procedures, and ideologies that govern how things get done (see Brigham 1987).

39. Martin Gilens writes that, based a covariance structure model analyzing survey data, he finds that "[r]acial attitudes are the most important source of opposition to welfare among whites" (1995, p.

994). Gilens finds that the most common whites' prejudice about African-Americans is that they lack a commitment to the work ethic.

40. In August of that year, the welfare reform law made noncitizen immigrants ineligible for certain federal public assistance.

41. About 927,000 immigrants were naturalized in fiscal years 1996 and 1997, and roughly 703,000 of these individuals reside in California, Florida, Illinois, New York, and Texas (see GAO Report 1999).

42. See text at *Cong. Rec.—House*, September 25, 1996, p. H11080, and discussion of this above at p. .

REFERENCES

Barrett, J. R., and D. Roediger. 1997. "Inbetween Peoples: Race, Nationality and the 'New' Immigrant Working Class." *Journal of American Ethnic History* (Spring): 3-44.

Belanger, M. 1999. "Immigration Policy Update." National Immigration Forum, February 16, 1999. At website of National Immigration Forum, www.immigrationforum.org.

Brigham, J. 1987. *The Cult of the Court.* Philadelphia: Temple University Press.

Brown, M. C., and B. D. Warner. 1992. "Immigrants, Urban Politics, and Policing in 1900." American Sociological Review 57: 293-305.

Brown, W. 1995. *States of Injury: Power and Freedom ini Late Modernity.* Princeton: Princeton University Press.

Calavita, K. 1996. "The New Politics of Immigration: 'Balanced-Budget Conservatism' and the Symbolism of Proposition 187." *Social Problems* 43 (August): 17-47.

Citrin, J., D. P. Green, C. Muste, and C. Wong. 1997. "Public Opinion Toward Immigration Reform: The Role of Economic Motivations." *Journal of Politics* 59: 858-881.

Espenshade, T., and K. Hempstead. 1997. "Contemporary American Attitudes Toward US Immigration." *International Migration Review* 30.

Espenshade, T. J., J. Baraka, and G. A. Huber. 1998. "Immigration Reform, Welfare Reform, and Future Patterns of U.S. Immigration." In *In Defense of the Alien, Vol. XX.* New York: Center for Migration Studies.

Feagin, J. R. 1997. "Old Poison in New Bottles: The Deep Roots of Modern Nativism." In *Immigrants Out! The New Nativism and the Anti-Immigrant Impulse in the United States.* New York: New York University Press.

Fix, M., and J. S. Passel. 1994. *Immigration and Immigrants: Setting the Record Straight.* Washington, DC: The Urban Institute.

Fragomen, A. T. 1997. "The Illegal Immigration Reform and Immigrant Responsibility Act of 1996: An Overview." *International Migration Review* 31 (Summer): 438-460.

Fraser, N., and L. Gordon. 1994. "A Genealogy of Dependency: Tracing a Keyword of the U.S. Welfare State." *Signs* (19): 309-336.

Fukuyama, F. 1994. "Immigrants and Family Values." Pp. 151-168 in *Arguing Immigration.* New York: Touchstone Publishers.

Gilens, M. 1995. "Racial Attitudes and Opposition to Welfare." *Journal of Politics* 57 (Nov.): 994-1014.

Gimpel, J. G., and J. R. Edwards, Jr. 1999. *The Congressional Politics of Immigration Reform.* Boston: Allyn and Bacon.

Gordon, L. 1995. *Pitied But Not Entitled: Single Mothers and the History of Welfare, 1890-1935.* Cambridge, MA: Harvard University Press.

Haney-Lopez, I. 1996. *White by Law : the Legal Construction of Race.* New York: New York University Press.

Little, C. 1998. "Continuing Problems at Krome Service Processing Center." Pp. 143-152 in *In Defense of the Alien Vol. XX*. New York: Center for Migration Studies.

Liu, L. 1994. "The Female Body and Nationalist Discourse: *The Field of Life and Death* Revisited." In *Scattered Hegemonies: Postmodernity and Transnational Feminist Practices*. Minneapolis: University of Minnesota Press.

McDonnell, P. 1999. "Proposition 187 Talks Offered Davis Few Choices." *Los Angeles Times*, July 30, p. A1.

Moore, K. M. 1999. "A Closer Look at Anti Terrorism Law: *American-Arab Anti Discrimination Committee v. Reno* and the Construction of Aliens' Rights." In *Arabs in America: Building A New Future*. Philadelphia: Temple University Press.

Moore, K. M., and S. R. Pelletier. 1999. "Weaving New Fabric: The Challenge of Immigration for Muslim/Christian Relations." *Islam and Christian-Muslim Relations* 10 (July): 177-196.

National Research Council. 1997. *The New Americans: Economic, Demographic, and Fiscal Effects of Immigration*. New York: National Academy Press.

Neiman, M., and K. Fernandez. 1998. "Dimensions and Models of Anti- Immigrant Sentiments: Causes and Policy Relevance." Paper presented at the Annual Meeting of the American Political Science Association, September 3-6, 1998, in Boston, MA.

Pan, P. P. 1999. "INS Shifting Policy on Immigrant Detention." *Washington Post*, August 9, p. A1.

Peffley, M., J. Hurwitz, and P. M. Sniderman. 1997. "Racial Stereotypes and Whites' Political Views of Blacks in the Context of Welfare and Crime." *American Journal of Political Science* 41 (Jan.): 30-60.

Perea, J. F. 1997. "The Statue of Liberty: Notes from Behind the Gilded Door." In *Immigrants Out! The New Nativism and the Anti-Immigrant Impulse in the United States*. New York: New York University Press.

Reich, R. 1991. *The Work of Nations: Preparing Ourselves for 21st Century Capitalism*. New York: A. A. Knopf.

Rohde, D. 1999. "Judge Rules Egyptian Linked to Terrorism Should Be Freed." *New York Times*, July 31.

Smith, R. 1997. *Civic Ideals: Conflicting Visions of Citizenship in U.S. History*. New Haven: Yale University Press.

Van Dijk, T. A. 1997. "Political Discourse and Racism: Describing Others in Western Parliaments." In *The Language and Politics of Exclusion: Others in Discourse*. Thousand Oaks and London: Sage Publications.

Vialet, J. 1998. "Welfare Entitlement: The Congressional View." In *In Defense of the Alien, Vol. XX*. New York: Center for Migration Studies.

Watkins, E. 1998. *Everyday Exchanges: Marketwork and Capitalist Common Sense*. Stanford, CA: Stanford University Press.

DOCUMENTS

CIR Report: Reports of the U.S. Commission on Immigration Reform, June 1995. Washington, DC: U.S. Government Printing Office.

Congressional Record-Extension of Remarks, March 29, 1996. "Immigration in the National Interest Act of 1995, Speech of Ed Pastor of Arizona in the House of Representatives, Friday, March 22, 1996." Pp. E506 passim. Also "Providing for Consideration of H.R. 2202, Immigration in the National Interest Act of 1995, Speech of Ed Pastor of Arizona in the House of Representatives, Wednesday, March 20, 1996." Pp. E496-497.

Congressional Record-House, Sept. 25, 1996. "Debate on Conference Report on H.R. 2202, Illegal Immigration Reform and Immigrant Responsibility Act of 1996." Pp. H11071-H11090.

Congressional Record-House, Dec. 6, 1995. Remarks of Lamar Smith, p. H14029.

Congressional Record-House, March 20, 1996. Remarks of Major Owens.

Congressional Record-House, July 31, 1996. "Not One Logical Reason for the President Not to Sign Congress' Third Welfare Reform Bill." 142 Cong Rec H 9383, p. H9383.

Congressional Record-Senate, April 25, 1996. "Debate on Immigration Control and Financial Responsibility Act [S.1664], pp. S4127-S4135.

Congressional Record-Senate, Sept. 27, 1996. "Debate on Conference Report to Accompany Illegal Immigration Reform and Immigrant Responsibility Act of 1996), pp. S11514.

Congressional Record-Senate, Sept. 28, 1996. Remarks of Alan Simpson, p. S11711.

GAO Report, June 1999. "Welfare Reform: Public Assistance Benefits Provided to Recently Naturalized Citizens." GAO/HEHS-99-102.

[6]

The Strange Career of the Illegal Alien: Immigration Restriction and Deportation Policy in the United States, 1921–1965

MAE M. NGAI

In January 1930 officials of the Bureau of Immigration testified about the Border Patrol before a closed session of the House Immigration Committee. Henry Hull, the commissioner general of immigration, explained that the Border Patrol did not operate "on the border line" but as far as one hundred miles "back of the line." The Border Patrol, he said, was "a scouting organization and a pursuit organization. . . . [Officers] operate on roads

Mae M. Ngai is an assistant professor of history at the University of Chicago. This article is adapted from *Illegal Aliens and Alien Citizens: Immigration Restriction, Race, and Nation, 1924–1965* (Princeton: Princeton University Press, forthcoming). Previous versions were presented at the Globalization Workshop, University of Chicago, May 2000; Legal History Colloquium, New York University Law School, November 2000; Political Science Seminar of the Graduate Faculty of New School University, February 2001; Law and Society Association, July 2001; and American Society for Legal History, November 2001. For comments and criticism she is grateful to workshop and conference participants and to Gabriel J. Chin, Eric Foner, Gary Gerstle, Neil Gotanda, Victoria Hattam, Nancy Morawetz, Gerald Neuman, Kunal Parker, Teemu Ruskola, Lucy Salyer, Amy Stanley, Leti Volpp, Aristide Zolberg, and Christopher Tomlins and the anonymous readers for *Law and History Review.* She thanks Aaron Shapiro and Deborah Cohen for research assistance. Research and writing were funded in part by the Social Science Research Council International Migration Program, the Samuel I. Goleib Fellowship at NYU Law School, and a Daniel Greenstone research grant from the Division of Social Sciences, University of Chicago. She gratefully acknowledges the Central Office of the U.S. Immigration and Naturalization Service in Washington, D.C., for allowing her access to its records and INS Historian Marian Smith for her generous assistance.

without warrants and wherever they find an alien they stop him. If he is illegally in the country, they take him to unit headquarters."[1]

George Harris, the assistant commissioner general, added that Congress had authorized the Border Patrol to arrest aliens without warrant in 1925. It is true, Harris said, that the law provided for arrest without warrant when an alien "enters in the presence or view . . . of the officer, but this does not necessarily mean that the officer must see the alien at the exact moment that he crosses the border into the United States. Entry is a continuing offense and is not completed . . . until the alien reaches his interior destination."[2]

Members of the House committee expressed concern that the Border Patrol, which was not a criminal law enforcement agency and had no statutory authority to execute search warrants, had defined its jurisdiction not just at the border but far into the nation's interior. This might extend not only one or two hundred miles but, theoretically, throughout the entire interior. If, as Hull said, "wherever [officers] find an alien, they stop him," how did the officers know the difference between an alien and a citizen? Indeed, what did it mean that Border Patrol officers could stop, interrogate, and search without a warrant anyone, anywhere, in the United States?

Yet if Congress was uneasy about the Border Patrol's reach, it had nearly assured such an outcome when it passed the Immigration Acts of 1921 and 1924, which for the first time imposed numerical restrictions on immigration. Because illegal entry is a concomitant of restrictive immigration policy, the quota laws stimulated the production of illegal aliens and introduced that problem into the internal spaces of the nation. Although unlawful entry had always resulted from exclusion, in the 1920s illegal immigration achieved mass proportions and deportation assumed a central place in immigration policy. The nature and demands of restriction raised a range

1. In 1891 Congress created the Immigration Bureau as part of the Department of Commerce and Labor (which became the Department of Labor in 1913). The Immigration Service was the Bureau's field organization; the Border Patrol was a division of the Service. In 1932 the Immigration Bureau and Naturalization Bureau merged to form the Immigration and Naturalization Service (INS). In 1940 Congress moved the INS to the Department of Justice.

Transcript, testimony before Executive Session of the House Committee on Immigration and Naturalization (hereafter "House Immigration Committee"), Jan. 15, 1930, file 55688/876–1, entry 9, Records of the Immigration and Naturalization Service, Record Group 85, National Archives (Washington) (hereafter "INS").

2. Ibid.; Act of Feb. 27, 1925 (43 Stat. 1049). The bureau's policy was an expansive interpretation of a 1916 federal court ruling, *Lew Moy et al. v. United States* (237 Fed. 50). In that case the court upheld the arrest of Chinese aliens two hundred miles north of the Mexican border on the grounds that the alleged act of conspiracy to smuggle had not yet been completed. Commissioner General of Immigration to the Secretary of Labor, *Annual Report* (hereafter *INS Annual Report*), fiscal year ending June 30, 1930, p. 36; "Immigration Border Patrol" (preliminary hearing, unrevised), March 5, 1928, Hearings before the House Immigration Committee, 70th Congress, First Session (Washington, D.C.: GPO, 1930), 5.

of problems for the modern state, which were at once administrative (how should restriction be enforced?), juridical (how is sovereignty defined?), and constitutional (do illegal aliens have rights?).

These questions had been answered with relative ease in the late nineteenth century, when illegal aliens comprised Chinese and other marginalized persons (such as criminals, the insane, and prostitutes) who could be summarily expelled from the United States. Upholding Chinese exclusion, the Supreme Court in the 1880s and 1890s located Congress's power to regulate immigration outside of the Constitution, in the nation's sovereignty, which power it deemed was absolute. The Court considered this necessary to protect the nation from foreign invasion, whether from armies during wartime or from foreign migrants during peacetime. The doctrine of plenary power privileged the nation's sovereignty absolutely over the rights of individual persons. Thus the Court declared that aliens have no right "to be and remain in this country, except by the license, permission, and sufferance of congress." In the era of numerical restriction, the exercise of this sovereign power over immigrants, especially those illegally present, gave rise to complex and troubling issues.[3]

This essay examines the advent of mass illegal immigration and deportation policy under the Immigration Act of 1924 and how these trends altered meanings of inclusion in and exclusion from the nation. It argues that numerical restriction created a new class of persons within the national body—illegal aliens—whose inclusion in the nation was at once a social reality and a legal impossibility. This contradiction challenged received notions of sovereignty and democracy in several ways. First, the increase in the number of illegal entries created a new emphasis on control of the nation's contiguous land borders, which emphasis had not existed before. This new articulation of state territoriality reconstructed national borders and national space in ways that were both highly visible and problematic. At the same time, the notion of border control obscured the policy's unavoidable slippage into the interior.

Second, the application of the deportation laws gave rise to an oppositional political and legal discourse, which imagined deserving and undeserving illegal immigrants and, concomitantly, just and unjust deportations. These categories were constructed out of modern ideas about social desirability, in particular with regard to crime and sexual morality, and values that esteemed family preservation. Critics argued that deportation was unjust in cases where it separated families or exacted other hardships that were

3. *Chae Chan Ping v. U.S.*, 130 U.S. 581 (1889); *Nishimura Eiku v. U.S.*, 142 U.S. 652, 659 (1892); *Fong Yue Ting v. U.S.*, 149 U.S. 698, 706, 723 (1893). See also Linda S. Bosniak, "Membership, Equality, and the Difference That Alienage Makes," *New York University Law Review* 69 (Dec. 1994): 1047–1149.

out of proportion to the offense committed. As a result, during the 1930s deportation policy became the object of legal reform to allow for administrative discretion in deportation cases. Just as restriction and deportation "made" illegal aliens, administrative discretion "unmade" illegal aliens.

Taken together, these trends redefined the normative basis of social desirability and inclusion in the nation. That process had an important racial dimension because the application and reform of deportation policy had disparate effects on Europeans and Canadians, on the one hand, and Mexicans, on the other hand. But, the disparity was not simply the result of existing racism. Rather, the processes of territorial redefinition and administrative enforcement informed divergent paths of immigrant racialization. Europeans and Canadians tended to be disassociated from the real and imagined category of illegal alien, which facilitated their national and racial assimilation as white American citizens. In contrast, Mexicans emerged as iconic illegal aliens. Illegal status became constitutive of a racialized Mexican identity and of Mexicans' exclusion from the national community and polity.

Deportation Policy and the Making of Illegal Aliens

The illegal immigrant cannot be constituted without deportation—the possibility or threat of deportation, if not the fact. The possibility derives from the actual existence of state machinery to apprehend and deport illegal aliens. The threat remains in the temporal and spatial "lag" that exists between the act of unlawful entry and apprehension or deportation (if, in fact, the illegal alien is ever caught). The many effects of the lag include the psychological and cultural problems associated with "passing" or "living a lie," community vulnerability and isolation, and the use of undocumented workers as a highly exploited or reserve labor force. Examining the policy and practice of deportation provides us not only with an understanding of how illegal immigration is constituted but also a point of entry into the experience of illegal immigrants, which, by its nature, remains largely invisible to the mainstream of society.[4]

Deportation was not invented in the 1920s, but it was then that it came of age. In a sense, legal provisions for the deportation of unwanted immi-

4. The official record is not without problems. Data on apprehensions and deportations do not represent all unlawful entries and are further skewed by policy decisions to police certain areas or populations and not others. On methodologies employed, see "Illegal Alien Resident Population," *INS Statistical Yearbook* (1998); see also Barry Edmonston, Jeffrey Passel, and Frank Bean, *Undocumented Migration to the United States: IRCA and the Experience of the 1980s* (Santa Monica, Ca.: Rand Corporation, 1990), 16–18, 27. I thank Neil Gotanda for suggesting that the racial concept of "passing" may be applied to illegal immigrants.

grants existed in America since colonial times, the principle having been derived from the English poor laws. A 1794 Massachusetts law, for example, called for the return of paupers to their original towns or "to any other State, or to any place beyond sea, where he belongs." The expense of transatlantic removal, however, meant that deportations to Europe rarely took place, if at all. The Alien and Sedition Laws (1798–1801) provided for the exclusion and expulsion of aliens on political grounds. But Americans quickly rejected the principle of political removal during peacetime and the nation operated without federal regulation of immigration for the better part of the nineteenth century. Unfettered migration was crucial for the settlement and industrialization of America, even if the laboring migrants themselves were not always free.[5]

In 1875 Congress legislated the first federal restrictions on entry when it banned persons convicted of "crimes involving moral turpitude" and prostitutes (a provision aimed at barring Chinese women from entry). During the 1880s the number of excludable classes grew to comprise the mentally retarded, contract laborers, persons with "dangerous and loathsome contagious disease," paupers, polygamists, and the "feebleminded" and "insane," as well as Chinese laborers. The litany of excludable classes articulated concern over the admission of real and potential public charges as well as late nineteenth-century beliefs, derived from Social Darwinism and criminal anthropology, that the national body had to be protected from the contaminants of social degeneracy.[6]

Still, the nation's border were soft and, for the most part, unguarded. Inspection at arrival sought to identify excludable persons and to deny them admission, but little could be done if they evaded detection and entered the

5. Gerald L. Neuman, *Strangers to the Constitution: Immigrants, Borders, and Fundamental Law* (Princeton: Princeton University Press, 1996), 19–43; Kunal Parker, "From Poor Law to Immigration Law: Changing Visions of Territorial Community in Antebellum Massachusetts," *Historical Geography* 28 (2000): 61–85. On migration and nineteenth-century economic development, see David Montgomery, *The Fall of the House of Labor* (New York: Cambridge University Press, 1987), 70–74; John Bodnar, *The Transplanted: A History of Immigrants in Urban America* (Bloomington: Indiana University Press, 1985), xviii–xix; Aristide Zolberg, "Global Movements, Global Walls: Responses to Migration, 1885–1925," in *Global History and Migrations,* ed. Wang Gungwu (Boulder, Col.: Westview, 1997), 279. On the transition from state to federal regulation of immigration, see Mary Sarah Bilder, "The Struggle over Immigration: Indentured Servants, Slaves, and Articles of Commerce," *Missouri Law Review* 61 (1996): 744–824.

6. Edward Hutchinson, *Legislative History of American Immigration Law, 1798–1965* (Philadelphia: University of Pennsylvania Press, 1981), 163–68. 22 Stat. 58 (first Chinese exclusion law, 1882); 22 Stat. 214 (Immigration Act of 1882); 23 Stat. 332 (Alien Contract Labor Law, 1885). On criminal anthropology, anti-Chinese coolieism, and late nineteenth-century anti-modernism, see Colleen Lye, "Model Modernity: The Making of Asiatic Racial Form, 1882–1943" (Ph.D. diss., Columbia University, 1999).

country. Subsequent discovery was commonly the result of being hospitalized or imprisoned, yet no federal law existed mandating the removal of alien public charges from the country. It was not until 1891 that Congress authorized the deportation of aliens who within one year of arrival became public charges from causes existing prior to landing, at the expense of the steamship company that originally brought them. Congress otherwise established no mechanism and appropriated no funds for deportation.[7]

Congress gradually extended the statute of limitation on deportation. The Immigration Act of 1917 added six excludable categories and harsher sanctions, extended the period of deportability to five years, removed all time limits for aliens in certain classes, and for the first time appropriated funds for the enforcement. The new harsh law was applied to immigrant anarchists and communists in a sweep of postwar vengeance against radicalism and labor militancy, culminating in the Palmer Raids in the winter of 1919–1920 when authorities arrested 10,000 alleged anarchists and ultimately deported some five hundred.[8]

The Red Scare notwithstanding, few people were actually excluded or deported before the 1920s. Between 1892 and 1907 the Immigration Service deported only a few hundred aliens a year and between 1908 and 1920 an average of two or three thousand a year—mostly aliens removed from asylums, hospitals, and jails. Deportation appears even less significant when one considers that some one million people a year entered the country in the decade preceding World War I. Congress and the Immigration Service conceived of and executed deportation as an adjunct to the process of exclusion, a correction to the improper admission of excludable aliens.[9] Perhaps most important, mere entry without inspection was insufficient grounds for deportation. The statute of limitation on deportation was consistent with the general philosophy of the melting pot: it seemed unconscionable to expel immigrants after they had settled in the country and had begun to assimilate.

A new regime in immigration policy, that of numerical restriction, commenced in the 1920s. This ended the historical policy of open immigra-

7. Hutchinson, *Legislative History*, 447.

8. Congress extended the statute of limitation for deportation to two years from time of entry in 1903 (32 Stat. 1213) and to three years in 1907 (34 Stat. 898). On the Palmer Raids, see William Preston, Jr., *Aliens and Dissenters: Federal Suppression of Radicals, 1903–1933* (Cambridge: Harvard University Press, 1963).

9. *Historical Statistics of the United States from Colonial Times to 1970* (Washington, D. C.: GPO, 1975), 105, 113; *INS Annual Report*, 1921, pp. 14–15; William Van Vleck, *Administrative Control of Aliens* (New York: Commonwealth Fund, 1932), 20. See also Jane Perry Clark, *Deportation of Aliens from the United States to Europe* (New York: Columbia University Press, 1931), 275.

tion from Europe. Political and economic developments, both national and global, influenced this shift. Anti-alien sentiment in the United States had grown since the mid-1880s, mostly in response to the social problems associated with mass migration from southern and eastern Europe—urban slums, disease, poverty, class conflict. More immediately, World War I had raised nationalism and anti-foreign sentiment to a high pitch. Immigration restriction was a core component of the politics of wartime nationalism and postwar reaction. There were structural influences, as well. By 1920 the system of mass industrial production had matured to a point where increased output derived from technological improvement, not continually increasing inputs of unskilled labor. More broadly, immigration restriction was part of a new global age. World War I marked the consolidation of the international nation-state system, based on Westphalian sovereignty, hardened borders, state citizenship, and passport controls.[10]

In 1921 Congress restricted immigration into the United States to 350,000 a year. The Immigration Act of 1924 further restricted immigration to 150,000 a year, less than 15 percent of the average annual immigration of one million before World War I.[11] Quotas were allocated to countries in proportion to the numbers that the American people traced their "national origin" to those countries, through immigration or the immigration of their forebears. I have discussed the racial dimensions of the national origin quota system elsewhere.[12] Relevant to this discussion is the law's other core feature, numerical restriction, and its concomitants, illegal immigration and deportation.

The passage of the quota laws marked a turn in both the volume and nature of unlawful entry and in the philosophy and practice of deportation.

10. John Higham, *Strangers in the Land: Patterns of American Nativism, 1860–1925,* 2d ed. (1955; New Brunswick, N.J.: Rutgers University Press, 1985), 204–7, 301; Montgomery, *Fall of the House of Labor,* 457–58; Saskia Sassen, *Guests and Aliens* (New York: New Press, 1999), 83–84; John Torpey, *The Invention of the Passport* (New York: Cambridge University Press, 2000), 111–21; Aristide Zolberg, "The Great Wall against China," in *Migration, Migration History, History: Old Paradigms and New Perspectives,* ed. Jan Lucassen and Leo Lucassen (Bern and New York: Peter Lang, 1997).

11. Act of May 19, 1921 (41 Stat. 5); Act of May 26, 1924 (43 Stat, 153); *Historical Statistics,* 105. Not all immigration was subject to numerical quota. Immediate family members of U.S. citizens could immigrate outside the quota limit, as "non-quota immigrants." Natives of the countries of the Western Hemisphere were not subject to quotas. At the same time, all Asians were excluded as "persons ineligible to citizenship." The quotas, then, were directly principally at European countries.

12. Mae M. Ngai, "The Architecture of Race in American Immigration Law: A Re-examination of the Immigration Act of 1924," *Journal of American History* 86 (June 1999): 67–92. See also Robert A. Divine, *American Immigration Policy* (New Haven: Yale University Press, 1957); Higham, *Strangers in the Land;* Desmond King, *Making Americans* (Cambridge: Harvard University Press, 2000).

In general, of course, legislators write laws to include sanctions against their violation. But in the Act of 1924 Congress evinced a wholly different approach toward deportation. The new law eliminated the statute of limitation on deportation for nearly all forms of unlawful entry and provided for the deportation at any time of any person entering after July 1, 1924, without a valid visa or without inspection.[13]

In addition, Congress for the first time legislated a serious enforcement mechanism against unlawful entry by creating a land Border Patrol. In 1929 Congress made unlawful entry a misdemeanor, punishable by one year of imprisonment or a $1,000 fine or both; and made a second unlawful entry a felony, punishable by two years imprisonment or a $2,000 fine or both. Deportation thus amounted to permanent banishment under threat of felony prosecution.[14]

The criminalization of unauthorized entry signaled a radical departure from previous immigration policy, which deemed deportation to be a civil, or administrative, procedure. That policy deprived aliens in deportation proceedings rights protected by the Fourth and Fifth Amendments, but it also protected deportees from criminal punishment.[15] The 1929 law made illegal entry a separate criminal offense; in effect, illegal immigrants inherited the worst of both propositions by making them subject to deportation, under which proceedings they still lacked Constitutional protections, and separate criminal prosecution and punishment. Criminal conviction also made future reentry impossible.[16]

The Immigration Act of 1924 and its attendant enforcement mechanisms spurred a dramatic increase in the number of deportations. A contemporary observed that the "extensive use of the power to expel" began in 1925 and that deportation quickly became "one of the chief activities of the Immigration Service in some districts." By 1928 the bureau was exhausting its funds for deportations long before the fiscal year ended. Carl Robe White, the assistant secretary of labor, told the House Immigration Committee that the department needed an annual budget of ten million dollars for deportations, more than ten times the appropriation for the previous year.[17]

13. Act of May 26, 1924, sec. 14. Those who entered before 1924 continued to be subject to deportation according to the terms of the Immigration Act of 1917.

14. Act of Feb. 27, 1925 (43 Stat. 1049); Act of March 4, 1929 (45 Stat. 1551).

15. *Fong Yue Ting v. U.S.,* at 708; *Wong Wing v. U.S.,* 163 U.S. 228 (1896); *Flora v. Rustad,* 8 Fed. (2nd) 335.

16. Between 1930 and 1936 the service brought over 40,000 criminal cases against unlawful entrants, winning convictions in some 36,000, or 90 percent, of them. Secretary of Labor, *Annual Report,* 1933, p. 45; *INS Annual Reports,* 1929–32; Secretary of Labor, *Annual Reports,* 1933–36.

17. Van Vleck, *Administrative Control,* 21; *INS Annual Report,* 1925, p. 9; White testimony in "Lack of Funds for Deportations," Hearings before the House Immigration Committee,

In 1927, in order to make expulsion more efficient, the Immigration Service allowed illegal aliens without criminal records to depart voluntarily, thereby avoiding the time and expense of instituting formal deportation proceedings. The number of aliens expelled from the country rose from 2,762 in 1920 to 9,495 in 1925 and to 38,795 in 1930.[18] The Immigration Service continued to deport public charges delivered to it by state institutions. But "aliens without proper visa" rapidly became the largest single class of deportees, representing over half the total number of formal deportations and the overwhelming majority of voluntary departures by the late 1920s.[19]

This shift in the principal categories of deportation engendered new ways of thinking about illegal immigration. First, legal and illegal status became, in effect, abstract constructions, having less to do with experience than with numbers and paper. Legal status now rested on being in the right place in the queue—if a country has a quota of *N*, immigrant *N* is legal but immigrant *N+1* is illegal[20]—and having the proper documentation, the prized "proper visa." These were not absolute, of course, as preference categories privileged certain family relations and qualitative indices for exclusion remained in force. However, the qualitative aspects of admission were rendered less visible as they were absorbed by the visa application process, which after 1924 took place at United States consular offices abroad. In addition to overseeing the distribution of quota slots, U.S. consuls determined the desirability of both quota and non-quota prospective migrants according to the submission of a "dossier," questionnaire and interview, and medical certification.[21] In 1924 the Immigration Service terminated medical line inspection at Ellis Island because medical exclusions were determined abroad. Thus, upon arrival, immigrants' visas were inspected, not their bodies. The system shifted to a different, more abstract register, which privileged formal status over all else. It is this system that created what we today call the "undocumented immigrant."

The illegal alien that is abstractly defined is thus something of a specter, a body stripped of individual personage, whose very presence is troubling, wrong. Moreover, this body stripped of personage has no rights. It is no coincidence that the regime of immigration restriction emerged with World War I. The war, by simultaneously destroying the geopolitical stability of Europe and solidifying the nation-state system, also created mil-

---

70th Congress, First Session, on HR 3, HR 5673, HR 6069; Jan. 5, 1928, Hearing no. 70.1.1. (Washington, D.C.: GPO, 1928), 10.

18. Historical Statistics, 114. Figures include deportation under formal warrant and voluntary departures.

19. *INS Annual Report,* 1931, pp. 255–56.

20. I am grateful to Kunal Parker for suggesting this illustrative formulation.

21. Act of May 24, 1924, Sec 7(b), (d).

lions of refugees and stateless persons, as well as denationalized and denaturalized persons during the postwar period.[22] Recalling Hannah Arendt, philosopher Giorgio Agamben tells us, "In the system of the nation-state, the so-called sacred and inalienable rights of man show themselves to lack every protection and reality at the moment in which they can no longer take the form of rights belonging to citizens of a state." Certainly the illegal alien appears in the same historical moment and in the same juridical no-man's-land that was created when the war loosened the links between birth and nation, human being and citizen.[23]

Second, the mere idea that persons without formal legal status resided in the nation engendered images of great danger. In 1925 the Immigration Service reported with some alarm that 1.4 million immigrants—20 percent of those who had entered the country before 1921—might already be living illegally in the United States. The service conceded that these immigrants had lawfully entered the country, but because it had no record of their admission, it considered them illegal. It warned,

> (I)t is quite possible that there is an even greater number of aliens in the country whose legal presence here could not be established. No estimate could be made as to the number of smuggled aliens who have been unlawfully introduced into the country since the quota restrictions of 1921, or of those who may have entered under the guise of seamen. The figures presented are worthy of very serious thought, especially when it is considered that there is such a great percentage of our population . . . *whose first act upon reaching our shores* was to break our laws by entering in a clandestine manner—all of which serves to emphasize the potential source of trouble, not to say menace, that such a situation suggests.[24]

Positive law thus constituted undocumented immigrants as criminals, both fulfilling and fueling nativist discourse. Once nativism succeeded in legislating restriction, anti-alien animus shifted its focus to the interior of the

22. Giorgio Agamben, *Homo Sacer: Sovereign Power and Bare Life* (Stanford: Stanford University Press, 1998), 130–31. See also Hannah Arendt, *The Origins of Totalitarianism* (New York: Harcourt Brace, 1979, 1951), 267–302. According to Agamben, refugees and stateless persons created by World War I included 1.5 million White Russians, 700,000 Armenians, 1 million Greeks, 500,000 Bulgarians, and hundreds of thousands of Germans, Hungarians, and Rumanians. France (1915), Belgium (1922), Italy (1926), and Austria (1933) denationalized persons of "enemy origin" and others deemed unfit for citizenship by reasons of birth, culminating of course in the Nuremberg citizenship laws and the Nazi concentration camps. Agamben points out, "One of the few rules to which the Nazis consistently adhered during the course of the "Final Solution" was that Jews could be sent to the extermination camps only after they had been fully denationalized (stripped even of the residual citizenship left to them after the Nuremberg laws)."

23. Agamben, *Homo Sacer,* 126.

24. *INS Annual Report,* 1925, pp. 12–13 (emphasis added).

nation and the goal of expelling immigrants living illegally in the country. The Los Angeles *Evening Express* alleged that there were "several million foreigners" in the country who had "no right to be here." Nativists like Madison Grant, recognizing that deportation was "of great importance," also advocated alien registration "as a necessary prelude to deport on a large scale." Critics of nativism predicted that "if every man who wears a beard and reads a foreign newspaper is to be suspected unless he can produce either an identification card or naturalization papers, we shall have more confusion and bungling than ever." [25]

Prohibition supplied an important cache of criminal tropes, the language of smuggling directly yoking illegal immigration to liquor-running. The California Joint Immigration Committee described illegal aliens as "vicious and criminal," comprising "bootleggers, gangsters, and racketeers of large cities."[26] Similarly, Edwin Reeves, a Border Patrol officer in El Paso during the 1920s, recalled, "Every fellow you caught with a load of liquor on his back . . . was a wetback." The *National Republic* claimed that two million aliens intent upon illegally entering the United States were massed in Canada, Mexico, and Cuba, on the "waiting lists" of smugglers.[27]

In this story, aliens were not only subjects—that is, the smugglers—they were also the objects, the human goods illegally trafficked across the border. In 1927 the Immigration Bureau reported that the "bootlegging of aliens" was "a lucrative industry second only to smuggling of liquor." It emphasized, "The bootlegged alien is by all odds the *least* desirable. Whatever else may be said of him: whether he be diseased or not, whether he holds views inimical to our institutions, *he at best is a law violator from the outset.*"[28] This view that the undocumented immigrant was the least desirable alien of all denotes a new imagining of the nation, which situated the principle of national sovereignty in the foreground. It made state

25. *Evening Express* (Los Angeles), Dec. 6, 1930, HR 71A-F16.2, in Records of the U.S. House of Representatives, RG 155, National Archives (Washington)(hereafter "House records"); Madison Grant, "America for the Americans," *Forum,* Sept. 1925, p. 354; *Survey,* March 15, 1929, p. 796.

26. Dept. of Labor Solicitor, "In re whether aliens who violate any of the provisions of the prohibition laws are subject to deportation," Sept. 17, 1924, file 54933/351–10 [entry 9], INS; McClatchy and Fisk to Johnson, Dec. 4, 1930, HR71A-F16.4, House records. It is worth noting that bootlegging itself was not a deportable offense. As vague as the term "crimes of moral turpitude" was, the Labor Department did not so classify violation of the Volstead Act.

27. Interview of Edwin M. Reeves by Robert H. Novak, June 25, 1971, transcript, tape no. 135, p. 5, Institute of Oral History, University of Texas, El Paso (microfilm); California Joint Immigration Committee, "Deportable Aliens," release #251, Jan. 24, 1930, Press releases and statements, CJIC Papers, Bancroft Library, University of California, Berkeley.

28. *INS Annual Report,* 1927, pp. 15–16 (emphasis added).

territoriality—not labor needs, not family unification, not freedom from persecution, not assimilation—the engine of immigration policy.

Territoriality was highly unstable, however, precisely because restriction had created illegal immigrants *within* the national body. This was not an entirely new phenomenon, but important consequences resulted from the different nature and scale of illegal immigration in the late 1920s. Illegal immigrants now comprised all nationality and ethnic groups. They were numerous, perhaps even innumerable, and were diffused throughout the nation, particularly in large cities. An illegal immigrant might now be anyone's neighbor or coworker, even one's spouse or parent. Her illegal status might not be known to her social acquaintances and personal intimates. She might not even be aware of it herself, particularly if it resulted from a technical violation of the law. She might, in fact, be a responsible member of society (employed, tax paying, and, notwithstanding her illegal status, law-abiding). Even if she were indigent or uneducated, she might have a family, social ties in a community, and interact with others in ways that arguably established her as a member of society.

The problem of differentiating illegal immigrants from citizens and legal immigrants signified the danger that restrictionists had imagined—to them, illegal aliens were an invisible enemy in America's midst. Yet their proposed solutions, such as compulsory alien registration and mass deportations, were problematic exactly because undocumented immigrants *were* so like other Americans. During the interwar period a majority of political opinion opposed alien registration on grounds that it threatened Americans' perceived rights of free movement, association, and privacy.[29] The Immigration Service had traditionally "never made any considerable attempt . . . to go out and look for aliens unlawfully in the country" and through the late 1920s remained reluctant to conduct mass raids, particularly in the north.[30] The problem of differentiation revealed a discontinuity between illegal immigration as an abstract general problem, a "scare" discourse used at times to great political effect, and illegal immigrants who were real people known in the community, people who had committed no substantive wrongs.

Yet, if illegal aliens were so like other Americans, the racial and ethnic diversity of the American population further complicated the problem of differentiation. We might anticipate that illegal aliens from Europe and Canada were perceived and treated differently from those of Mexican or

29. Organized labor, which was generally restrictionist, opposed alien registration on grounds that such information could be used against union activists. See sundry correspondence from union leaders to Congressmen in file HR69A-H3.5, House records.

30. I. F. Wixon, "Lack of Funds for Deportations," Hearings before the House Immigration Committee on H.R. 3, H.R. 5673, H.R. 6069, 70th Cong., 1st sess., 5 January 1928, 22–23.

Asian origin.[31] In fact, the racial dimensions of deportation policy were not merely expressions of existing racial prejudice. Rather, they derived from processes of territoriality and administrative enforcement that were not in the first instance motivated or defined by race.

We might approach this problem by considering the question of defining and controlling the border and by returning to Commissioner Hull's testimony that the Border Patrol did not operate "on the border line" but "back of the line." Contemporaries understood the distinction, if not the full implications. Writing about the Border Patrol in the Southwest, one author described apprehending aliens "at some distance back from the International Line" a "man-sized job." She explained, "To capture an alien who is in the act of crawling through a hole in the fence between Arizona and Mexico is easy compared with apprehending and deporting him after he is hidden in the interior, among others of his own race who are legally in this country."[32] The Border Patrol's capacious definition of its jurisdiction suggests that the nation's borders (the point of exclusion) collapsed into and became indistinguishable from the interior (the space of inclusion). But, this is not to say that the border was eliminated. Policies of restriction and deportation reconstructed and raised the borders, even as they destabilized them. History and policy also constructed the U.S.-Mexican and U.S.-Canadian borders differently. The processes of defining and policing the border both encoded and generated racial ideas and practices that, in turn, produced different racialized spaces internal to the nation.

The Border and the Border Patrol

Before the 1920s the Immigration Service paid little attention to the nation's land borders because the overwhelming majority of immigrants landed at Ellis Island and other seaports. The flow of immigrants into the country had been not only welcome but had been focused at fixed points that rendered

31. Chinese were the first illegal aliens and continued to be racially constructed as unalterably foreign. But they do not appear in deportation statistics or discourse because Chinese illegal immigrants mostly comprised persons who claimed to be U.S. citizens by native birth or descendants of those citizens. Deportation was exceedingly difficult because the fraudulent papers were actually official documents issued by the Immigration Service. See Madeline Y. Hsu, *Dreaming of Gold, Dreaming of Home: Transnationalism and Migration between the United States and South China, 1882–1943* (Stanford: Stanford University Press, 2000), chap. 3; Erika Lee, "Enforcing and Challenging Exclusion in San Francisco: U.S. Immigration Officers and Chinese Immigrant, 1882–1905," *Chinese America: History and Perspectives* 11 (1997): 1–15; Mae M. Ngai, "Legacies of Exclusion: Illegal Chinese Immigration during the Cold War Years," *Journal of American Ethnic History* 18 (Fall 1998): 3–35.

32. Mary Kidder Rak, *Border Patrol* (Boston: Houghton Mifflin, 1938), 17.

land borders invisible. One immigration director described the situation as the "equivalent to a circle with locked doors with no connecting wall between them."[33] A small force of the Customs Service and the Chinese Division of the Immigration Service jointly patrolled the Mexican and Canadian borders against illegal entry by Chinese. The Chinese patrol inspector, assigned to horseback detail or inspecting freight cars, occupied the loneliest and bottommost position in the hierarchy of the service.[34]

Immigration inspectors ignored Mexicans coming into the southwestern United States during the 1900s and 1910s to work in railroad construction, mining, and agriculture. The Immigration Bureau did not seriously consider Mexican immigration within its purview, but rather as something that was "regulated by labor market demands in [the southwestern] border states." The Bureau also described the Southwest as the "natural habitat" of Mexicans, acknowledging, albeit strangely, Mexicans' claims of belonging in an area that had once been part of Mexico. The Immigration Act of 1917 doubled the head tax and imposed a literacy test, erecting the first barriers to entry. But unlawful entry was limited, as the Labor Department exempted Mexicans from the requirements during the war. It was not until 1919 that Mexicans entering the United States were required to apply for admission at lawfully designated ports of entry.[35]

Before World War I, the U.S.-Canada border was also soft. In some ways it resembled the Mexican border: vast stretches were sparsely populated, economically undeveloped, and intemperate for many months of the year. As with the Mexican border, the first inspection policies instituted along the Canadian border in the 1890s aimed not to restrict Canadians but to deter Chinese and Europeans of the excludable classes who sought entry into the United States through the unguarded back door.[36] Throughout the nineteenth century, Canadians moved freely into the United States: Canadian farmers participated in the settlement of the American West, which movement preceded expansion to the Canadian West; and industry and manufacturing in Michigan and New England drew labor from Canada as

33. I. F. Wixon, "Mission of the Border Patrol," Lecture no. 7, March 19, 1934 (Washington, 1934), 2.

34. The Chinese Division was also called the Outside Division because it operated separately from the main Immigration Service. In general the Outside Division was understaffed and "not overloaded with talent." Clifford Perkins, *Border Patrol: With the U.S. Immigration Service on the Mexican Boundary, 1910–1954* (El Paso: Texas Western Press, 1978), 9, 75.

35. George Sánchez, *Becoming Mexican American* (New York: Oxford University Press, 1993), 52–53; *INS Annual Report,* 1919, pp. 24–25, 61; *INS Annual Report,* 1923, p. 16.

36. Marian Smith, "The INS at the U.S.-Canadian Border, 1893–1933: An Overview of Issues and Topics" (paper presented at the annual meeting of the Organization of American Historians, Toronto, April 23, 1999).

well as from Europe.[37] But Canadians assumed a different economic relationship to the United States than did Mexicans. In general Canadians did not comprise a major source of unskilled labor for American industry, largely because Canada itself suffered a labor shortage and relied on immigrant labor for its own economic development. For example, in the early twentieth century the sugar beet industry on both sides of the border—in Michigan, Wisconsin, and southern Ontario—recruited European agricultural laborers. After 1924, when European immigration to the United States declined, American sugar beet growers resorted not to Canadian labor but to Mexican and, secondarily, to Filipino labor.[38]

If both the Mexican and Canadian borders were soft until World War I, the passage of the quota laws in 1921 and 1924 threw the nation's contiguous land borders into sharp relief for immigration authorities. Although most European immigrants continued to land at seaports, contemporaries imagined that illegal aliens would overrun the land borders. One writer, believing that "the tide of immigration now beats upon the land borders—not upon the sea coasts—of the United States," asked, "can these long borders ever be adequately patrolled?"[39]

Indeed, illegal European immigrants entered the United States across both borders. Belgian, Dutch, Swiss, Russian, Bulgarian, Italian, and Polish immigrants enlisted in agricultural labor programs in the Canadian west, only to arrive in Canada and immediately attempt entry into the United States, at points from Ontario to Manitoba. An investigation by the Federal Bureau of Investigation in 1925 reported that "thousands" of immigrants, "mostly late arrivals from Europe," were "coming [into Canada] as fast as they can get the money to pay the smugglers." The most heavily traveled route for illegal European immigration was through Mexico. The commissioner general of immigration noted, "Long established routes from southern Europe to Mexican ports and overland to the Texas border, formerly patronized almost exclusively by diseased and criminal aliens, are now

37. *INS Annual Report,* 1934, p. 96; see also Bruno Ramirez, *Crossing the 49th Parallel: Migration from Canada to the United States, 1900–1930* (Ithaca: Cornell University Press, 2001), chaps. 1–3; Thomas A. Klug, "The Detroit Labor Movement and the United States-Canada Border, 1885–1930," *Mid-America* 80 (Fall 1998): 209–34; Gary Gerstle, *Working Class Americanism: The Politics of Labor in a Textile City* (New York: Cambridge University Press, 1989).

38. Testimony of T. G. Gallagher, Continental Sugar Co., Toledo, in "Immigration from Countries of the Western Hemisphere," Hearings before House Immigration Committee, 70th Congress, First Session, Feb 21–April 5, 1928, at 555–57; oral history interview with Rudolfo M. Andres by Helen Hatcher, June 27, 1981, file BA/NC81–Fil-004–HMH-1, Demonstration Project for Asian Americans (Seattle).

39. "The Eclipse of Ellis Island" (n.a.), *Survey,* Jan. 19, 1929, p. 480.

resorted to by large numbers of Europeans who cannot gain legal admission because of passport difficulties, illiteracy, or the quota law."[40]

By the late 1920s the surreptitious entry of Europeans into the United States declined. The threat of apprehension and deportation deterred some, but also alternate legal methods existed for circumventing the quota laws. Europeans could go to Canada and be admitted to United States legally after they had resided in Canada for five years. The evidence suggests that this was a popular strategy: the proportion of lawful admissions from Canada of persons not born in Canada increased from 20 percent in 1925 to over 50 percent in the early 1930s.[41] And, as European immigrants in the United States became naturalized citizens, they could bring relatives over legally as non-quota immigrants. In 1927 over 60 percent of the non-quota immigrants admitted to the U.S. were from Italy, with the next largest groups coming from Poland, Czechoslovakia, and Greece.[42]

This is not to say that illegal immigration of Europeans and Canadians stopped. The Immigration Service continued to deport illegal aliens to Europe and to Canada—deportations remained fairly constant at 6,000 to 8,000 a year through the early thirties. But the number of persons deported for surreptitious entry declined whereas the number deported for overstaying temporary visas increased.[43] In general, the Immigration Service was more concerned with the bureaucratic burden of processing the high volume of legal traffic crossing the U.S.-Canada border in both directions. It also relied on the 1894 agreement between the United States and Canada, which made Canadian rail carriers responsible for checking the status of passengers traveling to the United States, for deterring illegal entry from Canada.[44]

The service's work on the Canadian border was in sharp contrast to what the commissioner general described as the "high pitch" of its work along the U.S.-Mexico border.[45] During the late 1920s the number of illegal Mexican immigrants deported across the southern border skyrocketed—from 1,751 expulsions in 1925 to over 15,000 in 1929.[46] Deportations for

40. Walter Elcarr to Commissioner General, January 11, 1924; W. J. Egan to John H. Clark, March 25, 1924; John Clark to Commissioner General, March 27, 1924; file 53990/160A, box 792, accession 60A600, INS; W. F. Blackman, "Smuggling of aliens across the Canadian border," Jan. 21, 1925, file 53990/160C, ibid.; *INS Annual Report,* 1923, p. 16.

41. *INS Annual Report,* 1925, pp. 9, 18; *INS Annual Report,* 1929, p. 7; *INS Annual Report,* 1930, p. 13; *INS Annual Report,* 1931, p. 24; *INS Annual Report,* 1932, p. 17.

42. *INS Annual Report,* 1927, p. 12.

43. *INS Annual Reports,* 1924–1932.

44. *INS Annual Report,* 1925, p. 18. See also Smith, "The INS at the U.S.-Canadian Border."

45. *INS Annual Report,* 1925, p. 19.

46. After 1927, expulsions include both formal deportations under warrant and voluntary departures. *INS Annual Report,* 1928–1932; Secretary of Labor, *Annual Report,* 1933–1938.

entry without a proper visa accounted for most of the increase. Although Mexicans did not face quota restrictions, they nevertheless were confronted by myriad entry requirements, such as the head tax and visa fee, which impelled many to avoid formal admission and inspection.

Mexicans coming to the United States encountered a new kind of border. Notwithstanding the lax immigration procedures before World War I, the United States-Mexican border had had a long history of dispute. Born of war and annexation, it was contested literally from its first imagination, by the Mexican and American surveyors charged with drawing the boundary after the Mexican American war. Consolidating American sovereignty in the conquered territory was a protracted process, as armed skirmishes and rebellion along the border attended the appropriation of property and the imposition of American political institutions. After a decade of instability wrought by the Mexican Revolution and World War I, the border as a political marker became basically settled.[47]

During the 1920s immigration policy rearticulated the U.S.-Mexican border as a cultural and racial boundary, as a creator of illegal immigration. Federal officials self-consciously understood their task as creating a barrier where, in a practical sense, none had existed before. The service instituted new policies—new inspection procedures and the formation of the Border Patrol—that accentuated the difference between the two countries. As historian George Sánchez described, crossing the border became "a momentous occasion, a break from the past . . . a painful and abrupt event permeated by an atmosphere of racism and control—an event that clearly demarcated one society from another."[48]

Inspection at the Mexican border involved a degrading procedure of bathing, delousing, medical line inspection, and interrogation. The baths were new and unique to Mexican immigrants, requiring them to be inspected while naked, have their hair shorn, and have their clothing and baggage fumigated. Medical line inspection, modeled after the practice formerly used at Ellis Island, required immigrants to walk in single file past a medical officer.[49] These procedures were particularly humiliating, even gratu-

47. Leon Metz, *Border: The U.S.-Mexico Line* (El Paso, Tex.: Mangan Books, 1989), 20–40; Oscar Martínez, *Troublesome Border* (Tucson: University of Arizona Press, 1988), 17–21, 87.

48. Speech of John Farr Simmons, Chief of Visa Office, State Department, at Conference on Immigration, Williamstown, Mass. [1930], 7–9, file Sen71A-F11, box 93, Records of the U.S. Senate, Record Group 46, National Archives (Washington); Sánchez, *Becoming Mexican American,* 60–61.

49. Irving McNeil to J. W. Tappan, U.S. Public Health Service, Dec. 22, 1923; Inspector in charge to Supervising Inspector, El Paso, Dec. 13, 1923, file 52903/29, entry 9, INS. See also "Immigration Border Patrol," 31–32. Chinese immigrants landing at Angel Island were subjected to rigorous medical inspection and prolonged interrogation, but not mass bathing

itous, in light of the fact that the Immigration Act of 1924 required prospective immigrants to present a medical certificate to the U.S. consul when applying for a visa, that is, before travel to the United States. Medical line inspection at Ellis Island was eliminated after 1924, and at El Paso the service exempted all Europeans and Mexicans arriving by first class rail from medical line inspection, the baths, and the literacy test. Racial presumptions about Mexican laborers, not law, dictated the procedures at the Mexican border.

More than anything else, the formation of the Border Patrol raised the border. In the Mexican border district, the service first recruited patrol officers from the civil service railway postal clerk registers, but that proved to be a mistake, as they were generally unqualified and the service quickly exhausted the register.[50] Receiving a temporary reprieve from civil service requirements, the service hired former cowboys, skilled workers, and small ranchers as its first patrol officers. Almost all were young, many had military experience, and not a few associated with the Ku Klux Klan. "Dogie" Wright was a typical recruit. The son of a Texas Ranger, Wright had also been a ranger and a deputy United States marshal before he joined the Border Patrol in 1925.[51] Some patrolmen, according to Clifford Perkins, the first Border Patrol inspector in charge in El Paso, "were a little too quick with a gun, or given to drinking too much, too often"; many emulated the "rough but effective methods of the Texas Rangers."[52] Of thirty-four patrol inspectors in the El Paso district in 1927, only one was Mexican American. Pedro (Pete) Torres, a native of New Mexico, had a reputation as an "extremely valuable man on the river, for he thought like a Mexican and looked like one" and could "roam through Mexican neighborhoods without arousing suspicion." Torres had "no nerves at all," according to Perkins. "He may have been a little quick on the trigger, but his actions in every shooting match during which smugglers were killed always proved justified by the circumstances."[53]

Officials labored to create a professional enforcement arm of the Immigration Service out of such material. Perkins recalled a training program

---

and delousing. On Chinese inspection procedures, see Erika Lee, "At America's Gates: Chinese Immigration during the Exclusion Era" (Ph.D. diss., University of California, Berkeley, 1999).

50. *INS Annual Report,* 1925, p. 15.

51. Ibid.; Sánchez, *Becoming Mexican American,* 59; David Blackwell to SW Regional Commissioner, "Border Patrol 50th Anniversary," Jan. 19, 1954, in Edwin Reeves oral history file, Institute of Oral History, University of Texas, El Paso.

52. Perkins, *Border Patrol,* 95, 102.

53. Nick Collaer, Serial No. 58, Feb. 14, 1927, file 55494/25, box 3, accession 58A734, INS; Perkins, *Border Patrol,* 96.

comprising weekly lectures on investigative procedures, but training mostly took place on the job. Edwin Reeves said, "they just give you a .45 single action revolver with a web belt—and that was it." A civil service exam was soon instituted, which included math, writing an English essay, and demonstrating knowledge of Spanish "as spoken along the Mexican border." During the late 1920s turnover continued to average 25 percent within the first six months. A lack of professionalism plagued the force. In the El Paso district, drinking on the job, reading and socializing with friends while on duty, reckless driving, rumor mongering, and accepting gratuities from aliens were common problems.[54]

More important than unprofessional behavior, the Border Patrol's work assumed the character of criminal pursuit and apprehension, although officially it was charged with enforcing civil and not criminal laws and was not trained as a criminal enforcement agency. As discussed above, the service interpreted its authorization to apprehend illegal aliens without warrant to apply to anywhere within the interior of the nation. It also seized goods it believed were "obviously contraband or smuggled," a practice that the commissioner general acknowledged had dubious legal sanction.[55] During the Border Patrol's first five years of service, fifteen officers were killed in the line of duty, twelve in the Mexican border districts.[56]

As Border Patrol officers zealously pursued illegal aliens, smugglers, and criminals, the Immigration Service received complaints from white Americans who were interrogated by discourteous patrolmen or arrested without warrant. One citizen protested that the Border Patrol "enacted the role of Jesse James" on public highways. In 1929, in response to such adverse criticism, the service discontinued the "promiscuous halting of traffic" in the border area, acknowledging that it was "dangerous and probably illegal." A national conference of immigration commissioners and district directors held the same year devoted considerable attention to the conduct of Border Patrol officers and inspectors, including the lack of civility toward immigrants, bribery, and covering up misconduct. Official policy deemed "courtesy and consideration"—"good morning and a smile"

54. Perkins, *Border Patrol,* 96; Edwin Reeves interview, 5; David Blackwell to SW Regional Commissioner, "Border Patrol 50th Anniversary"; *INS Annual Report,* 1930, p. 37. El Paso district circulars by G. C. Wilmoth, on going to Mexico to drink alcohol, on and off duty, serial no. 2274, Sept. 2, 1924, reissued Feb. 16, 1928; on careless and reckless driving and failure to maintain vehicles, serial no. 4073, April 3, 1929; on reading or "entertaining friends by relating stories or jokes" while on duty, serial no. 4136, Nov. 21, 1929; on engaging in "useless and harmful talk to outsiders," serial no. 4133, Nov. 19, 1929; on taking gratuities from aliens, serial no. 4127, Oct. 1, 1929, file 55494/25–A, box 3, accession 58A734, INS.

55. Testimony of Henry Hull, Jan. 15, 1930, House Immigration Committee, INS.

56. *INS Annual Report,* 1930, p. 41.

and "I'm sorry"—as the "least expensive and perhaps the most useful" of the service's tools.[57]

Thus patrolmen were trained to act with civility, courtesy, and formality when dealing with Anglo citizens, ranch owners, immigrants arriving from Europe, and "high class tourists" from Canada.[58] But the quasi- and extralegal practices associated with rancher vigilantism and Texas Rangers suited the needs of the Border Patrol in the Southwest, particularly when it involved patrolling large expanses of uninhabited territory far removed from Washington's bureaucratic oversight.[59] The Border Patrol functioned within an environment of increased racial hostility against Mexicans; indeed, its activities helped constitute that environment by aggressively apprehending and deporting increasing numbers of Mexicans. The Border Patrol interrogated Mexican laborers on roads and in towns, and it was not uncommon for "sweeps" to apprehend several hundred immigrants at a time. By the early 1930s the service was apprehending nearly five times as many suspected illegal aliens in the Mexican border area as it did in the Canadian border area. The Los Angeles newspaper *La Opinión* believed the aggressive deportation policy would result in a "de-Mexicanization of southern California."[60]

Moreover, many Mexicans entered the United States through a variety of means that were not illegal but comprised irregular, unstable categories of lawful admission, making it more difficult to distinguish between those who were lawfully in the country and those who were not. Mexicans living in Mexican border towns who commuted into the United States to work on a daily or weekly basis constituted one category of irregular entry. The service counted these commuters as immigrants and collected a one-time head tax from them. It also required them to report to the immigration station once a week for bathing, a hated requirement that gave rise to a local black market in bathing certificates.[61]

57. Bisbee (Arizona) *Review*, Feb. 1, 1927; G. C. Wilmoth to Chief Patrol Inspectors, June 7, 1929, file 55494/25–A, box 3, accession 58A734, INS; D. W. MacCormack, "The Spirit of the Service," in U.S. Dept. of Labor, Bureau of Immigration, *Problems of the Immigration Service: Papers presented at a Conference of Commissioners and District Directors of Immigration, January 1929* (Washington, D.C.: GPO, 1929), 4.

58. "Immigration Border Patrol," 30.

59. According to Douglas Foley, the federal government "left [the] southern labor force to work out their own problems with local Texas Rangers, the Border Patrol, and hostile Anglos." Foley, *From Peones to Politicos: Class and Ethnicity in a South Texas Town, 1900–1987* (1977; Austin: University of Texas Press, 1988), 18.

60. Perkins, *Border Patrol*, 116; *La Opinión*, Jan 29, 1929, p. 1 (trans. from Spanish). In 1932 the INS counted 3,812 apprehensions along the Canadian border and 19,072 along the Mexican border. *INS Annual Report*, 1932, p. 44. The INS did not report comparable data in other years.

61. R. M. Cousar, Inspector in Charge at Nogales, circular, May 19, 1928, HR70A-F14.3, box 236, House records; on commuter classification, see *Karnuth v. US*, 279 U.S. 231 (1929);

Many other Mexicans entered legally as "temporary visitors" to work for an agricultural season and then returned to Mexico. According to one estimate, 20 to 30 percent of legal Mexican entrants during the 1920s and 1930s were classified as nonimmigrants—that is, as nonresident aliens intending to stay from six months to a year. The service did not require a passport or visa for such entry from Canada, Mexico, or Cuba, as part of a reciprocal arrangement with those countries. That policy served Americans with business in neighboring countries but was also available to seasonal laborers working in the United States. They had only to pay a refundable head tax. If they failed to depart within the time limit, they became illegal.[62] Immigration policy had thus constructed classifications of entry that supported local and regional labor markets but that were also perceived as opportunities for illegal immigration. The instability of these immigration categories made officials increasingly suspicious of Mexican immigrants.

It was ironic that Mexicans became so associated with illegal immigration because, unlike Europeans, they were not subject to numerical quotas and, unlike Asiatics, they were not excluded as racially ineligible to citizenship. But as numerical restriction assumed primacy in immigration policy, its enforcement aspects—inspection procedures, deportation, the Border Patrol, criminal prosecution, and irregular categories of immigration—created many thousands of illegal Mexican immigrants. The undocumented Mexican laborer who crossed the border to work in the burgeoning industry of commercial agriculture emerged as the prototypical illegal alien.

Administrative Law Reform and the Unmaking of Illegal Aliens

The illegal aliens deported during the late 1920s and early 1930s comprised both unauthorized border crossers and visa violators and those who entered lawfully but committed a deportable offense subsequent to entry. Each category included immigrants who had already settled in the country and acquired jobs, property, and families. These illegal immigrants had in ef-

---

INS Annual Report, 1930, p. 16; Lawrence Herzog, "Border Commuter Workers and Transfrontier Metropolitan Structure along the U.S.-Mexico Border," in *U.S.-Mexico Borderlands: Historical and Contemporary Perspectives,* ed. Oscar Martínez (Wilmington, Del: Scholarly Resources, 1996), 179; on the bath requirement, see José Cruz Burciaga interview by Oscar Martínez, Feb. 16, 1972, transcript of tape 148, Institute of Oral History, University of Texas-El Paso, 20–22.

62. "Immigration Border Patrol," 18; Lawrence Cardoso, *Mexican Emigration to the United States, 1897–1931* (Tucson: University of Arizona Press, 1980), 94; Paul Taylor, "Mexican Labor in the U.S.: Migration Statistics," *University of California Publications in Economics* 6.3 (July 31, 1929): 244.

fect become members of American society. But if their inclusion in the nation was a social reality, it was also a legal impossibility. Resolving that contradiction by means of deportation caused hardship and suffering to these immigrants and their families. It struck many as simply unjust.

Testifying before Congress in 1934, Nicholas Grisanti of the Federation of Italian Societies in Buffalo, New York, cited a typical case of an unjust deportation. An Italian immigrant had lived most of his life in Buffalo. He was married with three small children and was gainfully employed. But, Grisanti explained, "at some previous year he had taken as a boy a half bag of coal from the railroad tracks to help keep his family warm," for which crime he was convicted and given a suspended sentence. Years later, he went to Canada for a summer vacation. The Immigration Service considered his return a "new entry" and ordered him deported, on grounds that he had been convicted of a crime involving moral turpitude before "time of entry." His deportation was thwarted after a public outcry led acting New York Governor Herbert Lehman to pardon the "little offensive."[63]

In a sense, the protest against unjust deportations stemmed from the fact that European and Canadian immigrants had come face-to-face with a system that had historically evolved to justify arbitrary and summary treatment of Chinese and other Asian immigrants. It seemed that the warning sounded by Justice Brewer's dissent in *Fong Yue Ting* had come true. Justice Brewer had acknowledged that the absolute power of the state to expel unwanted aliens was "directed only against the obnoxious Chinese, but," he asked, "if the power exists, who shall say it will not be exercised tomorrow against other classes and other people?"[64]

Indeed, as early as 1920, in the aftermath of the Palmer Raids, legal scholars noted that alleged anarchists in deportation proceedings were deprived of their civil liberties according to the "methods applied in the Chinese deportation cases."[65] After 1924, not only anarchists but also Europeans who unlawfully entered the country were caught in the legal machinery designed for the "obnoxious Chinese."

Thus during the late 1920s and early 1930s a critique of deportation policy emerged among social welfare advocates and legal reformers. They did not directly challenge deportation as a prerogative of the nation's sovereign power, but they did search for ways to reconcile conflicting imperatives of national sovereignty and individual rights. During the early 1930s several legal studies called for administrative law reform in deportation.

63. U.S. Congress, Senate, Committee on Immigration, "Deportation of Criminals, Preservation of Family Units, Permit Noncriminal Aliens to Legalize their Status," 74th Congress, Second Session, Feb. 29, 1934, p. 122.

64. *Fong Yue Ting v. U.S.*, at 743, 737.

65. "Deportation of Aliens (Notes)," *Columbia Law Review* 20 (June 1920): 683.

These included *Deportation of Aliens from the United States to Europe,* by Jane Perry Clark, a Barnard political scientist; a report on deportation by the National Commission on Law Observance and Enforcement (Wickersham Commission); and *Administrative Control of Aliens: A Study in Administrative Law and Procedures,* by William Van Vleck, dean of George Washington University Law School. All three studies based their findings on an examination of actual deportation cases and other administrative records of the Immigration Service.[66]

Clark, Van Vleck, and the Wickersham Commission reached essentially the same two general conclusions. First, they believed deportation policy was applied in arbitrary and unnecessarily harsh ways, resulting in great personal hardship on individuals and in the separation of families, with no social benefit. Second, in terms of procedure, they concluded that deportation policy frequently operated in the breach of established traditions of Anglo American jurisprudence, especially those concerning judicial review and due process. As Lucy Salyer has shown, during the late nineteenth and early twentieth century the federal courts generally upheld the summary character of immigration proceedings. This was despite the principle established by the Supreme Court in 1903 in the *Japanese Immigrant Case* that aliens in immigration proceedings had rights derived from "fundamental principles that inhere in due process of law." By the 1920s aliens had won only a few procedural rights, among them the right to an administrative hearing and the right to counsel.[67] But critics found even these gravely lacking, or undermined by the lack of other procedural safeguards, and cited a broad range of abuses. The Wickersham Commission noted the danger at hand: "The very investigations to see whether suspected persons are subject to deportation, by their nature, involve possible interference of the gravest kind with the rights of personal liberty . . . These investigations are not public, and they often involve American citizens."[68]

Specifically, critics charged, aliens were often "forcibly detained." The boards of special inquiry, which conducted formal deportation hearings, were often one-man tribunals, with the immigration inspector often appearing simultaneously as arresting officer, prosecutor, and judge.[69] The boards

66. Clark, *Deportation of Aliens;* U.S. National Commission on Law Observance and Enforcement, *Report on the Enforcement of the Deportation Laws of the United States* (Washington, D.C.: GPO, 1931) (hereafter "Wickersham Report"); Van Vleck, *Administrative Control.*

67. Lucy Salyer, *Laws Harsh as Tigers: Chinese Immigrants and the Shaping of Modern Immigration Law* (Chapel Hill: University of North Carolina Press, 1995), 172–83; *Japanese Immigrant Case* (*Yamata v. Fisher*), 189 U.S. 86 (1903).

68. Wickersham Report, 29.

69. Van Vleck, *Administrative Control,* 26, 90–95; Wickersham Report, 65, 157–58, 170–71.

operated without rules of evidence, readily admitting hearsay, opinion, anonymous letters, and "confidential information." The alien also bore the burden of proof "to show cause . . . why he should not be deported." One study found that only one-sixth of aliens in deportation proceedings had legal representation, ranging from 1 or 2 percent along the Mexican border to 20 percent in New York City.[70]

Moreover, the service interpreted the statute in ways that grossly stretched the law's meaning in order to justify grounds for deportation. For example, it interpreted "entry without proper inspection" to cover not only aliens who circumvented inspection but also instances where the examining inspector had failed to ask a question that would have revealed the alien's excludability.[71] The greatest abuse surrounded the application of the provision "liable to become a public charge at time of entry," or "LPC," which, Clark said, was "shaken on deportation cases as though with a large pepper shaker." The service deported immigrants who committed minor crimes or violated norms of sexual morality, such as bearing children out of wedlock, which were not deportable offenses, on grounds that they were "LPC before entry." In other words, the Immigration Service considered lapses or misfortune subsequent to entry to be the teleological outcome of a prior condition, which it adduced by way of retroactive judgment.[72]

Finally, immigrants under warrants of deportation had few avenues of appeal. The Labor Department's board of review, which made recommendations to the secretary of labor, had no statutory authority. Judicial review was extremely rare because the federal courts historically practiced great restraint in immigration cases, having progressively narrowed the grounds for judicial review in Chinese exclusion cases over the years. During the late 1920s and 1930s the courts heard fewer than three hundred writs of habeas corpus in deportation cases and found nearly 70 percent of them in favor of the Immigration Service.[73]

The legal critique of deportation policy evinced the preoccupations of legal realism during the years between the two world wars: a rejection of categorical thinking and a desire to transform differences of kind into differences of degree; the privileging of experience over formal logic; and, consequently, a belief in the need for administrative discretion in the emerging regulatory state.[74] According to the legal critics, deportation policy

70. Van Vleck, *Administrative Control,* 99–100, 107; Clark, *Deportation of Aliens,* 324; Kohler, *Immigration and Aliens,* 413; Wickersham Report, 107–8.

71. Van Vleck, *Administrative Control,* 237.

72. Clark, *Deportation of Aliens,* 309; Van Vleck, *Administrative Control,* 97–98, 119–25.

73. *INS Annual Report,* 1928–1932; Secretary of Labor, *Annual Report,* 1933–1936.

74. Morton Horwitz, *The Transformation of American Law: The Critique of Legal Orthodoxy, 1870–1960* (New York: Oxford University Press, 1992), 189, 199.

seemed to be law gone amok. They believed that the problem perhaps came less from politics than from the administration of law based on rigid categories without room for discretion or experience. Because the main thrust of the criticisms concerned problems in procedure and enforcement, administrative law reform provided an alternative, less contentious route for reforming deportation policy than the more overtly political tack taken by liberal social welfare and immigration advocates. The latter had few friends in Congress during the Depression, when work was scarce and there were renewed calls for restriction and deportations. In fact, the gaze of administrative law reformers was aimed not so much at Congress as it was toward the judiciary, where they believed progress might be made in more clearly defining the limits of executive power in matters of deportation.[75]

Yet embedded in the arguments for administrative law reform was a powerful political critique. That critique challenged the eugenical premises of immigration policy, that is, the idea that social undesirability derived from innate character deficiencies, which were perceived to be rooted biologically in race, gender, or "bad blood." In a sense, administrative law reform was a stalking horse for a broader cultural challenge to nativist politics, challenging, in particular, late nineteenth- and early twentieth-century theories about social degeneracy and, more specifically, ideas about gender roles, sexual morality, and crime. These normative standards of social desirability and moral fitness for citizenship continued to define the qualitative standards for immigrant admission and deportation in the Immigration Act of 1924, even as they were eclipsed by the law's new emphasis on numerical restriction. In the late 1920s and 1930s legal critics challenged the application of these qualitative standards in deportation cases.

The trend may be discerned from a reading of William Van Vleck's treatise, *Administrative Control of Aliens,* published in 1932. *Administrative Control* followed several lines of criticism that challenged traditional ideas about female dependency and sexual morality. Van Vleck cited several cases in which the Immigration Service had ordered women deported as LPC because they were without male support, even though the women were employed and self-supporting. In one case, the service deported a woman whose husband became ill with tuberculosis fourteen months after they arrived in the U.S., on grounds that she was dependent on her husband—even though she was employed. Van Vleck cited other cases of single mothers supporting their children or living with other relatives. He recognized that the family was a diverse institution that included female-headed households and extended families.[76]

75. *The Nation,* April 29, 1931, p. 463; Note, "Statutory Construction in Deportation Cases," *Yale Law Journal* 40 (1931): 1283.

76. Van Vleck, *Administrative Control,* 126–27, 136–37.

Van Vleck also opposed the state assuming the role of sex police, stating, "[T]here appears from time to time evidence of a tendency on the part of some of the immigration officers to regard themselves as charged with the duty and the authority of exercising a general supervision of conduct and morals over our alien population." He evinced unease at the deportation of aliens on grounds of fornication, adultery, lewd and lascivious carriage, and other sexual activities. In some of these cases aliens were deported because state laws considered their transgressions to be crimes of moral turpitude; others were judged as LPC at time of entry.[77]

In line with modern thinking that considered crime environmentally, Van Vleck judged adultery and other moral transgressions to be social problems, not indications of deficiencies in character. He criticized as flawed reasoning the conclusion that "violations of the moral code by young men and women" were "evidence of 'criminal tendencies' or of a 'weak moral nature,'" which rendered them LPC at time of entry. He cited as an example the case of a young immigrant woman who had two illegitimate children during the first two years of residence in the United States. He said, "Evidence in the record tend[s] to show that before her entry . . . she had been well behaved and had lived quietly with her mother. . . . In fact, her morals were entirely controlled by outside forces."[78]

At another level, the issue of sexual morality was linked to notions about family privacy. Deportation cases involving adultery and other crimes of immorality were almost always connected to angry relatives or jealous suitors who had contacted authorities.[79] In a turn from Progressive-era thinking that advocated state intervention in the family, Van Vleck deplored the use of LPC in cases of "family rows leading to unproved accusations by angry spouses, parents, or relatives."[80] (These cases also indicate the heightened sensitivity among immigrants that individuals could use the power of the state to intervene in personal disputes—"calling Immigration," as it were.)

The idea of the family's privacy was connected to its sanctity. One of the most tragic consequences of deportation, Van Vleck argued, was the separation of families. He pointed out, "If [the deported alien] is a poor man his wife and children have not the money to follow him. Even if they have the money and do follow him, this may mean the expatriation of American citizens."[81] Similarly, Max Kohler, a former assistant attorney

77. Ibid., 119, 125, 236.

78. Ibid., 124–25.

79. A district immigration director told Clark that a majority of deportation cases stemmed from so-called "grudge reports." Clark, *Deportation of Aliens,* 324.

80. Van Vleck, *Administrative Control,* 124.

81. Ibid., 29.

general who represented many immigrants, invoked the Supreme Court's 1923 ruling *Meyer v. Nebraska* to oppose the separation of family by immigration restrictions. In *Meyer* the court claimed that the scope of individual liberty included the right of individuals "to marry, establish a home and bring up children . . . without interference from the state," anticipating the Supreme Court's decision decades later that located in *Meyer* the precedent for defining privacy to be a fundamental right.[82]

While Kohler posited family unity in fundamental terms of personal liberty, most reformers constructed a more conditional context for family rights. They utilized a cost-benefit analysis, which weighed violations of the immigration law that were technical or not substantively harmful to the public good against family separation that resulted either in the forced expatriation of dependents (often United States citizens) or in leaving them without support, making them public charges. The proverbial poor man's theft of a loaf of bread or sack of coal became a favorite of reform discourse. In this telling, family trumped both the original crime and the looming deportation. The family here was cast in the traditional patriarchal mode, in which the male head of the household is heroic because he breaks the law and risks imprisonment for his family's welfare. But Van Vleck's narrative also depicted unmarried women with children as legitimate families that were worthy of preservation. The trope of stealing to feed one's family ranked loyalty to one's family above one's obligation to the state. Van Vleck extended this idea of loyalty to protect family members who suffered from moral lapses.

Van Vleck's views were not isolated but articulated a trend among legal scholars and in the federal courts as well. In 1931 *Yale Law Journal* noted a trend in the federal circuit courts of appeal that recognized the "severe consequences" of restricting judicial review in matters of exclusion and expulsion. These cases suggested the need for "a more exacting construction of the due process rights of an alien and a more restricted construction of the statutory grounds upon which deportation orders may be based." The journal noted that courts were throwing out LPC cases that were "obviously grotesque." In one case the court overturned an order to deport a self-supporting Swedish woman living in California on grounds of a mis-

82. Kohler, *Immigration and Aliens,* 38; *Meyer v. Nebraska,* 262 U.S. 390 (1923); *Griswold v. Connecticut,* 381 U.S. 479 (1965). In *Immigration Commissioner of Port of N.Y. v. Gottleib,* 265 U.S. 310 (1924), the Court rejected the argument that family unification could override the quota law. However, Congress acknowledged the primacy of family unity by giving non-quota status to the wives and minor children of U.S. citizens in the Immigration Act of 1924. On the Supreme Court's use of *Meyer* to invent a tradition in support of family rights, see Martha Minow, "We the Family: Constitutional Rights and American Families," *Journal of American History* 74 (Dec. 1987): 959–83.

demeanor involving moral turpitude (cohabitation) and LPC. In a remarkable recognition of gender equality, the court said that, "as to her lapses [from virtue], not amounting to prostitution, the petitioner stands exactly in the same position before the court as would a man who was similarly charged. . . . [The] petitioner then may not be excluded on this ground, unless the paramour, if an alien, could be excluded under the same circumstances." By the early 1930s the Immigration Service tempered its use of LPC. The trend benefited Europeans and Canadians, who had comprised the vast majority of LPC deportation cases. The deportation of Europeans and Canadians as LPC dropped from a high of nearly 2,000 in 1924 to fewer than 500 in 1932.[83]

During this period the courts made other refinements in deportation law. They clarified that conviction of a crime "before entry" referred to crimes committed outside the United States before the immigrant's first entry into the country. Other cases eliminated criminal misconduct from the public charge category according to Judge Learned Hand's reasoning that public charge suggested "dependency not delinquency" and that LPC should not be used to deport people for petty crimes that were not deportable offenses. Echoing Justice Brewer's dissent in *Fong Yue Ting,* Judge Hand likened deportation to exile, "a dreadful punishment, abandoned by the common consent of all civilized people."[84]

The appeal to prevent family separation was particularly effective in areas where European immigrants were numerous and had some political influence. In New York many convicted felons received executive pardons after they served their prison terms, in order to prevent their deportation, including the Italian man in Buffalo who stole a half sack of coal when he was a boy. Governor Herbert Lehman granted 110 such pardons during his tenure.[85]

Although executive pardons and federal court rulings addressed some of the problems in deportation policy, these fell short of clarifying a uniform national policy. In the early 1930s the Immigration Service remained resistant to the idea that it should relieve aliens' families of hardship, citing its "plain duty of ridding the country of those uninvited guests who have 'crashed the gate.'" As for the "alleged hardship to the alien . . . or to his family," the

83. "Statutory Construction in Deportation Cases," 1236–37; Emma Wold, "Alien Women vs. the Immigration Bureau," *Survey,* Nov. 15, 1927, p. 217; *INS Annual Reports,* 1925–1932.

84. *Browne v. Zubrick,* 45 F. 2d 931 (CAA 6th 1930); *Iorio v. Day,* 34 F. 2d 920 (CAA 2d 1929); see also *Lisotta v. U.S.,* 3 F. 2d 108 (CAA 5th 1924); *U.S. ex rel. Klonis v. Davis,* 13 F. 2d 630 (CAA 2d 1926).

85. "Pardons and Commutations," *Public Papers of Governor Herbert S. Lehman,* 1933–1942.

service pointed out the primacy of "the hardships inflicted upon the American citizen and lawfully resident and law-abiding alien in their exposure to the competition in employment of opportunities of bootlegged aliens."[86]

In 1933 and 1934 liberals adopted a new legislative strategy for immigration reform, which proceeded simultaneously along two tracks: one that proposed to impose yet harsher sanctions on criminals and one that proposed to prevent family separation in cases that were "exceptionally meritorious." Legislation introduced in 1933 and 1934 linked the two issues within a single bill. This strategy gave reformers political cover by demonstrating their commitment to restriction and against criminals while arguing for compassion for "relatively harmless and deserving people."[87]

Just who were the criminals and who were the deserving, however, was under realignment. Since the Progressive era relativism and environmentalism had grown increasingly influential in thinking about criminal and moral deviance. There was also broader social support for the idea that people who made mistakes could be reformed. Speaking against the 1929 law that forever barred readmission after deportation, Jane Addams pointed out, "To make an old mistake indelible—to lay a dead hand on the future, is always of doubtful value." Thus petty crimes and sexual transgressions, once deemed evidence of innate character deficiency, could now be considered "more or less innocent [offenses] against the immigration law," falling below the bar set for deportation. Deportation for minor offenses was now considered punitive and unjust.[88]

The discourse on unjust deportation referred mostly to European immigrants and only occasionally to Mexicans. Ethnic Mexicans in the United States voiced the same concerns as did Europeans; for example, the Los Angeles Spanish-language newspaper *La Opinión* criticized the deportation of Mexicans who had ten years of residence in the U.S., businesses, and family.[89] But Mexicans remained marginalized from the mainstream of immigration discourse. Among Euro-American reformers, references to immigrants of good moral character were usually not racially explicit, but by definition such immigrants were unlikely to be Mexican because "Mexican" had been constructed as a negative racial category. More important, reformers did not call for leniency in cases of unlawful entry, because this was a core component of the system based on numerical restriction, *which*

86. *INS Annual Report,* 1931, pp. 13–14.

87. Secretary of Labor, *Annual Report,* 1934, p. 53.

88. Morton Keller, *Regulating a New Society: Public Policy and Social Change in America, 1900–1933* (Cambridge, Mass.: Harvard University Press, 1994), chaps. 3–4; Addams quoted in *Survey,* July 15, 1930, p. 347; *Interpreter,* April 1929, p. 76.

89. "Frequent Deportation of Mexicans," *La Opinión,* Jan. 30, 1929, p. 2 (translated from Spanish).

none of them directly opposed. In contrast to environmentalist and relativist notions of crime, the idea of transgressing the nation's sovereign space stood out as an absolute offense. Thus, while European immigrants with criminal records could be constructed as "deserving," Mexicans who were apprehended without proper documents had little chance of escaping either the stigma of criminalization or the fate of deportation.

Legislative and administrative reforms operated in ways that fueled racial disparity in deportation practices. In 1929 Congress passed the Registry Act, which legalized the status of "honest law-abiding alien[s] who may be in the country under some merely technical irregularity." The law allowed immigrants to register as permanent residents for a fee of twenty dollars if they could show that they had resided in the country continuously since 1921 and were of good moral character.[90] The law did not formally favor Europeans over Mexicans. But, of the 115,000 immigrants who registered their prior entries into the country between 1930 and 1940, eighty percent were European or Canadian. According to Berkeley economist Paul S. Taylor, many Mexicans qualified for an adjustment of status under the Registry Act but few knew about it, understood it, or could afford the fee.[91]

During the 1930s and 1940s the Labor Department instituted a series of reforms that addressed, albeit in limited ways, questions of due process in deportation proceedings and established administrative mechanisms whereby certain illegal aliens—mostly Europeans—could legalize their status. Immigration and administrative law reformers welcomed the administration of Franklin D. Roosevelt in 1933. Roosevelt's secretary of labor, Frances Perkins, was a New York Progressive-era reformer and the new head of the INS, Daniel W. MacCormack, was the first immigration commissioner who did not come directly from organized labor.[92] Perkins and MacCormack took seriously the criticisms that had been mounting against the Immigration Service's practices. The secretary noted that "much odium attached to the Service due to [its] policies and methods" in deportations.[93]

Perkins also appointed a civilian panel to investigate the practices of the INS. The Ellis Island Committee included northern urban elites noted for their charitable work among immigrants, like Mrs. E. Marshall Field and

90. *INS Annual Report,* 1925, pp. 12–13; Act of March 2, 1929 (45 Stat. 1551).

91. *INS Annual Report,* 1930–1932; Secretary of Labor, *Annual Report,* 1933–1940; Paul S. Taylor, "Mexican Labor in the U.S.: Dimmit County, Winter Garden District, South Texas," *University of California Publications in Economics* 6 (1930): 322.

92. On Perkins, see George Martin, *Madam Secretary: Frances Perkins* (Boston: Houghton Mifflin, 1976). MacCormack came from an elite New York family. He was a cousin of Eleanor Roosevelt, a banker, and former diplomat. I am grateful to Marian Smith for biographical information on MacCormack.

93. Secretary of Labor, *Annual Report,* 1934, p. 50.

Mrs. Vincent Astor, and immigrant advocates such as Max Kohler and Read Lewis of the Foreign Language Information Service. The committee's report, issued in March 1934, echoed the criticisms made by Van Vleck and the Wickersham Commission. In particular, it emphasized the need for administrative discretion to not deport in cases "deemed to involve extraordinary hardship, such as where deportation would involve the disruption of a family."[94]

In 1934 Perkins and MacCormack instituted a series of administrative reforms at the INS. One line of reform concerned procedures and due process. The INS discontinued the practice of arresting suspected aliens without warrant at places removed from the actual time and place of entry. It also mandated that the same officer could not conduct the preliminary examination and the final hearing.[95]

A second type of reform concerned the use of administrative discretion to grant relief from deportation for aliens for whom deportation would cause hardship. At one level, MacCormack undertook an intense effort to lobby Congress to pass legislation that provided for discretionary relief from deportation in "meritorious" cases. He stated, the "[immigration laws] are so rigid that at times they defeat their purpose and . . . sometimes result in extreme hardship and injustice both to the alien and to the innocent relatives of the alien." Giving discretionary relief was not a question of "sentimentality," MacCormack said, but necessary to prevent the creation of public charges.[96] MacCormack believed, moreover, that "illegal entry in itself is not a criterion on character." To the contrary, he said, "the mother who braces the hardship and danger frequently involved in an illegal entry for purpose of rejoining her children cannot be held by that sole act to be a person of bad character."[97]

But Congressional action would be slow in coming. Although Democrats now controlled Congress, the party's southern wing served as a conservative block against reform in immigration matters. In the context of economic emergency posed by the Depression, immigration reform was not high on Roosevelt's list of legislative priorities. Without statutory reform, Perkins and

94. *Report of the Ellis Island Committee* (New York [n.p.], 1934), 77, 87.

95. Secretary of Labor, *Annual Report,* 1934, pp. 50–52.

96. D. W. MacCormack, "Memorandum of the Commissioner of Immigration and Naturalization to the Committee on Immigration of the Senate and the Committee of Immigration and Naturalization of the House of Representatives, Relative to Certain Proposed Changes in the Immigration Law," April 24, 1934, p. 2; U.S. Senate, Committee on Immigration, "Deportation of Criminals, Preservation of Family Units, Permit Noncriminal Aliens to Legalize their Status," 74th Congress, Second Session, Feb. 24, 29, March 3, 11, 1934, pp. 16, 198.

97. "Deportation of Criminals," 218–19.

MacCormack creatively used provisions of existing law to suspend deportations and to legalize the status of certain illegal immigrants in hardship cases. This involved a two-step procedure whereby the secretary of labor granted the illegal alien a waiver from deportation and allowed him or her to depart to Canada and to reenter the U.S. as a legal permanent resident.

The secretary granted waivers by invoking an obscure clause of the Immigration Act of 1917, the Seventh Proviso to Section 3, which stipulated that "aliens returning after a temporary absence to an unrelinquished United States domicile of seven consecutive years may be admitted in the discretion of the Attorney General and under such conditions as he may prescribe." Congress intended the Seventh Proviso as a hardship measure for aliens who were temporarily out of the country when the Immigration Act of 1917 was passed and who, for reasons often technical in nature, were excludable upon their return.[98] Perkins's innovation was to use the concept "returning after a temporary absence" to apply to aliens who had not yet departed and to include in its scope illegal aliens who "have lived here a long time." By invoking the Seventh Proviso to waive deportations Perkins reverted to the central principle of pre-1924 immigration policy inherent in the statute of limitation on deportation, the idea that immigrants who have settled in the country should not be expelled.[99]

The process of readjustment of status was known as the "pre-examination" procedure. Since 1933 the INS had granted letters to legal aliens going to Canada for short visits assuring them of reentry, providing that they were first examined and found admissible by immigration inspectors. It began as a gesture of courtesy that allowed legal aliens departing temporarily to avoid the necessity of applying for a formal reentry permit. The Canadian authorities also required written assurance that the visitors would not remain in Canada. The practice became known in INS parlance as "pre-examination"—that is, inspection for readmission before departure.[100]

In 1935 pre-examination was extended to illegal immigrants to facilitate

98. Immigration Act of 1917 (39 Stat. 874). The 1917 act included twelve provisos, or exceptions, to the law's rules of exclusion. See Senate Report 352, 64th Congress, First Session, p. 6, on the Seventh Proviso as a hardship clause. See also Letter, Frances Perkins to Rep. Dave Batterfield, Jr., Sept. 17, 1940, file Immigration, General, 1940, box 66, Secretary's General Subject Files, Records of the Dept. of Labor, RG 174, National Archives (College Park) (hereafter "Perkins papers").

99. Perkins to Batterfield; Memorandum, Attorney General to Rufus Holman, Jan. 4, 1943, p. 4, file 55819/402D, box 75, accession 58A734, INS.

100. Memoranda, A. M. Doig, Acting District Director Detroit to Commissioner General, Sept. 7, 1933; MacCormack to District Directors, Newport [VT], Buffalo, NY, Detroit, Grand Forks [ND], and Seattle, Dec. 18, 1933, file 55819/402, box 75, accession 58A734, INS. Pre-examination as described here is distinguished from the INS policy of "pre-inspection," which refers to inspection abroad before emigration.

their legalization. A formal agreement between the U.S. Department of State and Immigration Service and their Canadian counterparts detailed procedures whereby an immigrant in the U.S. without a visa could be "pre-examined" for legal admission, leave the country as a "voluntary departure," proceed to the nearest American consul in Canada, obtain a visa for permanent residence, and reenter the United States formally as a legal admission.[101]

The INS thus suspended state territoriality in order to unmake the illegal status of certain immigrants. Although the whole procedure was a bureaucratic arrangement, the INS and State Department would not simply issue new documents granting an alien's legal status. The alien had to cooperate by physically leaving and reentering the country, to enact a voluntary departure and a legal admission. Some aliens failed to understand the necessity of the performance (or could not afford to make the trip to Canada) and wondered why, if it was willing to adjust their status, the INS would not simply leave them alone.[102]

The pre-examination program was an ad-hoc procedure, which officials made up as they went along, both broadening and narrowing its scope. Eventually it was routinized and written into the Code of Federal Regulations.[103] It was initially meant for immigrants who had a U.S.-citizen spouse or children and whose illegal status resulted from technical error. This was an uncontroversial political calculus in which preventing hardship for citizens easily trumped deportation for trivial causes. But "hardship" proved to be an elastic concept, another version of the notion of "deserving." It was quickly extended to certain types of criminal cases, or, more precisely, to certain criminals. A typical case involved Mrs. Lillian Joann Flake, who was charged with theft in 1918 and 1922 and larceny (shoplifting) in 1930. A native Canadian, she lived in the U.S. for more than seventeen years and had a husband and daughter in Chicago. In another case, the INS argued on behalf of Carlos Reali, an Italian, "in view of the fact that the alien is married to a native of the United States and that there are three American-born children." His record, added the INS, was good, notwithstanding his acquiring a visa by fraud and perjury in 1924. The INS vacated Flake's, Reali's, and hundreds of others' orders of deportation, allowing them to depart the country voluntarily and obtain a legal visa for readmission.[104]

101. Dept. of Immigration and Colonization [Canada], Official Circular no. 31, Feb. 23, 1935; MacCormack to A. L. Jolliffee, Commissioner of Immigration [Canada], Oct. 21, 1935, file 55819/402, INS.

102. Letter, Perkins to Mrs. Roosevelt, Jan. 27, 1939, file "Immigration-Deportations 1939," box 69, Perkins papers.

103. 8 CFR pt. 142.

104. Letter, James Houghterling to Sen. James Lewis, April 20, 1938, file 55819/402B, box 75, accession 58A734, INS; I. F. Wixon to Secretary of State, Nov. 8, 1937, file 55819/402A, ibid.

Restrictionists in Congress criticized the secretary for "granting waivers to lawbreakers" and "exerting unusual efforts to protect and keep without our borders hundreds of deportable foreigners branded as criminals." One angry senator counted 119 such cases in 1937 and a congressman cited nearly seven hundred cases in 1940. Perkins defended the practice, stating that in most cases the crimes committed "amounted only to violations of law committed many years ago and were counterbalanced by long periods of good moral conduct and useful service in the community."[105]

In 1940, when Congress moved the INS from the Department of Labor to the Department of Justice, the INS continued the pre-examination program. In 1943, defending the use of the Seventh Proviso, the attorney general stated that the "American sense of justice and fair play" ought to "respect [the alien's] rehabilitation and not to brand and treat him as a criminal perpetually."[106] Although the attorney general claimed that the INS did not grant waivers to criminals convicted of serious offenses, in fact Seventh Proviso and pre-examination cases included those involving fraudulent naturalization, larceny, bigamy, rape, even manslaughter. The only cases that were denied relief appear to be those involving alleged anarchists and smugglers.[107]

"Hardship" also extended beyond cases involving aliens with a U.S.-citizen spouse or child. By the early 1940s suspension of deportation and pre-examination were available to aliens with a legally resident alien relative, those with long-term residence in the U.S., and "exceptionally meritorious" cases, the latter constituting a general loophole.[108] The expanding grounds for eligibility suggest a policy grounded in the idea that what mattered most was not the immigrant's formal status but his or her presence and ties in the community. This was a remarkable acknowledgment that undercut the premises of restriction and territoriality.

Significantly, however, the privilege of pre-examination became restricted to European immigrants. Asiatics did not qualify, because they were categorically excluded from immigration on grounds of racial ineligibili-

105. Sen. Robert Reynolds to James Houghterling, April 4, 1938, file 55819/402B, box 75, accession 58A734, INS; "Seven Hundred Deportable Aliens Sheltered by U.S. Labor Department," *Congressional Record*, Oct. 10, 1940, pp. 20424–28; Perkins to Batterfield, Sept. 17, 1940.

106. Attorney General to Sen. Rufus C. Holman, Jan. 4, 1943, file 55819/402D, INS.

107. I. F. Wixon to Secretary of State, Nov. 8, 1937; "Summary of cases listed on page 47 of the State Dept. Appropriation Bill, 1939, with particular reference to the nature of the crimes involving moral turpitude in connection with which the Seventh Proviso to Section 3 of the 1917 Act was invoked by the Secretary of Labor," file 55819/402A, INS; "Seven Hundred Deportable Aliens Sheltered by U.S. Labor Department."

108. Five or more years of residence was required for those without citizen or legally resident alien spouse, parent, or minor child; one year of residence was required of the latter. Memorandum, Savoretti to A. R. Mackey, March 27, 1946, file 55819/402D, INS.

ty.[109] Mexicans were not initially excluded. After MacCormack formalized the pre-examination procedure, INS El Paso district director Grover Wilmoth implemented the procedure for Mexican hardship cases. But in 1938 he became stonewalled by the American consul in Juárez, William Blocker, who argued that those applying for visas at Juárez "were of the laboring class, some of them actually on relief." They should, he said, "unquestionably" be denied visas. In fact the INS Board of Special Inquiry had ruled in Canadian pre-examination cases that receipt of relief during the Depression, when no work was available, was not evidence of LPC. Blocker deliberately slowed the work of processing visas for Mexican pre-examination cases to only a handful a month in order to frustrate Wilmoth's efforts to grant relief to Mexican cases.[110]

I found no evidence that Wilmoth's higher-ups in the INS argued with the State Department for a fair application of the policy; rather, the INS seems to have quickly scuttled the program for Mexicans.[111] It clarified that the "general pre-examination procedure is limited to certain aliens—relatives of U.S. citizens—desiring to proceed to *Canada.*" Later documents conspicuously referred to the program as the "Canadian pre-examination procedure." Thus, initially, Mexicans were excluded not explicitly but by a lack of propinquity, by their distance from Canada, where physical departure and reentry were performed. In 1945 the INS explicitly restricted pre-examination to "other than a citizen of Canada, Mexico, or any of the islands adjacent to the U.S." This policy appeared to be race-neutral in that it applied to all countries with contiguous borders to the U.S., but in fact it was meant to categorically deny relief to Mexicans and Caribbean migrants. Because pre-examination involved permission for temporary entry into Canada to acquire the U.S. visa, it was irrelevant to Canadians, who did not need special permission to enter Canada.[112]

The racism of the policy was profound, for it denied, *a priori,* that de-

109. Perkins apparently wished to help Asians but the law tied her hands. For example, see the case of Ramkrishana Sakharan Jivotode, in letter, Perkins to Josephus Daniels, April 22, 1940, file Immigration-Deportation, 1940, box 67, Perkins papers.

110. Memoranda, G. C. Wilmoth to Commissioner General, Nov. 3, 1938; William Blocker to Secretary of State, Nov. 3, 1938; Wilmoth to Commissioner General, Nov. 29, 1938, file 55819/402C, box 75, accession 58A734, INS.

111. MacCormack died suddenly in 1937. It is possible that, had he lived, he would have fought for a universal application of the pre-examination program.

112. G. C. Wilmoth to all inspectors in charge and chief patrol inspectors, El Paso District (draft) [1938], file 55819/402C (emphasis in original); formal application form [1942] and Part 142 of Immigration Regulations, 1943, file 55819/402D; Ugo Carusi to Tom Clark, Oct. 15, 1945, ibid.; U.S. Senate, Report of Committee of the Judiciary, "Immigration and Naturalization Systems of the U.S.," 81st Congress, Second Session, Senate Report 1515, April 20, 1950 (hereafter "Senate Report 1515"), p. 604.

portation could cause hardship for the families of non-Europeans. In stressing family values, moreover, the policy recognized only one kind of family, the intact nuclear family residing in the United States, and ignored transnational families. It failed to recognize that many undocumented male migrants who came to the United States alone in fact maintained family households in their home country and that migration remittance was another kind of strategy for family subsistence.

For Europeans, however, the policy was clearly a boon. In fact, pre-examination became an official and routine procedure for adjusting the status of Europeans who were not legally present in the United States.[113] By the early 1940s pre-examination was used to help adjust the status of refugees from European fascism who had entered the United States in the 1930s by way of tourist or visitor visas.[114] Pre-examination continued with only two brief interruptions until the practice was terminated in 1958. The data indicate that between 1935 and 1959 the INS processed nearly 58,000 pre-examination cases and granted approval in the vast majority of them.[115]

Apart from pre-examination, the INS began to suspend orders of deportation after 1940, when Congress gave the attorney general authority to grant discretionary relief as part of the Alien Registration Act. Discretionary relief appears to be a concession granted in exchange for alien registration, which had been long opposed but passed as a wartime measure. The 1940 law allowed for the suspension of deportation in cases involving aliens of good moral character if deportation would result in "serious economic detriment" to the alien's immediate family. It excluded alien anarchists, convicted narcotics dealers, and the "immoral classes," the latter comprising prostitutes and the mentally ill. "Good moral character" did not pre-

113. The INS created special forms for applications in January 1941 (I-55, I-255, and I-155). For a description of the application procedure, see Common Council for American Unity, "An Immigration Summary: Outstanding Facts about the Admission, Exclusion, and Deportation of Aliens," June 1941, pp. 20–21.

114. Henry L. Feingold, *The Politics of Rescue: The Roosevelt Administration and the Holocaust, 1938–1945* (New Brunswick, N.J.: Rutgers University Press, 1970), 17; Divine, *American Immigration Policy,* 103–4.

115. For pre-examination data, see *INS Annual Reports* 1942–1959; see also Senate Report 1515. Pre-examination was suspended in 1940 for about one year, as a wartime "internal security" precaution. See Attorney General to Sen. Rufus C. Holman, Jan. 4, 1943. It was reinstituted but then discontinued in 1952 because the McCarran Walter Act (66 Stat. 163) provided statutory relief for illegal aliens who entered by way of fraud or misrepresentation, who were otherwise admissible, and who had immediate family in the U.S. Sec. 241(f), amended 71 Stat. 640 (1957). Pre-examination was reinstituted again in 1955 as a remedy to the flood of private legislation brought by illegal aliens whom the INS denied relief under 241(f). However, Congress imposed narrower grounds for pre-examination, limiting it to persons who had acquired eligibility for non-quota status as the spouse or child of a U.S. citizen. See *INS Annual Report* 1955. Since 1961 relief in fraud cases has been at the Attorney General's discretion. 75 Stat. 657 (Act of Sept. 26, 1961), now 8 USC 1182(i) (2000).

clude having a criminal record, but referred to "reputation which will pass muster with the average man [that] need not rise above the level of the common mass of people."[116]

The INS suspended the deportations of several thousand aliens a year from 1941 through the late 1950s.[117] An internal Justice Department study of 389 randomly selected cases conducted in 1943 revealed that 45.8 percent involved seamen, 18.3 percent involved visitors (visa overstays), and 10.5 percent involved border crossers. The overwhelming majority (73 percent) was of European origin (mostly German and Italian). Only 8 percent of the cases involved Mexicans.[118]

As for alien registration, the 1940 law required fingerprinting and yearly registration of all aliens resident in the United States. While clearly a wartime measure, the INS took pains to reassure immigrants that their loyalty was not under question, calling registration an "inventory" or a measure of prudence dictated by national security. This was, perhaps, aimed at securing the cooperation of the nation's four million foreign-born residents. But the nativism that had fueled earlier demands for compulsory alien registration was now displaced by more pluralist views. Speaking in Los Angeles in August 1940, Assistant Secretary of Labor Marshall Dimock explained alien registration as part of the nation's "defense program," but emphasized that national unity was the key to the nation's security. Americans must be vigilant "to discourage any tendency toward setting a particular group from others" based on differences of religion, color, economic status, or alienage. The "blue-eyed, flaxen haired farmer from Wisconsin, Minnesota, and the Dakotas," he said, "who in scores of cases have lived here most of their lives but who for one reason or another are not technically Americans . . . are as good Americans as we are." And, in what was becoming a familiar rhetorical move, Dimock underscored his call to embrace these noncitizens with a call for vigilance against undesirables. "Our immigration laws are being enforced as vigilantly as possible," he said. "We are constantly tightening up our border defenses against undesirable aliens; we have strengthened our deportation machinery; and in cooperation with other designated agencies we have armed ourselves to cope with subversive activities."[119]

In general, despite various reforms, change was limited and slow. Dis-

116. Act of June 28, 1940 (54 Stat. 670). For discussion on "good moral character" in suspension of deportation cases see Senate Report 1515, p. 596.

117. Published data for 1941–1960 indicate a total of 34,632 suspensions of deportation. See *INS Annual Reports,* 1941–1960.

118. Memorandum, Helen F. Eckerson, Statistical Unit to L. Paul Winings, General Counsel, March 12, 1946, file 55819/402D.

119. Transcript of speech by Marshall Dimock, "Security Within," delivered to Veterans of Foreign Wars, Los Angeles, August 27, 1940; file "Immigration-Naturalization," box 66, Perkins papers.

cretionary relief from deportation became incorporated into immigration law in the Immigration and Naturalization Act of 1952.[120] But throughout the 1950s and early 1960s, almost no progress was made in matters of due process and judicial review. The INS exempted itself from the Administrative Procedures Act (APA), which Congress passed in 1946. The Supreme Court ruled in 1950 (*Wong Yang Sung v. McGrath*) that deportation proceedings were of a judicial character requiring a fair hearing and ordered the INS to adhere to the terms of the APA, notably the separation of functions, that is, that the investigating inspector (prosecutor) could not be the hearing officer (judge). The INS reported a drop in the number of deportations of illegal Mexican immigrants from 16,903 in 1949 to 3,319 in 1950, as a result of the *Sung* decision. But Congress acted quickly to nullify *Sung* and to restore the INS's ability to deport efficiently by granting the INS statutory exemption to the APA. Indeed, if during the New Deal and World War II immigration officials showed an interest in administrative reform in areas of due process, their successors were generally impervious to it.[121]

Conclusion

Numerical restriction legislated in the 1920s displaced qualitative reasons for inclusion and exclusion with criteria that were at once more abstract and arbitrary—the quota slot and the proper visa. Previously, territoriality had been exercised to exclude people not deemed fit to be part of the nation. In the 1920s qualitative norms of desirability remained in the law as grounds for inclusion and expulsion but, as we have seen, they were employed in deportation cases less often than was the rule of documentation and, moreover, they were applied irregularly and with considerable discretion. As qualitative norms receded in importance, territoriality—defining and policing the national space—became both the means and the ends of immigration policy.

120. The basic terms of the Seventh Proviso were incorporated into Sec. 212(c) of the Immigration and Naturalization Act of 1952, 66 Stat. 163. It remained in the law until 1996, when it was eliminated. Suspension of deportation was incorporated into Sec. 244(a) of the INA. It remains in law although the grounds for it are now very narrow.

121. Administrative Procedures Act, Act of June 11, 1946 (60 Stat. 237); *Wong Yang Sung v. McGrath,* 339 U.S. 33; Marion Bennett, *American Immigration Policies* (Washington: Public Affairs Press, 1963), 90–91; Act of Sept. 27, 1950 (64 Stat. 1044). Congress repealed the exemption in 1952 and wrote provisions into the McCarran-Walter omnibus immigration act to effect the same results. On the "unmistakable purpose to exempt immigration hearings from the procedural requirements of the APA," see President's Commission on Immigration and Naturalization, *Whom We Shall Welcome* (Washington, D.C.: GPO, 1953), 159.

However, Americans increasingly believed that deportation, initially imagined for the despised and dangerous classes, was undemocratic and unjust when applied to ordinary immigrants with homes and families in the United States. Hence during the 1930s and early 1940s statutory and administrative reforms attempted to ease the tension between sovereignty and democracy that immigration policy had created. Family values and environmentalist views of delinquency and morality paved the way for reform, while race directed its reach.

Thus it became possible to unmake the illegality of Italian, Polish, and other European illegal immigrants through the power of administrative discretion. Of course, not all illegal European immigrants were legalized, but a rough estimation suggests that between 1925 and 1965 some 200,000 illegal European immigrants, constructed as deserving, successfully legalized their status under the Registry Act, through pre-examination, or by suspension of deportation. The formal recognition of their inclusion in the nation created the requisite minimum foundation for acquiring citizenship and contributed to a broader reformation of racial identity, a process that reconstructed the "lower races of Europe" into white ethnic Americans.[122]

By contrast, walking (or wading) across the border emerged as the quintessential act of illegal immigration, the outermost point in a relativist ordering of illegal immigration. The method of Mexicans' illegal entry could thus be perceived as "criminal" and Mexican immigrants as undeserving of relief. Combined with the construction of Mexicans as migratory agricultural laborers (both legal and illegal) in the 1940s and 1950s, that perception gave powerful sway to the notion that Mexicans had no rightful presence on United States territory, no rightful claim of belonging.

The basic principle of immigration law doctrine that privileged Congress's plenary power over the individual rights of immigrants remained intact. The contradiction between sovereignty and individual rights was resolved only to the extent that the power of administrative discretion made narrow exceptions of the sovereign rule. In the context of immigration law that foregrounded territoriality and border control, and in the hands of immigration officials operating within the contingencies of contemporary politics and social prejudices, that discretion served to racialize the specter of the illegal alien.

122. See generally Matthew Jacobson, *Whiteness of a Different Color* (Cambridge, Mass.: Harvard University Press, 1998); James Barrett and David Roediger, "In-between People: Race, Nationality, and the 'New Immigrant' Working Class," *Journal of American Ethnic History* 16.3 (Spring 1997): 3–44; Ian F. Haney López, *White by Law: The Legal Construction of Race* (New York: New York University Press, 1995).

[7]

When States Prefer Non-Citizens Over Citizens: Conflict Over Illegal Immigration into Malaysia

KAMAL SADIQ
University of California–Irvine

Why would a state encourage illegal immigration over the opposition of its citizens? According to the theories of immigration and citizenship, we should expect exactly the opposite: that states will monitor, control, and restrict illegal immigrants' access to citizenship on behalf of its citizens, as has been the experience of most countries. I use my research on Filipino immigration to Sabah, Malaysia to show how Malaysia utilizes census practices and documentation to incorporate an illegal immigrant population from the Philippines. Illegal immigrants play an electoral role in Sabah because of the loosely institutionalized nature of citizenship, a feature common to many other developing countries. Our examination of Malaysia reveals several elements of illegal immigration and citizenship that are common to migratory flows in other developing countries. I conclude by showing how this case is generalizable and what it tells us about illegal immigrant participation in the international system.

Immigrants can and do alter political outcomes in their host states; this much has been acknowledged in the scholarship on comparative politics and international relations. But the conventional wisdom has never acknowledged that *illegal* immigrants can alter political outcomes by means of *voting*. This is for the simple reason that national- and state-level voting has always been thought to be the most protected privilege of citizenship in the post-World War II international system—a privilege that illegal immigrants by definition cannot enjoy.[1]

The purpose of this article is to demonstrate that the conventional wisdom, insofar as it purports to apply to developing countries, is wrong. The common assumption of comparativists and IR scholars that all democratic states protect the privilege of national- and state-level voting for their citizens cannot be sustained in

Author's note: I thank Stephanie Di Alto, Tom Donahue, Lloyd Rudolph, Susanne Rudolph, Saskia Sassen, and three anonymous reviewers for their comments on previous drafts. My thanks are also due to Wayne Cornelius and his staff for hosting me for a year as a visiting research fellow at the Center for Comparative Immigration Studies, UCSD.

[1] See, inter alia, Marshall and Bottomore (1996), Brubaker (1992), and Smith (1997). Citizenship has always been safeguarded such that all 'outsiders,' of whatever sort, were denied the right to vote until the middle of the twentieth century. For example, women and certain classes of people were denied the franchise in many developed states at the turn of the twentieth century, notably the United States, as Roger Smith has brilliantly documented (see *Civic Ideals*, 1997). The right to vote at the national level is, according to Carmen Tiburcio, 'granted only to citizens, that is nationals with full political rights, and aliens are left outside the electoral process entirely' (Tiburcio, 2001:190). She cites the constitutions of individual states to show that only citizens can vote in national elections in Austria, Belgium, Brazil, Canada, Denmark, Greece, Hungary, Israel, Monaco, Norway, Poland, Portugal, Switzerland, Turkey, Thailand, the U.K., and the U.S., among many others (189–190).

the face of empirical evidence from the developing world. This evidence demonstrates that illegal immigrants in developing states are voting in large numbers because—for various reasons that I shall describe below—they are able to illegally procure documents that allow them to enjoy all the privileges of citizenship. Moreover, many of these states lack the police capacities to combat document fraud and have not even developed the administrative systems necessary to properly document nationality in the first place. These facts present major problems for democracies and democratizing states that need to delimit their *demos* in an era of increasing globalization.

Weak documentation systems leave states open not only to illegal entry of economic migrants, terrorists, and other criminals via document fraud, but to massive electoral fraud as well, which has serious implications for the conduct of democratic politics. By acquiring and possessing seemingly legal documents that "prove" juridical membership in a state, a non-citizen[2] can easily acquire citizenship status. I shall call this process through which citizenship status is ascribed to a non-citizen *documentary citizenship*.

This process has important implications for our understanding of international security. Since September 11, there has been an intensification of border controls and a tightening of visa regulations. The prospect of a worldwide trend of increasing documentary citizenship thus raises serious security concerns regarding flows of people as tourists, travelers, illegal workers, businesspersons, and students. If, as this article demonstrates, illegal Filipinos can easily acquire Malaysian citizenship documents, then what prevents Al-Qaeda terrorists from doing the same? Foreign terrorist groups in "neutral" states such as India, Malaysia, Thailand, and the Philippines could fraudulently acquire the paperwork for the citizenship of these states and then obtain legitimate visas to enter United States or any other target country. Alternatively, they could use documents from "neutral" states to enter other "neutral" states (such as those in Eastern Europe or Central and Latin America) before making an attempt to enter the United States or any other target country. In fact, cities such as Delhi and Bangkok are major centers for fraudulent passports and other paperwork that enable illegal immigrants to enter the restricted borders of West European or North American states. Therefore, what are the implications of documentary citizenship for "the war on terrorism" and on the increasing human mobility that is part and parcel of globalization?

Through a detailed case study of immigration into Malaysia, I shall describe and explain the emergence of documentary citizenship, a growing reality in many developing countries in which illegal immigrants acquire citizenship documents that many of the native[3] rural poor lack. Even more striking is that in the Malaysian case, not only does documentary citizenship enfranchise illegal immigrants, but also the political participation of these individuals alters political outcomes in favor of governments that enable illegal immigrants to acquire proofs of citizenship and the ability to vote.[4]

Here it may be asked whether my case is unique or exemplifies a broader phenomenon. Malaysia is not a unique case. It is illustrative of the problems of migration and citizenship faced by many developing countries.[5] Malaysia is like many

[2] Non-citizen includes the following categories: legal immigrant, illegal immigrant, refugee, and tourist.

[3] 'Natives' are individuals whose ancestors were born in the country.

[4] An anonymous reviewer drew a parallel between what is happening today in Malaysia and the United States during the nineteenth century; some illegal European immigrants to America in this period stepped off the boats and were immediately permitted to vote by ethnic political machines. This occurred even as indigenous populations (Native Americans) were denied basic citizenship rights. The parallel is illuminating; however, the distinction between citizen and immigrant—and regulatory structures for dealing with these two categories—only became deeply institutionalized after World War II. This article covers the period from the 1970s until September 11, 2001.

[5] My dissertation compares voting in India by illegal immigrants from Bangladesh with voting by illegal Filipinos and Indonesians in Malaysia. States in Latin America, Sub-Saharan Africa, and other Asian states such as Pakistan and Thailand could serve as fruitful subjects for future inquiry into the phenomenon of illegal immigrant voting.

developing states in that it is a multiethnic developing country where citizenship is not well institutionalized and the arrival and incorporation of illegal immigrants from neighboring countries is possible through varieties of fake documentation or real documentation falsely obtained. These similarities make it extremely likely that documentary citizenship is a widespread phenomenon that can be found, for instance, in Pakistan, where Afghan refugees are exercising political rights; in India, where hundreds of thousands of Bangladeshis are continually accused of voting; in Cameroon, where Nigerians have illegally acquired documents of citizenship; in Ghana, where Togoans are illegally gaining access to citizenship; in the Ivory Coast, where political participation of illegal immigrants from Burkina Faso has caused violence; and in South Africa, where illegal immigrants from neighboring countries are accused of accessing citizenship through illegal means.

The fact that illegal immigrants in Malaysia receive the same privileges as citizens[6] adds a new dimension to the literature on citizenship that focuses on the social, political, and economic rights of citizens (Kymlicka, 1995; Marshall and Bottomore, 1996), highlighting gradations of immigrant membership (Schuck and Smith, 1985; Joppke, 1999), and the literature that views the erosion of the state because of global processes as creating a new form of membership not tied to the nation-state (Soysal, 1994; Jacobson, 1997; Sassen, 1998). None of this literature deals with documentary citizenship. Moreover, local Malay authorities were constantly being accused of encouraging illegal immigration from the Southern Philippines and Indonesia to Sabah, a region in East Malaysia.[7] At a time when both the European Union and North America were erecting immigration barriers, Malaysia was facilitating the entry of illegal immigrants.[8] Taken as a whole, these practices contradict the conventional wisdom about immigration, especially illegal immigration (Stalker, 1994).

So, why would a state give non-citizens preference over native citizens? Why is being native not enough? These facts are in direct contrast to what most scholars know about Malaysia: that it is a multiethnic country with successful preferential policies for its natives—the "sons of the soil."[9] Yet, by encouraging illegal immigration, Malaysia was

[6] Illegal immigrants, mainly from Indonesia, are exercising social, economic, and even political rights in West Malaysia (Kassim, 1998). Azizah Kassim (285), a leading scholar of immigration into Malaysian, says that 'estimates on illegals in the *Peninsula* vary from between 300,000 and one million,' indicating the difficulty in measurement. Over the years, illegal immigrants have gained access to Malaysian citizenship; in fact, Malaysian authorities have accused many Indonesian immigrants of being politically active in radical Islamic groups. Given that a number of Indian plantation workers and other native groups (e.g., Orang Asli) in West Malaysia are without citizenship documents, West Malaysia parallels some of the features of my empirical case from Sabah in East Malaysia. Weakly institutionalized citizenship is a common feature of people living in regions with high poverty (or particular ethnic groups afflicted with poverty) and inhospitable areas of the interior—common to both East and West Malaysia.

[7] West Malaysia is over 1,000 miles from Sabah, a regional state in East Malaysia, and is separated from it by the South China Sea. It takes about two and a half hours to reach Sabah from West Malaysia by airplane.

[8] Now it is true that, after September 11, 2001, the Malaysian authorities cracked down on illegal immigration after Malaysia became a partner in the war on terrorism (*The New York Times*, 2002:A3). Immigrant groups in Malaysia are suspected of having links to rebel groups in the Southern Philippines and of supporting Islamic extremist groups within Malaysia—facts that gained salience after the events of September 11. But this transitory focus on deportation of immigrants was not at odds with the purpose of encouraging illegal immigration from the 1970s until September 11, because the ruling Malay-dominated parties had already achieved their demographic goals—many illegal immigrants had already become citizens. Furthermore, Sabah's geographic position and traditional immigrant networks are such that Indonesian and Filipino illegal immigrants who are deported can return to Sabah within days and acquire 'citizenship' documents easily. Public shows of deportation of Muslim illegal immigrants from West or East Malaysia conceal the fact that these illegal immigrants can and do return very soon, and that their networks ensure their access to citizenship. With estimates of approximately one million illegal immigrants each for Sabah and West Malaysia, the ease of access to citizenship through documentation, and the complicity by sections of the state, Malaysia provides a contrast with the experience of developed states such as those in the EU.

[9] Articles 153 and 161 of the Constitution have been used to promote the 'special rights' of Malays and the natives of Sabah—the 'sons of the soil.' Article 153 of the Constitution speaks of the responsibility of the state "to safeguard the special position of the Malays and the natives of the states of Sabah and Sarawak."

privileging non-citizens over citizens in certain situations. According to the various theories of immigration and citizenship cited above and the common experience of most countries, we should expect exactly the opposite: that states will monitor, control, and restrict immigration from another country rather than encourage illegal immigration (Cornelius, Martin, and Hollifield, 1994; Koslowski, 2000). These theories postulate that citizenship is about exclusion, or, to use Rogers Brubaker's term, "social closure" (Brubaker, 1992:21–34). Accordingly, in the modern international system, closure of territorial boundaries and political exclusion of non-citizens is essential to systemic stability. As Hannah Arendt (1968:278) argued, "sovereignty is nowhere more absolute than in matters of "emigration, naturalization, nationality, and expulsion." It is at the threshold of a state's membership and its territorial boundaries that the rules of entry and residence apply; the national interest is the interest of citizens only. The state, so it is said, belongs to the citizenry. Therefore, in matters of national- and state-level suffrage, military service, and positions in public office, legal citizenship is a sine qua non. For example, the President of the United States and of Indonesia must be a native-born citizen as must the Prime Ministers of Malaysia and Sweden. Many states debar naturalized citizens from public office. Most militaries defending territorial boundaries against security threats are comprised only of citizens.[10]

It is true, as some scholars have observed, that there has recently been a dramatic increase in the rights and privileges granted by many developed states to immigrants,[11] but at no time have these states opened national and state level voting, or high public offices, to non-citizens. Public office is considered a matter of state security, since access to it would allow entry into the guarded domains of foreign, defense, and security policy. States make their fundamental foreign and security policies based on recommendations by elected officials who are accountable to the voting citizenry and are assumed to represent the *demos* that the state regulates.[12] In short, citizenship continues to be—and is assumed by the conventional wisdom to be—the highest and most protected form of membership in a state because it ensures legal, political, and social priority for a citizen over all other persons within the polity. This assumption is fundamental to most of the literature on immigration, which, not surprisingly, is overwhelmingly dominated by cases from Western Europe and North America.[13]

The phenomenon of documentary citizenship, which I observed firsthand in Malaysia, reveals this assumption to be mistaken, at least insofar as it is applied to developing states. Illegal immigrants, I observed, were taking part in elections in Malaysia even as many natives continue to have no documents proving their citizenship. Illegal immigrants were being welcomed and *afforded the rights of citizens by*

[10]Critics may point to the enlistment of resident aliens in the U.S. armed forces as contradicting my assertion. While resident aliens have historically been drafted into the U.S. military, they do so under the expectation that as loyal Americans they will pursue naturalization and become citizens. See Jennings (2002) and Lopez (2003). Most militaries continue to be manned by citizens, in fact potential recruits are carefully screened for citizenship and nationality.

[11]Specifically, the influx of immigrants into Western Europe prompted the states of that region to extend inclusive policies in social and economic spheres to immigrants over time (Koslowski, 2000:72–94). The extension of citizen-like rights such as a local franchise for immigrants in some developed states became an index of the collapse of the distinction between citizen and immigrant. The Netherlands and some Nordic countries granted immigrants the right to vote in local elections (Rath, 1990:127). Since states have anciently associated voting with *de jure* citizenship, the extension of this right, along with many other rights and privileges traditionally enjoyed only by citizens, was seen as a reformulation of the traditional conception of the state under pressures of globalization and international human rights norms (see Jacobson, 1997; Sassen, 1998).

[12]Naturalized citizens can go on to become elected officials, but naturalization entails meeting stringent eligibility requirements.

[13]Recent contributions by Sassen (1999), Castles and Davidson (2000), and Koslowski (2000, 2002) have challenged traditional notions about immigration and its impact on world politics, but these too have ignored the phenomenon of illegal immigrant voting.

sections[14] *of the Malaysian state* over the opposition of many native citizens. Illegal immigration to Malaysia from the Philippines and Indonesia highlights the paradox of states actively admitting illegal immigrants.

In this article, I explore the motives that drive state actors to adopt these policies of encouraging illegal immigration, and how these state practices are managed by migrants. I will show how the state uses illegal immigrants from neighboring countries to "Malayize" or homogenize Malaysia. In short, the authorities at the center collaborate with their regional partners to utilize census practices and documentation to incorporate an illegal immigrant population from the Philippines. The motive for such practices is to use illegal immigrants as voters to assure political control by a Malay/Muslim party such as the United Malays National Organization (UMNO). At the individual level, illegal immigrants: (i) use the census by giving self-reports that deny their illegal immigrant status; and more importantly, (ii) use documents to prove citizenship and acquire citizen's rights, such as universal suffrage. The beneficiaries of such manipulation of ethnicity and migration at the subnational level are the parties that get the vote of these illegal immigrants, the officials, the local illegal entrepreneurs that sell citizenship documents, and finally, the illegal immigrants who not only become citizens with voting rights but also have access to affirmative action policies with their status as Bumiputera, or "sons of the soil."

I divide my analysis into the following sections. First, I outline the illegal immigration to Sabah, Malaysia, highlighting the visibility of the phenomenon, and discussing its impact on the state's changing ethnic composition. Next, I analyze the politics of estimation and classification of the illegal population emphasizing the use of easily manipulated census categories in facilitating immigrant incorporation—an outcome that sections of the federal and state government favor while the law disfavors it. The third section of this article highlights the lack of institutionalization of citizenship that makes possible the incorporation of illegal immigrants through varieties of documents. Importantly, "documentary citizenship" denotes the process by which illegal immigrants are incorporated into the state, get on the electoral rolls, and gain access to the rights of citizens. As a consequence, these *suffraged non-citizens* wind up being privileged over native, *non-suffraged citizens*. I follow this by scrutinizing the effects of illegal immigration and documentary citizenship on the political process by focusing on electoral politics. The use of illegal immigrants as voters advantages certain political parties, thus providing an insight into why the manipulation of migratory flows takes place. I conclude by examining whether Malaysia is a unique case, an outlier on the graph of immigrant incorporation. I show how this case is generalizable and why it requires us to rethink our current understanding of immigration and citizenship.

Illegal Immigration to Sabah

How "visible" is the presence of illegal immigrants in Sabah? Worried "locals" have this to say:

> Ours must be the only place in the world where illegals have the courage to walk about in the streets with impunity, commit crimes, use our over stretched government hospitals, steal our water, attend our schools and milk us of our resources in numerous ways. (*Daily Express*, 1999a)[15]

[14]By sections of the state I mean officials belonging to law enforcement, the immigration department, legislators, and others.

[15]A letter to the editor by "very concerned citizens."

Migration from the Sulu Archipelago in the Philippines to Sabah has a long history. Barter trade existed as early as the ninth century; today it is the cornerstone of a regional economic trade forum among Indonesia, the Philippines, Malaysia, and Brunei called BIMP-EAGA.[16] The first migrants to Sabah from the Sulu Archipelago arrived in the late fifteenth century when the Spanish began pushing southwards toward Sulu and Tawi-Tawi in the southern Philippines. As a result, members of ethnic groups such as the Suluk and the Bajau came to straddle the modern boundaries of Sabah, Malaysia, and the Southern Philippines. The second wave of migration is associated with the Mindanao insurgency in the Philippines; many refugees migrated to Sabah during 1970–1977. Thousands of Suluk and Bajau women, men, and children took small wooden boats (*kumpits*) to flee the war-torn southern provinces of the Philippines for the relative safety of Sabah. This wave of political refugees arrived in the East Coast of Sabah and settled in towns such as Sandakan, Tawau, and Lahad Datu. However, the number of 1970s refugees is small compared with the number of migrants since 1978.

It is this third phase, the post-1978 period, which witnessed a massive influx of illegal migrants. These immigrants cannot, however, be technically treated as refugees because the rebel Moro National Liberation Front (MNLF) in the Southern Philippines had signed a peace agreement with the Philippines government, reclassifying the region prima facie as peaceful.[17] Thus, the latest phase of immigration to Sabah was perceived by local observers in Sabah as the movement of mainly economic migrants seeking a better life rather than political refugees. Each wave of this historical immigration established networks in sections of the economy, society, and importantly for modern times, the government. New immigrants followed networks established by earlier arrivals of co-ethnics (see Koslowski, 2002).

One of the reasons why there is such unregulated flow of illegal immigrants is because of geographical proximity.[18] Sabah's coastline runs almost 250 miles and its proximity to several islands in the Philippine waters allows for easy travel across state boundaries. There are almost 200 small islands off Sabah's east coast, of which only 52 are inhabited. The Sulu Sea, a pirate's haven, separates Sabah from the Philippines and in some places it takes less than 20 minutes by boat to reach Sabah's waters from the Philippines (*Daily Express*, 2000a).

Today it is commonly known among Sabahans that the coastal town of Sandakan (in the eastern part of Sabah) is overwhelmingly Filipino, while Indonesians comprise the majority of residents in Tawau, a Sabah town that borders Indonesia. According to illegal immigrants in Sabah, it takes approximately 2 days to reach Kota Kinabalu, the capital of Sabah, from the Philippines by boat. In fact, one of the landing points is just below the Yayasan Sabah, a sky scraper housing the Chief Minister's office and other key Sabahan ministries dealing with immigration or security![19] For example, "Catherine," an illegal immigrant from the Philippines, came to Sabah 12 years ago after spending two nights on a boat.[20] She landed at Yayasan Sabah and later married a Muslim Filipino who was a legal worker, nominally converting to Islam. She says many Christian Filipino women convert to Islam, as conversion makes it easier to become "Sabahan." After a few years she "legalized" her presence through her husband's connections and is now a legal worker. Thus, it is probable that her achievement of legal status did not preclude extra-legal means to that end.

[16] Brunei, Indonesia, Malaysia, Philippines (BIMP); East Asian Growth Area (EAGA).

[17] As a consequence of this agreement, the head of the MNLF, Nur Misuari, became the Governor of the Autonomous Region of Muslim Mindanao in the Philippines.

[18] Even the United States with its large resources is unable to control illegal immigration. For a critical look at the effectiveness of immigration control measures on the U.S.–Mexican border, see Peter Andreas (2000).

[19] Based on the author's conversations with Filipino immigrants.

[20] Because of the sensitive nature of this research I will not reveal the names of some of my interviewees.

It is common for immigrants to become seemingly legal through fake documents. Labor operators or "towkays," for example, help to facilitate this semblance of legality. Most of these "towkays" who transport Filipino immigrants to Sabah are paid in Philippine pesos. The boats anchor in the night near the shore and immigrants carry their modest belongings (only small bags are allowed) on their heads while wading to the shore. Most immigrants already know of friends and relatives in the region; thus, these connections enable recent immigrants to establish themselves in "safe houses," from where they are directed to possible employers. The "towkays" receive part of the initial earnings of new immigrants as payment for their services.

Moreover, Christian immigrants often adopt Muslim names so as to more easily acquire documents. The Indonesian women, who are predominantly Muslim, have no such problems in assimilation or acceptance. Legalization, whether through government-instituted programs, or through marriages, bribery, or the granting of refugee status, is relatively easy for illegal immigrants. At every stage, there are co-ethnics—settlers from earlier waves of migration—who facilitate the acquisition and attainment of the rights of citizenship.

As immigrants settle, they move inwards and toward big towns on the West Coast. Both Indonesian and Filipino migrants have physical and cultural features similar to those of the Malays; the Indonesian language (Bahasa Indonesia)[21] is almost the same as Bahasa Malaysia, while Southern Filipinos speak dialects that have commonalties with Bahasa Malaysia. In major towns of Sabah, there are very visible pockets of illegal immigrant settlements such as Kampung BDC in Sandakan, Kampung Panji in Lahad Datu, Kampung Ice Box in Tawau, and Kampung Pondo at Pulau Gaya, Kota Kinabalu. According to some legislators, these settlements are security threats to Malaysia (*Daily Express*, 2000b).[22]

The public perception in Sabah is that an initial "trickle" of refugees has now turned into a "torrent" of immigrants. A range of figures is quoted on the number of illegal immigrants in the state. According to unpublished data for 1997 obtained from the state immigration department by Malaysian scholar Azizah Kassim (1998:282–285), there were only 120,719 registered alien workers in Sabah. According to the Malaysian census, between 1970 and 1980, the net immigration from Indonesia and the Philippines to Sabah was 45,000 Indonesians and 36,000 Filipinos (Department of Statistics, January 1983:58–59).[23] The total immigration to Sabah for the same period, after counting immigrants from other countries, was only 127,000 persons out of a total population of 950,000.[24] The 1991 census in Sabah identified 207,366 persons born in Indonesia and 161,533 persons born in the Philippines out of a total of 383,076 people born outside Malaysia (Department of Statistics, March 1995:144).[25] However, this is a distortion in at least one way—the Filipinos are a significant presence in Sabah now, while the official figures present the reverse picture.

Recognizing the problems of underestimation in state data, Azizah Kassim cites a former Chief Minister as estimating illegal immigrant numbers to be in the range of 400,000–500,000 (Kassim, 1998:285). Most leaders of the main opposition party, the Parti Bersatu Sabah (PBS),[26] give the figure of one million foreigners out of a

[21]The word "Bahasa" is Indian in origin and means "language" in Sanskrit.

[22]Wilfred Tangau, a member of Parliament, recently asked in Parliament whether the government would regard Kampung BDC in Sandakan, Kampung Panji in Lahad Datu, Kampung Ice Box in Tawau, and Kampung Pondo at Pulau Gaya, Kota Kinabalu, as security areas, owing to the large presence of illegal immigrants.

[23]See Table 5.3.

[24]See Table 5.2:58.

[25]See Table 4.1.

[26]PBS is the main Kadazandusun and Murut party. A confidential and comprehensive, almost census-like, project was carried out on these illegal immigrants when Parti Bersatu Sabah (PBS) was in power from 1985 to 1994: the *Transient Population Study* undertaken by the Chief Ministers' Department, Kota Kinabalu, 1988. The study covers statistics regarding immigration until the period 1988–1989. The author's personal copy.

current Sabah population of about 2.8 million.[27] Leaders of the Filipino community in the Philippines give similar estimates; their numbers in Sabah have passed the one million mark, making them the "biggest concentration of Filipino illegals in any part of the world" (*Philippine Daily Inquirer*, 1999).[28] This means that almost one in every three residents of Sabah may be a foreigner. Here "foreigner" would include both illegal migrants and legal workers.

What complicates the estimation issue further is that very often during "regularization" programs many illegal immigrants get "regularized" and therefore change their "illegal" status.[29] Over the years many have already made the transition from an illegal status to legal citizenship. Many illegal immigrants who are deported have been known to return to Sabah within a few months if not weeks or days. For example, Mustali, a 28-year-old Filipino who was recently arrested, had lived in Sabah since the age of 8 years (*Borneo Post*, 1999c).[30] Since then, he traveled between Malaysia and the Philippines with impunity, visiting his family several times in the Philippines. He has four children with him in Sabah; his wife returned to the Philippines to look after their older children who were being schooled in Jolo, Philippines. The judge ordered that Mustali, as an illegal immigrant, be jailed because he "had no respect for the laws of the country by going in and out of the country as though the Philippines and Malaysia were two different states in one country" (*Borneo Post*, 1999c; *Philippine Daily Inquirer*, 1999).

Illegal immigration is changing the ethnic makeup of Sabah in significant ways (see Table 1). At the beginning of the twentieth century, Kadazandusuns were the dominant ethnic group, comprising about 42 percent of the state population. They fell to 32 percent by the 1960 census, 29.9 percent by 1970, and then, to their alarm, by 1990 they had fallen to 19.6 percent (see Table 1). Similarly, Muruts have seen their share of decline from 4.9 percent in 1960 to 2.9 percent in 1990. Both of these non-Muslim groups overwhelmingly support the non-Muslim, non-Malay regional party, the PBS, which opposes the migration and settlement of illegal immigrants in Sabah.

In contrast, the UMNO, which derives its support from Muslim groups, has seen the ethnic makeup of Sabah change in its favor. The Muslim Malays have risen from just 0.4 percent of the population in 1960 to 6.2 percent of the population in 1990; the Indonesians have risen substantially from comprising only 5.5 percent of the population in 1960 to 21.3 percent in 1990; and the Filipinos, who had a negligible presence until 1960 (1.6 percent), represented 8.2 percent of Sabah's total population by the 1990 census. Continuing Filipino and Indonesian illegal immigration further increases the stock of various Muslim ethnic groups (Bajau, Bugis, Other Muslims, Suluks, etc.), while non-Muslim groups such as the Kadazandusun, Muruts or the Chinese are declining into demographic and political insignificance. The incorporation of illegal immigrants as citizens is critical to the changing ethnic demography and subsequent political map of Sabah.

Citizenship by Census

Illegal immigration produces a wide range of estimates concerning the magnitude of the immigrant population. As this section will demonstrate, manipulation of census categories is one mode of incorporating illegal immigrants into citizenship status. The census is a federal endeavor, but it is conducted with the cooperation of

[27]Interviews with Henrynus Amin, a prominent legislator of the native Parti Barsatu Sabah and their spokesman and other members of the party during my stay in Sabah in 1999.

[28]This is the first of a four part report on the Filipino illegal migration to Sabah conducted by correspondent Jerry Esplanade.

[29]Interview with Maximus Ongkilli, Vice President, PBS.

[30]The name of this illegal immigrant has been changed.

TABLE 1. Political Affiliation and Ethnic Group Representation in Sabah

	Political Party	*Ethnic Group*	*Census Years* 1960	1970	1980*	1991
Regional	PBS	Kadazandusun	32.0	29.9		19.6
		Murut	4.9	4.8		2.9
National	UMNO	Malay	0.4	2.8		6.2
		Bajau	13.1	11.8		11.7
		Other Muslims	15.8	13.5		13.6
		Indonesian	5.5	6.1		21.3
		Filipino	1.6	3.1		8.2
National	MCA	Chinese	23.0	21.4		11.5

Source: Based on Uesugi Tomiyuki (2000:37).
PBS, Parti Bersatu Sabah; UMNO, United Malays National Organization; MCA, Malaysian Chinese Association.
*The 1980 census collapsed all those who were not Chinese or Indians into a single category called Pribumi, thus making it impossible to obtain data for individual ethnic groups.

regional governments in Sabah. Census categories can be introduced and withdrawn according to the political goals of the dominant political party in Sabah. This section illustrates how ruling parties dominated by West Malaysian Muslims such as the UMNO use census categories to incorporate large-scale illegal immigration from the Philippines to Sabah. The political calculation to provide citizenship through census manipulation was part of a long-term goal to Malayize Sabah and ensure the political hegemony of Malay-based parties such as the UMNO. Reciprocally, the non-Malay Sabah party, the PBS, opposes categories that might allow the incorporation of illegal immigrants or might minimize their presence. Such census manipulation also provides incentives for self-reporting by illegal immigrants to fit in the Malay-Muslim categories such as Pribumi or Bumiputera.

Sabah's population is growing dramatically (see Figure 1).[31] It is experiencing an alarming annual growth rate of 5.5 percent (between 1981 and 1991) against the Malaysian average of 2.6 percent for the same period. Between 1991 and 1995, Sabah had an annual growth rate of 6.2 percent compared with the low Malaysian rate of 2.7 percent, and Sabah is projected to have a rate of 5.4 percent against the national average of 2.3 percent. Sabah's growth rate is almost three times that of other states.[32] According to the *Seventh Malaysia Plan* (1995–2000), Sabah will have an estimated 3.3 million people while the neighboring state of Sarawak will trail with a low 2.06 million. In fact, as recently as 1980, Sabah's population was smaller than Sarawak's. Sabah and Sarawak had, until recently, similar fertility rates and death rates. While Sarawak has higher in-migration from Peninsular Malaysia than Sabah, Sabah's annual population growth rates are three times that of Sarawak. The question of where the extra 1.3 million people came from when the population growth rates of both Sabah and Sarawak should have paralleled one another has become pre-eminently important to the "natives" of Sabah, according to Henrynus Amin, a prominent legislator of the native Parti Barsatu Sabah.[33] The obvious reference was to the rampant pervasiveness of illegal immigrants in the state.

[31]According to the *Population and Housing Census of Malaysia 1980* (13–14): "The figures for the years prior to the formation of Malaysia in 1963 are aggregates of the census figures for Peninsular Malaysia, Sabah, and Sarawak. For years where no census figures were available, the estimates were derived by using the intercensal growth rates of the region."

[32]Population growth rates for other states are shown by the bar graphs of Peninsular Malaysia covering all the states in West Malaysia, and the bar graphs of Sarawak, Sabah's neighboring state in East Malaysia—in each case the contrast with Sabah is striking.

[33]Interview, June 13, 1999.

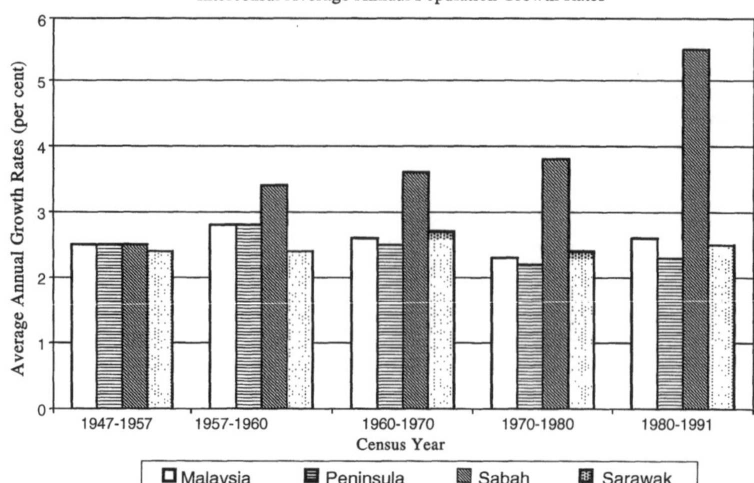

FIG. 1. Intercensal Average Annual Population Growth Rates
Sources: Population and Housing Census of Malaysia 1980, Vol.1 (Department of Statistics, Malaysia, January 1983), especially pp. 13–14; Population and Housing Census of Malaysia 1991, State Population Report, Sabah (Department of Statistics, Malaysia, March 1995). Note: Malaysia gained independence in 1963. Malaysian Peninsula is also known as West Malaysia while Sabah and Sarawak are in East Malaysia.

Although the state government estimated the population of Filipino refugees in the 1970s to be 70,000, the United Nations Commissioner for Refugees (UNHCR) estimated their numbers to be closer to 100,000 and the local community leaders in Sabah claimed a figure in excess of 130,000 (Kurus, Goddos, and Koh, 1998:161).[34] The state *Population and Housing Census* of 1991 estimates a figure of only 57,197. Controversy surrounds the changing categories used to classify and incorporate this "alien" population. Federal authorities, in collaboration with their regional partners—the United Sabah National Organization (USNO), Bersatu Rakyat Jelata Sabah (BERJAYA), and later the UMNO—created census categories that would deny or minimize illegal immigration. The category "Pribumi,"[35] or "sons of the soil," introduced in the *Population and Housing Census* of 1980, functioned to downplay the distinction between natives and immigrants since it was not a discrete category and included indigenous as well as immigrant groups. This category was introduced by a Sabah state government directive on October 7, 1982 (Regis, 1989:15–16).[36] It had the effect of collapsing all the indigenous groups classified under various headings in censuses conducted before 1980 and grouping them along with recent immigrants, thereby creating a large undifferentiated Malay stock. Pribumi was a political category as much as an all inclusive nomenclature in the census. Many groups, including immigrants from the Philippines and Indonesia who were included in the category "Others" in the 1970 census, are now subsumed under this category.

[34]This is a report by Bilson Kurus, Ramlan Goddos, and Richard T. Koh for the state think tank, Institute for Development Studies, recently published in *Borneo Review*, 1998.

[35]Pribumi means "native" and has the same meaning as the term Bumiputera (both words have roots in Sanskrit).

[36]Directive CMDC 503/60. While the nomenclature "Pribumi" was adopted by the center in the 1980 census, the directive to adopt it at the regional, Sabah level, was introduced in 1982.

By ignoring descent and ethnic boundaries between groups for classification purposes, the census facilitated the inclusion of illegal immigrants and their children who would qualify for citizenship and *Bumiputera* status since their parents would be classified as *Pribumi*. In the 1980 census, *Pribumi* accounted for as much as 82.9 percent of the Sabah population. The category *Pribumi*, much like the term *Bumiputera*, was a code for Muslims (Table 2). The category was officially dropped on April 24, 1985, after the opposition regional party, the PBS, came to power and made illegal immigration a major issue. By forcing the national census to back down, PBS was seeking to protect its regional interests who were mainly non-Malay local natives such as the Kadazandusuns and Muruts.

The reconfigured census of 1991 continued the incorporation but separated some of the immigrant groups out for illustrative purposes. In the *Population and Housing Census* of 1991, recent Filipino and Indonesian immigrants were placed in the category "non-Malaysian Citizens." From a total population in Sabah of 1,734,685 in 1991, the non-Malaysian Citizens numbered 425,175, which, after adjusting for underenumeration, is about 25.1 percent of the population (Table 2). This large percentage of non-citizens in Sabah's population excludes illegal immigrants who have self-reported themselves as Malay, Bajau, Suluk, or some Other Bumiputera category in the census. According to the explanatory notes and definitions of the 1991 census, citizenship "refers to the *self-identification* of an individual regarding his citizenship and was *not based on any official document*" (Department of Statistics, 1995:xxxi). Clearly, there was an incentive to self-report as a member of a Bumiputera group. The 1991 census would also exclude illegal immigrants who over the decade acquired Malaysian citizenship, either by naturalization or by fraudulent means.

Within the Malaysian Citizens category the breakdown was as follows (*Population and Housing Census 1991*:18–20): (i) Others numbered 32,210; (ii) Other Bumiputeras numbered 255,555 or 14.7 percent; (iii) Bajau's numbered 203,457 or 11.7 percent; (iv) Indonesians numbered 139,403 or 8 percent; and (v) Malays numbered 106,740 or 6.15 percent.

Why are Indonesians categorized as Malaysian citizens in the 1991 census? While some may have regularized their status from illegal to legal through marriage with a local, others might have benefited from the many "regularization" exercises that Malaysia conducts, which have the effect of legalizing and normalizing illegal

TABLE 2. Census Categories for Muslim Filipino Immigrants in Sabah

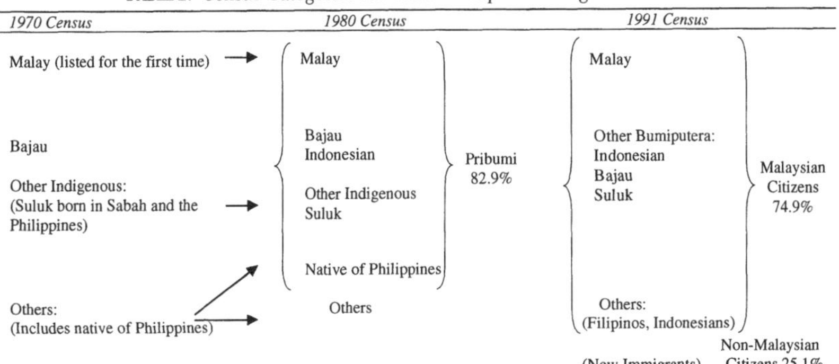

Sources: Population and Housing Census of Malaysia 1980, Vol.1 (Department of Statistics, January 1983), Population and Housing Census of Malaysia 1991, State Population Report, Sabah (Department of Statistics, March 1995). Patricia Regis, "Demography," Appendix 1 in Jeffrey Kitingan and Maximus Ongkili, *Sabah 25 Years Later: 1963–1988* (Kitingan and William, 1989).

immigrants. Malaysia is not unique in seeking to manage illegal immigration through regularization schemes.[37] This regularization paves the way for Filipinos and Indonesians alike to be eligible for naturalization as citizens. Therefore, in the census, Indonesians, a majority of whom are Muslim illegal immigrants, are listed under the "Others" category of "Malaysian Citizens" and constitute as much as 8 percent of the "Malaysian Citizens." Excluding the large Indonesian category, many of the sub-headings within "Malaysian Citizens" are meant to incorporate the large influx of illegal Filipinos into Sabah, Malaysia. Bajau, Malay, and Suluk are all "ethnic groups" that would neatly overlap with the recent illegal immigrants from the Philippines. Within the Bumiputera category, many subheadings include immigrant groups, formerly illegal, who are now "legal" citizens having spent decades in Sabah. A recent estimate in the *Monthly Statistical Bulletin Sabah* of October 1999 gives a total of 864,000 non-Malaysian citizens out of a mid-year population estimate of Sabah at 2,970,400. The percentage share of "non-Malaysian" has increased to 29.08 percent. "Others" constitute as much as 8.7 percent (259,200). It is clear that census terms such as Pribumi, Bumiputera, Bajau, Indonesian, Other Bumiputera, and Malay are code words for Muslims. This practice allows us to understand how *the census is in effect conferring citizenship upon various illegal immigrant groups*.

It is curious that 192,800 people (6.5 percent) in Sabah are categorized as Malays (Government of Sabah, 1999:9) when there are no records of large-scale migration of Malays from West Malaysia to Sabah after the initial migration of civil servants in the early years of the formation of independent Malaysia. This category includes armed forces personnel who are stationed in Sabah; yet the number of Malays is too high to be accounted for by the mere transfer of officers to Sabah. As Patricia Regis points out, "the term 'Malay' is being increasingly used as a generic term to describe traditionally Muslim groups who speak Malay" (Regis, 1989:417). She further states that "it is also likely that *a number of Indonesians may have claimed to be Malays in order to be indigenized*. In the census classification system for Peninsular Malaysia they are classified as Malays" (emphasis added). The same practice holds true for Muslim Filipinos.

Another category in the mid-year population estimates that raises questions is the group "Other Bumiputeras," which was negligible at one time but now has 393,300 people, or 13.2 percent of the state's population, listed under it. Filipino immigrants, whether through the connivance of elements in the state bureaucracy or through fraudulent documents, are being counted under "Other Bumiputeras," "Others," or "Malays," in the Malaysian Citizens category. In addition, the overwhelming majority in the "non-Malaysian" category are the fresh illegal Filipino and Indonesian immigrants.

The working and reworking of ambiguous census categories in recent years demonstrate the difficulty in accounting for such a large influx of illegal immigrants who have become citizens over time. It is also suggestive of a political strategy to absorb illegal immigrants. Complicity by sections of the state such as the bureaucracy, police, politicians, immigration officials, etc. has enabled the incorporation of illegal immigrants as citizens. The tension between Malay-Muslim sympathetic sections of Sabah and the non-Malay-based "sons of the soil" parties such as PBS helps explain the changing categories adopted to classify immigrants; Malay-based parties such as UMNO wanted to capture the illegal vote while the PBS wanted to neutralize their impact. However, there is incentive for mass self-(mis)reporting by

[37]Malaysia regularized about 320,000 illegal immigrants in 1992, the United States regularized 2,483,348 illegal immigrants in 1986, and Spain regularized 108,848 illegal immigrants in 1991 (Stalker, 1994:152). Italy, Spain, Greece, France, and the United States have conducted several regularization exercises whereby hundreds of thousands of illegal immigrants have become legal resident aliens who could become naturalized citizens after meeting residency requirements.

Filipino illegal immigrants, as Patricia Regis (1989) observes, regarding Indonesians claiming to be Malays. While the evidence from newspaper reports and from local conversations that the author had suggest that there is a political calculation behind classifying illegal immigrants as citizens, there is an obvious incentive for illegal immigrants from the Philippines to self-report themselves under any of the sub-categories falling under the generic term Pribumi or Bumiputera.

Furthermore, the dubious role of illegal immigrants as voters in national and state elections infuriates the non-Muslim local population. In order to analyze their roles as voters, we must first examine the crucial function that documents play in making citizens.

Citizenship by Documents

Most studies of immigration based on the experience of developed states in Western Europe or North America consider naturalization or extension of citizen like rights by states the only means for making immigrants full members of states (Koslowski, 2000:87–93). In turn, these studies assume that the acquisition of the most protected of citizenship rights—the franchise, the eligibility for public office, and military service—comes only with naturalization. I shall now demonstrate the nature of documentary citizenship, where the weakly institutionalized character of citizenship in developing states facilitates the entry of illegal immigrants and allows them to bypass naturalization and gain citizenship rights.[38]

Documentary citizenship is an informal device, a back channel, to many of the benefits associated with the narrower and more difficult path to legal citizenship. It expands and accelerates the incorporation of illegal immigrants into the citizenry of a state. More importantly, it allows many illegal immigrants access to political suffrage. Political suffrage, as we know it, is closely linked to legal citizenship since it opens the door to many protected domains of state activity such as the legislature and other public offices involved in defense, foreign, and security policy making. By transforming illegal immigrants into citizens, documents challenge the traditional view of the relationship between immigrants and the state.

Citizenship is not well institutionalized and defined in Sabah, Malaysia. Nor is Sabah alone in this—many developing countries, such as India, Indonesia, Bangladesh, Thailand, Ecquador, Paraguay, Nigeria, and Ghana among others, are weak on institutionalization of citizenship through documentation. The problems of estimation and classification in Sabah, discussed in an earlier section, are symptomatic of the fact that the use of legal documents is absent or only vaguely present among the "natives." This fact contrasts with the West European or American experience, where identity cards (ICs), passports, and documents are widely circulated and accepted as markers of citizenship (Torpey, 2000). Debates about national ID are related to a state's goal of controlling populations through surveillance. This Western "high modernism" (Scott, 1998) has enabled those states to minutely categorize and classify their populations. They can more readily monitor "foreigners" than can develop states such as Malaysia.

After independence, the Malaysian state sought to render "citizens" distinct from local populations. This effort was tied to its conception of a "nation." Who, the implicit question ran, "owned" the nation (Hall, 1999)? This debate over Malaysia's conception of nationhood is intertwined with that over illegal immigrants. Malaysia's effort to define and restrict citizenship is problematic because a large section of its population, as in so many developing countries, does not possess birth certificates or passports. Weakly institutionalized citizenship in Malaysia is the condition whereby some legally eligible natives have no documentary proof of citizenship

[38]As a status, documentary citizenship is distinguished from Tomas Hammar's "denizen" concept by the fact that "documentary citizens" acquire national level suffrage, as Hammar's denizens do not (Hammar, 1989:83–84).

while others have multiple documentary proofs of citizenship (issued by multiple state agencies). Since many natives do not have a standardized document such as the passport, a birth certificate, or a national IC, the state will not insist on a standard document for the exercise of an individual's civil, political, economic, or social rights. Another important aspect of weakly institutionalized citizenship is that some services provided by the government that require standardized documentation are unavailable to these sections of the population. This is especially true for urban areas. Inasmuch as illegal immigrants do, or hope to, gravitate toward urban areas, they are likely to have a greater incentive to acquire documents that prove their citizenship than are long-time inhabitants of difficult-to-reach areas, such as the interior of West Malaysia or the many islands of Sabah. On the other hand, since natives are accustomed to other natives either not possessing documents or, alternatively, having multiple documents, the distinction between legal and illegal is hazy. Coherent legality depends on monitoring, surveillance, and maintenance of certain state-established standard rules and regulations. However, given (i) the absence of proof of citizenship in some regions and, (ii) the varying nature of documentation in their other parts, it becomes impossible to firmly establish these rules and regulations under the condition of weakly institutionalized citizenship. It is difficult, based on paperwork, for authorities in developing states to monitor and distinguish those who are legal citizens from those who are not.

This brings us to an important question. Why is the weakly institutionalized character of citizenship in Malaysia important? Theories of immigration and citizenship assume that *the receiving state has standardized documentation for its population*, which permits citizens to be distinguished from immigrants—legal or illegal. In the real world, however, illegal immigrants are not so easily distinguishable from those locals who themselves do not carry any documents in many developing states. Even network analysis, which explains the process of immigration by illuminating how social and personal networks enable entry and settlement of immigrants, ignores the lack of standardized citizenship in countries like Malaysia. Additionally, illegal immigrants know that the local population in some parts of Malaysia has no documents and that settlement will therefore not likely be a major hurdle. Information flowing through networks of family, kin, and/or fellow-villagers ensures that illegal immigrants have reliable knowledge about their future host state. Illegal immigrants' confidence of not being detected during residence because the local population is also in a similarly weakly institutionalized condition facilitates their settlement.

A birth certificate is an essential document for obtaining a Malaysian IC, which is the main citizenship document. The IC is the basic document needed for entering the school system, exercising the franchise, and becoming eligible for licenses. Illegal migrants are poor people from neighboring countries who are seeking a more stable life. They therefore have a strong incentive to acquire citizenship documents by any means necessary. As illegal immigrants in a foreign country, they are often subject to harassment: while entering, while traveling, while seeking employment, while on the job, etc. Therefore, the search for "documents" is always a primary task for illegal immigrants. This functional aspect of documents, their practical consequences, and enabling power are completely ignored by scholars of international migration and politics.

In April 1999, an official of the National Registration Department (NRD) in Sabah complained that over two million people residing there did not possess birth certificates (*The Sun*, 1999). This is significant considering that the total population of Sabah is estimated to be about 2.8 million (Government of Sabah, 1998).[39] Many Sabah residents are born at home in villages or on remote islands and not in

[39] The mid-year population estimate for 1998 was 2,812,000 persons.

hospitals or maternity clinics, where birth certificates can be provided. Ignorance of the law, which requires registration certificates of birth and death, also causes the absence of citizenship-related documents. According to the Director General of the NRD, any birth must be reported at a NRD within 14 days; in case of problems, parents are allowed to register their child within 42 days (*Borneo Post*, 1999a). After that, the NRD requires evidence and has to interview parents to determine the child's citizenship. This is obviously a difficult process for natives living in the interior as well as the poor living in remote areas or islands, etc. The result was that almost 10,000 out of 500,000 babies born each year in Malaysia were not registered within the stipulated period (*Borneo Post*, 1999a). Before April 1987, no birth certificates were required for a Malaysian IC and the records show that most people did not possess birth certificates. Since then, however, the birth certificate has become an essential document for acquiring a Malaysian citizenship/IC. It is an offence to fail to obtain a Malaysian IC after the age of 12 years. There were 39,120 applications for ICs in 1998 from 12-year-olds alone throughout Sabah (*The Sun*, 1999). Therefore, it may take as much as 2–3 years before an IC is issued.

The NRD is "worried" about the possibility of people using other persons' birth certificates to acquire Malaysian ICs as well as the problem of "forged" ICs (*The Sun*, 1999). Immigrants say that it is quite easy to obtain an IC. A "blue" IC is for citizens only. But migrants can get a fake one for as little as 10 Ringgit ($2.63) (*Borneo Post*, 1999b).[40] The Registration Department seeks the help of community leaders, village chiefs, and other agencies to verify or to register people in remote areas who may not have birth certificates, and therefore, no ICs. However, the verification process itself can be corrupted with bribery and collusion of native chiefs and other local community leaders responsible for verification, thus resulting in issuance of "real" ICs for illegal immigrants. Complicating the issue of ICs is the problem of unclaimed Malaysian ICs. Malaysia has shifted to a new "high security" IC and as of February 1999, there were 52,320 new unclaimed ICs that were applied for since the beginning of 1991 (*The Sun*, 1999). There were 9,344 ICs from Kota Kinabalu (capital of Sabah), 7,143 from Sandakan (East Coast town bordering Philippines), 8,371 from Tawau (East Coast town bordering Indonesia), and 4,709 from Lahad Datu (West Coast town).

The non-possession of birth certificates or ICs by many natives, the slow process of acquiring birth certificates, the registration for everchanging new high security ICs, the conversion from old ICs to new ICs, the many cases of forged ICs, and the wrongful acquisition of ICs based on someone else's birth certificates—these have all created a citizenship card mess that allows illegal immigrants and various sections within Sabah to misuse the citizenship system for their own electoral benefit. Since it is difficult to physically distinguish a Malaysian Bajau from a Filipino Bajau or a Malaysian Bugis from an Indonesian Bugis—the language, physical features, and food habits are all the same—we may surmise that many illegal Bajau and Bugi immigrants possess one or more of these documents, which makes them eligible to vote in Malaysian elections. Otherwise, they can make use of fake papers since state agencies on the street cannot distinguish between fake and real documents.

This ambiguity in citizenship creates two new types of membership in weakly institutionalized developing countries, the distinctiveness of which the scholarly literature has yet to recognize—*suffraged non-citizens* and *non-suffraged citizens*. Suffraged non-citizens are the illegal immigrants and refugees who are beneficiaries of documentary citizenship; non-suffraged citizens are legal citizens who lack proper documentation of their status. The process I call *documentary citizenship* does not focus on rights and duties of citizenship per se, but rather on acquiring documents

[40]The Filipino laborer Amillusin Umar was jailed for 4 months for acquiring a high-quality fake IC. *The Borneo Post* and other local newspapers carry news about illegal immigrants every day. Much of the local news reporting is devoted to crimes committed by illegal immigrants.

that subsequently enable their holder to access state benefits and travel freely. In countries where citizenship is weakly institutionalized, citizenship is not defined by the exercise of social, political, and civil rights; instead, it is defined by the acquisition of documents and paper to prove one's membership. Furthermore, in a globalizing world, it is increasingly documentary citizenship that allows illegal migrants mobility across states and access to the privileges of a citizen in their host states. Sometimes it may give them access to two states if the immigrant has dual paperwork. It is the documentation, real or fake, which has become the major signifier of citizenship, a point missed by most scholars of immigration and citizenship.

Illegal Immigrants as Voters

In this section, I explain why the incorporation of illegal immigrants through manipulation of the census and the deceitful racket in citizenship documents occurs and how this incorporation is connected to the electoral politics of Sabah. Legalizing illegal immigrants becomes the preferred strategy of the dominant Malay parties when overt Malayization (through conversion, internal migration, etc.) does not proceed quickly enough.[41] The goal of the Malays, who dominate the federal government, is to change the demographic and political character of Sabah so that it becomes Malay Muslim-dominated, and because of cultural-religious commonalties, these immigrant Indonesians and Filipinos can easily be *Malayized* over time and will support Malay-Muslim parties.

The tacit support of fraudulent activities by sections in the federal government and by Malay elements in the state government produces a very insidious politics from within: a section within the state is trying to undermine the political rights of the major ethnic groups in a regional-state through migration. According to Herman Luping, (1994:444), a former Attorney General of Sabah: "the popular belief among Sabahans, of course, was that both UMNO and USNO (the premier Malay parties) leaders wanted these people (illegal immigrants) to stay in Sabah and become citizens so that they could swell the votes for their Muslim-based party." Contrary to the experience of other countries, it seems that the decision as to who will be the ruling government in Sabah is now being determined by the crucial illegal immigrant vote. What is lost is the distinction between citizens and immigrants.

It appears to Kadazandusuns and other natives that there is active involvement of some state officials in the process of "legalizing" illegal immigrants. In a recent court case (Harris Mohd Salleh vs. Ismail bin Majin) the petitioner, Dr. Chong, told the court how a number of senior UMNO (the ruling Malay party) members from Sabah were detained under the ISA for their involvement in the falsification of ICs (*Daily Express*, 1999b; *The Borneo Post*, 1999d).[42] The list included the UMNO Deputy Chief of Tawau, Shamsul Alang, as well as Datu Akjan, Jabar Khan, and Dandy Pilo, among others. Some NRD officers and businessmen were also detained under ISA for their part in this operation. According to Hassnar, a former ISA detainee and a participant in this operation, a total of 130,000 illegal foreigners were issued blue ICs in 1985 alone (*The Borneo Post*, 1999d).[43] Hassnar testified in court that he played a leading role in the operation, which was aimed at increasing the Muslim

[41]There were many attempts to convert Kadazandusun and other natives to Islam. The process was called "*masuk melayu*" or "entering Malayness." The "born again" Muslims were called *saudara baru*. I thank Herman Luping, a former Deputy Chief Minister as well as a former Attorney General of Sabah, for this information. See his book *Sabah's Dilemma*, 1994:530–535 and 564–567.

[42]The author was present in Sabah for a period when the court hearings on this matter were taking place. Dr. Chong went on to win part of his petition and the Likas constituency election result was nullified by the order of the judge on June 8, 2001. The judicial decision by the High Court judge was delivered despite pressure on him from "sources" to dismiss the petition. *Daily Express*, June 9, 2001.

[43]Hassnar was a former district native chief in Sandakan.

population in Sabah. He further alleged that this endeavor involved foreigners, government officers, and members of the ruling Barisan Nasional (BN) party.

Making citizens out of non-citizens has become a major industry in the state. With a potential market of 400,000 foreigners, the illegal IC business can be very lucrative (*Daily Express*, 1998).[44] Jeffrey Kitingan, a prominent Kadazandusun leader who was incarcerated under the ISA, says he was "privileged to meet fellow ISA detainees. . .who were directly involved in the *project IC*—businessmen, government servants and Indonesians" (Kitingan, 1997:23). A local daily reported the arrest of seven officials from the NRD under the ISA for their involvement in the issuance of fake ICs to foreigners (Kurus et al., 1998:174).

While the fake documentation business is partly driven by sheer profit motives, many non-Muslim natives allege that there are indicators of a deliberate political strategy of demographic change. For example, these officials are not put on trial because that would involve media and publicity, which risk the possibility of all the details of the "IC project" being made public in a court hearing. The ISA under which these persons are interned conveniently permits the government to hold these officials without trial and then release them after a few years. Current juridical practice permits the government to refrain from releasing reports or figures on these internments, as would be the case if these officials were charged in a court of law. Taken as a whole, these appear to be face-saving forms of support for a well-functioning citizenship card-making machinery. Jeffrey Kitingan (1997:23–24) alleges: "what the Malaysian Schemers are doing is tantamount to *selling out our birth rights to aliens*" (emphasis added).

Many Kadazandusuns and other natives feel that this deliberate strategy is a way of demographically overwhelming them. In an outburst after losing power in 1985, Harris Salleh, a former Chief Minister and one of the most prominent politicians of Sabah, acknowledged such a demographic strategy when he said:

> The Kadazans will become like the Sikhs are now in India, a race forever under suspicion by the majority race. There is no doubt that Sabah is moving towards being dominated by the Muslims who already make up more than 50% of the population. It all depends on the federal government, how fast the process continues. Remember we have nearly 300,000 Filipino and Indonesian refugees and workers here in Sabah and most of them are Muslims. Most have been here for many years and will become eligible for citizenship. They are happy living and working here and do not want to leave. . .the federal government can register any of the refugees in three hours, three days, three months or three years. There is no law stating the time and *if the federal government wants to alter forever the voting patterns of Sabah then it can do it as easily as signing the papers* (Raffaele, 1986:424–426; emphasis added).

The largely Muslim makeup of this illegal immigration into Sabah is viewed as an instrument for changing the voting pattern of Sabah to benefit Malay parties such as UMNO—the ruling Malay party of Peninsular Malaysia. The motive is to increase the UMNO's vote banks. The UMNO's obvious goal is to override the Kadazandusuns and Muruts[45] in favor of a coalition of Muslims groups represented

[44]Statement by Joseph Sitin Saang, Vice President of Parti Democratic Sabah (PDS).

[45]A recent report in the newspaper *Daily Express* quotes two researchers from University Malaysia Sabah making the same argument. W. Shawaluddin Hasan and Ramli Dollah argue that the "possession of original ICs via forged documents among the immigrants indirectly resulted in the group gaining control of the economic affairs, education, politics, and job opportunities and, *most importantly, the rights of the Bumiputeras*." They further said, "In this respect, we do not have the right anymore to question them because they have already become a part of the state natives because of the original and valid documents in their hands." See "Bumis are the Real Losers," *Daily Express* 2002. In this context, "Bumiputeras" means "Kadazandusuns and Muruts."

and led by UMNO. Just before the state elections, PBS submitted a list of 49,270 illegal immigrants who had been issued ICs enabling them to vote. A recent best-selling book about illegal immigrants[46] has identified hundreds of illegal immigrants who have fake ICs and may have voted in recent elections (Mutalib, 1999).[47] It lists their IC numbers, their affiliation to UMNO, provides the photographs of these individuals, and in some cases even lists their "foreign" passports (Mutalib, 1999).

These false-document-holding illegals who vote are called "phantom voters" in Sabah. I use the term *suffraged non-citizens* to capture the contradiction of non-citizens' voting. There are three kinds of *suffraged non-citizens* in Sabah according to the main opposition party (*Daily Express*, 1999c; *Borneo Post*, 1999e):

(i) foreigners who were illegally issued identification cards/receipts and were registered as voters in Sabah;
(ii) foreigners who were issued fake ICs or receipts bearing the names of others who appear on the electoral rolls; and
(iii) foreigners who were illegally issued fake identification cards/receipts bearing the name of dead voters whose names are still in the electoral rolls.

Here it may be asked what motivates these illegal immigrants to vote. Do they have rational, self-interested reasons to exercise the franchise? While UMNO benefits, what is the benefit for them? Besides gaining material benefits such as the distribution of water tanks, rice, money, and fishing nets of various sizes (many Filipino immigrants are excellent fishermen), an issue well covered by various local dailies during the elections (*Daily Express*, 1999d), there is the additional lure of access to better living conditions in Sabah, if one can secure Malaysian ICs. The IC comes with the expectation that these immigrants vote for their benefactors, which in Sabah happens to be the ruling Malay party—UMNO. Some of these "illegal" voters earn lucrative pay by working for the ruling party during elections, making billboards, mounting posters, distributing pamphlets, etc.[48] Also, connections with powerful members of the UMNO and other officials bring with them other privileges for these illegal immigrants. It is quite beneficial for these illegal immigrants to be involved in the Sabah elections.

In response to this involvement, the former Chief Minister of Sabah, Pairin, urged the government to stop allowing holders of temporary identity documents such as JPN 1/9, JPN 1/11, and JPN 1/22 to vote in elections (*The Borneo Post*, 1999f). JPN 1/9 is a document issued to new applicants of ICs, JPN 1/11 is issued to those who report a loss of IC, and JPN 1/22 is given to those who change their blue IC to the new "Bunga Raya" card (*Daily Express*, 1999e). All are temporary documents and yet persons with such documents are allowed to vote. Dr. Chong, a PBS candidate from the Likas constituency, submitted evidence alleging misuse of these temporary documents (*Borneo Post*, 1999g).[49] These were documents surrendered to him by anonymous individuals after the Sabah state elections in March 1999. In

[46]This book is titled *IC Palsu: Merampas Hak Anak Sabah.* IC Palsu means "False IC."

[47]The electoral role of illegal immigrants is corroborated by the author's conversations and interviews with both immigrants and local natives.

[48]Author's conversation with an illegal immigrant. It is not easy to get an illegal immigrant to acknowledge that she/he is illegal and voting.

[49]Copy in the author's possession. The evidence includes 18 pairs of receipts; each pair of receipts has the same photograph of a person bearing two different names and corresponding National Registration numbers that also appear on the electoral rolls. Among these 36 JPN receipts, three names with the corresponding IC numbers appear twice but with different photographs, different addresses, and dates of births. The news reports covering this issue include: (1) "Police report on fake documents," *The Borneo Post*, September 22, 1999:A5; (2) "Petitioner alleges illegality," *The Borneo Post*, September 22, 1999:A5; (3) "Sanctity of electoral rolls challenged," *The Borneo Post*, September 23, 1999:A4; (4) "Phantom voters influenced election," *The Borneo Post*, September 29, 1999:A1; and (5) "Flush out fake voters: Pairin to BN," *The Borneo Post*, September 23, 1999:A2.

Harris Mohd Salleh vs. Ismail bin Majin—a historic decision on the petition filed by Dr. Chong—the High Court declared the election result of the Likas constituency null and void, ruling that "non-citizens had cast their votes in the polls" (*Daily Express*, 2001). Accepting Dr. Chong's submission that the 1998 electoral rolls of the N13 Likas electoral seat were illegal since they contained names of illegal immigrants and persons who had been convicted for possession of fraudulent ICs, Judge Awang of the High Court wrote:

> The instances of non-citizens and phantom voters in the electoral roll as disclosed during the trial may well be the *tip of the iceberg* ... It is common knowledge that an influx of illegal immigrants has plagued Sabah for some years. It is a well known fact as it had appeared in the local dailies too frequently. . .(*Daily Express*, 2001; emphasis added).

The judge noted in his decision[50] how people convicted of possessing fake ICs in 1996 continued on the electoral rolls of Likas constituency in 1998.[51]

Natives' resentment of this phenomenon is understandable, considering that Article 119 (1) of the Malaysian Constitution accords the right to vote in any State or Parliamentary (national) election *only* to citizens (Percetakan Nasional Malaysia: 101). Furthermore, recent constitutional jurisprudence holds that non-citizens or those who have been convicted of possessing fraudulent citizenship documents are *ineligible* to vote (see Harris Mohd Salleh vs. Ismail bin Majin). In practice, illegal immigrants are enjoying political suffrage. For example, a female illegal immigrant confessed to having voted in the last five elections in Sabah, the first three times from Sembulan and the fourth and fifth times in a place called Kuala Penyu in Sabah (see *Borneo Post*, 1999h).[52] We can therefore assume that there are cases of Indonesian immigrants who have voted both in Sabah as well as in the elections in Indonesia if we consider that an estimated 1.4 million Indonesian immigrants voted in the 1996 Indonesian elections while still living in Malaysia (Kassim, 1998:285).

The Malaysian experience that this article documents highlights three remarkable features of international migration: (i) illegal immigrants can vote, (ii) documents enable their political participation as citizens, and (iii) parties and immigrants both have an interest in preserving the irregularities of documentation and collaborate to that end. Leading scholars of the mobility of labor and capital have pointed out the transnational character of such flows but have ignored the critical role that documents play in enabling the mobility and incorporation of labor (Sassen, 1998). In actual practice, voting and political participation are not products of some abstract group membership, but rather are products of the documents an individual holds, documents that are plentiful wherever there is illegal immigration. Around the world, documents, fake as well as real, are facilitating the incorporation and absorption of illegal immigrants into the state.

Conclusion

Malaysia, like most other states, restricts voting rights to citizens; however, distinctions between citizens and non-citizens are largely meaningless in developing

[50]This decision was an exception and not the rule and in his decision, Judge Awang draws attention to the pressure imposed upon him to throw out these petitions: "In my view it is an insult to one's intelligence to be given a directive over the phone that these petitions should be struck off without a hearing..." (*Daily Express*, 2001).

[51]These immigrants were (Harris Mohd Salleh vs. Ismail bin Majin, 1999):

Kassim Bin Ali	Identity card number H0508335
Anwar Identity	Identity card number H0512235
Kadir Labak	Identity card number H0454652

[52]The alien was identified as Sabturia and the news report identified her IC number.

countries such as Malaysia where citizenship is weakly institutionalized. Therefore, it becomes possible for illegal immigrants to gain access to social, political, and economic rights through false or falsely obtained documentation, a process I have called Documentary Citizenship.

Yet according to most studies of immigration politics, documentary citizenship should not be occurring, because they presume that when it comes to national and state voting, the lines between citizen and immigrant are sharply drawn. One has political suffrage; the other does not. But most developing countries have only recently begun to control migration and to certify identity. Many developing states with large rural populations are thin on documentation of any aspect of identity: there are no birth certificates, marriage certificates, or death certificates. The distinctions between citizens and immigrants do not matter for sections within the state that seek to change the ethnic composition of the region for political reasons. If conversion to Islam or internal migration from West Malaysia does not suffice, then immigration of fellow Muslims from Southern Philippines will. But in the eyes of the local natives of Sabah—the non-Muslim Kadazandusuns and the Muruts, who at one time formed the largest ethnic group(s) in the state—native groups have become foreigners in their own land. As natives, if they lack a birth certificate because they live in rural areas or in the interior (as many do), they cannot vote or become citizens. Yet a Filipino who takes a boat from Zamboanga in the Philippines and reaches Sabah with just a few hundred Ringgit can acquire a blue IC and the right to vote. By acquiring documentary citizenship, illegal immigrants can and do become a part of the electoral process in the host state, a right that, according to the laws of the state, should be restricted to real citizens.

The problem this article poses is this: the international system is based on distinct states having exclusive citizenries. According to international norms, a person can only belong to one state at a time. Concomitantly, naturalization is the only path to citizenship with full political rights. True, dual citizenship is increasing, but this is possible only with the permission of either one or both states. In sum, political exclusion of non-citizens is the basis of an international politics that equates national interest with the interest of citizens only. But if non-citizens and citizens *both* represent the state, then the traditional system of mutually exclusive citizenries will need considerable reconceptualization. Being an illegal immigrant is, in many developing countries, no different from being a citizen. In weakly institutionalized states, this is what we are witnessing. Non-citizens come through porous borders and reside in unmarked populations. Acquisition of documents, which is to say documentary citizenship, allows illegal immigrants the status of citizens. Possession of identical documents erodes the sharp distinctions between citizens and non-citizens, allowing both equal access to political rights. If illegal immigrants have access to political suffrage, they are able to determine who holds public offices, and thus indirectly to control national policies. In such circumstances, the notion of the national interest and the state's pursuit of it are thrown into crisis. The reality of both citizens and illegal immigrants competing on an equal footing to set the policies of states requires major rethinking of the role of illegal immigration in international politics.

References

ANDREAS, P. (2000) *Border Games: Policing the U.S.–Mexico Divide*. Ithaca: Cornell University Press.

ARENDT, H. (1968) *The Origins of Totalitarianism*. San Diego: A Harvest Book.

THE BORNEO POST (KOTA KINABALU) (1999a) September 29:A4.

THE BORNEO POST (KOTA KINABALU) (1999b) "RM 10 for fake IC," August 18: A3.

THE BORNEO POST (KOTA KINABALU) (1999c) "Illegal jailed after entering state since 1979," October 6:A3.

THE BORNEO POST (KOTA KINABALU) (1999d) "Conspiracy in issuing ICs to foreigners, " November 12:A4.

THE BORNEO POST (KOTA KINABALU) (1999e) August 21:A2.

THE BORNEO POST (KOTA KINABALU) (1999f) "Flush out fake voters: Pairin to BN," September 23:A2.

THE BORNEO POST (KOTA KINABALU) (1999g) "Police report on fake documents," September 22:A5.

THE BORNEO POST (KOTA KINABALU) (1999h) "Alien confesses voted in five polls." November 16:A1.

BRUBAKER, R. (1992) *Citizenship and Nationhood in France and Germany*. Cambridge: Harvard University Press.

CASTLES, S., AND A. DAVIDSON (2000) *Citizenship and Migration: Globalization and the Politics of Belonging*. New York: Routledge.

CORNELIUS, W., P. MARTIN, AND J. HOLLIFIELD, (ed.) (1994) *Controlling Immigration: A Global Perspective*. Stanford: Stanford University Press.

DAILY EXPRESS (KOTA KINABALU) (1998) May 20 (Internet edition). ⟨www.dailyexpress.com.my⟩

DAILY EXPRESS (KOTA KINABALU) (1999a) "Letter to the editor," August 1:20.

DAILY EXPRESS (KOTA KINABALU) (1999b) "Foreigners voted BN claim," September 29:1.

DAILY EXPRESS (KOTA KINABALU) (1999c) "Three categories of phantom voters: PBS," August 21:3.

DAILY EXPRESS (KOTA KINABALU) (1999d) November 17:2.

DAILY EXPRESS (KOTA KINABALU) (1999e) "Future generations will not forgive," October 8, 1999:4.

DAILY EXPRESS (KOTA KINABALU) (2000a) "No foolproof way of stopping more seizures," September 12 (Internet edition). ⟨www.dailyexpress.com.my⟩

DAILY EXPRESS (KOTA KINABALU) (2000b) 25 October (Internet edition). ⟨www.dailyexpress.com.my⟩

DAILY EXPRESS (KOTA KINABALU) (2001) "Its by-poll for Likas," June 9 (Internet edition). ⟨www.dailyexpress.com.my⟩

DAILY EXPRESS (KOTA KINABALU) (2002) "Bumis are the real losers," July 18 (Internet edition). ⟨www.dailyexpress.com.my⟩

DEPARTMENT OF STATISTICS (MALAYSIA) (1983) Population and Housing Census of Malaysia, Vol.1, January.

DEPARTMENT OF STATISTICS (MALAYSIA) (1995) Population and Housing Census 1991, State Population Report: Sabah, March.

GOVERNMENT OF SABAH (1998) Buku Tahunan Perangkaan (Cawangan Sabah: Jabatan Perangkaan Malaysia).

GOVERNMENT OF SABAH (1999) Monthly Statistical Bulletin Sabah, October.

HALL, R. B. (1999) *National Collective Identity: Social Constructs and International Systems*. New York: Columbia University Press.

HAMMAR, T. (1989) "State, Nation, and Dual Citizenship." In *Immigration and the Politics of Citizenship in Europe and North America*, edited by R. B. William. Lanham, MD: University Press of America.

Harris Mohd Salleh vs. Ismail bin Majin, Returning Officer, Election Petition No k5 and k11, 1999, High Court (Kota Kinabalu), 2001-3 MLJ 433; 2001 MLJ Lexis (Lexis Nexis).

JACOBSON, D. (1997) *Rights Across Borders: Immigration and the Decline of Citizenship*. Baltimore, MD: The Johns Hopkins University Press.

JENNINGS, C. (2002) "Accelerated Citizenship Available for Active Duty Personnel," *Navy Newsstand*, Story Number: NNS020827-18, August 27, 9:30:00 PM. ⟨http://www.news.navy.mil/search/display.asp?story_id=3295⟩

JOPPKE, C. (1999) *Immigration and the Nation-State: The United States, Germany, and Great Britain*. New York: Oxford University Press.

KASSIM, A. (1998) "International Migration and its Impact on Malaysia." In *A Pacific Peace: Issues and Responses*, edited by M. J. Hassan, pp. 273–305. Kuala Lumpur: ISIS.

KITINGAN, J. (1997) *The Sabah Problem*. Kota Kinabalu: KDI Publications.

KITINGAN, J., AND G. WILLIAM (1989) "Development of Administrative System in Sabah, 1963–1988." In *Sabah 25 Years Later: 1963–1988*, edited by K. Jeffrey and O. Maximus. Sabah: Institute for Development Studies.

KOSLOWSKI, R. (2000) *Migrants and Citizens: Demographic Change in the European State System*. Ithaca: Cornell University Press.

KOSLOWSKI, R. (2002) Human Migration and the Conceptualization of Pre-Modern World Politics. *International Studies Quarterly* **46**(3):375–399.

KURUS, B., R. GODDOS, AND R. KOH (1998) Migrant Labor Flows in the East Asian Region: Prospects and Challenges. *Borneo Review* **IX**(2):156–186.

KYMLICKA, W. (1995) *Multicultural Citizenship: A Liberal Theory Of Minority Rights*. Oxford: Clarendon Press.

LOPEZ, LAURA. (2003) "Sailors to Citizens," *Navy Newsstand* Story Number: NNS030522-04, May 22, 9:28 A.M. ⟨http://www.news.navy.mil/search/display.asp?story_id=7574⟩

LUPING, H. (1994) *Sabah's Dilemma: The Political History of Sabah: 1960–1994*. Kuala Lumpur: Magnus Books.

MARSHALL, T. H., AND T. BOTTOMORE (1996) *Citizenship and Social Class*. London: Pluto Press.

MUTALIB, M. D. (1999) *IC Palsu: Merampas Hak Anak Sabah*. Kota Kinabalu.

THE NEW YORK TIMES (2002) "Malaysia Deporting Indonesian and Philippine Workers," Friday, August 30:A3.

PERCETAKAN NASIONAL MALAYSIA (1997) *Federal Constitution*. Kuala Lumpur: Percetakan Nasional Malaysia Berhad.

PHILIPPINE DAILY INQUIRER (MANILA) (1999) "Filipino illegals swell in Sabah," October 30 (Internet edition). ⟨www.thefilipino.com/frames/philinq.htm⟩

RAFFAELE, P. (1986) *Harris Salleh of Sabah*. Hong Kong: Condor Publishing.

RATH, J. (1990) "Voting Rights." In *The Political Rights of Migrant Workers in Western Europe*, edited by L.H. Zig, pp. 127–157. London: Sage Publications.

REGIS, P. (1989) "Demography." In *Sabah 25 Years Later: 1963–1988*, edited by K. Jeffrey and O. Maximus. Sabah: Institute for Development Studies.

SASSEN, S. (1998) *Globalization and its Discontents*. New York: The New Press.

SASSEN, S. (1999) *Guests and Aliens*. New York: The New Press.

SCHUCK, P. H., AND R. M. SMITH (1985) *Citizenship Without Consent: Illegal Aliens in the American Polity*. New Haven: Yale University Press.

SCOTT, J. C. (1998) *Seeing Like a State: How Certain Schemes to Improve the Human Condition Have Failed*. New Haven: Yale University Press.

SMITH, R. (1997) *Civic Ideals: Conflicting Visions of Citizenship in U.S. History*. New Haven: Yale University Press.

SOYSAL, Y. (1994) *Limits of Citizenship: Migrants and Postnational Membership in Europe*. Chicago: University of Chicago Press.

STALKER, P. (1994) *The Work of Strangers: A Survey of International Labour Migration*. Geneva: International Labor Office.

THE SUN (KUALA LUMPUR) (1999) "Officially, these folks don't exist," April 19:A12.

TIBURCIO, C. (2001) *The Human Rights of Aliens Under International and Comparative Law*. The Hague, Kluwer Law International: Martinus Nijhoff Publishers.

TOMIYUKI, U. (2000) "Migration and Ethnic Categorization at International Frontier: A Case of Sabah, East Malaysia." In *Population Movement in Southeast Asia: Changing Identities and Strategies for Survival*, edited by K. -I. Abe and M. Ishii. Osaka: JCAS Symposium Series 10, Japan Center for Area Studies, National Museum of Ethnology.

TORPEY, J. (2000) *The Invention of the Passport: Surveillance, Citizenship and the State*. Cambridge: Cambridge University Press.

Part II
Transnationality

[8]

BETWEEN NATIONAL AND POST-NATIONAL: MEMBERSHIP IN THE UNITED STATES

*T. Alexander Aleinikoff**

This essay argues that the concept of post-nationalism does not precisely explain the American concept of citizenship. This is due to the strict construction of the nation state in American constitutional theory, the ineffective role of international human rights norms in American jurisprudence, and the extension of protection to non-citizens based on territorialist rationales. For these reasons, the author suggests that denizenship *is a more appropriate way of viewing the American citizenship model, and is one that explains how notions of personal identity can be transnational while still justifiable within traditional nation-state constructs.*

It has become fashionable to predict the decline of the nation-state at the hands of sub-national and supra-national forces. Ethnic minorities, transnational corporations, international organizations and Non-Governmental Organizations (NGOs) are rounded up as the usual destabilizing suspects. Increasingly, a new group is said to contribute to the weakening of the nation-state regime: trans-border migrants. Their movement—creates and maintains "transnational" communities that put pressure on the idea of loyalty to a single state. They may also form alliances with domestic minority groups who are demanding greater recognition—or autonomy—from the national government.

Migrants disturb national boundaries in another sense: they complicate notions of national membership. Settled immigrants (sometimes even unlawful immigrants) may make claims to some forms of "membership" rights, such as entitlements to national benefit programs and educational opportunities, protection under non-discrimination laws, and due process rights in deportation proceedings. These claims are generally put in domestic law terms; where possible, immigrants are likely to try to fit their claims within rights established by national constitutions and legislation. But increasingly, immigrants are invoking international legal norms that

* Professor of Law, Georgetown University Law Center. This paper was prepared for a conference on Integrating Immigrants in Liberal States, sponsored by the European Forum of the Centre for Advanced Studies at the European University Institute, May 8–9, 1998. I would like to thank Rainer Bauböck Linda Bosniak, Peter Spiro, Mark Tushnet, and Carlos Vázquez for providing important criticisms of an earlier draft of this paper.

protect "persons" (not just "citizens") as they assert claims to fair treatment and basic rights.

The recognition of moral and legal rights whose source is outside the nation-state but which are applicable within (or against the nation-state) has been termed an aspect of "post-national" membership. In an important work, Yasemin Nuhoğlu Soysal has examined post-national membership in Europe.[1] That continent may be the most fruitful location for such an inquiry: Europe has witnessed large-scale immigration in recent decades, and most of the states recognize the authority of the European Court of Human Rights to render decisions binding on national governments that are parties to the European Convention for the Protection of Human Rights and Fundamental Freedoms.[2] In this essay, I will consider the extent to which a "post-national perspective" may be applicable to concepts of membership and sovereignty in the United States. By "post-national perspective" I mean the claim that "national citizenship is losing ground to a more universal model of membership, anchored in deterritorialized notions of persons' rights."[3] The post-national perspective centers around the following claims:

(1) rights and privileges once reserved for citizens (the "national perspective") are now recognized on the basis of personhood;

(2) migration has been a motivating factor in this reconceptualization of rights (placing non-members in a position to assert newly defined membership claims);

(3) these rights claims find their source beyond the nation-state in international human rights norms and structures;

(4) the result is "deterritorialized" membership;

(5) the basis of state legitimacy is shifting from notions of (national) popular will to its respect for international human rights norms.[4]

---

1. *See* YASEMIN NUHOĞLU SOYSAL, LIMITS OF CITIZENSHIP: MIGRANTS AND POSTNATIONAL MEMBERSHIP IN EUROPE (1994); *see also* DAVID JACOBSON, RIGHTS ACROSS BORDERS: IMMIGRATION AND THE DECLINE OF CITIZENSHIP 2–3 (1996) (explaining the shift from state sovereignty to international human rights).

2. Sept. 3, 1953, 213 U.N.T.S. 221.

3. SOYSAL, *supra* note 1, at 3.

4. *See* JACOBSON, *supra* note 1, at 2–3:

> In the Euro-Atlantic core of the world order, in North America and Western Europe, the basis of state legitimacy is shifting from principles of sovereignty and national self-determination to international human rights. Increasingly, territorially delimited nations are not the

Together, these descriptions are understood to support a progressive narrative of the expansion of human rights to previously marginalized groups.

The post-national perspective has implications at the personal level as well. Traditionally, individuals have seen themselves primarily as members of one polity; but today, migration and the assertion of non-state-based rights are producing transnational or supra-national identities. Thus, we are said to be witnessing "the emergence of membership that is multiple in the sense of spanning local, regional, and global identities, and which accommodates intersecting complexes of rights, duties and loyalties."[5] Deterritorialized identities are usually seen as liberating—creating opportunities for new connections and communities, and establishing universal norms of just treatment.

I will argue that the post-national perspective is not an accurate depiction of U.S. models of rights and membership. To some degree there is an overlap between post-national models and the American tradition: rights and privileges have been extended to resident non-nationals in the United States. But the recognition of rights for non-nationals has not been based on norms that transcend the nation-state; rather, it is a core attribute of American constitutionalism, deeply embedded in the idea of the American state. International human rights norms play a surprisingly small role in U.S. discourse and jurisprudence. The post-national claim is correct to see migration as the wedge for the assertion of such rights, but such human rights discourses have had little traction in the United States. Finally, U.S. models of membership that extend rights to non-citizens are largely territorialized, making "denizenship"[6] a more accurate rendering of the American structure of rights than post-nationalism. I will conclude with some comments on post-nationalism at the personal level—suggesting that while personal identities are becoming more transnational, such multiplicity is

> only carriers of "universal humanity." All residents, noncitizens as well as citizens, can claim their human rights. In this process the state is becoming less constituted by "the people" while becoming increasingly constituted by international human rights codes and institutions. The state is becoming less a sovereign agent and more an institutional forum for a larger international and constitutional order based on human rights.

5. SOYSAL, *supra* note 1, at 166.

6. *See* TOMAS HAMMAR, DEMOCRACY AND THE NATION STATE: ALIENS, DENIZENS AND CITIZENS IN A WORLD OF INTERNATIONAL MIGRATION 106–124 (1990); *see also* RAINER BAUBÖCK, TRANSNATIONAL CITIZENSHIP: MEMBERSHIP AND RIGHTS IN INTERNATIONAL MIGRATION 65 (1994) (arguing that "denizenship" derives from an implicit contract, not simply subjection to a state's laws).

articulated primarily in the context of the nation-state (giving rise to an "inter-nationality" more than a post-nationality).

I. SOURCES OF RIGHTS AND CLASSES OF BENEFICIARIES: THE *BREARD* CASE AND BEYOND

On April 14, 1998, the State of Virginia executed by lethal injection Angel Francisco Breard, a 32 year-old citizen of Paraguay who had been residing in Virginia for 12 years. In 1992, Breard had been convicted of a brutal murder, stabbing his victim five times in the neck during a sexual assault. He testified at his trial that he had killed his victim because he had been under the influence of a satanic curse.

Imposition of the death penalty raises significant human rights issues. The United States is virtually alone among Western states in its preservation of the death penalty. A decade ago, the European Court of Human Rights held that it would be a violation of the European Convention on Human Rights for the United Kingdom to extradite a West German citizen to stand trial in Virginia in a capital case.[7] The U.N. Special Rapporteur on extrajudicial, summary or arbitrary executions called for a moratorium on the use of the death penalty in the United States following an investigative visit in 1997.[8] And Amnesty International, in a 1998 report on human rights abuses in the United States, singled out the death penalty for particularly harsh criticism.[9] But Breard's appeal of his conviction and sentence

7. *See* Soering v. United Kingdom, 161 Eur. Ct. H.R. (ser. A) (1989) (holding that long wait and uncertainty of punishment on death row violates European Convention on Human Rights' prohibition of inhuman or degrading treatment or punishment); *see also The Netherlands: Opinion of the Advocaat-General and Supreme Court Decision in* The Netherlands v. Short, 29 INT'L LEGAL MATERIALS 1375 (1990) (denying United States' extradition request of an American serviceman who killed his wife in the Netherlands to prevent defendant's possible exposure to death penalty). For a discussion of human rights and extradition, see John Dugard & Christine Van Den Wyngaert, *Reconciling Extradition with Human Rights*, 92 AM. J. INT'L L. 187 (1998).

8. *See Report of the U.N. Special Rapporteur*, ¶ 148, U.D. Doc. E/CN.4/68/1998/Add.3., 22 Jan. 1998, *cited in* AMNESTY INTERNATIONAL, UNITED STATES OF AMERICA RIGHTS FOR ALL 120 (1998) [hereinafter AMNESTY INTERNATIONAL]; *see also* U.N. GAOR, Hum. Rts. Comm., 50th Sess., Supp. No. 40 ¶¶ 266–304, U.N. A/50/40 (1995) (deploring the expansion of the death penalty at the federal level and its continued prevalence at the state level).

9. *See* AMNESTY INTERNATIONAL, *supra* note 8, at 99 ("International human rights standards seek to restrict the scope of the death penalty. They forbid its use against juvenile offenders, see it as an unacceptable punishment for the mentally impaired, and demand the highest legal safeguards for all capital trials. The USA fails to meet these minimum standards on all counts.").

did not assert a violation of international human rights norms. The American death penalty appears immune to such challenges.[10]

Breard did, however, eventually make a claim based on international law. In 1996, his lawyers filed a *habeas corpus* action in federal court asserting that his rights under the Vienna Convention on Consular Relations had been violated because he had not been informed of his right to contact a consular officer of Paraguay after his arrest and detention.[11] His argument was that consular officials might have urged him to accept a plea agreement, under which he could have received a life sentence, rather than go to trial and risk receiving a death sentence.

The federal courts rejected this claim, saying that he had waived his right to raise it during his appeal in state court. Meanwhile, Paraguay brought its own action against Virginia in federal court based on the Vienna Convention. It asked the court to return the situation to the *status quo ante*—that is, to nullify the conviction and the sentence. The lower courts held that the Eleventh Amendment prohibited a foreign country from suing a state in federal court.[12]

Following its loss in the lower court and receiving no help from the State Department in getting Virginia to change its decision (although the Department conceded that the treaty had been

---

10. *See also* Stanford v. Kentucky, 492 U.S. 361, 369 n.1 (1989) (rejecting argument of dissenting opinion that practices of other nations and provisions in human rights treaties condemning juvenile death penalties are relevant in determining constitutionality of death penalty for a 17 year-old).

For a case in which such a claim was raised—and failed, see *State v. Steffen*, No. C-930351, 1994 WL 176906, *4, *10 (Ohio Ct. App. May 11, 1994). There the court stated:

> In his fourth claim for relief, Steffen contended that his convictions and sentences were void or voidable because the Ohio death penalty is in violation of international law. Specifically, Steffen cited Articles 1, 2, 18, 25 and 26 of the American Declaration of the Rights and Duties of Man, to which the United States is a signatory. We have reviewed the various provisions of the American Declaration to which Steffen referred and find that the record does not demonstrate their violation. We note, moreover, that Steffen has presented absolutely no evidence and made no colorable argument supported by precedent from any human rights forum that his arrest, incarceration, trial and sentence violated international human rights norms to which the United States is bound either by customary international law, i.e., rights having acquired the status of jus cogens, or treaty.
>
> The trial court's dismissal of Steffen's fourth claim for relief was thus appropriate.

Id. at *4.

11. *See* Breard v. Greene, 528 U.S. 371 (1998); Vienna Convention on Consular Relations, Apr. 24, 1963, Art. 36(1), 21 U.S.T. 77, 596 U.N.T.S. 261.

12. *See Breard*, 523 U.S. at 373.

violated), Paraguay filed an action before the International Court of Justice on April 3, 1998. Six days later, the International Court of Justice (ICJ) issued an order stating that the United States "should take all measures at its disposal to ensure that Angel Francisco Breard is not executed pending the final decision in these proceedings."[13] The Legal Adviser to the State Department brought the order to the attention of the Governor of Virginia, and in an extraordinary letter, the Secretary of State personally requested the Governor to stay the execution pending the ICJ's consideration of the case.[14]

Meanwhile, Breard and Paraguay had appealed their cases to the U.S. Supreme Court. By the time the high court considered the cases, the ICJ had issued its order and Breard had been scheduled to be executed. The U.S. government, although not a party to the actions, filed a brief urging the Supreme Court to reject the appeals. This was contemporaneous with the Secretary of State's request to the Governor of Virginia that the execution be stayed. The U.S. government began its argument in the Supreme Court by noting that it took seriously its obligations under the Vienna Convention, then asserted that the Convention did not provide a remedy of nullifying state criminal convictions, that consular notification would in all likelihood not have changed the result, that Breard had waived the claim in any event, and that the matter should be handled state-to-state without Court intervention.[15] The government further stated that the Department of State had accorded Paraguay "the traditional remedy among nations for failure of consular notification: it has investigated the facts, determined there was a breach, formally apologized on behalf of the United States, and undertaken to improve compliance."[16] This "remedy," of course, provided little solace to Mr. Breard.

The Supreme Court denied the appeals. In a brief opinion, it held that Breard had defaulted his claim (assuming he had one); and even if the claim had been timely raised, it was "extremely doubtful" that the violation should result in overturning the conviction.[17]

The Court noted that "it is unfortunate that this matter comes before us while proceedings are pending before the ICJ that might

13. *See id.* at 374 (quoting ICJ order of April 9, 1998).

14. *See* Letter from Madeleine K. Albright, Secretary of State, to James S. Gilmore III, Governor of Virginia (April 13, 1998) (on file with author).

15. *See* Brief for the United States as Amicus Curiae at 12–13, Breard v. Greene, 523 U.S. 371 (1998) (Nos. 97-1390 & 97-8214).

16. *Id.* at 13.

17. *Breard*, 523 U.S. at 377.

have been brought to that court earlier."[18] Nonetheless, it concluded that Breard was not entitled to a remedy from U.S. courts.

The Court duly noted Secretary Albright's letter to the Governor of Virginia and closed by saying: "If the Governor wishes to wait for the decision of the ICJ, that is his prerogative. But nothing in our existing case law allows us to make that choice for him."[19]

The Governor did not wish to wait. He told the press:

> As governor of Virginia, it is my first duty to ensure that those who reside within our borders—both American citizens and foreign nationals—may conduct their lives free from the fear of crime.... In this case Mr. Breard received all of the procedural safeguards that any American citizen would receive. [Delaying the execution] would have the practical effect of transferring responsibility from the courts of the Commonwealth and the United States to the International Court.[20]

So Breard was put to death on the day the Supreme Court issued its opinion, and just five days after the ICJ's order requesting a stay.

There are different ways to read this narrative pertinent to the post-national claim. At first glance, the story is a flat denial of the claim: here a state violated international law and then ignored an order of the international court with the gravest of consequences—execution of a human being. The federal government—charged with enforcing international obligations—was left pleading with one of its own subunits (Virginia) to respect the ICJ. The Governor of Virginia stated that to respect international law would have been to violate his duties to the residents of Virginia, and would have actually given Breard *more* rights than those possessed by citizens of the United States (who cannot generally seek the assistance of a foreign sovereign in the course of a criminal proceeding). The U.S. government's inability to command fidelity to international law and the Governor's assertion that the legal claim based on international law was illegitimate and discriminatory is hardly a ringing endorsement of the post-national perspective.

But arguably there is something more here. Breard did raise a claim in the federal courts grounded in international law; and the United States government did not argue in the Supreme Court that international law did not apply or had not been violated.

18. *Id.* at 378.

19. *Id.*

20. Brooke A. Masters & Joan Biskupic, *Killer Executed Despite Pleas; World Tribunal, State Department Had Urged Delay*, WASH. POST, Apr. 15, 1998, at B1.

Furthermore, the Secretary of State specifically sought to forestall the execution on the ground that proceeding with the execution in the face of the ICJ order could "be seen as a denial by the United States of the significance of international law and the Court processes."[21] These are important concessions regarding the possible trumping power of international law. On this view, Breard's execution was not a failure to recognize international norms but rather a disagreement about what remedies are available if norms are breached.

But this more sanguine narrative merits closer scrutiny. What, after all, was the basis of the U.S. government's position that the Vienna Convention must be respected? According to the Secretary of State, the government was concerned that disrespect would have endangered U.S. citizens abroad who themselves might seek the protection of the Convention. On this view, the international law norm affirmed in the government's argument was not a human rights norm (it certainly was not the claim that the death penalty as practiced in the United States violates human rights law), but rather a means by which sovereign states order their affairs and protect their citizens in the pursuit of state interests.

The *Breard* case does not "disprove" the post-national claim. But it is powerful testimony that rights remain nationally based and defined, and that even those rights whose source is a "transnational community" frequently represent national interests more than the rights of personhood.

To say this, however, is not to accept the nationalist claim that rights and privileges are extended only to full members (i.e., citizens) of the American polity. Rather, American practice has long extended rights and privileges to non-nationals residing in U.S. territory. The Bill of Rights ostentatiously fails to apply its protections solely to citizens. It uses the words "person" or "the people" or other terms not tied to citizenship, such as "the accused," to define the beneficiaries of protection.[22]

The Supreme Court has regularly affirmed that most of the Constitution's protections extend to non-citizens.[23] After a careful

21. Letter from Madeleine K. Albright, *supra* note 14.

22. U.S. CONST. amend. IV ("The right of the people to be secure in their persons, houses, papers and effects, against unreasonable searches and seizures . . ."); *id.* amend V ("No person shall be held to answer for a capital, or otherwise infamous crime, unless on a presentment or indictment of a Grand Jury . . ."); *id.* amend. VI ("In all criminal prosecutions, the accused shall enjoy the right o a speedy and public trial . . .").

23. *See* T. Alexander Aleinikoff, *The Tightening Circle of Membership*, 22 HASTINGS CONST. L.Q. 915, 918–919 (1995); *see also* United States v. Brignoni-Ponce, 422 U.S.

examination of the role of citizenship in the American conception of rights and constitutionalism, Alexander Bickel concluded:

> I find it gratifying . . . that we live under a Constitution to which the concept of citizenship matters very little, that prescribes decencies and wise modalities of government quite without regard to the concept of citizenship. It subsumes important obligations and functions of the individual which have other sources—moral, political, and traditional—sources more complex than the simple contractarian notion of citizenship.[24]

While this constitutional tradition casts a long shadow on the nationalist claim, it does not lend support to the post-national claim because these rights and privileges find their source in national documents and institutions. Soysal is correct to note that "[o]riginally individual rights were defined and codified within schemes of national citizenship."[25] But her claim that "[t]oday . . . individual rights [are] expansively redefined as human rights on a universalistic basis and legitimized at the transnational level"[26] does not seem applicable to the United States. The rights of non-citizens are primarily based on direct application of the U.S. Constitution or statutory law.

I say *primarily* because international law—both treaty law and customary law—does play a role in the U.S. legal system. The Constitution declares that "all Treaties made . . . under the Authority of the United States shall be the supreme Law of the Land;"[27] and federal courts stand ready to enforce treaty rights against state and private action. But to be enforceable in court, such treaties must be "self-executing" or Congress must adopt legislation that makes the treaties applicable in U.S. courts. Human rights treaties are rarely held to be self-executing, and Congress in recent years has not chosen to make them enforceable in federal courts.[28] U.S. ratification of

---

873 (1975) (Fourth Amendment protection for non-citizens); Wong Wing v. United States, 163 U.S. 228, 238 (1896) (Fifth Amendment protection for non-citizens).

24. ALEXANDER M. BICKEL, THE MORALITY OF CONSENT 53–54 (1975).

25. SOYSAL, *supra* note 1, at 164; *see, e.g.* THE DECLARATION OF INDEPENDENCE para 2 (U.S. 1776) (affirming as "self evident" the proposition that "all men are . . . endowed by their Creator with certain unalienable rights.").

26. *Id.*

27. U.S. CONST. art. VI, § 2.

28. *See* Nadine Strossen, *Recent U.S. and International Judicial Protection of Individual Rights: A Comparative Legal Process Analysis and Proposed Synthesis*, 41 HASTINGS L.J. 805, 813 (1990); *see also* United States v. Aguilar, 883 F.2d 662, 680 (9th Cir. 1989) (Protocol Relating to the Status of Refugees not self-executing); Bertrand v. Sava, 684 F.2d 204, 218–19 (2d Cir. 1982) (same); Sei Fujii v. California, 242 P.2d 617, 620–21

human rights conventions has been accompanied by express declarations stating (1) that the convention is not self-executing,[29] and (2) that the United States accepts no obligations under the convention beyond protections already afforded by U.S. constitutional and statutory law.[30] As a result, as Thomas Buergenthal has noted, "it is becoming more and more difficult in the United States fully to transform international human rights obligations into directly applicable domestic law"—a trend that runs counter to developments in other Western states.[31]

Customary international law is potentially a source of human rights protection in domestic U.S. courts. Supreme Court decisions in the past appeared to provide generous reception of international law.[32] Nearly a century ago, the Court ruled that:

> International law is part of our law, and must be ascertained and administered by the courts of justice of appropriate jurisdiction as often as questions of right depending upon it are duly presented for their determination. For this purpose, where there is no

---

(Cal. 1952) (U.N. Charter not self-executing, therefore not binding on the court). On the meaning of self-execution, see Carlos Manuel Vázquez, *The Four Doctrines of Self-Executing Treaties*, 89 AM. J. INT'L L. 695 (1995).

29. *See, e.g.*, 136 Cong. Rec. S17486-01; S17491 (Oct. 27, 1990) (United Nations Convention Against Torture and Other Cruel, Inhuman, and Degrading Treatment not self-executing); 138 Cong. Rec. S4781-01, S4783 (International Covenant on Civil and Political Rights not self-executing).

30. *See, e.g.*, Resolution of Ratification Regarding International Convention on the Elimination of all forms of Racial Discrimination, 140 Cong. Rec. S7634 (June 24, 1994); Resolution of Ratification Regarding United Nations Convention Against Torture and Other Cruel, Inhuman, and Degrading Treatment, 136 Cong. Rec. S17486, S17491 (Oct. 27, 1990) ("The United States considers itself bound . . . only insofar as the term 'cruel, inhuman or degrading treatment or punishment' means the cruel, unusual, and inhuman or degrading treatment or punishment prohibited by the Fifth, Eighth, and/or Fourteenth Amendments to the Constitution of the United States."). A 1993 Human Rights Watch and American Civil Liberties Union report on U.S. compliance with the International Covenant on Civil and Political Rights concluded that the U.S. declarations, reservations and understandings to the Convention rendered ratification "an empty act for Americans: the endorsement of the most important treaty for the protection of civil rights yielded not a single additional enforceable right to citizens and residents of the United States." HUMAN RIGHTS WATCH & AMERICAN CIVIL LIBERTIES UNION, HUMAN RIGHTS VIOLATIONS IN THE UNITED STATES: A REPORT ON U.S. COMPLIANCE WITH THE INTERNATIONAL COVENANT ON CIVIL AND POLITICAL RIGHTS 2 (1993), *quoted in* Nkechi Taifa, *Codification or Castration? The Applicability of the International Convention to Eliminate All Forms of Racial Discrimination to the U.S. Criminal Justice System*, 40 HOW. L.J. 641, 653 (1997).

31. Thomas Buergenthal, *Modern Constitutions and Human Rights Treaties*, 36 COLUM. J. TRANSNAT'L L. 211, 212 (1997); *see also* Louis Henkin, *U.S. Ratification of Human Rights Conventions: The Ghost of Senator Bricker*, 89 AM. J. INT'L L. 341 (1995).

32. *See generally* JORDAN J. PAUST, INTERNATIONAL LAW AS LAW OF THE UNITED STATES (1996).

> treaty and no controlling executive or legislative act or judicial decision, resort must be had to the customs and usages of civilized nations. . . .[33]

Furthermore, the Court has applied a general interpretive norm, dating from an 1804 decision by Chief Justice Marshall, that "an act of congress ought never to be construed to violate the law of nations, if any other possible construction remains. . . ."[34] But in modern times courts have rarely concluded that international human rights norms are applicable or binding as a formal legal matter, particularly when they conflict with statutory law.[35]

Soysal and Jacobson are correct to suggest that international human rights law claims have generally arisen in cases involving non-nationals. In the U.S. context this is so because the Supreme Court has not applied general constitutional norms to most immigration regulation.[36] Thus, from time to time, non-citizens have invoked international human rights protections in challenges to U.S. immigration policies. These cases have raised claims regarding, for example, conditions of detention,[37] forcible abduction of non-citizens outside the United States for trial in the United States,[38] and refugee protection.[39]

But such claims have generally not received sympathetic treatment by the courts. Indeed, as Jordan Paust has noted, the modern approach of denying the applicability of customary international law has received its strongest statement in cases involving aliens—a development that turns the post-national claim on its head.[40] An

---

33. The Paquette Habana, 175 U.S. 677, 700 (1900).

34. Murray v. The Schooner Charming Betsy, 6 U.S. (2 Cranch) 64, 118 (1804).

35. *See, e.g.*, Bertrand v. Sava, 684 F.2d 204, 218–219 (2d Cir. 1982) (finding United Nations Protocol Relating to the Status of Refugees not self-executing). For some rare examples in domestic areas where international human rights norms have been held applicable, see *Jama v. United States Immigration and Naturalization Serv.*, 22 F. Supp. 2d 353 (D.N.J. 1998) (permitting suit against INS officials based on customary international law); Fernandez v. Wilkinson, 505 F. Supp. 787 (D. Kan. 1980) (finding indeterminate detention of Cuban refugee in federal prison violates Universal Declaration of Human Rights). The most important example is *Filartiga v. Pena-Irala*, 630 F.2d 876 (2d Cir. 1980). *See infra* text accompanying notes 40–44.

36. *See* T. Alexander Aleinikoff, *Federal Regulation of Aliens and the Constitution*, 83 AM. J. INT'L L. 862 (1989).

37. *See Jama*, 22 F. Supp. 2d 353; *Fernandez*, 505 F. Supp. 787.

38. *See* United States v. Alvarez-Machain, 504 U.S. 655 (1992).

39. *See* Sale v. Haitian Centers Council, Inc., 509 U.S. 155 (1993); *see also* United Mexican States v. Woods, 126 F.3d 1220 (9th Cir. 1997) (claiming that the murder conviction of Mexican national violated Vienna Convention on Consular Relations, Bilateral Consular Convention, and International Convention on Civil and Political Rights).

40. *See* Jordan J. Paust, *Customary International Law in the United States: Clean and Dirty Laundry*, 40 GERMAN YRBK. OF INT'L L. 78 (1998); *see also* Joan Fitzpatrick &

example is a case involving Cuban nationals in the United States who had been convicted of criminal offenses and whom the United States sought to deport to Cuba at the end of their terms of incarceration. Cuba would not accept their return, so they spent a number of years in Immigration and Naturalization Service detention. The Cuban nationals claimed that their long-term detention by the INS violated customary international human rights law. But a federal court of appeals rejected the claim, agreeing with several other courts of appeals that had ruled in similar circumstances that "international law is not controlling because federal executive, legislative, and judicial actions supersede the application of these principles of international law."[41]

A notable exception to the argument that international human rights norms are of limited utility in U.S. courts involves claims brought under the Alien Tort Claim Act (ATCA).[42] This statute, enacted in 1789, grants federal district courts jurisdiction to hear civil cases brought by an alien for "a tort . . . committed in violation of the law of nations or a treaty of the United States."[43] The statute lay dormant for almost two centuries until the watershed case of *Filartiga v. Pena-Irala.*[44] In that case, Dr. Filartiga and his daughter (citizens of Paraguay living in the United States) brought a damage action against Pena-Irala, who had been Inspector General of Police in Asuncion, Paraguay and was then present in the United States. The Filartigas alleged that the police had kidnapped and tortured to death Filartiga's seventeen year-old son in retaliation for Filartiga's political activities. The court held that the "law of nations" includes customary international law and that official torture, under modern standards, violates customary international law. Thus the court permitted the case to proceed, concluding that "[o]ur holding

---

William M. Bennett, *A Lion in the Path? The Influence of International Law on the Immigration Policy of the United States*, 70 WASH. L. REV. 589, 627 (1995) ("It is profoundly disturbing that contemporary U.S. immigration policy, in a number of respects, falls short of international standards. Even more troubling is the absence of international law as a relevant factor in immigration policy discourse.").

41. Gisbert v. United States Attorney Gen., 988 F.2d 1437, 1447–48, *amended*, 997 F.2d 1122 (5th Cir. 1993); *see* Galo-Garcia v. INS, 86 F.3d 916, 918 (9th Cir. 1996) (finding customary international law regarding safe haven inapplicable in proceeding before U.S. immigration authorities, given comprehensive federal scheme of regulation).

For a lower court case willing to consider international law in immigration proceedings, see *Caballero v. Caplinger*, 914 F. Supp. 1374, 1379–80 (E.D. La. 1996), which interpreted constitutional norms in light of customary international law and human rights treaties, condemning arbitrary detention of aliens.

42. 28 U.S.C. § 1350.

43. *Id.*

44. 630 F.2d 876 (2d Cir. 1980).

today, giving effect to a jurisdictional provision enacted by our First Congress, is a small but important step in the fulfillment of the ageless dream to free all people from brutal violence."[45]

Filartiga was viewed by many scholars as a breakthrough in the application of human rights norms in domestic cases.[46] But these extravagant hopes have gone largely unfulfilled.[47] Courts have been hesitant to declare most international human rights part of an enforceable customary international law.[48] More importantly, it is not obvious how the *Filartiga* case advances the post-national claim. The case involved a suit by a non-citizen against a non-citizen for events that happened outside the United States. The fact that a federal court permitted the lawsuit to proceed says little about the basis of legitimacy of the American state vis-a-vis its treatment of residents of its territory.

In sum, non-citizens enjoy a wide array of constitutional and statutory rights in the United States that are frequently asserted in U.S. courts. But international human rights law plays, at best, a limited role in the protection of the rights of persons—aliens or citizens—in the United States.

The controversy surrounding California's Proposition 187 nicely illustrates the point. Frustrated by years of lax federal enforcement, concerned about rising welfare and education costs, and worried about the race and ethnicity of immigrants, the people of California adopted Proposition 187 on November 9, 1994, with the intent of deterring the entry and residence of undocumented aliens

---

45. *Id.* at 890.

46. *See, e.g.*, Richard B. Lillich, *Invoking International Human Rights Law in Domestic Courts*, 54 U. CIN. L.REV. 367 397–402 (1985).

47. *See* Strossen, *supra* note 28, at 822 ("Despite some predictions that *Filartiga* heralded a trend toward wholesale domestic incorporation of customary international human rights law, that development has not yet materialized.") (footnotes omitted). For a case recognizing an ATCA claim, see *Hilao v. Estate of Marcos (In re Estate of Ferdinand Marcos, Human Rights Litig.)*, 25 F.3d 1467 (9th Cir. 1994) (brought by victims and families of victims of torture, summary execution, and disappearances in the Philippines).

48. *See, e.g.*, Jean v. Nelson, 727 F.2d 957, 964 n.4 (11th Cir. 1984) (en banc), *modified*, 472 U.S. 846 (1985) (rejecting amicus argument that continued detention of Haitian plaintiffs constituted arbitrary and indefinite punishment); Tel-Oren v. Libyan Arab Republic, 726 F.2d 774, 795–796 (D.C. Cir. 1984) (Bork, J., concurring) (rejecting cause of action based on international common law brought by survivors of a bus attack by the PLO). In an important development, a district court has permitted a case to proceed under the ATCA brought by alien detainees against INS officials for cruel, inhuman and degrading treatment. *See* Jama v. United States Immigration and Naturalization Serv., 22 F. Supp. 2d 353 (D.N.J. 1998). The court dismissed a claim against the INS on grounds of sovereign immunity, but let the case go ahead against individual INS officers. The case is significant because it is a use of the ATCA against the federal government, not a foreign official. It remains to be seen whether it will survive on appeal.

in the state. Proposition 187 barred undocumented migrants from public schools (in direct contravention of a Supreme Court decision[49]), prohibited them from receiving most forms of social welfare, and mandated that state law enforcement officers, teachers, doctors, and other social workers notify the INS if they believed a person was in the United States illegally. Opponents strenuously objected to nativist and racist statements made in support of Proposition 187.[50] Some immigrant groups and religious organizations argued that the measure violated notions of human dignity and constituted unjust treatment of undocumented migrants. But this was not a position pressed by most of the opponents.[51] And in the ensuing litigation challenging Proposition 187, human rights talk was nowhere to be found. Rather, the lawyers appealed to traditional constitutional grounds of equal protection and federal preemption and persuaded a court to issue an injunction preventing the proposition's implementation.[52]

One answer to the argument made in this section is that by focusing on the enforceability of legal norms, I have missed the discursive power of human rights claims to spark political action and change government conduct.[53] Harold Koh[54] reports these kinds

49. *See* Plyler v. Doe, 457 U.S. 202 (1982) (Texas statute authorizing local school districts to bar resident undocumented children from public schools violated the Equal Protection Clause).

50. *See* Kevin R. Johnson, *An Essay on Immigration Politics, Popular Democracy, and California's Proposition 187: The Political Relevance and Legal Irrelevance of Race*, 70 WASH. L. REV. 629, 650–58 (1995) (discussing the campaigns for and against the initiative).

51. *See* Linda Bosniak, *Opposing Prop. 187: Undocumented Immigrants and the National Imagination*, 28 CONN. L. REV. 555, 567–569 (1996).

52. *See* League of United Latin American Citizens v. Wilson, 908 F. Supp. 755 (C.D. Cal. 1995); *see also* League of United Latin American Citizens v. Wilson, 997 F. Supp. 1244 (C.D. Cal. 1997) (holding Congress's Personal Responsibility and Work Opportunity Reconciliation Act preempted portions of Proposition 187).

For a counterexample consistent with Soysal's thesis, consider the recent filing of a complaint by the ACLU and the California Rural Legal Assistance Foundation before the Inter-American Commission on Human Rights, asserting that INS border enforcement activities violate the Charter of the Organization of American States and the American Declaration of the Rights and Duties of Man. *See* PETITION TO THE INTER-AMERICAN COMM'N ON HUMAN RIGHTS OF THE ORG. OF AM. STATES 4, Feb. 9. 1999 (on file with author).

53. The fact that a treaty is not self-executing means primarily that it is not enforceable in courts. Under international law, a duly ratified treaty is binding on the executive branch. Thus, before Congress enacted the Omnibus Consolidated and Emergency Supplemental Appropriations Act, § 2242, Pub. L. 105-277, 112 Stat. 2681, slip law at 822 (1999), executing the Torture Convention, the Department of Justice had recognized that it was bound by the Convention's provisions prohibiting return of a person to a country where he or she is likely to be tortured. *See* 62 Fed. Reg. 10,312, 10,316 (1997); Office of Gen. Counsel Memo, May 14, 1997, *reprinted in* 75 Interp. Rel. 375 (Mar. 16, 1998).

54. *See* Harold Hongju Koh, *The "Haiti Paradigm" in United States Human Rights Policy*, 103 YALE L.J. 2391 (1994).

of results in his discussion of the *Alvarez-Machain*[55] case. In that case, the Supreme Court held that Alvarez-Machain's forced abduction from Mexican territory by U.S. agents did not violate the U.S.-Mexican extradition treaty and therefore did not divest U.S. courts of jurisdiction to try him. The decision prompted severe criticism, triggering congressional hearings, a Department of Justice review of procedures, and OAS and UN opinions that the conduct violated international law. Alvarez-Machain was acquitted of the criminal charges, and thereafter filed a civil suit against the federal officers who had kidnapped him.[56] Eventually, the U.S. and Mexico reached an agreement to amend their extradition treaty to prohibit trans-border kidnapping.[57]

Other examples of NGO reports, press conferences, and public demonstrations abound. Of particular note is the release of an Amnesty International report in October 1998 on human rights abuses in the United States.[58] The Amnesty report does not simply focus on treatment of non-citizens (although it devotes more than a few pages to those issues). It condemns police brutality, prison conditions, and operation of the death penalty as violations of the human rights of American citizens.[59]

While these examples are well-known and significant in terms of shaping public perceptions and, sometimes, government conduct, they are still far from proving the post-national claim that the legitimacy of the state is now conceived of in terms of its respect for international human rights. Perhaps the *Breard* case shows that the federal government takes seriously its international law obligations, even if it was unable to persuade the governor of Virginia to take seriously an order from the International Court of Justice. But respect for international law is not the same as a shift in the basis of state legitimacy. Indeed, if anything, *Breard* appears to demonstrate the dominance of nationally-based legal norms (which, as have been described, include protections for aliens) over international standards and processes.

55. Alvarez-Machain v. United States, 504 U.S. 655 (1992).

56. *See* Alvarez-Machain v. United States, 107 F.3d 696 (9th Cir. 1997) (refusing to dismiss claims under Federal Tort Claims Act and the Torture Victim Protection Act).

57. *See* Koh, *supra* note 54, at 2405–06.

58. *See* AMNESTY INTERNATIONAL, *supra* note 8 (1998).

59. *See id.*

II. THE CLAIM OF DETERRITORIALIZED MEMBERSHIP

In the preceding section, I have suggested that non-citizens receive significant rights protections based on domestic legal sources. These protections apply to all aliens present in the United States.[60] Furthermore, permanent resident aliens ("greencard holders") are generally protected by federal and state labor and health laws and are eligible for a wide array of social programs in the United States (although they were excluded from means-tested programs by the 1996 immigration legislation, described below). Thus, the membership rights of aliens under U.S. law are largely *territorially-based*.[61] This is surely a broader conception of rights than the citizens-only view of the nationalist model, but it does not fit easily with the "deterritorialized" membership claims of the post-national perspective.

As Soysal notes, Tomas Hammar and others have referred to this territorially based membership model for settled immigrants as "denizenship."[62] But she suggests that this concept, which "remain[s] within the confines of the nation-state model," is an inadequate description:

> [T]he incorporation of guestworkers is no mere expansion of the scope of national citizenship, nor is it an irregularity. Rather, it reveals a profound transformation in the institution of citizenship, both in its institutional logic and the way it is legitimated. To locate the changes, we need to go beyond the nation-state.[63]

Again, from the national perspective, it is true that extension of rights to non-citizens represents a fundamental shift in approach. But the "incorporation" of immigrants in terms of membership rights has been and continues to be the rule—the logic, if you will—of the American membership system. At least since the adoption of

60. *See* United States v. Balsys, 119 F.3d 122 (2d Cir. 1997) (recognizing aliens' privilege against self-incrimination); GERALD L. NEUMAN, STRANGERS TO THE CONSTITUTION: IMMIGRANTS, BORDERS, AND FUNDAMENTAL LAW 52–71 (1996) (discussing the rights of aliens in the United States).

61. Perhaps the high-water mark of protection of resident aliens is *Plyler v. Doe*, 457 U.S. 202 (1982). See *supra* note 49.

62. SOYSAL, *supra* note 1, at 138–39; *see* HAMMAR, *supra* note 6, at 735–47; William R. Brubaker, *Membership without Citizenship: The Economic and Social Rights of Noncitizens*, *in* IMMIGRATION AND POLITICS OF CITIZENSHIP IN EUROPE AND NORTH AMERICA 145 (William R. Brubaker ed., 1989); *see also* T. ALEXANDER ALEINIKOFF, BETWEEN PRINCIPLE AND POLITICS: THE DIRECTIONS OF U.S. CITIZENSHIP POLICY (1999) (describing "lawful-settlement-as-membership model"); Bauböck, *supra* note 6, at 65.

63. SOYSAL, *supra* note 1, at 139.

the Fourteenth Amendment in 1868, immigrants have been protected by the Constitution and federal laws against unfriendly state regulation. And the welfare state established in the twentieth century had generally been understood to benefit lawful immigrants as well as citizens.[64] (That understanding was seriously challenged by the round of anti-immigrant legislation enacted in the mid-1990s. But that legislation, disentitling lawful immigrants from most means-tested social programs, shows that if any movement is taking place in United States membership models, it is a drift more towards the nationalist model than towards the post-national model.)[65]

Soysal recognizes that politics in Western states in the 1990s seem to run counter to the post-national claim.[66] She argues that:

> [t]hese seemingly paradoxical affinities articulate an underlying dialectic of the postwar global system: While nation-states and their boundaries are reified through assertions of border controls and appeals to nationhood, a new mode of membership, anchored in the universalistic rights of personhood, transgresses the national order of things.[67]

She further notes that the "national order of things" is also destabilized by sub-national groups asserting "nationhood." Together, these "recontextualizations of 'nationness' within the universalistic discourse of human rights" are said to "blur the meanings and boundaries attached to the nation and the nation-state."[68]

There is much to this description. The boundaries of nation and nation-state are blurring to some degree, and the reassertion of aggressive nationalism may well, in part, be a response to challenges to the state from above and below, an increase in dual nationality, and diasporic politics activated by governments of "sending" countries. But it is difficult to describe developments in the United States as a reaction to the pressure of human rights discourse. Rather, the controversy in the United States plays out largely in terms of multiculturalism and assimilationism, fractionalization and unity. This is a fight that goes on primarily among native (citizen) groups, although immigration is commonly alleged to contribute

64. *See* Graham v. Richardson, 403 U.S. 365 (1971) (holding that a state's restriction on eligibility of legal aliens for public assistance violates the Equal Protection Clause).

65. *See* Aleinikoff, *Tightening Circle of Membership*, *supra* note 23.

66. *See* SOYSAL, *supra* note 1, at 156.

67. *Id.* at 159.

68. *Id.* at 162.

to the "balkanization" of America. Thus right-wing politics stresses a revaluation of citizenship as a way to command assimilation to a common (read: Anglo/White) culture, and seeks to redefine the American model of membership from denizenship to citizenship. Notions of personhood play a role in the resistance to such a move; but it is a personhood rooted in and protected by constitutional norms and American traditions, not an international human rights regime.[69]

III. POST-NATIONAL AMERICANS?

The blurring of borders may occur at the individual as well as the state level, producing a sort of post-modern malaise of unrootedness and "ambiguously identified" persons.[70] "In immigrant societies," Michael Walzer writes, "people have begun to experience what we might think of as a life without clear boundaries and without secure or singular identities."[71] Frequent movement across borders or the existence of communities experiencing a continuous flow of newcomers may challenge the creation of stable, rooted associations. Individuals may end up living in what is in effect a transnational community, straddling two worlds but at home in neither; or they may find no community at all, being simply the sum of their own particularistic circumstances, attachments and proclivities.

Do these bleak depictions accurately capture the (admittedly complicated) nature of modern identities? It is certainly true that many of us have multiple attachments and some of these attachments cross national borders. It is not obvious, however, that this state of affairs produces anomie or a post-modern neurosis. On the contrary, it appears that human beings are rather adept at living in more than one world, bringing the insights of one to bear on another, or compartmentalizing their lives into separate spheres. Let me give an example.

About a year ago, friends of mine traveled to Russia to adopt a Russian baby in an orphanage. They brought the baby home, and soon thereafter had a ceremony in their home. It was a double ceremony, commemorating her entry into two communities: membership in the Jewish people and citizenship in the United States.

---

69. *But see* Stanford v. Kentucky, 492 U.S. 361, 389–90 (1989) (Brennan, J., dissenting) (stating that widespread prohibition of execution of juveniles in other nations shows contemporary attitudes towards capital punishment that should influence interpretation of prohibition against cruel and unusual punishment).

70. *See* MICHAEL WALZER, ON TOLERATION 87 (1997) (discussing a post-modern toleration model).

71. *Id.*

The first ceremony (*brit habat*) was presided over by a rabbi, who noted that in recent years Jewish parents of daughters felt the need for a ceremony similar to the traditional *brit milah* (ritual circumcision) accorded Jewish boys. *Brit* translates as "covenant"; the ceremony signifies entry into the Jewish community and the taking on of the responsibilities that that entails. So the baby was blessed and given a Jewish name—the name of a number of ancestors of the parents, some of whom had come to the United States from Russia several generations before.

Then a second ceremony began. The U.S. Commissioner for Immigration, a friend of the parents, performed a naturalization ceremony, making the baby a citizen of the United States. The Commissioner said to the baby: "the naturalization oath is like making a promise, a promise to be loyal to this country and obey her laws. In return, America promises to welcome you as an equal member of the whole family of American citizens who enjoy the freedoms, rights, privileges and protections of the Constitution and the laws of this great land." The baby was asked to raise her right hand and repeat the following words (she clasped a tiny American flag in her left) as her parents recited the oath for her: "I will love and be true to the United States; I will support its Constitution; obey its laws; respect its flag; and defend it against all enemies."

Here were two ceremonies, two covenants, two different kinds of extended family created at the same time. The example, I think, shows that the opposite of a single, fixed identity is not necessarily a loss of bearings or radical personal confusion. The two identities—Jew and U.S. citizen—are deeply significant to their relevant communities; but the assembled family and friends did not see a contradiction (or even a tension) between them. Rather, there was a sense of double rootedness, a sense of the strengthening of individual identity by making it "thicker."

IV. THE FUTURE?

The future is likely to look like the present, only more so. Immigration to the United States is likely to remain at or around record levels; cross-border ties among immigrant and ethnic groups will continue to flourish; the number of dual citizens will continue to increase; foreign states will increasingly seek to influence or respond to their diasporas present in the United States. Immigration will have a significant impact on U.S. demographics, pushing Hispanics ahead of African Americans as the largest minority group in the near future and more than doubling the Asian American population over the next half century.

These trends may appear troubling to some, portending a further weakening of U.S. sovereignty and an undermining of a cohesive citizenship. But I think the nation-state (at least the American nation-state) is not at risk. Rather than witnessing the dawning of a post-national era, we are more likely to see the growth of what I will term "inter-nationalism." By this I mean a thickening of relations between domestic and foreign populations (through immigration, dual nationality, freer trade and travel, the communications revolution) that will occur *within* the regime of nation-states. States will remain the primary locus of law—including international law, which will be enforced through national legal organs.[72]

My concept of inter-nationalism is drawn from Anne-Marie Slaughter's theory of "transgovernmentalism."[73] She contrasts transgovernmentalism with the models of liberal internationalists (who see the rise of world government, with centralized rulemaking, hierarchical authority, universal membership) and, to use her term, the "new medievalists" (who see an end of the nation-state, stressing the rise of supra-, sub- and non-state actors). Slaughter's transgovernmentalism recognizes the continuing primacy of states, but sees states as "disaggregating into [their] separate, functionally distinct parts"—courts, regulatory agencies, executive departments—that "network[] with their counterparts abroad, creating a dense web of relations that constitutes a new, transgovernmental order."[74]

Inter-nationalism points to similar cross-border relations on the personal level.[75] The resulting "dense web of [human] relations" is likely to have important implications for states, some welcome and others not. On the positive side, such ties may foster trade and commerce, may support diversity in the arts, cuisine and ideas, may reduce international tensions by increasing contact and understanding. Inter-nationalism is also likely to give strength to claims for recognizing the rights of immigrants, as insider/outsider lines

72. As Rainer Bauböck has suggested to me, this statement should be qualified in the case of Europe where the European Court of Human Rights has some authority to enforce international human rights norms against national governments.

73. *See* Anne-Marie Slaughter, *The Real New World Order*, FOREIGN AFF., Sept.–Oct. 1997, at 183, 184 (criticizing traditional versions of a new world order in favor of a transgovernmental vision). I want to thank Catherine Gwin for calling my attention to Slaughter's insightful article.

74. *Id.* at 184.

75. I am not suggesting an analogy between inter-state relations and internationalism as experienced on a personal level. But I am noting parallel developments here: As a state thickens ties with another state by creating bonds between constituent parts, it is not giving up sovereignty to an international regime. On the contrary, such ties may reinforce each state's "stateness." So too an individual or groups may have ties to two states that affirm membership in each and do not necessarily forge a new transnational identity or community.

become less clear and states come to recognize that they are both senders and receivers of immigrants.[76]

Less helpfully, a thickening of ties among cross-border populations can create tensions between states. For example, states may be concerned about dual citizens voting in two countries, or they may seek to act to protect the interests of their nationals residing in other states. Resolving such issues will require state-to-state negotiation and coordination, and perhaps the establishment of international norms and new supra-national arrangements.

While international human rights may play a significant role in these developments—fostering both domestic and international rights talk—there is little reason to believe that the traditional basis for state legitimacy is, or will be, shifting. Neither transgovernmentalism at the state level nor inter-nationalism at the personal level suggests the need for new models of legitimacy or membership. Governmental powers and individual rights may continue to be articulated within a national structure, even as those structures adapt to thicker cross-national relations.

Inter-nationalism is likely to produce two policy strategies in the United States. Those on the right will increase their demands that immigrants "go national"; thus, they will push an anti-multicultural, anti-bilingual education agenda and perhaps seek to stem increases in levels of dual nationality. Those on the left will urge new incorporation programs, such as English and job training, and will support stronger antidiscrimination measures. Ethnic communities in the United States are likely to push for greater rights for co-ethnic immigrant populations here. Importantly, none of these strategies represents a "national" or "post-national" model. The basis of individual rights—which will continue to extend to resident aliens—will be presence in U.S. territory, and the definition of those rights will be found in domestic legal documents.

On the personal level, individuals will not see themselves as citizens of the world or as citizens of only their own solipsistic private domains, although they may well affirm ties to several communities (including, perhaps, more than one national community). Inter-nationalism means that these relationships will be structured within the regime of states, and indeed such relationships may put pressure on that regime to be more open to plurality and movement across borders. To return to the conversion/naturalization narrative, it appears that dual, overlapping memberships are possible and can be mutually supporting. Thus, there is nothing inevitable about either the hopelessness of postmodernism or the out-of-state experience of post-nationality. Put another way, to be bilingual is neither to speak

76. *See* Bauböck, *supra* note 6, at 65.

Esparanto nor a private language that no one else can understand. The future may not be a post-national world, but it will be a rich one, full of interesting and complicated relations in which the legitimacy of the American state will be based primarily on its dedication to democratic principles and its respect for U.S. constitutional rights and values.

[9]

Cultural logics of belonging and movement:

Transnationalism, naturalization, and U.S. immigration politics

SUSAN BIBLER COUTIN
University of California, Irvine

ABSTRACT
In the United States, unprecedented high numbers of naturalization applicants, the adoption of restrictive immigration policies, changing demographics, and the 1996 presidential election coalesced in the mid-1990s to make naturalization simultaneously a high priority and problematic. Salvadorans who had immigrated during the 1980s and who were still struggling for the opportunity to naturalize were caught up in these dynamics. A juxtaposition of their struggles against exclusion and of naturalization ceremonies' rhetoric of inclusion elucidates complex and paradoxical connections between naturalization and transnationalism. [*immigration, naturalization, transnationalism, politics, identity, the United States, El Salvador*]

As a nation of immigrants in which nativism flourishes (Higham 1974; Sánchez 1997), the United States has long had a complex relationship with the migrants who enter its territory. Migrants are desired as laborers but are excluded from certain public benefits (Calavita 1996; Huber and Espenshade 1997), praised for contributing to society but suspected of maintaining disparate loyalties (Calavita 2000; Chavez 2001; Starn 1986), seen as evidence that the United States is superior to other nations yet condemned as a challenge to national sovereignty (Sassen 1996), and both celebrated and denigrated for weaving diverse cultural heritages into the national fabric (Johnson et al. 1997; Perea 1997). In the mid-1990s, these tensions came to the fore in searing debates over where to place legal and other boundaries around those who would be included in the nation. In California, Proposition 187, which required educators, physicians, and other service providers to identify and report suspected illegal aliens, was overwhelmingly approved by the California electorate (see Martin 1995). In 1996, Congress passed the Illegal Immigration Reform and Immigrant Responsibility Act (IIRIRA), which stiffened border enforcement and made it more difficult for undocumented immigrants to legalize their presence. Other restrictive immigration measures, such as denying citizenship to the U.S.-born children of undocumented immigrants, were also considered (Chock 1999). At the same time, these more restrictive immigration policies, unprecedented numbers of naturalization applicants, changing demo graphics, and the 1996 presidential election coalesced to make naturalization a national priority (Baker 1997).[1] Thus, in 1996, President Clinton launched Citizenship USA, a drive to naturalize one million legal permanent residents in a single year. By the mid-1990s, the U.S. Immigration and Naturalization Service (INS) was holding mass naturalization ceremonies in which as many as 2,000-5,000 legal permanent residents simultaneously took the oath of citizenship. Both the adoption of restrictive measures and the celebration of naturalization shed light on the meanings of exclusion from and inclusion in the U.S. polity.

These seemingly contrary trends—the adoption of restrictive policies and the promotion of naturalization—are linked to what scholars have described as a disjuncture between the realities of global interdependancy, on the one hand, and the official models of incorporation in countries such as the United States, on the other hand (Guarnizo 1998; Portes 1997). The adoption of restrictive policies may be a response to the increased international movements of persons, goods, and ideas that accompany globalization. As financial systems and labor markets become global, corporations move to take advantage of differentials in labor costs and workers move from capital-poor to capital-rich countries to take service-sector and other jobs (Hamilton and Chinchilla 1991; Harvey 1989; Kearney 1986; Menjívar 2000; Ong et al. 1994; Sassen 1991). Migrant workers become, in a sense, resources for their countries of origin. Not only do many send remittances to family members back home (Menjívar et al. 1998), but they also become a focus of transnational political organizing with some potential to influence policies in both their countries of residence and origin (Guarnizo 1998; Itzigsohn 2000). Naturalization drives can be key to such organizing, as naturalization confers voting rights and can further ethnicity- or nationality-based politicking. Nonetheless, in the United States, official models of naturalization presume that immigration consists of leaving one society and joining another (making a "clean break"; cf. Smith 1998; Yngvesson 1997) and that naturalization creates equivalent and generic citizen–subjects. Moreover, for migrants' decisions to naturalize to be seen as voluntary (and therefore legitimate), one has to presume a sort of free market of citizenship, in which migrants select the nation whose social system best permits them to develop their personal talents. Such presumptions ignore the international relationships and inequities that propel migration, downplay the incommensurability of migrants' histories, and legitimize immigration systems that constitute some migrants as illegal and therefore exploitable (Jenkins 1978; but see Delgado 1993).

To examine the seeming disjuncture between transnationalism and nation-based forms of membership, I juxtapose the U.S. immigration history of Salvadorans and the celebration of Americanization, choice, and nation-building that characterized mass naturalization ceremonies held in Los Angeles in 1996 and 1997. Many Salvadorans wanted to naturalize but, in part because of the adoption of more restrictive policies in 1996, were not eligible to do so. These two contexts are interlinked in numerous ways. Salvadorans—among whom I have been doing fieldwork since the mid-1980s—began entering the United States in large numbers following the onset of the Salvadoran civil war in 1980. A relatively recent and initially largely undocumented immigrant group, Salvadorans experienced the difficulties of living in the United States without legal status or with temporary legal status (for instance, permission to remain in the country while an asylum application was pending). These migrants' experiences of exclusion led many to desire not only legal permanent residency but also naturalization, as a means of guaranteeing their rights in the United States, securing the ability to travel internationally (particularly, to reenter the United States if they left), acquiring a greater political voice, and improving their ability to petition for the legalization or immigration of family members. During the mid-1990s, Salvadoran community organizations in the United States therefore promoted naturalization and voter registration on the part of eligible immigrants. Immigrants' anxiety over their legal rights—an anxiety that was widespread during the mid-1990s because of California Proposition 187 and IIRIRA—fueled these naturalization drives and was one factor leading to record numbers of naturalization applicants during that period. Despite the political context, the naturalization ceremonies that actually produced large numbers of new citizens during that time attributed naturalization to immigrants' desire for Americanization, their choice of the United States over their country of origin, and the need of the United States to be renewed through immigrants' enthusiasm and "new blood." Examining the rhetoric of the ceremonies therefore reveals the disconnect between the assumption that naturalization is about Americanization, choice, and nation-building and the broader context that led immigrants to naturalize in large numbers—and that also prevented some would-be citizens from naturalizing.

By juxtaposing Salvadorans' struggles for U.S. residency with the rhetoric of mass naturalization ceremonies, this article makes three contributions to analyzing the disjuncture between transmigration (Schiller et al. 1995) and national membership. First, though they seem incommensurable, national forms of membership can be put in service of transnational goals. Thus, Salvadoran activists' promotion of naturalization and voter registration sought not only to increase Latinos' political clout in the United States but also to affect U.S. immigration policies in ways that would aid El Salvador. Moreover, given the trends toward dollarization and dual nationality in Latin America and increasing dependency on migrant labor in the United States (Portes et al. 1999), naturalization can be a way of furthering international integration rather than merely transferring migrants' allegiance from one nation to another. Second, this juxtaposition suggests that immigrants' full legal inclusion is limited by the forms of personhood that citizen–subjects can recognizably assume. Naturalization ceremonies celebrate the creation and incorporation of new citizen–subjects, but these subjects are created by (ritually) erasing histories and rendering difference generic. Such moves may contradict both migrants' understandings of their own identities and the ethnicity- and nationality-based organizing that promotes (and seeks to benefit from) naturalization. Third, although it presumes the sovereignty and choice-making capacity of both the naturalizing subject and the nation-state that naturalizes, naturalization can be linked to a lack of alternatives and to interdependency. Thus, individuals may naturalize not only out of a desire to become Americans but also because they feel that, as noncitizens, their rights are in jeopardy. As this article will

American Ethnologist ▪ Volume 30 Number 4 November 2003

demonstrate, although the disjuncture between nation-based forms of membership and transnational linkages is profound, there are also ways in which each of these cultural logics serves or is redefined by the other.

My analysis begins with the case of Salvadoran immigrants, focusing on how the politics of immigration reform prioritized and defined naturalization for some would-be citizens. Next, I examine the ritual and rhetoric of naturalization ceremonies, identifying disjunctures between the broader context that fueled the celebration of naturalization in the mid-1990s and the models of subjecthood, nationhood, and citizen–state relations that were ritually enacted as new citizens were produced. Finally, I reexamine these disjunctures, linking my analysis of the case of Salvadorans and the rhetoric of naturalization ceremonies to the literature on the gap between national memberships and global interconnections. This reexamination reveals that, although the logics of national membership and of global interdependencies are at odds, transnational interconnections can promote and be furthered by individuals' placement in the very national membership categories that deny these interconnections.

Migration and exclusion: The case of Salvadorans

Migration from El Salvador to the United States is a good example of both the ways that global forces compel movement and the ways that nation-based categories restrict membership. Migration between El Salvador and the United States is embedded in geopolitical, economic, and sociocultural ties between the two countries. Perhaps the most significant of these ties is U.S. support for the Salvadoran government during the 1980–92 Salvadoran civil war. During the 1980s, the Reagan administration defined the conflict in El Salvador as part of a broader struggle between communism and democracy and provided over $1 million a day to assist Salvadoran forces in their fight against guerrilla insurgents. Some observers attribute the prolongation of this conflict, which soon reached a military stalemate, precisely to U.S. support. By 1985, political violence had displaced 27 percent of the Salvadoran population (Kaye 1997), and reports published during the mid- to late 1980s estimated the Salvadoran population in the United States at 500,000 to 800,000 (Aguayo and Fagen 1988; Ruggles et al. 1985), and even as high as one million (Montes Mozo and Garcia Vasquez 1988). In addition to military support, investment and development aid from the United States to El Salvador has been extensive (Hamilton and Chinchilla 1991). As Saskia Sassen (1989) has pointed out, investment and development aid facilitate migration by displacing workers from their traditional occupations, paving the way for ties between potential migrants and potential employers (e.g., U.S. managers who might seek nannies or other workers) and familiarizing workers with the country from which investment or development aid originates. Such ties have also forged strong social and cultural connections between the United States and El Salvador. In short, geopolitical concerns, capital flows, the transnationalization of labor markets, cultural diffusion, and social interconnections have contributed to migration from El Salvador to the United States.

Migration between El Salvador and the United States also exemplifies the gap between global forces that compel movement and nation-based categories that restrict membership. Although their movements are embedded in processes that transcend national boundaries, Salvadoran immigrants have been treated by the U.S. government as members of a single nation—El Salvador—and therefore regarded as aliens. Because of the difficulties of obtaining visas, most Salvadorans who immigrated to the United States during the war years did so without the permission of the U.S. government. The Reagan administration defined these migrants as deportable economic immigrants rather than as persecution victims who deserved asylum in the United States. In 1986, only 2.6 percent of the asylum applications filed by Salvadorans were approved, in contrast to higher approval rates for applicants fleeing communist countries.[2] By the early 1990s, continued human rights abuses in El Salvador and the *American Baptist Churches v. Thornburgh* (ABC) lawsuit, which charged that the U.S. government discriminated against Salvadoran and Guatemalan asylum seekers, garnered Salvadorans the right to apply for asylum under special rules and 18 months of Temporary Protected Status (TPS), followed by several years of Deferred Enforced Departure Status (DED). These temporary statuses, however, did not permit recipients to leave and reenter the United States (without first obtaining special authorization from the INS), become legal permanent residents, naturalize, or petition for relatives to immigrate. In the mid-1990s, restrictionist sentiment in the United States grew, producing IIRIRA, which made legalization more difficult for undocumented immigrants.[3] The approximately 300 thousand Salvadorans and Guatemalans who had applied for political asylum through the ABC settlement agreement found that they were not only unlikely to obtain asylum (because of peace accords that ended civil conflict in both countries) but other avenues of legalization also were closed or greatly restricted. In 1997, Congress passed the Nicaraguan Adjustment and Central American Relief Act (NACARA), which restored these migrants' eligibility for a form of legalization known as suspension of deportation.[4] Nonetheless, according to one estimate from the INS asylum division, it could take as long as 20 years to adjudicate all of the applications for U.S. residency under NACARA. In the meantime, these applicants are still aliens who lack permanent membership in the U.S. polity.

Their experiences of transnational migration and legal exclusion have shaped Salvadoran immigrants' senses of their actual and desired positioning within the United

States. My description of their understandings is based on fieldwork conducted in Los Angeles between 1995 and 1997, a period when restrictionist sentiment peaked and immigration reform was implemented. Fieldwork entailed observing the legal services programs of three major Central American community organizations in Los Angeles, attending some 129 proceedings in U.S. immigration court, following Salvadoran immigrants' campaigns for legal permanent residency, and interviewing 90 legal service providers, community activists, and Central Americans with pending legalization claims. Here I draw on interviews with members of the latter two groups. The activists were predominantly Salvadorans who had supported popular struggles in El Salvador, immigrated during the civil war, and participated in solidarity work in the United States. Most activists were legal permanent residents or naturalized U.S. citizens; a few of the younger activists were U.S.-born Salvadoran college students. Most of the activists also were men, although I made a point of seeking interviews with Salvadoran women who had assumed leadership roles in the solidarity movement or in advocacy work on behalf of Central American immigrants. I met Central Americans with pending legalization claims through community organizations and through several immigration attorneys who worked for nonprofit organizations. Most of these interviewees had immigrated to the United States during the civil war and had applied for political asylum through the ABC settlement agreement. A few had immigrated too late to qualify for the ABC settlement or had missed application deadlines. Some interviewees with pending cases had sympathized with the left during the civil war, a few with the right, and most with neither side in the conflict. My sample of individuals with pending legalization claims was fairly evenly divided between men and women; most did low-income work in construction, childcare, housecleaning, the garment sector, and the service industry.

Regardless of their prior political affiliations, Salvadoran interviewees feared that they would never be regarded as full members of the U.S. polity. Citing the passage of California Proposition 187 and widespread anti-immigrant sentiment, interviewees complained that Latinos were being blamed for social problems that were not of their making. To illustrate the obstacles that Latinos faced in securing acceptance, several interviewees told me of a local mayor whose Hispanic appearance and dilapidated vehicle had led INS officials to conclude that he was an illegal alien. Interviewees linked immigration and racial discrimination to economic marginalization, noting that immigrants and Latinos (categories that they saw as interconnected) took the lowest paying and least desirable jobs. Interviewees who had held professional positions in El Salvador described the economic deprivation they had suffered on immigrating. Gregorio Orozco, who had been a professor in El Salvador and who, at the time of our interview, worked as a janitor in Los Angeles, saw marginalization as spatialized along class and racial lines. Describing Latinos as "second-class citizens," Gregorio criticized the overcrowding and disrepair of buses and other public services in his neighborhood of North Hollywood, as compared with Beverly Hills. Overwhelmingly, interviewees characterized restrictive immigration policies and anti-immigrant sentiment as directed against minorities in general rather than immigrants in particular.

Although they feared that it might not secure their *full* inclusion in the United States, interviewees saw naturalization as potentially strengthening their ties with their communities of origin. Thus, paradoxically, naturalization, which is accomplished by formally renouncing ties to another state, can reinforce transnational connections. Interviewees—most of whom stated that they would like to naturalize, if permitted to do so—said that they wanted U.S. citizenship to gain the freedom to travel internationally, the ability to petition for undocumented relatives, the right to vote, and better retirement benefits. Some pointed out that, as legal residents or U.S. citizens, they would be better connected to families and communities abroad than they were as asylum applicants who jeopardized their applications if they left the United States. One asylum applicant stated, "The day that I receive [legal permanent residency] papers, that very day, I'm catching a plane to go to El Salvador again. It's been 11 years since I've seen my parents." Few interviewees saw legalization primarily as choosing the United States over El Salvador. Even those who saw their futures in the United States depicted this vision as a de facto reality rather than as an overt choice. For instance, one ABC asylum applicant told me, "I think that if I have been living here for 12 years, I work here, I pay my taxes, then I live *here.* I don't have anything to do with El Salvador. I have to do with here, where I work, with this country."

Moreover—and consistent with the globalization literature's emphasis on the forces that compel movement—most interviewees suggested that they had had no alternative but to immigrate and then to seek permanent residency and U.S. citizenship. Given the violence and economic devastation of the Salvadoran civil war, it is not surprising that many interviewees characterized migration as a necessity. One activist, for example, insisted, "We [Salvadorans] didn't want to be here just because we want to, [because] we love the United States, or just because you can go to Disneyland. . . . So you came here for a necessity. Either, you leave your country, or you're going to be one of the statistics of the deaths." Interviewees also stated that the difficulties of living without papers had made them apply for TPS and political asylum.[5] One asylum applicant, for example, explained why he had applied for TPS instead of remaining undocumented: "It was not a question of choosing or not choosing, it was something that had to be done. Because one couldn't be hidden forever." Both activists and nonactivists noted that the more restrictive immigration policies adopted in

American Ethnologist ▪ Volume 30 Number 4 November 2003

1996 had sharpened distinctions between U.S. citizens and legal permanent residents and had made naturalization necessary to safeguard legal rights. As one Salvadoran asylum applicant put it, "The way things are going, in the future, the [legal permanent] residents will be treated like illegals."

Although naturalization has largely been construed legally as a transfer of allegiance, interviewees' descriptions of their relationships to the United States and to El Salvador articulated an *additive* model of citizenship. According to this model, national membership is not exclusive, individuals can acquire multiple citizenships, and these multiple ties can be both meaningful to individuals and manifested through social practices and relations. Thus, as they sought to acquire permanent residency and citizenship in the United States, many interviewees (but not all—see above and see Mahler 1998) also maintained an identification with El Salvador. One member of a Salvadoran organization that is promoting citizenship and civic participation commented, "Becoming citizens, we don't lose anything. We remain Salvadoran at heart." Such comments depicted legal citizenship as a formality that could leave other measures of membership and identity untouched. Interviewees suggested, for example, that regardless of legal citizenship, "Salvadoranness" was an immutable fact of nature, conferred by birth on Salvadoran soil, relationship to Salvadoran family members, and having Salvadoran blood.[6] One young man (who was a naturalized U.S. citizen) told me, "A Salvadoran is born, not made. Being Salvadoran is your culture, your family, your grandmother who is still in El Salvador and who writes all the time." These comments suggest that interviewees, many of whom hoped one day to naturalize, saw U.S. citizenship as *adding to* rather than replacing their national allegiances. In fact, El Salvador permits dual citizenship, so naturalization does not strip Salvadorans of their former allegiance—although not all interviewees were aware that this is the case. Such dual (or multiple) identities and affiliations are common among recent immigrants, who, regardless of their geographic mobility (Popkin 1999), orient their lives around multiple local and national realities (Goldring 1998; Guarnizo 1997, 1998; Schiller and Fouron 1999; Smith 1998).

To obtain permanent residency, counter restrictionist immigration policies, and promote the well-being of their families and communities in El Salvador, Salvadoran immigrant community organizations promoted naturalization, voter registration, and alliances with other ethnicity- and nationality-based groups in the United States. At numerous meetings of community organizations in 1996 and 1997, I heard activists urge Central Americans to encourage eligible relatives to apply for naturalization. At a meeting with ABC class members in 1996, a staff member of the Association of Salvadorans of Los Angeles (ASOSAL) explained this strategy. The speaker told those present that "20,000 people became citizens here in Los Angeles last month" and that individuals from ASOSAL had gone to the swearing-in ceremonies to register the new citizens to vote. He stressed, "We can't vote because we aren't citizens yet, but this is a way for us to register our opinions and to increase our impact."[7] The staff member noted that one of the people who went along to register voters had never applied for TPS or DED and "didn't have a single paper, not even a social security card. But, by registering voters, this person had an impact." Another ASOSAL staff member reinforced the speaker's analysis, commenting, "We need Salvadorans who are citizens. Those who are citizens are key to our efforts."

As they promoted naturalization and voter registration, Central American community groups also engaged in ethnicity- and nationality-based organizing. Several organizations, for example, floated the idea of asking the Los Angeles City Council to name a particular neighborhood in Los Angeles Little El Salvador or Little Central America. Like Korea Town, Chinatown, and Little Tokyo, such an ethnicization or nationalization of public space would legitimize Central Americans' claims to local—and thus legal—residency. Similarly, some community organizations have sought to institutionalize the annual Central American Independence Day parade. Like Take Back the Night marches or Catholic and Protestant processions in Belfast (Feldman 1991), parades can claim both territory and time. Both of these claims are explicit in an ASOSAL staff member's description of the Central American parade: "[Mexico]'s independence is on the 16th, and only the Central American countries are on the 15th. And in East L.A. [the Mexican community], they focus on that date, and on this side, where the Central American community supposedly is, we focus on the 15th." Similarly, another activist stressed the importance of "institutionaliz[ing] certain dates for our community. . . . Within a few years it would be good if there were a couple of days that were recognized in the city as 'Days of So-and-So.' So that we can succeed getting these celebrated in the schools and elsewhere." In fact, because of the efforts of a new organization, the Salvadoran American National Association (SANA), the L.A. City Council has declared August 6, *el día del salvadoreño,* Salvadoran Day. Activists also sought to create Salvadoran voting blocks and to identify Salvadorans who could run for public office.

Securing immigration benefits for the U.S. Salvadoran population was, at least in part, a transnational political strategy. Claims to space, presence, and membership rights not only sought to increase Central Americans' political clout in the United States but also to affect El Salvador. During the 1980s, Salvadorans sought refugee status in the United States both as a means of preventing deportations and to obtain U.S. recognition of human rights abuses being committed in El Salvador. Activists hoped that such recognition would make it difficult for the U.S. government to send assistance to the Salvadoran government and that, without such assistance, the war would end with either a negotiated settlement or a guerrilla victory. After the signing of peace accords, community activists continued to seek legal residency, but as immigrants rather than as refugees. Activists argued that permanent residency would prevent potentially destabilizing mass deportations and permit Salvadorans to continue to support their family members and home communities by working in the United States. This argument was made not only by Salvadoran activists but also—and perhaps more remarkably—by Salvadoran officials. Well aware of the economic significance of the U.S. Salvadoran population, which in 2000 sent $1.7 billion in remittances to El Salvador, Salvadoran officials have also urged U.S. officials to grant permanent residency to Salvadoran immigrants and have encouraged Salvadorans to take advantage of legalization opportunities such as ABC and NACARA.

The immigration strategies pursued by Salvadoran immigrants, activists, and officials are far from unique. Researchers have noted that discrimination has led migrants to identify with their countries of both residence and origin (Goldring 1998; Schiller and Fouron 1999) and to naturalize as a means of securing rights in the United States (Guarnizo 1998). Like that of El Salvador, the governments of other countries of emigration (such as Mexico, Haiti, and the Dominican Republic) have encouraged their citizens to legalize in the United States (Foner 1997; Guarnizo 1997) and have lobbied the U.S. government for immigration benefits for their citizens (Popkin 1999). At the same time, these governments have redefined citizenship in ways that permit their citizens to have dual or multiple allegiances and have developed policies and programs to incorporate émigrés into national life "at home" (Goldring 1998; Guarnizo 1997, 1998; Guarnizo and Smith 1998; Landolt et al. 1999; Smith 1998). The prevalence of such strategies suggests that sending states are defining émigrés as resources that can provide much needed infusions of U.S. dollars and can sometimes influence U.S. policies vis-à-vis their countries of origin (Guarnizo 1998). These processes, which, according to some scholars, make states transterritorial (Goldring 1998; Guarnizo 1998; Schiller and Fouron 1999; Smith 1998), have given naturalization new meanings. Rather than signaling a clean break in allegiance from one country to another, naturalization can add a national affiliation to preexisting ones, preserve migrants' abilities to remit, and give sending countries a voting constituency through which to influence U.S. policy makers. Why then, did naturalization become a national priority in the United States even as restrictive immigration measures were being adopted? What does naturalization mean to the receiving nation?

Naturalization as a national priority

In the mid-1990s, a number of factors converged to make naturalization a priority in the United States. First, by mid-1995, most of the 2.7 million individuals who legalized through IRCA had completed the five-year residency requirement that made them eligible for citizenship (Paral 1995). Second, restrictive immigration measures, such as IIRIRA and other reforms that limited noncitizens' access to public benefits may have spurred the naturalization of immigrants who otherwise would have remained legal permanent residents (Paral 1995; Sánchez 1997).[8] Third, community organizations around the United States promoted naturalization through drives that included lessons on civics, assistance in completing applications, and preparation for examinations and interviews (Immigrant Policy Project of the State and Local Coalition on Immigration 1996). Fourth, the Mexican government considered and eventually adopted constitutional changes that permitted dual nationality (Guarnizo 1998). This development encouraged Mexican immigrants, who have traditionally naturalized at lower-than-average rates, to apply for U.S. citizenship. Fifth, in 1992, the INS instituted a green card replacement program. Some green card holders may have chosen to naturalize rather than to replace their green cards (Immigration and Naturalization Service 1999).

By 1995, the INS was facing a processing backlog of 700,000 naturalization applications (Immigrant Policy Project of the State and Local Coalition on Immigration 1996), and applicants were experiencing waits of six months to more than a year between submitting their applications and taking the oath of allegiance (see also NatzNews 1998). Immigrant rights groups complained that the INS was directing too many of its resources to border enforcement and too few to naturalization. In response to these pressures, President Clinton launched Citizenship USA, an effort to naturalize one million citizens in 1996. As part of this effort, the INS streamlined its naturalization procedures, exempting certain elderly legal permanent residents from English language tests, holding citizenship interviews at community organizations' offices, and generally promoting naturalization. This naturalization drive was successful, as 1,044,689 individuals were naturalized during 1996. In contrast, during the previous five years, the average number of individuals naturalized per year was 357,037 (Immigration and Naturalization Service 1999). The naturalization drive was not uncontroversial, however. Republican Party leaders accused Clinton of simply trying to create more Democratic voters before the November 1996 presidential election. Errors in the processing of applications—such as its failure to review the criminal records of all naturalization applicants—led the INS to reexamine its procedures, limit the entities authorized to fingerprint individuals filing INS forms, and revoke some new citizens' naturalization (Wilgoren 1998). Community organizations came under fire for allegedly completing and mailing in voter registration cards for individuals who had not yet naturalized. The 1996 election of Loretta Sanchez to the U.S. House of Representatives was (unsuccessfully) challenged by her opponent, Robert

American Ethnologist ▪ Volume 30 Number 4 November 2003

Dornan, on the grounds that some of the votes Sanchez received were cast by immigrants who were not yet naturalized. In 1997, the number of individuals naturalized dropped significantly, to 598,225, even though the number of naturalization applications filed in 1997 was 1,412,712, up from 1,277,403 in 1996 (Immigration and Naturalization Service 1999).

This overview of naturalization trends, in conjunction with the foregoing description of migrants' legalization strategies, explains why naturalization came to be a national priority, albeit a controversial one. It does not convey, however, how the ceremonies that actually produced new citizens addressed the anxieties regarding racial and ethnic discrimination, migrants' rights, and international interdependency that, in part, fueled these ceremonies. I therefore turn now to the rhetoric of these ceremonies, noting the remarkable *absence* of explicit reference to the broader political context in which they occurred. In essence, the issues that concerned Salvadorans who desired to naturalize disappeared within the ceremonies themselves. Despite this absence, the ceremonies' attention to diversity, valorization of choice, and insistence on the sovereignty of the receiving nation suggest that, like Salvadoran immigrants' struggle against legal exclusion, these ceremonies were part of broader debates over the meanings of difference, membership, and the nation. The contrasts between the logics of belonging put forward by Salvadoran interviewees and by U.S. officials during these ceremonies illustrate the disjuncture between transnational migration and nation-based models of membership.

Naturalization ceremonies

I first attended a mass naturalization ceremony in February 1996, when Salvadoran community activists asked me to join them outside the Los Angeles Convention Center to help newly naturalized citizens register to vote.[9] In nine ceremonies taking place over three days, some 30 thousand new citizens were naturalized. Imagine the setting. The already clogged freeways that converged near downtown Los Angeles were further congested by as many as 5,000 naturalization applicants and their family members attempting to arrive for an 8:00 a.m. ceremony. After parking in crowded parking structures, candidates raced to the proper convention hall, a huge facility usually used for conferences or trade expositions, where they lined up at a doorway labeled *New Citizens*. Security guards checked their appointment notices and directed accompanying family members to the visitor section, which was partitioned off by yellow security tape. The new citizens were ushered to their seats, where each found a little U.S. flag and a booklet containing a copy of the citizenship oath and the U.S. Constitution. The only decoration in the room was a giant U.S. flag, and the only signage pointed to the restrooms. Soon, the new citizens were directed to turn in their green cards at one of the numbered tables that lined the walls of the room. Meanwhile, family members in the visitor section strained with video cameras to glimpse the applicants. This part of the process took over an hour, as the 2,000–5,000 candidates for citizenship filed up to the tables and back to their seats.

Suddenly the tedium was interrupted by the sound of a gavel. A court clerk announced, "Please rise, this court is now in session." A motion to admit the candidates to citizenship was quickly made by an INS official and granted by a judge, and the new citizens cheered, applauded, and, on cue, waved their flags. The oath of allegiance was administered, and the judge and an INS official made remarks. Any members of the armed forces who were naturalizing were singled out for commendation. The new citizens watched a video extolling the United States, and an INS official led all present in singing the national anthem. The clerk led the new citizens in the pledge of allegiance, and the ceremony concluded. The visitors were ushered out so that the new citizens could receive their naturalization certificates, after which they emerged from the convention center to face well-wishers, vendors hawking souvenirs, and volunteers carrying clipboards with voter registration forms.

During 1996 and 1997, I attended ten such naturalization ceremonies at the L.A. Convention Center. Although this may appear to be a small sample, these ceremonies were fairly standardized, and I found that there were occasions when the same judge officiated and gave the same speech that he or she had given previously. Six judges presided over these ten ceremonies: a white woman, a Chinese American man, and four white men. One was the son of an immigrant, another was a naturalized U.S. citizen, and two stated that their families had been in the United States since the signing of the U.S. Constitution. As rituals, these ceremonies—like the term *naturalization* (Anderson 1983:145)—were remarkable. They fluctuated between the tedium of bureaucratic processing and the mysticism of a religious conversion. To examine how these rites produced citizens—and the nation—I turn now to the rhetoric of the ceremonies themselves. I focus on (1) how ceremonies tried to create similarity out of difference; (2) ways that ceremonies contrasted "birth" and "choice" as two methods of becoming American; and (3) how ceremonies configured nations as members of an international community. These three problematics emerged as central themes within the ceremonies and also are germane to broader debates over the degree to which immigrants assimilate, the bases for conferring citizenship, and the relationship between immigration and national sovereignty.

Identity and difference

One focus of naturalization ceremonies was the meaning of diversity. Diversity is linked to the disjuncture between transnationalism and the nation-state in that, if migrants are transnational beings—as Salvadoran interviewees asserted—then presumably they maintain some degree of foreignness, adding U.S. nationality to their preexisting allegiances. On the other hand, state-based categories of membership have traditionally been assumed to be exclusive, and in the United States, "difference" has taken the form of a private ethnic affiliation rather than a public national one. According to Greenhouse, negotiating the public and private meanings of *difference* requires

> the mythicization of identities—for example, ethnic and racial identities—as categorical personifications of "difference." This mythic operation, which in the United States makes key differences generic, and generic in the same way, is what makes a construction such as "the melting pot" (for example) conceivable. [1996:217; see also Chock 1995]

Applying this insight to the conferral of citizenship through law rather than through birth suggests that in these ceremonies naturalization privatized, homogenized, and tamed what might otherwise be characterized as disruptive foreign differences and thus created generic public citizens (see also Asad 1990; Gilroy 1987). In other words, naturalization—in the United States, at least—is simultaneously a ritual denaturalization, a stripping away of the public, legal character of difference defined as membership in a foreign state. Such denaturalization reconstitutes difference as private and therefore as a source of commonality or something that everyone has. Naturalizing difference makes it possible for foreigners to acquire new and equivalent legal personae.

Officials at these ceremonies frequently remarked on the diversity of the new citizens. For example, scanning the crowd, one judge commented, "I see that many of you come from so many different countries around the world." This remark suggested that difference is transparent, something that can be read or seen by any observer. In contrast, an INS official who addressed those assembled described diversity through statistics, stating, "You represent 123 nations throughout the world. This is the testimony to the diversity of our nation, and especially the Los Angeles area. That's when you consider that there's approximately one hundred eighty-eight countries throughout the world. You represent over three-fourths of the nations." This official's use of the term *represent* was significant. This term suggested both that protocitizens' public personae were linked to their citizenship and that the nations that were represented (three-fourths of the world) were convinced of the superiority of the United States, an idea that will be explored further below.

Diversity and difference seemed to be a source of anxiety to some officials. While giving instructions about how to turn in green cards, one official commented, "The American way is to do things in order. If we wanted mob violence, we wouldn't become citizens." Through his use of the term *we*, this official seemed to be speaking for the new citizens, much as a teacher speaks for students (e.g., "We don't throw our pencils on the floor now, do we?"). Moreover, given that these ceremonies occurred only four to five years after the L.A. riots (see Gooding-Williams 1993), references to mob violence evoked the alleged potential disruptiveness of diversity (see Greenhouse 1996). Echoes of the Rodney King incident were also clear in the following comment from a judge: "Today, we have, right here in southern California, one of the most important challenges that this country has ever had. And that is, how do we get along?" Commenting that "southern California is so different from when I was a boy," the same judge noted that the second largest population group of many nations was found in Los Angeles rather than in the territories of those nations. By drawing attention to the diversification of Los Angeles rather than the Americanization of immigrants, this judge implied that the United States might be colonized instead of colonizer. Urging the new citizens to "love their differences," this judge depicted southern California as the experiment on which the fate of the world depended: "If we cannot live here in southern California, the world is never going to progress. It will continue in its old ways, and civilization will never raise its [standards]."

Given such anxiety about the potential disruptiveness of diversity, one task of naturalization ceremonies was to make difference a source of unity. To accomplish this task, officials told immigrants who had formerly "represented" their nations that their public allegiance was now to the United States. Differences—which officials listed as consisting of language, culture, and foods—were relegated to a domestic sphere, to be remembered and passed on to children. Once in the private sphere, these differences were homogenized and made part of both familial and national heritages. For example, one judge told the new citizens that when a Muslim immigrant had married his daughter, it had added to his family's traditions. The judge then jumped from his family to the nation, stating, "[This is] just another extension of what we're doing here today. We're bringing new people, we're bringing new strengths. We're gonna blend them together." As *heritages*, differences became a source of unity. One judge explained that everyone has "an American story. They're all interesting, they're all different. . . . [But] each illustrates the same principle." The unifying principle of these stories, the judge elaborated, is "why we came." By defining new citizens according to their allegedly unified motive for immigrating—namely, the search for a better life—instead of their different national origins, naturalization ceremonies erased both difference and history. Such erasures were explicit in judges' comments. To give but one example: "Would it make any difference whether they [my ancestors] came from Vietnam, from Japan, or from Mexico, Canada, Yugoslavia? I don't see why. They're all Americans.

American Ethnologist ▪ Volume 30 Number 4 November 2003

. . . It doesn't matter where they come [from], it does not matter when."

Erasing difference and history made it possible for judges to define the public sphere as an arena of equality. Judges evoked not only Rodney King but also Martin Luther King Jr. One judge, for example, predicted that the children of immigrants would "seek a world in which nobody cares what nation you are, nobody cares what your religion is, nobody cares what your skin color is, nobody cares about those things. What they care about is what kind of person you are." Of course, the very necessity of such a quest suggested that, in fact, public life was not characterized by equality. A judge raised this possibility by telling the new citizens two anecdotes from his childhood that were related to discrimination. The first anecdote described how the judge's parents had punished the judge's brother for showing disrespect to an African American man who was a trash collector, and the second recounted how the judge's parents had reprimanded the judge himself for failing to intervene when other boys wrote the letter "J" on the vehicle of a Japanese American man during World War II. The judge used these anecdotes not to warn new citizens that they might encounter discrimination but, rather, to demonstrate that the United States values equality. Through such anecdotes, judges invoked the construct of the citizen who is "equal before the law" (Collier et al. 1995) and therefore legally identical to every other citizen. Officials at naturalization ceremonies depicted such public equality or sameness as a means of overcoming divisiveness. One INS official, for example, told the new citizens, "You are a unit of new citizens. Take that unity back to the community."[10]

The emphasis of naturalization ceremonies on public equality defined citizenship as generic—a claim that contrasts sharply with Salvadoran interviewees' fears that they would never be regarded as fully American. Judges and officials stated, for example, that one person's citizenship was interchangeable with that of another. For instance, officials assumed the authority to speak for the U.S. citizenry as a whole, saying, "On behalf of the citizens, I congratulate you." Officials also implied, through the use of terms such as *we* and *fellow citizens*, that their own citizenship was no different from that of the new citizens. Immediately after administering the oath, one judge told the new citizens—who had previously been characterized by *diversity*—to take a moment to "congratulate each other, your neighboring citizens!" Difference had been made alike through naturalization. The generic nature of this likeness was made clear by one judge's attempt to overcome the impersonality of the mass ceremony. Stating that he wished he could greet every new citizen individually, he told his audience that if one of them ever met him in the street after the ceremony, that person should walk up to him and say, "Hello citizen!" The term *citizen* would be sufficient to name both the judge and the person the judge had naturalized. Another judge ritually created generic citizenship by having all of the new citizens yell out the names of their places of origin on the count of three. When this produced an unintelligible shout, the judge explained, "That little exercise illustrates a point, and that point is that no one person was able to outshout the other. And when you shout out your names in unison, it all blended in. And that's what America is all about." As the public voice of the new citizens is blended and rendered homogeneous, it is only in private (where no one else is shouting) that differences can be articulated.

Officials at naturalization ceremonies depicted the transformation of national diversity into generic citizenship as a quasi-mystical experience. The new citizens, judges suggested, were united by a feeling, a unique sensation, almost a spirit. One judge, who was himself a naturalized citizen, described this feeling as follows: "I felt from the outset, as I believe you feel, that unique sensation of freedom upon the taking of the oath. I saw, as I believe you will see in succeeding years, that the promise of America is not empty. It is real, it is vibrant, it is challenging. It reaches out and embraces you all." The transformation from legal permanent resident to citizen, in other words, had been animated by a spirit: the promise of America. Officials' remarks emphasized the transformative nature of naturalization ceremonies. Now that the new citizens had partaken of this spirit, they were reborn and could proselytize to others. One judge recommended that the new citizens "continue this feeling, to foster it to your children and your friends." Such references to a mysterious feeling experienced during naturalization suggested a conversion, a sense of Americanness, and a spirit that united all present with each other, officials, and other citizens. Judges frequently referred to new citizens' presumed high emotions (e.g., "You ought to be very, very happy, very emotional now"). Officials also expected the new citizens to remember the date of their naturalization, much as one remembers a birth date. One official invited the new citizens to "imagine, if you will, how your lives will be changed by your new citizenship." The most concrete example of this change that officials could provide, however, was that with citizenship, those present could vote and serve on juries.[11] To understand officials' references to the spirit that allegedly unites new citizens, it is necessary to examine how officials contrasted citizens by choice with citizens by birth.

Blood and choice

Like diversity, choice is central both to naturalization ceremonies and to the disjuncture between transnationalism and nation-based membership categories. The literature on globalization emphasizes the structures in which migrants are situated and tends to depict migrants "as passive subjects, coerced by states and marginalized by markets" (Smith 1998:201). Although Salvadoran interviewees did not depict themselves as passive, these migrants did emphasize that, because of political and economic difficulties in their countries of origin and legal restrictions in the United States, they had no alternative but to migrate and then seek legal status. In contrast, the ability to make choices is central to naturalization as a legal process. Choices that are coerced rather than freely taken are not legal, and the citizenship oath itself concludes "I take this obligation freely, without any mental reservation or purpose of evasion, so help me God." Defining new citizens as people who can choose makes it possible to recognize them as subjects of liberal law who have the capacity to realize their human potential through the rights and protections afforded by national membership (Collier et al. 1995). Ceremonies' emphasis on choice also speaks to mid-1990s debates over measures of worthiness. Advocates of restrictive immigration measures argued that migrants exhibited illegitimate forms of agency, that migrant women, for example, sneaked across the U.S.–Mexico border to have U.S.-citizen children and collect welfare (see Perea 1997). Some also questioned whether the mere fact of being born on U.S. soil made the children produced through "illegitimate" agency deserving of U.S. citizenship (see Chock 1999). In contrast, by emphasizing the *mutuality* of choice (new citizens and the nation choose each other), naturalization ceremonies suggested that the naturalizing citizens had demonstrated their worthiness and that, far from compromising national sovereignty, incorporating the deserving reinvigorated the nation.

During ceremonies, officials emphasized that naturalized citizens were both equivalent to and different from citizens by birth. Citizens' equivalency derived from their common generic citizenship. Officials stated, for example, that there was "only one class of citizens" and that those who spoke English with an accent were no less American than other citizens. Their difference lay in the means by which each had acquired citizenship. One judge used the analogy of adoption to explain this distinction: "I compare this to, perhaps, a child born in a family, a child by birthright is within the family. Then there are those children who are as a matter of course outside the family, but adopted into the family.... You are the adoptees of this country, and this country has adopted you. You really have adopted this country."[12] Officials left no doubt in new citizens' minds about whether adopting or being born into U.S. citizenship was superior. One judge, who stated that it is the naturalized citizens who were held in the "highest esteem," explained, "We [citizens by birth] do not have to do anything, we do not have to make a decision. However, you have made a choice. . . . You made an active choice to give up your citizenship of birth and to join us."[13] The fact that they had to make this choice, officials suggested, meant that the new citizens would not take their citizenship for granted: "You chose to come here. So when you compare myself to yourself, for all those citizens who were born here. We were given that birthright. We take everything for granted." In contrast, officials explained, new citizens were filled with "the immigrant spirit" that made them "totally different from those people who remained here for years and years and years and forgot." New citizens were therefore, according to officials, the most authentic Americans—"much more American," as one judge put it—in that their lives encapsulated the history of the nation.

In valorizing *choice*, officials also indicated that to naturalize, those who chose U.S. citizenship had to first be judged and found deserving. In other words, naturalization gave not only immigrants but also the nation a choice in allocating citizenship. Judges frequently praised naturalizing immigrants for having traveled distances, overcome obstacles, and made sacrifices. Such comments defined citizenship as a reward that immigrants earned, in contrast to the gift that the native-born received regardless of their worthiness.[14] The example set by individuals who had earned citizenship allowed officials to reaffirm the United States as a land of opportunity in which dreams could be fulfilled. Stories of the self-made man (and at the ceremonies I attended, it was always a man) abounded during these proceedings. Judges recounted their own family members' immigration experiences, such as an immigrant coming to the United States with nothing and later becoming a professor at an Ivy League university, or a father who came to the United States with nothing, sold fruit in the streets for a living (a practice that has now been criminalized—see Rocco 1997:119), and launched nine children on successful careers. One judge explained the lessons of such stories: "No one in America is going to tell you artificially what your utmost achievement can be. We are empowered to defeat naysayers who say we can't do it. Because we can. We can, because we are Americans. In America, that old saying, 'The sky's the limit,' is truer now than ever." Amidst such celebrations of opportunity and self-sufficiency, however, appeared veiled warnings against applying for welfare. One judge, for example, admonished the new citizens to teach their children "to never ever think first of someone else taking care of them."

By demonstrating their worthiness and choosing to naturalize, immigrants reproduced the history of the nation. One judge connected the rebirth of citizens to the rebirth of the nation, commenting, "Immigrants meet the challenge of this country we live in from the day of its birth until today." Another judge depicted new citizens as a renewing force: "We welcome your fresh appreciation of what citizenship in this country really means. We welcome your zeal, your eagerness, and your determination to become good loyal citizens. You are indeed a stimulating force, which cannot help but bring a new luster to the image of America." In such comments, the *we* of fellow citizens is replaced with a we–you distinction, according to which the old citizens are associated with a somewhat tarnished America that the new citizens can polish. This judge went on to equate immigration with a blood transfusion, stating, "New citizens are the

American Ethnologist ▪ Volume 30 Number 4 November 2003

new blood of America, and we need it." It is interesting that the nation needs immigrants' blood, which presumably would be foreign. Once naturalized, however, this blood is seemingly purer or stronger than native blood. From whence does this need for new blood arise?

A nation of immigrants

The apparent dependence of the United States on continual transfusions of immigrant blood is, in these ceremonies at least, connected to the complex claim that the United States is a nation of immigrants—a claim that ignores both forced immigrants, such as enslaved Africans, and Native Americans, whose "citizenship" has been "reserved." According to the "nation of immigrants" construct, the erasure of previous public difference and the choice for the United States produce a clear-cut shift in new citizens' allegiance. As R. C. Smith notes,

> In the citizenship model, membership in a nation state and in the national political community are seen to be coterminous and exclusive; one can be a member of only one state and nation at a time. . . . Given this definition of membership in a community, immigration necessarily involves an "uprooting" (Handlin 1951) and "clean break" with the country of origin. [1998:199]

Clean breaks make naturalization a rebirth of sorts, giving new citizens a quasi-biological connection to the United States (Bauböck 1994; Stolcke 1997). The infusion of new citizens' blood, of those who can be self-made men, affirms that the United States is a land of opportunity and therefore superior to other nations. As a "nation of immigrants," the United States is presumed to be the top choice of deserving individuals who could have chosen to stay in their country of origin or to go elsewhere. According to this logic, immigration occurs not because of global interconnections that compel movement but, rather, because the distinctiveness of the U.S. way of life draws those who can appreciate the opportunities offered by this nation. The United States is thus an experiment, even a model for others, but still simply one among an array of nations that offer potential migrants different options.

Judges sometimes treated both naturalization and the space of the convention center qua courtroom as metonymic with the nation (see also Coutin 2000).[15] One judge, for instance, commented, "What we have in this room is this country itself. This is the United States of America right here in this room. This is what we have from border to border, ocean to ocean." In this comment, the space and populace of the nation were equated with the room and assembly, respectively. This positive rendering of diversity can be read against another judge's comment that large numbers of people from many nations reside in southern California. Although a courtroom and naturalizing citizens could be equated with the country, such contrasts suggested that southern California might be becoming the territory of other nations. This latter possibility, which resembles the notion of "trans-territorialization" put forward by scholars of transnationalism, was largely unremarked, however, given the celebration of Americanization that predominated in naturalization ceremonies. The spatialization of the courtroom as the nation in certain ways paralleled the spatialization of identity that permitted and forbade naturalization itself. For example, to naturalize, immigrants had to be physically present in the United States, just as, to naturalize, candidates for citizenship had to be physically present in the courtroom when the oath was administered. "Presence" was clearly a legal construct, as indicated by an official's warning that if the new citizens accidentally sat in the visitor section during the ceremony, they would not be naturalized and would have to attend another ceremony to be sworn in.

Officials conveyed the meaning of the "nation" to the new citizens in part through a music video that was shown during the ceremony. The video featured the music of the Lee Greenwood country-western song "God Bless the U.S.A.," accompanied by images of national greatness. The video began with a shot of a white man (Greenwood?) sitting on a tractor in the middle of a field and looking pensive, as Greenwood sang, "If tomorrow all the things were gone I'd worked for all my life, and I had to start again with just my children and my wife" (Greenwood and McLin 1993:244)—a situation that was probably not unusual among immigrants. The video continued with shots of national monuments, landscapes (coasts, mountains, prairies, and fields), citiscapes, fighter jets, the U.S. flag, the moon landing, and the Olympic torch. The only people who appeared—and their appearances were brief—were astronauts on the moon and disembarking from the space shuttle, the man on the tractor, and Bruce Jenner winning the decathlon. The near absence of people in the video was striking, given judges' speeches about the meanings of ethnic and cultural diversity. The U.S. flag was a recurring image—the one that was planted on the moon was replicated by the small flags that the new citizens waved and the giant flag that adorned the wall of the convention center. By celebrating such national achievements as placing people on the moon, winning world sports competitions, and conquering territory, the video suggested that new citizens had joined a truly great nation. Moreover, the lyrics, which celebrate the freedom that would allow a man who has lost everything to rebuild his life, reiterated the notions of opportunity and progress that were explicit in officials' speeches. The moon landing, with the planting of the U.S. flag, evoked continued expansionism, the last frontier.[16]

By advocating patriotism, naturalization ceremonies told immigrants who to root for in the future.[17] The words of the oath of allegiance depicted naturalization as transferring new citizens' loyalties exclusively from one nation to another: "I hereby declare on oath that I absolutely and entirely renounce and abjure all allegance and fidelity to any foreign prince, potentate, state or sovereignty, of whom or which I have heretofore been a subject or a citizen." Yet some of the loudest applause in the ceremony occurred when INS officials enumerated the top five nations represented in the ceremony. When Mexico—which was number one at all of the ceremonies that I attended—was announced, the applause grew to a crescendo of loud cheering.[18] Such public and national partisanship, much like Salvadoran interviewees' discussions of citizenship as additive and naturalization as furthering transnational ties, would seem to contradict the "generic" nature of naturalized citizenship.

Officials also used immigration itself to suggest that immigrants were "voting with their feet" for the United States over their countries of origin. One judge, for example, commented, "This country has all of that [freedom, opportunity] to offer to its people. And that's why people keep coming to the gates of our country asking to enter it." In words reminiscent of the American Jeremiad (Bellah 1975; Bellah et al. 1985; Bercovitch 1978), judges described the United States as "a beacon for truth," "that shining example of democracy on earth," and something that "lights up the earth." These comments implied that the rest of the world would like to come to or even be the United States, if only it could. Judges also connected immigration to manifest destiny. One judge credited immigrants with having spread the country "from coast to coast," and another instructed citizens, "You have become a citizen of a country that is still growing to the fulfillment of its destiny." These comments linked the growth of the national populace through immigration to territorial growth and national mission. This mission, according to judges, was "to build a more perfect America. And hopefully, solutions to peace on earth." Naturalizing citizens and thus incorporating and disarming difference could be seen as part of efforts to Americanize peoples, markets, and territory abroad. One judge urged immigrants to "be infectious, like a disease" in convincing others to emulate the United States—a comment that acknowledged the possibility of resistance, however misguided, to Americanization.

Despite lofty rhetoric about equality, inclusiveness, and choice, naturalization ceremonies hinted at structures of state power that defined identity and that might be responsible for record rates of naturalization. In requiring residents to turn in their green cards, for example, officials reminded their audiences that these documents were government property rather than individual possessions. Clearly, the government that could issue or recall such documents could also confer or deny particular statuses. By celebrating the rights that new citizens would acquire on naturalization, judges emphasized that the state grants rights through social membership. After idealistic speeches, each ceremony ended with these words: "Ladies and gentlemen, please be seated and await further instructions regarding the distribution of your certificates. This court session is now adjourned." Such references to the *need* to document citizenship link these ceremonies to the broader context—including other, less celebratory court hearings that deny status and order immigrants deported—in which these rites occurred. To conclude, let me return to these disjunctures in light of such linkages.

National disjunctures and linkages

Naturalization ceremonies put forward logics of migration, membership, and the nation that are linked in complex ways to the models that Salvadoran immigrants and activists have developed in response to human rights violations and economic problems in El Salvador and to legal exclusion in the United States. Sameness–difference, choice–nonchoice, and sovereignty–interdependency are key to these logics. First, during naturalization ceremonies, officials ritually erased public, legal elements of difference to constitute new citizens as equivalent juridical subjects of the United States. In this multicultural formulation, difference could be celebrated as a source of commonality, a background, a presumed shared history of immigrating to the United States in search of a better life. "Difference" was also relevant to Salvadoran interviewees, who, like recent migrants from other nations, suggested that as categories, "citizen" and "American" connote whiteness and that, regardless of their legal citizenship, members of ethnic minority groups would always be seen by some as less than full citizens. Moreover, Salvadorans, including Salvadoran officials, expressed or promoted dual identities, according to which, rather than being a clean break, naturalization adds U.S. citizenship to migrants' preexisting Salvadoran nationality.

Second, the emphasis on choice during naturalization ceremonies suggested that the United States simply attracted immigrants as a matter of course because of its superior way of life. The fact that migrants had made the choice to naturalize and that the United States had agreed that they were deserving affirmed the mutual wisdom of the relationship being formed between new citizens and the nation. "Nonchoice" (which does not mean a lack of agency) was key to Salvadoran migrants' accounts of migration and of their subsequent quest for legal status. These accounts demonstrate an awareness of the structures and relationships that shape human action. Thus, migrants attributed their original entry into the United States to political violence, economic necessity, and the need to support family members in El Salvador. Their decisions to apply for legal status and their desire for as-yet-unobtainable U.S. citizenship were linked at least in part to the exclusion they experienced as noncitizens. Furthermore, Salvadoran migrants' and officials' campaigns for U.S. residency for the Salvadoran immigrant population stressed ongoing social, political, and

American Ethnologist ▪ Volume 30 Number 4 November 2003

economic ties between the United States and El Salvador, including the U.S. need for immigrant labor. This logic links migration to interdependancy, rather than solely to individualistic quests for opportunity and self-advancement.

Third, naturalization ceremonies depicted continued immigration as demonstrating the superiority of the United States as a *sovereign* nation. If the best and the brightest sought out the opportunities that the United States offers when they could have chosen to remain in their countries of origin or to migrate elsewhere, then clearly, the United States was the best among an array of nations from which migrants could choose. Such an account of migration would seem to justify U.S. efforts to spread its way of life to other countries through modernization and democratization. "Interdependency" was key to Salvadoran interviewees' models of movement and belonging. In fact, Salvadoran officials' and activists' immigration-related strategies characterized the dispersal of the Salvadoran citizenry in ways that resembled scholars' use of the term *transterritorialization*.[19] In other words, instead of representing a loss of Salvadoran citizens, migration made El Salvador transnational, provided it with a source of remittances, and gave Salvadorans greater potential to influence U.S. policies vis-à-vis El Salvador. In contrast to naturalization ceremonies' emphasis on distinct citizenries and competing national systems, these strategies focused on transnational ties and multiple and overlapping allegiances.

Despite these disjunctures between naturalization officials' and Salvadoran interviewees' logics of belonging and movement, juxtaposing these logics reveals ways that nation-based categories of membership can serve transnational ends. One such connection is that although legal status officially defines an individual as a member of a particular nation, individuals may seek such status to better access resources in both their country of residence and of origin. Both U.S. immigration law and international law pertaining to migrants presume that individuals have a single, clear-cut nationality (Bosniak 1991; Marrus 1985). Nonetheless, studies of migrant communities have noted that these groups span borders and attend to multiple national realities (Hagan 1994; Kearney 1998; Levitt 2001; Rouse 1991). *Transmigration* was coined by Schiller et al. (1995) to refer to the way that, rather than leaving one society and joining another, migrants now develop and maintain ties to multiple societies. Hometown associations (Popkin 1999; Smith 1998) have received particular attention as examples of institutions that are key to transnational identities, and border studies has emerged as a field that examines transnational zones that both supersede and are defined by national boundaries. Consistent with my argument here, some have suggested that, regardless of their transnational orientations, migrants seek legal status not only as part of the settlement process (a process that may include coming to identify with their new country of residence) but also as a form of political expediency (Hagan 1994). Migrants need legal status *both* to access those opportunities that, in the United States, at least, are restricted to citizens and to legal permanent residents *and* to obtain travel documents that permit them to further develop their connections with their countries of origin.

Recognizing that legal status can better connect migrants to their countries of origin suggests that debates over whether or not transnationalism is rendering national forms of membership obsolete are misplaced. Regarding this debate, Soysal (1994) notes that in Europe, instead of being restricted to nationals, rights are increasingly being granted to individuals on other bases, such as their humanity (see also Bauböck 1994; Bosniak 2000; Hammar 1990) or their membership in a supranational entity, the European Union. In contrast, Wilmsen and McAllister (1996) argue that far from becoming obsolete, ethnicity and nationalism have been increasingly reasserted in recent decades. Immigration policies, which, in receiving nations, have tended to become more restrictive (Freeman 1992), have been singled out as phenomena that seem to defy the trend toward globalization (Cornelius et al. 1994). Some have attempted to reconcile these competing positions by pointing out that globalization simultaneously can strengthen local identities (Kearney 1995), as communities market themselves and their products as somehow unique or different from other areas (Maurer 1997), and can break down national boundaries, as distant groups are caught up in common structures and processes (Ong 1999). Robertson (1995) used the term *glocalization* to convey the simultaneity of such seemingly incompatible events. Similarly, my analysis of U.S. immigration politics in the 1990s suggests that even national categories of membership can be given transnational meanings (see also Maurer 1998). Thus, restrictive immigration policies can derive from nation-based models of membership and of international relations while simultaneously making the acquisition of citizenship key to transnational organizing.

Given that legal status can facilitate transnational organizing efforts, "difference," which was a focus both of Salvadoran interviewees' criticisms of discriminatory policies and naturalization ceremonies' celebrations of Americanization, can both be erased in the acquisition of legal subjecthood and used as a basis for political organizing. With the rise of the modern nation-state, the more abstract citizen–state relationship replaced what had been a more concrete (in theory at least) subject–sovereign tie.[20] Citizenship therefore has a generic quality: All citizens are presumed to be in an equivalent position vis-à-vis the state as a legal entity (Collier et al. 1995; Coutin 1993). In the United States, immigrants who undergo naturalization acquire this generic and equivalent quality, even as their histories distinguish them from those who are citizens by birth. Naturalization mimics citizenship by birth, and vice versa, in that citizens by birth are presumed to have accepted the authority of the Constitution (see Foucault 1977), as have naturalized citizens, and naturalization imbues new citizens with an identity or quasi-biological connection to the United States, as does birth.[21] Nonetheless, as feminists and critical race theorists have pointed out, citizenship in the United States is never fully generic (see, e.g., Matsuda et al. 1993; Nelson 1984; Sapiro 1984; Williams 1991), given that legal citizenship does not guarantee equal rights to women, ethnic minorities, and other marginalized groups. In fact, both "whiteness" and "maleness" have been prerequisites for citizenship historically (Augustine-Adams 2000; Goldberg 2001; Haney López 1996; Salyer 1995), and the citizenship of economically marginalized individuals is sometimes questioned (Marshall 1950). Similarly, critical uses of the term *naturalize* draw attention to the ambiguity that is intrinsic to naturalization: That which is natural is supposed to be given or intrinsic, yet naturalization constructs as *natural* something that, originally at least, was not.[22] If naturalized citizens *appear* to be the equivalent of citizens by birth, and if naturalization *appears* to turn alienage into commonality, then what happens to the differences that naturalization erases?[23] They become remainders that lead the authenticity of naturalized identities to be questioned but that also enable migrant groups to use ethnicity and nationality as a basis for political organizing. Such groups' refusals to consign "difference" to the private sphere, where it becomes a source of commonality, challenges the requirement that public citizenship assume a generic form.

Recognizing the incommensurability of migrants' histories gives the nation multiple pasts and positionings. Creating a nation requires simultaneously creating a national history (Anderson 1983). In the United States, this history centers on immigration. National histories celebrate the idea that beginning with the Pilgrims, immigrants have come to the United States in search of freedom and opportunity, and, through capitalizing on opportunity, have recreated the nation (Bellah et al. 1985; Bercovitch 1978). Within this narrative, immigration (and naturalization) is a mutual choice—immigrants choose the nation that offers them opportunity, and the nation chooses those immigrants who are capable of maximizing these opportunities (Chock 1991). For the arrival and incorporation of new immigrants to be considered a choice, however, both the nation and the immigrant must be sovereign beings (Bauböck 1994). Yet, migrants move because of political repression, economic dislocation, and family obligations (Hamilton and Chinchilla 1991; Kearney 1986; Menjívar 2000; Sassen 1988, 1989); they legalize, in part, to protect their rights in their countries of residence. Similarly, nations admit migrants, either officially or unofficially, because of a dependence on foreign, often unskilled, labor (Bach 1978; Jenkins 1978; Sassen 1991). It is therefore possible that both immigration and naturalization are fueled by the very conditions—nonchoice, interdependency—that national narratives deny (Coutin et al. 2002).[24] Acknowledging this possibility means recognizing that alongside the nationalistic history of the United States as a nation of immigrants are other, less-celebratory histories, involving labor exploitation, racism, and foreign intervention. The "nation of immigrants" construct, for example, ignores the forcible migration–importation of African slaves, for whom naturalization consisted of being defined as natural beings outside the boundaries of civil society.[25]

In sum, because the political struggles of the excluded and the ceremonies that award citizenship to the deserving are two moments within broader processes and logics of movement and belonging in the contemporary United States, there are deep interconnections between the notions of sameness–difference, choice–nonchoice, and sovereignty–interdependency that are linked to naturalization and to transnationalism, respectively. The dual or multiple identities that make migrants publicly different can be furthered by the acquisition of generic U.S. citizenship, which permits greater freedom of movement internationally.[26] The record numbers of naturalization applicants in the mid-1990s may have been partially due to community groups' efforts to mobilize legal permanent residents and U.S. citizens as part of ethnicity- and nationality-based political campaigns. Indeed, it is likely that such campaigns had some impact on the 2000 elections, in which anti-immigrant rhetoric was replaced by Democratic Party efforts to pass the Latino and Immigrant Fairness Act (LIFA) and Republicans' successful effort to pass the Legal Immigrant and Family Equity Act (LIFE).[27] Naturalization is not only a choice to acquire U.S. citizenship but also a response to a set of circumstances that, in the mid-1990s, included anti-immigrant sentiment and the adoption of more restrictive immigration policies. Nationality- and ethnicity-based organizing is significant not only to U.S.-based activists but also to foreign governments that have urged their nationals to seek legal status in the United States. Such strategies prevent potentially destabilizing deportations, create an empowered constituency that may have the ear of U.S. policy makers, promote the transterritorialization of states, and give other nations access to sources of remittances. Furthermore, prioritizing naturalization and authorizing other forms of temporary or permanent legalization may acknowledge U.S. obligations to and dependence on migrant labor. In short, there are ways that naturalization, which places individuals in national categories, serves transnational ends.

The complex and contradictory relationships between transnationalism and nation-based membership may be linked to the long-standing ambivalence toward immigration in the United States. Perhaps it is not surprising that restrictive immigration policies adopted in the mid-1990s were accompanied by a drive to formally include more foreign-born individuals in the nation. Prioritizing naturalization can be

American Ethnologist ▪ Volume 30 Number 4 November 2003

seen as an effort to eliminate or domesticate the foreign, but it also can be viewed as an acknowledgment of the presence and the rights of those individuals, as well as of the needs of immigrant-sending countries. The adoption of restrictive measures was followed, after all, by discussions of some form of guest worker, legalization, or amnesty program. Yet, following the attacks on the World Trade Center towers and the Pentagon on September 11, 2001, there has been a renewal of caution and a return to more restrictive measures. It may now be more difficult for immigrants to assert a right to simultaneously be fully recognized members of U.S. society and maintain loyalties to and ties with their countries of origin. Clearly, this mix of acknowledging interdependency and mutuality, on the one hand, and of asserting national boundaries and rights, on the other hand, will play out differently at different historical moments.

Notes

Acknowledgments. The research on which this article is based was supported by National Science Foundation Law and Social Science Program Grant SBR-9423023. I wrote the draft of this article while I was a visiting scholar at the Center for Multiethnic and Transnational Studies (CMTS) at the University of California, and I am grateful to CMTS and to its director, Dr. Michael Preston, for their support. My understanding of naturalization benefited from conversations with Phyllis Chock, Carol Greenhouse, Richard Perry, and Jen Kihnley. My analysis also is informed by recent collaborations with Bill Maurer and Barbara Yngvesson. Susan Sterett, Carol Greenhouse, Phyllis Chock, Tom Boellstorff, Mindie Lazarus-Black, Susan Hirsch, Christine Harrington, Virginia Dominguez, and the anonymous *AE* reviewers provided very helpful comments on the draft of this article. Tom Boellstorff suggested the phrase "cultural logics of belonging and movement," which I have used in the title of this article. I would also like to thank the religion group, funded by Global Peace and Conflict Studies at the University of California, Irvine, for its support. Drafts of this article were presented at the University of Southern California's Center for Religion and at New York University's Institute for Law and Society. Last, I am indebted to the many individuals who agreed to be interviewed for this project, as well as to the Central American Resource Center, El Rescate, and the Association of Salvadorans of Los Angeles.

1. The high numbers of naturalization applicants were due in large part to the 1986 amnesty program, a component of the 1986 Immigration Reform and Control Act (IRCA), which permitted certain seasonal agricultural workers and individuals who had lived in the United States continuously and illegally since January 1, 1982, to apply for legal permanent residency. After five years of legal permanent residency, the individuals who legalized through IRCA became eligible to apply for naturalization.

2. The United States Committee for Refugees reported that between 1983 and 1986,

> [asylum] applicants from Iran had the highest approval rate . . . , 60.4 percent, followed by the Soviet bloc countries, Romania (51.0), Czechoslovakia (45.4), Afghanistan (37.7), Poland (34.0), and Hungary (31.9). Among the countries with the lowest approval rates were El Salvador (2.6), Haiti (1.8), and Guatemala (0.9). [1986:8]

3. IIRIRA eliminated or restricted preexisting methods of legalization. Under the act's regulations, asylum applications had to be filed within one year of applicants' entry into the United States, individuals who petitioned for their relatives had to meet new deeming requirements, individuals who were illegally present in the United States and who left the country faced new bars to legal reentry, and the requirements for legalizing on the grounds that one has lived in the United States and established roots were heightened. See ACLU Immigrants Rights Project et al. (1996) for further details.

4. Winning a suspension case requires proving (1) seven years of continuous residency, (2) good moral character, and (3) that deportation would cause extreme hardship to the applicant or to a U.S. citizen or legal permanent resident relative of the applicant.

5. Of course, there may be a significant population of Salvadoran immigrants who do not seek or desire legal status. Given that I met most interviewees through community organizations that provided legal services to the undocumented, my sampling methods did not enable me to reach such individuals.

6. In fact, the U.S.-born children of Salvadoran citizens are eligible for Salvadoran citizenship, and my interviews with Salvadoran officials indicated that the Salvadoran government is eager to inculcate a sense of Salvadoran identity among U.S. Salvadoran youth.

7. This strategy is premised on the idea that new citizens and recent immigrants share certain opinions and perspectives and that if more new citizens actually vote, there is a greater chance of promoting policies that favor immigrants.

8. Welfare reform, which made even legal immigrants ineligible for most federal benefits, was adopted in 1996. That was the same year that California voters passed Proposition 209, which eliminated affirmative action. This proposal was followed in 1998 by the Unz initiative, which dismantled bilingual education in California.

9. This voter registration drive was activists' response to anti-immigrant initiatives, such as California Proposition 187. Reasoning that immigrants would have more political clout if they could vote, numerous Central American groups, including ASOSAL, the Organization of Salvadoran-Americans (OSA), and the Central American Resource Center (CARECEN), sent volunteers—some of whom were undocumented—to help newly naturalized Spanish-speaking citizens fill out voter registration cards. These groups were not alone in seeking to register new voters. Representatives of both the Democratic and Republican Parties—including a man dressed as Uncle Sam—sought to register new citizens.

10. Such references to equality, unity, and inclusiveness might have been welcome to immigrants who had been targeted by Proposition 187, welfare reform, and other restrictive measures. One recently naturalized Salvadoran immigrant, however, assessed the ceremony's message as follows: "The whole ceremony tells you you have the right to sit on the grass. Not, 'Let's change the country from the barrio on up.' "

11. Tomas Hammar (1990) argues that there are three gates through which immigrants pass on the road to naturalization. The first gate regulates entry into the country, the second gate regulates presence and social participation, and the third gate regulates full political rights. Using his terminology, before naturalizing, immigrants pass through the first and second gates, thereby securing almost complete social membership before obtaining citizenship itself.

12. As described by the judge, this adoption was mutual. It occurred not only because the parent country was in search of children but also because the children actively sought out parents.

13. Despite the oath of citizenship, naturalized citizens from countries that allow dual nationality might not, in fact, give up their citizenship of birth.

14. Because citizenship was depicted as a reward that immigrants had earned, it is not surprising that naturalization ceremonies in some ways resembled both graduation ceremonies and school assemblies. One official's comments to the new citizens made this analogy explicit: "It's always a happy occasion for us to be here. It's almost like a graduation ceremony." The flag-waving of the naturalized citizens reminded me of graduates who throw their caps during commencement. When giving instructions, officials sometimes treated the new citizens like schoolchildren. One official, for instance, announced to the new citizens, "We're going to be dismissing you by groups" and then had members of each of the designated groups rehearse this procedure by raising their hands when called. Officials also occasionally used infantilizing terminology, such as saying that they didn't want to have any "boo-boos" when the new citizens filed over to the INS tables, or asking the naturalizing immigrants to say, "Bye-bye, green cards!" Another official asked the visitors not to stand on their seats to take pictures during the ceremony. Certain elements of the naturalization ceremony, such as the pledge of allegiance, are also daily rituals in public schools.

15. As Shapiro notes, "Modern citizenship is situated primarily in the juridical network of the (imaginary) international system of state sovereignties.... The territorial state remains the dominant frame for containing the citizen body, both physically and symbolically" (2001:118).

16. In my experience, the crowd responded enthusiastically to the video. People sitting near me, for example, commented that the video gave them goose bumps.

17. Not surprisingly, naturalization ceremonies were unabashedly patriotic. Judges urged the new citizens to consider serving in the armed forces, to "stand tall" for the United States, and to practice patriotism on a daily basis. One man sitting near me was so moved by the ceremony that he resolved to bring his children the next time that someone in his family naturalized. The ceremonies were heavily publicized. Press crews filmed certain ceremonies, local papers covered these events in both English and Spanish, and at least one ceremony was transmitted to schoolchildren in the Philippines via satellite. Both officials and judges cited the many freedoms that U.S. citizenship provided, including freedom of movement, speech, and assembly. Officials' examples of how new citizens could demonstrate their patriotism—such as paying taxes, not littering, voting, and serving in parent–teacher associations—were surprisingly prosaic, given the lofty rhetoric about feelings, freedoms, and national missions. Nonetheless, the ceremonies inspired the crowd to cheer for the United States, on at least this one occasion.

In this sense, these rites were analogous to sporting events—particularly international ones. One judge, for instance, commented that the naturalization ceremony was "no different than my attending the opening ceremony at the Olympics in Atlanta just a couple of weeks ago, as I sat there and watched a parade of nations come by." This reference to nations reiterated the difference that naturalization could not quite overcome. Sports analogies were also clear in other aspects of the ceremonies, such as the images of the Olympic torch and Bruce Jenner in the Lee Greenwood video and the waving of national flags, which occurs during soccer matches as well as naturalization ceremonies. One official similarly instructed the new citizens to do the "immigration wave" by rising in turn when he called their sections. Of interest, journalists sometimes also use sports analogies to flesh out immigrants' allegiances. In one news story about the 1986 Immigration Reform and Control Act, a journalist asked a young man who was applying for legalization whether he would root for a Mexican soccer team or a U.S. soccer team. See Coutin and Chock 1995 and Mathews 1986.

18. At the ceremonies that I attended, the other top nations were Vietnam, El Salvador, the Philippines, Korea, and Iran.

19. For instance, the Salvadoran vice president observed during a conference in San Salvador in August 2000, "We have become an emigrant people." An official in the Salvadoran Ministry of Foreign Relations similarly told me that El Salvador has become "a completely transnational society now" and that to confront this situation, every ministry was being required to develop a plan for addressing the needs of Salvadorans in the exterior.

20. On the corporality of the sovereign, see Kantorowicz 1957. I am grateful to Susan Sterett for bringing the relevance of this source to my attention.

21. Bauböck explains that the term *naturalization*

> can be understood to define the receiving group as a natural one and to require that new members change their nature.... In France and England from the 14th to the 18th century the native-born are seen to be *natural* subjects of a sovereign and naturalization signifies a *natural* way of obtaining a similar status by residing permanently in a country, acquiring property and obeying its laws. [1994:44–45]

See also Stolcke 1997.

22. Feminists and critical race theorists, for example, have used the term *naturalize* to draw attention to the processes that make socially and historically constructed categories and practices appear natural and impossible to change. Thus, Yanagisako and Delaney define naturalizing power as "ways in which differentials of power come already embedded in culture.... Power appears natural, inevitable, even god-given" (1995:1).

23. The possible disloyality or multiple loyalities of naturalized citizens and of other immigrants has troubled those concerned about large-scale immigration to the United States. The World War II internment of the Japanese (Salyer 1995; Starn 1986) and the post–September 11, 2001, questioning of Arab Americans' loyalties are cases in point. Diasporic peoples, who claim loyalties to deterritorialized nation-states (Basch et al. 1994; Bosniak 2000), have not always been well received by their countries of residence. Some analysts of immigration argue that the United States already tolerates and even encourages a degree of cultural and ethnic diversity that makes governance difficult. Peter Schuck and Rainer Münz note that in the United States

> many restrictionists . . . fear that the country has lost its capacity to absorb migrants as a consequence of government multicultural policies, including bilingual classes aimed at reinforcing ethnic and cultural identities and affirmative action policies.... They argue that these policies, along with a cultural norm that legitimates the maintenance of group identities, is further fragmenting a society already divided along racial lines. [1998:xx]

24. I do not mean to suggest that migrants lack agency. See Coutin 1998 for a discussion of this issue.

25. I am grateful to Tom Boellstorff for reminding me of this form of naturalization.

26. Legal permanent residents also enjoy considerable freedom of movement internationally. To maintain their eligibility for naturalization, however, legal permanent residents must have been physically present in the United States for at least six months out of each year for five years. Moreover, legal permanent residents do not travel with the U.S. passports that may afford easier entry into certain countries.

27. LIFA had three provisions: (1) parity for beneficiaries of the 1997 Nicaraguan Adjustment and Central American Relief Act, (2) the restoration of 245(i), a program that permitted the recipients

American Ethnologist ▪ Volume 30 Number 4 November 2003

of family visa petitions to adjust their status in the United States in exchange for paying a fine, and (3) updating of the registry date, which would have permitted the legalization of large numbers of immigrants. LIFE was more limited in scope and primarily benefited certain recipients of family visa petitions and members of class actions suits filed in relation to the 1986 amnesty program.

References cited

Aguayo, Sergio, and Patricia Weiss Fagen
1988 Central Americans in Mexico and the United States: Unilateral, Bilateral, and Regional Perspectives. Washington, DC: Center for Immigration Policy and Refugee Assistance, Georgetown University.
ACLU Immigrants Rights Project, Catholic Legal Immigration Network, Immigrant Legal Resource Center, National Immigration Law Center, and National Immigration Project of the National Lawyers Guild
1996 Background Materials: The 1996 Immigration Law. Los Angeles: National Immigration Law Center.
Anderson, Benedict
1983 Imagined Communities: Reflections on the Origin and Spread of Nationalism. Rev. edition. London: Verso.
Asad, Talal
1990 Multiculturalism and British Identity in the Wake of the Rushdie Affair. Politics and Society 18(4):455–480.
Augustine-Adams, Kif
2000 Gender States: A Comparative Construction of Citizenship and Nation. Virginia Journal of International Law 41(1):93–140.
Bach, Robert L.
1978 Mexican Immigration and the American State. International Migration Review 12(4):536–558.
Baker, Susan González
1997 The "Amnesty" Aftermath: Current Policy Issues Stemming from the Legalization Programs of the 1986 Immigration Reform and Control Act. International Migration Review 31(1):5–27.
Basch, Linda, Nina Glick Schiller, and Cristina Szanton Blanc
1994 Nations Unbound: Transnational Projects, Postcolonial Predicaments, and Deterritorialized Nation-States. Langhorne, PA: Gordon and Breach.
Bauböck, Rainer
1994 Transnational Citizenship: Membership and Rights in International Migration. Aldershot, UK: Edward Elgar.
Bellah, Robert N.
1975 The Broken Covenant: American Civil Religion in Time of Trial. New York: Seabury.
Bellah, Robert N., Richard Madsen, William M. Sullivan, Ann Swidler, and Steven M. Tipton
1985 Habits of the Heart: Individualism and Commitment in American Life. New York: Harper and Row.
Bercovitch, Sacvan
1978 The American Jeremiad. Madison: University of Wisconsin Press.
Bosniak, Linda S.
1991 Human Rights, State Sovereignty and the Protection of Undocumented Migrants under the International Migrant Workers Convention. International Migration Review 25(4):737–770.
2000 Citizenship Denationalized. Indiana Journal of Global Legal Studies 7(2):447–510.
Calavita, Kitty
1996 The New Politics of Immigration: "Balanced-Budget Conservativism" and the Symbolism of Proposition 187. Social Problems 43(3):284–305.
2000 The Paradoxes of Race, Class, Identity, and "Passing": Enforcing the Chinese Exclusion Acts, 1882–1910. Law and Social Inquiry 25(1):1–40.
Chavez, Leo R.
2001 Covering Immigration: Popular Images and the Politics of the Nation. Berkeley: University of California Press.
Chock, Phyllis Pease
1991 "Illegal Aliens" and "Opportunity": Myth-Making in Congressional Testimony. American Ethnologist 18(2):279–294.
1995 Culturalism: Pluralism, Culture, and Race in the Harvard Encyclopedia of American Ethnic Groups. Identities 1(4): 301–323.
1999 "A Very Bright Line": Kinship and Nationality in U.S. Congressional Hearings on Immigration. PoLAR: Political and Legal Anthropology Review 22(2):42–52.
Collier, Jane F., Bill Maurer, and Liliana Suárez-Navaz
1995 Sanctioned Identities: Legal Constructions of Modern Personhood. Identities 2(1–2):1–27.
Cornelius, Wayne A., Philip L. Martin, and James F. Hollifield
1994 Controlling Immigration: A Global Perspective. Stanford: Stanford University Press.
Coutin, Susan Bibler
1993 The Culture of Protest: Religious Activism and the U.S. Sanctuary Movement. Boulder: Westview Press.
1998 From Refugees to Immigrants: The Legalization Strategies of Salvadoran Immigrants and Activists. International Migration Review 32(4):901–925.
2000 Legalizing Moves: Salvadoran Immigrants' Struggle for U.S. Residency. Ann Arbor: University of Michigan Press.
Coutin, Susan Bibler, and Phyllis Chock
1995 "Your Friend, the Illegal": Definition and Paradox in Newspaper Accounts of U.S. Immigration Reform. Identities 2(1–2): 123–148.
Coutin, Susan Bibler, Bill Maurer, and Barbara Yngvesson
2002 In the Mirror: The Legitimation Work of Globalization. Law and Social Inquiry 27(4):801–843.
Delgado, Hector
1993 New Immigrants, Old Unions: Organizing Undocumented Workers in Los Angeles. Philadelphia: Temple University Press.
Feldman, Allen
1991 Formations of Violence: The Narrative of the Body and Political Terror in Northern Ireland. Chicago: University of Chicago Press.
Foner, Nancy
1997 What's New About Transnationalism? New York Immigrants Today and at the Turn of the Century. Diaspora 6(3): 355–376.
Foucault, Michel
1977 Discipline and Punish: The Birth of the Prison. Alan Sheridan, trans. New York: Pantheon.
Freeman, Gary P.
1992 Migration Policy and Politics in the Receiving States. International Migration Review 26(4):1144–1166.
Gilroy, Paul
1987 "There Ain't No Black in the Union Jack": The Cultural Politics of Race and Nation. Chicago: University of Chicago Press.
Goldberg, David Theo
2001 States of Whiteness. *In* Between Law and Culture: Relocating Legal Studies. David Theo Goldberg, Michael Musheno, and Lisa C. Bower, eds. Pp. 174–194. Minneapolis: University of Minnesota Press.
Goldring, Luin
1998 The Power of Status in Transnational Social Fields. *In* Transnationalism from Below. Michael Peter Smith and Luis

Eduardo Guarnizo, eds. Pp. 165–195. New Brunswick, NJ: Transaction.
Gooding-Williams, Robert, ed.
1993 Reading Rodney King/Reading Urban Uprising. New York: Routledge.
Greenhouse, Carol J.
1996 A Moment's Notice: Time Politics across Cultures. Ithaca: Cornell University Press.
Greenwood, Lee, and Gwen McLin
1993 God Bless the U.S.A.: Biography of a Song. Gretna, LA: Pelican Publishing.
Guarnizo, Luis Eduardo
1997 The Emergence of a Transnational Social Formation and the Mirage of Return Migration among Dominican Transmigrants. Identities 4(2):281–322.
1998 The Rise of Transnational Social Formations: Mexican and Dominican State Responses to Transnational Migration. Political Power and Social Theory 12:45–94.
Guarnizo, Luis Eduardo, and Michael Peter Smith
1998 The Locations of Transnationalism. *In* Transnationalism from Below. Michael Peter Smith and Luis Eduardo Guarnizo, eds. Pp. 3–34. New Brunswick, NJ: Transaction.
Hagan, Jacqueline Maria
1994 Deciding to be Legal: A Maya Community in Houston. Philadelphia: Temple University Press.
Hamilton, Nora, and Norma Stolta Chinchilla
1991 Central American Migration: A Framework for Analysis. Latin American Research Review 26(1):75–110.
Hammar, Tomas
1990 Democracy and the Nation State: Aliens, Denizens and Citizens in a World of International Migration. Aldershot, UK: Avebury.
Handlin, Oscar
1951 The Uprooted. Boston: Little, Brown.
Haney López, Ian F.
1996 White by Law: The Legal Construction of Race. New York: New York University Press.
Harvey, David
1989 The Condition of Postmodernity. Cambridge: Blackwell.
Higham, John
1974[1963] Strangers in the Land: Patterns of American Nativism, 1860–1925. New York: Antheneum.
Huber, Gregory A., and Thomas J. Espenshade
1997 Neo-Isolationism, Balanced-Budget Conservatism, and the Fiscal Impacts of Immigrants. International Migration Review 31(4):1031–1054.
Immigration and Naturalization Service
1999 Statistical Yearbook of the Immigration and Naturalization Service. Washington, DC: Immigration and Naturalization Service.
Immigrant Policy Project of the State and Local Coalition on Immigration
1996 Immigrant Policy News . . . The State-Local Report 3(1). Washington, DC: Immigrant Policy Project of the State and Local Coalition on Immigration.
Itzigsohn, José
2000 Immigration and the Boundaries of Citizenship: The Institutions of Immigrants' Political Transnationalism. International Migration Review 34(4):1126–1154.
Jenkins, J. Craig
1978 The Demand for Immigrant Workers: Labor Scarcity or Social Control? International Migration Review 12(4):514–535.
Johnson, James H., Jr., Walter C. Farrell Jr., and Chandra Guinn
1997 Immigration Reform and the Browning of America: Tensions, Conflicts and Community Instability in Metropolitan Los Angeles. International Migration Review 31(4):1055–1095.
Kantorowicz, Ernst H.
1957 The King's Two Bodies: A Study in Mediaeval Political Theology. Princeton: Princeton University Press.
Kaye, Mike
1997 The Role of Truth Commissions in the Search for Justice, Reconciliation, and Democratisation: The Salvadorean and Honduran Cases. Journal of Latin American Studies 29(3): 693–716.
Kearney, Michael
1986 From the Invisible Hand to Visible Feet: Anthropological Studies of Migration and Development. Annual Review of Anthropology 15:331–361.
1995 The Local and the Global: The Anthropology of Globalization and Transnationalism. Annual Review of Anthropology 24:547–565.
1998 Transnationalism in California and Mexico at the End of Empire. *In* Border Identities: Nation and State at International Frontiers. Thomas M. Wilson and Hastings Donnan, eds. Pp. 117–141. Cambridge: Cambridge University Press.
Landolt, Patricia, Lilian Autler, and Sonia Baires
1999 From Hermano Lejano to Hermano Mayor: The Dialectics of Salvadoran Transnationalism. Ethnic and Racial Studies 22(2):290–315.
Levitt, Peggy
2001 The Transnational Villagers. Berkeley: University of California Press.
Mahler, Sarah J.
1998 Theoretical and Empirical Contributions toward a Research Agenda for Transnationalism. *In* Transnationalism from Below. Michael Peter Smith and Luis Eduardo Guarnizo, eds. Pp. 64–100. New Brunswick, NJ: Transaction.
Marrus, Michael R.
1985 The Unwanted: European Refugees in the Twentieth Century. New York: Oxford University Press.
Marshall, T. H.
1950 Citizenship and Social Class, and Other Essays. Cambridge: Cambridge University Press.
Martin, Philip
1995 Proposition 187 in California. International Migration Review 29(1):255–263.
Matsuda, Mari J., Charles R. Lawrence III, Richard Delgado, and Kimberle Williams Crenshaw
1993 Words That Wound: Critical Race Theory, Assaultive Speech and the First Amendment. Boulder: Westview Press.
Mathews, Jay
1986 Home Is Where the Heart Is: Mexican Immigrants Arrive Looking over Their Shoulders. Washington Post, May 2: H5.
Maurer, Bill
1997 Recharting the Caribbean: Land, Law, and Citizenship in the British Virgin Islands. Ann Arbor: University of Michigan Press.
1998 Cyberspatial Sovereignties: Offshore Finance, Digitial Cash and the Limits of Liberalism. Indiana Journal of Global Legal Studies 5(2):493–519.
Menjívar, Cecilia
2000 Fragmented Ties: Salvadoran Immigrant Networks in America. Berkeley: University of California Press.
Menjívar, Cecilia, Julie DaVanzo, Lisa Greenwell, and R. Burciaga Valdez
1998 Remittance Behavior among Salvadoran and Filipino Immigrants in Los Angeles. International Migration Review 32(1): 97–126.
Montes Mozo, Segundo, and Juan Jose Garcia Vasquez
1988 Salvadoran Migration to the United States: An Exploratory Study. Hemispheric Migration Project. Washington, DC:

American Ethnologist ▪ Volume 30 Number 4 November 2003

Center for Immigration Policy and Refugee Assistance, Georgetown University.

NatzNews
1998 NatzNews Vol. 7, April 17. Washington, DC: Immigration and Naturalization Service, Office of Naturalization Operations.

Nelson, Barbara J.
1984 Women's Poverty and Women's Citizenship: Some Political Consequences of Economic Marginality. Signs 10(2):209–231.

Ong, Aihwa
1999 Flexible Citizenship: The Cultural Logic of Transnationality. Durham, NC: Duke University Press.

Ong, Paul, Edna Bonacich, and Lucie Cheng
1994 The New Asian Immigration in Los Angeles and Global Restructuring. Philadelphia: Temple University Press.

Paral, Rob
1995 Naturalization: New Demands and New Directions at the INS. Interpreter Releases 72(27):937–943.

Perea, Juan F., ed.
1997 Immigrants Out! The New Nativism and the Anti-Immigrant Impulse in the United States. New York: New York University Press.

Popkin, Eric
1999 Guatemalan Mayan Migration to Los Angeles: Constructing Transnational Linkages in the Context of the Settlement Process. Ethnic and Racial Studies 22(2):267–289.

Portes, Alejandro
1997 Immigration Theory for a New Century: Some Problems and Opportunities. International Migraton Review 31(4):799–825.

Portes, Alejandro, Luis E. Guarnizo, and Patricia Landolt
1999 The Study of Transnationalism: Pitfalls and Promise of an Emergent Research Field. Ethnic and Racial Studies 22(2): 217–237.

Robertson, Roland
1995 Globalization: Time-Space and Homogeneity-Heterogeneity. *In* Global Modernities. Mike Featherstone, Scott Lash, and Roland Robertson, eds. Pp. 25–44. London: Sage.

Rocco, Raymond
1997 Citizenship, Culture, and Community: Restructuring in Southeast Los Angeles. *In* Latino Cultural Citizenship: Claiming Identity, Space, and Rights. William V. Flores and Rina Benmayor, eds. Pp. 97–123. Boston: Beacon Press.

Rouse, Roger
1991 Mexican Migration and the Social Space of Postmodernism. Diaspora 1(1):8–23.

Ruggles, Patricia, Michael Fix, and Kathleen M. Thomas
1985 Profile of the Central American Population in the United States. Washington, DC: Urban Institute.

Salyer, Lucy E.
1995 Laws Harsh as Tigers: Chinese Immigrants and the Shaping of Modern Immigration Law. Chapel Hill: University of North Carolina Press.

Sánchez, George J.
1997 Face the Nation: Race, Immigration, and the Rise of Nativism in Late Twentieth Century America. International Migration Review 31(4):1009–1030.

Sapiro, Virginia
1984 Women, Citizenship, and Nationality: Immigration and Naturalization Policies in the United States. Politics and Society 13(1):1–26.

Sassen, Saskia
1988 The Mobility of Labor and Capital: A Study in International Investment and Labor Flow. New York: Cambridge University Press.
1989 America's Immigration "Problem": The Real Causes. World Policy Journal 6(4):811–831.
1991 The Global City: New York, London, Tokyo. Princeton: Princeton University Press.
1996 Losing Control? Sovereignty in an Age of Globalization. New York: Columbia University Press.

Schiller, Nina Glick, Linda Basch, and Cristina Szanton Blanc
1995 From Immigrant to Transmigrant: Theorizing Transnational Migration. Anthropological Quarterly 68(1):48–63.

Schiller, Nina Glick, and Georges E. Fouron
1999 Terrains of Blood and Nation: Haitian Transnational Social Fields. Ethnic and Racial Studies 22(2):340–366.

Schuck, Peter H., and Rainer Münz, eds.
1998 Paths to Inclusion: The Integration of Migrants in the United States and Germany. New York: Berghahn Books.

Shapiro, Michael J.
2001 For Moral Ambiguity: National Culture and the Politics of the Family. Minneapolis: University of Minnesota Press.

Smith, Robert C.
1998 Transnational Localities: Community, Technology and the Politics of Membership within the Context of Mexico and U.S. Migration. *In* Transnationalism from Below. Michael Peter Smith and Luis Eduardo Guarnizo, eds. Pp. 196–238. New Brunswick, NJ: Transaction.

Soysal, Yasemin Nuhoglu
1994 Limits of Citizenship: Migrants and Postnational Membership in Europe. Chicago: University of Chicago Press.

Starn, Orin
1986 Engineering Internment: Anthropologists and the War Relocation Authority. American Ethnologist 13(4)700–721.

Stolcke, Verena
1997 The "Nature" of Nationality. *In* Citizenship and Exclusion. Veit Bader, ed. Pp. 61–80. New York: St. Martin's Press.

United States Committee for Refugees
1986 Despite a Generous Spirit: Denying Asylum in the United States. Washington, DC: American Council for Nationalities Service.

Wilgoren, Jodi
1998 Thousands in Crackdown Face Loss of Citizenship. Los Angeles Times, February 2: A1, A13.

Williams, Patricia J.
1991 The Alchemy of Race and Rights. Cambridge, MA: Harvard University Press.

Wilmsen, Edwin N., and Patrick McAllister, eds.
1996 The Politics of Difference: Ethnic Premises in a World of Power. Chicago: University of Chicago Press.

Yanagisako, Sylvia, and Carol Delaney, eds.
1995 Naturalizing Power: Essays in Feminist Cultural Analysis. New York: Routledge.

Yngvesson, Barbara
1997 Negotiating Motherhood: Identity and Difference in "Open" Adoptions. Law and Society Review 31(1):31–80.

accepted March 12, 2003
final version submitted March 31, 2003

Susan Bibler Coutin
Department of Criminology, Law and Society
University of California, Irvine
Irvine, CA 92697
scoutin@uci.edu

[10]

The constitution of a European immigration policy domain: a political sociology approach

Virginie Guiraudon[1] *

ABSTRACT At the 1999 Tampere summit, EU member states committed themselves to developing a comprehensive immigration and asylum policy. Although directives harmonizing border controls or anti-discrimination instruments have been adopted, it remains an incomplete and complex European policy area. This article seeks to explain the timing, form and content of this new domain. It combines the insights of March and Olsen's 'garbage can' model with a sociological approach that emphasizes power competition among actors in the same field. Diverse actors have seized upon EU opportunities. Law and order officials in charge of migration control seeking to gain autonomy in intergovernmental settings linked their action to the single market and transnational crime. NGOs providing expertise to Commission units seeking competence in non-economic areas jumped on the 'social exclusion' bandwagon by proposing anti-discrimination legislation. These developments – superimposed on policies regarding free movement of workers and services – are thus often contradictory and adhocratic.

KEY WORDS Amsterdam Treaty; anti-discrimination policy; bureaucratic politics; 'garbage can' model; immigration and asylum; policy frames and venues.

While 'first generation' European Community (EC) policies such as the common agricultural policy are under fire, new policy domains are emerging in the European Union (EU) framework. At the 1999 Tampere summit, EU leaders declared that the development of a comprehensive immigration and

*EDITOR'S NOTE An earlier version of this article was presented as a paper to the 2001 EUSA conference and was awarded the prize for the best 2001 EUSA conference paper.

The prize selection committee (Dorothée Heisenberg, James Hollifield, George Ross) noted that Guiraudon's paper 'captures the complexity of contemporary EU policy formation in the immigration area ... [and] is remarkable for its recognition and mastery of different streams of policy-making over time. It foregrounds real EU politics in an unstable, constantly changing set of institutional arenas without imposing artificial social science parsimony. Reading the paper we enter the EU as it is, not as we would like it to be in our *a priori* models. Guiraudon's refreshing theoretical quest instead goes toward the sociology of organizations, borrowing from March and Olson's "garbage can" approach.'

asylum policy was a top priority and the EU's next large-scale enterprise after the single market and European monetary union (EMU).[2] Three years later, the June 2002 Seville summit was still largely dedicated to immigration as European leaders invoked populist electoral breakthroughs in various European elections to step up the 'fight against illegal migration'.

The official narratives behind the development of this common policy have taken two forms. Before 1992, the predominant discourse within the 'Schengen laboratory' and the 'ad hoc immigration group' was that free movement within the EC required compensatory measures at the external borders lest Europe become a 'sieve'. This political version of the 'spillover' theory of integration was largely replaced in the 1990s by a more securitarian perspective (Bigo 1996), as the number of asylum-seekers and persons displaced by war rose. 'Asylum shopping' and 'immigration risks' were now common 'problems' that could best be dealt with through co-ordination. The view here resembles liberal intergovernmentalism, which poses that major member states co-operate to upgrade common interests and reduce transaction costs.

The reconstruction of the rationale behind the rise of immigration on the political agenda masks the complexity and incompleteness of current EU-level policies and considers them to be an inevitable solution to a commonly defined problem. They postulate a rationality long criticized when analysing national policy processes. Among them, March and Olsen (1989) focused on situations of organized anarchy whereby the elements of decision-making are thrown into the process as they appear as in a 'garbage can'. The elaboration of an EU immigration policy presents similarities with their model.

My main claim is that, regarding both immigrant and migration control policy, only one side of the debate 'venue shopped' at the international level to pursue their own ends, primarily to escape domestic adversaries. In the case of migration control, bureaucrats sitting in interior ministries sought to regain the discretion taken away by courts and the leeway lost to inter-ministerial arbitrage. Regarding immigrant policy, the domestic challenge came from electoral politics that forestalled policy change and innovation. The migration policy domain cannot be understood as the bargaining outcome among states with a coherent or aggregated set of preferences on these issues. Instead, only one 'camp' in the national policy field went transnational, and this article provides an account of the ways they did so.

It thus examines the dynamics of the constitution of this policy domain to better apprehend its timing, form and content. After setting out the analytical framework that focuses on power struggles among groups seeking legitimacy (I), I turn to the main chapters of the story so far: the bureaucratic rivalry that led to Title IV of the EU Treaty and the incorporation of Schengen via protocol at Amsterdam which sets the frame for a common immigration and asylum policy (II); the rivalry of non-governmental organizations (NGOs) that carved out a space for EU policy in the area of migrant incorporation, which resulted in Article 13 on anti-discrimination and a 'race directive' in 2000 (III); and, finally, the parallel activities of the European Court of Justice (ECJ) and the Commission Trade directorate in the area of freedom of services that affect migration flows within and into the EU.

I. THEORETICAL AND CONTEXTUAL PREMISES

The story of the rise of immigration on the EU policy agenda is that of governmental and non-governmental actors arriving on the European scene to escape domestic constraints and open up new spaces for action. In this motley crew, we find law and order officials from Interior, Justice and Foreign Affairs ministries, international NGOs, activists and Commission *fonctionnaires* from different directorates. Although each came to believe that there should be a European immigration policy, they exploited different policy venues and frames resulting in a set of policy instruments involving varying degrees of supranationalization and distinct decision-making rules. These groupings are not monoliths. National and EU bureaucrats, NGOs compete among their own kind as much as they fight among themselves in a struggle for legitimacy and autonomy. In this respect, the Bourdieusian notion of 'field' (Bourdieu 1981) is helpful since it focuses on the power struggles within each group of actors (see also Favell 2000).

This actor-oriented approach generates several research questions: why did certain groups decide to 'go transnational'? Who were they competing with at the national and transnational level? Why did certain groups gain a monopoly of expertise in the European sphere? What policy venues and frames did they exploit? What opportunities could they seize upon (allies in EU institutions or member states, actors in other policy areas, treaty revisions, changes in the global economic or strategic context)? The empirical study of these mobilization strategies explains the particular timing, form and content of EU policies that affect both migration flows and the conditions of immigrant minorities in Europe. In other words, our approach should be able to explain:

- when international co-operation started and when competence was shifted to the EU (*timing*);
- why certain rules and procedures for EU decision-making were adopted (*form*);
- why a particular policy toolbox was adopted (*content*).

The insights of public policy studies can be fruitfully combined with that of political sociology to grasp the development of a European policy domain.[3] March and Olsen suggest that, although the choices made by the various self-interested actors can be said to be rational from their perspective, one should not reconstruct a non-linear policy process as inevitable. Contingencies and reversals closed certain paths and cleared others along the way. The 'garbage can' model underlines that interests, institutions, ideas, problems and solutions appear in the process in no preordained sequence as 'exogenous streams flowing through a system' (Olsen 2001: 191),[4] yet, as we will see, the order in which each element appears has a bearing on the eventual outcome.[5]

I build upon the public policy agenda-setting literature, including John Kingdon's work (1995) which was directly influenced by the garbage can model and Frank Baumgartner and Bryan Jones's concept of policy frames and venues (1993). If a solution is defined before a problem is identified, issue framing will be crucial to reconstitute a 'causal story' (Stone 1989). Similarly, the success of a particular frame will depend upon windows of opportunities. This implies that, once actors have decided to shift their strategies to a European policy venue, their ability to do so will depend on the availability of relevant frames and their seizing of opportunities.

In methodological terms, I have consequently favoured a genealogical approach that starts before the rise of immigration on the European agenda. To capture the cross-national and cross-sectoral dynamics of EU policy-making, I chose a comparative approach. I focused on immigration politics in three founding members of Schengen (France, Germany and the Netherlands) since the 1970s to apprehend the relative position and constraints of national migration policy players before and during the start of European co-operation. To understand the choices and the fate of the various groups that mobilized transnationally and that of EU institutional actors, I interviewed the national civil servants in charge of immigration issues in international forums and also conducted research in Brussels among NGOs and EU institutional actors.

Before analysing the scope of EU immigration policy, the contours of national policy-making in this area should be drawn. Migration as a policy issue was never confined to a single ministry since it had implications for labour, economics, foreign affairs, social affairs and internal affairs (etc.). In federal systems, the division of labour is even more complex. There is no tradition in Europe of 'immigration ministries' as there is for agriculture or defence. Immigration is a transversal issue where cross-sectoral conflicts often arise. Cross-national convergence was significant in the 1990s, yet there remain different models of incorporation, different priorities in migration control based on previous colonial and labour market histories or geopolitical position. Therefore, for immigration scholars, the question regarding the policy sectors and the national models and priorities that prevail in the European sphere is a fascinating one. Not all sectoral and national interests were weighed in the policy process and not all actors were deemed legitimate to set the agenda.

The shift of competence to the EU greatly narrowed the scope of migration-related policies. With regard to migration control, the European Economic Community (EEC) was limited by the treaty to the free movement of EC workers, later EU citizens, although the ECJ has extended some aspects of free movement to the families of Community nationals and to citizens of countries that have signed association treaties with the EC such as Turkey. One of the possible routes that an EU policy could still take but has not, in spite of a 1997 Commission proposal,[6] is to extend free movement to resident third-country nationals.

Instead, migration management in the EU context is focused on preventing unwanted migration, through visa policy and carrier sanctions, the establishment of buffer zones on the east of Europe, the constitution of a database of inadmissible aliens (the Schengen Information System) and of asylum-seekers' fingerprints (EURODAC). European asylum policies aim at preventing migration with accelerated procedures for examining asylum requests, a common definition of a refugee, the notion of 'safe third country' and the 1990 Dublin Convention which organized a system to determine which contracting party is responsible for examining an asylum request.

Regarding immigrant policy at the EU level, it has taken two forms. First, the Commission funds projects for the integration of workers and anti-racism, or gives grants to cities and regions that target initiatives at ethnic minorities. Second, in the Amsterdam Treaty, an article on anti-discrimination has been added and two directives have since been approved: one covers all forms of discrimination in employment, and the other counter-discriminations on the grounds of race and ethnic origin in many spheres.[7] To understand why these particular outcomes and not others such as the extension of free movement or EU citizenship to third-country nationals can be observed, I now turn to the history of EU mobilization around migration, asylum and anti-discrimination.

II. IMMIGRATION AND ASYLUM: BUREAUCRATIC RIVALRY AND SECURITY FRAMES

'When policemen replace diplomats': the emergence of intergovernmental co-operation on migration control

'Quand les policiers succèdent aux diplomates': the title of this French Senate report (Turk 1998) sums up in a nutshell the increasing involvement of law and order personnel at the European level since the early 1980s and, among them, civil servants in charge of migration management.

Migration control experts took advantage of new organizational models: the transgovernmental working groups on security-related issues such as the 1970s Trevi group. These groupings with varied membership were flexible, informal and secretive. This built trust among officials who set the agenda of transgovernmental co-operation by emphasizing the kind of technical solutions that required their expertise. They became inevitable interlocutors at the first negotiation stage, that of the Schengen Implementation Agreement (SIA). While the 1985 Schengen agreement only contained three articles on immigration, the issue came to dominate the discussion of the four Schengen groups in charge of the SIA. During the 1985–90 period when the SIA was drafted, inter-ministerial quarrels in the founding Schengen countries flourished. Michel Portal at the French Ministry of Interior recalls that 'the inter-ministerial conflicts were and still are considerable, terrible, especially when the political leaders totally lost interest'.[8] Vendelin Hreblay, a negotiator from the French police, admits that Foreign Affairs ministries – and in Germany the Chancellery – were progressively ousted by Justice and Interior ministries (1998: 28).[9]

Given that an international agreement was being negotiated and that Foreign Affairs ministries deliver visas through consulates abroad (visa policy being a cornerstone of European co-operation on remote border control), there was no *a priori* reason to expect a monopoly of Interior and Justice personnel. Notwithstanding, their domination accounts for the security-oriented content of the SIA and subsequent decisions. It also explains the emphasis on technical issues, border control and surveillance technologies such as the Schengen Information System.

Migration control bureaucrats went transnational at that particular moment because they had seen their action increasingly constrained in the early 1980s (Guiraudon 2000a). First, landmark court decisions in the main European receiving countries that date from the late 1970s had circumscribed administrative discretion. They established in particular the right to normal family life and to secure residence for long-term residents. In effect, governments could no longer prevent family reunification, diminish the 'stock' of legal residents except by financial incentives as the new Kohl government did in 1983, and certain categories of foreigners could no longer be expelled. This period also saw the first major clashes between agencies in charge of the integration of settled foreigners and those in charge of migration control. The incentive to seek new policy venues sheltered from national legal constraints and conflicting policy goals thus dates from the beginning of the 1980s (see Guiraudon 2000c on this case of 'venue shopping'). This explains the timing of transgovernmental co-operation and its character: an emphasis on non-binding decisions and secretive arrangements. Rather than creating an 'international regime', i.e. a constraining set of rules with monitoring mechanisms (Ruggie 1982), national civil servants sought to avoid domestic legal constraints and scrutiny.

In 1990, only some elements of March and Olsen's 'garbage can' were to be found in the migration policy domain at the European level. 'Solutions' had been devised before 'problems' had been defined. The solution was police co-operation and reinforced controls. The problem that these means were meant to address soon became apparent after the end of the Cold War in the form of an influx of asylum-seekers in Germany and many emotional debates over immigration in other core member states, largely covered in the media which prophesized 'tides' of 'bogus refugees'. International migration was also added to the list of transnational phenomena considered by a plethora of experts as the 'new threats' which replaced Cold War ideology: Islamic fundamentalism, global mafias and terrorism (Huysmans 2000).

While the 1980s had seen the emergence of a particular group of policy actors seeking to further their *interests* in transgovermental forums on migration and asylum, *ideas* and *institutions* were still in their infancy. The ideas that framed intergovernmental co-operation hinged on linking migration and crime and considering that they constituted the dark side of 'globalization' requiring a supranational response. The lack of an alternative policy frame can be attributed not only to the end of the Cold War security paradigm but also to economic slump and high unemployment, which demobilized business interests, which traditionally lobby for openness. These conjectural elements should not be neglected in understanding why migration became a 'security' (as opposed to a labour market) issue in the 1990s.

The institutional framework set up at the EU level with the creation of a Third Pillar on Justice and Home Affairs (JHA) confirmed that European co-operation allowed Justice and Interior personnel to regain a certain margin of manoeuvre and can be described as flexible multilateralism. One full group (GD1) of the K4 committee of the Third Pillar was dedicated to asylum, visa and migration yet the framework required unanimous decisions by the Council and remained outside the community legal order, thereby excluding the ECJ and the European Parliament. The Commission did not have a right of initiative and thus could not play its agenda-setting 'entrepreneurial' role.

Although a small task force was set up within the General Secretariat of the Commission to liaise with the Council on JHA migration discussions, they did not come from the units that had always defended the rights of third-country nationals (the Employment and Social Affairs and the Internal Market Directorate-Generals (DGs)), which task force personnel considered 'old-fashioned' and 'maximalist'. According to Wenceslas de Lobkowicz of the task force, they wanted to leave the field to the discretion of member states and avoid debates over sovereignty (1994). Jean-Louis de Brouwer, now head of the Commission unit 'External Borders, Immigration and Asylum', also points out that 'one need[ed] to talk to the big players, the ministers of Interior of the member states who usually are political heavyweights in their respective governments'.[10]

From Maastricht to Amsterdam, the JHA Council only agreed on one joint position on the common definition of a refugee and on five legally binding joint actions, for instance, on school travel for third-country national children and airport transit procedures. The lack of formal agreements has been attributed to the complicated decision-making structure of the Third Pillar. Yet, it is the same large member states (France, Germany) most concerned with immigration that stalled the process by insisting on labyrinthine procedures and unanimous voting, thus undermining Ugur's intergovernmentalist account of the upgrading of common interests in the face of massive asylum requests (1995). The only operative agreements, the 1990 Dublin and Schengen agreements, were in fact adopted outside the EU framework and their implementation delayed respectively until 1997 and 1995.

Moreover, a number of parallel forums on migration and asylum were set up during this period, making the 'Third Pillar' one of many other venues: among them and aside from the Schengen executive committee, Intergovernmental Consultations on Asylum, Refugees and Migration Policies, the Vienna Club (Germany, Austria, Switzerland, France and Italy), the Vienna Group and Budapest process, the Central European initiative, the Ad Hoc Committee of experts for identity documents and the movement of persons, the Council of Europe Committee of Experts on the Legal Aspects of Territorial Asylum, Refugees, and Stateless People, the UN Commission on Crime Prevention, and the Organization for Security and Co-operation in Europe (OSCE). The institutions of the EC were not considered as the legitimate set of institutions to develop common policies, thus contradicting the neo-functionalist account of a spillover of the creation of the EC single market.[11]

The diplomats strike back? Amsterdam and beyond

The decisions to shift co-operation on migration into the Community framework and incorporate Schengen via protocol during the last stage of the Amsterdam negotiations came as a surprise. The Commission negotiating team headed by Michel Petite won a battle if not the war in Amsterdam. Interior officials were taken aback since they themselves were unclear about the content of the Schengen *acquis*, 3,000 pages of various legal standing. They did not want the *acquis* published and given a legal character. The Treaty actually came into force in May 1999 before member states had agreed on its content and its incorporation.

To understand the Amsterdam outcome, one must remember that ministries of Foreign Affairs negotiate treaty revisions in the EU. They were not concerned with the consequences of the Schengen protocol, a task that their colleagues sitting in Interior and Justice ministries would have to undertake.[12] Having seen their negotiating role diminished during the Schengen process, Foreign Affairs were keen to rein in transgovernmental processes dominated by law and order civil servants which had multiplied and run amok. By neglecting the Third Pillar and preferring the Schengen group, the bureaucrats in the Schengen founding member states had unwittingly contributed to that outcome. They could not count on the support of later Schengen members such as Italy or Greece who had not been treated as equal partners. Among the three founding Schengen members studied, only the Dutch favoured a 'communitarization' of asylum and immigration. Given that the interests of the larger member states (France and Germany) were better preserved in a flexible multilateral setting such as Schengen, the Dutch preference for the inclusion of Community actors and a more constraining framework should not be surprising. Even less so given that the French in particular had bullied the Dutch in the Schengen context over drugs policy.

Notwithstanding, the German and French delegations successfully lobbied for provisions that limited the role of EC institutions in the new Title IV of the Amsterdam Treaty on the progressive establishment of an 'area of freedom, security and justice'. The Germans obtained unanimous voting in the Council of Ministers and, under French pressure, the role of the ECJ was circumscribed. The application of preliminary rulings to the ECJ in areas covered by Title IV is restricted since only courts of last instance will be able to use Article 177. Furthermore, the Court of Justice cannot rule on national measures adopted in relation to the crossing of borders to safeguard internal security, and its rulings 'shall not apply to judgments of courts or tribunals of the Member States which have become *res judicata*'. The defended position reflects the original motivation of intergovernmental co-operation, which was to avoid judicial scrutiny that had undermined migration control policy at the domestic level.[13]

It remains puzzling that the state most concerned with the issue (Germany) did not wish to shift competence to the Community or 'lock in' commitments, and lobbied for unanimity, given that their priority was refugee 'burden-sharing'.[14] We know that, during negotiations, like-minded officials and national governments do not share the same 'preferences' (Lord and Winn 2000) and here it seems that the German Interior officials' reluctance to depart from a Schengen model of secretive inter-bureaucratic co-operation led to a sub-optimal outcome for Germany, the main recipient of asylum-seekers and displaced persons. Yet this only points to the lack of domestic co-ordination on the issue in the German case. This is why the Interior–Foreign Affairs–Chancellery rivalry that dated from the Schengen negotiations still mattered at Amsterdam. It led to what Andrew Moravcsik has termed an 'aggregation failure' whereby the emergence of a coherent national position out of disparate demands is blocked, a situation that, in his view, allows supranational entrepreneurs to play the role of 'two-level network manager' (1999: 283): here the rejoicing Michel Petite who could claim victory for the policy shift from the Third to the First Pillar, although with limitations on the role of EC institutions.

Amsterdam has also not solved the question of 'opt-outs'. Amsterdam consecrates the idea of a *Europe à la carte*. The UK, Northern Ireland and, consequently, the Republic of Ireland have opted out of the new area of freedom, security and justice. Denmark, albeit a member of Schengen, is not bound by the new title and co-operates only on visa policy – a legal nightmare since it requires the signing of a separate Danish–EU treaty every time a decision is taken.

Since Amsterdam, developments suggest that, given the rules of the game, the logic of the policy process has not drastically changed. The Commission 2000 Communication on a community immigration policy resubmitted texts that had been discussed under the Third Pillar framework.[15] It faces competition from member states that have a right of co-initiative. Typically, the country that holds the Presidency of the Union uses this platform to push its pet projects to satisfy its domestic electoral interests. Law enforcement measures such as those proposed by the French Presidency in the fall of 2000 have been more successful than those emphasizing migrants' rights. The French proposals on carrier sanctions, expulsion of third-country nationals or the fight against smuggling were adopted in May 2001 under the Swedish Presidency, while the latter had to accept a much watered down version of its own text on temporary protection status to ensure passage.

What has been confirmed is the importance of migration in the foreign relations of the EU. For instance, all concerned parties agree that the JHA *acquis* has gone up the agenda in the accession negotiations in which Justice and Interior ministers take a large part (Lavenex 2001). Ten per cent of PHARE funding (130.7 million Euros in 2000) goes to JHA issues, half of which concern border issues (House of Lords Select Committee on European Union 2000, part 3, p. 4). 'Preventing migration at the source' has become an EU mantra.[16] It has resulted in an number of initiatives including the Dutch-inspired cross-pillar High-Level Working Group (HLWG) set up in December 1998. The latter drew up action plans for the six main countries of origin of unwanted migrants in Europe to assess, *inter alia,* the possibility of readmission agreements, 'safe returns' and 'transit zones'. The HLWG's 1999 report stressed the 'general recognition that a cross-pillar and comprehensive approach [was] needed' and stated that 'the expertise of the Member States needs to be made available in various policy fields'.[17] The group's 'trans-pillar' approach seemed to herald a new era when the prevailing 'prevention-by-policing' policies would be accompanied by policies that addressed the root causes of migration. Yet, the country reports simply restated the six 'action points' set out by the JHA K4 Committee in March 1998 regarding immigration from Iraq in which Turkey was expected to prevent Iraqis from arriving in the EU.

Thus, although diplomats at Amsterdam took their revenge on Interior and Justice personnel, the latter still dominate and are becoming more involved in diplomatic forums. For instance, in February 2000, during the negotiations of the revision of the fourth Lomé Convention between the EU 15 and seventy-one African, Caribbean and Pacific countries, Interior ministers insisted that a clause of readmission of illegal migrants be included in the final text at the risk of blocking the agreement.

In sum, transgovernmental co-operation allowed law and order officials to gain autonomy and devise policies without accommodating judges or conflicting sectoral interests. They successfully defined a frame that equated migration with transnational security threats and favoured intergovernmental secretive forums. Over time, they were perhaps too successful and, after Amsterdam, they have to co-operate with EU institutions and publish their decisions. They do remain key players.

III. PRO-MIGRANT FORCES GO TRANSNATIONAL TOO: NGO RIVALRY AND THE SOCIAL EXCLUSION PARADIGM

In 1985, when the first Schengen agreement was signed, the Commission issued new guidelines on migration (CEC 1985) and argued that European integration entailed a better access to rights for foreign residents. In July, it adopted a Decision setting up a procedure for prior consultation of new policy in this area. Five member states contested the move and the ECJ annulled the Decision in 1987.[18] The Commission's competence was confined to the free movement of EU citizens. Yet, this did not deter the Commission unit that had been pushing for this change and pro-migrant transnational organizations such as the Churches' Commission for Migrants from carving out a space for the defence of the rights of ethnic minorities in Europe.

The unit (D.4) within the Commission Directorate for Employment and Social Affairs now called 'Free Movement of Workers, Migrant Integration and

Anti-racism' was created in 1958 to handle issues related to free movement of labour and later handled many budget lines related to the integration of migrants and refugees and, since 1986, anti-racism.[19] Annette Bosscher, the head of the unit until the late 1990s, and Giuseppe Callovi, who later moved to other directorates, firmly believed that European integration should go hand in hand with the integration of non-Europeans.

Their unit has faced many challenges, given the thin treaty basis for its actions. Its 'institutional activists' (Ruzza 1999) had to find other bases for intervention. As Adrian Favell recalls:

> as a 'political' as opposed to 'economic' agenda began to differentiate itself in the Commission's corridors, certain DGs less powerfully placed in the central drive towards EMU, seized on alternative European 'public interest' agendas, following the path pioneered by the highly active and progressive-minded DG XI (Environment).
>
> (Favell 2000: 167)

Indeed the attitude of civil servants in the Employment and Social Affairs DG resembled the 'purposeful opportunism' (Cram 1997) found in other directorates whereby larger policy agendas are instrumentalized to increase their scope for action.

A few individuals committed to a progressive agenda in fairly marginal parts of the Commission could become 'policy entrepreneurs' (Geddes 2000a, 2000b) precisely because their activities were sheltered from public scrutiny. Daniel Cohn-Bendit, a Member of the European Parliament (MEP) who once headed the Frankfurt Bureau for Multicultural Affairs, has thus analysed the situation: 'Europe is full of promises for the future because the Commission and the Parliament are not exposed to immediate electoral pressures.'[20] Similarly, the successful initiatives in the area of immigrant policy concerned a few Commission insiders and small NGO structures that may have publicly decried the 'democratic deficit' yet practised top-down élite politics.

The first opportunity before Maastricht was to build upon the notion of 'European citizenship' that was meant to herald a 'people's Europe' and the end of the 'democratic deficit'. To help mobilization on this agenda, the Commission sought to increase its legitimacy as a spokesperson for 'civil society' by engineering an official channel of interest representation. In 1991, the European Commission acting upon an initiative of the European Parliament founded the Migrants' Forum that spoke for 130 migrant associations that held an annual general assembly. Yet, the Migrants' Forum failed to find common ground (Kastoryano 1994; Geddes 1998).[21] Turks and Moroccans vied for control of the organization, with the Moroccans eventually winning out and giving the organization a Francophone cast that set it apart from the largely Anglophone NGO world of Brussels. The Forum's activists also had different conceptions of citizenship and cultures of contention depending on the nation states in which they had settled.

In any case, using the concept of citizenship to further the rights of third-country nationals failed in 1992. The gap between EU and non-EU citizens widened when the Treaty on European Union granted special rights to EU citizens residing in other member states such as local voting rights. Both the Commission and the Brussels-based NGO Migration Policy Group (MPG) refocused their agenda.[22] They jumped on the bandwagon of the EU war on 'social exclusion' (Article 137 of the Treaty of Amsterdam). Commission documents insist that migrants and their descendants are prime victims of social exclusion and that NGOs know best how to fight it.[23] Social exclusion encompasses a wide range of programmes and the MPG promptly responded to this signal by linking migrant integration in the 1996 Intergovernmental Conference (IGC) to this agenda rather than to the debates on European citizenship, which had focused the energies of the Migrants' Forum (Geddes 2000b). Indeed, the 'social exclusion' frame benefited pre-existing transnational networks that could draw upon their credentials and expertise in the area of anti-discrimination.[24] In fact, the Starting Line Group (SLG) founded in 1992 by academic and NGO legal experts and co-ordinated by the MPG to draft an anti-discrimination article for the pre-Amsterdam IGC included members from national anti-discrimination boards: the British Commission for Racial Equality and the Dutch National Bureau against Racism.

Citizenship or social exclusion, EU citizenship for third-country nationals or anti-discrimination policies? In the NGO battle for legitimacy, the SLG supported by the MPG clearly had the organizational structure, and the local and legal knowledge to successfully lobby for its anti-discrimination agenda while the Migrants' Forum with its cumbersome structure remained focused on citizenship. Moreover, the SLG matched EU technocratic standards. The anti-discrimination clause project was reminiscent of Article 119 and the 1976 Equal Treatment Directive on gender equality in a very Euro-correct way. Leading up to the 1996 IGC, initiatives that showed a gentler, kinder Europe were welcome. The timing was ripe for the SLG initiative. With Commission officials, they were able to informally set the agenda at the 1996 IGC, thereby confirming accounts of Amsterdam negotiations that build upon Kingdon's model, such as Mark Pollack's (1999), and those that focus on the importance of 'policy framing', such as Mazey and Richardson's (1997).

Policy framing was key because, if the problem is defined as 'social exclusion', the range of solutions is wide. As Andrew Geddes has pointed out:

> it can be advantageous that the terms inclusion and cohesion are vague and their meanings unclear because it implies that the quest for inclusion is likely to be able to sustain itself in the long term and potentially be institutionalized at the European level.
>
> (Geddes 2000a: 224)

Like 'sustainable development', 'social inclusion' is an objective that one can hardly oppose. 'Anti-discrimination' for its part presented the advantage of not being solely targeted at migrants. Article 13 protects people with disability, the elderly and other groups – a plus given that measures specifically protecting migrants are a hard sell. Most member states that did not want to shift competence on immigrant policy to the EU level nevertheless did because they were led to believe that in fact the issue was social exclusion of a number of groups.

The ambiguity of the 'anti-discrimination' frame also partly explains the rapid adoption of the so-called 'race directive' in June 2000 (directive 2000/43/EC) seven months after the Commission's proposal – 'a record for the adoption of a piece of Community law requiring substantial legislative changes at national level' (Tyson 2001: 112). The directive also required a unanimous decision in the Council and had an inter-sectoral character that implied inter-ministerial co-ordination making it a 'least likely case'. The single factor most often mentioned by the Council Social Affairs working group interviewed in Brussels is Jorg Haïder.[25] France was most vocal at condemning the Austrian government for integrating the Freedom Party in February 2000. Ironically, their enthusiasm towards a directive that resembled Dutch or British tools for integrating ethnic minorities stemmed from an event, the success of a far-right leader who had praised the Waffen SS, that easily fitted the French conception of anti-racist measures as a means of fighting ideas inspired by Nazi Germany. In a classic 'Baptist-bootlegger coalition' situation, the German delegation was also extremely co-operative lest it be associated with the Austrians. The initial policy linkage between the anti-discrimination package and the Austrian far right ensured the passage of a directive.

Just as law and order officials, NGOs expanded the realm of competence of the EU to include immigrant-related issues. Their agenda had more chances of succeeding through lobbying techniques sheltered from public scrutiny than at the national level where public opinion, media coverage and the mobilization of anti-immigrant parties made the advancement of migrant rights unlikely. Even in the Council, negotiations focused on reaching compromises on technical issues and legal wording rather than on the normative underpinnings of immigrant policy and can be contrasted to the emotional partisan debates observed in many European countries. This closed venue of debate allowed policy change in favour of migrants that is arduous in open national venues.

IV. INDIRECT POLICY EFFECTS: MIGRATION AND FREEDOM OF SERVICES

Beside conscious efforts to mobilize around migration at the European level, one must take into account decisions by EU institutions and transnational non-state actors that indirectly bear on migration flows to complete the complex and contradictory set of EU rules that affect migration within and into the EU.

The ECJ has traditionally been concerned with extending its jurisdiction. The Court has had to strike a balance between expanding EC competence and remaining within the legitimate bounds of its sphere of duty (economic rights rather than people's rights and EC citizens rather than non-EC citizens). Therefore, its jurisprudence on third-country nationals has not been based on human rights but on freedom of services or association treaty provisions. In the Rush Portuguesa decision of 27 March 1990 (C-113/89, ECR I-1417), the ECJ reiterated that the provisions for the suppression of restrictions to the freedom to deliver services entailed that a company could move with its own staff. If the company employs third-country nationals, member states cannot refuse them entry to protect their labour market on the grounds that immigration from non-EU states is a matter of national sovereignty.

The Court decision was in line with the drive towards the single market, which resulted in the 1993 liberalization of service provision. It stirred a controversy in Germany given the important number of posted workers in the construction industry denounced by trade unions as a form of 'social dumping'. Indeed, no comprehensive supranational regulation has been passed on the social and wage conditions applicable to posted workers. Instead, a 1996 directive has allowed member states to apply a minimum level of national regulations to these posted workers and the Commission has proposed two directives to implement this derived right of third-country nationals (*OJ* 1999 C 67/9).

Meanwhile, at the Trade Commission directorate, developments suggest that the mobility of personnel in the services sector will be extended at the global level and thus affect flows into the EU. Co-optation strategies are at work between the Trade Commission staff and business interests. One particular non-governmental forum supported by the Trade Commission is the European Services Forum (ESF), an official NGO in the Seattle EU delegation whose focus is to support the Commission's viewpoint during the General Agreement on Trade in Services (GATS) negotiations. At a conference of the ESF under the patronage of the Commission, Trade Commissioner Pascal Lamy expressed this sentiment: 'I particularly welcome the participation of ... NGOs. The key to the success of the ESF is that it is a *forum*, open to all stakeholders, including civil society.'[26]

Pascal Lamy has experience in setting up 'partnerships' that short-circuit member states since this was a key strategy of Jacques Delors when Lamy was his *chef de cabinet* (Ross 1995). Lamy's reference to civil society is misleading. In fact, the ESF, based at UNICE, the European employers' federation, includes thirty-six European trade federations and fifty EU-based international companies in sectors such as banking, insurance, telecommunications, postal services, aviation, shipping, tourism, retail, legal services, accountancy, management consulting, architecture, engineering, IT services, publishing, audiovisual, energy and environmental services.

Part of their agenda is lobbying against 'barriers to the movement of people' and in particular the 'complex, cumbersome, and time-consuming procedures to obtain work permits and visas' (ESF 2000) and they favour a GATS visa or passport.[27] The adversaries are clearly identified: the ESF managing director describes them as 'the understandably defensive interests of WTO Member Countries' immigration and labor market developments officials' (Kerneis 2000).

At an MPG meeting on this issue organized in Brussels in March 2001,[28] immigration officials' jaws dropped in silent disbelief when they heard multinational corporations proposing 'their' passport. The meeting also showed that strange bedfellows emerge at the European level. European pro-migrant NGOs are not used, as are their American counterparts, to engaging in client politics with business interests (on the US case, see Freeman 2001). Yet there seems to be a fast learning curve, which is fostered by the MPG's 'transatlantic dialogue' with US think-tanks. Strategic alliances between NGOs and business interests are signs that some of the actors in our story are trying to co-ordinate their scripts to seize upon the opportunity of the new economic climate and the older free movement and neo-liberal agenda of European integration.

CONCLUSION

The coexistence of conflicting discourses that do not speak to one another, competition among like-minded actors, diverse modes of decision-making (depending on their level of supranationalization), in a period of numerous and rapid EU constitutional changes explains the adhocratic and contradictory character of law-making in EU immigration-related policies.

Both in the case of migration and asylum and that of anti-discrimination policies at the EU level, we observe parallel dynamics. First, a group of actors vie to become the legitimate policy interlocutors against other similar groups: interior civil servants vs. their foreign affairs counterpart, MPG and the SLG vs. the Migrants' Forum. Each group has a pre-formatted set of policy solutions based on their expertise: policing for the former, anti-discrimination for the latter. They succeeded by momentously seizing upon an emergent broader policy frame: immigration officials built upon the post-1989 new security agenda while NGOs joined calls for the fight against 'social exclusion' during the 1996 IGC. They were helped by their adversaries' weaknesses or errors, respectively the lack of supervision of other key ministries whose attention was fixed on the fall of the Berlin Wall when Schengen was being negotiated, and the structural and chronic problems of the Migrants' Forum. It is telling that *initially* there was little supervision of these experiments that grew on the margins of the core market-driven project of European integration.

Our goal has been to account for the particular timing, form and content of the immigration policy domain. Our focus on the actors who prevailed and the interests that they represented explains the content and form of the European immigration policy domain. Immigration officials sought to avoid national judicial constraints and conflicting bureaucratic views that were experienced in the early 1980s. They consequently favoured a secretive intergovernmentalism where they could exclude other ministries and escape judicial monitoring. Similarly, they have privileged informal co-operation and 'soft law'. Their own professional identity explains the bias towards control and policing. Pro-migrant groups knew that, as in a national context, the institutions most receptive to defending migrant interests are restricted venues of debate sheltered from electoral fallout such as social administrations and courts. They found European 'functional equivalents' in the Commission and the ECJ and have focused on legal solutions such as the inclusion of Article 13 in the Treaty. At the European level, small lobby-like structures are the most efficacious which explains the success of the Dutch–British activists and therefore the emphasis on anti-discrimination. Success only came once they could co-ordinate with Commission officials, who had first sought to build upon free movement to expand their competence and later had tried to foster a more representative assembly.

The timing of the constitution of the immigration policy domain itself depends on the windows of opportunity constituted by the emergence of new frames, changes in the strategic or economic context, or constitutional openings such as IGCs or Schengen negotiation working groups. In this respect, this is not a straight 'path-dependent' account. Today's winners may yet face challenges if the context changes or at the next constitutional moment. Notwithstanding, they have accumulated a legitimacy capital and the policy domain has been institutionalized in a way that cannot be easily undone. For instance, we have seen that the diplomats' 'revenge' at Amsterdam has not altered the predominance of Interior and Justice interests in the management of EU migration policy.

It cannot be denied that following 9/11 and the concert of European leaders' calls for a European border police prior to the Seville summit, a security/restrictive take may prevail. For politicians, this is a convenient way of shifting blame and responsibility. Yet, few concrete decisions were taken at Seville and harmonization is slow and EU measures have not resulted in a decrease in illegal immigration. In the end, this strategy may be as dangerous as 'activating xenophobia' at the national level. Populist parties, which are generally both anti-immigrant and anti-EU, will be further strengthened by the failure of European leaders to support more proactive immigration and integration policies.

Address for correspondence: Virginie Guiraudon, Chargée de recherches au CNRS, CRAPS, Faculté de droit, 1 place Déliot, BP 629, F-59024 Lille cedex, France. Tel: 33 3 20907451. Fax: 33 3 20907700. email: vguiraudon@mailsc.univ-lille2.fr

NOTES

1 The author thanks Martin Schain and participants of the 2001 EUSA meeting who commented on an earlier version of this paper, Andrew Moravcsik for his incisive reading, as well as the two anonymous referees for their insightful suggestions.

2 Before 2004, the Council should unanimously adopt measures on asylum, refugees and displaced persons, on the absence of any controls on persons crossing internal borders and on external border control (including rules on visas for stays of less than three months), and on the free travel of third-country nationals within the

EU for short-term stays. After 2004, measures should be adopted with respect to refugee 'burden-sharing', and the harmonization of the conditions of entry and residence, standards for the issue of long-term visas and residence permits, or the right of residence for third-country nationals wishing to stay in EU states other than their country of residence.

3 For a fuller treatment of the application of political sociology to EU studies, see Guiraudon (2000b).

4 'The central idea of the garbage can models is the substitution of a temporal order for a consequential order' (March and Olsen 1986: 17) and thus our research paid particular attention to temporal ordering.

5 Given the recent debate in the *American Political Science Review* on the 'garbage can' (see Bendor *et al.* 2001 and the reply by Olsen 2001), I clarify that my reference to Cohen *et al.*'s famed 1972 article respects the spirit of their work: the metaphor was not meant as 'the' theory but rather as 'a' model to 'comprehend some features of decision-making ... to extend, rather than replace, understandings gained from other perspectives' (March and Olsen 1986: 12).

6 Proposal for a Council Act establishing the convention on rules for the admission of third-country nationals to the member states. COM/97/0387 final – CNS 97/0227 [Doc 597PC0387].

7 Respectively, Council Directive 2000/43/EC of 29 June 2000 [*Official Journal* L 180, 19/07/2000, pp. 22–6] and Council Directive 2000/78/EC of 27 November 2000 [*O. J.* L 303, 02/12/2000, pp. 16–22].

8 Interview with Michel Portal, chef de bureau, Sous-Direction de la Circulation Transfrontière et des Visas, Ministry of Interior, Paris, December 1994. Also interviews with M. Malwald, German Federal Ministry of Interior, Bonn, April 1995, with Jürgen Haberlandt, German Federal Ministry of Interior, Berlin, June 1995, and with Nicolas Franzen, Immigration and Naturalization Department, Ministry of Justice, The Hague, February 1995. The lack of political leadership was heightened by glasnost and Germany's unwillingness to build a wall to its east.

9 Transport ministries had also signed the original 1985 agreement and later disappeared.

10 Interview, General Secretariat of the European Commission, Brussels, March 1999.

11 See Guiraudon (2000c) for a fuller analysis of alternative explanations.

12 Interview with Michel Petite, chief negotiator for the 1996 IGC, European Commission, Cambridge, MA, April 1999.

13 Stetter (2000) refers to these decisions as 'principals' seeking to prevent 'agency loss' when delegating authority. I would add that, once delegation had occurred against their views, migration bureaucrats did indeed seek to limit agency loss but that the rules and procedures adopted to do so seem to have been counterproductive given what he views as the motivation for shifting competence, which, again, was not the *ex ante* preferred option for French and German officials.

14 For a thorough test of alternative theories of EU burden-sharing in this area, see Thielemann (2002).

15 COM(2000) 757 final, 22/11/2000.

16 COM(2000) 757 final, 22/11/2000, section 2.1 'partnership with countries of origin'.

17 Press release, 'Final Report of the High-Level Working Group on Asylum and Migration', 18/9/1999.

18 See 9 July 1987 decision in joint cases 281, 283–5, 287/85, Rec. 1987, 3023.

19 The Unit administers about 10 million ECUs for refugee integration, 6 million for migrants, and 7 million for anti-racism every year. A 1995 report assessing 200 of the 560 projects on migrant integration that DG V funded between 1991 and 1993 demonstrates that only 32 (16 per cent) were migrant-led (CEC 1995: 10). NGOs, churches, trade unions, etc., made up the rest of the beneficiaries. After

1995, Brussels-based NGOs that had submitted 2.6% of the proposals received 6.8% of the total funding – a clear success (CEC 1998).

20 Interview, Brussels, May 1995.

21 After several mismanagement crises, the Forum has been suspended.

22 The MPG staff acknowledged that supranational competencies that would affect diverse national concepts of citizenship or change nationality law were anathema to member states (Hix and Niessen 1996).

23 See *Guidelines on Preparatory Measures to Combat Social Exclusion* (CEC 1998).

24 French or German national activists were interested in citizenship issues yet were rarely present among the personnel of pro-migrant Brussels NGOs.

25 Interviews in Brussels with Claire Aubin, Social Affairs attaché, French permanent delegation to the EU, 5 December 2001, Porfirio Silva, Social Affairs attaché (in charge of presiding Social Affairs and Employment Council working group), Portuguese permanent delegation to the EU, 6 December 2001, John Kittmer, Social Affairs attaché, British permanent delegation to the EU, 6 December 2001.

26 Speech given at the conference 'The GATS 2000 Negotiations: new opportunities of trade liberalization for all services sectors', Hotel Sheraton Brussels Airport, Brussels (Zaventem), 27 November 2000.

27 The idea of a 'GATS visa' emerged in 1993 at the end of the Uruguay Round and is understood as a passport for different categories of natural persons permitted entry under the schedule of commitments at the horizontal and sectoral levels like Information and Communication Technologies (ICTs), business visitors, contract personnel.

28 Transatlantic Workshop on High Skilled Migration (Brussels, 5–6 March 2001).

REFERENCES

Baumgartner, Frank and Jones, Bryan (1993) *Agendas and Instability in American Politics*, Chicago: Chicago University Press.

Bendor, Jonathan, Moe, Terry and Shotts, Kenneth (2001) 'Recycling the garbage can: an assessment of the research program', *American Political Science Review* 95(1): 169–90.

Bigo, Didier (1996) *Polices en réseaux. L'expérience européenne*, Paris: Presses de la Fondation Nationale de Sciences Politiques.

Bourdieu, Pierre (1981) 'La représentation politique: éléments pour une théorie du champ politique', *Actes de la recherche en sciences sociales* 36/37: 3–24.

CEC (Commission of the European Communities) (1985) *Orientations pour une politique communautaire des migrations*, COM(85) 48 def. Brussels: CEC.

CEC (Commission of the European Communities) (1995) *Assistance Given to Migrant Associations*, Brussels: DG V.

CEC (Commission of the European Communities) (1998) *European Year Against Racism Directory of Projects*, Brussels: DG V.

Cohen, Michael, March, James and Olsen, Johan (1972) 'A garbage can model of organizational choice', *Administrative Science Quarterly* 17 (March): 1–25.

Cram, Laura (1997) *Policy-Making in the European Union: Conceptual Lenses and the Integration Process*, London and New York: Routledge.

European Services Forum (ESF) (2000) *Second Position Paper on the Temporary Movement of Key Business Personnel*, Brussels: ESF, 24 October. Available at www.esf.be

Favell, Adrian (2000) 'L'Européanisation ou l'émergence d'un nouveau "champ politique": le cas de la politique d'immigration', in Virginie Guiraudon (ed.), *Sociologie de l'Europe: élites, mobilisations et configurations institutionnelles*, special issue of *Cultures et conflits* 38(9): 153–85. Available at www.conflits.org

Freeman, Gary (2001) 'Client politics or populism? The politics of immigration reform in the United States', in Virginie Guiraudon and Christian Joppke (eds), *Controlling a New Migration World*, London: Routledge, pp. 65–95.

Geddes, Andrew (1998) 'The representation of "migrants' interests" in the European Union', *Journal of Ethnic and Migration Studies* 24(4): 695–713.

Geddes, Andrew (2000a) 'Thin Europeanisation: the social rights of migrants in an integrating Europe', in Michael Bommes and Andrew Geddes (eds), *Immigration and Welfare. Challenging the Borders of the Welfare State*, London: Routledge, pp. 209–26.

Geddes, Andrew (2000b) 'Lobbying for migrant inclusion in the European Union: new opportunities for transnational advocacy?', *Journal of European Public Policy* 7(4): 632–49.

Guiraudon, Virginie (2000a) *Les politiques d'immigration en Europe. Allemagne, France, Pays-Bas*, Paris: L'Harmattan.

Guiraudon, Virginie (2000b) 'L'espace sociopolitique européen, un champ encore en friche?', in Virginie Guiraudon (ed.), *Sociologie de l'Europe: élites, mobilisations et configurations institutionnelles*, special issue of *Cultures et conflits* 38(9): 7–37. Available at www.conflits.org

Guiraudon, Virginie (2000c) 'European integration and migration policy: vertical policy-making as venue shopping', *Journal of Common Market Studies* 38(2): 249–69.

Hix, Simon and Niessen, Jan (1996) *Reconsidering European Migration Policies*, Brussels: Churches' Commission for Migrants in Europe.

House of Lords Select Committee on European Union (2000) *Seventeenth Report on Enlargement and EU External Frontier Controls*, London: House of Lords, published 24 October.

Hreblay, Vendelin (1998) *Les accords de Schengen. Origine, fonctionnement, avenir*, Brussels: Bruylant.

Huysmans, Jef (2000) 'The European Union and the securitization of migration', *Journal of Common Market Studies* 38(5): 751–77.

Kastoryano, Riva (1994) 'Mobilisations des migrants en Europe: du national au transnational', *Revue européenne des migrations internationales* 10(1): 169–81.

Kerneis, Pascal (2000) 'Letter to Pascal Lamy dated 8 November 2000', Brussels: ESF. Available at www.esf.be

Kingdon, John (1995) *Agendas, Alternatives and Public Policies*, 2nd edn, New York: HarperCollins.

Lavenex, Sandra (2001) 'Migration and the EU's new eastern border: between realism and liberalism', *Journal of European Public Policy* 8(1): 24–42.

Lobkowicz, Wenceslas de (1994) 'Intergovernmental cooperation in the field of migration – from the Single European Act to Maastricht' in Joerg Monar and Roger Morgan (eds), *The Third Pillar of the European Union: Cooperation in the Fields of Justice and Home Affairs*, Brussels: European University Press, pp. 99–122.

Lord, Christopher and Winn, Neil (2000) 'Garbage cans or rational decision? Member governments, supranational actors and the shaping of the agenda for the IGC', *Current Politics and Economics of Europe* 9(3): 237–56.

March, James and Olsen, Johan (1986) 'Garbage can models of decision making in organizations', in James March and Roger Weissinger-Baylon (eds), *Ambiguity and Command. Organizational Perspectives on Military Decision Making*, Marshfield, MA: Pitman, pp. 11–35.

March, James and Olsen, Johan (1989) *Rediscovering Institutions. The Organizational Basis of Politics*, New York: Free Press.

Mazey, Sonia and Richardson, Jeremy (1997) 'Policy framing: interest groups and the lead up to the 1996 Intergovernmental Conference', *West European Politics* 20(3): 111–33.

Moravcsik, Andrew (1999) 'A new statecraft? Supranational entrepreneurs and international cooperation', *International Organization* 53(2): 267–306.

Olsen, Johan (2001) 'Garbage cans, new institutionalism, and the study of politics', *American Political Science Review* 95(1): 191–8.
Pollack, Mark (1999) 'Delegation, agency and agenda setting in the Treaty of Amsterdam', *European Integration online Papers* (EIoP) 3/6 at http://eiop.or.at/eiop/texte/1999-006a.htm
Ross, George (1995) *Jacques Delors and European Integration*, Oxford: Oxford University Press.
Ruggie, John (1982) 'International regimes, transactions, and change: embedded liberalism in the postwar economic order', *International Organization* 36(2): 379–415.
Ruzza, Carlo (1999) 'Normal protest: social movements and institutional activism'. Unpublished ms.
Stetter, Stefan (2000) 'Regulating migration: authority delegation in justice and home affairs', *Journal of European Public Policy* 7(1): 80–103.
Stone, Deborah (1989) 'Causal stories and the formation of policy agendas', *Political Science Quarterly* 104: 281–300.
Thielemann, Eiko (2002) 'Between interests and norms: explaining burden-sharing in the European Union'. Paper for the UACES Workshop on European Burden-Sharing and Forced Migration, London: LSE, 12 January.
Turk, Alex (rapporteur) (1998) *Quand les policiers succèdent aux diplomates. Rapport d'information 523 (97–8) de la Commission des lois du Sénat*, Paris: Sénat.
Tyson, Adam (2001) 'The negotiation of the European Community Directive on Racial Discrimination', *European Journal of Migration Law* 3: 111–229.
Ugur, Ehmet (1995) 'Freedom of movement versus exclusion: a reinterpretation of the "insider–outsider" divide in the European Union', *International Migration Review* 29(4): 964–99.

Final version accepted for publication 9/10/02

Part III
Family and Identity

[11]

"Who Is a Homosexual?": The Consolidation of Sexual Identities in Mid-Twentieth-Century American Immigration Law

Margot Canaday

This essay uses court records to trace the federal government's attempts to regulate homosexuality among immigrants in the mid-twentieth century, asserting that such attempts illustrate the state's struggle to make homosexuality visible, to produce a homosexuality that could be both detected and managed. I focus on the process by which two competing paradigms for understanding homosexuality (status and conduct) were consolidated into a single model in which homosexual identity could be deduced from homosexual acts. Federal officials and the courts initially treated homosexuality as a form of conduct, most commonly deporting homosexual aliens for having committed crimes of moral turpitude. Later, these same government entities relied on status provisions, deporting immigrants charged with homosexuality as aliens "afflicted with psychopathic personality." While the "psychopathic personality" terminology supported the notion that the homosexual was a kind of person rather than a set of behaviors, it also depended upon psychiatrists to support the claim that homosexuals were by definition psychopathic. When many psychiatrists distanced themselves from that idea, the government refused psychiatric opinion that differentiated psychopaths from homosexuals by arguing that these terms connoted legal-political rather than medicalized identity categories. While this conception arose out of a conservative impulse by immigration officials and the courts to fix homosexuality as identity so that it could be regulated (by bureaucrats rather than psychiatrists), I argue

---

Margot Canaday is a Ph.D. candidate in history at the University of Minnesota. This piece was written with the support of the Social Science Research Council Sexuality Research Fellowship Program, funded by the Ford Foundation. The author would also like to acknowledge Greta Krippner, Sandy Levitsky, Mary Strunk, Kim Heikkila, members of Elaine Tyler May and Lary May's dissertation group, Sara Evans, Barbara Welke, Anna Clark, and Lisa Disch, all of whom provided helpful feedback on various drafts of this essay.

that the emphasis on legal-political identity categories licensed a conception of the homosexual as a kind of citizen that had some emancipatory as well as repressive effects.

For all orderly processes, we must in some way classify . . . man.
—Dr. Dahlgren, U.S. Public Health Service, 1959

In 1994, the U.S. Armed Services adopted the don't-ask/don't-tell policy. Ostensibly an improvement over an outright ban on homosexual service-members, the new policy proposed to discharge soldiers for engaging in homosexual activity, but not for the simple fact of being gay or lesbian. In contrast to the preexisting policy, don't-ask/don't-tell claimed to punish conduct but not status. But critics of the new policy have argued that the distinction between conduct and status has never been maintained in practice. Rather, the military infers homosexual conduct from homosexual status. "Doing things that make your commander think you are gay—like making pro-gay statements, or cutting your hair a certain way, or not fitting the gender stereotype of the sex you belong to," explains legal scholar Janet Halley, "can be the basis for an inference that you have engaged in or might someday engage in homosexual conduct" (1999, 2).

The don't-ask/don't-tell policy is based on the idea that homosexual identity reveals a propensity to act because homosexual acts are themselves considered a symptom and confirmation of homosexual identity. Critics of don't-ask/don't-tell have responded to the policy as though it were an even more illogical departure in the state's attempt to regulate homosexuality. Yet while certainly misguided, don't-ask/don't-tell is not really a departure. Rather, the policy follows a template now in existence for nearly half a century. The seemingly illogical don't-ask/don't-tell policy could be adopted in 1994 because the notion that homosexual acts confirm homosexuality as identity had been established as a given years before. This essay examines a much earlier case of state policy making—mid-twentieth-century American immigration law—and focuses on the process by which two competing paradigms for understanding homosexuality (status and conduct) were consolidated into a single model in which homosexual identity could be deduced from homosexual acts.

I construct my argument by exploring tensions between status and conduct in the first generation of federal court cases dealing with homosexuality among immigrants.[1] I begin by examining the passage of the 1952 Immigra-

1. I believe that I have compiled a complete sample of all cases dealing with homosexuality among immigrants from the end of World War II to 1969. I used several methods to locate cases: (1) I searched law review articles for relevant cases; (2) I searched the Federal Digest Index; (3) I conducted a Lexis search; and (4) I used *Hein's Cumulative Index* to locate published administrative (Board of Immigration Appeals) decisions. This search yielded 14 published Board of Immigration Appeals Cases and 13 federal court cases, including two of which were heard by the Supreme Court. For those two cases, I also consulted *Supreme Court Records and Briefs*. For the federal court cases, in addition to obtaining the opinion, I obtained trial

tion and Nationality Act (also known as the McCarran-Walter Act), which contained two anti-homosexual provisions. One provision was based on *conduct* and treated homosexuality as a behavior; it barred from entry immigrants who had committed unspecified "crimes of moral turpitude." A second provision relied on the notion that the homosexual was a type of person; it barred immigrants based on *status* by excluding homosexuals as *persons* "afflicted with psychopathic personality." Initially, as the court cases examined in the following pages reveal, Immigration and Naturalization Service (INS) officials and the courts relied more on the conduct provisions of the law, deporting immigrants who engaged in homosexual acts as having committed crimes of moral turpitude. But this strategy was not without its liabilities. From a practical viewpoint, criminal law charges entitled a defendant to certain procedural protections. Moreover, crimes of moral turpitude were defined by state criminal statutes, which varied in their treatment of homosexual behavior and thereby usurped some of the federal power to control immigrants.

The status provision of the law was not hamstrung by state criminal laws and therefore provided a better foundation for a uniform federal response to homosexuality. Accordingly, and as the court cases analyzed below demonstrate, as time went on INS officials and federal judges increasingly emphasized the psychopathic personality provision of the 1952 McCarran Walter Act. Yet while the government used the psychopathic personality clause to exclude immigrants based on *status*, immigration officials frequently relied on *conduct* (often criminal charges) as evidence of status. That conduct underlay these status charges enabled immigrants and their lawyers to demand some of the protections of criminal law or to refuse the status altogether, calling on an older regime of sexual identity that severed acts from personhood by insisting that occasional conduct did not make one homosexual.[2]

I go on to argue that government officials trumped these efforts by anchoring homosexual status in psychiatric definitions. The psychopathic personality provision secured homosexuality as a coherent identity by cloaking it in the mantle of scientific authority. But the ambiguity written into the law—*psychopathic personality* was used in the text of the statute, but not the word *homosexual*—would profoundly affect the state's attempts to manage immigrants charged with homosexuality. The law as it was written in 1952 vested the power of the state in medical experts because it depended upon psychiatrists to support the claim that homosexuals were by definition psychopathic.[3]

court records from the appropriate branch of the National Archives and Records Administration.

2. On this older regime, see Chauncey 1994.

3. In 1952, the year that the McCarran-Walter Act was passed, psychiatry seemed like a reliable ally. In that year, the American Psychiatric Association (APA) included homosexu-

Those charged with enforcing the anti-homosexual provisions of the immigration law came to regret the law's dependence on psychiatry. In the 1950s and 1960s, psychiatry was a liberalizing profession. Greatly influenced by Kinsey's ideas, many psychiatrists didn't share the same investments as the courts, the Congress, and the INS in the nexus between homosexuality, sickness, and subversion.[4] When many psychiatrists refused to testify in immigration cases that homosexuals were psychopathic, state authorities were left in the awkward position of rejecting expertise in the age of experts.[5] I then conclude that the INS and the courts increasingly reclaimed authority from psychiatrists by asserting that homosexuality and psychopathic personality were, in fact, legal and not medical terms.[6]

This essay traces the government's attempt to regulate immigrants at midcentury, asserting that such attempts illustrate how state authorities struggled to make homosexuality visible, to produce a homosexuality that could be both detected and managed. At issue was a tension between homosexual acts and homosexual personhood. "Who [is] a homosexual?" pointedly asked one immigrant's lawyer in defense of his client (*Boutilier v. INS* 1967, Supreme Court Records and Briefs, 9). Was homosexuality a kind of conduct—a crime that carried with it the procedural protections of criminal law? Or was homosexuality a status—a kind of person? And if the latter were true, how was one to ascertain that status with any certainty? Was a homosexual necessarily a psychopathic personality? If homosexuals were not psychopathic, as many psychiatrists argued in the 1950s, did that mean that homosexual immigrants should be allowed in the country?

Immigrants and their defenders consistently pointed to the contradictions between the status and conduct provisions of the law, destabilizing homosexuality as identity by asserting either that homosexual conduct did not make one homosexual or that homosexuals were not psychopathic, and

ality on its first formal list of mental illnesses. Homosexuality was classified by the APA among the "sociopathic personality disturbances," characterized by the "presence of profound pathology" (see Murdoch and Price 2001, 110).

4. Grob documents growing political and social liberalism within psychiatry in the 1950s and 1960s. This liberal orientation affected mainstream psychiatry and was exhibited in such institutions as the Group for the Advancement of Psychiatry, the National Institute for Mental Health, and even the American Psychiatric Association (see Grob 1991, 275–77).

5. "In the postwar era, the prestige of psychiatry reached unprecedented heights," writes Gerald Grob. "The public's affinity for psychological explanations and professional assistance enhanced the role and authority of practitioners" (Grob 1991, 273).

6. This wasn't the first time that the government and scientific expertise were in tension. David K. Johnson writes of the conflict between the government and scientists in the nuclear age: "But it was no accident that the first federal employee fired for homosexuality to launch a sustained fight with the government was a scientist. It reflected the growing power of the federal government in the sponsorship of scientific research and the growing discontent within the scientific community over the government's security program, whose secrecy requirements clashed with the free flow of ideas necessary to the scientific method. With the secrets of the atomic bomb supposedly holding the key to America's future, those concerned about America's defenses were particularly suspicious of the scientists and intellectuals upon whom they now had to depend" (Johnson 2000, 288).

therefore not covered by the law. Ultimately, these attempts failed. By the late 1960s, federal authorities relied almost exclusively on the notion that homosexuality defined a kind of person (revealed through homosexual acts), and further, they refused psychiatric opinion that differentiated psychopaths from homosexuals by arguing that these terms connoted legal-political rather than medicalized identity categories. While this strategy for dealing with homosexuality among immigrants arose out of a conservative impulse by immigration officials and the courts to fix homosexuality as identity so that it could be regulated (by bureaucrats rather than psychiatrists), I argue in a concluding section that the emphasis on legal-political identity categories licensed a conception of the homosexual as a kind of citizen that had some emancipatory as well as repressive effects.

I. THE 1952 MCCARRAN-WALTER ACT

The anti-homosexual provisions of the McCarran Walter Act cannot be understood apart from the Cold War context of 1950s America. Historians consider the 1950s to be the nadir of homosexual life in America. After the fall of China to communism, the successful Soviet detonation of an atom bomb, and the conviction of Alger Hiss, Senator Joseph McCarthy sought to destroy the Truman administration by charging that it had been infiltrated by both communists and homosexuals. In 1950, the Senate conducted a massive investigation into "sex perverts" in the federal government, resulting in Eisenhower's executive order barring homosexuals from federal employment, countless firings, and even more security investigations. The military also purged homosexual personnel from its various branches—as many as 3,000 each year by the late 1950s (D'Emilio 1992). But what began as a partisan attack on the Truman administration became, over the course of the decade, a much more widespread belief that homosexuals were, like communists, not only unnatural but dangerously subversive. According to this view, both communists and homosexuals could easily blend into the mainstream, where they corrupted the bodies and minds of the young and launched a full scale attack on American political and social institutions, including gender and familial arrangements (D'Emilio 1992, 64).[7] The dominant political and cultural ethos of the decade held that homosexuals posed a serious threat to the American way of life.

Historians have explained the homosexual "kulturkampf" of the 1950s as a reaction to the way in which World War II both created the conditions for a massive expansion in homosexual subcultures across the nation and

7. For a fascinating analysis of the homosexual content of the masculinity crisis in Cold War political culture, see Cuordileone 2000, 515–45.

destabilized gender roles more generally.[8] "The anti-homosexual campaigns of the 1950s," John D'Emilio writes, "represented but one front in a widespread effort to reconstruct patterns of sexuality and gender relations shaken by depression and war" (1992, 68).[9] The *kulturkampf* arose not only because homosexual populations were more visible than ever before, but also in reaction to the idea that homosexuality might not be confined to any population at all. Alfred Kinsey's 1948 study, *Sexuality in the Human Male*, asserted that there was no such thing as a homosexual person, but only homosexual acts. Moreover, Kinsey presented the startling statistic that some 37% of American men had engaged in homosexual contact to the point of orgasm.[10]

The notion that homosexuality was a behavior and not a category of identity was profoundly threatening as it raised the specter of homosexuality lurking within all Americans. But homosexuality became an obsession with state authorities in the 1950s, not just because it was potentially so widespread, but because of the unique function that homosexuality served in 1950s political culture. The paranoid rhetorical linkages between communism and homosexuality suppressed political dissent by tarring some with the brush of pollution and thereby marginalizing them from the political life of the nation.[11] The rhetorical exclusion of homosexuals from the polity not only marginalized those on the left, it also created an excluded figure against which a citizenry supposedly now unified along racial and class lines could define itself.[12]

Given the association between homosexuality, communism, and foreign subversion, it is hardly surprising that the state's need to render homosexuality visible would emerge in especially profound terms in immigration law.[13] The 1950 congressional hearings on the employment of sex perverts in the federal government were undoubtedly a catalyst for the adoption of anti-homosexual provisions in immigration law. Indeed, historian Randolph Baxter suggests that the new immigration provisions were championed by Herbert O'Conor, who had served on the 1950 congressional committee

8. William Eskridge Jr. refers to this period as a *kulturkampf* (1999).

9. On the relationship between sexuality and postwar political culture, see also May 1999.

10. "What is a homosexual?" asked a confused reporter for *Time* magazine in 1958, reporting on a study of British prisoners doing time for unnatural acts. Many of the prisoners did not engage in homosexual acts exclusively, the reporter noted, and there appeared to be no hormonal or other physical difference between these subjects and "normal" men (*Time* 1958).

11. See Cuordileone's essay on cold war political culture.

12. On the way in which the ideology of the liberal consensus concealed racial and class differences, see Gerstle 1994, 1043–73. On the relationship between homosexuality and American political culture, see Courdileone 2000; May 1999; Johnson 2000; D'Emilio 1983; and Baxter 1999.

13. Interestingly, cases involving immigrants were the first cases heard by the Supreme Court that involved homosexuality and individuals, as opposed to publications (Murdoch and Price 2001, 87).

investigating the infiltration of homosexuals into the federal government (Baxter 1999, 541).

Initially, the Senate Committee on the Judiciary advocated the use of explicit language in the new immigration bill, and proposed legislation that barred immigrants who were "psychopathic personalities" or "homosexuals and sex perverts" (Senate 1950, 345). But after consulting with the Public Health Service (PHS), Congress dropped explicit language barring homosexuals. While conceding that the psychopathic personality terminology was "vague and indefinite," the PHS asserted that it was "sufficiently broad" to cover homosexuals (House 1952, 46; Senate 1952, 9). The PHS report to Congress stated that "psychopathic personalities" who are "ill primarily in terms of society and the prevailing culture . . . frequently include those . . . suffering from sexual deviation" (House 1952, 46–47). With this assurance, Congress kept only the psychopathic personality terminology, dropping the words "homosexual" and "sex pervert" from the proposed legislation, but then noting in a report that "this change of nomenclature is not to be construed in any way as modifying the intent to exclude all aliens who are sexual deviates" (Senate 1952, 9).

Representative Emmanuel Cellar criticized the use of psychopathic personality as overly vague.[14] "It's as broad as a barn door," he exclaimed during congressional hearings. "What does it mean? . . . We are revising the code to clear away [these] barnacles." But Representative Cellar was similarly critical of any attempt to ban the entry of homosexuals and sex perverts:

> Now I am not an expert on this, but how in the world is the inspector going to determine whether the person before him is homosexual? He certainly would have to do it in one of two ways, by investigation or by test. Is he going to have "test girls" or "test boys"? . . . Every inspector would have to have a volume of "Dr. Kinsey" with him. . . . How could you find out? It is a hard nut to crack. (Senate and House 1951, 361–62)

Cellar's tirade reflected the increasingly widespread belief that homosexuals, like communists, could easily slip into the country undetected. The PHS acknowledged that detecting homosexuality was a matter of some difficulty. It was easy enough, the PHS's report to Congress stated, when homosexuality manifested itself in unusual dress or behavior. But more typically, a history of homosexuality had to be obtained from the individual, "which he may successfully cover up." Psychological tests might help uncover homosexuality, the report stated hopefully, even when individuals were unaware

14. Emmanuel Cellar was, interestingly, one of the leaders of the anti-restrictionists in the House. Along with Senators Lehman and Humphrey in the Senate, Cellar "attacked the continuation of the quota system as an incorporation of a philosophy of racism not unlike that of Nazi Germany" (see LeMay 1987, 104).

of the condition in themselves. The PHS report also lamented, however, that no laboratory tests could reliably determine homosexuality in every case. Still, the psychopathic personality clause made the inspectors' task a little easier, because "in those instances [where] the disturbance in sexuality may be difficult to uncover, a more obvious disturbance in personality may be encountered which would warrant a classification of psychopathic personality or mental defect" (House 1952, 46–47). The vagueness of the psychopathic personality provision in the law, in other words, gave it some additional power to vet homosexuals, who, Public Health Service officials believed, most likely possessed some form of mental illness besides their sexual aberration.

The McCarran-Walter Act, an omnibus immigration bill reaffirming the national origins quota system, was finally passed in 1952 over President Truman's veto.[15] The relatively uncontroversial psychopathic personality provision barred the entry of any person who at the time of entry acknowledged being or was found to be homosexual. The law required that suspected homosexual aliens be sent to a PHS official to be examined. After a brief examination (usually an interview), the PHS official issued a "Class A" certification to the INS. "This certificate subsequently constituted the sole evidence for exclusion or deportation at the . . . hearing," according to legal scholar Shannon Minter (1993, 778).[16]

At the time the McCarran-Walter Act was enacted, many jurists, legislators, and immigration officials assumed that the "psychopathic personality" provision simply updated language in the 1917 Immigration Act that barred the entry of "constitutional psychopathic inferiors."[17] Constitutional psychopathic inferiors were—according to a 1918 Public Health Service manual for alien examination—"the moral imbeciles, the pathological swindlers,

15. Truman objected to the bill's renewal of national origins quotas. The bill included some liberalizing provisions. It repealed the racial ban on Asian citizenship. It further created an Asian Pacific Triangle and allotted an annual quota of 100 for each country within it (for a total of 2,000 per year). After Congress passed the bill over Truman's veto, the president appointed a special commission on immigration. The commission's report "Whom Shall We Welcome?" laid the groundwork for revisions in immigration law enacted by the 1965 Immigration Act (see LeMay 1987, 104–7).

16. The inspection process was not new in 1952. As early as 1891, Congress mandated medical inspection of all immigrants by the Marine Hospital Service (later called the Public Health Service). For a history of immigrant inspection, see Kraut 1994.

17. For example, from congressional hearings in 1951: "Homosexuals and perverts are excluded . . . under the term 'constitutional psychopathic inferiority'" (Senate and House 1951, 677). Judge Frank of the Second Circuit of the Court of Appeals was one exception. In *United States of America v. Roberto Flores-Rodriguez,* Frank agreed with the majority that Flores-Rodriguez, who had been twice convicted of soliciting men in public washrooms, should be deported, but he disagreed with the majority's reasoning. Flores-Rodriguez had applied for a visa before the McCarran-Walter Act went into effect, but the majority argued that he should have been excluded anyway as a constitutional psychopathic inferior under the terms of the 1917 Immigration Act. Frank was uncertain that the congressional ban on homosexual immigrants in 1952 could be read back into the 1917 legislation without further research (*United States of America v. Flores-Rodriguez,* 1956 [Frank, J., concurring], discussed below).

the defective delinquents, many of the vagrants and cranks, and persons with abnormal sexual instincts" (Public Health Service 1918, 45). But despite the inclusion of this last group, the psychopathic inferior clause was used only rarely against aliens who engaged in same-sex sexual behavior or who exhibited signs of gender nonconformity. If those aliens were to be excluded or deported, and this was not always the case, it was more often as aliens who were likely to become public charges, or as aliens who had committed crimes of moral turpitude.[18]

Accordingly, the moral turpitude clause augmented the psychopathic personality provision in the 1952 legislation. Long used against immigrants who were found to have engaged in homosexual activity, the moral turpitude clause had "deep roots" in the law, and some version of the provision had been on the books since 1891 (*Jordan v. DeGeorge* 1951, 223, 227). Since the 1930s, courts had defined moral turpitude as "an act of baseness, vileness, or depravity in the private and social duties which a man owes to his fellow men . . ." (*Ng Sui Wing v. United States* 1931, 755–56). Under the McCarran-Walter Act, the moral turpitude provision excluded from admission aliens convicted of a crime of moral turpitude or "who admit having committed a crime involving moral turpitude or acts which constitute the essential elements of such a crime." Additionally, aliens could be deported if they were convicted within five years of entry of a crime of moral turpitude and sentenced to confinement for a year or more, or convicted of two crimes of moral turpitude at any time after entry and regardless of sentence (Harms 2001).[19] While neither the Congress nor the courts have ever enumerated a list of crimes that constitute moral turpitude, homosexual acts have long been considered to belong to this class (Minter 1993, 783–91).

18. I do not mean to imply by this that gender nonconformists and those who acted on or experienced same-sex desire were never targeted by immigration officials prior to 1952. What my own research has found is that gender/sex deviants were much more likely to be excluded or deported as public charges or as persons who committed crimes of moral turpitude than as constitutional psychopathic inferiors. Further, my research shows that economic and social resources had a much greater bearing on whether sex/gender deviants would be deported in the early–twentieth century than at midcentury. Moreover, it wasn't homosexual aliens that the state was protecting itself against in the early years of the twentieth century. Rather, persons who engaged in sodomy, persons with abnormal genitalia, and persons who flouted normative gender conventions were all lumped together (along with the feeble minded, the syphilitic, the insane, and many others) as degenerates.

19. Homosexuality was also a factor in naturalization cases. In order to be eligible for naturalization, an alien must have legally entered the United States and lived in the United States for five years. During that period, the petitioner must have demonstrated that he or she was a person of "good moral character." A conviction for a crime of moral turpitude during the five-year period would bar a finding of good moral character. So would evidence of homosexuality. For a discussion of homosexuality and naturalization issues, see Sedlak 1984. *Matter of Schmidt* is a fascinating naturalization case; unfortunately, trial records do not seem to exist. In Schmidt, a lesbian who sought naturalization testified to having a series of sexual relationships with women. "Citing a New Jersey Court that found few 'behavioral deviations . . . more offensive to American mores than homosexuality,' the New York court dismissed the woman's petition for citizenship despite the fact that her behavior was private and violated no law" (Minter 1993, 794). See also, *In re Schmidt* 1968.

II. FEDERAL COURT CASES

Most homosexual immigrants came into contact with the INS at mid-century because they had been caught in the snares of state law enforcement.[20] After an alien's arrest—sometimes for a public sex act, but more often for loitering in public parks or bathrooms—public authorities were supposed to contact the INS. They did so irregularly, and sometimes it wasn't until an alien left the country on a family visit or vacation and then reentered the country that the INS became aware of criminal charges that might indicate homosexuality.[21] Once the INS uncovered a potential violation of immigration law, it conducted an investigation. At the conclusion of the investigation, a special inquiry officer issued a decision. Immigrants had to appeal these decisions administratively to the Board of Immigration Appeals (BIA) before taking their cases to the federal courts.

As would be true with most federal cases involving homosexuality and immigration, the first of these cases appealed to the federal courts shifted clumsily between conduct and status provisions of the immigration law. Roberto Flores-Rodriguez, an unmarried Cuban, was arrested for disorderly conduct on a visit to New York City in September of 1950. According to the police report, Flores-Rodriguez loitered at the men's toilet at Duffy's Square, and moved "from one urinal to several others . . . manipulate[d] the exposed and naked parts of his person, to wit, his penis, to the view of others, and . . . motion[ed] with his head in the direction . . . of several others in said toilet." Flores-Rodriguez was sentenced by the City Magistrate's Court to thirty days imprisonment, but the sentence was suspended and Flores-Rodriguez was allowed to return to Cuba (*United States v. Flores Rodriguez* 1956, 405).

20. There are very few cases in the 1950s and 1960s where immigrants were turned away as psychopathic personalities at the point of initial inspection. Rather, almost all cases involve immigrants who were convicted of a morals offense and were subsequently deported. This is due in part to the fact that after 1925, immigrant inspection was no longer conducted at U.S. ports of entry, but at consular offices abroad. This fact has rendered the inspection process invisible to historians and meant, as Mae Ngai has observed, that it was visas that were examined at U.S. ports of entry, not physical bodies. The exporting of the inspection process shifted the focus of INS officials from exclusion to deportation (Ngai 2001). Indeed, in the 27 immigration cases I have found that deal with homosexuality between the end of World War II and 1969, all but a few are deportation cases.

21. See, for example, published BIA cases. In *Matter of J* and *Matter of K*, the INS was contacted after each alien's arrest. In the *Matter of* G. R., G. R. had been in the country for 30 years and convicted four times in Los Angeles for lewd vagrancy. It wasn't until he left the country for Mexico and then reentered the country that immigration officials tried to deport him. Leaving the country made aliens especially vulnerable—and not only those who were technically deportable when they left the country. Under immigration law, returning after even a short trip constituted an entry. Because exclusion provisions were more far-reaching than deportation proceedings, those immigrants "reentering" after a trip abroad experienced heightened vulnerability. This understanding of an entry would be overturned by the *Fleuti* decision, discussed below (*Matter of J* 1946, 533–35; *Matter of K* 1949, 578; *Matter of G. R.* 1953, 18–22; *Matter of S* 1959, 409–17).

Two years later, Flores-Rodriguez appeared at the Consulate in Havana to apply for an immigration visa. When asked if he had ever been arrested or convicted, Flores-Rodriguez said no. His visa was granted, and he entered the United States as a permanent resident, settling in New York City. In June of 1954, Flores-Rodriguez was again arrested and convicted of disorderly conduct. His 30-day sentence was of minor consequence except that it brought his case to the attention of immigration officials who ordered Flores-Rodriguez deported on the grounds that his entry had not been valid because he failed to disclose his 1950 conviction for homosexuality.

Because Flores-Rodriguez's difficulty with the INS was the result of his criminal conviction for disorderly conduct, his deportation initially rested on the conduct-based moral turpitude provision of the law. Flores-Rodriguez appealed his deportation on these grounds, arguing before the Board of Immigration Appeals that because disorderly conduct, under New York state law, was an *offense* rather than a crime his failure to disclose was not material. (He could not be deported for a *crime* of moral turpitude, in other words, when he had been convicted of an *offense* and not a crime.) The BIA initially agreed. But after the INS filed a motion for reconsideration, the BIA reversed itself (*United States v. Flores-Rodriguez* 1956, Trial Records). Flores-Rodriguez then appealed his deportation to the Second Circuit of the Court of Appeals, which heard his case in 1956.

Given the BIA's initial ruling, much of the Second Circuit's decision was devoted to proving that Flores-Rodriguez had, in fact, committed a *crime* of moral turpitude under the immigration law. Despite the holding of New York state courts that an "offense" of disorderly conduct was neither "crime" nor "misdemeanor," the Second Circuit held that "an Act of Congress should not be necessarily circumscribed" by the New York courts. How odd it would be, the court reasoned, for an alien convicted of the *crime* of disorderly conduct in Washington, D.C., to be deported, while an alien convicted of the *offense* of disorderly conduct in New York would be allowed to remain. Congress, the Second Circuit wrote, had clearly expressed its disapproval of behavior like that of Flores-Rodriguez, and therefore could not have intended such a result (*United States v. Flores-Rodriguez* 1956, 410).

Because the offense/crime distinction weakened the conduct charge against Flores-Rodriguez, the government's brief in the case bolstered the conduct charge with a status charge. Flores-Rodriguez had applied for his visa before the passage of the McCarran-Walter Act, so the government argued that had Flores-Rodriguez revealed his 1950 arrest to the consulate, he might have been excluded as a "constitutional psychopathic inferior" or as a mental defective under the 1917 immigration act. The ruling opinion acknowledged that the government, in lodging its charge that Flores-Rodriguez was a constitutional psychopathic inferior, had "offered no evidence, whatever . . . to the effect that a homosexual who solicits unnatural acts in a public place comes within that category." But the Second Circuit reasoned that because Flores-Rodriguez had admitted being a homosexual to the investigating INS officer in 1955, "together with the fact of defendant's conviction which in itself was evidence of homosexual tendencies of an extremely offensive and exhibitionistic nature," Flores-Rodriguez was potentially subject to exclusion as a constitutional psychopathic inferior. His failure to disclose his 1950 arrest was therefore material to his entry, the Second Circuit ruled, upholding the deportation order for Flores-Rodriguez (*United States v. Flores-Rodriguez* 1956, 405, 410).[22]

In his concurring opinion, Judge Frank voiced his discomfort with the majority's ruling, as he feared that the intent of the 1952 Act was being read back into the 1917 legislation.[23] Before coming to the conclusion that the constitutional psychopathic inferiority clause was meant to include homosexuals, Judge Frank argued, "we should have asked the government to assist us by . . . supplying us with such data as, by diligent research, it might discover" (*United States v. Flores-Rodriguez* 1956, 405, 413–14 [Frank, J., concurring]). Because no such research was conducted, both the U.S. attorney and the Second Circuit emphasized the antisocial nature of Flores-Rodriguez's acts, thereby implying that the particular public expression of his homosexuality qualified him as a psychopathic inferior. This linkage between homosexuality and psychopathy rested on the long-standing notion that psychopaths were unable to control antisocial impulses and to adapt to the norms of the communities in which they lived. Hence the government's brief in the case noted that "Defendant is not merely homosexual," but that "his illness has twice manifested itself in public anti-social behavior" (*Flores-Rodriguez* 1956, Trial Records, 23). The Second Circuit further observed that a deviate who solicited an unnatural act as Flores-Rodriguez had, "will find it extremely difficult to adapt himself and to become a useful member of the American community" (*United States v. Flores-Rodriguez* 1956, 405, 412).

This discussion of psychopathy and the related shift from conduct to status provisions of the law—the shift, in other words, from the notion that homosexuality was a behavior to the idea that the homosexual was a kind of person—thus introduced citizen-motifs into the discussion of an alien's potential deportation. Psychopaths were problematic as citizens precisely

22. Flores-Rodriguez later retracted his admission of homosexuality, attributing his misstatement to nervousness. He stated that he was worn down by the interrogation: "I was ready to cry, I was all broken up" (*U.S. v. Flores Rodriguez* 1956, Trial Records, 41a).

23. Some historians and legal scholars have fallen into a similar trap. Legislators in the 1950s claimed that they were updating the 1917 provision barring "constitutional psychopathic inferiors" (CPI) with the "psychopathic personality" clause. Historians have used this as evidence that the CPI provision was used against homosexuals in the early–twentieth century. However, my own research has shown that this was rarely the case. If "sexual degenerates" were to be deported, it was likely to be under moral turpitude or public charge provisions. Moreover, the CPI clause was most often used against aliens (like Flores-Rodriguez) who entered the country before the passage of the McCarran-Walter Act but came to the attention of the INS after the enactment of that legislation. See also *Matter of LaRochelle* 1965, 436–43.

because they flouted convention, according to William Alanson White, a leader of the American mental hygiene movement. "The individual who manifests a kind of conduct that is calculated to tear down the existing conventions, to deviate greatly from the normal conduct of the community," White wrote, "has to be relegated to some place other than a position of free citizenship" (Minton 2002, 55). Later, immigrants held for deportation under the 1952 act who more closely conformed to societal mores would use this same logic to challenge the notion that homosexuals were by definition psychopathic—and they would call on psychiatric expertise to bolster this claim. While this development still had not materialized in 1956, Judge Frank issued a prescient warning: "I think it a mistake," he wrote, "for my colleagues needlessly to embark—without a pilot, rudder, compass or radar—on an amateur's voyage on the fog enshrouded sea of psychiatry" (*United States v. Flores-Rodriguez* 1956, 405, 412 [Frank, J., concurring]).

Frank's warning was based on the lack of clarity in the 1917 Immigration Act concerning the definition of constitutional psychopathic inferiority. Perhaps heeding his warning, in several subsequent cases in which an alien's entry occurred before the enactment of the McCarran-Walter Act (and the adoption of the psychopathic personality provision), neither the INS nor the courts attempted to use the constitutional psychopathic inferiority clause, relying solely on the conduct provisions of the law. Many of these cases involved, like the Flores-Rodriguez case, disorderly conduct convictions in states where that conviction was an offense and not a crime (and hence not covered as a crime of moral turpitude). In these cases, the courts followed Flores-Rodriguez in asserting that "deportation is solely a federal power" and that the federal courts were not required to "slavishly follow state law" (*Babouris v. Esperdy* 1959, 621; *Babouris v. Murff* 1958, 503). Like Flores-Rodriguez, Robert Wyngaard, a Dutch immigrant residing in Washington, D.C., had been convicted for an offense of disorderly conduct in New York City. His counsel argued that it was not clear that Wyngaard's conviction fell within the vaguely defined moral turpitude provision, not only because it was an offense and not a crime but also because of widely disparate reactions to homosexuality—between state and federal governments and within society at large. Could Wyngaard have committed moral turpitude, his attorneys asked, "in view of the fact that consensual homosexual behavior is not a crime universally or in the District of Columbia . . . [and] in light of current knowledge [that such conduct] . . . is not regarded as necessarily vile or depraved, and the fact that under New York law the offense here is regarded as merely a minor breach of the public peace?" (*Wyngaard* 1961, Trial Records, 9, 16).[24]

24. Wyngaard's counsel argued that debate existed about what homosexuality was (congenital anomaly, psychiatric disorder, constitutional, acquired, a matter of taste, or a sexual outlet), but that "current thinking among authorities seems unanimous that consensual homosexual relations among adults is not an activity which society should punish." Surely, Wyn-

However lenient New York state (or society in general) was in its attitude towards homosexuality, the D.C. District Court and the D.C. Circuit followed the Second Circuit's decision in *Flores-Rodriguez*. "The Second Circuit very cogently argues that what constitutes a crime involving moral turpitude is a Federal question," the D.C. District Court argued, "and is not dependent on the manner in which State law classifies the violation of law" (*Wyngaard v. Rogers* 1960, 527). But the repeated court challenges as to what constituted crimes of moral turpitude proved the point of one federal judge, who argued that the moral turpitude clause "hampers uniformity" (Wyngaard 1961, Trial Records, 12).

The psychopathic personality provision did not seem to share the same liabilities. Under the psychopathic personality clause, federal immigration officials and federal courts could decide—based on state convictions for offenses like disorderly conduct—that an alien was a psychopathic personality. As such, the clause enhanced the power of the federal government to remove aliens charged with homosexuality from the country, regardless of how homosexual offenses were treated at the state level. The status provision of the act bolstered the power of the federal government over immigrants not only because it reasserted federal authority over state law, but because status charges in general were vague and not easily refuted.[25] The moral turpitude provision subjected aliens to deportation if they were convicted within five years of entry of a crime of moral turpitude and sentenced to confinement for a year or more, or convicted of two crimes of moral turpitude at any time after entry. The psychopathic personality provision only required, by contrast, that one seem to be homosexual. Sometimes aliens were deported as psychopathic personalities who were not technically deportable under the moral turpitude clause.

The first federal court case to rely on the psychopathic personality provision was *Ganduxe y Marino v. Murff* in 1959. As would be true with most psychopathic personality cases, the charge depended on the alien's conduct—a single minor conviction—as evidence of status. In *Ganduxe*, the court successfully shifted the focus from Ganduxe's acts to the presumption that such acts confirmed his homosexuality, and by extension, his status as a psychopathic personality. The facts in the case closely paralleled those of Flores-Rodriguez. Ganduxe was a Cuban alien who had been arrested and convicted during a 1953 visit to New York City for loitering for "the purpose of inducing men to commit acts against nature." Like Flores-Rodriguez, he concealed the conviction when applying for his visa at the consulate in

---

gaard's brief overstated the unanimity of such tolerance. But the point that homosexuality was not universally condemned was bolstered by the fact that Wyngaard's public act of fellatio resulted in a conviction for disorderly conduct, a minor crime regarded by New York statutes as "quasi criminal" (*Wyngaard* 1961, Trial Record, 23).

25. This was true of other status provisions in law—for example, vagrancy laws and the clause in immigration law focused on those who were likely to become a public charge.

Cuba. He had been living in the United States for one year when the Immigration Service served Ganduxe with an order to show cause as to why he should not be deported.[26] At an investigatory hearing, Ganduxe testified that he was not a homosexual. Ganduxe offered to be examined by the Public Health Service, since as his lawyer argued, "It is a medical question and not a factual question on whether or not a person is or is not afflicted with psychopathic personality." When the government refused his offer, Ganduxe presented a letter from a board-certified psychiatrist who stated that Ganduxe was neither a psychopath nor an overt homosexual, further ascribing the alien's arrest to alcohol and "linguistic difficulties." Moreover, the psychiatrist wrote, "Mr. Ganduxe claims that his interests are heterosexual ones and that he is unofficially engaged to a girl residing in Cuba." Apart from the conviction, Ganduxe's brief to the court stated, "There was no affirmative evidence in the record that the appellant is homosexual" (*Ganduxe* 1960, Trial Records, and *Ganduxe* 1959Trial Records). Ganduxe's lawyer concluded that his client's case differed in this respect from *Flores-Rodriguez*.

When Ganduxe's case was appealed to the district court, the government did not have to prove that Ganduxe actually was a psychopathic personality or a homosexual. The government only had to make the case that Ganduxe had lied about something that was material to his entry. Ganduxe's lawyer had argued that materiality required not just the possibility of a refusal of the visa but "the probable existence of a ground of inadmissibility." Given that the government had failed to show that Ganduxe was a psychopathic personality—and ignored the opinion of Ganduxe's doctor that he was not—Ganduxe's counsel was skeptical that the alien's misrepresentation was, in fact, material to his entry (*Ganduxe* 1959, Trial Records).

"Materiality is a matter of degree," the district court concluded, ruling in favor of Ganduxe's deportation, and contrasting his case with that of another alien, not deported, who had failed to disclose her residence in Russia for fear she would be barred entry as a communist. "Disclosure of residence in Russia for a year and a half is not nearly so likely to result in a refusal of a visa on the ground of membership in the Communist party," the court wrote, "as pleading guilty to loitering to solicit homosexual acts is to result in refusal of a visa on the ground that the alien is afflicted with psychopathic personality, i.e.: is a homosexual" (*Ganduxe y Marino v. Murff* 1959, 565).[27]

26. It is unclear from the record what triggered the INS's action at this time. Probably another arrest (*Ganduxe y Marino v. Murff* 1959, 565).

27. The Second Circuit affirmed per curium (*Ganduxe y Marino v. Esperdy* 1960, 330). The distinction the court made between homosexuality and communism suggests that even while closely linked in political discourse, they could be separated in the law's application. See also *Matter of Alfonso-Bermudez*, in which the BIA canceled the deportation order for an alien who had been twice convicted of crimes of moral turpitude (involving homosexuality) but whose family had a strong history of anti-communism and who himself had been involved in anti-Castro activities in Cuba (*Matter of Alfonso-Bermudez* 1967, 225–27).

Ganduxe's case demonstrates how even minor acts could be taken as evidence of psychopathic personality. The defendant in the contrasting case had spent 18 months in Russia. Ganduxe had been in a public restroom for 20 minutes. He had not been charged with homosexual acts, or with soliciting acts, but with *loitering* to solicit homosexual acts. The crime of loitering was trivial—he was fined $25—except in so far as it revealed Ganduxe as a homosexual person. Perhaps Ganduxe understood this dynamic when he defended himself not only by denying the crime but also by arguing that the crime was not a reliable indicator of his personhood. It is also possible that Ganduxe genuinely understood himself as heterosexual. According to the sexual regime operative among Latino immigrants in New York City in the 1950s, even had Ganduxe engaged in homosexual acts, it would not have compromised his own heterosexual status as long as he performed the masculine role in sexual relations.[28] The court's ruling rejected such logic by linking homosexual acts to homosexuality as identity and thereby pathologizing both. There were then fewer and fewer ways to engage in homosexual sex acts and still maintain a normative sexual identity, as those acts were increasingly construed by the court as the outer symptoms of a pathological or perverse personhood. This shift rendered immigrants whose culture provided a different understanding of acceptable sexual expression especially vulnerable.

As the universe of normative sexuality became more restricted, with homosexuality increasingly construed as an identity to be confirmed by acts, some aliens barely resisted the charge of homosexuality but argued instead that homosexuality did not make one psychopathic. In doing so, they often turned to medical and/or mental health professionals as allies. Sara Harb Quiroz was stopped at the U.S.-Mexico border after a family visit, according to historian Eithne Luibheid, because her short hair and trousers made her look like a lesbian to the immigration official who stopped her (Luibheid 1998, 483).[29] After an initial attempt to deny her homosexuality, Quiroz admitted to the INS "that she had homosexual desires for at least a year. . . .

28. Meaning that he was either the penetrator in anal sex, or was fellated in oral sex. The sexual regime among Latinos in New York City in the 1950s mirrored that of Italians in early twentieth-century New York. Latinos (especially Puerto Ricans) were often trade—i.e., *straight* men whose masculinity protected them from the stigma of homosexuality when they had sex with *queer* men (Chauncey 2002).

29. There are only two lesbians cited in the literature: that of Quiroz, and *In re Schmidt* (cited above). This does not mean that lesbians were not targeted for deportation. Luibheid reports a conversation with Quiroz's lawyer in which he states that the immigration officer who spotted Quiroz at the border was known to have been responsible for the exclusion or deportation of hundreds of women for sexual deviation (1998, 483). Male aliens were most often vetted by immigration officials because they had been caught engaging in some kind of public sexual behavior. It is my belief that lesbians were far less likely than men to come to the attention of the INS for criminal offenses, and probably relatively more likely to be vetted because of appearance. Also women undoubtedly had fewer resources to hire lawyers to fight deportation and are probably less present in court cases for this reason.

[and] had homosexual relations on numerous occasions over this period of time with two women . . . with weekly frequency" (Lubheid 1998, 493). When her case reached the federal courts in 1961, Quiroz asserted that her homosexuality did not make her a psychopathic personality. Quiroz's lawyer argued that Congress had not defined psychopathic personality, and even if Congress had the (doubtful) power to relegate the question to the Public Health Service, the latter body had not stated that the psychopathic personality terminology *always* included sexual deviates (*Quiroz* 1961, Trial Records, 5). "Since law is silent on the criteria or definition of a psychopathic personality," Quiroz's attorney wrote, "the only alternative to which law can turn is medicine." The brief cited the evidence presented by two doctors at the INS hearing, who argued that while it was clear that Quiroz was a homosexual, it was not similarly obvious that she was a psychopathic personality. Remarkably, one of these doctors was a Public Health Service surgeon who testified that while PHS regulations included all homosexuals as psychopathic personalities, he was not certain that Quiroz was "medically a psychopathic personality." The other doctor—a psychiatrist—testified that Quiroz's traits of "trustworthiness, conscientiousness, and hard work . . ." indicated that she was not a psychopathic personality (*Quiroz* 1961, Trial Records, 3–5).[30]

Highlighting Quiroz's role as a useful member of her community was an attempt to reverse the discourse that associated psychopaths with those utterly devoid of the characteristics of good citizens. Perhaps because the psychiatrist's emphasis on strong work habits would not have carried as much weight in Quiroz's case as they might have for a male immigrant, the attempt failed, and the Fifth Circuit rejected Quiroz's appeal.[31] Presented with evidence from the two doctors that homosexuals were not necessarily considered psychopathic personalities by the medical profession, Judge Jones quoted Judge Frank's concurring opinion in *Flores-Rodriguez* that it was a mistake "to embark . . . on the fog enshrouded sea of psychiatry." Ironically, courts cited Frank's opinion, according to legal scholar Shannon Minter, "to bypass the ambiguities of clinical discourse about homosexuality and use convictions of homosexual offenses as proof of a 'psychopathic personality' under the 1952 Act."[32] Almost as soon as the courts began to rule on cases

30. Moreover, Quiroz's lawyer added that his client had not been "convicted of any acts of moral turpitude."

31. While Quiroz had a young daughter, little attempt was made to depict Quiroz as a good mother—which probably would have been a much more effective way for her to claim that she bore the traits of a good citizen (and was therefore not a psychopath). Her lawyer only mentioned Quiroz's daughter briefly, arguing that the child would suffer if deprived of the government benefits on which she depended.

32. *Flores-Rodriguez* was cited in many of the cases that followed for an important reason. The court found Flores-Rodriguez excludable under two provisions: moral turpitude and as a constitutional psychopathic inferior. Judge Frank disagreed with the latter charge in his concurring opinion, arguing that it was not clear that the term included homosexuals and that the court should not venture into the arena of psychiatry. Shannon Minter writes, "Ironi-

that involved the psychopathic personality charge, then, they distanced themselves from the discipline of psychiatry. Judge Jones then cited the legislative history of the act which stated that Congress's adoption of the PHS terminology *psychopathic personality* in no way modified congressional intent to exclude homosexuals. "Whatever the phrase 'psychopathic personality' may mean to the psychiatrist, to the Congress it was intended to include homosexuals and sexual perverts," Jones wrote. "It is that intent which controls here" (*Quiroz v. Neelly* 1961, 906–7).[33]

Amid a string of unfavorable decisions for aliens charged as psychopathic personalities during this period, George Fleuti's case stands out. Atypically, the Ninth Circuit in Fleuti treated homosexuality as conduct, and argued, in essence, that had Fleuti been able to interpret the hopelessly vague psychopathic personality clause he could have avoided the behavior that made him a homosexual. Fleuti, a Swiss alien, worked as the front office manager at the Ojai Valley Inn and Country Club. He had been living in the United States since 1952 and had also done administrative hotel work in Los Angeles (*Rosenberg* 1963, Supreme Court Records, 4). He was convicted in 1953 as "willfully and lawfully a dissolute person" and in March of 1956 for an act of oral copulation (*Rosenberg* 1963, Supreme Court Records, 42). It wasn't until another arrest (later dismissed) in November of 1958, that the INS began deportation proceedings on moral turpitude grounds (*Matter of Fleuti* 1965).[34]

In the spring of 1959, an investigator from the INS obtained a statement from Fleuti that he had engaged in homosexual relations about once a month for 22 years. Fleuti explained the circumstances surrounding his 1956 arrest:

> In Switzerland, whenever I and one of my friends performed homosexual relations, we did it in private rooms or apartments. We . . . were

cally, the disagreement between the majority opinion and the concurrence in *Flores-Rodriguez* allowed courts greater flexibility in interpreting the two Acts [1917 and 1952 immigration legislation] and actually made the exclusion of homosexuals easier. In cases governed by the pre-1952 law, courts could cite the majority opinion's psychiatric rationale to authorize using a homosexual offense as evidence of 'constitutional psychopathic inferiority,' under the 1917 Act." In cases governed by the 1952 act, as noted above, Frank's concurrence bolstered the court's rejection of psychiatric opinion, which complicated the relationship between homosexuality and psychopathic personality (Minter 1993, 789–90).

33. Luibheid reports that Quiroz had "one last card to play." Two months after the court of appeals ordered her deportation, Quiroz married Edward Escudero and filed a motion to reopen her case. "The motion filed on her behalf requested the right to reopen her case so as to 'present evidence of her marriage and full rehabilitation . . . that . . . applicant is prepared to prove that she is, at this time, a normal individual and no longer a psychopathic personality.'" The attempt failed. The INS ordered her deported anyway, since her rehabilitation had no bearing on her condition at the time of entry (Luibheid 1998, 498–99).

34. He was also arrested as a lewd vagrant in November 1958. That charge was dismissed, but it is probably what brought his case to the attention of INS officials, since he was first investigated in April of 1959 (*Rosenberg* 1963, Supreme Court Records, 43–49).

> never caught or arrested. In Los Angeles, I was unfortunate enough that I did it in a park and was arrested. Ever since that . . . I have felt that the United States Immigration might be looking for me because I heard that such things were reported to Washington, so I have been very careful. (*Rosenberg* 1963, Supreme Court Records, 75)

When the examining officer concluded that Fleuti was not deportable on moral turpitude grounds on a technicality, the INS used testimony from the investigation to request a reopened hearing on psychopathic personality grounds.[35] During the reopened hearing, Fleuti denied the truth of the statements he had made to the INS investigator, but affirmed that he had been examined by a PHS surgeon who had certified him as a psychopathic personality.[36] That doctor, who conceded that he had no formal psychiatric training, noted that he had based that determination on "the history and documentation of the, shall we say, arrest" (*Rosenberg* 1963, Supreme Court Records, 63). When pressed further, Dr. Dalhgren conceded that he had "'no strong feeling' as to whether, 'according to traditional medical terms' respondent would be considered a psychopathic personality" (*Rosenberg* 1963, Supreme Court Records, 7). Fleuti also presented a letter from his psychiatrist, a Dr. Harvey, which stated that Fleuti's sexual deviation was under control and that Fleuti "seems to have traits of a better than average citizen, in the sense of hard work, general morality, and honesty" (*Rosenberg* 1963, Supreme Court Records, 4). Dr. Harvey stated that Mr. Fleuti had long recognized his homosexual interests and had his first homosexual experience at age 26. "However," Harvey wrote, "his socio-economic relationships have been consistently good according to my history." The psychiatrist observed that Fleuti "did not frequent homosexual hangouts, had no evident interest in youths, manifested no irresponsible trends, and had his main social contacts with respected members of the community." Fleuti had a greater interest in homosexual relations than was typical, but his overall sex drive was not strong, he had engaged in heterosexual relations up to 1959, and he was not, according to Fleuti's doctor, "a sociopath, a psychopath, or a person of constitutional psychopathic inferiority." In a remark clearly intended to highlight Dahlgren's lack of psychiatric expertise, Dr. Harvey concluded, "I do not think that another psychiatrist with adequate training

35. The examining officer concluded that the charge that Fleuti was "willfully and unlawfully a lewd and dissolute person" did not involve moral turpitude because of a 1953 BIA decision that lewd vagrancy was a condition and not a crime. Because the latter charge of sexual perversion was a misdemeanor that carried no sentence, Fleuti was not deportable on moral turpitude grounds (*Rosenberg* 1963, Supreme Court Records, 43).

36. That examination consisted of a review of Fleuti's medical history: "both as to medical illnesses, questions in regard to his sexual practices were asked, and there was a review of the records accompanying Mr. Fleuti, and it included x-ray, neurological report and urinalysis" (*Rosenberg* 1963, Supreme Court Records, 63).

and experience will be likely to disagree with my findings" (*Fleuti v. Rosenberg* 1962, 652, 657).

In ordering Fleuti's deportation, the special inquiry officer noted that Fleuti's deportation as a psychopathic personality was supported by Fleuti's own admissions as well as the certification of the Public Health Service (*Rosenberg* 1963, Supreme Court Records, 45). The logic that made Fleuti a psychopathic personality was incredibly circular: The INS cited the PHS certification, and the PHS doctor who made the certification had, when question by Fleuti's lawyer about medical disagreements about the term, cited the authority of the PHS manual. "We have to use certain terminology—and the rest of the world may not agree," the doctor explained, "we are so ordered; therefore we do" (*Fleuti v. Rosenberg* 1962, 652). The Board of Immigration Appeals upheld the order, and Fleuti appealed his case to the federal courts.

In his appeal to the Ninth Circuit, Fleuti's attorney argued that the deportation order was a violation of his due process because the term *psychopathic personality* was "void for vagueness." That legal concept prohibited punishment for any conduct that could not reasonably be understood to be proscribed. The court observed that Fleuti's deportation had relied on conduct both before and *after* his entry to the country to determine that he was a psychopathic personality. Because Fleuti seemed to exercise choice in post-entry homosexual behavior (based on the fact that his psychiatrist testified that he could control his homosexual urges) "it follows that if, by reason of vagueness, the statute failed to advise him that homosexual practices conclusively evidence a 'psychopathic personality,' Fleuti was substantially prejudiced." The Ninth Circuit observed that the PHS surgeon and Fleuti's own doctor disagreed as to the meaning of the term *psychopathic personality*, the PHS (in its report to Congress) conceded that the term was "vague and indefinite," and experts in general disagreed about its meaning. Based on this confusion, the Ninth Circuit concluded that the psychopathic personality provision, "when measured by common understanding and practices, does not convey sufficiently definite warning that homosexuality and sex perversion are embraced therein." The court ordered Fleuti's deportation canceled on the grounds that the statute was void for vagueness (*Fleuti v. Rosenberg* 1962, 652). In doing so, it implicitly affirmed the underlying premise of Fleuti's brief that homosexuality was a form of conduct—hence the notion that if properly warned, Fleuti would not have engaged in such behavior.

Fleuti's court battle was far from over. The government appealed the case to the Supreme Court, where its strategy was to reassert the idea that homosexuality was a condition or status rather than a behavior. The government argued that the statute was not void for vagueness because Congress was "not seeking to regulate conduct but to prescribe standards for admission to the United States." Fleuti was being deported, the government argued, not for post-entry conduct but for *condition at entry*. The void-for-vagueness doctrine, intended in the immigration context to ensure that aliens had adequate warning about conduct for which they could be deported, was inapplicable to Fleuti. The doctrine, government counsel argued, "was not a device to enable persons having defined characteristics . . . or suffering from specified physical or mental diseases or defects, to conduct themselves so as to avoid making these conditions manifest" (*Rosenberg* 1963, Supreme Court Records, 10, 32).

The Supreme Court declined to address the void-for-vagueness issue and instead vacated the lower court's ruling on other grounds.[37] But in letting the Ninth Circuit's ruling stand, at least Chief Justice Earl Warren had been influenced by the ambiguity of the medical testimony in the case. "It was conceded by the government doctors," Warren wrote in a note to himself, "that all homosexuals are not medically psychopaths" (Murdoch and Price 2001, 93). After the Fleuti decision was remanded, the INS ordered Fleuti's deportation, asserting that he had been a *constitutional psychopathic inferior* at the time of his entry in 1952. (Like Flores-Rodriguez, Fleuti's original entry occurred before the passage of the 1952 McCarran Walter Act).[38] The order for deportation was finally canceled in 1965 when the Board of Immigration Appeals ruled, in a fascinating opinion, that it did not find compelling evidence that Fleuti was a homosexual:

> Respondent has been employed in a responsible position for the past 11 years by one employer who thinks very highly of him, that he has a history of devotion to family and interest in others, that he has sought psychiatric help and has his problem under control, that apart from these arrests resulting in convictions on two occasions, he has not been in trouble with the authorities, that he is well regarded by people who have known him over an extended period of time . . . . While the records reveals that respondent has an inclination toward homosexual-

37. Under immigration law, leaving the country and returning after even a short trip constituted an entry. In Fleuti's case, when he was charged with being afflicted with psychopathic personality at the time of his entry, his entry comprised an afternoon visit to Mexico. (Because his original entry to the country occurred before the passage of the McCarran-Walter Act, he could not have been charged as afflicted with psychopathic personality at the time of *that* entry. The INS would later try to deport him as a constitutional psychopathic inferior at the time of his original entry). But the Supreme Court ruled that Fleuti's three-hour excursion from the country in 1956 did not constitute an entry and vacated on this ground. "We do not think Congress intended to exclude aliens long resident in this country after lawful entry who have merely stepped across an international border and returned 'in about a couple hours.' " The Court defined an entry as "an intent to depart which can be regarded as meaningfully interruptive of the alien's permanent residence." Such an intent might be inferred from the length of time the alien was absent, purpose of the trip, and/or whether or not the alien had to procure travel documents (*Rosenberg v. Fleuti* 1963, 449, 457, 458). This ruling became the basis of the "Fleuti doctrine," according to El Paso immigration lawyer Albert Armendariz Sr. (telephone conversation with Armendariz, December 2001).

38. In its ruling, the Supreme Court noted that "since respondent's homosexuality did not make him excludable by any law existing at the time of his 1952 entry, it is critical to determine whether his return from a few hours in Mexico was an entry in the statutory sense." This was critical acknowledgment of the shaky legal ground that underlies attempts to exclude homosexuals as constitutional psychopathic inferiors (*Rosenberg v. Fleuti* 1963, 449, 452).

ity, it appears to be one respondent can control and that he had it under control before he entered. *Therefore, we cannot find that the record establishes that he was a homosexual at the time of that entry*. (*Rosenberg v. Fleuti* 1963, 449, 452, emphasis mine)[39]

What, then, according to the court, made one a homosexual? Fleuti's sexual acts—unlike Ganduxe's or Quiroz's—were mitigated by other facts that seemed to suggest to the Board that Fleuti led an upstanding and moral life. In contrast to the image of the out-of-control psychopath, Fleuti's homosexual urges were well under control. Moreover, he had severed not only sexual but social contacts with other homosexuals. Fleuti exhibited many of the traits of a good citizen: He was productively employed, a responsible family member who cared for his dependents, well thought of by his associates, and not least, both Northern European and male. Interestingly, such traits did not suggest to the BIA that Fleuti was a good homosexual. They suggested instead that he was *not* a homosexual (*Matter of Fleuti* 1965). The BIA's ruling destabilized homosexuality as identity by challenging the idea that such identity bore any necessary relationship to homosexual acts.

Following *Fleuti*, *Lavoie v. Immigration and Naturalization Service* further jeopardized government efforts to regulate homosexuality among immigrants. Lavoie, a Canadian alien, entered the United States in 1960. After Lavoie pled guilty to an arrest for a homosexual act in a Woolworth's store in 1961, the INS began an investigation. Lavoie told an INS investigator that he had first become aware of homosexual feelings when he was in the Royal Canadian Navy, and he admitted to frequent homosexual encounters but more than 30 heterosexual acts as well. During hearings before a special inquiry officer, the government's own psychiatrist, Public Health Service surgeon Beittel, testified that from a *psychiatric* point of view, Lavoie was *not* a homosexual but a "sexual deviate manifested by auto-eroticism and homo-eroticism." The testimony of Lavoie's own psychiatrist, a Dr. Diamond, was vexing for the INS. He stated that respondent was not a psychopathic personality, but suffered from a neurotic conflict over sex. Diamond initially refused to fix homosexuality as identity, testifying that "homosexuality is not an appropriate medical term . . . [and] there is no such diagnosis as homosexuality." But he then reversed himself, arguing that while Lavoie clearly manifested sexual confusion, he bore none of the traits of a "true" homosexual:

No molesting of children, no interest in adolescents, no sustained relationships "with some abnormal individual in any perverted way," no

39. This was the last attempt the INS made to deport Fleuti. In 1975, Fleuti became a naturalized citizen. Fleuti's attorney stated that the INS couldn't deny Fleuti his naturalization because Fleuti had "more than five years of good moral character. No more arrests. He was very cautious. It was like walking a tightrope" (Murdoch and Price 2001, 98).

> feminine characteristics, no love affairs with men. The homosexual "experience[s]" were "extremely superficial, extremely casual" and "in between the scattered homosexual contacts he has had perfectly normal relationships with women." (*Lavoie* 1966, Trial Records, 13).

Thus, ultimately, Diamond did fix homosexuality as identity, but he defined it not in terms of sex acts but, rather, in terms of emotional attachments. Consequently, he might have considered Lavoie a "true" homosexual—and hence problematic for the INS—*if* Lavoie had developed emotional bonds with his sexual partners. Homosexuals, in Diamond's framework, were men who loved other men, but not necessarily men who sought out other males for casual sex. The special inquiry officer rejected this notion, returning instead to the familiar argument that homosexual acts confirmed homosexual status. "A person who [has] engaged in homosexual acts twelve to twenty-four times a year for a period of at least eleven years," the special inquiry officer wrote, is "a sexual deviate irrespective of the mental condition which [causes this]" (Trial Records Lavoie 1966, 13).

Lavoie then appealed to the BIA, which remanded the case so that the psychiatric issues could be reconsidered in light of the Public Health Service's *Manual for the Medical Examination of Aliens* and further testimony could be taken as to "what pattern determines a . . . homosexual." But, at the reopened hearing, psychiatric testimony remained unchanged. "A good deal of their testimony only served to confuse me," the special inquiry officer wrote, "[but] I did get out of it that they agreed that the phrase 'psychopathic personality' has no precise medical meaning and that 'homosexual' is not a medical term." Having found in the PHS manual a reference to psychopathic personality as a "legal term;" the officer firmly rejected the relevance of psychiatric testimony. "If, as testified to by the medical experts, 'psychopathic personality' and 'homosexual' are not medical terms," he reasoned, "any testimony concerning such conditions is without the scope of their special competence and is of little value in resolving the issue" (*Lavoie* 1966, Trial Records).

While the INS may have felt that it had effectively dismissed the psychiatric testimony, Lavoie's lawyers resurrected it again when his case reached the Ninth Circuit.[40] Lavoie's opening brief established that the government psychiatrist had stated that Lavoie might be neurotic and not homosexual and that this doctor finally reached his "diagnosis" of psychopathic personality with "grave doubts" and "under [the] compulsion of a government manual" that he believed needed revision. "Like the government doctor in *Fleuti*," the brief argued, Dr. Beittel was "*required* to so certify *anyone* who is a sex deviate." The government's case was clearly weakened by such

40. The government was represented in the case by Solicitor General Thurgood Marshall.

testimony from within its own ranks, and the Ninth Circuit followed *Fleuti* in holding that psychopathic personality was void for vagueness in its application to homosexuals (*Lavoie v. INS* 1966, 27, 28; and *Lavoie* 1966, Trial Records, 5, 11).[41]

Fleuti and *Lavoie* unsettled many of the "givens" on which federal regulation of homosexuality among immigrants rested. In the 1967 *Boutilier* decision, immigration officials and the courts made a determined attempt to reassert those givens: first, the notion that homosexuality designated a kind of person, and second, that homosexual persons were psychopaths and hence covered by the immigration law. In the face of psychiatric disagreement about the nature of homosexuality, the latter effort would require the court to find another foundation on which to establish homosexual identity. That foundation would be the law itself.

Canadian national Clive Michael Boutilier had been living in the United States for eight years when he applied for naturalization in 1963. During that process, Boutilier completed an affidavit which disclosed a 1959 sodomy charge that had been changed to simple assault and then dismissed. As a result of this admission, Boutilier was questioned by the INS in great detail about his entire sexual history, including the 1959 charge (*Boutilier* 1967, Supreme Court Records, 4). Boutilier told the investigator that he had engaged in homosexual acts approximately four times a year both before and after his entry to the United States, and that he had also engaged in occasional heterosexual acts. Immigration officials also obtained information from Boutilier that he had lived for some time with a man with whom he had occasional sexual relations and that, after a psychiatric examination, he was classified as 4F by the Selective Service System.[42] Information from the investigation was submitted to the Public Health Service, which reviewed the materials and certified that Boutilier was a psychopathic personality at the time of his entry. At his hearing, Boutilier declined to be examined by PHS doctors but submitted evidence from two psychiatrists who declared that Boutilier was not a psychopathic personality. The special inquiry officer ruled Boutilier deportable as a person afflicted with psychopathic personality at the time of his entry, revealing the conflict between INS and psychiatric definitions that would recirculate in various courtrooms and legal briefs (*Boutilier* 1967, Supreme Court Records; and *Boutilier v. INS* 1966, 488, 491).

When Boutilier's case made its way to the Second Circuit in 1966, the majority opinion supported the INS's attempt to label Boutilier (and all homosexuals) as psychopathic, regardless of medical opinion. The court asserted that homosexuals were defined by the legislative history of the McCarran-Walter Act as psychopathic personalities. "Congress utilized the

41. The case was not finally resolved until after the *Boutilier* decision. See footnote 48.

42. The 4F categorization indicated that one was unfit for military service.

phrase 'psychopathic personality' not as a medical or psychiatric formulation," the majority wrote, in a by-then familiar argument, "but as a legal term of art designed to preclude the admission of homosexual aliens into the United States" (*Boutilier* 1967, Supreme Court Records; *Boutilier v. INS* 1966, 488, 491).[43]

In his dissent, Judge Moore argued that Congress could not have intended the psychopathic personality language to exclude *all* homosexuals. He pointed to Kinsey's finding that 37% of American men had at least one homosexual experience. "To label a group so large 'excludable aliens' would be tantamount to saying," Judge Moore reasoned, "that Sappho, Leonardo da Vinci, Michelangelo, Andre Gide, and perhaps even Shakespeare were they to come to life again would be deemed unfit to visit our shores." Moreover, he continued, "so broad a definition might well comprise more than a few members of legislative bodies." Moore raised the possibility that homosexuals were not necessarily, like psychopathic personalities, persons whose "sexual deviation put [them] into repeated conflict with the authorities." Rather, some homosexuals—not least legislators and famous writers and artists—might be contributing members of society. The assertion certainly seemed true of Boutilier who was, Moore observed, "young, intelligent, responsible," and "who has worked hard . . . and is respected in his work" (*Boutilier v. INS* 1966, 488, 491).

The argument in the Supreme Court followed similar contours.[44] Boutilier's legal team employed a variety of legal strategies to make the case that the psychopathic personality provision did not apply to him. An amicus brief filed by the Homosexual Law Reform Society of America included dozens of letters from prominent medical and scientific experts—Margaret Mead, Ruth Benedict, Harry Benjamin, and John Money among them—which asserted that homosexuals were not by definition psychopathic.[45] The brief charged the government not with ignoring science but rather with manipulating it. "In labeling the homosexual as . . . a psychopathic personality, we have not discovered a classification of disturbed persons," the amicus

43. Interestingly, a 1967 law review article observed that *unpublished* cases from the Board of Immigration Appeals treated psychopathic personality as "a medical term requiring expert medical diagnosis." This was a "significant divergence" from the published BIA cases, which treated psychopathic personality as a legal term of art encompassing homosexuality. "These unreported decisions are in obvious conflict with the reported cases . . . . It seems that the Board of Immigration Appeals desires to have precedential consistency in its reported cases, and still allow itself to do justice in individual cases by refusing to report cases that conflict with those already reported" (Byrne and Mulligan 1967, 335–36).

44. Solicitor General Thurgood Marshall urged the justices to take the *Boutilier* case to resolve a conflict between the Second Circuit's decision in the case and the Ninth Circuit's decision in *Lavoie* (on the void-for-vagueness issue). The next time the Supreme Court handed down a full-length, signed opinion on a case involving homosexuality was the *Bowers v. Hardwick* decision in 1986 (Murdoch and Price 2001, 106, 275–76).

45. The brief also pointed to similar positions taken in the writings of Alfred Kinsey, Evelyn Hooker, Sigmund Freud, and Richard Kraft von Ebbing.

brief explained. "Rather, we have created such a classification in the purposeful but unscientific pursuit of certain non-medical ends." Boutilier's lawyer strongly rejected the lower court's dismissal of scientific opinion, asserting that psychopathic personality was a medical term whose definition should be left to psychiatrists rather than administrators. As evidence, Boutilier's counsel observed that the clause was included in the statute in a section with other medical exclusions, such as epilepsy. And, as Boutilier's brief explained, "respondent and the court are . . . . in the ambivalent position of denying that a medical opinion is required to find that petitioner was a psychopathic personality at the time of entry" and simultaneously basing his deportation on the "the pro forma certification of the U.S. Health Service." It was contradictory, in other words, to turn to the doctors of the PHS to legitimize the deportation of aliens for homosexuality, while ignoring the opinion of broader medical experts (*Boutilier* 1967, Supreme Court Records, 14, 9).

In addition to the argument that Boutilier was a homosexual but homosexuals were not psychopathic personalities, Boutilier's legal team mounted the contradictory but subversive argument that Boutilier might not have been a homosexual at all. As evidence of this, Boutilier's heterosexual experiences were cited, as was the frequency of occasional homosexual contact among American men in general. "In no event can Boutilier be classed as homosexual without violating part of his history," concluded psychiatrist Clarence A. Tripp, "and/or forcing him into a category that would include a sizable population of the whole white American population." General lifestyle issues as well seemed to disrupt the construction of Boutilier as a homosexual. Psychiatrist Montague Ullman noted that in addition to the petitioner's strong work record, he had moved back home with his mother. Boutilier went to Mass and spent most nights at home. "He occasionally goes bowling," Ullman concluded (*Boutilier v. INS* 1967, Supreme Court Records, 15).

This attempt to problematize Boutilier's homosexuality was part of a larger strategy to disrupt the notion that homosexuality was a category of identity that could be deduced from homosexual behavior. Boutilier's brief addressed the issue:

> The source of the evil lies in an apparent belief that there is some kind of recognizable human being that is a homosexual, like one might recognize a red-head. . . . By and large homosexuality is a kind of behavior, evidently very wide spread, and not the manifestation of a particular kind of person. (*Boutilier v. INS* 1967, Supreme Court Records, 10)

Boutilier's writ to the Supreme Court adopted a similar tone. "Who is a homosexual?" the brief asked. One who engaged in both homosexual and heterosexual acts? One time? Or many times? One who was drawn to such practices as experimentation? One who was drawn to such behavior compulsively? (1967, 6).

The facts in *Boutilier* resisted the fixing of homosexuality as identity because while the petitioner had admittedly engaged in homosexual behavior, he did not *seem* like a homosexual. Boutilier engaged in homosexual acts, but he also had occasional heterosexual sex. Only very rarely did Boutilier have sex in public places. He had no criminal record and had only come to the attention of the government by his own admissions when he attempted to naturalize. And, indeed, he bore many of the markers of a good citizen—he was a hard worker who lived with his mother, attended Mass, and even went bowling—a hobby so quintessentially American that political scientist Robert Putnam has used it as a metaphor for engaged civic community (Putnam 2000). Indeed, no other immigrant besides George Fleuti so fully claimed the mantle of good citizenship. Fleuti did this so successfully that it entirely displaced his homosexuality. But that Boutilier's counsel could make similar arguments was not incidental to his whiteness and his maleness—traits which, of course, he shared with Fleuti.[46]

If the contradictions that Boutilier posed as a homosexual man were engaged, they were truly threatening. They challenged the notion that homosexual aliens were an identifiable group who must be refused entry because they did not belong in the American body politic, and instead raised the possibility that homosexuality might be an occasional act among aliens who otherwise had the potential to become good citizens. Boutilier's legal team had opened a dangerous space between homosexual acts and homosexual identity, between conduct and status. In the face of this threat, it is hardly surprising that the Supreme Court would move to close that gap, restabilizing homosexuality by fixing it as an identity that could be deduced from sexual acts. In the final view of the Court, homosexuals were a type of people, not a set of free-floating practices from which no conclusions about identity could be drawn. "Congress commanded that homosexuals not be allowed to enter," the Supreme Court asserted, collapsing all distinctions between psychopathic personality and homosexuality. "The petitioner was found to have that characteristic and was ordered deported." In further rejecting the void-for-vagueness argument, the Supreme Court asserted that Boutilier was deported not based on conduct but on his status at time of entry.[47] But if the Court clearly made the argument that the homosexual

46. In sharp contrast to early-twentieth-century immigration cases, where homosexuality was a mark of racial degeneration often associated with immigrants from places other than northwestern Europe, race seems strangely unmarked in these midcentury cases. I think this may have something to do with the rhetorical function of homosexuality in cold war political culture as an excluded group that was used to cement the notion of a unified citizenry, in part by minimizing racial differences. But even while fairly unmarked at the discursive level, race was still operative in these midcentury cases. Fleuti and Boutilier were able to claim good citizenship in a way that other immigrants (from Cuba and Mexico) were not.

47. *Boutilier* thus resolved the void-for-vagueness issue from *Fleuti*.

was a kind of person, it also importantly rejected the medical terms on which homosexual identity had historically been based. The Court described homosexuality as a legal-political identity category and noted that the question of Boutilier's deportation was a "purely legal" rather than a medical decision (*Boutilier v. INS* 1967, 118, 122–24). By its assignment of a legal rather than a medical valence to psychopathic personality cases, the Supreme Court authorized Congress and federal bureaucrats to decide who was a homosexual and how that category would be regulated.[48] In his dissenting opinion, Justice Douglas protested the Court's move, asserting that Congress wanted psychiatric expertise to guide these immigration decisions. "We cruelly mutilate the [McCarran-Walter] Act," he wrote, when instead "we make the word of the bureaucrat supreme" (*Boutilier v. INS* 1967, 118, 135 [Douglas, J., dissenting]).[49]

III. TOWARD A HOMOSEXUAL CITIZENRY

As the example of the don't-ask/don't-tell policy with which I began this essay demonstrates, it is now taken for granted that homosexuality is an identity that is betrayed by homosexual acts. This paper has examined midcentury immigration law in order to trace the process by which this assumption was first operationalized in state policymaking. Federal immigration cases from the 1950s and 1960s reveal that the interdependence of conduct and status is not unique to the don't-ask/don't-tell policy, but rather

48. The Lavoie case was not finally resolved until after *Boutilier*. After the Ninth Circuit found the psychopathic personality provision void-for-vagueness, the government appealed to the Supreme Court. The Supreme Court argued that the void-for-vagueness issue had been settled by *Boutilier*, but it remanded the case so that the lower court could consider other issues (387 U.S. 572 [1967]). The issue that had been raised in the meantime (in *Woodby*) was that "no deportation order may be entered unless it is found by clear, unequivocal, and convincing evidence that the facts alleged as grounds for deportation are true" (*Lavoie v. INS* 1969, 732). In light of *Woodby*, the court of appeals then remanded the case to the INS. The BIA reheard the case, noting that the facts were remarkably similar to *Boutilier* in that the latter also "had a long-continued . . . history of homosexual relations prior to entry and had also engaged in heterosexual relations on several occasions." The BIA ruling found that the record clearly established that Lavoie was a homosexual at the time of his entry. "Evidence as to post-entry conduct added nothing to the finding of inadmissibility but was merely corroborative but does not constitute a basis for the finding of inadmissibility or excludability," the Board wrote (*Matter of Lavoie* 1968). Finally, Lavoie appealed to the Ninth Circuit Court of Appeals, which ruled that despite the fact that both psychiatrists expressed doubt that Lavoie was a homosexual, *Boutilier* was controlling. "Each was a person who, in common opinion, would be regarded as a homosexual. [Psychiatric testimony is] irrelevant, in view of the meaning which the Supreme Court in *Boutilier* gave to the pertinent statute" (*Lavoie v. INS* 1969, 732). The court's phrase "in common opinion" is revealing. It not only suggests an emphatic refusal of psychiatric expertise but also has resonances of a postwar tradition linking homosexuality with an effete intellectualism.

49. In doing so, the majority took a step toward the "therapeutic state" in which, according to psychiatrist Thomas Szsaz, psychiatry became a tool of administrators and bureaucrats who were "both a party to a controversy and its judge" (1963, 216–17).

emerged with the federal government's earliest attempts to manage homosexuality. As is now true with soldiers who serve under don't-ask/don't-tell, the chimera of a conduct/status distinction heightened the vulnerability of immigrants to federal policing in the 1950s and 1960s. When the state did not have enough evidence to deport an alien on moral turpitude charges—charges that required that one be convicted of an actual crime, in some circumstances, twice—the state could use such conduct as evidence of status.[50] Tightening the causal link between conduct and status—asserting in other words that one who had homosexual sex was a homosexual—foreclosed the introduction of other kinds of evidence into the evaluation of one's status, of the kind of person one was, and of the kind of citizen one would make. It was irrelevant if an alien also engaged in heterosexual sex, took care of elderly parents, was a reliable employee, or went bowling.

This made the psychopathic personality provision very powerful, and partially explains why the INS seemed to rely more heavily on the charge as time went on. But the emphasis on the psychopathic personality clause was strategic for other reasons as well. Unlike the moral turpitude provision, the psychopathic personality clause made homosexuality refer to a kind of person rather than a form of behavior. Not only was it easier to regulate a person than a random act, but cold war political culture seemed to require an outsider figure that could be used to banish dissenters and to unite a diverse citizenry around the mythology of consensus.[51] "The ties among the non-deviant citizens," observed attorney Gilbert Cantor in the amicus brief he wrote in *Boutilier* on behalf of the Homosexual Law Reform Society of America, "are strengthened by their common opposition to the rejected and excluded" (*Boutilier* 1967, Supreme Court Records, 16).

Yet Judge Frank had warned as early as 1956 that it was "unwise" for

50. Under the McCarran-Walter Act, aliens convicted of a crime of moral turpitude were excluded. The act also subjected aliens to deportation if, within five years of entry, they were convicted of a crime of moral turpitude and sentenced to confinement for a year or more, or convicted of two crimes of moral turpitude at any time after entry. Shannon Minter asserts that the moral turpitude clause supported deportations under the psychopathic personality charge. "Because the 'psychopathic personality' provision authorizes exclusion based on sexual orientation alone," she writes, "courts have readily found evidence of moral turpitude in convictions involving homosexual conduct even when offenders were charged under vague statutes that did not define the proscribed behavior and even when the conduct criminalized lacked the elements of violence or abusiveness present in other sexual crimes deemed to involve moral turpitude." Minter describes a BIA case in which the INS deported a man convicted under a vague "gross indecency" statute. The INS argued that "regardless of whether the statute defined an offense of moral turpitude, the conviction 'provided a substantial basis for concluding that the respondent was inadmissible on medical grounds' as a homosexual" (Minter 1993, 788).

51. The shift also reflected the particularly American veneration of individualism, which easily bled into a notion that homosexuality reflected individual identity and not sexual behavior per se. Jennifer Terry writes that "Americans privileged individual identity to a significantly greater degree [than Europeans], regarding it as the principal site for uncovering the causes of homosexuality and for intervening and guiding the individual toward a more harmonious balance with social norms" (Terry 1999, 10).

the courts in deciding immigration matters to "venture into the sea of psychiatry." Frank was perceptive. Relying on the psychopathic personality clause meant vesting the authority of the national state in medical experts, who would change their minds as science developed. "The meaning and precise content [of the psychopathic personality terminology]," legal scholar Marc Bogatin has written, "was susceptible to a certain amount of modification as the state of medical knowledge evolved" (Bogatin 1981, 373). And certainly, the inclusion of dozens of statements by psychiatrists in the amicus brief to the Supreme Court in *Boutilier* demonstrated that medical professionals were not reliable partners in the state's enforcement of normative heterosexuality.

When it asserted that psychopathic personality was a legal and not a medical term, the Court both reasserted the control of administrators over that of psychiatrists and froze homosexuality as identity by fixing it "with a single, unchanging meaning" (Bogatin 1981, 373).[52] The Court also mandated that status would be, as Janet Halley has written of the military, determined in the public sphere by law; and that legal words would designate, according to Rogers Smith, "the existence of a political 'people' . . . in ways integral to individuals' sense of personal identity as well" (Halley 1999, 33; Smith 1997, 31). The Court's move was fundamentally conservative—designed to both police nonconformist sexual behaviors and make them decisive indicators of identity. Boutilier's legal team resisted the Court's attempt to consolidate homosexuality as a kind of person: "The world is not divided into sheep and goats," the alien's brief to the Supreme Court stated, quoting Kinsey. The "living world is a continuum in each and every one of its aspects," including sexuality (*Boutilier* 1967, Supreme Court Records, 50). But even though Boutilier's counsel had tried to draw on that fluidity to suggest that Boutilier did not fit within the given legal categories, harnessing a stable identity would have some empowering effects for sex/gender nonconformists like Boutilier.

In the years between *Flores-Rodriguez* and *Boutilier*, the courts and the INS had won the battle to define homosexuality as an identity rather than a behavior. But the victory was partial at best, because in failing to maintain the support of psychiatrists, the INS and the courts failed to establish the

52. Congress similarly acted to redistribute power from psychiatrists to bureaucrats when it replaced the "psychopathic personality" provision with a clause barring the entry of "sexual deviates" in the 1965 Immigration Act. Interestingly, this tightening of the ban against homosexual immigrants occurred in the context of immigration legislation that Michael LeMay has called a "civil rights" bill because it eliminated many racist provisions in immigration law, including the national origins quota system (1987, 14). The act also continued the support of the 1952 Act for family reunification. The McCarran-Walter Act had for the first time permitted quota-free entrance of alien wives, husbands, and children of U.S. citizens (Trelles and Bailey 1979). A major goal of the 1965 act was to "preserve the family unit and reunite families" (LeMay 1987, 111). Thus, in addition to excluding homosexuals, immigration policy during these years shored up the heterosexual family.

homosexual individual as diseased. Asserting that homosexuals were defined by legal-political rather than medical categories would have ambivalent effects: It gave the state a way to win these cases, but in shifting the terrain from medical to political-legal identity categories, it simultaneously licensed a concept of the homosexual individual as potential citizen. And as much as the courts' rulings during these years envisaged the homosexual as a kind of anti-citizen, some who found themselves defined by the law as homosexual (as well as the lawyers and jurists who supported them) would redeploy these concepts in strategic ways.

Indeed, the notion that homosexuals could be good citizens circulated throughout many of the cases dealing with homosexuality among immigrants during these years. Justice Douglas, dissenting in *Boutilier*, wrote that "it is common knowledge that in this century homosexuals have risen high in our own public service—both in the Congress and in the Executive Branch—and have served with distinction" (*Boutilier v. INS* 1967, 118, 129). Dr. Norman Reider sent a letter in support of Boutilier's brief, which stated that "homosexuals can be as honest, courageous, contributory to society, and trustworthy as heterosexuals" (*Boutilier* 1967, Supreme Court Records, 73). Dr. Isadore Rubin, editor of *Sexology Magazine*, similarly observed in support of Boutilier's case that homosexuals were found in all professions and walks of life and were making great social contributions. "To deny persons otherwise qualified as citizens the privilege of citizenship on the basis of homosexual behavior per se," Rubin wrote, "is to deprive our nation of important human resources as well as to commit an injustice against them." And then Rubin concluded, "Unless there is a place for [homosexuals] in the Great Society, there will never be a great society in any sense" (*Boutilier* 1967, Supreme Court Records, 74, 85). Quiroz's record of responsible employment, Fleuti's association with reputable members of the community and his closeness to his family, Boutilier's attendance at church and his participation in community rituals like bowling all suggest the centrality of rhetorical strategies that pictured these aliens as capable of assimilation as good American citizens.[53]

The conception of homosexuals as potentially good citizens that circulated in immigration cases only rarely produced positive outcomes for aliens facing deportation during these years, but the shift in the discursive terrain had an impact outside the arena of the courtroom. To take just a couple of

53. In *Tovar v. Immigration and Naturalization Service*, a married Mexican alien residing in California was arrested three times for patrolling public restrooms and each time convicted for lewd vagrancy. A special inquiry officer initially determined that Tovar was deportable but then granted a suspension of his deportation, finding that he was a person of good moral character. Presumably, this finding was based on the fact that Tovar supported a wife (in poor health) and three children of his wife's niece. The Board of Immigration Appeals and the Ninth Circuit Court of Appeals rejected the suspension and ordered Tovar deported (*Tovar v. INS* 1966, 1006; *Tovar* 1966, Trial Records).

examples: Psychiatrist R. Masters's self-declared "evenhanded" account of homosexual life in America reported that homosexuals wanted to be regarded as "ordinary citizens" with a homosexual "bill of rights" that included the freedom to serve in the armed forces; the freedom to secure government employment; the freedom to marry, own property jointly, and take advantage of tax breaks; and the freedom of the press, among others. Masters's list alluded to one of the foundational documents of the American republic and touched on some of the major components of American citizenship: military service, employment, marriage, property ownership, and tax paying (Masters 1962, 115–46).

Donald Webster Cory, a homosexual man writing under a pseudonym, also employed citizen motifs in his midcentury account of homosexual life. Homosexuals were a minority group that was not based on inborn characteristics, Cory wrote, but on a number of social-legal factors: "In the denial of civil liberties; in legal, extra-legal, and quasi-legal discrimination; in the assignment of an inferior social position; in the exclusion from the mainstreams of life and culture" (Cory 1951, 4–5, 14). Cory repeatedly identified homosexuality with democracy and noted that totalitarian societies had been the most repressive of homosexuals. In fact, Cory wrote, homosexuals were a "pillar of democratic strength" and "no force will be able to weave these groups into a single totalitarian unity which is the unanimity of the graveyard." Moreover, having been denied basic freedoms, Cory argued, homosexuals would be champions of freedom (Cory 1951, 69, 233–35, 240–43).[54]

The Mattachine Society and other homophile groups also claimed the mantle of good citizenship during these years. This was a point of contention in their collaborative relationship with Alfred Kinsey, who steadfast in his belief that homosexuality was a behavior, urged Mattachine leaders to "avoid 'the special pleas of a minority group'" (Minton 2002, 174).[55] The Mattachine Society of Washington claimed as its purpose "to act by any

54. Cory—who in the 1950s wrote eloquently of his personal struggle to accept his homosexuality—had become a reactionary 20 years later. When *The Homosexual in America* was reprinted in 1975, Cory, according to Henry Minton, "declared that, for the most part, the book no longer expressed the views of its author. . . . He believed that homosexuality was a mental illness marked by 'distress, loneliness, promiscuity, search for affection with little success, depression, [and] superficial gaiety'" (Minton 2002, 251).

55. Henry Minton examines the Mattachine Society's relationship with Kinsey in the context of a long history of homosexuals trying to achieve emancipation through science. Kinsey was an important ally but, according to Minton,

> was not a social revolutionary. Aside from conventional sexual mores, he did not question other sexual values, nor did he question the existing power structure with its inherent sexual and gender bias. As William Simon notes, his assumption of the essential naturalness of virtually all types of sexual expression encouraged a bland sexual liberalism. Thus, in the case of homosexuality, he was insensitive to the politically heuristic value that a collective homosexual identity could provide as a source of resisting oppression. In fact, he strongly argued against the need to categorize people according to sexual identity. Rather than homosexual people, there was only homosexual behavior. (Minton 2002, 168)

lawful means . . . to secure for homosexuals the right to life, liberty, and the pursuit of happiness, as proclaimed for all men by the Declaration of Independence and . . . the basic rights and liberties established by the word and spirit of the Constitution of the United States" (Johnson 2000, 320). [56] In accordance with this aim, the Mattachine Society of Washington called its main publication *The Homosexual Citizen.*[57] Both Mattachine insiders and those who feared the organization wondered about the possibility of a homosexual voting bloc that might carry "tremendous political power" (Masters 1962; Cuordileone 2000, 536).

All of this is not to say that the courts discovered or created the notion of homosexuality as a fixed, legal-political identity that lent itself so ably to this rhetoric of homosexual citizenship. That construct was partly a response to the public displays of military and civil service purges during the early 1950s, which pictured homosexuals as soldiers and civil servants and ensured that debates about homosexuality would be debates about citizenship as much as disease or crime. In attempting to regulate homosexuality among immigrants, the Congress, administrative agencies, and especially the courts both reflected larger cultural currents and helped to consolidate this notion of homosexuals as potential citizens. But the notion that homosexuals were a type of people with a legal-political identity had unintended consequences. In using law to constitute status in the way they did, in using legal words to designate the people, the courts, the Congress, and the INS probably had little idea that they were lending authority to a burgeoning gay rights movement that continues to this day to base its claims on a legal-political conception of homosexuals as potentially good citizens.[58] But at the same time, gay rights movements cannot themselves escape the ambivalent legacy of fixing homosexuality as identity and thereby surrendering themselves to regulation by state authority.

56. Johnson argues that the emphasis of the Washington Mattachine on claiming the rights of citizenship was unique (2000, 294). My own review of other chapters of the organization suggests that it was a common goal.

57. In a reflection of the effectiveness of the Mattachine's use of citizen/minority group rhetoric (and a fascinating reversal of the court's articulation in immigration cases that the homosexual was a kind of person), the Civil Service Commission responded to the Mattachine's challenge to the firing of federal homosexual employees by denying "the very existence of homosexual individuals, stating that the adjective 'homosexual' could only be applied to actions. 'We see no third sex, no oppressed minority or secret society,' the Civil Service Commission wrote in a memo to the Mattachine Society of Washington" (Johnson 2000, 329). The Civil Service Commission was on the defensive by 1965, because D.C. Court of Appeals Judge David Bazelon ruled in *Scott v. Macy* that the CSC had to explain how immoral conduct related to occupational fitness. Bazelon's progressive position may have been an outgrowth of his association with several psychiatrists (including Evelyn Hooker) as a member of the National Institute of Mental Health's Taskforce on Homosexuality (Johnson 2000, 322, 338–39).

58. Indeed, to return to the don't-ask/don't-tell policy, it is the very success of the gay rights movement in mobilizing this conception that has now made it politically untenable for the military to appear to punish homosexual identity.

REFERENCES

Baxter, Randolph. 1999. "Eradicating This Menace": Homophobia and Anti-Communism in Congress, 1947–55. Ph.D. diss., University of California, Irvine.

Bogatin, Marc. 1981. The Immigration and Nationality Act and the Exclusion of Homosexuals: *Boutilier v. INS* Revisited. *Cardozo Law Review* 2:359–96.

Byrne, Thomas Jr., and Francis Mulligan. 1967. Psychopathic Personality and Sexual Deviation: Medical Terms or Legal Catch Alls—Analysis of the Status of the Homosexual Alien. *Temple Law Quarterly* 40:328–47.

Chauncey, George Jr. 1994. *Gay New York: Gender, Urban Culture, and the Making of the Gay Male World, 1890–1940*. New York: Basic Books.

———. 2002. A Different West Side Story: Latino Gay Culture and Urban Politics in Postwar New York. Lecture delivered 15 February, at the University of Minnesota, Minneapolis.

Cory, Donald Webster. 1951. *The Homosexual in America: A Subjective Approach*. New York: Greenberg.

Cuordileone, K. A. 2000. Politics in an Age of Anxiety: Cold War Political Culture and the Crisis of American Masculinity, 1949–1960. *Journal of American History* 87:515–45.

D'Emilio, John. 1983. *Sexual Politics, Sexual Communities: The Making of a Homosexual Minority in the United States, 1940–1970*. Chicago: University of Chicago Press.

———. 1992. The Homosexual Menace: The Politics of Sexuality in Cold War America. In *Making Trouble: Essays on Gay History, Politics, and the University*, 57–73. New York: Routledge.

Eskridge, William Jr. 1999. *Gaylaw: Challenging the Apartheid of the Closet*. Cambridge, Mass.: Harvard University Press.

Gerstle, Gary. 1994. The Protean Character of American Liberalism. *American Historical Review* 99:1043–73.

Grob, Gerald. 1991. *From Asylum to Community: Mental Health Policy in Modern America*. Princeton, N.J.: Princeton University Press.

Halley, Janet. 1999. *A Reader's Guide to the Military's Anti-Gay Policy*. Durham, N.C.: Duke University Press.

Harms, Brian C. 2001. Redefining Crimes of Moral Turpitude: A Proposal to Congress. *Georgetown Immigration Law Journal* 15:259–89.

Johnson, David K. 2000. The Lavender Scare: Gays and Lesbians in the Federal Civil Service, 1945–1975. Ph.D. diss., Department of History. Northwestern University, Evanston, Illinois.

Kraut, Alan. 1994. *Silent Travelers: Germs, Genes, and the "Immigrant Menace."* Baltimore, Md.: Johns Hopkins University Press.

LeMay, Michael. 1987. *From Dutch Door to Open Door: An Analysis of U.S. Immigration Policy Since 1820*. New York: Praeger.

Luibheid, Eithne. 1998. Looking Like a Lesbian: The Organization of Sexual Monitoring at the United States-Mexican Border. *Journal of the History of Sexuality* 8:477–506.

Masters, R. E. I. 1962. *The Homosexual Revolution: A Candid and Unbiased Appraisal of an Organized Minority Which Threatens to Become a Powerful Social and Political Force*. New York: Belmont Books.

May, Elaine Tyler. 1999. *Homeward Bound: American Families in the Cold War Era*. New York: Basic Books.

Minter, Shannon. 1993. Sodomy and Morality Offenses Under U.S. Immigration Law: Penalizing Lesbian and Gay Identity. *Cornell International Law Journal* 26:771–818.

Minton, Henry. 2002. *Departing from Deviance: A History of Homosexual Rights and Emancipatory Science in America*. Chicago: University of Chicago Press.
Murdoch, Joyce, and Deb Price. 2001. *Courting Justice: Gay Men and Lesbians v. the Supreme Court*. New York: Basic Books.
Ngai, Mae. 2001. Making and Unmaking Illegal Aliens: Deportation Policy and the Production of U.S. Nation-State Territoriality, 1920–1930. Paper delivered at the Annual Meeting of the American Society for Legal History, 9 November, Chicago, Illinois.
Public Health Service. 1918. *Manual for the Mental Examination of Aliens*. Washington, D.C.: Government Printing Office.
Putnam, Robert. 2000. *Bowling Alone: The Collapse and Revival of American Community*. New York: Simon and Schuster.
Sedlak, Eric. 1984. *Nemetz v. INS:* The Rights of Gay Aliens under the Constitutional Requirement of Uniformity and Mutable Standards of Moral Turpitude. *International Law and Politics* 16:881–912.
Smith, Rogers M. 1997. *Civic Ideals: Conflicting Visions of Citizenship in U.S. History*. New Haven, Conn.: Yale University Press.
Szasz, Thomas. 1963. *Law, Liberty, and Psychiatry: An Inquiry into the Social Uses of Mental Health*. New York: McMillian.
Terry, Jennifer. 1999. *An American Obsession: Science, Medicine, and Homosexuality in Modern Society*. Chicago: University of Chicago Press.
Time Magazine. 1958. What Is a Homosexual? 16 June, p. 44.
Trelles, O., and J. Bailey. 1979. *Immigration and Nationality Acts, Legislative Histories, and Related Documents*. Buffalo, N.Y.: Hein.
U.S. House. 1952. Revising the Laws Relating to Immigration, Naturalization, and Nationality. 82d Cong., 2d. sess. H. Rept. 1365.
U.S. Senate. 1950. The Immigration and Naturalization Systems of the United States. 81st Cong., 2d sess. S. Rept. 1515.
———. 1952. Revision of Immigration and Naturalization Laws. 82d Cong., 2d sess. S. Rept. 1137.
U.S. Senate and U.S. House. 1951. Joint Hearings Before Subcommittees of Committees of Judiciary. Revision of Immigration, Naturalization, and Nationality Laws. 82d Cong., 1st sess.

CASES

Babouris v. Esperdy, 269 F.2d 621 (2d Cir. 1959).
Babouris v. Murff, 175 F. Supp 503 (S.D.N.Y. 1958).
Boutilier v. Immigration and Naturalization Service, 360 F.2d 488 (2d Cir. 1966); 387 U.S. 118 (1967).
———. 1967. Supreme Court Records and Briefs.
Fleuti v. Rosenberg, 302 F.2d 652 (9th Cir. 1962).
Ganduxe y Marino v. Esperdy, 278 F.2d 330 (2d Cir. 1960).
———. 1960. Trial Records at the National Archives and Records Administration.
Ganduxe y Marino v. Murff, 183 F. Supp 565 (D.N.Y. 1959).
———. 1959. Trial Records at the National Archives and Records Administration.
In Re Schmidt, 56 Misc. 2d 456 (N.Y. Sup. Ct. 1968).
Jordon v. DeGeorge, 341 U.S. 223 (1951).
Lavoie v. Immigration and Naturalization Service, 360 F.2d (9th Cir. 1966); 418 F.2d 732 (9th Cir. 1969).

———. 1966. Trial Records at the National Archives and Records Administration.
Matter of Alfonso-Bermudez. 1967. 28 I & N Dec. 275.
Matter of Fleuti. 1965. 26 I. & N. Dec. 308.
Matter of G. *R*. 1953. 14 I. & N. Dec. 18.
Matter of J. 1946. 7 I. & N. Dec. 533.
Matter of K. 1949. 10 I. & N. Dec. 575.
Matter of LaRochelle. 1965. 26 I. & N. Dec. 436.
Matter of Lavoie. 1968. 29 I. & N. Dec. 224.
Matter of S. 1959. 20 I. & N. Dec. 409.
Ng Sui Wing v. United States, 46 F. 2d 755 (7th Cir. 1931).
Quiroz v. Neelly, 291 F.2d 906 (5th Cir. 1961).
———. 1961. Trial Records at the National Archives and Records Administration.
Rosenberg v. Fleuti, 374 U.S. 449 (1963).
———. 1963. Supreme Court Records and Briefs.
Tovar v. Immigration and Naturalization Service, 368 F.2d 1006 (9th Cir. 1966).
———. 1966. Trial Records at the National Archives and Records Administration.
United States v. Flores-Rodriguez, 237. F.2d. (2d Cir. 1956).
———. 1956. Trial Records at the National Archives and Records Administration.
Wyngaard v. Kennedy, 295 F.2d 184 (D.C. Cir. 1961).
———. 1961. Trial Records at the National Archives and Records Administration.
Wyngaard v. Rogers, 187 F. Supp. 527 (D.D.C 1960).

[12]

The Limits of Citizenship: Migration, Sex Discrimination and Same-Sex Partners in EU Law*

R. AMY ELMAN
Kalamazoo College

Abstract

This article addresses the paradoxical politics of heterosexism within European Union (EU) policy through a critical consideration of matrimony as the primary legitimating link between EU nationals and third-country spouses. It also emphasizes the discrimination experienced by same-sex couples to whom the protection and privileges of marriage are unavailable and questions efforts to extend state-sanctioned unions to same-sex partners. Indeed, it argues against the presumption that relationships (whether spousal, cohabitational, sexual or familial) provide justifiable criteria for citizenship and the privileges associated with it. The article has theoretical implications for those studies in which the themes of citizenship, immigration, family, sexuality and social exclusion are central.

I. Introduction: Paradoxical Citizenship

Sexuality has long been a subtle catalyst for defining and amending nationality, citizenship and migration. Sexuality's imposing influence on social arrangements is so pervasive that it is often ignored or naturalized. To discern the ways sexuality sustains and/or precludes membership in national and

*Research for this project was supported, in part, by the Center for Western European Studies at Kalamazoo College under Title VI. The author would like to thank Lisa D. Brush, Peter L. Corrigan, Mark A. Pollack, John Peterson, and her anonymous reviewers for their critical comments.

transnational communities, this article examines the codified bias toward marital relationships and the resulting social exclusion faced by gay men and lesbians within the European Union (EU). It begins with a brief summary of EU policy regarding citizenship and (im)migration more generally, and then focuses on the particular obstacles to free movement that gay and lesbian EU nationals encounter. This focal point reveals that the equivalence in the treatment between lesbians and gay men has been employed to conceal sexual inequality and nullify the promise of current anti-discriminatory measures. The article concludes with an exploration of whether and how the second-class citizenship status of lesbians and gay men can be subverted through existing state and union policies.

In 1992, the Maastricht Treaty extended the offer of EU citizenship to Member State nationals: 'Every citizen holding the nationality of a member state shall be a citizen of the Union' (Art. 8(1) EC). Union citizenship entitles a person to free movement within all Member States. Though the guarantee of free movement for economic purposes dates from the Community's inception, the recent attachment of this right to the Article on citizenship is significant. It suggests a desire to reaffirm the ability of Member States to determine the acquisition of this transnational status. EU citizenship is, after all, premised on nationality, an identity determined by state, not Union, policy. Nationality is, by definition, tied to states. Scholars of citizenship have therefore noted that, technically speaking, EU citizenship is not citizenship at all (e.g. Guild, 1997; O'Leary, 1996a, b; Tanca, 1993). Citizenship presupposes an individual's direct allegiance to her or his nation-state. In contrast, under Union citizenship the Member State remains the necessary intermediary between the individual and the (transnational) Community (Tanca, 1993, p. 272). The nationalist roots of power over citizenship mean that Member States retain significant influence over Union migration. Assessments pointing to the declining importance of states in transnational contexts of interdependence may be overstated to the extent that they ignore such residual national power.

Numerous migration scholars focusing on race and ethnicity have observed the paradoxical effect of European unity. The greater integration of Europeans (within the European Community) has strengthened conventional conceptions of nationality that fuel 'fortress' Europe (Cesarani and Fulbrook, 1997, p. 3; Kofman and Sales, 1992).[1] In this article I argue that the case of sexuality is analogous. The paradoxical effect of the rhetoric of increased tolerance that

[1] For example, it is now commonly acknowledged that xenophobia has risen steadily throughout Europe (Commission, 1997). In 1997, a special *Eurobarometer* opinion poll on racism and xenophobia (47.1) revealed that of the 16,241 people questioned across the Member States, 33 per cent openly described themselves as 'quite racist' or 'very racist'. No comparable data have been collected since. At the closing conference on the 1997 European Year Against Racism, then Commission President Jacques Santer said that the poll revealed a 'worrying and unacceptable banalisation of the expression of racist sentiments'

facilitates European integration has in fact elevated conventional lifestyles and legitimized heterosexism. Oddly, such bias is particularly evident in programmes undertaken to diminish sexual equality where emphasis has shifted from discussions of 'women's double burden' to gender neutral guidance on 'reconciling family and working life'. Interest tilts exclusively to the preservation and promotion of heterosexual family units, rhetorical acknowledgements of 'non-traditional households' notwithstanding. Financed by the Commission, programmes offer 'practical and attractive training materials for groups discussing gender roles within the family', round-tables facilitate support to self-employed spouses and (heterosexual) men are encouraged to take paternity leave (Commission, 1999, p. 21).

This article addresses the paradoxical heterosexism of EU policy through three main analytic strategies. One principally involves disentangling the threads of discrimination based on gender from those based on sexuality. Sorting through the combination of sexism and heterosexism in recent Member State and Community law reveals one dimension of the paradox. A second strategy problematizes marriage as the primary legitimating link between EU nationals and their third-country spouses. Finally, matrimony highlights three forms of discrimination: the disadvantages women face under conventional notions of family and citizenship, the disadvantages cohabiting couples face in a system that privileges state-sanctioned unions, and the specific discrimination against same-sex couples to whom the protections and privileges of marriage have not been available. An analysis that reckons fully with all three dimensions of the matrimonial bias in Member State and Community law leads inexorably to the conclusion that anti-discrimination strategies must radically question the presumption that relationships (whether spousal, cohabitational, sexual or familial) provide justifiable criteria for citizenship and the privileges associated with it. To date, even the most recent and ambitious efforts undertaken to mitigate discrimination do not do this.

II. Obstacles to Nationality and Citizenship

The subtleties of sexualized discrimination are revealed, in part, through a discerning view of the ways in which nationality is itself constituted and maintained. 'Those aspiring to membership of the state must be or become members of the nation', according to Rogers Brubaker. Brubaker continues: 'If not (presumptively) acquired through birth and upbringing, such nation-membership must be earned through assimilation' (1998, p. 133). 'Assimila-

(Commission, 1998, p. 5). The success of Haider's far right Freedom Party in Austria's national election is one of the most recent examples of this troubling situation.

tion' may be achieved through prolonged residence. Thus, for example, 'Any child born in France to foreign parents acquires French nationality when he is 18 if, at this date, he is residing in France and if he has habitually done so for 5 years since the age of 11' (Loi 98-170, 16 March 1998).[2]

Though thoughtful analysis has been extended to the determination of national identity through birth, descent, and/or residence (Brubaker, 1998; Kofman and Sales, 1992; Soysal, 1994; Yuval-Davis, 1997), considerably less attention has been given to the ongoing (heterosexist) assumptions and social structures that influence (sexual) reproduction. Yet, throughout the EU the status of parenthood (e.g. *Kerkhoven* v. *The Netherlands*), like that of spouse (e.g. *Netherlands* v. *Reed*) is predominantly, if not exclusively, heterosexual.[3] With the limited exception of Denmark since July 1999 (Jenson, 1999), all Member States currently refuse adoption to same-sex *couples*. In England, gay and lesbian partners are challenging policy that permits them to adopt children but not *qua* couple (Black, 2000). And while the Netherlands may soon permit same-sex couples to adopt, there is a stipulation that they may do so only if the child has 'nothing to expect' from the original parent(s) (Waaldijk, 1999). In a Europe where 'artificial' insemination by donors for lesbians is expressly forbidden (in, e.g., Austria, France, Sweden and Denmark) and same-sex partners are prohibited from adoption, analysing the pervasive consequences of heterosexism is not an exercise in abstraction but perhaps a step towards social change.

Current restrictions governing adoption and insemination throughout the European Union support the long-held patriarchal 'principle of legitimacy' whereby 'no child should be brought into the world without a man – and one man at that – assuming the role of sociological father' (Malinowski, 1962, p. 63). To date, no EU provision forcefully prohibits this standard and other manifestations of heterosexist discrimination. My point is that the heterosexual dimension of national maintenance cannot be underestimated. Serious social consequences are evident in comparative rates of suicide that indicate

[2] This is the author's translation. The original French text can be found at «http://www.legifrance.gouv.fr/html/frame_codes_lois_reglt.htm»

[3] In *Kerkhoven*, a lesbian couple claimed they and their son had been discriminated against on the basis of 'his birth and status in comparison with legitimate children' (19.05.92, No. 15666/89, unpublished case cited in Wintemute, 1995, p. 123). The Commission responded that 'as regards parental authority over a child, a homosexual couple cannot be equated to a man and a woman living together' (19.05.92, No. 15666/89, unpublished case cited in Wintemute, 1995, p. 123). In Case 59/85 *Netherlands v. Reed* [17.4.86, ECR 1283], an unmarried heterosexual British couple moved to the Netherlands where the man had obtained a temporary post and his companion, Ms Reed, was unable to find employment. When Reed applied for a residence permit to stay with her partner, she was rejected. In an effort to stay, she sought to have her cohabiting relationship of five years recognized as 'spousal'. The Court responded by refusing to extend the term 'spouse' (in Regulation 1612/68/EEC) to unmarried cohabitants. Tamara Hervey writes: 'Rejection of a dynamic interpretation, reflecting social diversity in the member states, has the result of excluding all but those families which conform to the dominant norm' (1995a, p. 105).

that the risk among young gays and lesbians is much higher than that for heterosexual youth (van der Veen and Dercksen, 1993, p. 114, n. 140). While several scholars have discussed the willingness of citizens to die for their state (e.g. Walzer, 1970) fewer appear to mourn those whose alienation from the state may be manifest in suicide.

Political inclusion has typically entailed a cultural assimilation premised in heterosexuality. Marriage is, thus, the principal route of legal entry into the Union for heterosexual third-country immigrants (Lutz, 1997, p. 103; Staring, 1998). This is particularly interesting when one considers that marriage rates in all Member States declined by almost one-third between 1960 and 1995 (*Eurostat,* 1996).

Without denying the vast differences between states concerning access to citizenship and nationality (Brubaker, 1989), Member States remain strikingly similar in the special provisions they maintain for the foreign spouses of their nationals. Through matrimony, foreign spouses are typically entitled to an array of privileges including, but not limited to, rights of residence, the possibility of acquiring their partner's nationality, shared child custody and the preferential status extended to spouses and/or family for purposes of free movement.

Endeavours to extend similar entitlements (e.g. legal partnerships) to Member State homosexuals and their partners have sometimes met with additional affirmations of matrimony's heterosexual character. For example, in 1993, Germany's Constitutional Court ruled that the right to marry (and the ensuing socio-economic benefits) is, without exception, a heterosexual prerogative. Although the exclusively heterosexual character of matrimony has been challenged on a piecemeal basis (*Agence France Presse*, 1993), the overarching principle remains the relevant precedent within Germany and throughout the EU. At the level of the EU itself, moreover, 'spousal' relationships are legally recognizable only through marriage (*Netherlands* v. *Reed*) which, to date, remains exclusively heterosexual. However, the Netherlands is soon expected to pose an exception.

Precluded from lawful matrimony to one another within their Member States, gay and lesbian EU nationals are faced with legal obstacles that undermine their ability to establish intimate, cohabiting relationships (to say nothing of extended families) with third-country nationals. Their heterosexual counterparts do not face these additional obstacles. For example, marital privileges (e.g. maintaining legal residency for third-country partners) provide a buffer against pressures from which lesbian and gay EU nationals are unprotected. Thus, lesbians and gay men not only lose the social support offered their married counterparts; they also face the destructive pressures from which matrimony shields heterosexuals. The relationship double standard in Union policy renders lesbian and gay EU nationals second-class citizens.

III. Obstacles to Free Movement

European integration has been accomplished, in part, through the mutual recognition of privileges accorded exclusively to heterosexual EU nationals, their spouses and families. The 1968 Regulation (1612/68) on freedom of movement provides workers of EU nationality the right of family reunion without which, it has been understood, workers would find the option of movement onerous. Yet, in spite of this regulation, only 1.5 per cent of 370 million EU nationals avail themselves of this right (High Level Panel, 1997, p. 6). The preamble to that regulation states:

> Whereas the right of freedom of movement, in order that it may be exercised, by objective standards, in freedom of dignity, requires that equality of treatment shall be ensured in fact and in law in respect of all matters relating to the actual pursuit of activities as employed persons and to the eligibility of housing, also that obstacles to the mobility of workers shall be eliminated, in particular as regards the worker's rights to be joined by his family and the conditions for the integration of that family into the host country.

Intra-European workers are thus entitled to be joined by their dependent relatives, descendants (under 21) and spouses, irrespective of their nationality.

Though the Union has refused to regard cohabitants (including those who are heterosexual) as 'spouses' deserving of these rights of integration (*Netherlands* v. *Reed*), it has yet to provide an exact definition of those additional relations that constitute 'the family'. Indeed, settling on a definition would be difficult as the operationalization of the concept varies considerably across the Member States (Hantrais, 1999).

Nonetheless, numerous policies, secondary legislation and European Court of Justice (hereafter the Court) rulings have privileged conventional conceptions of family premised on blood and marriage (Hervey, 1995a). In cases where same-sex partners of European Union nationals were denied the right to immigrate and live with their lovers as 'family', the Court refused them redress. In *X. & Y.* v. *UK*,[4] it offered the explanation that while homosexual partners may be entitled to respect for their privacy, their relationships are incomparable to heterosexual partnerships and thus fall outside the acceptable scope of 'family life'. Moreover, the Commission concluded that because lesbian and gay couples are comparable only to one another, and both are rejected as 'family', sex discrimination was not at issue (Wintemute, 1995, p.

[4] (No. 9369/81) [03.05.83, 5 EHRR 601 at 602].

122), a position that persists (e.g. in the Court's ruling in *Grant* v. *South-West Trains*[5]). The Commission's ability to detect a 'modern evolution of attitudes towards homosexuality' (in Wintemute, 1995, p.110) did not temper its conservative inclinations nor did it allow it to observe a similar shift in attitudes regarding 'family'. Years later, in 1996, when the Commission established a High Level Panel on the Free Movement of Persons, it was challenged to alter its anachronistic perceptions and policies.

The High Level Panel declared that 'the "family group" is undergoing rapid change' in ways still formally unrecognized by the EU (1997, p. 42). In view of these changes, the High Level Panel 'recommends, on the basis of the case-law of the European Court, that if a Member State grants rights to its own unmarried nationals living together, it must grant the same rights to nationals of other Member States...' (1997, p. 4). This recommendation, though seemingly progressive, is unlikely to mitigate heterosexism. First, as will be noted below in our discussion of *Grant*, current case law provides little foundation for the ambitious claims of gay and lesbian activists seeking legal recognition for their partnerships and/or families. Second, the Panel's position provides no protection to those EU nationals moving from Member States with cohabitation rights to those that have none. Legislative efforts to militate against the adoption of lowering 'equal treatment' standards are unlikely to assuage concern because they are restricted to employment and occupation.[6] Third, the report is ambiguous about how best to resolve such disparities and whether they are even susceptible to Community action. It acknowledges that obstacles to free movement result from the 'disparity of national legislation' in matters relating to 'personal and family status' (1997, p. 10). However, the report calls for respect of the very different personal and family practices that it acknowledges could be 'denounced as discriminatory by certain people' and concludes that the solution to such 'societal problems' rests 'exclusively, or at least primarily' with the Member States (1997, p. 10). In sum, the Panel recognizes the indirect obstacles to free movement that result from restrictions on entry and residence for 'certain persons' but proffers no suggestions that would specifically appear to provide redress (for gays and lesbians).

The occasional formal recognition of same-sex couples within Member States notwithstanding, gay and lesbian partners are barred from the marital privileges that facilitate freedom of movement. Because their relationships have not been recognized by the Community as falling within the accepted parameters of legal relationships (i.e. 'relative', 'family' or 'spouse'), gay and lesbian European Union nationals have limited access to migration and other

[5] Hereafter *Grant*. Case C-249/96, *Grant* v. *South-West Trains Ltd* [17.2.98], found at «http://www.cura.eu». This case will be discussed in greater detail below.
[6] See Art. 7 in *COM* (99) 565 final, *Proposal for a Council Directive Establishing a General Framework for Equal Treatment in Employment and Occupation*, 25.11.1999.

citizenship rights afforded their heterosexual counterparts throughout much of Europe (Stychin, 1998; Tanca, 1993, p. 283). Moreover, as the case of Sweden will make clear, this difficult condition persists for even those nationals from Member States that have extended some legal recognition to homosexual partners.

Same-sex partners from Sweden moving to other Member States (with the exception of Denmark) have, for example, found that they suddenly had the status of strangers to each other. In France, 'the government, which allows Swedish heterosexuals to register their partnership in their embassy in Paris, banned same-sex partners from doing so despite the legality of the move on Swedish soil' (International Lesbian and Gay Association, 1996, p. 2). In addition, the Council's General Secretariat denied a household allowance to a Swedish employee, Sven Englund, whose same-sex marriage it refused to recognize. And, in *D.* v. *Council,*[7] Europe's Court of First Instance endorsed the Council's defiance, reasoning that the regulations governing EU civil servants refer exclusively to civil marriage in the conventional sense of the term. The Council is not, therefore, obliged to extend a household allowance to the same-sex (Swedish) male couple. Allowances are an exclusive privilege for heterosexual spouses. The Swedish government is appealing against this decision on the grounds that (its) national law (and not Community law) stipulates the notion of marriage and recognizes Englund's relationship. As suggested earlier, the High Panel's proposal that Member States that grant rights to their own unmarried, cohabiting nationals must extend the same rights to nationals of other Member States fails to provide remedy in this and similar instances. It is now for the Court, as the final arbiter of European Union law, to resolve this matter. Those who have previously appeared before it, such as Cherie Booth (Counsel for Lisa Grant) and Judge Michael Elmer (Advocate General in *Grant*), are doubtful that the Court can be persuaded to reverse its course in the near future.[8] Still, whatever the eventual outcome, the Council's history on household benefits may signal its reluctance to mitigate discrimination against gays and lesbians more generally. This possibility is especially worrisome given the Council's potential prominence in alleviating discrimination as defined in the Amsterdam Treaty (Duff, 1997).

The right to free movement carries with it the stated desire to abolish obstacles to the exercise of that benefit. It remains uncertain whether the continued exclusion of gays and lesbians from the rubric of 'family' constitutes an impediment sufficiently discriminatory to warrant Union intervention. Alternatively stated, the conditions that hinder the exercise of gay and lesbian

[7] Case T-264/97, *D.* v. *Council*, [28.01.99], found at «http://www.cura.eu».

[8] Both Booth and Elmer shared their views at a King's College conference entitled 'Legal Recognition of Same-Sex Partnerships: A Conference on National, European and International Law' (3 July 1999). The Court is arguably Europe's 'least accountable institution' (Caldeira and Gibson, 1995).

migration often result from (indirect) heterosexist discrimination that is, as yet, unrecognizable in state or Community law as constituting harm to gay men and lesbians specifically and the larger Community as a whole.

IV. Obstacles to Equal Treatment

According to Community law, discrimination entails a difference in treatment for similarly situated persons under conditions where differentiation is unjustifiable. In *Ruckdeschel*, for example, the Court found that 'similar situations shall not be treated differently unless differentiation is objectively justified'.[9] The project of European equality requires comparison. Unfortunately for gays and lesbians, the Court has been adamant in its refusal to regard same-sex relationships as comparable to intimate heterosexual relationships (Wintemute, 1995, Ch. 5). Because they are not 'similarly situated', it cannot be 'discrimination' when gay men and lesbian EU nationals are penalized for not conforming to norms of heterosexual cohabitation and intimacy. This principle is explicit in *Grant.*

In *Grant*, a British lesbian employee (Lisa Grant) objected to her company's denial of travel benefits to her British same-sex partner while providing the same concessions for opposite sex partners regardless of marital status. Invoking Art. 141 (then Art. 119), Grant insisted that the company's refusal of benefits constituted sex discrimination. The Court had previously recognized concessions as falling within the definition of pay (*Garland* v. *British Rail Engineering*[10]) and a colleague of Grant had previously enjoyed his travel concession (worth approximately £1,000 per year) for his unmarried woman partner. The Court, through its own calculations of comparison, rebuffed Grant's claim and reasoned: 'travel concessions are refused to a male worker if he is living with a person of the same sex, just as they are refused to a female worker living with a person of the same sex' (para. 27).

The Court's comparison of a lesbian with a hypothetical gay man is reminiscent of the Court's conduct over a decade earlier in *X. & Y.* v. *UK.* At that time, when deciding a complaint of discrimination brought by a gay male couple, the Court invoked an imagined lesbian couple. In both, the Court established that because lesbians and gay men can be equally ill treated, their condition does not trigger a judgment of 'discrimination' based on sex, a ruling that conceals the favoured treatment extended to heterosexuals. This sleight of hand substitutes spurious gender equivalence for a serious consideration of the unfairness of heterosexual privilege. In the most recent case, a more compel-

[9] Case 117/76, *Ruckdeschel & Co.* v. *Hauptzollamt Itzoe* [19.10.77, ECR 1753].
[10] Case 12/81, *Garland* v. *British Rail Engineering* [09.02.82, ECR 359].

ling comparison could have been made between Lisa Grant and her (heterosexual) male colleague whose unmarried female partner received travel concessions denied Grant's lover. Grant's lawyers argued that 'the mere fact that the male worker who previously occupied her post had obtained travel concessions for his female partner, without being married to her, is enough to identify direct discrimination based on sex' (paras. 16–17).

The Court's imposition of an imaginary gay comparandus in *Grant* reaffirmed its inaction and concretized its position that 'stable relationships between two persons of the same sex are not to be regarded as equivalent to marriages or stable relationships outside marriage between two persons of the opposite sex' (para. 35). As Mark Bell observed, 'it is undoubtedly this aspect of the judgment which is the most damaging to those supporting equal rights irrespective of sexual orientation' (1999, pp. 71–2). A summary and analysis of this trend follow.

The Court's suggestion that the partners of gays and lesbians do not deserve equal treatment and respect is as disappointing as its emphasis on 'stability' is bewildering. Scholars have observed that even marriages that are 'for all practical purposes dead and buried, can still be the basis for a dependent residence right of the spouse of the worker' (D'Oliveira, 1993, p. 300). For the Community, the quality of any relationship has long been unimportant; its legality is what has mattered (e.g. *Diatta*).[11] Moreover, Bell rightly notes that the Court chose to ignore the increasing trend among a number of its Member States to extend legal recognition to same-sex relationships (1999, p. 72). Still, as Robert Wintemute sagely cautions, one must not rush to an uncritical embrace of 'European consensus' analysis that emphasizes the importance of trends. He observes that 'it seems to amount to protection only to those human rights that have been endorsed by a substantial majority of majorities'. He concludes, 'thus, there is no protection for a "European minority" against a "European majority" that rejects recognition of a right … ' (1995, pp. 138–9).

At the time of *Grant*, seven of 15 Member States had moved to blunt discrimination against gays and lesbians through the adoption of policies that extend official recognition of and privileges to same-sex relationships. While such steps may have invalidated some aspects of heterosexism by providing a measure of relief to certain same-sex couples, these reforms can still prove

[11] Case 267/83 *Diatta* v. *Land Berlin* [13.02.85, ECR 567]. This case involved a Member State national separated, though not formally divorced, from his third-country wife. The Court ruled that the woman was, despite the collapse of the relationship, still entitled to the protections of Community law *until* the marriage was formally annulled. The ruling indirectly grants the EU national husband control over expulsion of his third-country wife. Once divorced, she ceases to be a member of the family for purposes of Community law (Hervey, 1995a, p. 106). This issue was addressed by the High Level Panel which suggested that Community provisions 'should be amended so as to recognize a right of residence for the divorced spouse who is a third-country national' (1997, pp. 60–1).

remarkably disappointing with regard to the practicalities of (im)migration. For example, in 1999 France recognized homosexual unions by entitling same-sex couples to some of the benefits enjoyed by married couples in the areas of income tax, housing and social welfare. However, such legal recognition stopped short of granting immigration rights to the foreign partners of French gays and lesbians, a position that prompted some activists to regard such unions as 'fake' (Daley, 2000). By contrast, since 1997, foreign same-sex partners of British citizens could immigrate; though, for two years, they faced stringent standards of demonstrating 'commitment' (Home Office, 2000; Watson, 1997). Same-sex couples had to demonstrate that they had been living together for four years, an exceptionally difficult criterion for many long-standing couples to meet (Verkaik, 2000; Watson, 1997). Though the recent relaxation of the requirement to two years provides some relief, marriage is still exclusively an option for heterosexual cohabitants intent on relatively swift and easy access to migration. It is, however, interesting that cohabitation policy may have a discriminatory effect against heterosexual couples not wanting to marry because the right to remain as an unmarried partner of a person settled in the United Kingdom extends only to couples 'legally unable to marry' (Home Office, 2000, Section 3.1). Nonetheless, gays and lesbians are still challenged with violating residence requirements that typically forbid non-EU nationals from living in Britain for more than several months each year.

Those lesbians and gays that do obtain longer legal residence (through, e.g., special work permits) frequently discover that British law affords them no legal protection against discrimination in either housing or employment. As Sonya Andermahr explains: 'Britain is contradictory in having one of the most visible and active gay and lesbian communities in Europe, yet some of the most draconian and discriminatory legislation' (1992, p. 117; see also Cooper and Herman, 1995). Indeed, in 1988, Section 28 of the Local Government Act singled out lesbian and gay lifestyles for legal disapproval. To date, local authorities are prohibited from 'intentionally promoting homosexuality'. Such conditions, among countless others, clearly suggest that heterosexist discrimination remains legally sanctioned (Tatchell, 1992; Waaldijk and Clapham, 1993) – even within national contexts that appear to be moving in a direction that would seemingly subvert it.

As the British and French examples amply demonstrate, the state's recognition of same-sex partnerships is no guarantee of equality before the law. The Netherlands is an additional case in point. Up until January 2001, when the Dutch will legalize gay and lesbian marriages, Dutch lesbians and gay men could register their relationships with other Dutch nationals, but the state extended neither joint pension benefits nor equal inheritance taxes to these couples (Schuyf and Krouwel, 1999, p. 168). Moreover, like France, the Netherlands refused same-sex foreign partners access to immigration. The government attributed its refusal to the fact that same-sex partnerships and marriages lack legal standing within most other Member States (Waaldijk, 1998, p. 10). While the government's position may have been politically objectionable (and even suggested a race to the bottom), it was an empirically valid contention. The Dutch now claim they will defend their unique position.

Policies pertaining to the recognition of and benefits for same-sex partners vary between Member States. Europe's reluctance to intervene favourably generates significant concern among some elements within Europe's diverse lesbian and gay communities (see Adam *et al.,* 1999). Still others find that issues relating more directly to class override their concerns with relationship status. Reflecting on Ireland, Leo Flynn notes that the country's Gay and Lesbian Network (GLEN) focuses on poverty and health-related issues. Prioritizing poverty and health concerns has meant that 'a focus on partnership laws or legal recognition of partners has not been a significant item on the agenda to date' (1999, p. 4). In addition, the political aspirations of lesbians and gay men appear to differ. Writing from Germany, Judith Rauhofer observes a definitive split between gays and lesbians concerning 'registered partnerships' (1998). While it seems that many German gay men favour codification of same-sex relationships, Rauhofer suggests that lesbians remain 'too critical of the institution of "marriage" to actually claim it for themselves' (1998, pp. 73–4, 79). Recent statistics from within those Member States that have legalized registered partnerships would appear to substantiate her claim. In all such states, more men than women have registered their relationships (Waaldijk, 1999).

For most European social movements, the successful assertion of claims at the Union level can obviate the need for local campaigns within all 15 Member States just as losing may obliterate any local victories that movements may have already accrued. However, the special difficulty for gay and lesbian movements is that their claims for justice often challenge policy areas where states maintain sovereignty and the EU refuses to intervene (e.g. marital policies). As Virginia Harrison has pointed out, 'Community case law indicates that the Court will avoid making far-reaching decisions which challenge important institutions such as marriage and the family' (1996, p. 280 n. 58). In consequence, lesbian and gay activists are forced repeatedly to assert claims within all Member States while knowing that progressive policy gains within any one state rarely transfer to other national contexts, a condition amply demonstrated up until now by migrating Swedish nationals.

V. Community Remedy for Discrimination

The politics of EU policies pertaining to heterosexism are complicated (Stychin, 2000). As recently as 1990, the Community denied it had any competence to adjudicate claims on behalf of gays and lesbians. The Commission asserted, 'the Community has no powers to intervene in possible cases of discrimination practised by Member States against sexual minorities'. Indeed, it observed redress was best offered elsewhere: 'the fundamental rights of sexual minorities are protected by other international instruments' (Clapham and Weiler, 1993, p. 28), a curious claim for a Community that has typically prided itself on its own higher standards of human rights. The Community missed an immense opportunity to demonstrate its affirmation of human rights. Instead, its efforts may be characterized as sluggish and inconsistent.

In January 1997, only 18 months after adopting the Roth Report affirming gay and lesbian rights, the European Parliament's Committee on Legal Affairs refused to adopt the demand of equal treatment for lesbian and gay EU civil servants. This action resulted in the denial of benefits to same-sex couples that are currently enjoyed by married couples where the Commission employs only one partner. Such benefits include, but are not restricted to, bereavement leave, pensions and joint health insurance. Exclusion from such benefits can cause significant financial hardship, particularly for lesbians who, as women workers in Europe, are likely to earn 20 per cent less than their male counterparts (International Lesbian and Gay Association, 1998, p. 18). Marion Oprel, co-president of EGALITE, an advocacy group for lesbian and gay Eurocrats, said that 'homophobia has once again reared its ugly head and in an institution we had believed to be free of it' (EGALITE Press Release, 28 January 1997, p. 1).

As gay and lesbian movements mobilized within and across Member States, they precipitated an increased awareness and sensitivity to heterosexism that the institutions of Europe could no longer ignore. Thus, the European Parliament was persuaded to alter its course only a month after it had disappointed EGALITE. And, within months following tortuous negotiation over whether and how to prohibit discrimination, including that directed against gay and lesbian EU citizens, the Member States adopted the Amsterdam Treaty. It defines discrimination as bigotry based on disability, sex, age and 'sexual orientation'. The text, Art. 13, reads:

> Without prejudice to the other provisions of this Treaty and within the limits of powers conferred by it upon the Community, the Council, acting unanimously on a proposal from the Commission and after consulting the European Parliament may take appropriate action to combat discrimination based on sex, racial or ethnic origin, religion or belief, disability, age or sexual orientation.

The Treaty's distinction between discrimination premised in sex and that based on sexual orientation could be read two ways. It can be read as an effort to extend official recognition to the distinct injustice(s) of heterosexism, a positive step toward fulfilling the agendas of gay and lesbian activists. On the other hand, the language of 'sex' and 'sexual orientation' may be read as redundant or worse – as a means of differentiating discrimination against gays and lesbians from sex discrimination. The latter interpretation is particularly disturbing because, as Harrison explains: 'discrimination against a person for having a partner of the same sex is discrimination on the ground of gender' (1996, p. 275) and could, thus, be prohibited under existing equality law (e.g. Art. 141). That is, as under the logic of *Grant* and *X. & Y.* v. *UK*, lesbians and gay men are 'equally' excluded from the privileges extended to those conforming to normative heterosexual gender expectations to the extent to which they have same-sex partners. While the language of sexual orientation may remedy this discrimination, as Jacqueline Stevens observes, 'the exclusion of homosexual marriage from kinship possibilities renders marriage an institution that reproduces "heterosexuality" but not necessarily "gender".' After all, 'the state does not determine the content of the female "wife's" and male "husband's" roles' (1999, pp. 221–2). Moreover, this issue is separate from the specific discrimination against women as women that is also experienced by lesbians. Indeed, differentiating between sex discrimination and prejudice premised on 'sexual orientation' is particularly difficult for lesbians as these oppressions are often profoundly interconnected. Nonetheless, it is precisely this distinction between 'sex discrimination' and 'sexual orientation discrimination' that is likely to endure.[12]

The Treaty's requirement that the Council must reach a unanimous vote on a Commission proposal before it 'may take appropriate action' to blunt discrimination tempers the reach of the clause, regardless of readings given to 'sexual orientation'. By declining to assert that the Council 'shall' endeavour to take action, concern grew that passivity would prevail in the presence of prejudice. In February 2000, the Commission was presented with a Declaration from the European Network Against Racism at an official conference that the Commission had organized to combat racism at the Union level. The signatories called for an Intergovernmental Conference (IGC) decision that would enable qualified voting within the Council and a codecision procedure with the Parliament on measures proposed under Art. 13.

[12] Asked whether she saw herself working with others to combat the differing forms of discrimination covered in Art. 13, Parliament's new Equality Division chief, Elvy Svennerstål, insisted that sex discrimination is 'totally different' and that it 'has to be treated separately'. Though it is impossible to know if this assertion results from sensitivity to the gender-specificity of discrimination or from a desire to avoid confronting heterosexism, lesbians are nonetheless vulnerable (Svennerstål, interview with author, 28 July 1999, European Parliament).

Despite the efforts taken to strengthen the reach of Art. 13 in ways that would diminish discrimination, several factors make it unlikely that the Community will change course, particularly on issues involving discrimination against gay men and lesbians. The Community has been reluctant to provide swift redress for heterosexist discrimination. The Parliament has been ambivalent regarding same-sex benefits. *Grant* set a new disappointing precedent, and the decision of the Court of First Instance in *D* v. *Council* (Case T-264/97) affirmed heterosexual privilege. Indeed, until recently, the Council has had little incentive to change matters given that the Treaty itself lacks sufficient clarity, precision and strength to have effect (Guild, 1999, p. 4, n. 13).

With the above-noted obstacles in mind, the Commission itself recognized the need to strengthen the Amsterdam Treaty and therefore proposed the adoption of legislation and a Community Action Programme to Combat Discrimination (2001–2006).[13] The proposed directive to implement Art. 13 focuses on establishing a general framework to promote equal treatment at work. In claiming to combat inequities associated with work, the EU is able to evade action against sexual orientation inequality elsewhere (e.g. 'family' and 'spousal' rights). Moreover, having insisted that the 'Community is already active in the fight against discrimination', the Commission reasons that 'responsibility for implementing the fight against discrimination rests principally with the Member States'.[14] These members are expected to adopt the laws, regulations and administrative procedures necessary to comply with the new law by 31 December 2002.

VI. Conclusion

Considering the small inroads and a multitude of shortcomings of Community-oriented efforts, gay and lesbian activists within some states have demonstrated greater interest in pursuing legal reform through national legislatures than through EU institutions (Bell, 1999, p. 80). For example, though British activists turned to Europe prior to Amsterdam in the hope that Europe's political actors were more supportive of and receptive to their claims (Stychin, 1998, p. 136), in the Treaty's aftermath their prior domestic orientation was reinforced. Britain's prominent gay and lesbian lobby, Stonewall, reasoned that Community 'legislation can be passed only if all the Member States agree

[13] *COM* (99) 565 final, *Proposal for a Council Directive Establishing a General Framework for Equal Treatment in Employment and Occupation*, 25.11.1999; *COM* (99) 567 final, *Proposal for a Council Decision Establishing a Community Action Programme to Combat Discrimination 2001-2006*, 25.11.1999, p. 3.

[14] *COM* (99) 567 final, p. 3.

to it unanimously. This is so unlikely to happen that we might as well forget it. What is needed is for the British parliament to legislate' (in Bell, 1999, p. 82).

Unfortunately, however, the legal recognition of same-sex partnerships garnered through numerous national legislatures (including Britain) has failed to facilitate full citizenship rights, including freedom of movement (as promised by Regulation 1612/68). Indeed, one may wonder whether the 'commitment' such legal partnerships inspire inhibits the search for superior solutions to the concrete problems their recognition was designed to eliminate. For example, rather than seeking the extension of health care to the sexual partners of (and/or those 'related' to) insured employees, the ethically ambitious project would entail mobilization for guaranteed access to quality health care for all, regardless of their cohabiting status (Rieder, 1992). The legal theorist Ruthann Robson warns that the promotion of domestic partnerships 'tacitly promises lesbians protection if we conform our relations to traditional family values and threatens persecution if we do not' (1994, p. 989).

The state's recognition of same-sex relationships entails regulation, to say nothing of the ominous potential of its agencies in later discriminating against the very couples that trusted the authorities enough to register in the first instance. The history and destructive capacity of states should not be ignored (Arendt, 1979; Rubenstein, 1975). If states were nearly as benevolent as such faith implies, such registered recognition would be unnecessary. Those seeking the eradication of heterosexism focus less on ending the particularized privileges of (heterosexual) couples than on embracing the illusion of stable domesticity in an effort to secure equivalent advantages. Note that Lisa Grant's objection was not that benefits were given to the spouses and lovers of her heterosexual co-workers. Rather, she demanded that she and her lesbian partner be granted the same privileges. Grant's position was not unusual. In their efforts to end discrimination, lesbian and gay movements throughout Europe have recently called for the 'recognition of lesbian and gay relationships and families as *equally valid to heterosexual relationships and families* within laws and social policies pertaining to the family, parenting, the care of children, adoption and fostering, and immigration' (International Lesbian and Gay Association, 1998, p. 26, my emphasis). In March 2000, the European Parliament responded with a resolution that calls upon Member States (as well as accession countries) to recognize registered same-sex partnerships if they have not already done so (International Lesbian and Gay Association, 2000).

Feminist theorists have long decried the exclusive and oppressive characteristics of marriage (e.g. Barrett and McIntosh, 1982; Hodgkinson, 1988). Marriage and marriage-like relationships are now commonly presumed to afford a venue (*vis-à-vis* nation-states and/or the Community) in which one can secure and support egalitarian goals. This approach may prove misguided, especially as it ignores the potential avenue of redress that sexual discrimination law could afford. A greater emphasis on sexual equality may be premised on a principle of equal treatment that predates Amsterdam and therefore does not require a condition of unanimity to take effect.

The continued exclusion of gays and lesbians from the rubric of 'family' may best be countered not by begging for inclusion but, instead, through resort to truly equal treatment. That is, movements could insist that 'equal treatment' means that there shall be no discrimination (directly or indirectly) whatsoever on the grounds of marital or family status. In pursuing this more radical 'equal treatment' position, lesbians and gay men could free themselves from the burden of demonstrating the equivalence and/or merit of their (intimate) relationships. In seeking justice, for example, Sven Englund (and his Swedish legal counsel) could pursue an innovative challenge to the Council's heterosexism by insisting that marital benefits (and by extension, marital comparators) are inherently prejudicial. Concomitantly, those interested in social change must not relinquish the demand to know the basis by which (any) couples constitute a preferential class, deserving of socio-economic benefits and rights denied others. As Stevens notes, the most fundamental structures of the modern state rest on the rules regulating marriage and immigration and these are 'what make possible the power relations associated with nationality, race, and family roles' (1999, p. xv). She thus concludes that until this is understood, 'it is clear that piecemeal approaches to eradicating certain inequalities will not work' (1999, p. xv).

Bartering over privileges rather than demanding their eradication has proved strategically ineffective. It represents a lapse of political judgement and a lack of ambition. 'Gay and lesbian politics that focus on merely sharing rights and privileges that come out of the heterocentric system deny … the opportunity to make a difference' (Rauhofer, 1998, p. 74). In the context of European integration, heterosexism will be more effectively undermined through its repudiation rather than through the extension of its privileges.

Correspondence:
R. Amy Elman
Department of Political Science
Center for Western European Studies
Kalamazoo College
Kalamazoo, MI 49006, USA
email: elman@kzoo.edu

References

Adam, B. D., Duyvendik, J. W. and Krouwel, A. (eds) (1999) *The Global Emergence of Gay and Lesbian Politics: National Imprints of a Worldwide Movement* (Philadelphia: Temple University Press).

Agence France Presse. (1993) 'Gay Couples Can't Marry in Germany, Court Rules'. 13 October. «http://lexis-nexis.com/universe» accessed 16 July 1998, p. 1.

Andermahr, S. (1992) 'Subjects or Citizens? Lesbians in the New Europe'. In Ward, A., Gregory, J. and Yuval-Davis, N. (eds) *Women and Citizenship in Europe* (Exeter: Trentham Books/EFSF), pp. 111–22.

Arendt, H. (1979) *The Origins of Totalitarianism* (New York: Harvest/HBJ Books).

Barrett, M. and McIntosh, M. (1992) *The Anti-social Family* (London: Verso).

Bell, M. (1999) 'Shifting Conceptions of Sexual Discrimination at the Court of Justice: from *P.* v. *S. to Grant* v. *SWT*'. *European Law Journal*, Vol. 5, No. 1, March, pp. 63–81.

Black, E. (2000) 'UK to Accept Adoption by Gay Couples'. *ILGA Euroletter 79* (April) «http: www.qrd.rdrop.com:80/qrd/orgs/ilga/euroletter/79-04.00», accessed 16 June 2000.

Brubaker, R. (1989) *Immigration and the Politics of Citizenship in Europe and North America* (Lanham, MD.: German Marshall Fund of the United States and University Press of America), pp. 131–64.

Brubaker, R. (1998) 'Immigration, Citizenship, and the Nation-State in France and Germany'. In Shafir, G. (ed.) *The Citizenship Debates: A Reader* (Minneapolis: University of Minnesota Press).

Caldeira, G. A. and Gibson, J. L. (1995) 'The Legitimacy of the Court of Justice in the European Union: Models of Institutional Support'. *American Political Science Review*. Vol. 89, No. 2, pp. 356–76.

Cesarani, D. and Fulbrook, M. (eds) (1997) *Citizenship, Nationality and Migration in Europe* (London: Routledge).

Clapham, A. and Weiler, J.H.H. (1993) 'Lesbian and Gay Men in the European Community Legal Order'. In Waaldijk, K. and Clapham, A. (eds), pp. 7–72.

Commission of the European Communities (1997) *The European Institutions in the Fight Against Racism* (Luxembourg: OOPEC).

Commission of the European Communities (1998) *1997 European Year Against Racism: Closing Conference Report* (Luxembourg: OOPEC).

Commission of the European Communities (1999) *Interim report on the implementation of the medium-term Community Action programme on equal opportunities for men and women (1996–2000)* (Luxembourg: OOPEC).

Cooper, D. and Herman, D. (1995) 'Getting the "Family Right": Legislating Heterosexuality in Britain, 1986–91'. In Herman, D. and Stychin, C. (eds) *Legal Inversions: Lesbians, Gay Men, and the Politics of Law* (Philadelphia: Temple University Press), pp. 162–79.

Daley, S. (2000) 'French Couples Take Plunge That Falls Short of Marriage'. «http://www.nytimes.com.../europe/041800france-marriage.html», accessed 18 April 2000, pp.1–4.

D'Oliveira, H. (1993) 'Lesbians and Gays and the Freedom of Movement of Persons'. In Waaldijk, K. and Clapham, A. (eds), pp. 289–316.

Duff, A. (1997) *The Treaty of Amsterdam: Text and Commentary* (London: Federal Trust).

EGALITE Press Release (1997) 'MEPs Withhold Equal Treatment For Gays And Lesbians'. «http://qrd.rdrop.com/qrd/world/eur ...p. rejects. lindholm.report», accessed 28 January 1997, pp. 1–3.

Eurostat (1996) *Social Portrait of Europe* (Luxembourg: OOPEC).

Flynn, L. (1999) 'Can the Transition to Individual Protection be Extended to Recognition of Relationships?: Same-Sex Couples and the Irish Experience of Sexual Orientation Law Reform'. Paper presented at the 'Legal Recognition of Same-Sex Partnerships: A Conference on National, European and International Law' (London: King's College).

Guild, E. (1997) 'The Legal Framework of Citizenship of the European Union'. In Cesarani, D. and Fulbrook, M. (eds) *Citizenship, Nationality and Migration in Europe* (London: Routledge), pp. 30–54.

Guild, E. (1999) 'Free Movement and Same-Sex Relationships: Existing Law and Article 13EC'. Paper presented at the 'Legal Recognition of Same-Sex Partnerships: A Conference on National, European and International Law' (London: King's College).

Hantrais, L. (1999) 'What is a Family or Family Life in the European Union?' In Guild, E. (ed.) *The Legal Framework and Social Consequences of Free Movement of Persons in the European Union* (The Hague: Kluwer Law International), pp. 19–30.

Harrison, V. (1996) 'Using EC Law to Challenge Sexual Orientation Discrimination at Work'. In Hervey, T. and O'Keeffe, D. (eds) *Sex Equality Law in the European Union* (New York: Wiley), pp. 266–80.

Hervey, T. (1995a) 'A Gendered Perspective on the Right to Family Life in European Community Law'. In Neuwahl, N. and Rosas, A. (eds) *The European Union and Human Rights* (London: Martinus Nijhoff).

Hervey, T. (1995b) 'Migrant Workers and their Families in the European Union: The Pervasive Market Ideology of Community Law'. In Shaw, J. and More, G. (eds) *New Legal Dynamics of European Union* (Oxford: Oxford University Press).

High Level Panel (1997) *Report of High Panel on Free Movement of Persons.* «http://europa.eu.int/comm/internal_market/en/people/hlp/hlphtml.htm», accessed 16 June 2000, pp. 1–63.

Hodgkinson, L. (1988) *Unholy Matrimony: The Case for Abolishing Marriage* (London: Columbus Books).

Home Office Immigration and Nationality Directorate (2000) *Immigration Directorate's Instructions* (Ch. 8, Section 7).

International Lesbian and Gay Association (1996) *ILGA Annual Report.* «http://www.casti.com/FQRD/assocs/ilga/report96.html», accessed 5 August 1996, pp.1–5.

International Lesbian and Gay Association (1998) *Equality for Lesbians and Gay Men: A Relevant Issue in the Civil and Social Dialogue* (Brussels: ILGA-Europe).

International Lesbian and Gay Association (2000) 'European Parliament Calls Again for Respect for Human Rights of Lesbians and Gay Men'. *ILGA Euroletter 78* (March) «http: www.qrd.rdrop.com:80/qrd/orgs/ilga/euroletter/78-03.00», accessed 16 June 2000.

Jenson, S. (1999) 'Adoption Rights to Danish Gay or Lesbian Couples – Partnership Law Changed'. *ILGA Euroletter 70* (May) «http: www.casti.com/FQRD/assocs/ilga/euroletter/70.html», accessed 25 May 1999.

Kofman, E. and Sales, R. (1992) 'Towards Fortress Europe?'. *Women's Studies International Forum,* Vol. 15, No. 1, pp. 29–39.

Loi no. 98-170, 16 March 1998. Articles 19-1; 21-7; 21-11. «http://www.legifrance.gouv.fr/html/frame_codes_lois_reglt.htm», accessed 16 July 1998, pp. 1–2.

Lutz, H. (1997) 'The Limits of European-ness: Immigrant Women in Fortress Europe'. *Feminist Review*, No. 57, pp. 93–111.

Malinowski, B. (1962) *Sex, Culture and Myth* (New York: Harcourt).

O'Leary, S. (1996a) *European Union Citizenship: Options for Reform* (London: Institute for Public Policy Research).

O'Leary, S. (1996b) *The Evolving Concept of Community Citizenship – From the Free Movement of Persons to Union Citizenship* (The Hague: Kluwer Law International).

Rauhofer, J. (1998) 'The Possibility of a Registered Partnership under German Law'. In Moran, L. J., Monk, D. and Beresford, S. (eds) *Legal Queeries: Lesbian, Gay and Transgender Legal Studies* (New York: Cassell), pp. 68–80.

Rieder, I. (1992) 'Lesbianism in the House of Europe'. In Ward, A., Gregory, J. and Yuval-Davis, N. (eds) *Women and Citizenship in Europe* (Exeter: Trentham Books/EFSF, pp. 107–10).

Robson, R. (1994) 'Resisting the Family: Repositioning Lesbians in Legal Theory'. *Signs: Journal of Women in Culture and Society*, Vol. 19, No. 4, pp. 975–96.

Rubenstein, R. (1975) *The Cunning of History: The Holocaust and the American Future* (New York: Harper Books).

Schuyf, J. and Krouwel, A. (1999) 'The Dutch Lesbian and Gay Movement'. In Adam, B. D., Duyvendik, J. W. and Krouwel, A. (eds), pp. 158–63.

Soysal, Y. N. (1994) *Limits of Citizenship: Migrants and Postnational Membership in Europe* (Chicago: University of Chicago Press).

Staring, R. (1998) '"Scenes from a Fake Marriage": Notes on the Flip-side of Embeddedness'. In Koser, K. and Lutz, H. (eds) *The New Migration in Europe: Social Constructions and Social Realities* (Basingstoke: Macmillan), pp. 224–41.

Stevens, J. (1999) *Reproducing the State* (Princeton: Princeton University Press).

Stychin, C. F. (1998) *A Nation by Rights: National Cultures, Sexual Identity Politics, and the Discourse of Rights* (Philadelphia: Temple University Press).

Stychin, C. F. (2000) '*Grant*-ing Rights: the Politics of Rights, Sexuality and European Union'. *Northern Ireland Legal Quarterly*, Vol. 51, No. 4, Summer, pp. 281–302.

Tanca, A. (1993) 'European Citizenship and the Rights of Lesbians and Gay Men'. In Waaldijk, K. and Clapham, A. (eds), pp. 267–88.

Tatchell, P. (1992) *Europe in the Pink: Gay & Lesbian Equality in the New Europe* (London: Gay Men's Press).

Van der Veen, E. and Dercksen, A. (1993) 'The Social Situation in Member States'. In Waaldijk, K. and Clapham, A. (eds), pp. 131–62.

Verkaik, R. (2000) 'Brazilian Lover Will Test Rights for Gay Migrants'. *Independent*, 24 April, p. 7.

Waaldijk, K. (1998) 'Dutch Government Decides Against Same-Sex Marriage – But In Favor Of Adoption By Same-Sex Couples'. *ILGA Euroletter 57* (February) «http:www.casti.com/FQRD/assocs/ilga/euroletter/57.html», accessed 4 June 1998, pp. 8–11.

Waaldijk, K. (1999) 'What Legal Recognition of Same-Sex Partnership Can Be Expected in EC Law, and When? – Lessons from Comparative Law'. Paper presented at the 'Legal Recognition of Same-Sex Partnerships: A Conference on National, European and International Law' (London: King's College).

Waaldjik, K. and Clapham, A. (1993) *Homosexuality: A European Community Issue* (London: Martinus Nijhoff).

Walzer, M. (ed.) (1970) *Obligations: Essays on Disobedience, War and Citizenship* (Cambridge, MA: Harvard University Press).

Watson, M. (1997) 'Immigration Rules'. *ILGA Euroletter 54* (October) «http: www.casti.com/FQRD/assocs/ilga/euroletter/54.html», accessed 4 June 1998, p. 4.

Wintemute, R. (1995) *Sexual Orientation and Human Rights: The United States Constitution, the European Convention, and the Canadian Charter* (Oxford: Clarendon Press).

Yuval-Davis, N. (1997) *Gender and Nation* (London: Sage).

[13]

Inequality Near and Far: Adoption as Seen from the Brazilian Favelas

Claudia Fonseca

Focusing on child circulation among the urban poor in Southern Brazil, this article considers the parallels and divergences between local practice, national legislation, and global policy involved in legal adoption. Following a brief ethnographic account of child circulation among working-class families in Porto Alegre, Brazil, the analysis focuses on *adoção à brasileira* (clandestine adoption) as one of the ways in which the Brazilian poor bypass legal bureaucratic procedures in order to adjust the State apparatus to their needs. Finally, the comparative analysis of Brazil and North America centers on the evolution of adoption law and policies. Our approach highlights the variant experiences of family and legal consciousness according to class and national identity, while at the same time considering the political inequality implied in the hierarchization of different cultural repertoires.

In a recent book on international adoption, the social worker responsible for describing the situation in Brazil underlines the superior quality of overseas adopters. Brazilian nationals, judging from the number of children returned to the court, "lack a serious attitude toward adoption." The author mentions factors such as poor financial conditions and unstable family structures that may explain this lack of seriousness, but, in her opinion, the real motive (and key to a solution?) lies in the fact that Brazilians don't pay anything for the adopted child: "In contrast, expenses for foreigners are huge, and the adoptive ties turn out to be strong and lasting" (Silva 1995:126).

These comments serve as a springboard for the subject of my article: Brazilian adoption practices, placed within a globalized context. They speak of a problem that is central to my concerns—the so-called "gap" between law and actual behavior.[1]

I would like to thank Chantal Collard and Françoise-Romaine Ouellette for their thoughtful suggestions to this article, as well as the Anthropology Department of the Université de Montréal, which provided an amicable setting for my sabbatical year. Direct all correspondence to Claudia Fonseca, PPG Antropologia Social, Universidade Federal do Rio Grande do Sul, Av. Bento Gonçalvez 9.500, Porto Alegre (91.500), RS, Brazil (e-mail: claudiaf2@uol.com.br).

1 For a critical overview of the "gap studies" of the 1970s, see Sarat & Silbey (1988).

However, inverting the question that this social worker implicitly poses ("Why can't Brazilians measure up to international norms of adoption?"), I ask how is it that Brazilian laws, often touted as being on the forefront of progressive international legislation, give so little heed to local values and social dynamics? In fact, in this article, I hope to convince readers that it is no surprise that foreign adopters conform more closely to Brazilian legal directives than do national candidates, since the laws, rather than being based on and adapted to an accurate assessment of local reality, derive from the abstract principles that dominate international debates.

The possibly reprehensible character of this fact derives from two hypotheses. First, these abstract principles are not the neutral product of consensual humanitarian interests. They are, instead, the fruit of ideological power struggles and are inevitably shaped by the hegemonic narratives that reflect, above all, First World contexts and values (Silbey 1997). Following this line of thought, the very popularity of legal adoption that seems to have recently swept the globe—from President Clinton's speech in which Americans are urged to adopt the 500,000 children in foster care[2] to the Brazilian child welfare services' listing of adoptable children on internet sites—may be considered part of a hegemonic narrative in which this particular form of child placement is presented as the "obvious" remedy for the ills of the world's children. The criticism of hegemonic narratives on adoption having been elaborated elsewhere (see, e.g., Yngvesson 2000; Selman 2000; Fonseca, forthcoming), I will dwell in this article on a second hypothesis, which is that in many countries distinct values and patterns of family organization, including non-mainstream forms of adoption, exist on a widespread basis. To illustrate, I rely on ethnographic research in Brazilian favelas, arguing that to socialize and ensure the survival of younger generations, lower-income families have traditionally resorted to the informal placement of children in different, substitute households, and that the dynamics of this "circulation of children,"[3] with its emphasis on extended family networks, have been not only ignored but also disavowed by legislators and social workers alike. Thus, I suggest, adoption laws have evolved in a way that simply does not make sense to a good many people. This supposition not only would explain the "lack of seriousness" of local adopters but also would raise doubts about another fundamental issue in the adoption process: the treatment of birth parents in

[2] I am referring to the 1997 speech President Clinton made during the signing of the Adoption and Safe Families Act.

[3] The "circulation of children" is a generic term that permits the comparative analysis of different forms of child placement found throughout the globe and at different moments in history. On this subject, the work of anthropologists such as Carroll (1970), Goody (1982), and Lallemand (1993) has provided fundamental inspiration.

the legal procedures that render their child available for adoption. Having worked with the sort of poverty-stricken families from which most adoptable children are drawn, I concentrate my aim on this latter element: the understanding and possible misconceptions members of the birth family and, in particular, birth mothers have of the legal adoption process.

My approach is not entirely original. I have drawn inspiration from the abundant literature that points out discrepancies between state law and particular community practices concerning child welfare.[4] Commenting on the tendency of Hawaiian state services to remove native children from their clan-like kinship networks to place them in non-Hawaiian (white and Japanese) families with a more mainstream way of life, Judith Modell (1997) furnishes a recent example of how state policies, geared toward middle-class family values, have at times discriminated against minority groups. Her study reveals how Hawaiians, in the name of a distinct cultural heritage,[5] seize upon the very weapons offered by the court—Western legal discourse—to protect the right to raise their children in what might seem, according to official state criteria, substandard homes. Native Americans, Canadian Inuits, and Australian aborigines are among the many groups who have likewise proved competent in appropriating the political strategies of modern government to stem the flow of children extracted from their communities, whether by missionaries or adoptive parents, to be raised and educated in another way of life (Fournier & Crey 1997; Slaughter 2000). One could no doubt include many of these examples in what Merry (1997) describes as "legal vernacularisation," a process whereby colonized minorities, in their bid for human rights, reinterpret and transform Western law according to their own legal conceptions.

In the Brazilian case I examine here, this sort of "legal vernacularisation" appears to be distinctly lacking. Not only were the birth mothers I dealt with ill-versed in their own individual rights, but also their heterogeneous racial backgrounds (African, Native American, Polish, Portuguese) provided them with no evident common identity through which to articulate their resistance. Indeed, these women were seen, and, in general, saw themselves as nothing other than "poor"—raising doubts in many people as to whether they had any "culture" at all.

Failing to consider certain forms of cultural specificity among the urban poor, state authorities may proceed untroubled with the removal of children from what they consider problematic

[4] See, e.g., the special issue of the *International Journal of Law, Family, and Policy* on the principle of a "child's best interests" (1994, vol. 8).

[5] To evoke native Hawaiian cultural heritage, Modell highlights key concepts in the local kinship system: *hanai*, a sort of adoption, based not "on genealogy but on generosity, not on biology but on belonging," and *ohana*, the clan system, with emphasis on "the coming together of people who assume responsibility for and loyalty to one another" (1997:159).

families. The consistent refusal to entertain the possibility of alternative family patterns leaves them no other option than to label many households "disorganized"—a diagnosis that can only contribute to the breakdown of existing dynamics. My proposal, to reframe the analysis in terms of local kinship values, complicates this picture. Such an approach need not imply romantic pleas for traditional purity, nor the idealization of practices such as child circulation, which, like any other social dynamic, can be fraught with conflict, internal contradictions, and, in some particular cases, may even justify energetic state intervention. Nonetheless, my approach does imply the existence of non-mainstream logics that however foreign to the hegemonic narrative make sense to certain sane and intelligent people, and—what's more—may actually work to their benefit in ways unimagined by convention-bound state authorities.[6]

By my emphasis on the specificity of family practices and values among Brazilian favela residents, I do not mean to produce the image of separate and isolated cultural spheres. On the contrary, I hope to demonstrate the interlinking processes that—from local practice to national legislation and global policy—influence family related values. This perspective, inspired in the notion of "stratified reproduction" (Colen 1995), concentrates on how different cultural repertoires interweave, clash, or complement one another according to the particular historical circumstances. The scrutiny of cultural difference, furthermore, is inseparable from considerations on the political and social inequality that cause certain sets of values to be presented as superior to others.

To achieve my aim, I first present the setting and a brief ethnographic account of child circulation among working-class families in Porto Alegre, Brazil. Having set the background, I zero in on those elements of the traditional system that most resemble legal adoption, drawing attention to *adoção à brasileira* (a sort of clandestine adoption) as a way in which the Brazilian poor bypass legal bureaucratic procedures in order to adjust the state apparatus to their needs. The active participation of birth mothers in the placement of their children is contrasted with the prevalent national policy of plenary adoption, which, by its insistence on secrecy in the adoption process, leaves biological kin completely out of the picture. Finally, I suggest that, despite enthusiastic adherence to international campaigns on children's rights, recent Brazilian policies of state intervention, rather than becoming more sensitive to local-level "alternative" family practices, demonstrate increasing indifference.

[6] For more on the political significance of cultural difference, see Yanagisako & Delaney (1995), Comaroff & Comaroff (1999), and Santos (1999).

Continuity and Change in the Brazilian Context

Porto Alegre, with its 1,500,000 inhabitants (and counting a metropolitan population double that amount), is the capital city of Rio Grande do Sul, Brazil's southernmost state. With quick access to the nearby countries of Argentina and Uruguay, the area is known for its relatively high standard of living, sporting certain social indicators (low infant mortality and high literacy, for example) closer to those of First World countries than to the Brazilian northeast.[7] At the end of the 1990s, however, even after more than a decade of relatively efficient administration by the Workers' Party, 10 to 15% of the Porto Alegre population had a per capita income of under US$40 a month.

When I began my research in Porto Alegre in 1981 conditions were even worse. Public agents—social workers, nurses, or domestic aides—in the city's working-class neighborhoods were few and far between, leaving the bulk of the urban poor to their own devices. Poor people lived in informally segregated residential areas, from which they made daily forays into middle- and upper-class neighborhoods, whether as workers or beggars; however, aside from an occasional nun doubling as a social worker, I seldom saw representatives of the state entering these zones. The particular favela I was then working in was known as "the lawless zone," since even the police were reputed to be afraid of penetrating the area. My estimate was that not more than a quarter of the adult couples with children were legally married. Most workers, being part of the informal economy, did not possess a social security number, and a great many of the older people had no identity documents, much less the legally required voter's registration card. True, in less poverty-stricken zones, there were schools (offering a maximum of four hours of daily instruction to local children) and public dispensaries, but it was a rare day when the teachers or health officers entered anyone's home. In other words, unless they committed a serious crime, the urban poor had contact with the state authorities when (and how) they chose to—which was not all that often.

It was in just such a context that I became aware of the circulation of children. In a first neighborhood of poverty-stricken squatters (rag pickers, beggars, and an occasional construction worker), approximately half of the women had placed a child, whether on a short- or long-term basis, with a substitute family or at the state orphanage. Five years later (1986), I began a second phase of research in a less-miserable working-class district inhabited by artisans, janitors, maids, bus drivers, and other lower-income employees, where better-off families had an average

[7] This fact no doubt explains in part certain discrepancies between my observations and those of Scheper-Hughes (1992).

income of about US$200 a month. Here, I encountered a surprising number of women who had at some time taken in a child to raise. A fine line divided "foster" from adoptive offspring, as many children who had embarked on a short sojourn just "stayed on" in their new home. All in all, in more than 120 households that I canvassed during my field research, I discovered nearly 100 people who, during their childhood, had transited among the households of godmothers, grandmothers, and other sorts of mothers *de criação*.[8] Of these, not one had been legally adopted.[9]

Since the 1964 coup d'état, the military regime had manifested its concern for children and youth through a state-run service, the Fundação Estadual de Bem-Estar do Menor (FEBEM), which, aside from sponsoring a series of private and philanthropic institutions, basically limited its action to the institutionalization of poor, orphaned, and refractory children. Much to my surprise, the slum-dwellers I was studying neither feared nor resented this agency. Instead, they used it to their own purposes.[10] There were an infinite number of reasons a woman might want to institutionalize a child: if, for example, she was going through a particularly bad financial period (which was often), she was without a place to live, or she remarried and her new companion refused to support the children she had had in previous unions. Parents might also use the threat of internment to keep their disobedient children in line.[11] If institutional authorities attempted to impose obstacles, alleging that the establishment was not meant to be a simple "boarding school," a woman could trump up more persuasive arguments, claiming, for example, that her child was in danger of rape by a new stepfather or a menacing neighbor (see Fonseca 1986). At any rate, the mothers I knew who had institutionalized a son or daughter generally considered the arrangement temporary and expected to bring the child home "as soon as things got better."

Women who later showed up at the orphanage, ready to resume their motherhood, sometimes after years of absence, would thus be stupefied when told that their child had been declared "abandoned" and given away in adoption. Even those who had signed a paper consenting to their child's adoption, did not seem

---

[8] The verb *criar* in Portuguese means both "to raise" and "to create." Kin ties formed by caring for one another are labeled "*de criação*." I have loosely translated the term here as "foster" relatives.

[9] According to a 1985 census taken in Brazil's major cities, 2.9% of the children under 18 were adopted, less than a third of them by legal means. Over half of these children had left their birth parents before the age of three (see Campos 1991).

[10] We should remember that in Rio Grande do Sul, the institution was minimally adequate—providing individual beds and regular meals to the interns, which was more than many children got in their homes. Furthermore, older children with no behavior problems were allowed to come home on weekends and holidays. See Blum (1998) for a similar use of state institutions by the poor in 19th-century Mexico.

[11] See Merry (1990) for examples in contemporary America of a similar use of juvenile court.

to grasp the idea that they had been permanently stripped of their motherhood and that the child had disappeared forever. From their point of view, they had left their children in the care of the institution in the same spirit they would have resorted to if they had left their children with a grandmother or neighbor. On occasion, these substitute mothers also insisted that the transfer of parental responsibilities should be permanent; but experience often proved them wrong. In the great majority of cases, the birth mother and child would eventually end up in contact, and the child would not be lost to its kin group. In the birth mother's confrontation with state authorities, the clash of different rationalities was glaringly evident.

During the 1980s, the Brazilian political scenario went through important changes. Emerging from 20 years of military dictatorship, the country witnessed with tolerance an effervescence of social movements: workers' strikes, invasions of housing projects, marches for land reform, and church-led neighborhood associations. With an increasing number of university-educated professionals, including social and community health workers, as well as a technologically more efficient state bureaucracy, there arose a demand for greater intervention in people's domestic affairs. The writing of a new constitution (completed in 1988) mobilized thousands of activists aiming at social reforms, who then turned their attentions specifically to the subject of children. Spurred on by the international attention given to the theme (events such as the 1989 United Nations Convention on the Rights of the Child) as well as the Brazilian government's desire to avoid unflattering publicity on its "street children," in 1990 the National Congress passed the Estatuto da Criança e do Adolescente, Law No. 8.069, July 13, 1990 (hereafter referred to as the 1990 Children's Code).

Touted as a document "worthy of the First World," in some respects "even more advanced than the United Nations Declaration on the Rights of the Child," the 1990 Children's Code was seen by many activists as a hallmark in the history of Brazilian children. Aside from guaranteeing to all children the right to "life, health, food, education, sports, leisure, preparation for a future profession, culture, dignity, respect, and liberty," it declared radical changes in institutional policies. Orphaned children were to be separated from juvenile offenders, allowing for each category to be placed in specialized and decentralized institutions adapted to their particular needs. No child was to be institutionalized (whether because of or despite their parents' pleas) merely for reasons of poverty. The quality of a child's home environment was to be monitored through local-level "Children's Tutelary Councils," made up of commissioners whose sole concern would be to guarantee the rights and conditions of children within their families, school, and public space.

Brazil, however, has a long history of passing "symbolic legislation" that has very little effect on its citizens' concrete behavior (Vianna 1996). In 1993 and 1994, curious as to the extent the changes in the political agenda had affected the lives of common citizens, I conducted a series of interviews with working-class families. The following accounts, used to convey ethnographic details of the circulation of children in Brazilian favelas, are drawn from this second phase of field research. Because so little time had passed since the enactment of the new Children's Code, my study did not ultimately reveal the new legislation's full impact on local populations. However, as one will see in the first example given below, it did demonstrate the presence of deep-rooted values linked to extended-family networks and a sort of "fosterage culture" that, four years after the new law, still appeared to be highly relevant to people's lives. And, as one may observe in the second example, it furnished insights into certain forms of legal consciousness linked to a baby's "clandestine" adoption. Through a birth mother's tale, one may not only come to imagine why, to certain actors, such a procedure might appear to be more attractive than proper legal adoption, one may also begin to wonder about the political factors bearing on adoption laws that have left this sort of mother so few options.

Inez's Mothers: Survival, Conflict, and Blood Ties

Inez was 38 years old when I met her. At the time, her husband was distributing newspapers while she worked as an attendant at the neighborhood day care center. As a preamble to her life story, she mentioned the odds she was up against during her early childhood: Nine of her 15 brothers and sisters had died in infancy. "My mother was very poor. She didn't get enough to eat so the babies would be born already undernourished." Inez was lucky enough to have been placed with her godmother, Dona Joana, early on. She explains: "They took me to visit my godmother and when it was time to go home, I grabbed onto a table leg, and nobody could pry me loose. So, they just let me stay on."

Despite being sterile, Dona Joana had always been surrounded by children, brought in by her activities as midwife and foster mother. Twenty years before Inez had entered her life, she had acquired a son, an "abandoned" child whom she had illegally registered as though he were her own flesh and blood. For a short period, this son became Inez's stepfather, making the (then) little girl a sort of granddaughter in the three-generation household. However, for a good part of her childhood, Inez had called the elderly woman who cared for her neither "Godmother" nor "Grandmother," but "Mother." When eventually Inez's birth mother, long since separated from Dona Joana's son and living elsewhere, demanded her daughter's return, the conflict had to be settled in court.

In fact, disputes are not uncommon; the coexistence of different sets of parents is hardly pacific. In particular when a child transfer takes place because of a crisis situation in the mother's life, there is often a great deal of ambiguity about who is actually helping whom. Birth mothers will claim they have made a gift to another household, blessing it with the gracious presence of a child. Foster parents, for their part, often broadcast a different sort of discourse—insisting that they have accepted the caretaking "burden" in order to help out and implying that, in reward, they deserve to keep the child permanently. Considering the inadequacy (if not total lack) of old-age pensions among working-class individuals, the moral issue—to whom a grown child owes his or her loyalty—instead of waning, takes on increasing importance with time, and quibbling among different mothers is, to a certain extent, predictable.

Of course, a birth mother may clarify the ambiguous terms of informal child placements by paying the foster family for the child's upkeep, thus reaffirming her maternal status. However, in most cases, regular payment is hardly a viable option: If a woman cannot afford to support a son or a daughter in her own home, how is she to pay for the child's upkeep in someone else's? One may reasonably assume that Dona Joana—who earned her living as a foster mother, paid either by the state or directly by her wards' parents—was expecting to be financially compensated for taking in Inez and that it was precisely the non-payment of this debt that led Joana to claim maternal privileges. As in many other situations I observed, maternal status—with its emotional and long-term material benefits—would be seen by the child's caretaker as compensation for the unpaid debt.[12]

Therefore, it is no coincidence that Inez's mother, when recounting her version of the story, underlined the fact that Dona Joana was an elderly widow. In an evident attempt to reverse the flow of obligations, she presented the gracious company of her little girl as a sort of gift to this solitary woman. Her stance is made credible by the fact that in the neighborhoods where I worked children indeed appear to be cherished. Young, unmarried mothers, as well as widows and recently divorced women going through hard times, will often be bombarded with offers by people seeking to take babies and toddlers off their hands (see Fonseca 1985). Since, according to local values, both Inez's birth mother and foster mother had valid claims over the child, they

12 More than once, I saw babies held ransom by a doting foster mother for as little as one or two liters of milk. People claimed that this commodified aspect of child exchange was endorsed by the public courts that, in mediating disputes, would routinely establish a certain amount of financial compensation that a biological mother had to pay in order to regain custody of her child.

resorted to the court to resolve the question of the girl's legal custody. In this particular dispute, which must have taken place in the late 1960s, the court followed the child's (by then a preteen) preference, assigning her to her foster mother.

Notwithstanding the various conflicts that result from this "invented kinship," the bonds it forms appear to be more longlasting than the grudges. Well into old age, finding herself with no retirement benefits, no property, and incapable of making a living, Dona Joana was taken in by her former rival, Inez's mother, Maria. At the time of our interview, Dona Joana was reigning as proud grandmother over an extended household, which included at least four nuclear families (those of Maria and three of Maria's married children). The fact that she had no blood connection to the other members of the family appeared to trouble no one, exactly because her tie to this family was as unquestionable and enduring as a biologic fact. *Mãe é quem criou* (mother is whoever brings you up), her family members explained, using an adage known to all—one that states that to give food and lodging to another person carries with it all sorts of affective and symbolic consequences, creating in the case of child placement a bond not only between tutor and ward but also between the different adult partners of exchange.

The example of Inez and her family demonstrates how a child's placement may be used to cement or even create new social networks. A woman, for example, may expect to receive periodic aid from her brother in exchange for raising his children. A grandmother will see her own married children far more often if she is raising one of their offspring. By taking in a poor cousin or an orphaned nephew, an upwardly mobile relative will demonstrate to his kin group that he is not getting "uppity," nor does he intend to sever ties. Finally, the circulation of children also serves to expand the kin group to neighbors and unrelated friends, such as Dona Joana, as momentary affinities are transformed into life-long relationships through the sharing of parental responsibilities.

The placement of a child may well contain a utilitarian aspect. Women are often driven by sheer necessity to find substitute families for their children, but poverty does not explain the willingness with which people take in unrelated youngsters. It never ceased to amaze me how many, even very poor, households opened their doors to "help out" an extra child or young person.[13] As they say, "*Onde come um português, come dois, três*" ("Where there's food enough for one, there's food enough for two, three"). Amid so dynamic a play of household arrange-

[13] Donna Goldstein (1998) describes a Rio de Janeiro maid living in the favela who, besides raising her own children, took in four of her deceased sister's offspring as well as three of her ex-lover's children. Such a case would not be entirely uncommon in the neighborhoods where I worked.

ments, the question arises: How do people view the subject of kinship and personal identity?

The story of Inez's family underlines the socially forged nature of kinship; it also serves to illustrate the enormous weight attributed to blood ties. Of Inez and her six siblings, only the last two were raised by their biological parents. Nonetheless, the Sunday I arrived unexpectedly to interview Maria (the mother of this family), I found her at a backyard barbecue, surrounded by six of her seven living offspring. (The seventh, who had spent the night at Maria's, was having lunch with his parents-in-law). With no hesitation, they all chimed in to piece together their family romance. Two of them had been raised by Dona Joana. Another, carried off by his paternal grandparents, was chased down 20 years later by his brothers and sisters, who had simply followed a tip on where his father worked. Still another recounts how, as a baby, he endured the mistreatment of a negligent wet nurse, before being brought back to live with his mother and stepfather. The oldest brother had simply run away from home at age eight, "never to be seen again." In fact, all of Maria's children eventually found their way back, but the arrival of the oldest, after a ten-year silence, had become a sort of family saga. His sister recounts in vivid detail the day she ran into this 18-year-old youth, pushing his bike up the hill:

> *He waved me over and asked, "Listen, you don't happen to know a Dona Maria living around here? A woman with a whole lot of kids?" I said, "I guess you're talking about my mother. She's the only Dona Maria around here and she has a pile of children. I don't know if it's her, but I'll take you to see." I didn't pay much attention; I just left him with mom saying, "This boy says he wants to talk to you." But when I came back a couple of minutes later, my mother introduced us: "This is your brother."*

Six years later, this particular son was working as a night watchman and was still living (with his wife and two children) in a house he had built in his mother's backyard.

This story is far from exceptional. Innumerable times, I ran into a family ostensibly united—where the mother lived side-by-side with several married offspring with whom she interacted daily and celebrated the usual family rites—despite the fact that the children, spread out among different "mothers," had not grown up together. To explain this situation and reaffirm what, for this group, seems to be a fundamental belief in the biological connection, people (who moments before were telling me *mãe é quem criou*) now cited another proverb: *Mãe é uma só* (mother, there's but one). It is as though the tie between blood relatives, going beyond individual acts of volition, could not be broken. Birth mothers and adoptive mothers alike appeared to credit the belief voiced by one of my informants: "Even though that (six-year-old) boy doesn't know I'm his mother, I know I attract his attention every time he sees me. I feel it. . . . Because it's like my mom says, it's the blood—it's the drawing power of blood *(o sangue puxa)*." The symbolic nature of this bond dispenses with the necessity of a person's physical presence. Small children will be taught—through photos on the wall, or birthdays recalled—to remember their siblings who are living elsewhere. The bond also entitles apparent strangers to become sudden intimates. As Inez said, describing her re-encounter with one of her long-lost brothers: "When we met, I knew right away he was my brother. We hugged with all the emotion of brother and sister, even though we'd spent all those years apart."

Despite the strong emotion of such re-encounters, child circulation is often treated as a banal event by the various people concerned. In one example, a woman wanting to spend a weekend at the beach left her six-day-old daughter in the care of a neighbor. The unpaid babysitter, whose two adolescent children were just becoming independent, called in her sister to wet-nurse the child. A triangular sort of arrangement ensued that, when I met them in 1994, had lasted for at least eight years. As the foster mother said, "She sleeps and eats in my house, and I'm the one she calls mother." Called momentarily away from her playmates to speak to me, the eight-year-old endorsed her foster mom's story with apparent delight. "I have three mothers," she beamed, "The mother who nursed me, the mother who raised me, and the mother who gave birth to me."[14]

A good number of children claim to have set up their own arrangements. It is not unusual to hear an 8-year-old explaining, "Auntie asked me to visit, I liked it, so I told my mom I was just going to stay on." Adults will include in their life histories a list of various households in which they lived during childhood, with a predictable variety of commentaries. Some foster parents are remembered as wicked slave drivers, and some as fairy godmothers, but most are described in quite matter-of-fact terms. Many, many people will speak of two, three, and four "mothers" with no embarrassment or particular confusion.

Thus, as children scatter among different foster families, they acquire new parents and siblings. However, as historians and ethnographers throughout the globe have demonstrated (Collins 1992; Goody 1982; Lallemand 1993), such additions do not necessarily imply a rupture or replacement of previous relationships. Instead, just as with ritual kin (which adds godparents to a child's list of relatives), foster arrangements serve to enlarge the pool of significant others in a person's social universe. It is as though the child's social identity were "multi-layered" (Yngvesson 2000), revealing a perception of self that is inseparable from the various

[14] In Portuguese: *A mãe de leite, a mãe de criação e a mãe que me ganhou.*

relationships that form a background sociality to his or her existence.

* * *

The case of Inez well illustrates the comings or goings of children within the deep-rooted fosterage culture prevalent in many Brazilian working-class neighborhoods. There are moments, however, when children are given away on a permanent and irrevocable basis, much as in the system of legal adoption. With the following case, we come to know a woman who, faced with intolerable conditions, actually surrendered her maternal status. However, in stark contrast to legal plenary adoption as it is practiced in Brazil, this birth mother took an active role in the selection of her baby's adoptive family. The story of how she gave up her third-born child highlights how, working between local values and state mandates, the *favela* residents have fashioned a creative bricolage to ensure the reproduction of future generations.

Eliane's Story: Clandestine Adoption in Context

Eliane, a tall, thin black woman, received me in the front room of the little wooden house where she was living with her husband and four of her children. Between chuckles and sighs of exasperation, she had chatted with me for well over an hour about the exploits of her various offspring when suddenly she fell silent. Taking a long puff on her cigarette, tears welling in her steady gaze, she let out an almost inaudible whisper, "I forgot to tell you. Now that you mentioned adopted kids . . . I gave one away [pause] . . . I gave one away."[15]

Eliane tells a story not much different from that of many other mothers from the outskirts of the city. Her extended kin group had been able to absorb her first two unplanned children, but, still unmarried and living with her mother when she got pregnant a third time, Eliane had reached the limits of her family's endurance. Her third child was simply banished from the kin group before he was even born.

> *They were saying things like, "This child can't be my nephew, it can't be my grandson. It's a child of the night, of the partylife. It has no father." They just kept after me. All that revolted me. When you're pregnant, it's easy to get upset.*

The young woman had no hope of being able to pay a nonrelative to keep her child. Even were she to work, for example, as a maid, she could not expect to receive more than one or two minimum salaries (US$60–$120 a month), hardly enough to feed and pay for the day care of three children. (The government-allotted family allowance, available only to salaried workers,

[15] Whereas most women, like Dona Maria, will say they simply "left" (*deixei*) a child with a certain caretaker, Eliane explicitly states that she "gave" (*dei*) her child to someone else.

would add no more than a monthly US$6 per child.) She knew that many families—recently married couples with no children of their own, sterile women, and simply older couples whose children were all grown—would be on the lookout for a precious bundle such as she had to offer. But, especially when coveting the infant of a non-relative, the prospective parents were reluctant to share parental responsibilities, and even less willing to consider their parenthood of only temporary standing. In these circumstances, Eliane had little choice but to give her newborn child away.

We should remember that there is good reason to believe that the great majority of children given in adoption in Brazil have identifiable parents.[16] There is also reason to presume that many of these parents "consent" to give their children in adoption because of sheer poverty.[17] In other words, they are not embarrassed adolescents trying to cover up a sexual faux pas so they can start life anew. It therefore makes sense that, no matter how poor or unprepared they are, many women, like Eliane, seek an active role in the decisions affecting their child's future—first and foremost of which is the choice of surrogate parents.

Eliane thus went searching among relatives and acquaintances for her future child's adoptive parents and, shortly before giving birth, found what she was looking for. Her choice fell upon the baby's paternal aunt, a woman who, after years of trying for a pregnancy, had recently birthed a stillborn child. Eliane recalls the circumstances of this encounter with amazing detail: the hesitation, the tears, and the respect with which the potential mother treated her: "[*The adoptive mother*] said, 'Look Eliane, we don't want to force you.' She gave me liberty to do what I wanted." But, after a week's soul-searching and mutual support, the decision was made. As our narrator tells it, she went to the would-be mother's house, and the two women sat there crying—the baby between them, in his crib—until Eliane drew herself up to say, "No, you keep him."

It would be misleading to frame the analysis of this scene entirely in terms of individual maternal rights. A birth mother's decisions are enmeshed in a social fabric wherein other members of the extended family (particularly older women) are constantly giving opinions and exerting pressure to influence what many consider the collective rights and obligations over the group's offspring. Yet, in general, mothers occupy and, what's more, wish to occupy a central place in this process.

[16] Ferreira's study (2000) covering 12 years of adoption processes in Porto Alegre, shows that the mother was located in approximately 90% of the cases.

[17] In the 1985 study of over 150,000 Brazilian mothers who had separated from a child before its first birthday, the overwhelming majority said they had done so because of the "total absence of financial conditions" (Campos 1991).

A further point of interest illustrated by Eliane's story is that a birth mother's active concern for her children need not imply continued proprietary claims. Six years after having "given away" her child, this particular birth mother is enjoying a new, more prosperous phase in life. Her present husband earns a good living collecting junk and transporting goods with his horse-drawn cart. Eliane has her own house now, and has brought all her children to live with her—all but the one she gave away. Living in the same neighborhood as the adoptive parents, she is able to see her third-born faring well, and even occasionally visit his home, but she categorically rejects the idea of reclaiming him:

> *I always say, even if I won at the lottery, even if I was rich enough to pay back [the foster family], I wouldn't do that. What for? Sure, I could if I wanted. Wow! Just think of it, all my kids here together with me! But I wouldn't do that to them* [the adoptive parents]. *After six years! How could they avoid loving the child? For God's sake! It would be a crime.*

Whereas, before, the lack of money had obliged Eliane to give her child away, now, the financial aspect of her maternal rights reappears in the idea of ransoming her son. Her ties to the child are inalienable ("*o sangue puxa*"), but in order to activate these ties she must have money to pay back all those years of the adoptive mother's financial inputs. In other words, to reintegrate her child into her household, she must be able to provide much more than the bed, schooling, and regular meals she gives her other four children. At this point, only by cashing in on a winning lottery ticket could she hope to merit her "priceless child."[18]

However, Eliane is insistent that there are other concerns that are more important than any financial calculation. She clearly pictures the transfer of her son as a gift made to a couple "who had always dreamed of having a child." She also respects the attachment formed between her child and his new family: "As far as he's concerned, I'm no one. At least not his mother. When I go by to visit, he calls me 'auntie'." The value of the gift she made to the other couple is heightened by her feelings of sacrifice. These feelings are, nonetheless, contingent on her active participation in the adoption process.

We arrive now at the point in Eliane's story of central importance to this investigation. The adoptive parents of this woman's baby were not content with an informal oral contract made with the birth mother. In order to ensure the binding nature of this transaction, they went to the proper public authorities and obtained the child's birth certificate as though they had borne him. It was not, in fact, difficult for them to pose as the biological parents. Since hospitals do not require or even facilitate the issuing of birth certificates, parents are obliged to take the necessary

[18] Zelizer's study (1985) on the "priceless child" will be further discussed later.

measures, locating the appropriate office of registry and normally paying a fee. In such circumstances, it is not then surprising that, according to 1998 statistics, nearly one-third of Brazilian births were not registered within the legal deadline. The fact that many children acquire a legal identity only when they enter first grade or even many years later (when, for example, boys embark on their military service) makes it relatively easy to manipulate information on their birth register.

By participating in this sort of procedure (often referred to in the literature as "clandestine adoption," but known locally as *adoção à brasileira*),[19] Eliane and the adoptive parents of her child have technically committed a crime. All three have been guilty of what the law labels as "ideological falsity," punishable by up to six years in jail. However, the illegality of the act does not seem to intimidate most potential parents. According to some estimates, this form of adoption was, until recently, ten times more common than legal adoption,[20] and, what's more, it enjoyed the tacit support of a good many members of the judiciary. At the end of the 1980s, public television broadcasted a debate in which judges and lawyers spoke in favor of the "obvious nobility of spirit" that moved families to thus take in foundlings.[21] Although an occasional newspaper story might connect a clandestine adoption with baby-snatching, there are still serious sources pointing out advantages of the system.[22]

Such tolerance of technically illegal practices horrifies the professionals working at the public adoption board in Rio Grande do Sul and fuels criticisms from abroad on the purported corruption and possible commercialization linked to the adoption process. Nonetheless, a closer look at local dynamics suggest that *adoção à brasileira* is not necessarily an isolated practice. It fits into a longstanding behavior pattern of people who have traditionally lived on the margin of state bureaucracy; that is, of a working class that deploys "weapons of the weak" (Scott 1985) in order to exert a certain control over its conditions of existence.

---

19 Evidently, the informal name given this illegal practice carries with it a connotation of widespread acceptance.

20 Interview with a state judge, quoted in *Isto E,* 26 August 1990.

21 "Nobility" here is an important legal point since, according to Article 242 of the Penal Code, in cases where people have acted for recognizably noble motives, the punishment for clandestine adoption may be diminished or waived altogether.

22 E.g., in Weber's (1999) research on adoption in the state of Paraná, she found that while Brazilians who consult legal adoption services show a persistent preference for light-skinned babies, *adoção à brasileira,* carried out in general by lower-income people, tends to concern older children of darker color.

Historical Precedents

Students of Brazilian history point out that, since colonial times, the central government has had great difficulty in inciting even banal collaboration from its average citizens. From military conscription to jury service and vaccination campaigns, working-class groups have historically sidestepped state intervention in their daily affairs (Carvalho 1996). This independent spirit was, if anything, more pronounced in the sphere of family organization. Brazilians were proverbially averse to legal marriage (performed, until the 1889 Republic, by scarce and often corrupt church officials), and attempts to impose civil birth registration in the mid-19th century provoked such a reaction that in most parts of the country the measure was revoked within a year (Carvalho 1996; Meznar 1994). Notwithstanding the tenacious myth held by many social workers of a Golden Age of unified families,[23] female-headed households appear to have been extremely common since at least the beginning of the 19th century, accounting for as much as 40% of the population in certain urban neighborhoods (Ramos 1978). Out-of-wedlock births were relatively banal, and, in many day-to-day routines, stigma against unmarried mothers and bastards was hardly perceptible. In recognition of the number of people who fell between the cracks of the official norm, the law made official allowances for an unmarried man to exert paternal authority over, and leave his inheritance to, *illegitimate* sons and daughters (Kuznesof 1998; Venâncio 1986; Fonseca 1997).

In such a context, lower-ranking Brazilians found ingenious ways to get around, or at least to stamp their own values onto, the existing structures of the legal system. Meznar (1994), for example, recounts that particular historical conditions in the northern state of Paraiba (the abolition of slavery and a spurt on the agricultural market because of the 1870s cotton boom) brought officials to judge certain single women as unfit for motherhood, withdrawing their sons who were old enough to work and placing them as cheap farm labor with "respectable," land-owning tutors.[24] To preempt the system, a woman would negotiate the placement of her child with a suitable patron *before* the courts interfered. Some, widows in particular, would petition to foster their own child, agreeing to pay a monthly sum to be held in the youngster's name until he reached adulthood. (Whether payments were ever made is another matter.)

23 *Casa Grande and Senzala*, the seminal work of Gilberto Freyre on patriarchal, extended families among the ruling elite of colonial Pernambuco has been used and abused to support various (and often erroneous) theories on Brazilian families (see Corrêa 1982).

24 Girls who provided domestic service were not fought over in the same way and did not receive a monthly stipend.

The extraordinary realism with which mothers would evaluate the prevailing mood of the courts is evident in other modes of behavior that I registered while poring over Porto Alegre archives to examine child custody disputes of the early 1900s. Whereas, at the time, certain women were obliged to demonstrate utter chastity in order to maintain guardianship of their children, others would, on the contrary, underline their sexually promiscuous behavior, exactly to cast doubt on their ex-mate's paternal status. (One woman went so far as to bring in a policeman to testify she was a prostitute.) Since fathers, even of illegitimate offspring, had priority legal rights, a woman would frequently omit her companion's name on a child's birth certificate so as to guarantee her own authority. In at least one significant case, the child's paternal grandparents were registered on the birth certificate, while leaving the father's name out (Fonseca 1993).[25]

In both Meznar's (1994) and my study, one sees how the law produced unforeseen effects that may have even discouraged the formation of legally constituted family units. The conclusion to be drawn from such observations is *not* that working-class groups had some sort of pristine family patterns that were somehow corrupted by "external" laws; on the contrary, it is precisely that these family patterns have evolved in constant interaction with the various state laws. It is in this sense that I interpret more recent practices—such as clandestine adoption and even the way, during the 1980s, women would use the state orphanage as though it were a private boarding school—as part of a longstanding pattern of working-class family dynamics.

In each of these instances, lower-income people resort to legal means to exert their authority, guarantee the survival of their offspring, or protect their interests. They do so, however, not necessarily in utter reverence for the rules but rather in hopes of finding loopholes in their favor. Whereas such maneuvers have been identified with the working-classes elsewhere (see Merry 1990; Ewick & Silbey 1998), in Brazil there is evidence that people from all walks of life share a profound suspicion of the court system, counting on personal connections and individual cleverness rather than on the impersonal legal system to see justice done (DaMatta 1979). Furthermore, in common law regimes such as those found in Britain or the United States some effort is made to adapt laws to local practices and values, but in Brazil legislators have consciously espoused the idea of "symbolic legislation"—laws that, by providing a sort of blueprint for the ideal society, point out the direction social change will hopefully take. In such circumstances, the gap between, on one hand, the legal

[25] See Lazarus-Black (1994) for a similar analysis of law and paternal status in the Caribbean.

ideal and, on the other, the lived values held by a good number of lower-income Brazilians leaves many people little choice but to contrive strategies to adjust the laws to their reality.

The International Mood of National Laws

Whereas the social dynamics of lower-income families have indeed been influenced throughout history by national laws, the opposite does not seem to hold true. The evolution of Brazil's national legislation on child placement, for example, appears to be oriented by anything but local realities. Briefly, the present national policy is to promote plenary adoption as the progressive option for extremely poor, mistreated, and otherwise institutionalized children. This option not only ignores traditional circuits of fosterage and other forms of shared parental responsibilities but also in contrast to *adoção à brasileira*, eliminates any possibility of the birth mother's active participation in her child's placement.

The Legal Adoption Package: Equality Plus Exclusivity

Of course, following the philosophy set out in the 1989 UN Convention on the Rights of the Child, the overriding principle of Brazilian legislation concerning children is at present "the child's best interests." It is undeniable that in many ways the adoption laws have gradually introduced important reforms mandated by universally accepted values. Until recently, for example, Brazil's adoption law condoned discrimination against adopted children, institutionalizing social inequality within the household. The logic of inequality was inscribed in the very vocabulary used in better-off families where the same word (*criado*) was used to signify servant and foster (or adopted) child. During the 19th century, besides using their wards as cheap labor,[26] people could "adopt" a boy in order to send him to do military service instead of a biological son. The 1916 Civil Code, aimed at creating a certain uniformity throughout the national territory, reflected traditional biases. Adopted children, transferred from one adult to another by a simple notarized contract, could be returned to their parents (or public institution) with little fuss. They would have no inheritance rights whatsoever if their new parents had borne any "legitimate" children before the adoption, and only half the share of inheritance of any brothers and sisters who might be born after the adoption. It was not until the 1979 Children's Code that it became possible for adopted children to become permanent members of their new family, with full inheri-

[26] Historians have furnished ample evidence as to the association throughout the Americas between premodern adoptions and domestic service (Meznar 1994; Neff 1996; Blum 1998; Kuznesof 1998).

tance rights. Only in 1990, with the elimination of "simple adoption," was this privilege extended to all adopted children.

Significantly, together with the equality of adopted children, the other major change in Brazil's adoption legislation has been the gradual elimination of the child's birth family from the adoption process. Until the middle of the 20th century, an adopted individual maintained a sort of double filiation—sharing rights and obligations in his or her adoptive as well as biological family. Law 4.655 of 1965 was the first to frame the child exclusively in terms of membership in his or her new adoptive family. Following the sensitivities of the country's cosmopolitan elite, the law was inspired in the idea that adoptive families should "imitate nature" (Siqueira 1993). Since *naturally* a child had but one mother, adoption should signify a total rupture with the child's biological relatives.

Since the 1965 law theoretically pertained only to children under 7 years of age whose parents were dead or unknown, the erasure of a child's original genealogical ties provoked few reactions. However, with the enactment of the 1979 Children's Code, guidelines were laid down as to the treatment of living birth parents: Children could be adopted only if these parents had been stripped of authority or had expressly consented to the procedure. This "plenary adoption" was extended to all children under 7 years old who were found by the courts to be "in an irregular situation"—a condition that could include anything from those who were badly abused, abandoned, or being raised in a morally inadequate milieu to those who, because of parental omission, had been deprived of the essential conditions of subsistence, health, or schooling.

The amplitude of this category soon fell under attack, explaining why there is an explicit clause in the 1990 Children's Code declaring that poverty alone should under no circumstances justify the loss of parental authority. However, as many researchers have demonstrated (Cardarello 1998; Ferreira 2000), despite ostensive safeguards, most children withdrawn from their original families still come from homes in which parental neglect is barely distinguishable from the effects of dire poverty. Furthermore, as elsewhere in the world, the very language of Brazil's adoption law tends to deemphasize extended family arrangements common in working-class groups, relying instead on values imbedded in the "modern" nuclear family: kinship ties based on choice rather than social or biological givens; children perceived as autonomous identities, detachable and movable from one kin group to another; and the refusal of shared parental rights.[27]

[27] For critical analysis of the Western family values that permeate international discussions on child welfare, see Boyden (1990), Stephens (1995), Yngvesson (2000), and, particularly as they affect public policy on Brazilian street children, Hecht (1998).

One can only suspect that the consistently low socioeconomic status of birth parents has had a lot to do with the way their role has been progressively supplanted (rather than complemented) by their child's adoptive parents over the past 30 years. During the 1980s, in most regions in Brazil the name of an adopted child's biological parents was stricken from the birth certificate, thus rendering the state the official guardian of the "secret of (the child's) origin." With the 1990 Children's Code, and the consolidation of plenary adoption, the secret of the adopted child's origins became a definitive part of the Brazilian adoption process,[28] and the notion of plenary adoption, based on a distinctly middle-class family ideal, was declared the sole legal means of adopting a child.

Adoption as a Hegemonic Narrative

Just as in numerous other donor countries, it was to a great extent the increasing presence of *foreign* adoptive parents that led Brazilian policymakers to turn their attentions to the plight of the country's children and to refine policies concerning in-country adoption (Yngvesson 2000; Abreu 2002).

During the first three-quarters of the 20th century, it was quite possible for anyone, including a foreigner, to legally adopt a child without ever having seen a public authority. It was sufficient for a woman, after having first registered her baby, to sign a notarized document passing complete parental responsibility to a second party. With this document, the new parents could obtain a birth certificate in their name, guaranteeing their child a passport (Brazilian or of the parents' nationality) for travel abroad.[29]

As early as the 1970s, newspapers fueled the image of foreigners descending en masse to adopt Brazilian children, causing special clauses on intercountry adoption to be written into the 1979 Children's Code. Henceforth, adoption by foreign nationals had to pass through Juvenile Court. By the 1980s, Brazilian social planners were anxious to take measures that would not only check the "theft" of Brazilian children but would also counteract negative images dwelling on abandoned street children in the foreign press. It was at this point that *adoção à brasileira* began to be singled out as a backward practice, and concerted efforts were made to bring all adoptions, both national and intercountry, under the control of the Juvenile Courts.

[28] According to its terms (Children's Code Art. 47, §4) an adopted child's original birth certificate as well as the court proceedings are to be sealed unless unusual circumstances lead a judicial authority to reveal them.

[29] See *O Globo*, 14 August 1980, for a report on several Americans who were able to adopt children in this way.

After the enactment of the 1990 Children's Code, the flux of Brazilian adopted children toward foreign countries slowed down for a year or two, and there is some indication that even with the renewed impetus of the mid 1990s international adoption increasingly involved children who are black or handicapped or too old to be accepted in local homes. These trends bear the mark not only of international directives (aside from the 1989 U.N. Convention, see the 1993 Hague Convention on the Protection of Children and Co-Operation in Respect of Intercountry Adoption) but also of nationalists who see children as part of Brazil's national resources and resent the demeaning role of producing children to be "saved" by First World countries (see Abreu 1998). However, the impact of international influence should not be measured merely by the number of children sent abroad. Campaigns for *in-country* adoptions have never before been so vigorous. Recent nationwide movements for legal adoption have put posters on the walls of town halls and advertisements for available children on the Internet sites of state orphanages.

The important point here is that not only has adoption in Brazil become more centralized and rigidly defined, it has managed to expunge alternative state-sponsored, as well as traditional, forms of child placement. In Rio Grande do Sul, for example, state-coordinated fosterage, long considered a poor stepsister to adoption, is today practically non-existent.[30] The previous system of foster care that placed children in lower-income families (at the monthly cost of half a minimum salary—US$30—per child) is considered not up to present standards. To meet the standards laid out in the 1990 Children's Code, the state has replaced the old orphanages with a series of smaller units, which, at a monthly cost of over US$1000 per child, offer comforts approximating those of an upper-middle-class home (complete with swimming classes and horseback riding). At this price, the state has a strong incentive to limit the number of state-financed children; thus, juvenile authorities—taking as a parameter the naturalized nuclear family—tend to frame their policies in terms of either/or. *Either* the child stays in his or her birth family (where, presumably, biology compensates for poverty) *or* he or she is given to a new family through plenary adoption. In the latter case, the fact that the great majority of children are under 3 years of age spells out an inevitable rupture with the birth family.

[30] A 1994 study on child placement in the state of Rio Grande do Sul indicated that there were only 80 children in foster homes, against 350 in institutional care (not counting juvenile offenders), and 243 given in adoption (both national and international) that year (Cardarello 1996). During the 1990s, the program of substitute families was phased out, reducing the number of foster homes to four in January 2000.

Many of the poverty-stricken parents I dealt with evidently do not agree with either of these options. Like Dona Maria, at times they may feel that their children would be better off in another household, and so they seek allies among relatives and neighbors or even those in state-run programs who might share in child care responsibilities while not entirely usurping their identity as parents. Or, like Eliane, they may be willing to give their children permanently into the keeping of another family that they have helped choose and that they can keep track of from afar. Certainly, these "traditional" practices are not without their hitches, and they could invite state assistance and/or supervision. The possibility of abuse such as that documented in foster homes elsewhere must be taken into account.[31] However, there is every reason to believe that the less-publicized accounts of relatively successful foster parenthood (Cadoret 1995; Hoelgaard 1998) could prove equally relevant to the Brazilian case. Despite this fact, debate over such issues is practically non-existent. Foster families as well as birth families have been all too easily removed from the scene, leaving adoptive parenthood the single viable alternative for children in serious difficulty.

I suggest that the violence of inequality that until recently branded adopted children as inferior members of their new family has today been relocated in another relation written into the adoption procedure—that between birth parents and adoptive parents. Let us remember that child circulation in the favela traditionally involves adults of more or less equal status. In the working-class districts of Porto Alegre, it would be difficult to distinguish a class of child donors separate from a class of child recipients. Many women who as young mothers placed their children in a substitute family end up taking in somebody else's child to raise. The slight financial advantage enjoyed by foster and adoptive mothers is generally because of factors linked to the life cycle rather than to social stratification. Near-equal social status may explain why birth mothers in the local setting maintain a certain power of negotiation. Similarly, it is quite possible that the increasingly unequal status between birth and adoptive parents is a relevant factor in the progressive effacement of the former from the adoption process, and that the greater the inequality the stronger the tendency to be so. Considering this hypothesis, one would have reason to believe that birth mothers in intercountry adoption where socioeconomic and cultural differences are at their peak would have less power than ever. In the following and final paragraphs of this article, I will explore this possibility.

31 For just one of the frequent newspaper articles on the problems connected with abusive foster homes in the United States, see the *New York Times*, 27 October 2000, p. A18. Gailey (1998) offers an interesting study on abuse within foster as well as adoptive homes.

Inequality Near and Far

Cutting Birth Parents Out of the Picture

Although I did not engage in field work in the North American and European circuits, I draw on the abundant literature that exists on both national and international adoption in these receiving countries to add a comparative perspective to my analysis—one that proves particularly revealing with regard to power plays involved in adoption laws. Inspired by this comparison, I will suggest that, whether in Brazil or in First World countries, adoptive parents commonly feel uncomfortable about their child having another set of parents. They thus tend to dwell on images that justify total rupture with the donor parents—underlining their dire misery, highlighting their sacrifice, or emphasizing their need for protection (see, e.g., Gailey 2000). Such images present plenary adoption, with its clean-break principle, as a necessary—even inevitable—measure in adoption processes. Of fundamental interest, then, is the fact that in the North American context, political circumstances have permitted the growth of a countercurrent composed principally of birth parents and adoptees who question the closed nature of plenary adoption, which denies birth parents participation in their child's placement and bars children from ready access to information on their genitors. I argue that the conspicuous lack of any such movement in Brazil is linked to the birth parents' continued powerlessness, and to a great extent explains the tightening grip of plenary adoption in this context.

Literature on adoption practices in receiving countries furnishes rich insight, particularly on the vastly heterogeneous field of adoptive parents. For example, in Gailey's (1999) study of a small number of extremely affluent North Americans who adopted a child born overseas, she puts us in touch with one extreme of the spectrum. With an average annual income of US$110,000, her interviewees were distinctly better off than those who adopted children from within the United States, and, with two exceptions, they had few compunctions about linking their affluence to their right to parenthood. Not only did they tend to present this right as obvious—because of the wealth and social status they could provide a child—these adoptive parents also implied that, considering the high price they were willing to pay (an average of US$10,000 and up for costs involved), they expected high-quality goods: light-skinned babies in good mental and physical health.[32] Although no adoption agency, public or private, would explicitly give voice to such consumer logic, the

[32] Such attitudes echo those of certain North American couples who use prenatal testing with the intent of producing a perfect child (Rapp 2000).

child-saving rhetoric used by certain agencies may subtly imply that because of their financial security the well-off are not only (by definition) well-equipped to take in children, they practically have a moral obligation to do so. Descriptions on "huge numbers" of "homeless" or "abandoned" children (see, e.g., Bartholet 1993), despite occasional mention of inadequate social policies in sending countries, play on subliminal stereotypes concerning the birth parents' irresponsibility, absence of moral fiber (inability to "plan" their family), or lack of sexual constraint.

Certainly it would be unjust to reduce the heterogeneous field of adoptive parents to a single note. There are a good number of adoptive parents clearly moved by humanitarian impulses who reject moralistic discourses, emphasizing, on the contrary, the noble sacrifice of their child's "first" parents. However, even in such cases, social scientists have suggested that the insistence on images of "abandoned waifs" or even "gift children" is part of an individual and collective process of "misrecognition" designed to keep inconvenient ideas such as the possible existence of biological parents, social inequality, and commodity logic at bay (Ouellette 1995; Yngvesson 1998; Strathern 1992).

It is thus no coincidence that discussions on international adoption have generally focused on exceptional historical circumstances in which children have been orphaned or unequivocally abandoned by their parents. Korean War orphans, for example, are often cited as the first wave of foreign children to enter adopted homes in America. More recently, researchers have pointed out the disastrous consequences of totalitarian policies of population control that in the case of Ceausescu's Romania prohibited contraception and in the case of contemporary China imposed it with draconian measures (Kligman 1992; Johnson, et al. 1998). Finally, much has been said of Korean morality that marginalizes unwed mothers and their offspring, supposedly leaving no alternative but to arrange for children to be adopted outside the country.[33] However, relatively little has been said about Latin American children who, like many Third World "orphans," come from the singularly unglamorous circumstances of sheer poverty. The idea of "abandoned" and "homeless" children, which throughout the world pervades the adoption discourse, allows very little space for mothers such as these who are simply poor.

Imagining that a child's birth parents have died or that they were forced to anonymously abandon their child frees the adoptive parents of having to deal with the idea of living birth par-

[33] The video by Korean adoptee, Deann Borshay, "First Person Plural," in which the cineast rediscovers her birth family, lays to waste many of the stereotypes regarding "abandoned orphans."

ents.[34] Any number of reasons have been given why it is inevitable for birth parents to be cut out of the picture. One argument evokes the "foundling wheels" in Renaissance orphanages, a sort of rotating compartment in the porter's lodge where babies could be deposited by totally anonymous visitors.[35] Although today it is well known that many of the children left in these conditions were the legitimate offspring of poverty-stricken couples, advocates of secrecy dwell on the image of unwed girls who, had they not been given this alternative, would sooner have died or killed their babies than face the shame of bearing an out-of-wedlock child. More recently, debates have raged about whether or not having more than one set of parents will upset the adoptive child's normal psychological development (see Avery 1998). However, there is another pervasive—although often unspoken—argument for avoiding birth parents when they come from poverty-stricken areas—the fear that the child might be reduced to an object of barter.

Zelizer (1985), in her historical essay on "pricing the priceless child," furnishes important insights as to why there is such vehement denial of anything smacking of commerce in the adoption process. According to her analysis, Victorian reformers were faced with a paradox. Modern notions on the family provoked a growing sacralization of children, dictating that youngsters be withdrawn from paid labor and other profane influences of the economy's cash nexus. Yet, the more a child was revered, the more he or she gained in financial as well as symbolic value, thus giving rise to the equally modern notion of "the market of adoptable children." The turn-of-the-century imagination was peopled with rapacious intermediaries as well as venal mothers who were ready to auction their children off to the highest bidder; hence, the loathing of any contact between adoptive and birth parents, and the repeated call for public regulation of the adoption process.

If this account aptly describes the hegemonic narrative held by those sectors of the population with political clout, it does not necessarily reflect attitudes of less influential, lower-income groups from whose ranks come most adopted children. In this sense, a look at the past 30 years of American adoption procedures—in which political factors have, at times, permitted birth mothers to exert an influence—is highly revealing.

[34] As J. Modell states, the notion of a restricted conjugal household is so entrenched in the minds of North Americans that the very idea of sharing represents a fundamental violation of parenthood (1994:47; see also Wegar 1997).

[35] See Le Grand-Sebille (1996) and Fine & Neirinck (2000) on the recent legislative approval of the longstanding French practice that most closely resembles the foundling wheel: "accouchement sous X."

Changes in the Adoption Scene: North Versus South

In the United States, it would seem that "closure" in adoption procedures—including both secrecy (rather than simple confidentiality) of the child's judicial records and the no-contact principle (barring any contact between child-donors and child-receivers)—peaked in the late 1960s and early 1970s. The adopters' desire for exclusive parental rights coincided nicely with a new class of birth mothers—among which there were many middle-class girls who, caught in the crossfire of changing sexual mores, began giving birth to out-of-wedlock babies they were not ready to assume socially (Carp 1998). Soon afterward, with the advent of more efficient means of birth control and more tolerant attitudes toward extra-marital sex, this source of adoptable children dried up, and the pendulum of abandoning mothers swung back toward the poverty-stricken whose reasons for giving children up were of a different order, just as in the pre-war period.

Significantly, it is during the early 1970s that people's worries arose as to the number of transracial adoptions taking place. Spearheaded by the National Association of Black Social Workers (NABSW) and other black activist groups, this movement advanced certain arguments that have since fallen in disrepute: for example, those challenging the possibility that black children can experience adequate social and psychological development while growing up in white families. Other arguments, however, produced long-lasting policy changes, bearing particular relevance on the problem of inequality between birth parents and adoptive parents.

Activists pointed out that black families had long practiced adoption, and, in general, at a higher rate than white families (Stack 1996; Simon 1984). Nonetheless, distrust of bureaucratic procedures and fear of not meeting adoption agencies' stringent criteria led them to prefer informal circuits. Changes in legislation were thus proposed to encourage "in-group" adoption: financial requirements for adoptive parents were lowered; adoptive mothers were no longer asked to be fulltime homemakers; and certain material comforts (for example, a separate bedroom for exclusive use of the adopted child) were waived. Prominent among the innovations were an acceptance of single adoptive parenthood and the possibility of subsidized adoptions, especially in the case of "special needs" children.[36] Another important change in policy concerned the association of foster and adoptive homes. Transgressing previous barriers, "fostadopt" programs permitted foster families to adopt their wards, and prospective adopters were likewise allowed to foster a child while

[36] Gailey (1998) comments that in many agencies black children are systematically included in this category to encourage the adoption of these otherwise "difficult to place" cases.

awaiting pronouncement of the child's adoptable status. In the more-progressive sectors, adoption workers would no longer speak of "selecting" adoptive families, but of "preparing" families for the task (Modell 1994).

Adoptees who had been raised in middle-class families were also coming of age in the 1970s and demanding their right to know about their origins. They joined hands with birth mothers' associations to challenge what they considered the state's authoritarian monopoly on information surrounding the adoption process. Although it was generally agreed that judicial files should be confidential, available only to the concerned parties, court-controlled *secrecy* was seen as an abusive use of power. Furthermore, although controversies still rage over the issue, some form of "open adoption," associated by certain researchers with the empowerment and self-affirmation of birth mothers (Modell 1994; Carp 1998), seems to have come to stay. Today in 2002 there are literally hundreds of agencies adhering to the policy that a birth mother should not only be able to meet her child's adoptive parents but also participate in choosing them. The more enthusiastic advocates suggest that relations should not stop with one or two meetings, but that open adoption should entail "full disclosure of identifying information and . . . a commitment to lifelong relatedness."[37]

Considering that so many other political concerns have been globalized, one might expect the theme of open adoption to have also spread to Third World countries—those which, at the moment, provide the bulk of the world's adopted children. The fact that some of the first (and sometimes extra legal) intercountry adoptions involved a brief contact between birth parents and adoptive parents with, in most cases, no evident abuse (see Abreu 2002), leads one to believe that such a procedure should not be ruled out. However, this possibility does not seem to have occurred to most Third World policymakers. Yngvesson (2000), for example, holds that the "clean break" principle is increasingly dominating adoption as a global practice, and, according to my own observations as well as recent literature on the subject (Jaffe 1995), the "no-contact" principle appears to be spreading in Latin America—together with the increasing sophistication of government regulation. It is significant that international conventions have done little to alter this panorama. On the contrary, Article 29 of the 1993 Hague Convention on Protection of Children and Co-Operation in Respect of Intercountry Adoption, operating on traditional paternalistic principles, recommends a series of obstacles to the meeting of birth and adoptive parents. It is as though state regulation of adoption practices (no doubt, a

[37] "A Statement of Beliefs—Open Adoption," CHS Catholic Charities, Traverse City, Michigan. See Yngvesson (1997) for a first-person account of such proceedings.

necessary and salutary trend) had been delivered, part and parcel, with the total substitution of birth parents in the decision-making processes.

In Brazil, until recently, only an occasional birth mother who showed up at the adoption board having "changed her mind" might complain about the secrecy involved in the adoption process,[38] and, in general, such incidents had little influence on policy makers. However, as more and more children adopted by foreign families come of age and seek to discover their origins, this panorama may be changing. At the end of 1999, Brazilian national TV frequently carried programs on a foreign-reared adoptee's reencounter with his or her Brazilian birth family, and state adoption agencies reported they were being regularly approached by individuals from abroad, looking for their blood relatives. Today, the controversy over sealed birth records is thus emerging for the first time in Brazilian history (see, e.g., Nabinger & Crine 1997)—as a response, one might say, to consumer demands. Yet, the revelation of information appears to follow a one-way track. It only occurs when the adoptive family (never the birth family) takes the initiative in the desire to furnish necessary "background" elements for their child's development. Significantly, open adoption, which would involve the active participation of birth parents (much as in traditional practices of child circulation), remains an untouched issue.[39]

Of course, many officials contend that the "no-contact" principle stems precisely from a desire to protect birth mothers in sending countries against undue pressures from gift-laden strangers seeking to adopt their babies. However, it might be relevant to remember that in the United States those who most vehemently opposed the no-contact principle—mounting campaigns for open adoption and the disclosure of sealed documents—were birth mothers as well as grown adoptees backed by strong minority politics (Modell 1994; Wegar 1997). In such countries as Brazil, there appear to be no political movements ready to endorse birth mothers' rights, and a good number of the adoptees have been removed, through intercountry adoption, from the national political scene. In such circumstances, one can only wonder if the patronizing concern adoption agencies and legislators show toward local birth families, impeding any contact between

[38] Aside from mention of such cases in Fonseca (1986), Scheper-Hughes (1990), and Abreu (1998), the Brazilian newspapers frequently carry articles on just such incidents.

[39] Curious as to how sensitivities were evolving in Brazil, I took advantage of a recent (1999) seminar of Brazilian adoption workers to ask the audience if anyone present had worked with open adoption. My question drew a complete blank. It would appear my interlocutors did not have a clue about what the term meant. My impression was then confirmed by a quick search on the Internet. Among the nearly 100 sites in Portuguese concerned with adoption, not one contained any mention of open adoption. On the other hand, I found more than 4,000 sites in North America and Canada dedicated to this subject.

them and foreign adopters, is not inspired by the desire to simplify their work. By their demanding the birth mother's unconditional surrender of her child, the adoption services and potential parents may go about bargaining the terms of the youngster's future unhindered.

* * *

In this article, I have attempted to point out a series of processes. As I stated earlier, it is difficult to evaluate the impact of the new Children's Code, given the short time it has been in existence. Just as working-class populations have historically adapted their reproductive strategies to prevailing political conditions and social policies, one may reasonably guess that they will continue to find new and creative ways of adjusting their family patterns to the present context. Furthermore, the "impact" of the laws will probably to a large extent depend on extra legal factors. For example, were the Children's Code to be accompanied by a public policy to provide full-time schools with free or subsidized meals, child circulation might well recede, nudging working-class families in the direction of the nuclear family model imagined by state legislators. Lacking such policy changes, the heightening of child rights rhetoric might also scare off certain families, causing them to avoid government intervention by falling back upon traditional and not-always-efficient measures of child circulation and *adoção à brasileira*. Such assertions await further research for verification.

From the material set forth in this article, one can ascertain with reasonable confidence that national laws bear little mark of local realities. A comparison of Brazilian adoption policies with those of North Americans would show that "modern" options for child placement are much more varied than those offered in the 1990 Children's Code, and that the particular option inscribed in official legal policies depends very much on the balance of power among disputing blocks of birth parents, adoptive parents, and adoptees.

In terms of political influence, favela residents appear to be at the bottom rung of the global system of adoption. We should remember, however, as Starr and Collier (1989) have pointed out, that asymmetrical power relations are not always defined according to national borders. Ruling groups should be thought of in terms of a coalition of forces stretching through and beyond the nation. We know that the legal vulnerability of favela mothers' parental status has much in common with that of lower-income women in Western Europe and North America. In like fashion, there are many Third World adoption workers, such as the one cited in the opening paragraphs of this article, whose attitudes have more in common with upper-income adoptive parents in the prosperous regions of the globe than with local birth mothers.[40] By bringing to bear the relevance of "localized" family dynamics to the issue of adoption, and by pointing out the way these dynamics have been consistently shunted aside by apparently progressive legal reforms, I hope to raise doubts about certain hegemonic narratives, undermine the alliances that support them, and help to redirect the debate in a way that may facilitate dialogue between the unequal partners concerned in today's globalized forms of adoption.

References

Abreu, Domingos (1998) "Assim Falou 'o Povo': Adoção Internacional no Dizer Jornalístico," 2 *Cultura e Política*: 133–150. Fortaleza, Brazil: Editora da Universidade Federal do Ceará.

——— (2002) No Bico da Cegonha: Histórias da Adoção Internacional no Brasil. Riò de Janeiro: Relùme Dumará.

Avery, Rosemary J. (1998) "Information Disclosure and Openness in Adoption: State Policy and Empirical Evidence," 20 *Children and Youth Services Rev.* 57–85.

Bartholet, Elizabeth (1993) *Family Bonds: Adoption and the Politics of Parenting.* New York: Houghton Mifflin.

Bausch, Robert S., & Richard T. Serpe (1999) "Recruiting Mexican-American Adoptive Parents," 78 *Child Welfare* 693–715.

Blum, Ann S. (1998) "Public Welfare and Child Circulation, Mexico City, 1877 to 1925," 23 *J. of Family History* 240–71.

Boyden, Jo (1990) "Childhood and the Policy Makers: A Comparative Perspective on the Globalization of Childhood," in A. James & A. Prout, eds., *Constructing and Reconstructing Childhood: Contemporary Issues in the Sociological Study of Childhood.* London: Falmer Press.

Cadoret, Anne (1995) *Parenté Plurielle: Anthropologie du Placement Familial.* Paris: Harmattan.

Campos, Maria M. M. (1991) "Infância Abandonada—O Piedoso Disfarce do Trabalho Precoce," in J. S. Martins, ed., *O Massacre dos Inocentes: A Criança sem Infância no Brasil.* São Paulo, Brazil: Hucitec.

Cardarello, Andrea D. L. (1996) *Implantando o Estatuto: Um Estudo sobre a Criação de um Sistema Próximo ao Familiar para Crianças Institucionalizadas na FEBEM-RS.* M.A. Thesis Dept. of Anthropology, PPGAS-UFRGS (Porto Alegre).

——— (1998) "A Transformação de Internamento 'Assistencial' em Internamento por 'Negligência': Tirando a Cidadania dos Pais para dá-la às Crianças," 19(2) *Ensaios FEE* 306–30.

Carp, E. Wayne (1998) *Family Matters: Secrecy and Disclosure in the History of Adoption.* Cambridge: Harvard Univ. Press.

Carroll, Vern, ed. (1970) *Adoption in Eastern Oceania.* Honolulu: Univ. of Hawaii Press.

Carvalho, José Murilo De (1996) "Cidadania: Tipos e Percursos," 9 *Estudos Históricos* 257–424.

Colen, Shellee (1995) "'Like a Mother to Them': Stratified Reproduction and West Indian Childcare Workers and Employers in New York," in F.D. Gins-

[40] One may cite a certain Peruvian social worker advocating that, even if the foreign parents were not ideal, the adopted child "would still have a better chance for a decent life . . . in a country where children are not condemned by conditions to suffering" (in Jaffe 1995:187). One may also recall the opinion of a Colombian adoption worker who when turning down the petitions of loving, foster families who wish to adopt their wards explains that Western couples "possess superior moral qualities and parenting abilities, besides being better off materially than local applicants" (cited in Hoelgaard 1998:219).

burg & R. Rapp, eds., *Conceiving the New World Order: The Global Politics of Reproduction.* Berkeley: Univ. of California Press.

Collins, Patricia Hill (1992) "Black Women and Motherhood," in B. Thorne & M. Yalom, eds., *Rethinking the Family: Some Feminist Questions.* Boston: Northeastern Univ. Press.

Comaroff, John L., & Jean Comaroff, eds. (1999) *Civil Society and the Political Imagination in Africa: Critical Perspectives.* Chicago and London: Univ. of Chicago Press.

Corrêa, Mariza (1982) "Repensando a Família Patriarcal Brasileira," in *Colcha de Retalhos: Estudos sobre a Família no Brasil.* São Paulo: Brasiliense.

DaMatta, Roberto (1979) *Carnavais, Malandros e Heróis: Para Uma Sociologia do Dilema Brasileiro.* Rio de Janeiro: Zahar.

Ewick, Patricia, & Susan S. Silbey (1998) *The Common Place of Law: Stories From Everyday Life.* Chicago: Univ. of Chicago Press.

Ferreira, Kátia Maria Martins (2000) *Os Reflexos do Estatuto da Criança e do Adolescente na Justiça da Infância e Juventude de Porto Alegre—Análise Sociológica dos Processos de Destituição do Pátrio Poder.* M.A. Thesis, Dept. of Sociology, PPGS-UFRGS (Porto Alegre).

Fine, Agnès, & Claire Neirinck (2000) "Parents de Sang, Parents Adoptifs; Approches Juridiques et Anthropologiques de L'adoption, France, Europe, USA, Canada," (Special Issue) *Droit et Sociétés,* Paris.

Fonseca, Claudia (1985) "Amour Maternel, Valeur Marchande et Survie: Aspects de la Circulation d'enfants dans un Bidonville Brésilien," 40 *Les Annales ESC* 991–1022.

——— (1986) "Orphanages, Foundlings, and Foster Mothers: The System of Child Circulation in a Brazilian Squatter Settlement," 59 *Anthropological Q.* 15–27.

——— (1993) "Parents et Enfants dans les Couches Populaires Brésiliennes au Début du Siècle: Un autre Genre D'amour," 25 *Droit et Cultures* 41–62.

——— (1997) "Ser Mulher, Mãe e Pobre," in M. Del Priore, ed., *História Das Mulheres no Brasil.* São Paulo: Editora Contexto.

——— (forthcoming) "The Politics of Adoption." *Law & Policy.*

Fournier, Suzanne, & Ernie Crey (1997) *Stolen from Our Embrace: The Abduction of First Nations' Children & the Restoration of Aboriginal Communities.* Toronto: Douglas & McIntyre.

Gailey, Christine W. (1998) "Making Kinship in the Wake of History: Gendered Violence and Older Child Adoption," 5 *Identities* 249–92.

——— (1999) "Seeking 'Baby Right': Race, Class, and Gender in U.S. International Adoption," in Anne-Lise Rygvold, Monica Dalen, & Barbro Saetersdal, eds., *Mine, Yours, Ours . . . and Theirs: Adoption, Changing Kinship and Family Patterns.* Oslo, Norway: Univ. of Oslo.

——— (2000) "Ideologies of Motherhood and Kinship in U.S. Adoption," in Heléna Ragoné & Frances Winddance Twine, eds., *Ideologies and Technologies of Motherhood.* NY: Routledge.

Goldstein, Donna (1998) "Nothing Bad Intended: Child Discipline, Punishment, and Survival in a Shantytown in Riò de Janeiro, Brazil," in N. Scheper-Hughes & C. Sargent, eds., *Small Wars: The Cultural Politics of Childhood.* Berkeley: Univ. of California Press.

Goody, Esther (1982) *Parenthood and Social Reproduction: Fostering and Occupational Roles in West Africa.* London: Cambridge Univ. Press.

Hecht, Tobias (1998) *At Home in the Street: Street Children of Northeast Brazil.* Cambridge: Cambridge Univ. Press.

Hoelgaard, Suzanne (1998) "Cultural Determinants of Adoption Policy: A Colombian Case Study," 12 *International J. of Law, Policy, & the Family* 202–401.

Jaffe, E., ed. (1995) *Intercountry Adoptions: Laws and Perspectives of 'Sending' Countries.* London: Martinus Nijhoff.

Johnson, Kay, Huang Banghan, & Wang Liyao (1998) "Infant Abandonment and Adoption in China," 24 *Population Development Rev.* 469–510.

Kane, Saralee (1993) "The Movement of Children for International Adoption: An Epidemiologic Perspective," 30 *Social Science J.* 323–39.

Kligman, Gail (1992) "Abortion and International Adoption in Post-Ceausescu Romania," 18 *Feminist Studies* 405–19.

Kuznesof, Elizabeth Anne (1998) "The Puzzling Contradictions of Child Labor, Unemployment, and Education in Brazil," 23 *J. of Family History* 225–39.

Lallemand, Suzanne (1993) *La Circulation des Enfants en Société Traditionnelle. Prêt, Don, Échange.* Paris: Editions Harmattan.

Lazarus-Black, Mindie (1994) "Alternative Readings: The Status of the Status of Children Act in Antigua and Barbuda," 28 *Law & Society Rev.* 993–1007.

Le Grand-Sebille, Catherine (1996) "Naissances Marquées, Rituels Manqués," 19 *Gradhiva* 77–85.

Merry, Sally Engle (1990) *Getting Justice and Getting Even: Legal Consciousness Among Working-Class Americans.* Chicago: Univ. of Chicago Press.

——— (1997) "Legal Pluralism and Transnational Culture: The Ka Ho'okolokolonui Kanaka Maoli Tribunal, Hawai'i, 1993," in R. Wilson, ed., *Human Rights, Culture & Context.* London: Pluto Press.

Meznar, Joan (1994) "Orphans and the Transition from Slave to Free Labor in Northeast Brazil: The Case of Campina Grande, 1850-1888," 27 *J. of Social History* 499–516.

Modell, Judith S. (1994) *Kinship with Strangers: Adoption and Interpretations of Kinship in American Culture.* Berkeley: Univ. of California Press.

——— (1997) "Rights to the Children: Foster Care and Social Reproduction in Hawai'i," in S. Franklin & H. Ragoné, eds., *Reproducing Reproduction: Kinship, Power, and Technological Innovation.* Philadelphia: Univ. of Pennsylvania Press.

Nabinger, Sylvia, & A.M. Crine (1997) "L'enfant entre Deux Mondes," 10 *Nervure* 33–36.

Neff, Charlotte (1996) "Pauper Apprenticeship in Early 19th Century Ontario," 21 *J. of Family History* 107–24.

Ouellette, Françoise-Romaine (1995) "La Part du Don dans L'Adoption," 19 *Anthropologie et Sociétés* 157–74.

Ramos, Donald (1978) "City and Country: The Family in Minas Gerais, 1804–1836," 3 *J. of Family History* 361–75.

Rapp, Rayna (2000) *Testing Women, Testing the Fetus: The Social Impact of Amniocentesis in America.* New York: Routledge.

Santos, Boaventura de Sousa (1999) *Pela mão de Alice: O Social e o Político na Pó-Modernidade.* São Paulo: Cortez Editora.

Sarat, Austin & Susan Silbey (1988) "The Pull of the Policy Audience," 10 *Law & Policy* 97.

Scheper-Hughes, Nancy (1990) "Theft of Life," *Society* 57–62 (September/October).

——— (1992) *Death Without Weeping: The Violence of Everyday Life in Brazil.* Berkeley: Univ. of California Press.

Scott, James C. (1985) *Weapons of the Weak: Everyday Forms of Peasant Resistance.* New Haven: Yale Univ. Press.

Selman, Peter (2000) *Intercountry Adoption: Development, Trends, and Perspectives.* British Agencies for Adoption and Fostering (BAAF).

Silbey, Susan (1997) "Let Them Eat Cake: Globalization, Postmodern Colonialism, and the Possibilities of Justice," 31 *Law & Society Rev.* 207–35.

Silva, Daisy Carvalho (1995) "The Legal Procedures for Adopting Children in Brazil by Citizens and Foreign Nationals," in E. Jaffe, ed., *Intercountry Adoptions: Laws and Perspectives of 'Sending' Countries.* London: Martinus Nijhoff.

Simon, Rita J. (1984) "Adoption of Black Children by White Parents in the USA," in P. Bean, ed., *Adoption: Essays in Social Policy, Law, and Sociology.* New York & London: Tavistock.

Siqueira, Liborni (1993) *Adoção no Tempo e no Espaço.* Forense: Riò de Janeiro.

Slaughter, M. M. (2000) "Contested Identities: The Adoption of American Indian Children and the Liberal State," 9 *Social and Legal Studies* 227–48.

Stack, Carol (1996) *Call to Home: African Americans Reclaim the Rural South.* New York: HarperCollins.

Starr, June, & Jane F. Collier, eds. (1989) "Introduction: Dialogues in Legal Anthropology," in J. Starr & F. Collier, eds., *History and Power in the Study of Law: New Directions in Legal Anthropology.* Ithaca & London: Cornell Univ. Press.

Stephens, Sharon, ed. (1995) *Children and the Politics of Culture.* Princeton: Princeton Univ. Press.

Strathern, Marilyn (1992) *Reproducing the Future: Anthropology, Kinship, and the New Reproductive Technologies.* New York: Routledge.

Venâncio, Renato Pinto (1986) "Nos limites da Sagrada Família: Ilegitimidade e Casamento no Brasil Colonial," in Ronaldo Vainfas, ed., *História e sexualidade no Brasil.* Riò de Janeiro: Graal.

Vianna, Luiz Werneck (1996) "Poder Judiciário, 'Positivação' do Direito Natural e História," 9 *Estudos Históricos* 257–424.

Weber, Lidia N.D. (1999) *Lacos de Ternura: Pesquisas e Histórias de Adoção.* Curitiba: Juruá.

Wegar, Katarina (1997) *Adoption, Identity, and Kinship: The Debate Over Sealed Birth Records.* New Haven: Yale Univ. Press.

Yanagisako, Sylvia, & Carol Delaney, eds. (1995) *Naturalizing Power: Essays in Feminist Cultural Analysis.* New York: Routledge.

Yngvesson, Barbara (1997) "Negotiating Motherhood: Identity and Difference in 'Open' Adoptions," 31 *Law & Society Rev.* 31–80.

——— (1998) "States of Origin: Race, Roots and Nation in the Adoption of Children Transnationally." Presented at the annual meeting of the American Anthropological Association, Philadelphia.

——— (2000) "'Un Niño De Cualquier Color': Race and Nation in Intercountry Adoption," in J. Jensen & B. De Sousa Santos, eds., *Globalizing Institutions: Case Studies in Regulation and Innovation.* Aldershot: Ashgate.

Zelizer, Viviana (1985) *Pricing the Priceless Child: The Changing Social Values of Children.* New York: Basic Books.

Statutes

Adoption & Safe Families Act, Public Law 105–89 (H.R. 327, amending H.R. 867). Published in Congress, November 13, 1997; signed by President Clinton on November 19, 1997.

Código Civil Brasileiro [Brazilian 1916 Civil Code]. Lei n. 3.071 de 1 de Janeiro, 1916, Art. 368–378.

Código de Menores [1979 Children's Code], lei n 6.697 de 10 de Outubro de 1979.

Código Penal Brasil [Brazilian Penal Code], decreto-lei n 2.848 de 7 de dezembro, 1940, Art. 242.

Estatuto de Criança e do Adolescente [1990 Children's Code], lei n 8.069 de 13 de julho de 1990, Diário Oficial da Uniã de 16.07.1990.

Hague Convention on Protection of Children & Cooperation in Respect of Intercountry Adoption, adopted by the 17th Session of the Hague Conference on Private International Law (concluded May 29, 1993), I.L.M. 1134, Art. 29.

Lei n 4.655 de 2 de Junho de 1965.

United Nations Convention on the Rights of the Child. G.A. RES. 44/25, U.N. GAOR, 44th Session, Supp. No. 49, U.N. Doc. A/44/736 (November 20, 1989).

[14]

Tender Ties: Husbands' Rights and Racial Exclusion in Chinese Marriage Cases, 1882–1924

Todd Stevens

When Congress ended the immigration of Chinese laborers in 1882, the Chinese population was over 95% male. While there has been much disagreement about why so few women came, the more fruitful question may be to ask how Chinese women were able to immigrate to the United States at all. Central to their immigration were legal arguments for lawful Chinese immigrants—primarily merchants and native-born citizens—to bring their wives to the United States. Due to racial restrictions barring them from independent entry or marital naturalization, Chinese wives appealed to the uncodified gender privileges of their husbands in turn-of-the-century legal society: the natural right of a man to the company of his wife and children. In the face of a bureaucratic structure designed to sift immigrants by race, judges ruled that racial admission policies must conform to established gender privileges. The power of these arguments was tested in cases involving the deportation of Chinese women admitted as wives. While initially evading registration regulations for immigrants, Chinese women were unsuccessful at evading regulations concerning prostitution. This failure underscored the performative aspects of husbands' rights arguments, especially the image of the dutiful wife and husband and the class-based ideal of the elite merchant or citizen.

The standard that we apply to our inhabitants is that of manhood.

—President Calvin Coolidge, 1924 message to Congress

Todd Stevens is a Samuel A. Golieb Fellow in legal history at the New York University School of Law and a Ph.D. candidate in history at Princeton University. Many thanks to Dirk Hartog, Daniel Rodgers, Susan Naquin, Sean Wilentz, Dionne Searcey, Jesse Hoffnung-Garskof, Eduardo Elena, Donna Dennis, Sarah Igo, Lucy Salyer, Kitty Calavita, and Leti Volpp for their helpful comments and suggestions. Versions of this paper were presented at the Annual Conference of the American Society for Legal History.

It is not good for man to practice celibacy.

—Kenneth Fung, Executive Secretary of the Chinese American Citizens Alliance, testimony before the House Committee on Immigration and Naturalization, 4 March 1930

Historians generally agree on the importance of the gender imbalance in shaping Chinese American communities in the United States before World War II (Chan 1991a; Yung 1995, 69–77; Hing Ong 1993). The scarcity of women facilitated the rise of a bachelor culture, hindered the creation of Chinese American families in the United States, and led many men to return to China. The reasons that so few Chinese women immigrated to the United States had domestic as well as international roots: restrictive U.S. immigration laws, especially those concerning prostitution; the discriminatory climate for Chinese in the United States; and transnational family networks that required women to remain in China (Peffer 1992, 1999; McKeown 1999). While scholars disagree about the relative weight of each of these factors, the more fruitful question may be to ask how Chinese women were able to come to the United States at all. In terms of raw numbers, the population of Chinese women in America doubled from 1890 to 1920.[1] For answers, we must turn to the experience of Chinese men and women in American courts and the story of federal judges' struggle to tame the competing demands of racial exclusion and gender privilege.

Returning to the United States with his new wife in 1884, Too Cheong thought he had done everything necessary to secure her admission. Before leaving San Francisco for China, he had obtained a reentry certificate from the Treasury Department. The certificate stated clearly that he was a legal resident of the United States, having worked as a laborer in California from 1880 to 1883. That the marriage was legal was undisputed by all parties. Under U.S. law, the laws of the country in which a marriage takes place determined its validity. Too Cheong's marriage license confirmed that he and his bride, Ah Moy, had been legally married in China in 1883. While Ah Moy had never been to the United States before and thus had no reentry certificate, the law appeared to be on her side. Signed in 1880, article 2 of the latest treaty between the United States and China provided that "Chinese laborers who are now in the United States, shall be allowed to go and come of their own free will and accord, and shall be accorded all the rights, privileges, immunities, and exemptions which are accorded to the citizens and subjects of the most favored nations." And what was more of a right and privilege of the nineteenth-century husband than the "care and comfort" of his wife?

1. Based on U.S. Census figures, there were 3,868 Chinese women in the United States in 1890. In 1920, there were 7,748. In 1930, there were 15,152. From 1906 to 1924, 2,848 Chinese women entered as wives of citizens (Yung 1995, 293; U.S. House 1926, testimony of Guy E. Kelly).

Immigration officials, however, saw it differently. They ordered Ah Moy returned to China on the first available steamer leaving San Francisco. The same treaty that granted Too Cheong protection from discrimination had paved the way for the Chinese Exclusion Act (Exclusion Act) (22 U.S. Stat. 60). Passed in 1882 by an increasingly xenophobic Congress, the Exclusion Act prohibited the immigration of Chinese laborers to the United States for a period of 10 years. Yet the Exclusion Act mentioned nothing about the husbands, wives, or children of laborers already resident in the United States. Nonetheless, the inspector determined that Ah Moy was a Chinese laborer for purposes of the Exclusion Act. If Ah Moy's status was that of her husband's, he reasoned, then she should be treated as a Chinese laborer, a category of immigrant that was inadmissible without a reentry certificate. Despite his wife's detainment, Too Cheong had been allowed to enter and immediately filed for a writ of habeas corpus. The California Circuit Court stayed the deportation order and heard the case within the month (*Case of the Chinese Wife, In re Ah Moy* 1884).

On the surface, the case looked to be a simple matter of determining whether acts of Congress or international treaties took precedence when the one contradicted the other. Yet Justice Stephen Field and Judge Lorenzo Sawyer's opinions strayed far from questions of international law and veered between admissions of sympathy for the husband and speculations about the hordes of Chinese that might enter if the case were improperly decided. Their conclusions betrayed a similar ambivalence. The judges denied Ah Moy's appeal, but could not agree on the appropriate question: Was Ah Moy's status a function of her race, her marriage, or both? Judge Sawyer wrote that the case "presents one of the most important questions that can arise under the Chinese restriction act."

What caused such confusion and hyperbolic rhetoric? Unlike other cases concerning the due process of immigration hearings, Too Cheong's situation probed a gray area of immigration law. His lawyers confronted the judges with a Chinese man who demanded the legal privileges associated with those of all husbands.[2] Instead of challenging Congress's ability to make racial distinctions in immigration policy, Too Cheong wanted his wife to be exempted from the ban on Chinese immigration based on his rights as a California husband.

The tension between husbands' rights and racially based immigration laws would dog the proponents of Chinese exclusion and the judges deciding Chinese immigration cases for decades. Nineteenth-century definitions of coverture mandated that the care and comfort of a man's wife was so important to him and his children that her status should follow his. Most

2. In my article, I do not discuss the origin of the Chinese plaintiff's arguments. My dissertation takes up this issue with respect to the relationship between lawyers and their Chinese clients in Portland and Seattle from 1870–1925.

American men expected courts to view wives' property as under husbands' control. Husbands represented their wives' interests (Siegel 1994a, 1994b). In addition to the ability to legally represent their family, husbands claimed a natural right to their wives and children that informed areas of statutory ambiguity (Hartog 1997, 2000).

Too Cheong's argument that his rights—coverture and principles of family unity—trumped his wife's racial classification presented judges with a specific problem of both external and internal classification. Chinese marriage cases moved judges to imagine a hierarchy of identities: Was the man standing before them a husband or a Chinese person under the law? He could only be one or the other; never both. This hierarchy was similarly extended to a Chinese woman when judges asked whether she was a dutiful wife or an immigrant ineligible for naturalization and wholly subject to the state's power.[3] Judges' decisions were contingent, in part, on their own self-identification. Were they administrators of the immigration laws or guardians of a gendered male privilege?[4]

While a novel problem in immigration law, the parceling out of rights associated with marriage and family based on a litigant's race was nothing new. Judges denied coverture and husbands' rights to most nonwhite members of American society throughout the nineteenth century. Before the Civil War, Southern courts were unwilling to recognize slaves as husbands and their families as deserving of protection from separation (Burnham 1987; Morris 1996). Anti-miscegenation statutes undercut the right of husbands to marry whom they wanted and to control their households (Pascoe 1996; Osumi 1982). This national trend in civil rights litigation held out little room of hope for Chinese husbands and wives. The 1870s saw the rejection of Reconstruction egalitarianism and the restriction of federal interference with private violations of African Americans' civil rights (Smith 1997; Kaczorowski 1987). Over the next 25 years, the U.S. Supreme Court acceded to barriers to African American voting and the segregation of public facilities (Smith 1997, 347–409; Kennedy 1986). In immigration law,

3. The dualities judges encountered in deciding the fate of Chinese wives were part of the broader challenge of interpreting the Chinese Exclusion laws or distinguishing merchants from laborers. Focusing on the "front-end stage of legal decision making," Kitty Calavita describes how Chinese immigrants frustrated inspectors' attempts to sort Chinese immigrants by class by mimicking the "physical markers" and documentation of upper-class merchants (2000, 31, 40). This article adds to her line of analysis by highlighting the dualities expected of Chinese women and the power of accusations of prostitution to stigmatize women in the minds of judges and inspectors.

4. Readers of an earlier draft suggested that the subject of the project is the intersectionality of race and gender. See Kimberle Crenshaw 1991, 1989. And so it is. But the intersectionality that shapes my argument is not the one that examines the subject position of women of color in cases that put them in the impossible situation of choosing between sometimes-competing regimes of race and gender, but the intersectionality that judges experienced in their competing roles as administrators of racially based immigration laws and guardians of certain types of gender privilege. For another treatment of marriage as the intersection between gender and state policy, see Nancy Cott 2000.

the Exclusion Act was followed by five more immigration acts that progressively tightened the noose on Chinese entry into the United States and led to more universal restrictions in 1917 and 1924.[5] Federal judges validated Congress's plenary power to make whatever restrictions it deemed necessary with respect to new immigrants.

Yet, Chinese husbands and wives were increasingly successful at claiming the rights of family unity during the four decades after 1884. Here, husbands won, at least sometimes. This article tracks the evolution of arguments concerning husbands' rights and the difficulties they posed for federal judges in three types of cases over this period. Each section of the article will discuss one of the types. The first type—characterized by the efforts of Chinese laborers such as Too Cheong—ended with his case and did not present much of a problem for judges thereafter. While neither Judge Sawyer nor Justice Field doubted the "sacredness of that relation" or "the rights of the husband and father . . . to bring their wives and children with them," they were unwilling to allow an unforeseen argument about gender privilege to undermine the Exclusion Act. Field described Too Cheong and Ah Moy's marriage as a voluntary act, entered into with full knowledge of the potential consequences.[6] If he wanted to be with her, "he can return and protect his child wife in the Celestial Empire." Judge Sawyer was more open about his fears of undermining the exclusion laws. If Sawyer allowed her to enter based solely on her marriage to a permitted Chinese laborer, then, under "this right, the number of [female] Chinese laborers who are entitled to come to the United States will be greatly extended beyond the number who can enter by virtue of their own individual rights" (*In re Ah* Moy 1884, 786).

The second section considers the demands of Chinese men with stronger rights to legally travel back and forth from the United States to China. First merchants, and then a second generation of Chinese Americans, appealed to federal courts to admit their wives. A close reading of these lower-court opinions reveals judges struggling with their role as administrators or guardians. Presented with similar facts, judges in different district courts flip-flopped from blanket acceptance to irreversible rejection until the 1899 Supreme Court ruling in *U.S. v. Gue Lim*. The court in *Gue Lim* allowed the wives of merchants to enter based solely on their marriage to a person exempted from the exclusion laws. Soon after *Gue Lim*, the immigration officials extended this privilege to second-generation Chinese Americans who were American citizens by birth. Even during the "Gilded

5. Act of 5 July 1884, 23 U.S. Stat. 115; Act of 1 October 1888, 25 U.S. Stat. 47; Act of 5 May 1892, 27 Stat. 25; Act of 3 November 1893, 28 Stat. 7; Act of 18 August 1894, 28 U.S. Stat. 390; Act of 5 February 1917, 39 Stat. 874; Act of 26 May 1924, 43 Stat. 153.

6. The idea of marriage as a voluntary act parallels Field's reasoning in other cases involving freedom of contract (see McCurdy 1975).

Age of Ascriptive Americanism," these Chinese American husbands attained the rights of men in a patriarchal legal order (Smith 1997, 347).

The third type of case concerns the deportation of wives accused of being illegal immigrants. Post–*Gue Lim*, the legal status of Chinese wives remained contested and precarious due to the 1882 Exclusion Act's explicit denial of marital naturalization to Chinese persons. The judges' willingness to invoke gender privilege depended primarily on the extent to which the grounds for the wife's deportation disturbed the couple's claim of family unity. Thus, judges continued to identify Chinese women as covered by their husbands' status in deportation cases concerning the possession of residence certificates. Yet the same appeals to husbands' rights fell flat when applied to women accused of prostitution. By focusing on stereotypes of Chinese women's sexual licentiousness, immigration officials and prosecutors exposed the degree to which appeals to coverture rested on an image of a dutiful wife.[7] Judges' change of heart similarly revealed the ways in which they sorted Chinese women by class. Prostitutes could not be wives in part because only wealthy Chinese men could afford to bring their wives, and no wealthy man would have a prostitute for a wife.

The struggles of Chinese men born in the United States—native-born citizens—to shield their wives from restrictive immigration laws challenge previous descriptions of judges' response to the intersection of citizenship rights, gender, and race. The two leading portraits of citizenship during this period rely mainly on political theory to interpret judges' decisions. James Kettner (1978) describes a gradual opening and universalizing of citizenship privileges over the nineteenth century—the creation of a liberal state. Before the Civil War, citizenship was volitional, and after 1830, open to all white males regardless of property ownership. The Reconstruction amendments further expanded the citizenship pool by mandating native-born citizenship, favoring national over state citizenship, and removing racial barriers to African American citizenship. By contrast, Rogers Smith (1997) sees legislators and judges during the last part of the nineteenth century honing a normative vision of citizenship continually restricted by race and gender. The Reconstruction Amendments may have provided an aspirational ideal for those outside the protected class, yet ascriptive limitations dominated by the turn of the century. While this article is more in agreement with Smith's pessimistic vision, Smith fails to explore how ethnocultural norms were tied to gender roles that sometimes cut in contradictory directions.[8] The struggles of Chinese couples certainly reveal federal judges

7. For more on the image of Chinese women in the Anglo imagination, see Hirata 1984, 402–34; Yung 1995 26–37; 73–77; Peffer 1986, 28–46.

8. Nancy Cott (1988, 2000) explores the gender roles that pervade citizenship in her recent work on marriage and citizenship. For Cott, the relationship between marriage and citizenship before the 1922 Cable Act was one of gender subordination. Marriage was linked to citizenship, in part, because men's independent status was achieved through the depen-

actively building racial and gender categories and segmenting litigants' claims accordingly; the judges were just much less successful at maintaining stable hierarchies.

In the face of a bureaucratic structure designed to sift immigrants by race, judges ruled that racial admission policies must conform to established gender privileges. The disputes explored in this article reveal the unpredictable stresses on systems of racial exclusion: The rights of husbands to their families both qualified and distorted apparently straightforward laws.

THE UNFINISHED BUSINESS OF THE CHINESE EXCLUSION ACT

The passage of the Chinese Exclusion Act in 1882 sealed off the free immigration of Chinese laborers to the United States. Promoted as protecting the rights of American workingmen, the Exclusion Act was the first racially based immigration restriction in United States history. The racial logic of the Exclusion Act and its subsequent extensions wrote into law the logic of California's anti-Chinese movement: Chinese keep out! In the eyes of the California state legislature and the United States Congress, Chinese immigrants were not fit for the freedoms of American democracy.[9] Despite Congress's unambiguous opposition to further Chinese immigration, the Exclusion Act and its successors were less clear about the fate of the more than 100,000 Chinese Americans still residing in the United States.

For Chinese immigrants living in the United States, the primary consequence of the Exclusion Act was to call into question their ability to go back and forth to China. As of 1880, the Chinese population was 95%

dence of their wives. The point of view here is obviously crucial; for white women during a time of increasing political activity and an emerging discourse of women's suffrage and equality, the tying of citizenship status to notions of coverture in the 1855 and 1907 Immigration Acts represented giant leaps backward. Yet for certain Chinese American couples during this period, marriage and its relationship to coverture, while not able to bestow citizenship on Chinese women, functioned as a bulwark against separation and an immigration regime increasingly bent on preventing the creation of Chinese American families. See Cott 1998, 2000.

9. Much scholarship has focused on the mechanism of political organizing that led to the Chinese Exclusion Acts. Stuart Creighton Miller traces the negative images of Chinese people in the United States back to late-eighteenth-century international merchants. Looking at the formation of Dennis Kearney's Workingmen's Party in California, Alexander Saxton explores how working-class consciousness rested on designating Chinese immigrants as the universal and racialized enemy of all workingmen. Both these studies emphasize that in all its myriad forms, the anti-Chinese movement of the 1870s and 1880s was predicated on racial categories that motivated large segments of American society to support the Chinese Exclusion Act (Miller 1969; Saxton1971). For a dissenting view, see Gyory 1998. Leti Volpp further argues that perceptions of Chinese Americans, and Asian Pacific Americans as a group, as perpetual "foreigners" and racially unfit for participation in the U.S. political community continue to the present and have "rendered their [Asian Pacific American's] presumptive fitness for citizenship suspect" (Volpp 2001, 84).

male, the vast majority of whom were born in China and had immigrated to the United States from a cluster of counties in Guangdong Province. In response to the multiple civil wars, environmental disasters and increased competition from imported manufactured goods, villages in South China sent men to countries all over Southeast Asia as well as North and South America. Upon coming of age, men arranged with trading organizations (*huiguan*) based in their town to borrow money for the trip and find employment once they arrived. Whether they married before they left or on a visit home, most emigrants' wives remained in their husbands' home village to care for his parents and raise their children. Men would send a portion of their earnings home while they were abroad, with the expectation that when they had saved enough to either retire or purchase land, they might return.[10]

For most Chinese immigrants, going back and forth to China represented a lifeline to their families.[11] Although precise statistics are not available, early historians of the Chinese community estimated that more than one-third of Chinese immigrants were married before coming to the United States (Hsu 2000, 99; Coolidge 1909, 17–20; Culin 1887). Due to the scarcity of Chinese women in the United States, those who could returned to China to marry. Thus, for most Chinese men, traveling to China was an integral part of working in the United States. It was the only way for Chinese immigrants to see their families as well as start their own.

---

10. Conditions in China as well as the United States contributed to the gender imbalance in Chinese American communities. These gender imbalances were extreme relative to both non-Chinese immigrant communities in the United States and other overseas communities in the Chinese diaspora. On average, females represented between 10 to 20% of overseas Chinese populations before 1920.

In China, male sojourning traditions that bound wives to their husbands' family home were well established by the 1850s. The presence of wives in the husbands' home village tied men—and their remittances—to the village. Wives were also able to maintain traditions of ancestor worship and care for their in-laws while their husband was away. In nineteenth-century China, women typically had no right to divorce or remarry should they become unhappy with their marriage or their husbands' absence (see McKeown 1999; Mackie 1996, xx; Yung 1995, 19; Lyman 1968, 326). In the United States, the poor working conditions Chinese immigrants endured, including legalized discrimination and anti-Chinese violence, discouraged female Chinese immigration. In addition, laws prohibiting Chinese prostitutes generally hindered female Chinese immigration before and after the Exclusion Act (Peffer 1999, 1992). Yet, the increase in the percentage of native-born Chinese in the decades after the Exclusion Act highlights the importance of an exception for certain Chinese wives. In 1900, 10% of the Chinese population was born in the United States; by 1930, over 41% were. See table 8 in Yung 1995, 303.

11. A new study of the transnational community of Taishan details the close connection between Chinese immigrants to the United States and their home villages in China (Hsu 2000). Interviews with Chinese Americans on the Pacific coast in 1924 emphasize similar connections: "Can a man live in this country without a wife, never see the wife? We have got to go to China to see how our children are. We got to spend some money over there. I can't understand your new law in breaking the people as a family" (Survey of Race Relations 1923–25).

Within days of the passage of the Exclusion Act, the federal district court in San Francisco was deluged with cases of Chinese men denied entry upon returning from a visit to China. As legal residents of the United States under the Burlingame Treaty of 1868 and the Treaty of 1880, these men argued that they could not be denied entry for lacking a reentry certificate they could not have obtained; when these men left the United States, no certificates existed. One contemporary lawyer estimated that there were 12,000 men in such circumstances, which constituted over 10% of the total Chinese population in the United States (Fritz 1991b).

The federal courts were initially quite supportive of Chinese laborers' attempts to reenter the country. Appointed by the state legislature, the partisan Collector of Customs in San Francisco detained virtually all Chinese entrants without a certificate (Fritz 1991b). In one case, the collector would not allow a Chinese boatswain on an American steamer to re-enter the United States, even though he had never left the ship (*In re Ah Sing* 1882). Against vociferous public protests, Judges Sawyer and Hoffman turned their courtrooms into "habeas corpus mills," churning out 7,000 cases between 1882 and 1891 (Fritz 1988, 28–29). Holding that Chinese persons who had been in the United States before the passage of the Exclusion Act were entitled to reenter, the judges admitted and reviewed each person's evidence that they were a former resident. Too Cheong was one of these petitioners.

Congress responded in 1884 with the passage of a revised Exclusion Act (23 U.S. Stat. 115). The 1884 act strengthened the certificate requirements. But to no avail. While the Supreme Court continued to support Congress's right to determine what kinds of immigrants should be allowed to enter the United States, federal district judges upheld the right of Chinese laborers who had left before the return certificates were issued to offer other evidence of their previous residence (Fritz 1991b, 40–43; *United States v. Chew Heong* 1884). The 1888 Immigration Act put the issue to rest by prohibiting Chinese immigrants from reentering the United States, no matter what their previous standing (25 U.S. Stat. 476). The Supreme Court reaffirmed the 1888 act within the year (*Chae Chan Ping v. United States* 1899).

Under the 1888 act, the question posed by Too Cheong and Ah Moy became moot. Too Cheong could not have returned to the United States after marrying his wife in China. The 1888 Immigration Act targeted the Chinese still living in America. Chinese laborers were prohibited from going back and forth from China, and the Chinese population in the United States continued to steadily decrease as men returned to China. Those who stayed searched for ways to continue their long-distance families. One method of combating immigration restrictions was to change one's status under the immigration laws. While the 1888 law shut off any avenues for return for laborers, it left intact the right of protected classes, such as merchants, to come and go. This loophole helped the Chinese community survive, as men began to save money not just to return home, but to invest in a trading firm (and become a "merchant") to gain the right to return to China. While this option was only open to those who could earn sufficient funds, it gave Chinese men a chance to remain in the United States, visit their families and father children in China.[12] And if they were lucky enough to reenter in the right jurisdiction, they might even bring their families with them.

THE WIFE OF A MERCHANT

Merchants were the first Chinese immigrants to arrive in California. Merchants came initially as traders, and when gold was discovered in Sutter's Creek, they facilitated the immigration of thousands of Chinese laborers. Loaning money to prospective miners, arranging work contracts with employers in search of manual laborers, and selling the new immigrants imported Chinese foodstuffs, merchants were the wealthiest men in the Chinese community. They came to America to invest their capital—instead of discovering it with a pick and shovel—and take part in a family business. Organized into trading companies, merchants also formed the de facto government in urban Chinatowns. While the sandlot bigot might only see another "Chinaman," the leaders of the merchant associations (known on the West Coast as the Six Companies) represented the Chinese establishment. Their Western clothes, command of English, and high-priced legal counsel ensured that American judges could not miss this fact (Lyman 1974; McClain 1994; Lu 1994; Ma 1983).

The claims of merchants to bring their wives and children to the United States were much stronger than those men classified as Chinese laborers. Indeed, their right to come and go to China was never restricted.[13] In each treaty with China, merchants represented a protected class:

> Chinese subjects, whether proceeding to the United States as teachers, students, merchant or from curiosity, together with their body and household servants. . . shall be allowed to go and come of their own

12. The practice of seeking merchant status in order to travel back and forth to China and potentially bring their families was quite similar to those of other immigrants to the United States. For non-Asian immigrants, naturalization was the analogous response, a strategy they increasingly adopted to bring families to the United States when Congress tightened entry and residency standards.

13. Unlike laborers, merchants were exempted by the Exclusion Acts of 1882, 1884, 1888, and 1908 as well as the Immigration Act of 1924. The language in the Burlingame Treaty of 1868, which was carried over to the Treaty of 1880, was copied in each of the Exclusion laws. Merchants' special privileges resulted from Congress's interest in maintaining access for its own merchants and traders to sell American goods in China (McKee 1977).

> free will and accord, and shall be accorded all the rights, privileges, immunities and exemptions which are accorded to the citizens and subjects of the most favored nation. (22 U.S. Stat. 826 [1880])

The 1882 Exclusion Act essentially repeated this language with one condition, that "every Chinese person other than a laborer" who may legally come to the United States must obtain a certificate from the Chinese government stating the details of their profession (22 U.S. Stat. 58). Since the vast majority of immigrants came through Canton, the certificates became known as Canton certificates. For nonlaborers, the 1884 amendment mandated that the certificates issued by the Chinese government be verified by the American consul and include more particulars about merchants' businesses. The 1888 act similarly left the merchant exemption unchanged.

A merchant's right to come to the United States based on his profession instead of his previous residency, reinforced arguments based on coverture and parentage. Unlike cases involving laborers and their wives, especially after 1888, a merchant's wife benefited from interpretations that linked her and her children's status to that of her husband. Restrictive immigration laws did not invalidate the "equal treatment" clauses of the Treaty of 1880. If the judges were as sensitive to a man's right to his family as they claimed in cases involving laborers, they could not hide behind favoring congressional statutes over international treaties. How could a judge rule that a Chinese merchant could bring his "household servants," as promised in the Treaty of 1880, but not his wife and children?

In a decision written three months before the passage of the 1884 amendments, Judge Ogden Hoffman sided with a Chinese merchant. The case involved a group of merchants' children who had been issued Canton certificates. While Hoffman could have ruled these certificates fraudulent—the children "were in no sense merchants"—he reported that "it was not without satisfaction that I found there was no requirement of the law which would oblige me to deny to a parent the custody of his child, and to send the latter back across the ocean to the country from which he came" (*In re Tung Yeong* 1884). Speaking to the wider San Francisco public, he defended his reasoning in a wide range of Chinese immigration cases brought before his district court in northern California. Stating that the "rulings of the court have been very imperfectly reported by the press," he included a summary of decisions concerning Chinese "children brought to or sent by their parents or guardians in this city." The children were mainly 10 to 15 years old and were coming to the United States, as their parents testified, to go to school or begin working in the family business. Hoffman noted that the parents were almost all merchants, "sometimes of considerable substance, resident here," and entitled to their rights under the Treaty of 1880.

Judge Sawyer of the circuit court of California disagreed six months later. Although the intervening passage of the 1884 Act changed little with respect to the necessary certificates, Judge Sawyer found ample reasons why wives and minor children of merchants should now not be allowed to enter. Instead of a man's right to care and custody of his family, the judge emphasized the literal language of the statute. Congress meant "every Chinese person" to be all-encompassing. To introduce an exception for a merchant's wife and children, he reasoned, would "be legislating, rather than construing" (*In re Ah Quan* 1884, 187). While Sawyer agreed that wives "should be deemed to belong to the class to which the husband or father belongs," they were still required to have a certificate. The justification for this strict construction followed the logic of racial fear: To allow Chinese petitioners to introduce evidence other than a certificate would induce potential fraud and allow "anyone who might choose to father these minor children [to] bring any number of them hither" (*In re Ah Quan* 1884, 186).

Yet even Sawyer was not entirely insensitive to the merchants' position. Sawyer's insistence on using the certificates may have been simply a means to streamline the immigration process and reduce the number of Chinese immigrant habeas corpus cases on his docket.[14] Viewing the ruling as a guide to future cases, Sawyer promoted his construction as merely procedural, for "the husband, when he obtains a certificate for himself, can as readily obtain it for his wife and child" (*In re Ah Quan* 1884, 187). The problem, however, was what the certificate for a wife or child was supposed to say. The 1884 Act's language only covered merchants, students, and tourists (all presumptively adult male identities), and the information required on the certificates was intended to verify immigrants' vocational status. There was no mention of the wife and child of a member of the protected class. If Sawyer believed the act's provisions should be read strictly, how could a judge view a certificate stating that a woman was married to a merchant as a certificate of the sort that the act required?

This question was never answered, but a clue lay in the instructions on federal policy toward Chinese merchants' dependents issued by the solicitor of the Treasury Department. In 1889, collectors of customs were informed that the wife of a Chinese merchant who had never been to the United States before should be refused entry, regardless of whether her husband accompanied her. In a subsequent letter, Solicitor Hepburn explained his

14. Judge Sawyer used his decision to review the court's position on Chinese immigration in light of the July 1884 Act and propose that the new laws, if enforced strictly, might better regulate Chinese immigration and free the courts from the glut of cases. He argued that the 1884 Act did not change the ability of laborers who left before certificates were obtainable to enter the United States. But with regard to the minor children and wives of Chinese men allowed to enter, he still felt that "every person must have a certificate." Sawyer admitted that there might be difficulties until the word got out, but still believed that it would not "make any great difference, when the construction becomes known" (*In re Ah Quan* 1884, 187).

reasoning to Rev. Frederic Masters, superintendent of the Chinese Mission in San Francisco. Rev. Masters had protested the decision of the collector of customs to deny admission to the wife of a Chinese dentist. It was, he had written the solicitor, "unreasonable to expect the Chinese officials to furnish her with a certificate of her being the wife of a dentist" who was doing business in this country. "The proof," according to Masters, "is to be found here rather than there." The solicitor's response emphasized that neither the dentist nor his wife was a citizen (which, as we shall see, would have put the solicitor in an even deeper legal thicket). Therefore her "marital relation [did not] exempt her from the requirements of the [1884] statute" (*United States v. Mrs. Gue Lim* 1899, letter from Solicitor W. P. Hepburn, 26 July, 1890, in Brief of the U.S. Attorney).

The ambiguity of the statute and lack of a higher-court decision prompted each federal district court to issue its own decision on the admissibility of wives and children of Chinese merchants. A pair of decisions from the Oregon district court diverged from those of the California courts and permitted wives and children to enter based solely on their marital relation. In *In re Chung Toy Ho* (1890), Judge Matthew Deady ruled that the wife and child of a Chinese merchant living in Portland were exempt from the 1884 act. Like an early Judge Hoffman, Deady argued that Wong Ham's wife and child were simply not "the 'persons' contemplated by Congress in the passage of the Act." Four years later, another Oregon judge concluded that despite the fact that a merchants' marriage was invalid under United States laws, his wife could enter without a certificate because of the merchants' social standing, his good faith effort to follow the law, and his respectable lawyers (*In re Lum Ling Ying* 1894). While neither opinion was any more controlling than the California decisions, the reasoning of the Oregon judges displayed a willingness to sidestep the letter of the law in the interest of spousal unification.

Contending decisions multiplied as the 1890s wore on. In 1895, the new solicitor of the Treasury Department, F. A. Reeve, advised a collector to admit Tom Ah Bat, the son of a domiciled Chinese merchant, so he could be educated in an American school in Omaha, Nebraska. But in two subsequent opinions over the next 13 months, Reeve ordered young Chinese boys in similar circumstances to be deported (*United States v. Mrs. Gue Lim* 1899, letters from F. A. Reeve to J. G. Carlisle, 19 March 1896, 1 October, 1896; letter from F. A. Reeve to J. G. Carlisle, 7 September 1895, in Brief of the U.S. Attorney, 46–48). In 1897, a New York circuit court judge rejected the appeal of a young Chinese boy trying to join his father, a legally domiciled merchant (*In re Li Foon* 1897). San Francisco's federal district court took a similar view in 1888 in a case concerning the admission of the wife of an actor (*In re Wo Tai Li* 1888). Judge Hoffman, the family-values author of the decision in *In re Tung Yeong* (1884), rejected the appeal on the grounds that to admit evidence other than the certificate specified would reward the petitioner for neglecting to follow the law's instructions.

Two years later the United States Supreme Court finally agreed to take on a case involving the wife of a Chinese merchant. In May 1897, Mrs. Gue Lim arrived in Tacoma, Washington, with her husband, Fook Kee, a Chinese merchant with interests in Seattle. They had lawfully married in China the month before and were admitted by the collector of customs. Five months later, however, the collector apparently changed his mind and arrested Mrs. Gue Lim as having unlawfully entered the United States. She was brought before a United States commissioner who ordered her returned to China. Gue Lim's attorneys appealed the decision to the United States district court in Washington.

Judge Cornelius Hanford heard the case and admitted her. Ironically, Hanford structured his opinion around Judge Sawyer's reasoning in Ah Moy's case (*United States v. Mrs. Gue Lim* 1897). Hanford agreed with Sawyer that the "wife of a Chinese person has the same status as her husband, and belongs to the class he belongs, whether she is in fact a laborer or not." Mrs. Gue Lim was both part of the protected class Congress intended to allow to come and go freely and unable to acquire a certificate to identify herself as exempt from the immigration laws. And Congress could not have meant to create requirements that were impossible to perform. Thus, using the same logic that effectively excluded all Chinese women married to Chinese laborers, Hanford argued that those married to members of the protected classes should be allowed to enter.[15] The U.S. attorney's office in Washington appealed the case to the United States Supreme Court.

The brief of Assistant Attorney General Henry Hoyt gave an indication of the headway the Chinese merchants' arguments had made. The first sentence of the section entitled "Argument" began: "The United States at the outset disclaims any intention to contend against the fundamental and natural right of the valid wife and legitimate minor children of Chinese merchants, not being laborers, to come and remain in this country" (*United*

15. Hanford chose Sawyer's interpretation of the impact of marriage on the status of a Chinese alien instead of Field's (that the wife was still a distinct person as expressed in *Ah Moy*) based on the outcome of *United States v. Chew Heong* (1884). Chew Heong was a laborer who upon returning to the United States in late 1884 was denied entry based on the 1884 Act's stipulation that return certificates were the only permissible evidence allowed to prove prior residence. In the circuit court decision, Sawyer, along with the other lower court federal judges in northern California, found for Chew Heong because Chew had left before the return certificates were available and Congress could not have intended to exclude those who never had an opportunity to obtain a certificate. Having recently been elevated to the U.S. Supreme Court, Judge Field sat on the panel as a circuit justice and overruled his colleagues based on his desire to satisfy "the impatience in the public mind" and his unwillingness to allow any evidence other than the certificates. On appeal, the United States Supreme Court, reversed Field in favor of Sawyer's position. Citing the precedent in *United States v. Chew Heong* as more recent than *Ah Moy*, Hanford believed the court had enforced Sawyer's position on the types of evidence allowed in immigration proceedings and the impact of marriage on the status of a Chinese alien.

States v. Mrs. Gue Lim 1899, Brief of the U.S. Attorney, 6). While Hoyt tried to steer the issue back to contradictions between the Treaty and later Acts of Congress, he admitted that a husband's right to the company of his wife and children extended to Chinese men. Instead of stating that the law literally mandated that "every Chinese person" must have a certificate, the government argued that the impracticability of obtaining a certificate was a matter of degree. In response to Judge Deady's ruling in *In re Chung Toy Ho* (1890), Hoyt declared, "a trip back to China for the purpose of obtaining the certificate would involve serious inconvenience and possibly some hardship, but that course is not impracticable." The problem, once the discussion moved away from the literal language of the statute, was that neither Hoyt nor anyone else had any idea what that inconvenient certificate should say.

Caught between natural rights and the demands of racial exclusion, Hoyt's brief degenerated into determining who was to blame. Citing Field's advice in *Ah Moy*, Hoyt attempted to wish away the problem of these pesky litigants: "would it be so onerous for all the members of the separate families to withdraw to some other country or to return to China, and thus preserve the family relation." It would certainly have made Hoyt's job less onerous. Hoyt concluded by recommending that if Gue Lim and her husband, Fook See, felt abused by having to return to China and endure possible separation to obtain the correct certificate, they had only themselves to blame.

In contrast to its rulings on laborers under the Exclusion Act, in *Gue Lim* the Supreme Court found for the merchants and their wives and children. Justice Peckham stated that dependents may "enter by reason of the right of the husband and without the certificate mentioned in the Act of 1884." Citing the number and variance of the lower courts' decisions, Peckham did not elaborate. Instead, he reaffirmed the reasoning of an earlier district court opinion: *In re Chung Toy Ho* (1890). With respect to a Chinese merchant's wife and children, "the company of one and the care and custody of the other, are his by natural right; and he ought not to be deprived of either" (1890, 400).

Peckham's endorsement of husbands' rights for Chinese men led him to a new view of the mandates of the Exclusion Act. He stated that to abide by earlier decisions that required all persons to have a certificate was "to decide that the woman [Gue Lim] can not come into the country at all." Yet, to deny her admission was contrary to the spirit of the exclusion laws, which were aimed solely at the laboring class, and "never meant to accomplish the result of permanently excluding the wife under the circumstances of this case" (*United States v. Mrs. Gue Lim* 1899, 468).[16]

16. A clue to why Peckham believed that wives were not the laborers that Congress envisioned lay in the district court opinion he cites as explanation. In *In re Chung Toy Ho* (1890, 399), Judge Deady explains that the wife of a merchant could not possibly have been

While Peckham's language appears similar to earlier rulings that allowed exceptions to restrictive immigration laws based on an evaluation of Congress's intent, the victory in *Gue Lim* had achieved much more. Earlier victories for Chinese immigrants ventured into areas where Congress had not been explicit, such as whether laborers who had left the United States before the necessary readmission certificates were available could reenter without them (*United States v. Chew Heong* 1884). The ambiguity of the law allowed Chinese petitioners to claim their treaty rights to equal privileges where the immigration laws had not fixed differential treatment based on race. In *Gue Lim*, however, a member of the protected classes convinced the Supreme Court to admit his wife in the face of all-encompassing language excluding "all Chinese laborers" and "every Chinese person, other than a laborer" without a certificate. For judges faced with Chinese couples demanding their rights as husband and wife, gender norms challenged as much as they reinforced racial categories. The decision proved a beachhead for subsequent Chinese husbands to argue for their rights as men in American society.

THE SECOND GENERATION

The wives of most Chinese men living in America before the turn of the century remained in China. Yet some Chinese families did live in the United States both before and after the Exclusion Act. And these families had children who, after being educated in China, began to return to the United States in the 1890s. While the parents could not become naturalized citizens, their children were citizens by birth. The Fourteenth Amendment granted that any person born in the United States, regardless of parentage, was a citizen of the United States and the state in which they were born. Despite deferrals to the authority of the inspectors to evaluate Chinese immigrants' proof of citizenship, the courts insisted that Chinese with proof of their birth in the United States possessed the full rights of United States citizenship.[17] While subject to repeated harassment and possible

---

on the mind of the legislature with an aside about the role of women in his imagined middle-class Chinese household: "it is common knowledge that women are not laborers." For more on Deady, see Mooney 1984.

17. U.S. courts first addressed the question of Chinese persons claiming native-born citizenship in 1884 (*In re Look Ting Sing* 1884). Justice Field, writing for the Northern California Circuit Court, held that Look Ting Sing, born in San Francisco in 1873 and returning from a brief stay in China, was a full citizen under the Fourteenth Amendment and therefore outside the jurisdiction of the Chinese Exclusion Act. The Oregon circuit court seconded Field's reasoning four years later (*Ex Parte Chin King* 1888), and the Supreme Court settled the issue in 1898 (*U.S. v. Wong Kim Ark* 1898). Part of the reason that the issue kept coming to the courts was immigration officers' distrust of Chinese citizenship claims.

Perceptions of Chinese mendacity also limited the Supreme Court's support for the rights of Chinese citizens to enter the United States. In *Quock Ting v. United States* (1891), the

interrogation by immigration inspectors each time they returned to the United States, these young men and women could technically travel back and forth to China freely, just like white citizens.

Upon coming of age, some U.S.-born citizens of Chinese descent began to bring wives to the United States. While Chinese men possessed the full rights of U.S. citizen, they had no more statutory basis to bring their wives into the country than did Chinese merchants. Principles of coverture may have been imbedded in marriage and immigration laws, but so were racial markers. An 1855 federal statute provided that "any woman, who might be lawfully naturalized under the existing laws, married, or who shall be married, to a citizen of the United States, shall be deemed and taken to be a citizen" (10 U.S. Stat. 604).[18] This rule allowed most male immigrants to bring their wives to the United States simply by making the wives citizens by marriage. But for Chinese husbands, the 1855 law limited their ability to bring their wives to the United States because Chinese persons were banned from becoming naturalized citizens (*In re Ah Yup* 1878). As interpreted by the Supreme Court in 1868, the 1855 Act was specific to "free white women," thereby denying to Chinese women the possibility of U.S. citizenship by marriage (*Kelly v. Owen* 1868).[19]

Due to their status as racially ineligible for naturalization, wives of Chinese citizens also relied on the uncodified natural right of their husband to the company of his family. While marriage to a citizen of Chinese descent did not make a Chinese immigrant a citizen, the *Gue Lim* decision convinced the Treasury Department in 1900 that wives were allowed to enter. In response to a Chinese woman's appeal of an inspector's ruling, the Treasury Department permitted her to land based on "her right not to be separated from her husband, who is a citizen of the United States and is legally entitled to live in the country of his birth."[20] But the fight for the care and

Supreme Court ruled that a Chinese petitioner claiming citizenship could be denied even in cases with no contradictory testimony because "there may be such an inherent improbability in the statements of a witness as to induce the court or jury to disregard his evidence, even in the absence of any direct conflicting testimony." Beyond allowing judges substantial discretion in interpreting Chinese testimony, there was a discernible trend in the 1890s toward leaving questions of fact to local immigration officials who interviewed the witnesses. Congress codified this trend in the Immigration Act of 1907 (*In re Tom Yum* 1894; *Gee Fook Sing v. United States* 1892; *Lem Hing Dun v. United States* 1892; *United States v. Chung Fung Sun et al.* 1894; *Lee Sing Far v. United States* 1899; *Woey Ho v. United States* 1901).

18. The law did not work the other way around, as only men had the right to bestow citizenship in their spouse. In fact women lost their citizenship by marrying an immigrant man ineligible for naturalization until 1931 (*McKenzie v. Hare* 1915; Bredbenner 1998).

19. During the debates on the 1870 naturalization bill, which provided for African Americans to become naturalized citizens, Senator Charles Sumner attempted to remove any racial barriers to naturalization. His amendment was voted down specifically because it would allow Chinese resident aliens to become citizens (see Torok 1996). The 1882 Exclusion Act reaffirmed that Chinese persons could not become naturalized citizens.

20. It is unclear what immigration inspectors did before this document. After 1884, if a man convinced the inspector that he was born in the United States, he would be admitted. With respect to bringing his alien wife into the United States with him, I think the variety of

comfort of his family did not end for the citizen of Chinese descent once his wife had cleared customs. Once the couple entered the United States, the wife, by virtue of her naturalization status, was still subject to a host of increasingly draconian regulations that targeted Chinese immigrants. In fact, the test of a male Chinese citizen's ability to exercise the rights of husbands in the early twentieth century rested on his ability to keep his wife from being deported.

HUSBANDS' RIGHTS AND DEPORTATION

Just as Congress imagined a diverse parade of inadmissible immigrants to be stopped at the border, it instructed immigration officials to expel an expanding pool of objectionable immigrants already in the United States. Two categories of deportable immigrants bore heavily on Chinese women: those without residence certificate and prostitutes. Enacted in 1892, the Geary Act, stipulated that all Chinese laborers who did not possess a residence certificate would be deported upon a summary trial. The Geary Act's deportation provisions gave special weight to the category of "unlawfully in the United States"; certificate requirements meant that "any Chinese person or person of Chinese descent" had to justify his or her very presence in the United States to immigration officers.[21] Yet, despite the inclusive language of the statute, family-unification arguments convinced judges to exempt wives from the Geary Act. Gender-based arguments succeeded even if the woman had been living unmarried in the United States when the certificates were issued and had simply chosen not to apply. Yet when it came to accusations of prostitution, judges steadfastly refused to grant similar exemptions.

Arguments based on coverture relied heavily on the ability of Chinese couples to present themselves as dutiful husbands and wives. Armed with accusations of disloyalty and immorality, prosecutors convinced judges that Chinese prostitutes, whatever their marital status, were the kind of

decisions with regard to the fate of merchants' wives points to the same diversity for wives of citizens. The answer may have been conditional on who was conducting the inspection and whether they believed the couple's story. In 1892, the Office of Internal Revenue issued a ruling that allowed the wife of a citizen of Chinese descent to enter the country as long as there was sufficient proof of the marriage, but the rule was taken out of circulation in the next few years leaving some uncertainty as to its authority (*Tsoi Sim v. United States* 1902, Letter from H. A. Taylor to Collector of Customs, San Francisco, California, 19 October 1900, in Brief in Behalf of Appellant, 8; McKeown 1999, 85).

21. This might be described, in contemporary parlance, as "living in the United States while Chinese." Even native-born citizens of Chinese descent had to fear the Geary Act's deportation provisions considering the inspectors' mistrust of Chinese citizenship claims. The courts provided no relief in this regard. The Supreme Court repeatedly sustained Congress's power to regulate the entry and conduct of non-citizens (*Chae Chan Ping v. United States* 1889; *Fong Yue Ting v. United States* 1892).

immigrants that Congress intended to exclude. Racially based categories outweighed the objections of husbands and sons, regardless of the men's citizenship. The stigma of prostitution negated the possibility that these women deserved to be protected and remain with their families—even if the evidence consisted only of a "connection" to a brothel. The same was true for the husband. Allowing his wife to become a prostitute stripped him of any claim to have his wife remain in his home. He was a pimp, not a husband.[22] Family unification meant little to a judge who did not consider the woman a proper wife and the man a proper husband.

Tsoi Sim's case illustrated the distorting effects of husbands' rights when applied to new areas of law. Tsoi Sim was arrested in San Francisco on 20 April 1901, for being a female laborer of Chinese descent without a certificate. Despite having lived in California for almost 20 years, she was certainly in violation of the Geary Act and illegally living in the United States at the time of her marriage. Referring directly to the rights of her husband, however, Tsoi Sim's lawyers argued that the Ninth Circuit Court of Appeals should not treat her as just a laborer, but as the wife of a native-born citizen (*Tsoi Sim v. United States* 1902).

Born in China in 1879, Tsoi Sim had come to the U.S. in 1882 at the age of three, approximately one month before the passage of the Chinese Exclusion Acts. She lived and worked in California continuously from this date until her arrest. She married Yee Yuk Lum, on 16 November 1900, in California and resided with him as his "lawful, sole and only wife." While of Chinese descent, her husband was a United States citizen by birth. He worked as a laborer and, like her, had never registered under the Geary Act.

As Judge Hawley admitted in the first two paragraphs of his decision, precedent afforded him little guidance: "the case is a novel one, and is different in material respects from any of the Chinese cases heretofore considered by this court." With no "authoritative cases directly in point," Judge Hawley was forced to argue by "[a]nalogy of *other cases*—and especially the decisions of the courts, under the different statutes relative to the right of Chinese persons to come into the United States—and by independent reasoning (*Tsoi Sim* 1902, 922). A review of these "other cases" placed Tsoi Sim's case within the larger group of actions brought by both Chinese and non-Chinese married couples trying to avoid deportation or gain admittance into the United States.

Like *Gue Lim*, the appellants' brief tried to shift the discussion away from Congress's power over immigrants to the sanctity of the marital relation: "the right of the citizen husband to have and enjoy the society and

22. Images of Chinese husbands as pimps were reinforced by the stories of "rescue workers" who freed Chinese women from the brothels. The Chinese pimp became an iconic image in the popular literature on tong wars and the "dirty city" of Chinatown (see Pascoe 1990; Wong 1996).

company of whomsoever he may lawfully marry." Linking the couples' situation with the rights of all families, Tsoi Sim's lawyers insisted that "state and society in general is an interested party in promoting and protecting this relation." While she was not made a citizen outright by marriage, Tsoi Sim "acquired new rights which she never possessed before." With a flourish, the appellant's brief closed with a warning to the judges about the perils of second-class citizenship: if the court succeeded in deporting her and depriving her husband of his rights as a citizen, then "the founders of our great Republic fought and bled in vain, and our boasted 'liberty of the citizen' is but an idle dream" (*Tsoi Sim* 1902, Brief of Appellant, 10, 11, 33)."

Similarly, the brief of the U.S. Attorney highlighted the consequences of the judge's decision. Marriage could not cure Tsoi Sim's illegal status in the United States in part because "the United States would be deluged with Chinese, males and females, under 21 years of age, who belong to the laboring class and desire to come to the United States for the purpose of laboring" (*Tsoi Sim* 1902, Brief on Behalf of the United States, 6). Either Judge Hawley violated a husband's natural rights, or he aided in subverting the Exclusion Acts.

While the husband was not a party to the decision, Judge Hawley's decision emphasized that "his rights, as well as hers, are involved." Based on his status, she did not need a certificate to enter. Her marriage had changed her status "from that of a Chinese laborer to that of wife of a native-born citizen." Her life before the marriage was immaterial. Her attorneys had successfully moved the discussion away from Tsoi Sim and focused the judge's attention on her husband. A wife had the right "to live with her husband; enjoy his society; receive his support and maintenance and all the comforts and privileges of the marriage relations," regardless of her racial identity. With these definitions in hand, Judge Hawley interpreted the Geary Act as inapplicable to the wife of native-born citizen, despite the fact that "by applying the literal language of the statute, it might be held that she should be deported." If she could simply return to the United States as the wife of an American citizen immediately after being deported, then Congress could not have meant to include her.

The decision in Tsoi Sim was a resounding affirmation of the power of husbands' rights to exempt Chinese wives from apparently obvious immigration restrictions. Combined with the Treasury Department order in 1900, the decision left little doubt that if a couple could prove the husband's citizenship and their marriage, they could enter the United States. Beyond affirming the existing policies of the Treasury Department, *Tsoi Sim* proved that the wife of a citizen, despite being ineligible for naturalization, possessed some protection from regulations deporting Chinese immigrants. Viewing the victories in *Gue Lim* and *Tsoi Sim* through the lens of husbands' rights leads to a picture of judges in a variety of federal courts who were more pushed and pulled by arguments concerning the identity and character of the participants in question than constrained by procedure.[23]

WIVES OR PROSTITUTES

Despite the ruling in *Tsoi Sim*, judges refused to grant an exception for citizens' wives in cases involving allegations of prostitution. While similar on their face to the deportation provisions of the Geary Act, charges of prostitution attacked the core of husbands' rights arguments. How could a prospective wife (and a family) be worth protecting if she was also a prostitute? Exposés on prostitution in Chinatown made judges' decisions all the more difficult. Since the 1890s, female missionaries to the Chinese American community publicized the smuggling of young Chinese women into United States to work in underground brothels (Pascoe 1990). As the immigration restrictions grew tighter, smugglers used the exceptions for wives to evade entry and certificate requirements. Family unification arguments suffered, in part, because some of the married women being deported were in fact prostitutes.[24]

Chinese prostitutes had long been a symbol of the depraved and pestilential character of all Chinese women (Shah 1995, 33–34; Peffer 1986, 28–46; Hirata 1984, 402–34). As early as 1870, a California statute required a bond from steamship companies for all Chinese women brought to California (Statutes of California 1869–70, 330–32). Seven years before the passage of the Exclusion Act, the Page Law prohibited the importation of women for immoral purposes (18 U.S. Stat. 477 [1875]). While many subsequent immigration acts included provisions prohibiting immoral women, the 1907 Immigration Act marked a turning point by adding a deportation clause to previous controls. Section 3 of the act mandated that any female immigrant "found an inmate of a house of prostitution, at any time within three years after she shall have entered the United States, shall be deemed unlawfully within the United States and shall be deported."

While the 1907 act was aimed at intercepting prostitutes of all races, immigration officials had been clamoring for help in stopping the immigration of Chinese prostitutes specifically. After the first year of responsibility

23. Lucy Salyer describes federal judges as reluctant defenders of Chinese immigrants' right to appeal based on the constraints of judicial culture and procedure. Judges were "captured" by the due process requirements of the law, despite their agreement with the project of racial exclusion. Here, I am suggesting that judges' allegiance to patriarchal notions of marriage and family unity was, in some cases, the motivating factor in ignoring the racial mandates of immigration law (Salyer 1995; Smith 1997, 443–48).

24. The precise percentage of prostitutes who entered as wives in order to evade the immigration restrictions is unknown. Hirata estimated that between 21 and 50% of the Chinese women living in the United States were prostitutes. Since women primarily entered as native-born citizens or wives after 1882, the number of false marriages must have been significant (Hirata 1984, 432).

for Chinese immigration, the commissioner-general of immigration reported in 1901 that there were major obstacles to combating illegal Chinese immigration, including "their totally different standards of morality" (Commissioner-General of Immigration 1901, 460). Three years later, he implicated marriage as a vehicle to smuggle prostitutes into the country:

> One of the singular and unanticipated results of the increase of Chinese citizens of this country was shown by several appeals by the wives of such citizens against the excluding decisions of the officer in charge in San Francisco. The appellants were married at a consulate of the United States in China by a Methodist missionary to young Chinamen whom the courts had determined to be citizens by birth in this country. It was evidence that the wives had never seen their husbands until brought to the consulate to be married to them and that the purpose of such marriage was to bring appellants to this country to enter houses of ill-fame . . . they were admitted to pursue their intended shameless avocation should their husbands so require. (Commissioner-General of Immigration 1904, 87)

The commissioner-general's reports in 1906 and 1907 continued this rhetoric, even claiming that the marriages of the majority of Chinese women who entered as wives of citizens were fraudulent (Bredbenner 1998, 30).

Accusations of prostitution also resonated with larger trends of urban social reform and gender anxiety. The corrupting effect of the city on unsupervised young men and women was a long-standing concern for Progressive Era reformers (Boyer 1978). Congressional commissions investigated urban prostitution and the evils of the white slave traffic (U.S. House 1909; U.S. Senate 1909, 1910). The commissions were alarmed about the use of marriage to evade immigration laws by immoral women of every nationality. As much as Chinese women, European women of ill repute raised great concern because they could marry naturalized citizens outside the United States and be admitted without review (U.S. Senate 1910, 32). Even more alarming was the potential misuse of marital naturalization. Women eligible for naturalization, no matter what the accusation, could (and did) marry citizens while out on bail and become exempt from immigration regulations. Before the Nineteenth Amendment, judges placed a high value on the transformative effect of marriage to an American.[25] The 1909 senate

25. Again, the experience of Chinese women ran counter to the efforts of suffrage advocates. Chinese wives were not accorded the same protections from immigration regulations as wives of citizens, in part, because they could not claim dependent citizenship. Yet dependent citizenship was the very status that women's rights activists wanted to end. The irony continued into the 1920s, when Congress passed the Cable Act, granting women independent citizenship (apart from marriage). While not applicable to Chinese women ineligible for naturalization, the Bureau of Immigration used the Cable Act as a statutory grounding to argue that marriage to legal Chinese residents (citizens or merchants) should not exempt them from the 1924 Immigration Act. In other words, Congress's rejection of dependent

commission recommended additional powers for inspectors to arrest women "on sight" who were thought to be prostitutes, the removal of the three-year limitation on deporting prostitutes, and harsher penalties for perjury. Husbands' rights were on shaky ground when the terrain shifted from the need to keep families together to the protection of the public health.

In addition to the larger social and political environment, judges heard the prostitution cases during a shift in the balance of power between the courts and immigration officials. In a story well told by Lucy Salyer (1995), immigration officials during the ten years after *Gue Lim* were increasingly successful in restricting the courts' jurisdiction in cases brought by both immigrants and native-born citizens of Chinese descent. The dispute between the courts and immigration officials came to a head in a series of Supreme Court cases involving the courts' ability to review the citizenship claims of immigrants denied entry. Writing for the Court in *United States v. Ju Toy* (1905), Justice Holmes limited judges' ability to review all questions of fact decided by immigration inspectors. The decisions of the secretary of commerce and labor were final, even in cases where petitioners claimed United States citizenship.[26] The courts were only available in cases involving the denial of a fair and impartial hearing—a much lower standard than the due process standards of a judicial trial.

For Chinese citizens wanting to bring their wives into the country, the decision in *Ju Toy* undercut some of the gains of *Tsoi Sim*. While limiting judicial review did not touch the right of a Chinese woman to enter the United States based on her marriage to a citizen, it made the inspectors the only parties who could decide whether the husband was actually a native-born citizen and whether the wife was legally married to him. Without the protections afforded in a judicial trial, these were not idle hurdles, especially considering that most of the wives had never been to the United States and did not speak a word of English.[27]

Looe Shee's case was the first in which a married woman argued for an exemption from the act of 1907, but certainly not the strongest (*Looe Shee v. North* 1909). She had come over the border in El Paso in 1906, based on her marriage in Mexico to Lew Chow, a native-born citizen of the United States. In October 1908, the police arrested her in a San Francisco brothel, and the immigration inspectors claimed that she had been a prostitute for

---

citizenship for women should be regarded as a signal to judges that husbands' rights, a necessary dependent status relationship, should also be abandoned. See Bredbenner 1997 for an excellent description of the relationship between women's rights ideology and immigration policy.

26. The decision in *Ju Toy* overturned earlier decisions where the authority to hear an appeal of a petitioner claiming citizenship resided with the federal courts (*In re Tom Yum* 1894).

27. For an application of *Ju Toy* with respect to wives of Chinese citizens, see *Tang Tun v. Edsell, Chinese Inspector* (1912), especially the Supreme Court's refusal to review the immigration officials' findings of fact.

over a year. Her husband was nowhere to be found and was presumed dead. While this did not deter her from basing her claim to stay in the United States on her husband's citizenship, the absence of a husband in the courtroom surely did not help. Without a husband or children to consider, Judge Morrow of the Ninth Circuit Court of Appeals followed a Supreme Court decision that allowed probationary periods to determine if immigrants were among those classes to be denied entry (*Keller v. United States* 1909). He also made short work of Looe Shee's arguments that she had entered before the law was passed. Judge Morrow closed by emphasizing the necessity of banning diseased persons to protect the public health—a far cry from the sanctity of the hearth.

Arguments for husbands' rights lost again, the next time they appeared alongside charges of prostitution. Two years later, the same appellate court considered the case of Hoo Choy, a Chinese woman who had entered San Francisco with her husband, a citizen, and lived with him until her arrest for prostitution (*Hoo Choy v. North* 1910). The district case denied both her and her husband's writ of habeas corpus, claiming a lack of jurisdiction. The circuit court of appeals heard the case in conjunction with another one involving the deportation of a suspected prostitute who had been admitted as a native-born citizen (*Haw Moy v. North* 1910). Again writing for the court, Judge Morrow denied both applications in one paragraph. After reciting Hoo Choy's claim based on her husband's citizenship, he rejected any oversight role for the court other than to insure that Hoo Choy was given an opportunity to make a case before the immigration inspectors.

The result was the same even when the woman had just given birth to an American citizen. In 1912, the United States Supreme Court heard the case of Li A. Sim, a Chinese woman scheduled for deportation for being on the premises of a brothel (*Low Way Suey v. Backus* 1912). She was prosecuted under the more expansive 1910 amendment to the 1907 act, which broadened the scope of violations to include anyone who had any connection or role at all in a house of prostitution or even "where prostitutes gather." Unlike in earlier cases, Li A. Sim was given every opportunity to turn the case into a question of family separation rather than one of the immigration officials' capacity under the police power to cure a health problem. Her husband, Low Wah Suey, was both the petitioner and the joint appellant. Her son, born 12 days before her arrest (and thus a U.S. citizen), was a party as well. She denied that she was or had been a prostitute and contended that she had not been permitted to prove her innocence to the immigration inspectors.

In their brief, the couple's lawyers kept the spotlight on the husband's rights to his family. The case, they argued, should be distinguished from the *Looe Shee* decision and others because Low Wah Suey was alive, living with his wife, and in court demanding his rights. He should not be penalized any more than any other citizen for marrying a woman ineligible for naturalization because "his rights, which flow from citizenship, are not stopped and terminated because he marries a woman of the Chinese race" (*Low Way Suey* 1912, Brief in Opposition of Motion for a Rehearing). As in *Tsoi Sim* and *Gue Lim*, the Chinese couple insisted deportation would misconstrue Congress's intent. How could immigration laws operate on the wives of U.S. citizens, living in the United States and bearing their husbands' children? How could it be the "intent of these laws to separate husbands and wives"? Indeed, the authority of husbands' right emanated from an even greater realm than citizenship: "Those whom God hath joined together, Let no man put asunder."

The U.S. attorney's brief similarly replayed themes from *Gue Lim* and *Tsoi Sim*, with one notable exception: The woman in *Low Way Suey* was accused of violating a moral standard instead of a procedural one. The U.S. attorney reminded the justices that the law called for deportation; there was no mention of an exception for the wife of a citizen anywhere in the legislation concerning prostitutes. The Court's earlier interpretations of the immigration laws required that Li A. Sim be given "a fair opportunity to be heard," not a judicial trial. Statutory support for the concept that marriage changed the status of an immigrant was reserved only for a woman who "might be lawfully naturalized" (10 Stat. 604 [1885]). Finally, Li A. Sim did not act like a wife should and had thus forfeited any of her husband's unspoken natural rights to her company:

> If Li A. Sim had conducted herself properly, she would not, although an alien, have come within the operation of the immigration laws. But when she went or was put into a house of prostitution, it was not only in disregard of her duties as a wife, but in defiance of her duties as a wife. (*Low Way Suey* 1912, Supplemental and Reply Brief for Appellee upon Motion to Dismiss or Affirm, 13–14)

Writing for a unanimous Court, Justice Day's opinion demonstrated the power of an accusation of prostitution to stigmatize a woman and strip her of any privileges judges reserved for wives and mothers. After disposing of her procedural objections, he confronted the precedent of *Gue Lim* and Low Wah Suey's objection that the 1907 act was not intended to separate husbands and wives. He insisted that Li A. Sim was not brought before the Court as a wife; the charge of prostitution overshadowed and denied her refuge in coverture. The intention of the 1907 act and its amendments was to prohibit alien prostitution, and "a married woman is as objectionable as a single one in the respects denounced by law." Focusing on *her* conduct instead of *his* rights, the justice concluded that Li had voluntarily forfeited the protections accorded a wife. Her right to enter the United States and live with her husband and son "could have been retained by proper conduct on her part and was only lost upon her violation of the statute, she, being an alien, thereby forfeiting her right to longer remain in this country" (*Low Way Suey* 1912, Supplemental and Reply Brief for Appellee upon Motion to Dismiss or Affirm, 13–14).

Family unification arguments were also ineffective in subsequent deportation decisions concerning health regulations. In two cases regarding the exclusion of citizens' wives diagnosed by a medical inspector to carry "dangerous contagious diseases," judges were unwilling to make an exception for Chinese husbands. In both cases, the part of the 1917 immigration law that exempted wives and children of "naturalized citizens" (a code word for racially acceptable citizens) who were being held for treatment in a hospital was not extended to the dependents of native-born citizens.[28] Another section of the 1917 law further diminished the rights of appeal of those immigrants accused of prostitution by limiting their deportation hearings to only an "executive hearing." This set off a witch-hunt after 1921 when the Ninth Circuit Court of Appeals upheld the provision (Chan 1991b, 136–37; *Chin Shee v. White* 1916). When it came to questions of "defective" women, judges interpreted separating families as preserving the public health.

This focus on identity had a class element as well. Judges assumed that the women who were admitted as wives of merchants or American citizens were of a higher class than other Chinese women. According to the popular stereotypes about Chinese family life, Chinese husbands, especially upper-class men, cloistered their wives inside their houses (Lu 1994). Bound feet, a sign of an upper-class childhood, were an asset to women trying to persuade immigration officials that they were wives of Chinese men who could enter (Yung 1995, 24, 41–47). Thus, accusations of prostitution or sickness, with its attendant images of solicitation or lack of sanitation, implied a lower-class status that was incompatible with the exemption for the families of the "better" class of Chinese residents.[29]

28. Section 22 of the 1917 Immigration Act (39 Stat. 874) provided that the wives and children of naturalized citizens "shall be admitted without detention for treatment in a hospital." The statute's wording was a roundabout means of preventing husbands of races that had been denied the ability to acquire citizenship by naturalization, specifically Asians, to bring their wives into the United States. In both of the controlling decisions on the subject, the Court denied wives of Chinese citizens access to the hospital exception because their husbands were citizens by birth, instead of by naturalization. While the Court in *Chung Fook v. White* (1923, 1924) considered arguments by the Chinese couple that the rights of native-born citizens should be no different from those of naturalized ones, it held that Congress had the power to make such a differentiation and advised the couple to look to Congress instead of the courts for any remedy (*Chung Fook v. White* 1924).

29. The reasoning behind denying Chinese women accused of prostitution an exemption from the immigration laws was quite similar to Judge Deady's public/private dichotomy in *In re Chung Toy Ho* (1890), specifically that proper Chinese women do not work outside the home. The gender implication is that women were supposed to remain in the domestic sphere and those who did work in the public sphere, as working-class women or as prostitutes, were not ladies and therefore not deserving of protection that linked a husband and his wife.

In summary, the struggles of Chinese women to avoid deportation were a special case; they were ineligible for naturalization and remained immigrants no matter how long they lived and worked in the United States. For a Chinese woman, marriage to a citizen promised a defense, a legal argument, but not immunity from being deported as an unlawful immigrant. The story was much the same for other aliens. While this policy was controversial and contested, persons who had not become naturalized could be deported for a host of offenses.[30] In times of labor agitation, the Bureau of Immigration deported alien labor radicals, even though their deportation stranded spouses and children born in the United States. The difference, of course, was that most immigrants could become naturalized, and even beginning the process promised them a degree of protection. Thus, when the 1924 Immigration Act subjected the family members of most resident aliens to quotas, many resident aliens applied for naturalization in order to bring their relatives in as non-quota immigrants. Seventy-five percent of the citizens applying for visas for relatives in the years immediately after 1924 had been recently naturalized (see Bredbenner 1998, 265). Chinese couples did not have this option.

CONCLUSION

The hope that men's "tender ties" would lead them back to China propelled much of the unfinished business of the 1882 Chinese Exclusion Act. Congress legislated the theoretical end of Chinese immigration, but its efforts to discourage the Chinese men and women already living in the United States from remaining proved more difficult. Chinese marriage cases presented judges with the vexing problem of balancing racially based immigration restrictions with Chinese men's arguments for their rights as husbands. For the most part, the women in these cases could not be admitted of their own accord; they were not members of a protected class or citizens themselves. Instead of alleging discrimination based on the Fourteenth Amendment's protections for all persons, Chinese husbands sought exemptions from existing immigration laws based on their right to the company of their wives. Considering judges' unyielding support for Congress's power to exclude certain types of immigrants, this tactic achieved remarkable success in a series of decisions in the 1890s and early 1900s; at least initially, a Chinese woman's marital status trumped her racial classification.

30. The list of classes of deportable aliens by 1907 included prostitutes, the mentally retarded, those likely to become public charges, the insane, those with a contagious disease, paupers, and subversives. For an extended discussion of the debates surrounding deporting resident aliens both inside the government and in law journals, see Bredbenner 1998, 30–44, especially n.43.

While husbands' rights could not overcome the stain of accusations of prostitution, that should not overshadow the legal gains made by Chinese husbands and wives before the Immigration Act of 1924. Despite frequent challenges, the precedents set in *Gue Lim* and *Tsoi Sim*—the right of Chinese merchants and native-born citizens to bring their wives to the United States—remained in force for almost 25 years.[31] The practical exercise of this "right" was never easy. Chinese husbands had to document their status as a merchant under the immigration statutes or as a citizen born in the United States.[32] Wives had to prove the legitimacy of their marriage under the harsh questioning of immigration inspectors and in virtual isolation.[33] The commissioner of immigration reviewed the inspectors' decisions and could recommend a rehearing without substantive justification (*Mah Shee v. White* 1917; *Chew Hoy Quong v. White* 1918). And over this period, questions of fact were increasingly left to immigration authorities as courts retreated from judicial review of immigration cases.[34] Yet the ability to enter the United States remained. While Chinese wives might be deported under even the most flimsy associations or the judgment of a racist health inspector, most were able to come to the United States when Congress had closed virtually all other doors of entry.

The success of husbands' rights' arguments spilled over into related cases concerning the ability of children of permitted immigrants to enter the United States. In addition to securing the admission of minor children of domiciled merchants, the decisions in *Gue Lim* and *Tsoi Sim* allowed merchants and citizens to adopt minors on their visits to China and return with them to the United States (*Yee Won v. White* 1921; *United States ex rel.*

31. Cases concerning the procedural rights of alien wives of Chinese husbands allowed to enter the United States show *both* the bureaucratic struggles between courts and immigration inspectors and the generally accepted understanding that "actual" Chinese husbands and wives could enter (*Mah Shee v. White* 1917; *Chew Hoy Quong v. White* 1918; *Ex Parte Low Joe* 1922).

32. "That any Chinese person or person of Chinese descent arrested under the provisions of this act or the acts hereby extended shall be adjudged to be unlawfully within the United States unless such person shall establish, by affirmative proof, to the satisfaction of such justice, judge, or commissioner, his lawful right to remain in the United States" (*Case of the Chinese Merchant In re Low Yam Chow* 1882; § 3 of the Act of 5 May 1892, 27 Stat. 25).

33. Disputes over the validity of a Chinese couple's marriage were exacerbated by the practice of polygamous marriages among wealthy Chinese. Some traditional sojourning arrangements allowed a wealthy man to have wives in both China and his country of business: the first wife in China to bear children and maintain the family home and the second to accompany him in the United States. Immigration officials typically considered plural marriage invalid and grounds for exclusion. While Chinese men probably believed these second marriages to be valid under Chinese custom, they usually attempted to omit any mention of their first wife in dealings with the immigration officials (see *Lee Lung v. Patterson* 1902).

34. While this retreat was discernible, judges insisted that Chinese wives and minor children be given a fair and impartial hearing and allowed to communicate with their attorneys, hear the evidence against them, produce witnesses, and present evidence of their connection with their husband or father (see *Tang Tun v. Edsell* 1912; *Chin Yow v. United States* 1908; also see cases cited in note 31, above).

Soo Hoo Hong v. Tod, Commissioner of Immigration 1923, 692; *White v. Kwock Sue Lim* 1923, 734). While concerned that these adoptions would be used to circumvent the exclusion laws, judges held that adopted children should be treated the same as biological ones and admitted if under the age of 21.[35] To justify making another category of people exempt from the exclusion laws, judges returned to the rights of a man to his family: "The question is perhaps not so much concerning their right to enter as it is concerning his right to have them enter" (*Ex Parte Fong Yim et al.* 1905, 941). And like most loopholes, Chinese sons pushed the opening as wide as judges would allow. In the decade before the 1924 Immigration Act, the adopted sons of merchants and resident citizens tried to bring *their* wives and children back with them to the United States.[36] While always contingent, family unification arguments steadily widened the door for an ever-expanding universe of legal Chinese immigrants.

The 1924 Immigration Act signaled a new era of immigration restriction, but it did not free judges from disputes over exceptions for wives of legal immigrants. While the act did not specifically mention wives who were ineligible for marital naturalization, their omission as an exempt category prompted immigration officials to arrest wives of both citizens and merchants when they tried to enter. Within months of the act's passage, Chinese couples' appeals reached the appellate courts. In 1925, the Supreme Court held that only Chinese merchants' wives were exempt from the 1924 law (*Ex Parte Cheung Shee, Ex Parte Chan Shee* 1924; *Chang Chan v. Nagle* 1925). Marriage to a citizen no longer guaranteed Chinese women the right to enter the United States. Reflecting the importance of the ability to bring wives to the United States, the leading Chinese American citizens' associations reacted to the ruling by lobbying Congress to amend the act to include citizens' wives.

The House Committee on Immigration and Naturalization held three hearings on the issue (U.S. House 1926, 1928, 1930). Each time representatives from the Chinese community explained the perils of separating fami-

35. The children of U.S. citizens were citizens by the 1855 Immigration Act if the father had lived in the United States at some point. The adopted Chinese son of a citizen, while admissible before the Immigration Act of 1924, could not become a citizen by adoption. The sons of merchants were permitted to remain in the United States and travel back and forth to China even though their father had died (Act of 10 February 1855, 10 U.S. Stat. 604, 606; U.S. Rev. Stat. 351 § 1993 (1874); *Ex Parte Fong Yim et al.* 1905; *United States v. Lee Chee* 1915; *Woo Hoo v. White* 1917; *United States ex rel. Shue Quey v. Pierce* 1922; *Johnson, Commissioner of Immigration v. Shue Hong* 1924).

36. In *White v. Kwock Sue Lim* (1923), Judge Dietrich declined to admit an adopted son of a resident citizen whose wife had purchased the boy 15 years earlier in China. Citing the son's marriage to a woman in China who was pregnant with their child, the appellate judge ruled that the "tender ties" of family led back to China instead of the United States. Judge Dietrich supported his conclusion by insisting that the wife and child of the adopted son, Yee Won, would not be allowed to come to the United States because he was a laborer (*Yee Won v. White* 1921).

lies and denying "the natural right of a man to enjoy the companionship of his wife." Like they had in courtrooms since the 1880s, Chinese husbands made personal appeals to the congressmen.

> Put yourselves in our position. If you were separated from your wives and you could not bring your wife to where you were living and the only way of having the association of your wife is to go across the ocean ever so often, you would realize one of our hardships. (U.S. House 1926, 8: Testimony of George Fong)

Peter Soo Hoo, an electrical draftsman from Los Angeles, asked the committee if it intended to "compel us to live lives of celibacy or compel us to abandon our residence in the land of our birth and our citizenship?" (U.S. House 1926, 27). Congress finally responded in 1930 by amending the law to allow those married before 1924 to enter.

The 1930 legislation was a partial victory. More revealing of the enduring power of husbands' rights was the fate of the Chinese women who had tried to enter as citizens' wives during the previous six years. Due to the Supreme Court's ruling in *Chang Chan* (1925), no wives of citizens were admitted as legal immigrants between 1924 and 1930. Indeed, once the Supreme Court's decision came down, the district court judges returned the women to the custody of the local commissioner of immigration ostensibly for deportation (General Case Files 1925: *In re Lee Shee*, Case File 8893; *In re Jane Theng on the behalf of Leung Shee*, Case File 8923; *In re Jew Hong Fook on the behalf of Lock Shee*, Case File 8932; *In re Eng Shee*, Case File 8951; *In re Lee Shee*, Case File 9007; *In re Chin Hin*, Case File 9008; In re *George J. Mar on behalf of Poon Shee and Ma Sum Kew*, Case File 8990).

Yet none of them were sent back to China. In each case, the local commissioner-general of immigration permitted them to remain with their husbands—and, for many, with their newborn children—on $1,000 bonds.[37] Like earlier cases, the women's lawyers had appealed to the commissioner's emotions: "to return the woman—take her from her husband and children would be cruel and unfortunate, if not inhuman" (U.S. Department of Immigration and Naturalization 1924–30, 21 Aug. 1925, Case #2205/1-10, Box 188). And like the judges in *Gue Lim* and *Tsoi Sim*, immigration officials found a gray area for the women—"temporary admission"—and allowed them to remain in the United States pending indeterminate legislative action (U.S. Department of Immigration and Naturalization 1924–30, 25 June 1929, Case #2115/2-10, Box 182). In the six years before Congress amended the law, the bonds were renewed three times. As Justice Field articulated nearly 50 years before, it was the "sacredness of that

37. Thirty-five wives remained in the United States on bond: fifteen from Seattle, fourteen from San Francisco, two in Boston, and one or two in New York (U.S. House 1926, 20: Testimony of Guy Kelly).

relation"—its lack of codification—that captured the commissioners. Like the judges who Congress had finally nudged out of the process, the commissioners, when faced with a couple that gave a convincing performance as citizen and wife in the courtroom, found racial immigration restrictions more flexible than gender privileges.

REFERENCES

Bonacich, Bona,and Cheng, Lucie, eds. 1984. *Labor Immigration under Capitalism*. Berkeley and Los Angeles: University of California Press.

Bonner, Arthur. 1997. *Alas What Brought Thee Hither: The Chinese in New York, 1800–1950*. Madison, N.J.: Fairleigh Dickinson University Press.

Boyer, Paul. 1978. *Urban Masses and Moral Order in America, 1820–1920*. Cambridge, Mass.: Harvard University Press.

Bredbenner, Candice Lewis. 1998. *A Nationality of Her Own: Women, Marriage, and the Law of Citizenship*. Berkeley and Los Angeles: University of California Press.

Burnham, Margaret A. 1987. An Impossible Marriage: Slave Law and Family Law. *Law and Inequality* 5:187–225.

Calavita, Kitty. 2000. The Paradoxes of Race, Class, Identity, and "Passing": Enforcing the Chinese Exclusion Acts, 1882–1910. *Law & Social Inquiry* 25:1–40.

Chan, Sucheng, ed. 1991a. *Entry Denied: Exclusion and the Chinese Community in America, 1882–1943*. Philadelphia: Temple University Press.

———. 1991b. Exclusion of Chinese Women. In Chan 1991a, 94–136.

Chinese Historical Society of Southern California and UCLA Asian American Studies Center. 1994. *Origins and Destinations: 41 Essays on Chinese America*. Los Angeles.

Commissioner-General of Immigration. 1900–1930. *Annual Reports of the Commissioner-General of Immigration*. Washington, D.C.: Government Printing Office.

Coolidge, Mary. 1909. *Chinese Immigration*. New York: H. Holt.

Cott, Nancy F. 1998. Marriage and Women's Citizenship in the United States, 1830–1934. *American Historical Review* 103:1440–74.

———. 2000. *Public Vows: a History of Marriage and the Nation*. Cambridge, Mass.: Harvard University Press.

Crenshaw, Kimberle. 1989. Demarginalizing the Intersection of Race and Sex: A Black Feminist Critique of Antidiscrimination Doctrine, Feminist Theory, and Antiracist Politics. *University of Chicago Legal Forum* 139–68

———. 1991. Women of Color at the Center: Mapping the Margins: Intersectionality, Identity Politics, and Violence against Women of Color. *Stanford Law Review* 43:1241–99.

Culin, Stewart. 1887. China in America: Social Life of the Chinese in Eastern Cities of the United States. Annual Meeting of the American Association for the Advancement of Science, Philadelphia.

Fritz, Christian. 1988. A Nineteenth Century "Habeas Corpus Mill": The Chinese before the Federal Courts in California. *American Journal of Legal History* 32:347–72.

———. 1991a. Federal Justice in California: The Court of Ogden Hoffman, 1851–91. Lincoln: University of Nebraska Press.

———. 1991b. Due Process and Treaty Rights and Chinese Exclusion. In Chan 1991a, 25–56.

General Case Files. 1925. U. S. District Court for the District of Washington. Records of District Courts of the United States, Record Group 21. National Archives and Records Administration—Pacific Alaska Region, Seattle.

Gyory, Andrew. 1998. *Closing the Gate: Race, Politics, and the Chinese Exclusion Act*. Chapel Hill: University of North Carolina Press.

Hartog, Hendrik. 1997. Lawyering, Husband's Rights, and "The Unwritten Law." *Journal of American History* 84:67–96.

———. 2000. *Man and Wife in America: A History*. Cambridge, Mass.: Harvard University Press.

Hing Ong, Bill. 1993. *Making and Remaking Asian America through Immigration Policy, 1850–1990*. Stanford, Calif.: Stanford University Press.

Hirata, Lucy Cheng. 1984. Free, Indentured, Enslaved: Chinese Prostitutes in California in Nineteenth Century America. In Bonacich and Cheng 1984, 402–34.

Hsu, Madeline Yuan-yin. 2000. *Dreaming of Gold, Dreaming of Home: Transnationalism and Migration between the United States and China, 1882–1943*. Stanford, Calif.: Stanford University Press.

Kaczorowski, Robert, 1987. To Begin the Nation Anew: Congress, Citizenship, and Civil Rights after the Civil War. *American Historical Review* 92:45–68.

Kennedy, Randall. 1986. Race Relations Law and the Tradition of Celebration: The Case of Prof. Schmidt. *Columbia Law Review* 86:1622–61.

Kettner, James H. 1978. *The Development of American Citizenship, 1608–1870*. Chapel Hill: University of North Carolina Press.

Lee, Erika. 1998. At America's Gates: Chinese Immigration during the Exclusion Era, 1882–1943. Ph.D. diss., University of California, Berkeley.

Lu, Huping. 1994. Chinese Merchant Wives in the United States, 1840–1945. In Chinese Historical Society of Southern California and UCLA Asian American Studies Center. 1994.

Lyman, Stanford. 1968. Marriage and the Family among Chinese Immigrants to America, 1850–1960. *Phylon* 29:321–30.

———. 1974. Conflict and the Web of Group Affiliation in San Francisco's Chinatown, 1880–1910. *Pacific Historical Review* 43: 473–99.

Ma, Eve Armentrout. 1983. Urban Chinese at the Sinitic Frontier: Social Organizations in United States' Chinatowns, 1849–1898. *Modern Asian Studies* 17:107–135.

Mackie, J.A.C. 1996. Introduction. In Reid 1996, i–xx.

McClain, Charles. 1994. *In Search of Equality: The Chinese Struggle against Discrimination in Nineteenth-Century America*. Berkeley and Los Angeles: University of California Press.

McCurdy, Charles. 1975. Justice Field and the Jurisprudence of Government-Business Relations: Some Parameters of Laissez-faire Constitutionalism, 1863–1897. *Journal of American History* 61:970–1005.

McKee, Delber L. 1977. *Chinese Exclusion versus the Open Door Policy, 1900–1906*. Detroit: Wayne State University Press.

McKeown, Adam. 1999. Transnational Chinese Families and Chinese Exclusion, 1875–1943. *Journal of American Ethnic History* 18:73–110.

Miller, Stuart Creighton. 1969. *The Unwelcome Immigrant: The American Image of the Chinese, 1785–1882*. Berkeley and Los Angeles: University of California Press.

Mooney, Ralph James. 1984. Matthew Deady and the Federal Judicial Response to Racism in the Early West. *Oregon Law Review* 63:561–638.

Morris, Thomas D. 1996. *Southern Slavery and the Law*. Chapel Hill: University of North Carolina Press.

Osumi, Megumi Dick. 1982. Asians and California's Anti-Miscegenation Laws. In *Asian and Pacific American Experiences: Women's Perspectives*, ed. Nobuya Tsuchida. Minneapolis: Asian/Pacific American Learning Resource Center and General College, University of Minnesota, 1–37.

Pascoe, Peggy. 1990. *Relations of Rescue: The Search for Female Moral Authority in the American West, 1874–1939*. New York: Oxford University Press.

———. 1996. Miscegenation Law, Court Cases, and Ideologies of "Race" in Twentieth Century America. *Journal of American History* 83:44–69

Peffer, George Anthony. 1986. Forbidden Families: Emigration Experiences of Chinese Women under the Page Law, 1875–1882. *Journal of American Ethnic History* 6:28–46.

———. 1992. From Under the Sojourner's Shadow: A Historiographical Study of Chinese Female Immigration to America, 1852–1882. *Journal of American Ethnic History* 11:41–67.

———. 1999. *If They Don't bring their Women Here: Chinese Female Immigration before Exclusion*. Urbana: University of Illinois Press.

Reid, Anthony ed. 1996. *Sojourners and Settlers: Histories of Southeast Asia and the Chinese in Honour of Jennifer Cushman*. St. Leonards, Australia: Allen and Unwin.

Salyer, Lucy. 1995. *Laws Harsh as Tigers: Chinese Immigrants and the Shaping of Modern Immigration Law*. Chapel Hill: University of North Carolina Press.

Saxton, Alexander. 1971. *The Indispensable Enemy: Labor and the Anti-Chinese Movement in California*. Berkeley and Los Angeles: University of California Press.

Shah, Nayan. 2001. *Contagious Diseases: Epidemics and Race in San Francisco's Chinatown*. Berkeley: University of California Press.

Siegel, Reva. 1994a. Home as Work: The First Woman's Rights Claims Concerning Wives' Household Labor, 1850–1880. *Yale Law Journal* 103:1073–1219.

———. 1994b. The Modernization of Marital Status Law: Adjudicating Wives' Rights to Earnings, 1860–1930. *Georgetown Law Journal* 82: 2127–212.

Smith, Rogers. 1997. *Civic Ideals: Conflicting Visions of Citizenship in U.S. History*. New Haven, Conn.: Yale University Press.

Survey of Race Relations. 1923–25. Woo Gen, box 27, file 183. Hoover Institution of War, Revolution, and Peace; Stanford University, Stanford, Calif.

Torok, John Hayakawa. 1996. Reconstruction and Racial Nativism: Chinese Immigrants and the Debates on the Thirteenth, Fourteenth, and Fifteenth Amendments and Civil Rights Laws. *Asian Law Journal* 3:55–103.

U.S. Department of Immigration and Naturalization. 1924–30. Letters. National Archives Record Group 85, Chinese Exclusion Act Case Files, Seattle District. National Archives—Pacific Alaska Region.

U.S. House. 1909. White Slave Traffic, Illegal Importation, and Interstate Transportation of Alien Women and Girls for Prostitution, with minority report, H.R. 47, 61st Cong., 2d sess.

———. 1926. Admission of Wives of American Citizens of Oriental Ancestry, Hearings before the Committee of Immigration and Naturalization. 69 Cong., 1st sess. H419-1.

———. 1928. Wives of American Citizens of the Oriental Race, Hearings before the Committee of Immigration and Naturalization. 70th Cong., 1st sess. H477-2.

———. 1930. Wives of American Citizens of Oriental Race, Hearings before the Committee of Immigration and Naturalization. 71st Cong., 2d sess. H559-3

U.S. Senate. 1909. Importing Women for Immoral Purposes, 61stCong., 2d. sess. S. Doc. No. 196.

———. 1910. White Slave Traffic. 61st Cong., 2d. sess. S. Rep. No. 886.

Volpp, Leti. 2001. "Obnoxious to their Very Nature": Asian Americans and Constitution Citizenship. *Asian Law Journal* 8:71–87.

Wong, K. Scott. 1996. "The Eagle seeks a Helpless Quarry": Chinatown, the Police, and the Press: The 1903 Boston Chinatown Raid Revisited. *Amerasia Journal* 22:81–103.

Yung, Judy. 1995. *Unbound Feet: A Social History of Chinese Women in San Francisco.* Berkeley and Los Angeles: University of California Press.

CASES

Case of the Chinese Merchant In re Low Yam Chow, 13 F. 605 (1882).
Case of the Chinese Wife, In re Ah Moy, 21 F. 785 (1884).
Chae Chan Ping v. United States, 130 U.S. 581 (1889).
Chang Chan v. Nagle, 268 U.S. 346 (1925).
Chew Hoy Quong v. White, 249 F. 869 (1918).
Chin Shee v. White, 273 F. 855 (1916).
Chin Yow v. United States, 208 U.S. 8 (1908).
Chung Fook v. White, 287 F. 533 (1923), 264 U.S. 443 (1924)
Ex Parte Cheung Shee, Ex Parte Chan Shee, 2 F. 2d 995 (1924)
Ex Parte Chin King, 35 F. 354 (1888).
Ex Parte Fong Yim et al., 134 F. 938 (1905).
Ex Parte Leong Shee, 275 F. 364 (1921).
Ex Parte Low Joe, 287 F. 545 (1922).
Fong Yue Ting v. United States, 149 U.S. 698 (1892).
Gee Fook Sing v. United States, 49 F. 147 (1892).
Haw Moy v. North, 183 F. 89 (1910).
Hoo Choy v. North, 183 F. 86 (1910).
In re Ah Quan, 21 F. 182, 187 (1884).
In re Ah Sing, 13 F. 286 (1882).
In re Ah Yup, 1 F. 223 (1878).
In re Can Pon, 223 U.S. 673 (1912).
In re Chung Toy Ho, 42 F. 398 (1890).
In re Li Foon, 80 F. 881 (1897).
In re Look Ting Sing, 21 F. 905 (1884).
In re Lum Ling Ying, 59 F. 682 (1894).
In re Tang Tun; In re Gang Gong, 168 F. 488 (1908).
In re Tang Tun, et ux. In re Gang Gong, In re Can Pon, 161 F. 618 (1908).
In re Tom Yum, 64 F. 485 (1894).
In re Tung Yeong, 19 F. 184 (D. Cal. 1884).
In re Wo Tai Li, 48 F. 668 (1888).
Johnson, Commissioner of Immigration v. Shue Hong, 300 F. 89 (1924).
Keller v. United States, 213 U.S. 138 (1909).
Kelly v. Owen, 74 U.S. 496 (1868).
Lee Lung v. Patterson, 186 U.S. 168 (1902).
Lee Sing Far v. United States, 94 F. 834 (1899).
Lem Hing Dun v. United States, etc., 49 F. 148 (1892).
Looe Shee v. North, 170 F. 566 (1909).
Low Way Suey v. Backus, 225 U.S. 460 (1912).
Mah Shee v. White, 242 F. 868 (1917).
McKenzie v. Hare, 239 U.S. 299 (1915).

Quock Ting v. United States, 140 U.S. 417 (1891).
Tang Tun v. Edsell, 223 U.S. 673 (1912).
Tsoi Sim v. United States, 116 F. 920 (1902).
United States v. Wong Kim Ark, 116 U.S. 649 (1898).
United States ex rel. Shue Quey v. Pierce, 285 F. 663 (1922).
United States ex rel. in Soo Hoo Hong v. Tod, Commissioner of Immigration, 290 F. 689 (1923).
United States v. Chew Heong, 21 F. 791 (1884), 112 U.S. 536 (1884).
United States v. Chung Fung Sun et al., 63 F. 262 (1894).
United States v. Ju Toy, 198 U.S. 253 (1905).
United States v. Lee Chee, 224 F. 447 (2d Cir. 1915).
United States v. Mrs. Gue Lim, 83 F. 136 (1897), 176 U.S. 459 (1899).
White v. Kwock Sue Lim, 291 F. 732 (1923).
Wöey Ho v. United States, 109 F. 888 (1901).
Woo Hoo v. White, 243 F. 542 (1917).
Yee Won v. White, 256 U.S. 399 (1921).

[15]

Placing the "Gift Child" in Transnational Adoption

Barbara Yngvesson

In this article I focus on discourses of freedom and exclusive belonging that structure the conventions of giving in transnational adoption, and I examine state practices for regulating the production and circulation of children in a global market economy. I argue that while the gift child, like the sold child, is a product of commodity thinking, experiences of giving a child, receiving a child, and of being a given child are in tension with market practices, producing the contradictions of adoptive kinship, the ambiguities of adoption law, and the creative potential in the construction of adoptive families.

gratuitous 1. Given or granted without return or recompense; unearned.
2. Given or received without cost or obligation; free; gratis (*American Heritage Dictionary of the English Language*).

What would be a gift that fulfills the condition of the gift, namely, that it not appear as gift, that it not be, exist, signify, want-to-say as gift? A gift without wanting, without wanting-to-say, an insignificant gift, a gift without intention to give? Why would we call that a gift?

—Jacques Derrida, *Given Time*, 1992

Even if reversibility is the objective truth of the discrete acts which ordinary experience knows in discrete form and calls gift exchanges, it is not the whole truth of a practice which could not exist if it were consciously perceived in accordance with the model. The temporal structure of gift exchange, which objectivism ignores, is what makes possible the existence of two opposing truths, which defines the full truth of the gift.

—Pierre Bourdieu, *The Logic of Practice*, 1977

Research on which this paper is based was supported by the National Science Foundation (grant no. SBR-9511 937) and by faculty development grants from Hampshire College. I am grateful to the individuals who agreed to be interviewed for this project, to staff of Stockholm's Adoption Centre, without whose support and assistance it would not have been possible, and to Susan Coutin and Bill Maurer, with whom I have been collaborating on a related project.

Address correspondence to Barbara Yngvesson, Hampshire College, Amherst, MA 01002 (e-mail: byngvesson@hampshire.edu).

Complex Truths

A front-page story in the October 25, 1998, edition of the *New York Times* describes an open adoption in which Kim Elniskey chose Yvette Weilacker and her husband to adopt her newborn son. The story, illustrated by a picture of the future adoptive mother reaching out to touch the child in the arms of his birth mother, quotes Elniskey as saying, "I want you to feel that this is your baby, your family" (Fein 1998:1). The only intimation of tension between giver and receiver, and the force this might have in shaping the landscape of adoption and the experience of the adopted child, is the comment, made almost in passing, that "loaded" phrases such as "real parent" and "natural parent" have been replaced in the current climate of transparency surrounding adoption. The birth parent gives, relinquishes, and chooses; the adoptive parent receives. Together, they become "part of a clan."[1]

The fascination this story evokes—its representation of a selfless mother who gives her child away in order to create a family for him—is an effect of its moral ambiguity for the educated, white, middle-class audiences to whom it is directed. A mother who gives away her child is unthinkable. She gives the child away because she loves it so much, the story and its accompanying image imply; but the unspoken subtext—If she really loved the child, how could she bear to part from it?—is no less powerful a message in a moral economy in which becoming a woman is inseparable from the work of motherhood and the assumptions about nurturance this implies (Ginsburg 1989). A birth mother I interviewed several years ago, who had placed her infant son in an open adoption in 1993, described the shocked admiration of friends who told her she was "so brave," followed immediately by the cautionary statement, "I could *never* give away my child." This woman is still haunted by the sense that her gesture of love and trust was morally wrong, whatever her aspirations for her son, and that he will eventually condemn her for it, possibly hate her (Yngvesson 1997:55–56).[2]

What is one to make of the "gift child"? How are we to place such a child in a cultural universe where being given away by a mother is tantamount to abandonment, the worst fate that can be imagined for *any* child? In "Abandonment: What Do We Tell Them?" social worker and adoptive parent Jane Brown argues

---

1 Fein (1998:30), quoting Jim Gritter, director of Catholic Human Services in Traverse City, Michigan, who advocates adoption as a "collaborative experience."

2 See Modell (1999) for a discussion of the rhetoric of giving in open adoptions.

that the "a-word" should be abandoned in favor of more neutral language—"making an adoption plan," "placing" a child for adoption—which depict the motives of a mother in a way that is less injurious to the feelings of the adoptee (Brown 2000). For similar reasons, the rhetoric of giving has been criticized in how-to books on adoption, which suggest that placing the child is more of a piece with the birth mother's increased visibility in contemporary (American) society. The visible birth mother makes "a voluntary decision and a positive plan" for her child, rather than giving her child away (Melina 1989:26–27; 1998:94–95). Similarly, the giving nation is positioned differently in contemporary adoption rhetoric, as vigilant over the loss of its most precious national resources—children—rather than as a country that has only children to give away (Carlson 1994:256; Yngvesson 2000:185; Stanley 1997:1).[3] The rhetoric of giving and the experience of loss go hand-in-hand in these representations, in which alienation (the split subject, the fragmented nation) is an inevitable consequence of "giving." By contrast, child "placement"—understood as planned, consensual, and regulated by the nation-state—is celebrated by adoption professionals and policymakers.

In spite of efforts to reconceptualize the physical movement of a child between persons or nations as placement rather than gift, the gift child remains a powerful and persistent image in adoption discourse. I suggest that the reason this is so is related in part to the ambiguity of the concept—the difficulty of interpreting what gifts signify about the relationship (or absence of a relationship) between donor and receiver, an ambiguity that resonates with the experience of the adoptee, the adoptive family, and, in some cases, the birth family. Ambiguity, in turn, is a function of the traces gifts bear of their passage in the world—their movement from and to some*one* and some*place*, however vague the identity of the donor may be. By contrast, "placement" conveys a sense of grounding and permanence that is at odds with the experience of *being adopted*, of *giving in adoption*, or of *adopting*, verbs that imply a transformation of belonging and identity. A woman who wrote in response to the *New York Times* article with which I began, commented on this disjunction between language and experience:

> As an adult adoptee who has been struggling with her own feelings, I'd like to remind birth and adoptive parents that the question "why did your real mother give you away?" will haunt the adopted child no matter how trained we all become in using the "language of adoption"—for example, the term "birth mother" as a substitute for "real mother" or "natural mother."

[3] Nanuli Shevardnadze told the *New York Times* in 1997 that she was "categorically against foreign adoption," adding that "our nation's gene pool is being depleted" (Stanley 1997:1).

> Though your Oct. 25 front-page article claims that open adoptions make the process an "infinitely more transparent experience," the anxiety to cover the painful feelings of all parties is still obvious in the concern with controlling language. (Duckham 1998:A28)

In what follows, I examine the concept of the adopted child as gift and explore the difficulties of an interpretation of such gifts as "freely given." Building on Marilyn Strathern's (1988) discussion of giving relationships as "enchaining" giver and receiver, rather than freeing them, and drawing on the experiences of agencies, orphanages, adoptive parents, birth parents, and adoptees, I argue that the enchainments of adoptive kinship open up our understandings of family and identity, and the ideas about exclusive belonging these understandings assume. Practices of adoptive kinship that seek to counter the alienation of the child and the divisions of the adoptive family by imagining placement to be a consequence of voluntarism by a birth mother or of "choice" by prospective adoptive parents obscure the dependencies and inequalities that compel some of us to give birth to and give up our children, while constituting others as "free" to adopt them.[4] By examining the ways in which the gift of a child always leaves a trace and implies the potential for a return, I suggest how an adoptee's lived experiences of being given away may transform our understandings of personhood, identity, and belonging in an adopted world. However freestanding the child is "made" by adoption law, he or she can *never* be free of the "implicate field of persons" in which he or she was constituted as legally adoptable.[5]

Commodity Thinking

The emphasis on freedom in forging the relations of adoptive kinship is deeply embedded in adoption law, both at national and international levels. Adoption lawyer Joan Hollinger noted some years ago in a discussion of U.S. adoption law that "birthparents are said to 'bestow' their children directly upon the adoptive parents or to 'surrender' them to child-placing agencies. . . . 'Solicitation' of children is deplored" (1993:49). In Massachusetts, the birth mother is required by law to "voluntarily and unconditionally surrender" her child to the guardianship of the state or of the future adoptive parents (Yngvesson 1997:34). In California, a social worker who obtains a birth mother's consent

[4] Susan Wadia-Ells (1995) provides a moving account of her own coming to terms with the material reality confronting her adopted son's birth mother, and her sense of the "profound cultural arrogance" involved in the assumptions and practices surrounding what she had assumed to be the "incredible gift" of a child (1995:118–22).

[5] The phrase is Marilyn Strathern's (1997:298), in a discussion of the relationship of sociality to the production of persons in Melanesia.

to relinquish her child is required to ascertain that she is not "taking any medications that might alter [her] reasoning" (Interview, RP 11/16/94)—that is, the social worker must ensure that there is nothing that might inhibit the freedom with which the birth mother gives her consent to the adoption. International conventions, such as the *Hague Convention on Protection of Children and Co-operation in Respect of Intercountry Adoption* (Hague Conference, 1993) also emphasize that "persons, institutions and authorities have given their consent freely, in the required legal form, and expressed or evidenced in writing." The consents must "not have been induced by payment or compensation of any kind" (1993, Article 4).

Concern regarding the freedom of a birth mother from inducements that might jeopardize the validity of her consent is matched by the conceptualization of the institutions and/or parents who receive the child as receiving him or her gratuitously. Any payment must be characterized as a payment for services or as an "act of charity" to an orphanage or other child welfare institution, not as payment for a child (Hollinger 1993:49). As Hollinger notes, "The notion that adoption is not contractual is so powerful that it obscures the extent to which bargaining is intrinsic to a transfer of a child by a birthparent in exchange for a promise by adoptive parents or an agency to support and care for the child and thereby relieve the birthparent of these legal duties" (1993:49).

The centrality of freedom in the discourse of giving and receiving children in adoption is linked to a second key feature of adoption law, its finality. The laws of most adopting nations, whether they typically "give" children or "receive" them, require or state a preference for "strong" adoptions. In strong adoptions, the decision of a woman to surrender her child is irrevocable, and the adoption that follows creates a permanent and exclusive relationship of adoptive kinship that cannot be "undone."[6] In the United States, where adoptions are both unconditional and irrevocable (Hollinger 1993), efforts by adoptees, adoptive parents, and many birth mothers to secure legislation that would make adoption records public have had only limited success (Wegar 1997; Carp 1998; Verhovek 2000; Yngvesson & Mahoney 2000). The only way for adopted adults and the birth parents who "placed" them to discover how the adoption "plan" was made, and what led to the decision to make such a plan, is to work around laws that define the adoptive family as the *only* family of an adopted child. In Chile, an official who oversaw thousands of surrenders of children by women who could not keep them and who hoped to find homes for them through adoptions to Sweden

6 This term was used by a Swedish official commenting on a contested adoption involving a Colombian-born child (see p. 242).

and other nations in the 1970s and 1980s advised these women that "it will be like your child is dead to you" (Yngvesson 2003). International conventions urge "the termination of a pre-existing legal relationship between the child and his or her mother and father" (Hague Conference 1993, Art. 26) and suggest that receiving nations be permitted to "convert" an adoption that does not terminate such a relationship in the sending nation into an adoption that does so in the receiving nation (1993, Art. 27).

The combination of freedom to choose (to exit from a parenting relationship that is presumed to be natural and given) and closure (the new relationship is exclusive of other ties) are both dimensions of a global market economy in which commodity thinking defines the meaning of personhood. In commodity thinking, "persons are assumed to be proprietors of their persons (including their own will, their energies, and work in the general sense of directed activity)" (Strathern 1988:157). These "properties" of the person "belong" to them in a definitional sense and constitute the possessor "as a unitary social entity" (104). Moreover, "belonging" is understood as "an active proprietorship" (135). Persons "'are' what they 'have' or 'do.' Any interference with this one-to-one relationship is regarded as the intrusion of an 'other'" (158). Just as the individual is assumed to be the owner of his or her own person in commodity thinking, so too is society conceptualized as "owning" the properties (persons) that intrinsically constitute it. The transferal of a child from one "owner" to another unsettles this relationship of product to producer—of a nation to "its" citizens, a parent to "its" child, or a person to his or her "nature" (as Colombian or Korean, or as the "natural" child of a particular parent or parents). In commodity thinking, separation from this ground of belonging cannot help but produce an alienated (split) subject, which will always be pulled "back" to where it *really* belongs.

The idea of gratuitous bestowal of the child that is so central a feature of adoption law developed as a response to the perceived danger of producing an alienated subject. Baby-giving could be interpreted as "admirable altruism," because "we do not fear relinquishment of children unless it is accompanied by—understood in terms of, structured by—market rhetoric" (Radin 1996:139). But as Viviana Zelizer argues in her study of the sentimentalized or "priceless" child in America during the late-19th and early-20th centuries, baby-selling and baby-giving are part of the same system, a system in which licit markets depend on illicit ones to establish the value of "priceless" objects (1985:202–3). Indeed, a priceless (gift) child presents a legal quandary that is no less a cultural and social quandary: "How could value be assigned if price were absent?" (14). The adopted child embodies this quandary, in a world where the "fundamentally seductive idea of exchange" (Kopytoff 1986:72) leaves its trace on all entities, whether these are distinguished as "persons" or as "things." In her movement from one family (and one nation) to another in adoption, the child experiences (and symbolizes) the meaning of pricelessness "in the full possible sense of the term" (1986:75): "thrown away like a blade of grass" by her mother (to quote a 6-year-old girl adopted from China by American parents), she is embraced by someone who has "traveled to the ends of the earth" (Serrill 1991:41) to become her parent.

Price and Pricelessness

The interplay of value and the child's capacity to be thrown away is the central paradox of adoptability, one that is especially salient in the international arena. In India, for example, which together with Korea became one of the earliest nations to "give" children to the overdeveloped world in adoption, the value of physically abandoned, institutionalized children developed as part of an economy of desire in which heterosexual, Caucasian couples from Europe and North America sought to adopt them (Yngvesson 2000).

The desire to adopt children from Third World orphanages was not initially a function of infertility and the "scarcity" of healthy, white infants in Western nations, although this rapidly became a central consideration. Instead, this desire took shape as a dimension of development discourse (Escobar 1995) in a postcolonial world in which child adoption operated in conjunction with other forms of aid. In Sweden—which has the largest percentage of international adoptees per capita of any nation (approximately 40,000 in a nation of 39 million) and is widely regarded as a pioneer in the field—international adoption was regarded in the 1960s and early 1970s as a *responsibility* for socially conscious citizens.

Reaction to this sense of responsibility in what were to become "sending" or "giving" nations was mixed. As one woman who adopted her daughter from a Delhi orphanage in 1964 explained, "[W]e weren't exactly encouraged" by local officials. When she and her husband came to fetch their daughter at the orphanage, "they kept asking us, 'Why on earth are you doing anything like this?'"[7] At the same time, one of the earliest contact persons in India for Swedish adopters observed that "as an underdeveloped country, the only thing we [could] give away is children, you know?" (Yngvesson 2000:185).

As the numbers of children moving to the overdeveloped world in adoption increased steadily during the 1970s and a growing international movement to protect children's rights took shape (Therborn 1995), officials in sending nations began

[7] GA, interview, August 1999.

to voice concern about the potential for exploitation of children sent abroad in adoption.[8] These concerns provoked child welfare officials in India to hold a series of workshops, which continued into the late 1990s, with concerned adoption professionals from Western receiving nations. The workshops were sponsored by Sweden's Adoption Centre and the International Social Service Committee in Geneva, and were held at regional and international meetings of the International Council of Social Welfare. In 1981, workshop participants produced the "Bombay Guidelines," a document that defined the issues that were subsequently incorporated into a 1985 Indian Supreme Court Judgment, *Lakshmi Kant Pandey v. Union of India.* Justice Bhagwati, who presided over this landmark case, declared the Indian child to be a "supremely important national asset" on which the "physical and mental health of the nation is dependent" and which should be kept, whenever possible, in its nation of origin (*Lakshmi Kant Pandey* 1985:4–5). His judgment established a quota system for international adoptions, requiring that at least 50% of Indian children placed in adoption be placed domestically.

Justice Bhagwati's ruling was a key moment in the legal recognition of the value of internationally adoptable children as a national resource of the country that produced them (Carlson 1994:256), a moment that was contingent, however, on the experiences of Indian child welfare officials that destitute children had become "commodities [in] an export market."[9] By the early 1990s, when the Hague Conference on Protection of Children and Co-operation in Respect of Intercountry Adoption was convened with representatives of 66 sending and receiving nations, the most divisive issue separating senders from receivers was that of regulating an international market in adoptable children, while at the same time "placing" children in need of families in suitable homes.

The idea that legal adoption is a "market" is anathema to many adoptive parents, adoption agencies, and government officials in sending and receiving countries. But it is accepted as common (if sensational and often disturbing) sense by the public and many adoptees, some of whom comment ironically on their status as "Made in . . . Colombia [India, Korea, Nepal, Chile, and so forth]."[10] In a front page, three-part series featured in the *New*

[8] Adoptions from India to Sweden increased from 30 per year in the late 1960s to 300 to 400 annually between 1979 and 1985. For a discussion of trends during the growth period of international adoption, see Pilotti (1993).

[9] AD, interview, November 1995.

[10] In a performance by Swedish adoptees for adoptive parents at the biennial meeting of Stockholm's Adoption Centre in 1997, over 100 intercountry adoptees marched onto a stage wearing identical white shirts with a Swedish flag on the front, then turned to reveal the words "Made in Colombia" (and so forth) on the back of each shirt. This was an obvious reference to Swedish products that are made in the developing world but identified as uniquely Swedish by a small blue and yellow flag glued to the side or bottom.

York Times in the fall of 1998, one article titled "Market Puts Price Tags on Priceless" presents adoption as a baby bazaar in which the color, culture, and condition of a child are for sale and race determines fees (Mansnerus 1998:A14). While noting that the actual sale of children is illegal in the United States and internationally, the *Times* points out that many adoptions today maintain only the finest line between buying a child and buying adoption services that lead to a child. This view underscores Viviana Zelizer's argument that, in the United States (and, at the present time, internationally), adoption is a legal market in children, one that is entwined in complex ways with illegal markets to establish the value of an adoptable child (1985:202–3).

I suggest that what seems to be an irresolvable tension between the gift child and market practices that make her priceless is a function of the "double evocatory power" of gifts in commodity thinking (Strathern 1997:301). For an object to become a gift, it must be made freestanding: It must be broken free from a producer and constituted as "part of a[n anonymous] store on which others draw" (1997:302). Gifts, then, are alienable, like any other commodity. At the same time, once given, they become a means of building relationships; and relationships constituted through "giving" are interpreted as a function of love (1997:303). Gifts represent "the intimate altruism of transactions that typify personal relations outside the market . . . the wrapped present, the exhibited taste" (1997:301–2). This representation is only possible, however, if they are (imagined to be) "free" and "freely given." The compelled gift is an oxymoron, suggesting that the giver has been induced, seduced, or otherwise placed in a relationship of indebtedness to the receiver. Indebtedness enters time and history into what is envisioned as a timeless relation of love, a relation that endures in spite of all contingencies.[11]

Conceptualizing the relinquishment of a child for adoption as a gift constitutes the relations involved as family relations in an economy where family is imagined as "natural" and not contractual (Schneider 1968), the site of "love relations" (Coontz 1992:53), not of law. Indeed, the given child constitutes the adoptive family as "family," almost as though no adoption had taken place at all. It is precisely the complex identity of the adopted child as, on one hand, a "gift of love" that makes a family (complete), and, on the other, a "resource" that has been contractually alienated from one owner so that it can be attached to another, that produces the contradictions of adoptive kinship, the ambiguities of adoption law, and the creative tension in practices that surround the construction of adoptive families.

[11] See Hervé Varenne's (1977:188–9) discussion of the place of love in American kinship as a way of "relating to" people who are seen as fundamentally separate from the "self."

The Production of Adoptability

These considerations are central to placing the gift child in the context of transnational adoption, and especially to an explanation of the role of the state in these types of transactions. Documents such as the *Hague Convention* (Hague Conference 1993), the earlier *UN Declaration on Adoption and Foster Care* (1986), and the *Child's Right to Grow Up in a Family: Guidelines for Practice in National and Inter-country Adoption and Foster Care* (Adoption Centre 1997), as well as *Lakshmi Kant Pandey v. Union of India* (1985)—which established terms for the commodification of the child vis-à-vis the state—emphasize the rights of the child as a state resource and the state's obligation to protect this resource. In particular, these documents focus on "identity rights"—to a name, a nationality, and to be cared for by one's parents—that are essential in defining the resource status of the child: his or her ownership or belonging in or to a specific family or nation (Stephens 1995).

I suggest that while these rights are crucial protections in a global economy that promotes the circulation of children, to focus on them deflects attention from the role of the state in *producing* the physically abandoned child. Reconfigured as a "legal orphan" that is "available" for adoption, this child becomes a particular kind of "natural resource" for the state that has produced it. The role of the state in this form of production is both more subtle and more powerful than its role in producing identity rights. The transnational adoption of children cannot be explained without reference to state reproductive policies (Ceauşescu's pro-natalism, China's one-child policy, Korea's protection of patriarchal bloodlines), to the *violencia* of wars, kidnappings, and disappearances in which the state is a key player (in Colombia, Chile, Argentina, Honduras, and other Latin American nations, e.g.), and to the incentives for "giving" these children in adoption that are provided by conventions and agreements among cooperating states. Children's rights to an identity are constituted so that the mobility of certain children (who are defined as "adoptable" by the state) is facilitated (Hague Conference 1993, Art. 4), while the identities of all children are fixed so that they can *only* be thought in terms of a "State of origin" (1993:Preamble) and can only be defined in terms of exclusive "identity rights" that are authorized by the state.[12]

[12] A striking recent example of how state policy determines the mobility of children internationally is China's recent decision to change its adoption law, permitting domestic adoptions of children by families who already have one child (Johnson 2002 [herein]). Experience with India's regulation of international adoption in the mid-1980s suggests that such moves to encourage domestic adoption of "available" children transform the range of children considered adoptable abroad (and eventually, at home), in this way increasing the size and diversity of the pool of children available for adoption (see Yngvesson 2000 for an elaboration of this point).

The dual role of the state in producing a child whose right to "the full and harmonious development of his or her personality" entitles him or her "to grow up in a family environment, in an atmosphere of happiness, love and understanding" (1993:Preamble) even as it produces the conditions for the abandonment of children and determines the terms of their adoptability by other states illuminates once again the tension between giving and selling in commodity thinking, and the significance of marking the divide between state and market in these transactions. The adoptable child is not sold, but is given to other states in exchange for a donation of money, a transaction that creates an orderly (and hierarchical) relation of states to one another through the movement of valued resources (children) in adoption.

This orderly traffic is officially distinguished from a market in children (Hague Conference 1993, Art. 1), which is viewed as the source of alienation and loss for the adopted child. In the marketplace (of adoption), all that counts is money, and children become, in effect, *only* money, in this way losing "themselves."[13] The gift child, by contrast, does *not* lose him- or herself (according to national laws and international conventions), either because the move is erased (the child's belonging is transferred to a new family or country), or because the child's source of belonging (his or her national identity) moves with the child. The assumption that identity is inalienable and moves with the child is implicit in everyday depictions of adopted children as "Chinese," "Russian," "Colombian," and so forth. It can be seen as well in popular representations of adoption, such as the *New Yorker* cartoon that appeared a few years ago depicting two couples having dinner. One woman says to the other, "We're so excited. I'm hoping for a Chinese girl, but Peter's heart is set on a Native American boy" (7 July 1992). Here, the child moves, but "Chineseness," "American Indianness," "Koreanness," or "Colombianness" remains the same (or rather, these qualities are enhanced and constituted anew as immutable in this movement).

As this discussion suggests, it is the *circulation* of persons, as promoted or prevented by state policy, that establishes borders, belongings, and the right of a child to "an identity."[14] Indeed, studies of undocumented immigrants in the United States suggest that their mobility or immobility is constituted by agents of the state in ways that secure a traversal of boundaries (the official act of immigration or deportation) only when recognized by im-

[13] See Greenhouse et al. (1994:100) for a discussion of people with "dollar signs in their eyes"; and see Radin (1996:18–21, 136–48) for a discussion of children and market inalienability.

[14] See Elizabeth Grosz's discussion of this issue in *Space, Time and Perversion* (1995:131). Citing Massumi (1993:27–31), Grosz argues that "boundaries are only produced and set in the process of passage. Boundaries do not so much define the routes of passage: it is movement that defines and constitutes boundaries."

migration officials, regardless of when the immigrants physically entered or departed the country (Coutin 2000:29–34). Likewise, the idea that adoptees originate in one place or another and have or lack parents (they are legally abandoned or do not qualify as abandoned) is also constituted by state agents.[15] Mobility (and the traversal of boundaries this implies) is fundamental to modernity and the fixed identities this requires.[16]

If identity is grounded in movement rather than immobility, what does this suggest about the place of the gift child? If identity (and its associated rights) is contingent on the cut-offs mandated by adoption law, citizenship decrees (Coutin 2000), and other legal processes that establish rights by erasing pre-existing social and legal ties, how might "giving" a child in adoption refigure not only identities but the transactions in which identities take shape? To explore this question, I begin with a re-examination of the meaning of a gift.

Identity and Enchainment

The concept of "gratuitous transfer" of a child in adoption might be viewed as a legal and social fiction that "misrecognizes" the contractual nature of a process in which children are separated from one author and attached to another, in exchange for a promise to (exclusively) care for them. Marilyn Strathern, for example, argues that the alienability of gifts in a market economy is systemic—"[I]t is hardly admissible to decide that this particular transaction results in alienation, while that particular one does not" (1988:161). But as Pierre Bourdieu argues in *Outline of a Theory of Practice* (1977:3), this approach fails to take into account the limits of a standpoint that grasps practices "from outside, as a *fait accompli*," instead of situating itself "within the very movement of their accomplishment." In order to situate oneself within the movement of practices, attention must be directed to their temporal structure, a structure that differs depending on whether one is a participant or an observer. With regard to gift exchange, "[T]he observer's totalizing apprehension substitutes an objective structure fundamentally defined by its *reversibility* for an

[15] See Coutin & Yngvesson (2002) for a discussion of the parallels between adoptees on roots trips and deportees who have been forced "back" to a country they no longer consider their "own." In both cases there is a "back" but what constitutes such a place (and the desires and fantasies associated with it) is dependent on the role of the nation-state in producing a place from which each form of expatriate is exiled.

[16] Slavoj Zizek, in a reinterpretation of Marx's work on commodity fetishism, argues that the essential (unchanging) "nature" of an object is constituted in the act of exchange. Drawing on the work of Sohn-Rethel, Zizek argues that commodity exchange requires a fundamental "as if" ("*als ob*"): that the object exchanged is not subject to the uncertainties of time and the processes of generation and corruption that transform all objects in the world. Commodity exchange (and the transacting states that guarantee it) stamps the object exchanged with an unchanging essence, a kind of "immaterial corporality" that "endures all torments and survives with its beauty immaculate" (1989:18).

equally objective *irreversible* succession of gifts which are not mechanically linked to the gifts they respond to or insistently call for" (Bourdieu 1977:5). This suggests that the "full truth" of the gift of a child in adoption lies neither in the experienced truth of a cut-off from the past nor in the longing for reconnection, but in the capacity of such a gift to evoke "two opposing truths" (5) at the same moment:

1. The truth that identity is located in the inseparability of a child from an author, a concept of selfhood (or of nationhood) in which there is "an identity between owner and thing owned" and in which there is no place for the intervention of social others "except in the guise of supplanted authorship" (Strathern 1988:158). In this account of identity, legal adoption is a process that alienates a child from its "origins": the mother (nation) must give the baby *up* (Yngvesson 1997:53, quoting a birth mother), termination of parental rights is irrevocable, and legal adoptions cannot be "undone" (see case that follows). The finality of law in adoption—what Duncan (1993:51) describes as the principle of the "clean break"—reflects a specific cultural perspective on the child as property, but has come to dominate the practices of transnational adoption.
2. At the same time, and co-existing in painful tension with this finality, is a parallel truth that is both hard to hold onto and impossible to let go: that the identity of the adopted child is created in its exchange *among* partners (states, agencies, orphanages, and very occasionally, parents), neither of whom is the "author" of the child. This competing story about the gift child places the emphasis on *giving*, rather than on giving *away*, and requires that the connection between giver and receiver ("giving" nations and "receiving" nations) be kept open rather than shut down. Unlike commodity thinking—where the emphasis on single authorship means that the connection to "roots" is always in the foreground, constituting a pull on adopted children either to find their roots or replace them (but in any case to define only one set of roots as "real")—the given child cannot be alienated from roots, but can only "find" herself in the relationship *between* self and other, birth country and adopted country, birth parent and adopted parent. In this sense, the gift of a child in adoption enchains giver and receiver, even as it alienates a child from his or her "roots."

The concept of giving as enchainment creates forms of identity that are both more complex and inherently more divisible than the "in"dividuals created by the identity rights spelled out in the *Hague Convention*, the *UN Convention on the Rights of the Child*, and other legal instruments. Enchainment is a function of the link between persons and nations out of which the internationally adoptable child is born; it presumes a field that is not dissolved but strengthened with the passage of the child. This relational field connects rather than separates, and has implications for the confusions and ambiguities that surround the internationally adopted child's "identity." Adoptive identities, constituted in the "in-between" of nations, agencies, and orphanages, position the adoptee as simultaneously "placed and not stitched in place" (Hall 1997:50)—she "belongs" in Korea when she is in the United States or in Sweden, but is "American" or "Swedish" when she is in Korea (Trotzig 1996; von Melen 1998; Liem 2000). The simultaneity of fixity and non-fixity, and the placement in an in-between that this compels, forges identity for persons no less than for nations.

The adoption story below lays open the tension in the concept of a given child, elucidating the child's connection to market "forces" and to the longing for exclusive belongings these forces provoke. In this particular story, the tragedy that underpins so many adoptions is explicit. The story also makes plain both the fragility of connections which tie "identity" and belonging to one particular place and the power of the structures of feeling these connections incite, propelling people to challenge the law (even as they use it), to undo an adoption that cannot be undone and to create unexpected relationships across nations and across the more conventional family boundaries these nations seek to maintain.

Carlos Alberto/Omar Konrad[17]

On the night of December 9, 1992, Nancy Apraez Coral was kidnapped with her 11-month-old son, Carlos Alberto, from the home of her son's father in Popayan, a town in the district of Cauca in southern Colombia. The kidnappers were later identified as members of UNASE (Unidad Antiextorción y Secuestro), an anti-kidnapping unit connected with Colombian state security forces in Popayan. They were apparently searching for the father of Nancy's child, who himself was suspected of involvement in a recent kidnapping. When they did not find him, they took Nancy and her infant son instead.

Nancy was killed some time in the next 8 days. In the early morning of December 16, her baby boy was left, dressed warmly and with a bottle of milk, on a street in Pasto, a town about 300 miles south of Popayan, in the Andes near the Ecuadorian border. The child's cries were heard by Cecilia and Conrado España,

[17] The following discussion of this case appears as well in an earlier publication (Yngvesson 2000:173–8).

who took him in and later that morning notified the Colombian child welfare department, ICBF (Instituto Colombiano de Bienestar Familiar). According to a subsequent Colombian newspaper story, "[H]e was a precious child, swarthy [*trigueño*], robust, acceptably clothed and had a little white poncho" (Calvache 1995:12A). The child was picked up that evening by welfare officials, and subsequently placed in a foster home pending location of his family or a legal declaration of abandonment. The local newspaper, *Diario del Sur*, published his picture on its front page the following day, along with an account of his discovery by local residents (Calvache 1992:1).

Colombian law requires that efforts be made to locate a "lost" or "abandoned" child's family by placing a notice in the local or national mass media. If no family member appears to claim him, the child becomes available for domestic or international adoption. In this case, apart from the report in *Diario del Sur*, the effort to locate Carlos Alberto's family consisted of announcements on the local (Pasto) radio station on January 14, 15, and 18. When there was no response to these notices, he was declared legally abandoned on February 4, 1993, and was named Omar Conrado España, after the family who found him. Two months later, a Swedish couple was selected by ICBF as adoptive parents for the child, and on June 4, 1993, the adoption was completed in Colombia. The child left for Sweden with his new parents, and his adoption was officially recognized by the Swedish government on August 4, 1993. His new parents named him Omar Konrad Vernersson, retaining in his new legal identity the traces of the violent displacements that had shaped his brief life.

In September 1993, three months after the adoption of Omar Conrado and nine months after the kidnapping, the baby's maternal grandmother received an anonymous phone call telling her that her grandson had been abandoned at the town plaza in Pasto. When she arrived there and found no baby, she went from door to door with a picture of the child and eventually located the España family, who sent her to the ICBF. There she was told by the director of child welfare that her grandchild had been legally adopted, the adoption was final, and the record of the adoption was sealed, thus there was no possibility of locating the child (Calvache 1995:12a,1b).[18]

The grandmother hired a lawyer, who filed an appeal with the Pasto Superior Court to have the record opened, and the appeal was approved in February 1994. On June 9, 1995, the adoption was overturned by a Colombian court, which ordered the Colombian authorities (ICBF) and the adoptive family to return the child to his maternal grandparents. Sweden, however

[18] Colombian law requires that adoption documents be sealed (*reservados*, hidden or shut away) for 30 years (*Codigo del Menor*, Art. 114, 1990).

(representing the position of the Adoption Centre, which arranged for the adoption, and of NIA, the Swedish State Board for International Adoptions) did not recognize this action, arguing that since the child was now a Swedish citizen, a Colombian court decree could not affect his legal relationship to his Swedish adoptive parents. In Sweden, according to the Adoption Centre, "adoptions cannot be undone."

The child's grandmother visited Sweden in June 1995, with the assistance of Colombia's ASFADDES (Association of the Family Members of the Disappeared) and Norway's Council of Political Refugees. The Adoption Centre, under pressure because of widespread media publicity in both Colombia and Sweden, received the grandmother at its office in Stockholm, and facilitated a meeting between the grandmother, her grandson, and his adoptive parents. No agreement was reached, however, about the child's return, and the Colombian government said that it lacked the resources to pursue the case in Sweden.

In 1996, Amnesty International intervened on the grandmother's behalf by providing a lawyer for her, and she made a second trip to Sweden, where she visited her grandson and his adoptive parents at their home. During this visit, an unofficial agreement regarding visitation and the child's education was drawn up and eventually (in 1997) signed by the adoptive parents and the grandmother. The agreement specifies that the child is to remain with his adoptive parents, that his grandmother has visitation rights once a year, that the child is to take Spanish classes, and that when it is "suitable," the adoptive family will visit Colombia. These terms satisfied the Adoption Centre, which continued to affirm its position that it was in the best interest of the child (now six years old) to remain with his adoptive parents—"He has no other parents"—but conceded that "the biological maternal grandparents should continue to be the child's grandparents." This concession by adoption officials, together with the signed agreement between the parents and grandparents, blurs the concept of adoption as a "clean-break" process and tacitly contributes to the official endorsement of a model of family that is heterotopic (Foucault 1973), in that it suggests forms of belonging that disrupt the orders, divisions, and groupings of blood kinship and of exclusive national identities.[19]

This story illuminates the complications of any simple interpretation of parental "abandonment" of a child. It demonstrates the embeddedness of physical abandonment in the violence of the state and in the "pull" of international agreements and un-

[19] As Foucault argues, "*Heterotopias* are disturbing . . . because they make it impossible to name this *and* that, because they shatter or tangle common names, because they destroy 'syntax' in advance, and not only the syntax with which we construct sentences, but also the less apparent syntax which causes words and things to 'hold together'" (1973:xviii).

derstandings (such as those that underpin intercountry adoptions from Colombia to Sweden). Physical abandonment and the legal erasures that follow (and may provoke) this abandonment are central to the commodification of the adoptable child. While the routinization in processing that is implied by this story is not necessarily characteristic of other Colombian adoptions, it is nonetheless revealing of the erasures of belonging—the effacement of traces that would link the child to a specific social, cultural, and political surround—that have accompanied the emergence of adoption as a practice for creating families among infertile couples of the north and for managing a political or economic "excess" of children in the south.

These erasures of belonging—and the identities and histories they imply—have become a site of personal struggle for adoptees and their families, as well as an arena for ongoing policy negotiation between sending and receiving countries. This was particularly in evidence during the three years of the Hague Conference on Intercountry Adoption that culminated in the signing of the 1993 Convention. Negotiations at the Conference focused on reconciling the apparent "need" for the adoption of children transnationally with the reassertion of nationalisms, ethnicities, and identities grounded in a particular national soil—particularly with the proclamation of the key place of the child as a "natural" resource through which a claim to a "national" identity can be made.

In this sense, adoptions such as that of Carlos Alberto both challenge (and entrench ever more deeply) ideas of children's identity rights as tied to exclusive national belongings and as deeply rooted in the blood connections of one generation to another "through" time (Anderson 1983). The tenaciousness of Carlos Alberto's grandmother in pursuing her "right" to a relationship with her grandchild, and her skill in mobilizing both national and international groups in support of this right, together with the persistence of Sweden's Adoption Centre in affirming Omar Konrad's Swedish citizenship, the irrevocability of his adoption, and the applicability of Swedish, rather than Colombian law in this case, point to the complex ways in which identity rights may be deployed to secure a specific cultural embeddedness for a particular child.[20] At the same time, this case suggests the unexpected permutations of belonging that struggles over these contradictory rights may produce.

---

[20] The success of Carlos Alberto's grandmother in mobilizing international support for her right to a relationship with her daughter's son is surely connected, in part, to the publicity surrounding the efforts of the Mothers of the Plaza de Mayo in Argentina to establish their right to a relationship with grandchildren who had been "adopted" by agents of the state, following the murder of their parents. See Bouvard (1994) for a study of the Mothers.

Nevertheless, what is most interesting about this case is not its illumination of the contradictions of rights discourse, but the way it gestures toward a more complex adoption story than the familiar narrative of identity rights. In this more complex narrative, a child (and the parents/grandparents to whom he or she is connected and from whom he or she is separated) is at the same time alienated and enchained. The trace of enchainment is signaled in the implied continuity of mothering (or of parenting) that the terms "biological" grandmother and [adoptive] mother suggest, even as the distinction of the marked terms (*biological* grandmother, *adoptive* mother or parent) sets them apart from "real" mothering/parenting (Yngvesson 1997:73) and embeds in them the hierarchies and injustices of an economy in which the desire for a "real" family shapes the actions of both kinds of parents—the parents who adopted Carlos Alberto so they could have an "as if" real family, and his grandmother who fought for him so she could have a relationship with her "real" grandson (the biogenetic son of her biogenetic daughter). In this case, while the longing for conventional families is apparent, the "in practice" family has not been pinned down by law and is instead evolving over time in the relations among adoptive parents, birth grandparents, and adopted child.[21] This actual family is tacitly acknowledged in the unofficial agreement between grandparents and parents—one that defies the official clean-break policy that established this adoption as final (in accordance with both Swedish and Colombian adoption law)—and provides a blueprint for similar, more "open" relationships in the future.

As this example suggests, the "full truth" of the gift relation in adoption is in the simultaneity of closure and openness it represents, in its deferral of meaning, and in the play with time this deferral requires, as "the trace of something which still retains its roots in one meaning while it is, as it were, moving to another, encapsulating another" (Hall 1997:50). The tension between closure and openness in adoption can be found in legislation, such as the Hague Convention, that makes provisions both for cutting the adopted child off from his or her birth family and country (1993, Art. 26, 27) and for connecting the child to his or her "background" or "origin" (1993, Art. 16, 30). While the simultaneity of cutting off "the past" and of preserving it might be viewed as simply reflecting the power of commodity thinking and the alienability of identity it makes possible, it can also be seen as more than this. Indeed, it is the ambiguity of the gift in commodity thinking that gives the gift its power. It is all "a matter of style"—whether and how an exchange for the child is handled, whether the relations between nations and organizations is main-

[21] This is reminiscent of a birth mother in an open adoption who didn't want to "make a plan" for her relationship with the adoptive parents of her son, but felt they should "just basically leave it open."

tained, whether the records are open or sealed, whether the adoptee goes "back"—not only in relations between families but also in relations between nations, and in the ways adoptees experience the "pull" to return to the nations where they were born.

Inter/national Attachments

At the national level, the gift child of adoption and the donations the child provokes is one of the forms of exchange that creates an order of nations (see Malkki 1992), an order in which the child as gift is arguably a key symbolic resource. When we locate the child of one nation in the heart of another (in its middle-class families), we can forge the most intimate international ties (as in the adoption of Carlos Alberto). The repeated performance of these ties through continued adoptions, over time; their expansion in return visits by adoptees to their birth countries; and their formalization in policies that facilitate ongoing connections between adoptees and their birth countries (see discussion below), suggest strongly that adoption, both at the national and increasingly at the individual/familial level, is as much about enchainment and the multiple authorings and attachments this implies as it is about fixing a child to an identity.[22]

This enchainment is most apparent in the relations connecting representatives of Western adoption organizations with the officials of orphanages, child welfare organizations, and other institutions through which Third and Second World children are made adoptable to families in the North and West. These relations began as person-to-person connections and eventually developed as "a network of social workers, honorary secretaries of institutions, magistrates, doctors, and lawyers in various countries," which made possible "a cooperation built very much on personal trust and a shared belief that children fared better in families than in institutions" (Andersson 1991:7). These networks of cooperation are the operative mechanism that makes intercountry adoptions possible among established agencies and organizations approved by international conventions (the Adoption Centre in Stockholm, Holt in Eugene, WACAP in Seattle, Danadopt in Copenhagen, and so forth). Similar networks underpin the activities of so-called private operators and facilitators who negotiate for babies in the shadow areas cast by "Central Authorities" and by official adoption laws.

These networks and the transactions they make possible involve multiple reciprocities, dependencies, and commitments, including "donations" of several thousand dollars that are paid by First World agencies and parents to Third World orphanages and

---

22 Intercountry adoptees are referred to in some literature as "bridges" or as "little ambassadors" (Aronson 1997:103–4).

facilitators (but not to birth parents) in exchange for the gift of a child. Donations are explained in terms of the support they provide for the activities of the orphanage, and they are a key dimension of the reciprocity that defines southern orphanages and northern agencies as exchange partners. They are never defined as a per-child payment, or as "buying" a child. Indeed, some Colombian adoption homes are attempting to shift the terms of the donations so that they are paid on an annual basis, rather than on a per-child basis, so the appearance of impropriety is avoided. As the director of what is arguably the premier private adoption home in Colombia told a *Time Magazine* reporter in 1991, her organization "is not a business; it's total devotion to children" (Serrill 1991:46).

What never takes place in these exchange relations is a reversal of the flow of children in one direction and of donations in the other. In this sense, the enchainments of intercountry adoption, like those of other forms of gift exchange, function "*both* as relations of production *and* as ideologies . . . upon which mythologies are built" (Strathern 1988:146). Strathern (161) argues that "enchainment is a condition of all relations based on the gift." Legal adoption bears the traces of this condition, even as it is premised on the erasure of the mutual dependencies enchainment assumes.

The gift of a child in adoption bespeaks the potential for an enchainment that is unthinkable in commodity thinking but that exists as a kind of "shadow other" to commodity thought—it is the foreclosed relationship on which the exclusivity of commodity thought is contingent (see Butler 1993:8). Enchainment haunts the gift relationship of adoption with what sociologist Avery Gordon (1997:8) describes as a kind of "seething presence" that "act[s] on and often meddle[s] with taken-for-granted realities." Haunting, Gordon argues, "draws us affectively, sometimes against our will and always a bit magically, into the structure of feeling of a reality we come to experience, not as cold knowledge, but as a transformative recognition" (1997:8).[23]

What is transformative about the recognition of adoption as giving, and not simply as giving *up*, is the always unfinished quality of the exchange, its inherent incompleteness (in contrast to the inherent completeness of the identities of commodity thought), and the potential for a response that may exceed the alienation of the gift and the commodification of a child. This is so in spite of all the pressures—legal, social, political, bureaucratic, economic—for closure and for the reproduction of identical selves and national identities that this closure secures. From this perspective, the emphasis on identity rights in international agreements such as the 1989 *UN Convention on the Rights of the*

[23] See Mahoney & Yngvesson (1992) for a related approach to structures of feeling.

Child, the 1993 *Hague Convention*, and the 1997 *Guidelines for Practice on National and International Adoption and Foster Family Care* is as much about openings as it is about closures. It is not only about the right to an identity but about "the right to [a] . . . life story . . . which may be presented in many forms" (Adoption Centre 1997:2, 10), leaving open the possibility that a life story might connect the adoptee to *two* names, *two* nationalities (or more) and to multiple parents (as in the adoption of Carlos Alberto). A life story of this kind is less about "identity" than it is about "points of identification and attachment" (Hall 1996:5); and it is less about "wholeness" (Lifton 1994) than it is about doubleness, about splitting, and about holding the tension between identity and difference. The ways in which this tension manifests itself and the kinds of openings and closures that adoption stories entail are as diverse as the circumstances of physical abandonment that underpin the adoptability of a child.

Adoption is a hot topic these days, not so much because it transgresses familiar assumptions about what a family should be, but because it compels us to contemplate what commodity thinking produces, over and over again, as its most unsettling "frontier effect" (Hall 1996:3): not the alienation of self from author, but the possibility that there *is* no author, no "core" that owns the self (or to which the self belongs) other than the states of origin that produce (and then exchange) the adoptive child. The popular wisdom that adoptees will "find themselves" or "complete themselves" or become "whole" (Aronson 1997; Trotzig 1996; von Melen 1998; Lifton 1994) by returning "home" is one way in which the affirmation of "identity" takes place in this frontier zone. This is the flip side of Swedish adoptee Astrid Trotzig's observation that it is "annoying . . . to always be met with questions about me and my origins. [As though] it is not natural that I am here" (1996:62).

The idea that identification with a nation to which s/he belongs pulls the child "back" nicely captures the compelling quality of "the nation" as a root metaphor and the multiple ways the power of an "original" identity makes itself felt in the life of the adoptee.[24] For example, President Kim Dae Jung invited Korean adoptees from eight adoptive nations on an all-expense-paid visit to the Republic of South Korea in 1998. In a ceremony at the Blue House, held in their honor, the President apologized for South Korea's foreign adoptions (which until the mid-1990s regularly topped the lists of foreign adoptions to the United States, Sweden, and other receiving nations). He described South Korea as "filled with shame" over the practice; but he also pointed out that "no nation can live by itself" and urged adoptees to "nurture

[24] Liisa Malkki (1992:31) describes a similar "powerful sedentarism" in the lives of refugees. See also R. Radhakrishnan (1996).

[their] cultural roots" because "globalization is the trend of the times" (Kim 1998:16).

In a related move (one not directed specifically at adoptees, however), current government policy in India encourages close ties between India and its diaspora. For example, the Persons of Indian Origin Card, established in 1999, is intended to "make it easier for people of Indian descent sprinkled around the globe to travel to their familial homeland and invest in it" in ways that are "hassle-free" (Dugger 1999:4). The card is "part of a broader recognition by a growing number of countries that people who move abroad remain potentially valuable contributors in an economically interdependent world" (1999:4).

Doubling and the Politics of the "In-Between"

> "Because of my exterior, the foreigner, the unknown, is always with me."
> —Astrid Trotzig, *Blood Is Thicker Than Water,* 1996.

During the 1990s, as the push to open adoptions and search for roots mounted in intensity in countries of the overdeveloped world, and as the number of intercountry adoptions to the West from Asia, Eastern Europe, and Latin America continued to rise, intercountry adoptees who had arrived as infants or children in the 1950s, 1960s, and 1970s began to speak and write about their experiences of coming from one world and living in another. Their narratives reveal how complex their effort is to occupy the "in-between" constituted by the double evocatory power of a gift child (her capacity to evoke alienation and connection at the same time) and to resist pressures to resolve the opposing truths of gift exchange as a lived experience, into a single reality—what Jean-Luc Nancy (1991:76) describes as resolving "the play of the juncture" into "the substance . . . of a Whole."[25] The lived experience includes what R. Radhakrishnan (1996:175) describes as the "painful, incommensurable simultaneity" that accompanies efforts to inhabit a location where "the political reality of one's present home is to be surpassed only by the ontological unreality of one's place of origin."[26] In this concluding section, I draw on

[25] "By itself, articulation is only a juncture, or more exactly the play of the juncture: what takes place where different pieces touch each other without fusing together, where they slide, pivot, or tumble over one another, one at the limit of the other—exactly at its limit—where these singular and distinct pieces fold or stiffen, flex or tense themselves together and through one another, unto one another, without this mutual *play*—which remains, at the same time, a play *between* them—ever forming into the substance or the higher power of a Whole."

[26] Betty Jean Lifton (1994:57ff) also describes what she terms the "ghost kingdom" in which adoptees reside. Unlike Radhakrishnan's subtle exploration of the notion of a ghostly "location," however, Lifton regards this place as one that can be escaped, or come out of, by searching for and finding a birth parent. What Lifton misses is the constitution of this kingdom and its co-existence with one's "present home," by histories that cannot be erased by simply "finding" what seems to be lost. A search for a birth parent (or the

memoirs of adult adoptees in Sweden and the United States and on interviews conducted with adoptees in Sweden to explore what it means to inhabit this "ghostly" place.

Sara Nordin, who is now 34, was adopted from Ethiopia by Swedish parents in 1969, when she was one-and-a-half-years old. She recounts her experience of growing up black, in a special issue of the journal *SvartVitt* [*BlackWhite*] (1996:4-5) devoted to accounts by international adoptees. Nordin says that the meaning of the word "BLACK"

> has grown with each passing year, until I have finally understood that I am black. It is something big, personal and hard. It is a fact for me. The people who only see my color don't see all of me. The people who suggest that they can look beyond my color don't see all of me. When I try to gather together all the bits of myself, I easily lose myself. In colors and stories. In theories and dreams. When I walk by a mirror I see something exotic that I barely recognize from TV, newspapers and books. Sometimes it makes me happy, sometimes sad, and sometimes astonished. But most often the reflection in the mirror evokes questions that have no simple answers. I have tried to absorb [*ta till mig*] the "black" but then I have difficulty holding onto [*få med mig*] the Swedish. I have tried to absorb the "Swedish" but then I haven't understood what I see in the mirror [freely translated].

In an interview four years later, Nordin spoke of a particularly awkward situation (*en jobbig sits*) in which she found herself in the early 1980s when she was a teenager, a time when "I became almost an immigrant even though I felt myself to be extremely Swedish (*jättesvensk*). And the immigrants thought I was like them. And my Swedish friends thought I was like them. And I couldn't really decide where I belonged" (Interview, 8/22/99, freely translated).[27]

The ambiguities of identity and confusions of belonging experienced by Nordin in Sweden were intensified in the late 1990s when she returned to Addis Ababa. She explained in an interview that Addis "is not a place I would have chosen to live," apart from the fact that she was "from" there. "It wasn't terrible. It was poor, but the poverty wasn't catastrophic. And people were really nice." But she added that once she got back to Sweden, she had a diffi-

opening of adoption records) cannot undo the fundamental alienability of a unitary self that participation in a commodity economy assumes, and the unrealizable "wholeness" that such an economy always sets up as the heart's desire of those who "belong" to it.

[27] It might be argued that the centrality of race to Swedish identity is in inverse relation to official silence about race in that country. Thus, in Sweden, "[i]t is not fitting to describe immigrants in terms of race or ethnic minority groups. Even if there is a terminology for race (e.g., black or white skin color) and ethnic minority groups (e.g., Gypsies, Jews, Sami, etc.) in everyday language, no official concepts have been developed to register persons in such terms. It would be widely considered as discriminatory to ask a person about his or her 'race' in a survey or official questionnaire. The basic concepts used when officials classify immigrants' ethnic background are citizenship and country of birth" (Martens 1997:183).

cult (*jobbigt*) time. "It was hard there [in Ethiopia], but since I was alone I more or less shut off those feelings, just so I could manage. When I got home [to Sweden], it all caught up with me and everything seemed unfathomable. 'Why just me?' And all the children you see. 'What would have become of me if I had stayed there? Who was I while I was there?'" (Interview, 8/22/99, freely translated).

Amanda F., who is 29 and has visited her birth family in Ethiopia twice, describes what she experiences as a constant process of "doubling":

> I felt that a lot when we were there recently—that there is so much one has to relate to all the time. Here I have to relate to the fact that I look different and all that. And there I have to relate to the fact that I don't look different, but I *am* different. I don't know the language, I know almost nothing of what they are about or what they do. And so one has to relate to that also. There is a lot to keep track of. . . . It's hard, because when you are there everything is so real to you. As soon as you come here—after just a couple of weeks, Ethiopia feels so far away and they [her family] feel *really* far away. You have to struggle all the time to keep everything in mind and look at pictures. Although I have begun to feel clearer now, I mean I feel that they are my family and I love them. But we haven't lived together, so there are things that make it seem—I mean, we can't recover twenty years, it isn't possible, it has to start with now. (Interview, 8/22/99, freely translated.)[28]

Astrid Trotzig, adopted by Swedish parents in 1971, returned to South Korea when she was in her twenties, in hopes that she might find a place where it would feel "natural" to be. Instead, as with so many other intercountry adoptees who return to a homeland where they have never lived, what she encountered there was a powerful sense of loss. She found "no memories . . . which all of a sudden could well up from my subconscious, be remembered, be reborn here and now. . . . [N]othing [was] awakened other than melancholy" (Trotzig, 1996:214). Rather than finding a homeland, Trotzig found that "I have no home, nothing that constitutes both an outer and an inner homeland, a place where I belong [*hemvist*]. In Sweden I can never be fully integrated. My appearance is against me. In South Korea it's the opposite. I disappear in the crowd, people who see me think I am Korean, but inside I am in another place."

Experiences such as these reveal the impossibility of fully belonging in Sweden for these adoptees, whose names, skin color, facial configuration, or hair texture set them apart, tying them to a forgotten past that nonetheless infuses the present, separating adoptive parent from child, the Kingdom of Sweden from its "im-

[28] And see Amitav Gosh's (1988:194) description of people like his narrator's grandmother, who because "they have no home but in memory, learn to be very skilled in the art of recollection."

migrant" adoptees, and adoptees from the country of birth that made them "adoptable." This past will always haunt their present, dividing the identities of adoptees and challenging the unstable boundaries of nations that seek to absorb adoptees as citizens. At the same time, the constant presence of this "past" challenges the concept of identity as either divided or whole.

Deann Borshay Liem, whose autoethnographic film, *First Person Plural* (Liem 2000), has been aired to wide acclaim on U.S. television, was adopted from South Korea when she was eight years old. Liem's adoptive history was complicated by the fact that she was sent to her American parents with the false identity of another child. When she arrived, she attempted to explain that she already had a family in Korea and was not an orphan, but her new parents told her (and believed themselves) that this was a fantasy. Her adoption papers confirmed the deaths of her birthparents. Eventually, Liem recounts, she came to believe this story. She forgot Korea, forgot her home, forgot the path that led from her home to the orphanage, and lost her capacity to speak Korean. She became in most ways a typical American girl—prom queen, cheerleader, popular classmate, adored by her parents. After graduating from high school, however, Liem became increasingly depressed. Dreams of the orphanage, and the sudden appearance of her father's face "flying" into her car and around her kitchen, sent her back to the file of documents in her parents' house, where she found what had been previously overlooked: two pictures, one of Liem as a child with her name penciled on the back, the second of an unknown child. The second picture also bore her name.

Liem wrote to the orphanage in 1983, asking about the two pictures. Six weeks later, she received a letter from her brother confirming that she had a family in Korea and that her adoption had been a mistake. *First Person Plural* follows Liem and her adoptive parents on a journey to Korea, where they meet her birth family and she tries to come to terms with the significance of a "forgotten" past for her sense of belonging in the present. Especially traumatic for her is the realization over the course of this journey that although she has returned to her "real" mother in Korea, the only possibility of developing a relationship with this woman is to accept the fact that she is *not* her "real" mother. Indeed, Liem's film hints at the realization that the very question "Who is my real mother?" may be the wrong question. In spite of a past that lives in Liem's imagination, time is not reversible, the "gift" cannot be given back. There is no "return," only a new journey that embeds the implicate field of persons out of which Deanne Borshay Liem was born in new, inevitably painful, sometimes astonishing, ways.

Astrid Trotzig's sense that, as an adoptee, there is nothing that constitutes for her both an inner and an outer homeland, no "belonging" that is "beyond the reach of play" (Derrida 1978:279) is echoed in descriptions by other adoptees of an inner landscape that never quite fits with their lived experience but that becomes an enabling place, a site of "painful, incommensurable, simultaneity," through which they can make contact with a ghostly "past." This often vivid inner landscape, constituted from exclusions that construct the adoptee as "legally abandoned" by/in her homeland (family, nation), becomes a point of investment, a surface of desire, a site of temporary identification with a "past" that is a constant unknown presence.

An adoptee, now in his thirties and living in the United States, describes this "absent presence" as a life that has always run parallel to his everyday life but has never overlapped it. When he was asked by his adoptive mother if he would like to search for his birth parents, he answered that to do so would be like "removing an organ": he was so used to the doubled vision of an unknown interior life and a known life of the everyday that he couldn't imagine living without it.

This adoptee is "white," like his adoptive parents, and it is striking that, in the metaphor of doubling he uses, the unknown self is on the "inside," while his "outside" self is one that connects him to the familiar world he knows. For Korean, Ethiopian, Colombian, and other adoptees of color in contrast, the split is more likely to be experienced, as in Astrid Trotzig's case, as involving a familiar Swedish (American, Dutch, etc.) inside and an unknown exterior that connects them to a homeland that is not their home.

This kind of doubling and the doubled vision it bespeaks might be interpreted as simply a replication of the familiar story about alienation from roots and the split self this produces.[29] While the narratives of these adoptees speak about fragmentation and loss, they also seem to be pointing in the direction of what Stuart Hall describes as "not the so-called return to roots but a coming-to-terms with our 'routes'" (1996:4, quoting Paul Gilroy), a sometimes agonizing process that is captured in Sara Nordin's struggle to "absorb the 'black'" while holding onto the Swedish, and to absorb the Swedish while at the same time understanding "what I see in the mirror."

This process of holding onto points of identification that are contradictory builds on the exclusions of commodity thinking but produces a "constantly shifting frontier" (Balibar 1991:44) rather than an "identity." This shifting frontier emerges from the

[29] An anonymous reviewer of this article pointed to the relevance for my discussion here of Nahum Chandler's discussion of "double consciousness" in his essay on W. E. B. Dubois (1996:250). Chandler describes the sense of double consciousness as a "pivotal recognition" in Dubois' (1975) [1940] *Dusk of Dawn: An Essay Toward an Autobiography of a Race Concept*, one which was "self-consciously and strategically apprehended as a path of inquiry and understanding" (Chandler 1996:251).

adoptee's experience of not fully belonging anywhere and of being suspended between mutually exclusive places and conditions. "Roots trips," depending on how they are enacted, allow a kind of retracing of the "routes" through which the adoptee moved from one condition to the other, and may provide the material context (the enabling surfaces) for a desire that is not so much about a "return" to origins that cannot be found, but about the "mandate . . . to live 'within the hyphen' and yet be able to speak" (Radhakrishnan 1996:175–76). This hyphen, for many adoptees, is a space "between two humanities which seem incommensurable, namely the humanity of destitution and that of 'consumption,' the humanity of underdevelopment and that of overdevelopment" (Balibar 1991:44). Adoptees cannot serve as "bridges" between these incommensurable humanities (Aronson 1997:104–6), but may be able to bear witness to the tension between them.

References

Adoption Centre (1997) *The Child's Right to Grow up in a Family: Guidelines for Practice in National and Intercountry Adoption and Foster Family Care.* Bangalore, India: Adoption Centre.

Anderson, Benedict (1983) *Imagined Communities.* London: Verso.

Andersson, Gunilla (1991) "Intercountry Adoptions in Sweden: The Experience of 25 Years and 32,000 Placements." Sundbyberg, Sweden: Adoption Centre.

Aronson, Jaclyn C. (1997) *Not My Homeland: A Critique of the Current Culture of Korean International Adoption.* Unpublished senior thesis, Dept. of Social Science. Hampshire College, Amherst, MA.

Balibar, Etienne (1991) "Racism and Nationalism," in E. Balibar & I. Wallerstein, eds., *Race, Nation, Class: Ambiguous Identities.* New York: Verso.

Bogard, Howard E. (1991) "Who Are the Orphans? Defining Orphan Status and the Need for an International Convention on Intercountry Adoption," 5 *Emory International Law Rev.* 571–616.

Bourdieu, Pierre (1977) *Outline of a Theory of Practice.* Cambridge: Cambridge Univ. Press.

Bouvard, Marguerite Guzmán (1994) *Revolutionizing Motherhood: The Mothers of the Plaza de Mayo.* Wilmington, DE: Scholarly Resources.

Brown, Jane (2000) "Abandonment: What Do We Tell Them?" 2 *Adoption Today* 5:32–34.

Butler, Judith (1993) *Bodies That Matter: On the Discursive Limits of Sex.* New York: Routledge.

Calvache, Jaime Eliecer (1992) "Caso de un niño conmueve a habitantes del Javeriano," *Diario del Sur,* Pasto, Colombia, 17 Dec., p. 1.

——— (1995) "Abandonado en Pasto y hallado en Suecia," *Diario del Sur,* Pasto, Colombia, 1 Sept., p. 12a.

Carlson, Richard R. (1994) "The Emerging Law of Intercountry Adoptions: An Analysis of the Hague Conference on Intercountry Adoption," 30 *Tulsa Law J.* 243–304.

Carp, E. Wayne (1998) *Family Matters: Secrecy and Disclosure in the History of Adoption.* Cambridge: Harvard Univ. Press.

Chandler, Nahum D. (1996) "The Figure of the X: An Elaboration of the Duboisian Autobiographical Example," in S. Lavie & T. Swedenburg, eds.,

Displacement, Diaspora, and Geographies of Identity. Durham, NC: Duke Univ. Press.

Coontz, Stephanie (1992) *The Way We Never Were: American Families and the Nostalgia Trap*. New York: Basic Books.

Coutin, Susan (2000) *Legalizing Moves: Salvadoran Immigrants' Struggle for U.S. Residency*. Ann Arbor, MI: Univ. of Michigan Press.

Coutin, Susan, & Barbara Yngvesson (2002) "Roots, Trips, and Deportations: Reconfiguring Belonging, Place, and Return" (unpublished ms.).

Derrida, Jacques (1978) *Writing and Difference*. Chicago: Univ. of Chicago Press.

——— (1992) *Given Time: 1. Counterfeit Money*. Peggy Kamuf, trans. Chicago: Univ. of Chicago Press.

Du Bois, W. E. B. (1975) [1940] *Dusk at Dawn: An Essay Toward an Autobiography of a Race Concept*. CPW. H. Aptheker, ed. Millwood, NY: Kraus-Thomson.

Duckham, Janet (1998) "Letter to the editor," *New York Times*, 27 Oct., p. A28.

Dugger, Celia W. (1999) "India Offers Rights to Attract Its Offspring's Cash," *New York Times*, 4 Apr., p. 4.

Duncan, William (1993) "Regulating Intercountry Adoption: An International Perspective," in A. Bainham & D. S. Pearl, eds., *Frontiers of Family Law*. London: John Wiley & Sons.

Fein, Esther B. (1998) "Secrecy and Stigma No Longer Clouding Adoption," *New York Times*, 26 Oct., pp. 1, 30–31.

Foucault, Michel (1973) *The Order of Things*. New York: Vintage Books.

Ginsburg, Faye D. (1989) *Contested Lives: The Abortion Debate in an American Community*. Berkeley: Univ. of California Press.

Gordon, Avery F. (1997) *Ghostly Matters: Haunting and the Sociological Imagination*. Minneapolis: Univ. of Minnesota Press.

Gosh, Amitav (1988) *The Shadow Lines*. Delhi, India: Ravi Dayal.

Greenhouse, Carol J., Barbara Yngvesson, & David M. Engel (1994) *Law and Community in Three American Towns*. Ithaca: Cornell Univ. Press.

Grosz, Elizabeth (1995) *Space, Time, and Perversion*. New York: Routledge.

Hall, Stuart (1996) "Who Needs 'Identity'?," in S. Hall & P. du Gay, eds., *Questions of Cultural Identity*. London: Sage Publications.

——— (1997) "Old and New Identities, Old and New Ethnicities," in A. D. King, ed., *Culture, Globalization and the World System*. Minneapolis: Univ. of Minnesota Press.

Hollinger, Joan H. (1993) "Adoption Law," 3 *The Future of Children* 43–61.

Kim, Dae Jung (1998) "President Kim Dae Jung's Speech: October 23, 1998, at The Blue House," 1 *Chosen Child* 5:15–16.

Kopytoff, Igor (1986) "The Cultural Biography of Things: Commoditization as Process," in A. Appadurai, ed., *The Social Life of Things*. Cambridge: Harvard Univ. Press.

Liem, Deann Borshay (2000) *First Person Plural*. Ho-He-Kus, NJ: Mu Films.

Lifton, Betty Jean (1994) *Journey of the Adopted Self: A Quest for Wholeness*. New York: Basic Books.

Mahoney, Maureen A., & Barbara Yngvesson (1992) "The Construction of Subjectivity and the Paradox of Resistance: Reintegrating Feminist Anthropology and Psychology," 18 *Signs* 44–73.

Malkki, Lisa (1992) "National Geographic: The Rooting of Peoples and the Territorialization of Identity among Scholars and Refugees," 7 *Cultural Anthropology* 24–44.

Mansnerus, Laura (1998) "Market Puts Price Tags on Priceless," *New York Times*, 26 Oct., pp. 1, A16–17.

Martens, Peter (1997) "Immigrants, Crime, and Criminal Justice in Sweden," M. Tonry, ed., *Ethnicity, Crime, and Immigration: Comparative and Cross-National Perspectives*. Chicago: Univ. of Chicago Press.

Massumi, Brian (1993) "Everywhere You Want to Be. Introduction to Fear," in B. Massumi, ed., *The Politics of Everyday Fear.* Cambridge & London: MIT Press.

Melina, Lois R. (1989) *Making Sense of Adoption: A Parent's Guide.* New York: Harper & Row.

——— (1998) *Raising Adopted Children.* New York: HarperCollins.

Modell, Judith S. (1994) *Kinship with Strangers: Adoption and Interpretations of Kinship in American Culture.* Berkeley: Univ. of California Press.

——— (1999) "Freely Given: Open Adoption and the Rhetoric of the Gift," in L. L. Layne, ed., *Transformative Motherhood: On Giving and Getting in a Consumer Culture.* New York: New York Univ. Press.

Nancy, Jean-Luc (1991) *The Inoperative Community.* Minneapolis: Univ. of Minnesota Press.

Nordin, Sara (1996) "Mer eller mindre svart" [More or less black]; 1 *SvartVitt* 4–6 (Stockholm, Sweden).

Pilotti, Francisco (1993) "Intercountry Adoption: Trends, Issues, and Policy Implications for the 1990s," 1 *Childhood* 165–77.

Radhakrishnan, R. (1996) *Diasporic Mediations: Between Home and Location.* Minneapolis: Univ. of Minnesota Press.

Radin, Margaret Jane (1996) *Contested Commodities.* Cambridge: Harvard Univ. Press.

Schneider, David M. (1968) *American Kinship: A Cultural Account.* Chicago: Univ. of Chicago Press.

Serrill, Michael S. (1991) "Wrapping the Earth in Family Ties," *Time International,* 4 Nov., pp. 41–46.

Stanley, Alessandra (1997) "Hands Off Our Babies, a Georgian Tells America," *New York Times,* 29 June, pp. 1, 12.

Stephens, Sharon (1995) "Children and the Politics of Culture in 'Late Capitalism'," in S. Stephens, ed., *Children and the Politics of Culture.* Princeton: Princeton Univ. Press.

Strathern, Marilyn (1988) *The Gender of the Gift.* Berkeley: Univ. of California Press.

——— (1997) "Partners and Consumers," in Alan D. Schrift, ed., *The Logic of the Gift: Toward an Ethic of Generosity.* New York: Routledge.

Therborn, Göran (1996) "Child Politics: Dimensions and Perspectives." 3 *Childhood* 29–44.

Trotzig, Astrid (1996) *Blod är tjockare än vatten* [Blood is thicker than water]. Stockholm, Sweden: Bonniers Förlag.

Varenne, Hervé (1977) *Americans Together: Structured Diversity in an American Town.* New York: Teacher's College Press.

Verhovek, Sam H. (2000) "Debate on Adoptees' Rights Stirs Oregon," *New York Times,* 5 Apr., pp. A1, A14.

von Melen (1998) *Samtal med vuxna adopterade* [Conversations with adult adoptees]. Stockholm, Sweden: Raben Prisma.

Wadia-Ells, Susan (1995) "The Anil Journals," in S. Wadia-Ells, ed., *The Adoption Reader: Birth Mothers, Adoptive Mothers and Adoptive Daughters Tell their Stories.* Seattle, WA: Seal Press.

Wegar, Katarina (1997) *Adoption, Identity and Kinship: The Debate Over Sealed Birth Records.* New Haven: Yale Univ. Press.

Yngvesson, Barbara (1997) "Negotiating Motherhood: Identity and Difference in 'Open' Adoptions." 31 *Law & Society Rev.* 31–80.

——— (2000) "'UnNiño de Cualquier Color': Race and Nation in Intercountry Adoption," in J. Jenson & B. de Sousa Santos, eds., *Globalizing Institutions: Case Studies in Regulation and Innovation.* Aldershot, England: Ashgate.

——— (2003) "'Going Home': Adoption, Loss of Bearings, and the Mythology of Roots," *Social Text* 74, Special Issue on Transnational Kinship.

Yngvesson, Barbara & Maureen A. Mahoney (2000) "'As One Should, Ought, and Wants to Be': Belonging and Authenticity in Identity Narratives," 17 *Theory, Culture and Society* 77–110.
Zelizer, Viviana A. (1985) *Pricing the Priceless Child: The Changing Social Value of Children.* Princeton: Princeton Univ. Press.
Zizek, Slavoj (1989) *The Sublime Object of Ideology.* London: Verso.

Statutes Cited

Codigo del Menor, Decreto 1310 del 1990 (junio 20). Republica de Colombia. Santafe de Bogotá: Ecoe Ediciones.
Hague Conference on Private International Law, Final Act of the Seventeenth Session, May 29, 1993, 32 I.L.M. 1134.
Lakshmi Kant Pandey Vs. Union of India (Writ Petition Crl. No. 1171 of 1982. Decided on 27 Sept. 1985).
United Nations (1986) *Declaration on Social and Legal Principles Relating to the Protection and Welfare of Children, with Special Reference to Foster Placement and Adoption, Nationally and Internationally,* G.A. Res. 41/85, U.N. GAOR, 41st Sess., Annex at art. 5.
——— (1989) *Convention on the Rights of the Child,* G.A. Res. 44/25, U.N. GAOR, 61st plen. mtg., Annex at art. 21.

Part IV
Refugees and Asylum-Seekers

[16]

Minors or Aliens? Inconsistent State Intervention and Separated Child Asylum-Seekers

JACQUELINE BHABHA*

'These minors are, after all, children'[1]

'... unaccompanied children of tender years encounter a stressful situation in which they are forced to make critical decisions. Their interrogators are foreign and authoritarian. The environment is new and the culture completely different. The law is complex. ... In short, it is obvious to the Court that the situation faced by unaccompanied minor aliens is inherently coercive ...'[2]

1. Introduction

Refugee children, placed as they are at the intersection of two particularly vulnerable populations – refugees and children – have a strong claim to international concern and attention. This has long been recognized. Indeed in the early days of international protection of both children and refugees, they had, one might say, pride of place – their distinctive needs were quite clearly and specifically addressed. It was concern over the special problems facing refugee children during and following war, that led to the submission of the original draft of the 1924 Declaration of the Rights of the Child to the League of Nations, the precursor to the 1989 Convention on the Rights of the Child.[3] And the first international refugee definition, in the 1946 Constitution of the International Refugees Organization (IRO) to regularize the status of World War II refugees, included as one of four categories of refugee unaccompanied

* Executive Director, University Committee on Human Rights, Harvard University.

[1] Per Judge Chapnick, Ontario Superior Court of Justice in *Gao (Litigation Guardian of) v Canada (Minister of Citizenship and Immigration)* Docket 00-CV-102960, Judgment 27 July 2000.

[2] Per District Judge Rafeedie, *Perez-Funez v District Director, INS* 611 F. Supp. 990 (D.C. Cal. 1984), 24 January 1984.

[3] Guy Goodwin-Gill, 'Unaccompanied Refugee Minors: The Role and Place of International Law in the Pursuit of Durable Solutions', 3 *International Journal of Children's Rights* (1995), 405–416, 413.

children who were war orphans or whose parents had disappeared.[4] Interestingly, international recognition of the particular needs of refugee children[5] thus predates attention to the specificities of women refugees by about 40 years.[6]

By contrast with this early period, more recent international attention to the distinctive situation of children as refugees and asylum seekers has been scant.[7] In international debates about migration and refugee protection, until very recently, the issue has been largely ignored.[8] Accompanied children have tended to be subsumed within their family's asylum applications, even if they have a strong case of their own;[9] separated[10] children have been largely invisible, mired in confusion over the relative importance of welfare

[4] Atle Grahl-Madsen, *The Status of Refugees in International Law* (A.W. Sijthoff, Leyden. 1966), Vol. 1, 135.

[5] For an example of early UNHCR involvement in problems relating to separated children, following the Hungarian uprising of 1956, see UNHCR, *The State of the World's Refugees 2000* (OUP, Oxford. 2000), 34.

[6] The first official consideration of the special situation of refugee women occurred in 1985, in EXCOM Conclusion No. 39 (XXXVI), 1985 (Refugee Women and International Protection).

[7] A notable scholarly exception is Everett M. Ressler, Neil Boothby and Daniel J. Steinbock, *Unaccompanied Children: Care and Protection in Wars, Natural Disasters and Refugee Movements* (New York, Oxford: Oxford University Press, 1988) [hereafter Ressler et al., Unaccompanied Children]. See also (ed.), J. Doek, H. van Loon and P. Vlaardingerbroek, *Children on the Move: How to Implement their right to Family life* (The Hague, Boston, London: Martinus Nijhoff, 1996) section on International Refugee Children, pp. 97–122. For other more recent work on separated children see generally Jacqueline Bhabha and Wendy Young, 'Not Adults in Miniature: Unaccompanied Child Asylum Seekers and the New U.S. Guidelines', 11(1) *International Journal of Refugee Law* (1999), 84–125. For an excellent recent survey of the situation and needs of separated child asylum seekers in Europe see Ruxton, *Separated Children Seeking Asylum in Europe: A Programme for Action* (Stockholm: Save the Children and UNHCR. 2000) [hereafter Ruxton, Separated Children].

[8] See International Organization for Migration, *Migrant Trafficking and Human Smuggling in Europe: A review of the evidence with case studies from Hungary, Poland and Ukraine* (IOM, Geneva, 2000) [hereafter IOM, Migrant Trafficking] 105.

[9] For examples of several Canadian cases where the persecution faced by the child influenced the grant of refugee status to the family as a whole see Geraldine Sadoway, 'Refugee Children Before the Immigration and Refugee Board', 35 *Immigration Law Reporter* 106, 109.

[10] Children who are outside their country of origin without their families have in the past generally been referred to as 'unaccompanied' children. However many such children are not unaccompanied throughout their journeys or stays abroad – they may be escorted by family acquaintances, co-villagers or clansmen, they may be in the custody of paid smugglers or agents, or they may be under the control of traffickers or organized criminal networks. Accordingly, following the Separated Children in Europe Programme, the term 'separated' is preferred here, see Ruxton, *Separated Children.*

protection and immigration control concerns,[11] often denied recognition as refugees[12] in favour of a lesser status[13] or a limbo of indeterminacy.[14] At the same time in international debates about the protection needs of particularly vulnerable, displaced children, attention has tended to focus on cases where the travel itself is clearly exploitative, and where the child migrant is a passive victim – children forcibly trafficked for sex or labour exploitation, child soldiers recruited into armed conflict, babies sold for international adoption.[15] From both the migration and the child rights perspectives, separated child asylum seekers have tended to be neglected.

2. Numbers of Separated Child Asylum Seekers

This lack of consistent attention to the issue is notable given the magnitude of the problem. Though comprehensive demographic data for the global refugee population do not exist, refugee populations are shown to roughly mirror the

11 Human Rights Watch, *United States – Detained and Deprived of Rights: Children in the Custody of the U.S. Immigration and Naturalization Service* December 1998 Vol. 10 (4) G.

12 According to Amnesty International, separated refugee children in the UK are discriminated against compared with adult refugees: Amnesty International, *Most Vulnerable of All: The Treatment of Unaccompanied Children in the UK* (Amnesty International, London, 1999), 5 [hereafter AI, Most Vulnerable]. There is also evidence of disparity in the treatment accorded to accompanied and separated children, with the latter group faring considerably worse, see Geraldine Van Bueren, *The International Law on the Rights of the Child* (Martinus Nijhoff, Dordrecht, Boston, London, 1995), 372.

13 Ruxton, Separated Children, 11.

14 This is particularly true in the US situation, where children's asylum cases frequently take years to be determined. One child interviewed 2 years after arriving in the US gave this account of his legal situation: 'I had a bad lawyer. I hope my new lawyer is better. I have a court hearing coming up in October. I have been to court 4 times. My first lawyer ditched me, because I couldn't pay the fee. When I went to court the lawyer didn't show up, so the judge continued the case till October. I have a second lawyer now, but my cousin owes this lawyer $700 and he is not quite sure how it will be paid'. Interview conducted by Celeste Froehlich, author's research assistant, in New York, August 2000 [hereafter Froehlich interviews].

15 See for example reports by Ms. Ofelia Calcetas-Santos, Special Reporter on the sale of children, child prostitution and child pornography, A/CN.4/1999/74; A/CN.4/1999/71/Add.1. One exception to this is the Recommendation of 21 October 1994 on the application to refugee children and other displaced children of the Hague Convention of 29 May 1993 on Protection of Children and Co-operation in Respect of Intercountry Adoption. This recommendation reflects recognition of the special problems that arise in the adoption of separated children and addresses relevant issues, such as whether a child is 'adoptable', and whether repatriation to family is feasible. H van Loon, 'How can the Rights of Separated Children be Realised? – the role of the Hague Conventions, in UNHCR and Save the Children Sweden, *Documentation of the European Conference 'Children First and Foremost – Policies towards Separated Children in Europe* (Stockholm: SCF and UNCHR. 2000) [hereafter SCF and UNHCR, Documents], 58.

home region's population as a whole.[16] Children therefore represent at least half of the world's refugee population. A widely repeated figure is that women and children constitute 80% of the world's refugee population.[17] According to UNHCR, two to five percent, or approximately a quarter of a million, of such children are separated from their families, either as a result of the chaos of displacement or because their parents have sent them away.[18] The number of children who reach the shores of western countries is relatively small. Nevertheless available evidence suggests that significant, and probably growing numbers of separated children seeking asylum are arriving in Western Europe and North America.[19] According to the Separated Children in Europe Program, a minimum of 25,000 separated children applied for asylum in Europe in 1999, and 'the numbers have increased considerably in most countries in the last 2–3 years, especially in Western Europe'.[20] The UK figures show that over five times the number of separated children applied for asylum in 1999 as did in 1995.[21] The picture is probably similar in the US and Australia, though, surprisingly, no official statistics are available in either country.[22] In Canada, the number of separated children applying for asylum

[16] T. Spijkerboer, *Gender and Refugee Status* (Ashgate, Aldershot, 2000), 17, citing work of Monica Boyd.

[17] Ibid., 15.

[18] UN High Commissioner for Refugees (UNHCR), The State of the World's Refugees, p. 28 (1995). It is important to keep in mind that these statistical estimates vary, dependent in part on the fact that agreement on the definition of 'separated' or the age of majority does not exist.

[19] The statistical information is persuasive and probabilistic rather than conclusive – a reflection of the vicious circle that since the situation of separated children has not been carefully attended to, until recently most states did not record information about their arrival and status determination. See IOM, *Migrant Trafficking*, 31. According to the Separated Children in Europe Project, there are 'roughly 100,000 [separated] children in Europe at any one time; unless and until they claim asylum, many remain "hidden" to public authorities', Ruxton, *Separated Children*, 22.

[20] Personal communication from Kate Halvorsen, researcher with Separated Children in Europe Program, 5 January 2001. On file with the author.

[21] 595 in 1995, and 3345 in 1999. Home Office Immigration Research and Statistics Service (Asylum and Appeals Section) personal communication 12 December 2000. Because of the defects in the system of identification of separated minors, it is likely that official statistics significantly underestimate the numbers, see AI, *Most Vulnerable*, 21–22.

[22] According to INS spokesman Ross Bergeron, the INS handles 4,000 unaccompanied minors a year. CISNEWS [Center for Immigration Studies News; www.cis.org; 1522 K St. N.W., Suite 820, Washington DC 20005; center@cis.org], 13 January 2000. INS data record that 4,607 separated children were taken into custody in 1999 (Sen. Feinstein question during Ashcroft confirmation hearings sschmidt@lirs.org 30 January 2001); compared to 4,295 'custody occurrences' of children occurred between October 1997 and July 1998; at the end of July 1998 the INS had 479 children in detention. Data quoted in *Detained and Deprived of Rights: Children in the Custody of the U.S. Immigration and Naturalization*

nearly quadrupled between 1993 and 2000, and grants of refugee status nearly doubled between 1997 and 1999.[23]

If children constitute over 50% of the world's refugee population, and separated children constitute two to five percent of that population, then one would expect separated children to account for no more than 2.5% of the asylum seeking population in western receiving states. Given their special vulnerability, their lack of power over family resources and the difficulties of embarking and arranging for travel alone, one might in fact expect a lower proportion of separated child asylum-seekers in countries far away from home. According to one study, this is indeed the case for women asylum-seekers (a comparable group to children in respect of some of these factors) – they are under-represented in the numbers of refugees.[24] But for separated children the opposite appears to be true. The proportion, at least in Western Europe according to the figures above, is double the expected ratio, or more: according to the Separated Children in Europe program, separated children account for between 5 and 15% of the general asylum-seeking population; in 1999 separated children applying for asylum in the UK represented nearly 5% of the total pool of asylum applicants.[25]

Given the scale and social salience of the issue, there is a serious absence of consistent statistical data.[26] But on the basis of the available evidence it is reasonable to hypothesize that separated children are over-represented amongst asylum seekers today. Given our assumptions about children's dependence and lack of autonomous agency, this is remarkable and counterintuitive. It is also widely ignored and urgently calls for attention.

Service, Human Rights Watch 3 (December 1998). According to John Pogash, Acting director of the Juvenile Affairs Division of the Immigration and Naturalization Service (hereafter INS) 'It is impossible to keep numbers for all the unaccompanied minors apprehended by the service'. Personal communication, 12 December 2000. The Australian Department of Immigration and Multicultural Affairs responded to the author's request for statistics on separated children seeking asylum on 31 January 2001: 'The statistics section are unable to provide statistical data on unaccompanied minor settler arrivals to Australia by eligibility category – refugee or other'. On file with the author.

23 370 in 1993, 1415 in 2000. Reference Services, Library, Citizenship and Immigration Canada, personal communication, 21 December 2000. The figures for asylum applications for separated children show a near consistent increase between 1993 to 2000, but interestingly the figures for the 3 years from 1990 – 1992 are 3 times higher than the figure for 1993 (possibly due to a very large influx of Romanian orphans).

24 According to this study, women are under-represented among asylum applicants in western countries; the suggested explanation is that this is because resources for fleeing are primarily allocated to men. Spijkerboer, *Gender and Refugee Status*, 26.

25 3345 out of 71,000 applications, i.e. 4.7%. Home Office Immigration Research and Statistics Service, *Asylum Statistics United Kingdom 1999*, October 2000.

26 For example the US, Australia, Germany, France, Italy and Austria, inter alia, do not disclose official figures of separated child asylum seekers.

3. Causes of Increase in Migration of Separated Child Asylum Applicants

No comprehensive study exists of the causes of this high and increasing number of separated child asylum applicants, as distinguished from the general escalation in the numbers of refugees and asylum applicants worldwide.[27] It seems clear, that, in the main, children seeking asylum flee for the same reasons as adults – to escape war, persecution, ethnic strife and civil upheaval. The main countries of origin of separated child asylum seekers match those primarily generating adult refugee flows: former Yugoslavia, China, Sri Lanka, Somalia.[28] What factors would account for the increase in the migration of these separated children over and above those that apply to the general migration situation? In the absence of conclusive research on the topic, one can only speculate. One factor is the changing nature of contemporary war, the fact that civilians, and especially vulnerable civilians, are increasingly targeted and affected. Children are no longer just innocent bystanders caught in the crossfire of armed conflict, but are subject to calculated genocide, forced military conscription,[29] gender-based violence, torture,[30] and exploitation.[31] Indeed it has been suggested that in the newly emerging world order, childhood is increasingly being obliterated as a protected space. [32] It is estimated that in the last decade, over one and a half million children have been killed, 5 million have been forced to live in refugee camps and over 12 million have lost their homes. Of these many have

[27] There is an excellent small scale study of the reasons for and travel routes of 218 separated children who arrived in Western Europe, see Wendy Ayotte, *Separated Children Coming to Western Europe: Why they Travel and How they Arrive* (Save the Children Fund. London, 2000). The study found that out of 448 'movement reasons' for the 218 children, 104 were due to armed conflict, 94 were for Refugee Convention reasons and 77 were because of separation from parents.

[28] Immigration and Refugee Board, CRDD, Claims Finalized: Unaccompanied Minors, Canada – private communication, on file with the author; Home Office Immigration Research and Statistics Service (Asylum and Appeals Section) on file with the author; S. Ruxton, *Separated Children*, 13; compare with J. Morrison, *Trafficking and Smuggling*, 27–28.

[29] It is estimated that there are between 250,000 and 300,000 child soldiers today, some as young as 5 years old. Amy Beth Abbott, 'Child Soldiers – The Use of Children as Instruments of War', *Suffolk Transnational Law Review*, Summer 2000, 499.

[30] Amnesty International, *Hidden scandal, secret shame: torture and ill treatment of children* (London: Amnesty International, 2000).

[31] 'The Impact of Armed Conflict on Children', United Nations (November 1996). See also Geraldine van Bueren, 'Opening Pandora's Box: Protecting Children Against Torture or Cruel, Inhuman or Degrading Treatment or Punishment', 17 *Law and Policy* 377, 389 (1995) [hereafter 'Pandora's Box'].

[32] S. Stephens, 'Introduction'. In: S. Stephens (ed.), *Children and the Politics of Culture* (Princeton University Press, Princeton. 1995), p. 20 [hereafter Stephens, Children].

lost or become separated from their families. Children appear to have been affected more than any other demographic group.[33] As a result they may be disproportionately forced to seek refuge away from home.

Second, the growing difficulty of claiming asylum in developed states because of stringent visa requirements, checks on carriers, militarized borders and other escalating immigration controls has led to increased dependence by asylum seekers on the professional travel services of smugglers and traffickers.[34] According to one expert, '[it] seems likely that a very large number – perhaps the majority – of asylum seekers arriving in Central or Western Europe have been smuggled or trafficked'.[35] This certainly influences the demographic composition of the refugee pool and may well account for the increase in the proportion of separated children. A distinction needs to be made between the factors impinging on the numbers of separated children in the smuggling and in the trafficking context.[36] Smuggling services, where asylum seekers consensually contract to be transported to safety for a fee, are costly, sometimes exorbitantly so. The fee for transport from the Fujian province of China to the US currently stands at approximately $ 50,000.[37] Preliminary research carried out by the University of Chicago on the factors influencing families to send children alone to seek asylum suggests that families who are unable to afford smuggling fees for more than one member to seek asylum, may be increasingly choosing to send a child.[38] There are

33 Ruxton, *Separated Children*, 20.

34 For definitions which have recently received widespread international support see Protocol to Prevent, Suppress and Punish Trafficking in Persons, Especially Women and Children, supplementing the United Nations Convention against Transnational Organized Crime A/55/383, Annex II art 3; Protocol against the Smuggling of Migrants by land, Sea and Air, supplementing the United Nations Convention against Transnational Organized Crime, A/55/383, Annex III, art 3. See also Morrison, *Trafficking and Smuggling*.

35 Morrison, *Trafficking and Smuggling*, 24.

36 The distinction between these two forms of organized migrant transport has recently been codified in the Protocols to the UN Convention on Transnational Organized Crime, see note 34 above. There are two critical distinguishing variables: consent versus coercion, and the absence or presence of an exploitative intent. Smuggling is consensual and non-exploitative, trafficking is coercive and exploitative. The distinction is not clear-cut, and is particularly problematic when applied to children because of the difficulty of establishing the child's ability to validly consent even in the smuggling context. But the distinction is nevertheless useful for identifying different types of organized migration situations, with quite different human rights implications.

37 E. McCormick and J.H. Zamora, 'Slave Trade still alive in US', *San Francisco Examiner*, 13 February 2000.

38 Certainly there are some smugglers or 'snakeheads' as they are called in China who specialize in children. Associated Press, 'Child Traffickers executed in China', 26 April 2000 (reporting that 2 members of a 16 member gang that had smuggled 26 children, one of whom had died in the process, were sentenced to death).

various reasons for this: the child may be chosen as the preferred survivor, either because of his or her greater vulnerability or because of aspirations for a better future for the child:[39] 'When my Mom talked to me about coming to the United States, I disagreed with her very strongly, but then she started to cry. She begged me. I didn't want to disappoint her, so eventually I agreed to go. They want me to have a good future. They are my parents so I have to obey them'.[40] Or the child might represent the family's best choice because of the potential to get an education and eventually more remunerative employment: 'When my parents decided I should come here . . . I knew I would have a hard time, and I wasn't sure I wanted to go. But then I changed my mind again and agreed to come here for the well being of my family . . . My parents said I can go to school for now. They want me to stay in school for a half year or longer, so I can learn English. But they also want me to start working, when I get used to life here. They also said that if I become more educated, I'll make more money, because I'll be able to get a good job'.[41] There is also some evidence that a child's reduced likelihood of deportation from the receiving state compared to an adult enters into the calculation – smugglers may suggest to families that money spent on sending a child is a better and more secure investment:[42] 'The latest trend [in Fujian, China] is for people in the village to borrow money from their neighbours or relatives at a very high interest rate in order to send their kids away'.[43]

By contrast with smuggling, trafficking networks coerce or trick asylum seekers into travelling, in order to subject them to sexual or other forms of slavery-like exploitation, on arrival in the receiving state. Refugee populations, dispossessed, unemployed, uprooted from family support systems, represent a fertile catchment area for trafficking organizations because of their susceptibility to being tricked and induced to accept offers of transport and work elsewhere. Forced prostitution, bonded labour, forced marriage are increasingly common outcomes of such trafficking arrangements.[44] It is clear that refugee children, young girls in particular, are especially targeted by

[39] These seems to have been a factor in the massive migration of separated Vietnamese children, UNHCR, *The State of the World's Refugees 2000*, 94.

[40] Interview with 18-year-old Chinese girl, Case 1, Froehlich interviews.

[41] Interview with 17-year-old Chinese boy in New York, Case 2, Froehlich interviews.

[42] J. Bhabha, 'Lone Travelers: Rights, Criminalization and the Transnational Migration of Unaccompanied Children', 7 *University of Chicago Law School Roundtable* (2000), 269–294, 282.

[43] Froehlich interviews, Case 1.

[44] Report of the Special Rapporteur on violence against women, its causes and consequences, Ms. Radhika Coomaraswamy, on trafficking in women, women's migration and violence against women, submitted in accordance with Commission on Human Rights resolution 1997/44, E/CN.4/2000/68.

organised criminal networks specializing in trafficking for sexual or labour exploitation.[45] Children are sought after because they cater to a particular demand in the booming global sex trade, both because of special sexual proclivities and because of reduced AIDS risks. Often they are ensnared by drug offers that lead to dependency on a steady income, typically from crime or prostitution. As a result of this combination of factors, a growing number of refugee children are trafficked into receiving states; it is likely that many apply for asylum, sometimes at the instigation of the traffickers at the point of entry. So in both the smuggling and trafficking contexts, there are reasons why the numbers of separated child asylum applicants might be growing disproportionately to the general pool of applicants.[46]

Finally, the forces of globalization may contribute to the growth in numbers of separated child asylum seekers. Structural adjustment policies and the disintegration of traditional sources of security and employment are placing growing numbers of children at risk,[47] children who have to shoulder adult burdens, indeed often stand in for absent or dysfunctional adults[48] – they become miniature adults with enhanced longevity. At the same time global travel has become more accessible, communication systems have brought images of different life styles and options across the globe and a small but growing number of children may now be deciding to seek out survival possibilities elsewhere, exercising independent choices to flee human rights violations inflicted on them by their families or by their societies at large.[49] The violations include a wide range of persecutory behaviours – children who have been physically or sexually abused or rejected by their families, the threat of unwanted female genital circumcision, forced marriage, subjection

[45] Communication from the Commission to the Council and the European Parliament, *Combating trafficking in human beings and combating the sexual exploitation of children and child pornography* COM (2000), 854 final. Estimates of the scale of the problem of trafficking vary wildly, and no disaggregated figures for refugees or children, let alone separated refugee children, are available; the United Nations estimate that 4 million persons, the majority women and children, are trafficked every year, the US government estimate that at least 50,000 women and children are trafficked into the US every year.

[46] Frank Viviano, 'Global Mob cashes in on human cargo' *San Francisco Chronicle* A1 (16 February 1999).

[47] UNICEF, *Poverty and Children: Lessons of the 90s for Least Developed Countries* http://www.unicef.org/pubsgen/poverty-ldcs/

[48] United Nations Development Program, *Human Development Report 2000* (Oxford University Press, New York, 2000), pp. 73–88. For a related point in the context of developed states where welfare is being cut back, See M. John, 'Rights in a Free Market Culture'. In: Stephens (ed.), *Children*, p. 134.

[49] For a good example of this sort of entrepreneurial transnational initiative by children see the five part Time Magazine series, P. Cuadros, 'Ramon's Journey: A kid in No-Man's Land', *Time.Com*, 4 June 2001.

to oppressive cultural or religious norms, persecution as street children, children fleeing gang violence, bonded labour. Children may be more able and willing to take independent initiatives that involve long distance travel now than in a less globalized era. A growing awareness of children's rights may also play a part.

4. State Intervention

State involvement in the migration of separated children is not a new phenomenon. Since the mid nineteenth century, western states have, through overseas refugee resettlement and sponsorship programs, been involved in facilitating the migration of war orphans, and other groups of children without familial or community support or whose well-being was of concern to the international or philanthropic community.[50] However, until the last decade or so, state intervention was concentrated on children whose transport was organized or accepted by the receiving state. By contrast states appear to have paid little attention to the voluntary or self-propelled migration of separated refugee children, whose journeys were organised by their families, their communities or by the children themselves. As a 1985 Canadian government background paper succinctly stated: 'There is no mechanism or procedure in place where the federal government could admit and provide for the needs of unaccompanied minors as independent applicants'.[51] Deferring to the primary role of parents or guardians as providers and protectors, states generally tended to acquiesce in families' choices regarding their children's future and only to step in, in an ad hoc manner, where such familial involvement was absent or defective. The assumption seems to have been that where the migration was to benefit the separated child, and where supportive family or community structures were in place, there was no need for state interference in the post-entry situation. Over the last ten years, however, this generally laissez-faire attitude has been replaced by a more interventionist approach.

This interventionism has been inconsistent, at times even contradictory. In part this is a reflection of the absence of concerted attention to the problem, the invisibility of separated children as a focus of consistent policy: instead of centralized and coordinated decision making, different ad hoc approaches have coexisted. This is apparent within current US practice. In some cases, separated children are promptly handed over by the authorities into the

[50] Ressler et al., Unaccompanied Children; P. Bean and J. Melville, *Lost Children of the Empire* (Unwin Hyman, 1989).

[51] Settlement Branch, Canadian Employment and Immigration, 'Unaccompanied Minors – refugees, designated classes, special programs: a background paper', May 1985, Para I (c). Unpublished document on file with the author.

custody of distant relatives (the case of Elian Gonzalez springs to mind), in other cases, children are detained when close relatives are available to care for them.[52] In some cases detained children are even used as baits to catch parents suspected of being in the country illegally.[53] Even similarly situated children can receive opposite treatment: two 17 year old boys, smuggled together from China, and arrested by INS agents on the island of Guam, both testified in court against the smugglers who had beaten them during their trip across the world. One boy was represented by a lawyer and was granted asylum, the other boy was unrepresented and lost his asylum claim.[54] Inconsistency is not just a feature of US practice: in Canada, two cases of separated Chinese child asylum seekers who arrived as stowaways and claimed asylum had opposite outcomes: in one case the child said he knew nothing about the arrangements to smuggle him to Canada to seek asylum, and he was granted asylum; in the other case the child said he knew what was planned and went along with it because of filial piety or obedience to his parents wishes – he lost his case.[55] These examples suggest an arbitrary system for dealing with separated children's claims.

5. The Tension between Immigration Enforcement and Welfare Protection Concerns

But randomness is not an adequate or full explanation. An additional reason for the policy inconsistency is that state intervention has been pulled in different directions because of a clash between two opposing normative frameworks – immigration control preoccupations on the one hand, and welfare protection (including child's rights) concerns on the other. Immigration control concerns focus on the child's alien and irregular status. Here children, like adults, are viewed as illegal migrants, who have chosen, or consented to, the evasion of immigration controls in order to gain access, who have lied, knowingly made use of false documents, who are coming to study or work without permission; from this point of view children's minority is a disqualification or, at best, an irrelevance – as the director of Save the Children commented, these children are assumed to be "bogus" before they are

[52] A. Chardy, 'INS tightens policy to prevent future Elian – type custody cases', 22 April 2001, *Miami Herald*.

[53] D. Montero, 'Feds use kids as bait to snare immigrant parents', *The New York Post*, 29 January 2001.

[54] Sen. Feinstein's introductory remarks to Unaccompanied Alien Child Protection Act 2001, 29 January 2001, personal communication by sschmidt@lirs.org.

[55] Personal communication, Geraldine Sadoway.

assumed to be in need of help'.[56] A clear example of this approach is the US Government's treatment of the several hundred separated children who were part of the large Haitian exodus to the US in 1994, at the height of military repression in Haiti. Many were forcibly repatriated without any consideration of the fate awaiting them. An investigation of the effect of government policy on the children concluded: '... the repatriation experience of these children has without exception been extremely harsh. One girl had been repatriated on the alleged basis of the willing support of her father, though in fact her father died years ago (as she consistently stated). Another 12-year-old boy found himself completely abandoned within hours of his arrival at Port-au-Prince ... two of the children had been homeless since their repatriation. [At the time of the report] they [were] still living on the streets with no money, no shelter, and no family'.[57]

It is often claimed that these children are 'really' much older and can be treated as adults, that they are not children like 'our' children, but rather manipulative impostors.[58] The traumatic quality of their life experience is so at odds with decision makers' conceptions of what constitutes 'childhood', that the category 'child' is viewed as inapplicable to this class. Heightened skepticism and hostility rather than compassion are thus, paradoxically, typical official responses. Like street children in other contexts, they are viewed as 'people out of place', more rather than less suspect for being displaced and detached from firm anchoring in familiar social settings.[59] In one egregious UK case, a 17 year old boy detained in an adult jail had his application for bail rejected because the special adjudicator found there were no compassionate circumstances: his ruling might have been different, he stated, if the child had been much younger or suffering from Downs Syndrome.[60] Separated children thus frequently fall through the cracks when it comes to representation – it is assumed that they need no special care; they are more likely to receive inadequate representation and to be victimized by incompetent or negligent legal representatives. Central American children, routinely removed and returned across the US southern border, are viewed

56 R. Paveley, 'Charity wants fairer treatment of asylum-seeking children', Press Association (UK) 20 November 2000.

57 Florida Rural Legal Services of Miami, *Not in their Best interest: A report on the US Government's Forcible Repatriation of Guantanamo's Unaccompanied Haitian Children* 2 May 1995.

58 Where several children recount similar incidents, they may be considered to have 'cooked up' the story together, rather than to be corroborating each other – see M. John, 'Rights in a Market Free Culture'. In: Stephens (ed.), *Children*, p. 131.

59 S. Stephens, 'Introduction'. In: S. Stephens (ed.), *Children*, p. 20.

60 AI, *Most Vulnerable*, 73.

in that light, as petty criminals who need to be ejected,[61] where the main problem is lack of parental supervision or care. To quote a senior US INS official, 'these kids are run-aways or throw-aways'.[62] Days after the world's media were focused on the case of Elian Gonzalez,[63] two Haitian children aged 8 and 9, also shipwrecked en route to the US, were returned to Haiti, despite their mother having been taken ashore in the US for medical treatment and consideration of an asylum claim.[64] Chinese, Sri Lankan, Albanian, and Indian children, especially when their travel is facilitated by smugglers, are also viewed with suspicion, as illegal immigrants choosing to defy immigration controls.[65] The child's participation in the migration decision leads to a finding of culpability. The Canadian example of the Chinese child who was refused asylum because he admitted having consented to being smuggled exemplifies this approach. Advocates report cases where children, without the benefit of legal advice, are threatened with prolonged imprisonment if they make a claim to remain in the country, and as a result frequently agree to 'sign the papers' and relinquish rights to challenge removal or refusal of entry.[66]

By contrast welfare protection concerns privilege the child's minority – the child is viewed as a child first, and an asylum seeker or alien second.

[61] Of the 809 Mexican children who entered the U.S. in the fiscal year 1999–2000, 619 were sent straight back. *Chicago Tribune*, 5 March 2000. Local INS offices are not required to report the numbers of these child 'border-crossers' to central INS, personal communication from John Pogash, INS acting juvenile director.

[62] Personal communication.

[63] The case of Elian Gonzalez was exceptional in many ways. Not only did it attract unprecedented media and political attention because of the powerful and well-connected anti-Castro Cuban lobby in Florida. It also highlighted the particular issues raised in cases of unaccompanied child asylum seekers where a parent opposes the application for asylum. In this, rare situation, decision-makers need to carefully balance the parent's rights to make decisions about his or her child's future with the child's right to asylum from persecution. For a careful analysis of the legal issues raised by this situation, suggesting that a parent's wishes should only be overridden on proof of clear and convincing risk of severe and irreversible harm to the child, see Peter Margulies, 'Children, Parents, and Asylum' 15 *Georgetown Immigration Law Journal* (2001), 289.

[64] CISNEWS 17 January 2000. In response to protests about discriminatory treatment, U.S. officials eventually said the children would be allowed to rejoin their mother in the US, while her asylum claim was being considered.

[65] See argument put forward by the government in the case in *Bian v Canada (Minister of Citizenship and Immigration)* Federal Court of Canada, Trial Division, Docket: IMM-1640-00, Judgment 11 December 2000, Para 8.

[66] See criticism of this practice in *Perez-Funez v INS* 611 F. Supp. 990 (D.C.Cal. 1984) (16 year old Salvadorian plaintiff alleged he was not informed of any legal alternatives after being detained and was led to believe his failure to consent to voluntary departure would result in a long jail sentence and return to El Salvador nonetheless).

The emphasis here has traditionally been on the child's incapacity, status as victim, claim to special protection. The approach is consistent with the view of children as particularly vulnerable, dependent, legally incompetent.[67] For children this special consideration is a double-edged sword: eligibility for beneficial extra protection brings with it skepticism about competence, reliability, access to 'knowledge'.[68] The analogy here is to the position of groups such as the physically disabled, the mentally ill or the elderly – groups whose difference from a competent adult norm has to be registered and accommodated to by extra protections. As already mentioned, this approach is longstanding in international policy. Though the Refugee Convention itself makes no special age-based provisions[69] – age is no more a ground for establishing a fear of persecution than gender – UNHCR has consistently stressed the need for a protectionist approach. In so doing it reflects precisely the ambivalent position towards children just described. Several EXCOM conclusions take up the special protection needs of refugee children.[70] The UNHCR handbook, published in 1979, devotes seven paragraphs to the issue.

On the one hand, in line with the thinking that urges extra benefits for children because of their minority, the handbook urges states to adopt 'a liberal application of the benefit of the doubt' when considering the well-foundedness of a minor's fear of persecution.[71] So, decision-makers are invited to suspend their normal evaluative procedures and replace them with an approach that is more generous to the asylum applicant. They are also encouraged to take into account fears other than those of the child applicant when coming to a decision: 'The circumstances of the parents and other family members, including their situation in the minor's country of origin, will have to be taken into account. If there is reason to believe that the parents wish their child to be outside the country of origin on grounds of

[67] For a good example of the introduction of child protection concerns into decision-making about separated children see *X v Minister for Immigration and Multicultural Affairs and Another; Y v Minister for Immigration and Multicultural Affairs and Another* 164 A.L.R. 583 (1999).

[68] M. John, 'Rights in a Market Free Culture'. In: S. Stephens, *Children*, p. 131.

[69] With the small exception of family reunion provisions, see G. Goodwin-Gill, 'Protecting the Legal Rights of Refugee Children: Some Legal and Institutional Possibilities'. In: J Doek, Hans van Loon and P. Vlaardingerbroek (eds.), *Children on the Move: How to Implement their Right to Family Life*. The Hague, Boston, London: Martinus Nijhoff, 1996, p. 97.

[70] Bhabha and Young, *Not Adults in Miniature*, 90.

[71] Office of the United Nations High Commissioner for Refugees, *Handbook on Procedures and Criteria for Determining Refugee Status* (UNHCR, Geneva. 1979) Para 219 [hereafter UNHCR Handbook].

well-founded fear of persecution, *the child himself may be presumed to have such a fear*'.[72]

On the other hand, however, the skepticism, indeed suspicion about children as independent rights bearers and agents, is reflected in a cautionary approach to claims made by minors who are not considered 'sufficiently mature'. The handbook divides minors into three sets of dichotomized categories; child/adolescent, mature/immature, under 16/over 16. It is not clear how the first set maps onto the other two, since the terms are not defined. However, 'maturity', rather than calendar age or developmental category, seems to be the key consideration. The Handbook states: 'It can be assumed that – in the absence of indications to the contrary – a person of 16 or over may be regarded as sufficiently mature to have a well-founded fear of persecution. Minors under 16 years of age may normally be assumed not to be sufficiently mature. *They may have fear and a will of their own, but these may not have the same significance as in the case of an adult*'.[73] This approach is problematic. It establishes a norm, without a clear basis for exercising discretion ('minors under 16 ... may normally be assumed ...'). It invokes the Handbook's interpretation of the 'well-founded fear' requirement of the refugee definition in Art 1(a) of the Refugee Convention, as consisting of two discrete components, a subjective element ('fear') and an objective element ('well-foundedness').[74] And it then proceeds, in the case of children, to subordinate the objective to the subjective component; thus, a child's well-founded fear of persecution is considered an unreliable emotional response, to be accorded less significance than an adult's.[75] However, this interpretation of 'well-founded fear' has long been questioned by scholars and courts, who have challenged both the feasibility and propriety of evaluations of subjective states of mind as a basis for asylum. As one scholar put it, 'the frame of mind of the individual hardly matters at all. Every person claiming ... to be a refugee has 'fear' ... of being persecuted in the sense of the present provision, irrespective of whether he jitters at the very thought of his return

[72] UNHCR *Handbook* Para 218 (emphasis added). The Handbook does not address the opposite situation, where a separated child seeks asylum against the wishes of a parent who wishes to have his or her lack of fear imputed to the child, as in the Elian Gonzalez case. This possibility illustrates the point that the substitution of the parent's fear or lack of fear for the child's is not necessarily beneficial to the child; it depends on the circumstances, including whether the assessment of harm facing the child is shared by parent and child, or – in the case of a very young child – by parent and guardian (or assessor of the child's 'best interests'). For an interesting reflection on these issues see P. Margulies, note 63 above.

[73] UNHCR *Handbook*, Para 215 (emphasis added).

[74] UNHCR *Handbook*, Para 37–38.

[75] The Handbook's reference in the section quoted to 'fear and ... will', indicates that not only the emotional response but also the decision-making choices of children may be considered less significant.

to his home country, is prepared to brave all hazards, or is simply apathetic or even unconscious of the possible dangers'.[76] As a result the 'two-pronged "subjective" and "objective" assessment has been functionally converted to a single objective standard'.[77] If state of mind is irrelevant to the assessment of the merits of an asylum claim, then there is no justification for distinguishing between an adult and a child applicant on this basis. And even if one were to take the subjective component of fear as being part of the evidentiary picture relating to the asylum claim, it is not clear that children, as a category are in fact more fearful than adults; some research on the recruitment and indoctrination of child soldiers in contemporary wars suggests the opposite.[78] Finally, variation within the category 'child' or 'adult' is likely to be at least as great as between the two categories – people's subjective responses to traumatic situations are conditioned by a wide range of factors, of which age is only one. There seems no justification for according less significance to the fear or will of a child than that of an adult.

More recently international jurisprudence on the rights of children has received new prominence and acceptance, through the widespread ratification of the 1989 UN Convention on the Rights of the Child. Though the convention's force is limited by the fact that it allows states considerable latitude and discretion in formulating mechanisms for implementation, it nevertheless plays a critical normative role in establishing agreed benchmarks for the treatment of children. The Convention stipulates that a child's 'best interests' shall be a 'primary consideration' when decisions about the child are taken.[79] Moreover, children who are refugees or seeking asylum, have a specifically articulated right to 'appropriate protection and humanitarian assistance'.[80] In addition to this traditional protective concern, however, the Convention has added a new dimension to states' responsibilities towards children. It requires that the child must be considered a subject with the right to express his or her own views, and to have those views taken into account, with 'due weight [given] in accordance with the age and maturity

76 A. Grahl-Madsen, *The Status of Refugees in International Law* (A.W. Sijthoff, Leiden. 1966), 174. I am grateful to T. Spijkerboer for drawing my attention to this paragraph.

77 J. Hathaway, *The Law of Refugee Status* (Butterworths, Vancouver, 1991), 71.

78 'Children at both ends of the gun', UNICEF *Impact of Armed Conflict on Children* at www.unicef.org/graca/kidsoldi.htm.

79 Art. 3. Several Scandinavian aliens laws specifically draw attention to this principle. Ruxton, *Separated Children*, 6. The Swedish Aliens Act Chapter 1, sec 1 provides: 'In cases where a child is involved, special attention shall be given to what is required bearing in mind the child's health and development and the best interest of the child otherwise'. Cited in M-I Kingvall, 'Swedish Policies towards Separated Children', in UNCHR and SCF, Documentation, 11.

80 CRC Art. 22.

of the child'.[81] This additional strand requires states to consider children's agency more directly – to view children as having the potential to make decisions about themselves, and the right to have those decisions attended to. In the refugee context, such agency can include political activism, consent to embarking on travel to seek refugee status, refusal to abide by oppressive norms or familial abuse. Because it presents the child as at least in part a competent agent and decision-maker, this approach is in tension with the passive victim protectionist approach. Presenting the child as an active participant in the process of seeking flight can also lead to a child's migration motives being called into question.

6. Inconsistent State Policies

These two approaches, the immigration enforcement and the child rights approach, coexist in a state of tension which is reflected both in current policies towards separated child asylum seekers and in court decisions concerning them. I consider these in turn. Many examples of inconsistent policies can be given. The EU Council's 1997 resolution on 'unaccompanied minors who are nationals of third countries'[82] is a good illustration. On the one hand the resolution upholds member states' rights to 'refuse admission at the frontier to unaccompanied minors, in particular if they are without the required documentation and authorizations', and to detain children at the border pending a decision[83] – a position which seems to completely equate the treatment of separated children with adults; on the other the resolution sets out minimum guarantees for these minors, including the appointment of a legal guardian, and stresses, given their particular vulnerability, the need to process minors' asylum applications 'as a matter of urgency'.[84]

Examples of inconsistent policies within 3 western countries can be cited to exemplify the issue. In 1994, the UK followed UNHCR's call for special attention to the needs of separated child asylum seekers; it established a Refugee Council Panel of Advisers for Unaccompanied Refugee Children, to provide children with independent support. Advisers perform a welfare role, assisting and counseling separated children as they navigate the immigration, educational, health and welfare systems that confront them. Moreover the government has adopted a firm policy against the detention of separated child asylum seekers, in the face of considerable criticism of past practice: a 1998 survey by the Panel for Unaccompanied Refugee Children

81 CRC Art. 12.

82 OJ C221 (1997).

83 Art. 2.

84 Art. 4.

had found that separated children were 5 times more likely to be detained than adults: 5% of unaccompanied asylum-seeking children compared with only 1% of asylum-seeking adults.[85] Social services departments, rather than immigration or law enforcement agencies, are responsible for the care and control of separated children from the point of entry in the UK onwards. But, though this system has much to commend itself, there are several lacunae, where an immigration enforcement approach still dominates. The Panel of Advisers lacks statutory force; the advisers are not guardians. As a result there is no clear allocation of legal responsibility for the child. Moreover the system for identifying separated child applicants is unsatisfactory; despite the policy change some children are still misidentified as adults and treated accordingly – they fall through the safety net and end up in detention and or inadequately represented; others are deported or removed without adequate legal safeguards.[86]

As with the UK experience, Canada's approach to separated children seeking asylum is inconsistent. Canada was the first country, in 1996, to produce special procedural guidelines on child refugee claimants, calling for the appointment of a 'designated representative' to play a guardian-like role for each child refugee claimant,[87] outlining child-sensitive procedures for eliciting and evaluating a child's testimony and emphasizing the need for refugee determinations to reflect the best interests of the child. As Nurjehan Mawani, Chair of the Canadian Immigration and Refugee Board pointed out: 'The emphasis on the best interests of the child reinforces the treatment of children as individuals and not as a rigid, undifferentiated class. Every child is different. What is in the best interest of one child may not be in the best interest of another'.[88] The designated representative is responsible for the appointment of a lawyer to represent every separated child. Yet, despite this protectionist infrastructure, the situation facing separated children seeking asylum in Canada is at best confusing. Legal aid inadequacies result in a lack of real advocacy in many cases – frequently underfunded attorneys pay scant attention to the particular complexities of children's asylum claims; according to a leading child asylum advocate, 'many children fall through the cracks of representation'.[89] Even where children are awarded refugee status,

[85] Minutes of House of Commons meeting on 'Children in Detention and the Issue of Age Assessments', 29 May 1998, on file with author, cited in Bhabha and Young, *Not Adults in Miniature*, 88.

[86] AI, *Most Vulnerable*.

[87] Immigration Act R.S.C. 1985 c.1–2, s 69(4).

[88] Statement by Nurjehan Mawani, Chair, Immigration and Refugee Board, at Canadian Bar Association Annual Meeting/Commonwealth Law Conference (Vancouver, B.C., 26 August 1996), 4.

[89] Geraldine Sadoway, personal communication, 4 February 2001.

they encounter great hurdles and delays in receiving 'landed' or permanent resident status that is the gateway to the full panoply of welfare, health and education benefits. Many cases remain in limbo for years, such as the case of a 2 year old Somali child who, 6 years later, is still awaiting a final determination of her asylum application (with consequent disqualification from welfare benefits and full health coverage).[90] To add to this, recently Canadian authorities have started detaining some separated children, even where there is no dispute as to their minority. One judge, hearing a *habeas corpus* application by twelve adolescent minors who had already been in immigration detention for over six months at the time of the hearing, remarked: 'I am deeply troubled by the length of time these minors have been detained and by the conditions of their detention ... It appears that our immigration system is not equipped at the present time to deal properly with the detention of unaccompanied minors'.[91] The judge contrasted the length of the children's detention with the average of 18 days for adult immigration detention in jails and 8 days in holding centers. Child welfare officers expressed concern for the detained minors' physical and mental health: 'They reported that most of the youth presented as depressed, suffering from sadness and anxiety. Most reported health problems including loss of sleep, dizziness, fainting, bleeding gums. All wished to see a Mandarin speaking doctor. Many of the young women had difficulty obtaining an adequate supply of sanitary napkins, and some of the detainees were without basic necessities such as toothpaste and soap ... Reading materials were almost non-existent, consisting of just one book ... Almost all of [the minors] have lost weight and become increasingly withdrawn and timid. They have been visited by a doctor only once, and this doctor did not speak any of the languages spoken by the minors. This, despite the fact that a Mandarin speaking doctor had agreed to treat the children'.[92] Detention is justified as necessary to avoid flight risk, and sometimes, surprisingly, as a means of 'protecting' children from traffickers and smugglers.[93] This official stance clearly contradicts Canada's obligations under the Convention on the Rights of the Child. As a state party with a relatively

90 Ibid.

91 *Gao (Litigation Guardian of) v Canada (Minister of Citizenship and Immigration)* 2000 Carswell Ont. 2646, Docket 00-CV-192960, Judgment 27 July 2000.

92 Ibid. Para 7–8.

93 These arguments have been used both in the US and Canada: 'In those instances where particular juveniles have engaged in delinquent behaviour, are escape risks or have a need for greater safety and security – for example, when they might be harmed by smugglers or their families ransomed – they are placed in secure settings' Doris Meissner, former INS commissioner, *USA Today* 28 February 2000, at 18A. Infact in the 1999 fiscal year only 19% of the 1958 cases of children placed in secure detention concerned children chargeable or convicted as delinquents. *Detention Watch Network News* 4 April/May 2000. See also *Gao*

robust record of international law enforcement, this is particularly regrettable. The Convention states that separated children seeking asylum are entitled to 'receive appropriate protection and humanitarian assistance';[94] moreover 'In cases where no parents or other members of the family can be found, the child shall be accorded the same protection as any other child permanently or temporarily deprived of his or her family environment for any reason'.[95] So discrimination against non-citizen children separated from their family is specifically prohibited. In addition to these general protections for children seeking asylum, the Convention's approach to imprisonment of children is unequivocal: detention is a punitive and extreme measure to be used as little as possible. Art. 37 (b) states: 'No child shall be deprived of his or her liberty unlawfully or arbitrarily. The arrest, detention or imprisonment of a child shall be used only as a measure of last resort and for the shortest appropriate period of time'.

Perhaps the clearest example of the inconsistent treatment of separated child asylum seekers, amounting to no less than a contradiction, is the US approach. The immigration enforcement framework is most evident, because, unlike the previous countries described, the authority responsible for the care and custody of separated children is also the body responsible for enforcing immigration control – the INS. No social services agency has a direct statutory responsibility. The INS's dual role in respect of separated children gives rise to a clear conflict of interest, and to serious rights violations. About 90% of separated children seeking asylum are unrepresented – a situation which is tantamount to a radical denial of access to any refugee protection for most children, given the legal complexities, the child's lack of skills and confidence, and the insurmountable obstacles of an unfamiliar environment and separation from familial support. No public funding for representation for child asylum seekers exists; as a result these children are dependent on *pro bono* advocates, many of whom are completely inexperienced (it is common for complex child asylum cases to be young associates' or law school legal clinic students' first experience of court advocacy) or a few non-profit organizations, which typically have one or two paid staff lawyers to represent hundreds of applicants. Another unjust aspect of the US system, which reflects the INS's central role, is the routine detention of separated child asylum seekers. The staff working in the detention facilities are INS employees, but they are also the children's carers. As a result children's confidentiality is severely compromised, the detention center staff's ability to

v Canada Para 29. Some European countries have adopted a similar approach – see Ruxton, Separated Children, 55.

[94] Art. 22 (1).

[95] Art. 22 (2).

advocate on behalf of the children is strictly limited, and many basic welfare entitlements for detained children, apart from access to legal advice, such as health care and adequate education, are severely neglected. This conflict of interest and the problems it gives rise to, have long been criticized by advocacy groups.[96]

Detention is one of the clearest examples of an immigration enforcement policy.[97] In the US separated children seeking asylum are routinely detained, some for very long periods (up to 2 years) and some in very punitive settings. According to INS records, in the 1999 federal fiscal year, there were about 4,600 children under 18 in its custody. Of these 1958 or 19% were in 'secure facilities' – i.e. juvenile jails, where the INS detained children are held alongside juvenile offenders. Conditions in these facilities are harsh and violate minimal standards for children, especially those who are not charged with any criminal wrongdoing. Children, some under 10 years old, are placed behind multiple layers of locked doors, surrounded by barbed wire; they are strip-searched, placed in solitary confinement for punishment, forced to wear prison uniform and handcuffed and shackled when they are transported to court or from one facility to another; there are punitive disciplinarian regimes. In one jurisdiction, detention center staff routinely confiscate children's shoes and prohibit outdoor play for children who have had an unsuccessful asylum hearing, or have received news that a planned family reunion will not take place[98] – flight risk or disciplinary misdemeanors are the reasons given. Two recent incidents in another area illustrate the punitive approach adopted: in one case, 2 siblings were moved from the ordinary detention wing to the correctional wing (alongside juvenile offenders) and forced to sit side by side in a corridor for 9 hours without moving or talking to each other, as

[96] Recently, collaborating with legislators, they have produced a bill currently before the Congress, Senator Feinstein's *Unaccompanied Alien Child Protection Act 2001*, which would eliminate this conflict by separating the child welfare function (to be allocated to a new Children' Services Office) from the immigration control role, S. 121.

[97] Increasing numbers of states are detaining separated child asylum seekers, as attitudes to immigration in developed states become increasingly hostile and exclusionary. In Australia child rights bodies have expressed concern about the detention of such children in inappropriate settings See statement by Danny Sandor, president – Defence for Children International, Australia, calling for a specialist external panel to be established to review detention of separated child asylum seekers in Australian immigration detention centers, *http://members.dynamite.com.au/dci-aust/index. Html* 28 November 2000. The immigration authorities do not seem to recognize separated child asylum seekers as an issue of public concern: no official figures for the numbers arriving or applying for asylum exist. Personal communication from Statistics Section, Department of Immigration and Multicultural Affairs, Australia, 31 January 2001. On file with the author.

[98] Personal communication, Meredith Linsky, staff attorney, Pro Bar Texas, 3 February 2001.

punishment for misbehaving. In another case a child was moved into the correctional wing as a punishment because the detention officer decided he had been lying.[99] No due process protections apply. Conditions in the correctional wing are described by Human Rights Watch in relation to the case of a 15 year old asylum seeker from China: 'Xiao Ling was placed in a secure detention wing with juvenile offenders. This particular facility houses violent offenders, including children accused of murder, rape and drug trafficking. . . . Despite having no criminal record, Xiao Ling was kept [at this facility] for several months and assigned a small concrete cell. It was completely bare except for bedding, and a bible in a language she could not read. Xiao Ling was forbidden to wear her own clothes or keep any personal possessions in her cell'.[100] Another example of the immigration enforcement approach to separated child asylum seekers is the use of detention of children as a bait to ensnare relatives with irregular migration status.[101]

At the same time as it detains growing numbers of separated children and subjects them to harsh treatment, the US is a leader in encouraging revision of the legal framework for adjudicating claims by child asylum seekers. It is the first country to produce a substantive, rights based set of 'Guidelines for Children's Asylum Claims'. These guidelines go beyond the UNHCR, UK and Canadian procedural policies, because they incorporate substantive legal standards to address the particularities of children's persecution in the context of US asylum law. For example, the guidelines state: 'The harm a child fears or has suffered . . . may be *relatively less* than that of an adult and still qualify as persecution . . . The types of harm that may befall children are varied . . . . In addition to the many forms of persecution an adult may suffer, children may be particularly vulnerable to sexual assault, forced labor, forced prostitution, infanticide, and other forms of human rights violations such as the deprivation of food and medical treatment. Cultural practices, such as FGM, may under certain circumstances constitute persecution'. These standards reflect a protectionist bias. The Convention on the Rights of the Child (which the US has not ratified) is cited and clearly informs the analysis of the specificity of children's persecution. And yet, as if to highlight the contradictory position of the US, (its interest in evolving a child-centered approach to persecution and at the same time its exceptionalist stance towards

99 Personal communication, Wendy Young, staff attorney, Women's Commission for Refugee Women and Children, 3 February 2001.

100 Jo Becker, 'Children in Detention suffer denial of basic human rights', *Detention Watch Network News* 4 April/May 2000.

101 For example the US authorities refused to release an 11 year old from detention into the custody of his permanent resident aunt to trap his mother, who they suspected of working illegally in the US. Douglas Montero, 'Feds use kids as bait to snare immigrant parents', *The New York Post*, 29 January 2001.

international human rights norms) the introduction to the guidelines contains the following remarkable comment: 'the internationally recognized 'best interests of the child' principle is a useful measure for determining appropriate interview procedures for child asylum seekers, *even though it does not play a role in determining substantive eligibility under the U.S. refugee definition*'. Why the best interests principle should apply to procedural matters, but not to establishing what counts as persecution of a child is not explained.[102]

7. A Dual view of the Child: Inconsistent Judgments in Separated Child Asylum Seeker Cases

The tension between the two opposing normative frameworks does not only produce inconsistent state policies; it also affects the judicial approach to separated children as asylum seekers. Given the large and growing numbers of separated child asylum seekers reaching developed states, it is remarkable how limited the jurisprudence on such cases still is. The absence of proper access to legal procedures in most countries is a large part of the explanation – very few children are in the privileged position of securing sufficient evidence and instructing lawyers. Despite procedural recommendations or guidelines to the contrary, children are regularly subjected to hostile and adversarial questioning, which is intimidatory and discourages further pursuit of a legal claim. As one advocate vividly put it: 'Just as we would cringe at the thought of pitting a 250 pound adult male against a 70 pound boy in a physical fight, we should recognize that children are not equipped to spar with the intellectual and verbal skills of adults in the hearing room. This is true even for children who are able to converse intelligently and who appear mature in many respects. The result of this incapacity to testify may be that the child is unable to provide the necessary evidence in support of his or her own claim'.[103]

Even those who do assemble substantial evidence of persecution and get legal representation, often receive a grossly inadequate service – at best lawyers who are under funded and overloaded,[104] at worst lawyers who are

[102] For the opposite approach see the interesting judgment of Gibson J in *Bian v Canada*: 'the values reflected in international human rights law [such as the Convention on the Rights of the Child] may help inform the contextual approach to statutory interpretation and judicial review', Para 16.

[103] G. Sadoway, 'Refugee Children before the Immigration and Refugee Board', 35 *Immigration Law Reporter* (1997), 117..

[104] Organizations such as Pro Bar in Texas, the Florence Project in Arizona or the Midwest Immigrants Rights Center in Chicago function on a proverbial shoestring, representing many hundreds of applicants.

hired by smuggling networks, who never see their client, and whose sole interest in the case is to get the child out of detention and into an exploitative workplace to repay their smuggling debt.[105] As a child commented: 'The lawyer my snakehead hired was in San Francisco, but he called me up saying he could not be my lawyer anymore, because he was being investigated for connections to the smugglers. I was happy when I got this phone call, because I think my lawyer didn't respect me'.[106] So only a tiny minority of separated children get a lawyer who will conscientiously and thoroughly advocate on their behalf. In addition, scholarly and practitioner attention to the specific nature of child asylum claims and to a child-specific approach to persecution is in its infancy. The refugee definition, though age neutral, has yet to be consistently applied to the circumstances of child applicants.[107] A 1994 UK case illustrates this point. A 15-year-old child from Iran applied for asylum on the basis of physical abuse from her father. The record suggests that there was evidence of alcohol-related 'extreme violence'. Though she was accepted as a credible witness by a special adjudicator, the Immigration Appeal Tribunal rejected her application, inter alia because it held she could have relied on the Iranian authorities for protection and 'neither gender nor violence within a family is sufficient to create a social group'. Nowhere in the record is there any mention of the fact that the applicant was a child,[108] nor is there any discussion of whether extreme child abuse could constitute persecution.

For the minority of separated children who do get access to diligent legal representation, the normative conflict between different approaches to separated children influences their chance of a successful asylum claim. On the one hand, reflecting a traditional child welfare approach, children are viewed as passive victims of harms inflicted by others, who need and deserve refugee protection; on the other hand, reflecting the exclusionary concerns of immigration control, they are viewed as knowing, even willing participants in illegal migration practices.

As a result case law is inconsistent. The welfare protection approach motivates findings of refugee status for children who are defenseless and vulnerable if they can prove they are victims of persecution. This includes

[105] One especially notorious example of a 'smuggler's lawyer' is Robert Porges, who was listed as the attorney representing many detained separated child asylum seekers. Porges was arrested in September 2000 on a 44 count federal indictment, charging that the $13.5 million he had accumulated in 7 years of practice, was the result of working closely with 'snakehead' smuggling rings. G. Rayman, 'Human Smuggling – Lawyer charged in schemes to sneak Chinese into country', *Newsday*, 21 September 2000.

[106] Case 1, Froehlich interviews.

[107] Bhabha and Young, *Not Adults in Miniature*; AI, *Most Vulnerable*.

[108] *Sec of State for Home Dept v Fatemah Firouz Ranjbar* HX/70912/94 (11105); UNHCR case ref: CAS/GBR/56.

cases of children who flee their homelands to escape being targeted for the same political, religious or ethnic persecution that leads adults to flee. In some cases, though the persecution alleged is not child specific, the fact that the asylum applicant is a child is central to the court's reasoning. An example is the case of a 17-year-old Ethiopian girl, who lost her father, mother and brother as a result of persecution by the communist regime that overthrew Haile Selassie. In reversing the Board of Immigration Appeal's refusal of asylum and remitting the case for reconsideration, the US Ninth Circuit Court of Appeals emphasized the particular vulnerability of a child: 'the fact that [the appellant] did not suffer physical harm is not determinative of her claim of persecution: there are other equally serious forms of injury that result from persecution. For example, when a young girl loses her father, mother and brother – sees her family effectively destroyed – she plainly suffers severe emotional and developmental injury'.[109] In other cases minority is largely irrelevant – similarly placed adults would also qualify. The case of two 11 and 13 year old Tamil Sri Lankan brothers who obtained refugee status in Canada after being targeted as LTTE guerilla recruits[110] is an example.

A child welfare approach also supports findings of refugee status for children who flee child specific persecution, where their minority is a relevant part of the persecution claim, indeed an asset rather than a disqualification. Sometimes the child's persecution is related to both familial and societal circumstances. Two recent US cases exemplify this. In one the US Board of Immigration Appeals awarded asylum to a Honduran child who had been persistently tortured by his stepfather from the age of 3, and faced becoming a street child if returned to Honduras; the decision cited U.S. state department reports that 'the police are responsible for torturing street children and a number of extra judicial killings'.[111] In another an immigration judged granted asylum to a 16-year-old Chinese girl fleeing a forced marriage arranged by her parents 'for money according to feudal practices'.[112] Other successful asylum claims of child specific persecution include cases based on recruitment as a minor into the international sex trade,[113] conscription

[109] *Kahssai v INS* 16 F.3d 323,3 29 (9th Cir.).

[110] See *Sooriyakumaran v Canada (Minister of Citizenship and Immigration)* 156 F.T.R.285 (1998) IMM-4099-97.

[111] BIA, *Martinez Mejia, Juan Carlos* A# 76-312-250, 20 January 1999.

[112] Executive Office for Immigration Review, Chicago, Decision by Immigration Judge Zerbe dated 18 October 2000 #A76-512-001.

[113] Y.C.K. (re) [1997] C.R.D.D.No. 261 No. V95-02904 (concerning 18 year old Ukrainian unwittingly drawn into the international sex trade by illicit traffickers; granted asylum as a member of the particular social group of 'impoverished young women from the former Soviet Union recruited for exploitation in the international sex trade'). See also *In Re Ji-Zhu Mai* where the US Board of Immigration Appeals dismissed an appeal by the INS who challenged

as a child soldier[114], physical violence as a street child,[115] child abuse by a parent.[116]

Sometimes a human rights standard is introduced to challenge cultural arguments about child rearing practice or family customs in the country of origin. Thus a U.S. court granted refugee status to a child 12 year old Indian girl who was physically abused by her parents and then sold to traffickers for domestic service in the US: the court argued that, though 'standards for child treatment vary among cultures and families, and . . . indeed, gradations of child treatment exist which reasonably include disciplining a child and requiring a child to work . . . the treatment suffered by the applicant is beyond the limits of acceptable rearing practices to such an extent that it rises to the level of persecution'. The court found that the child's persecution was on account of membership in the particular social group of 'Indian children sold or abandoned by their parents'.[117] Another example of this approach is a Canadian case concerning a 13-year-old Chinese boy who claimed asylum after being smuggled into Canada following arrangements made between his parents and smugglers. The asylum claim was based on the child's fear of persecution if returned to China, because the fines the family would incur on account of the child's illegal exit and the onerous debts to the smugglers meant that the child had a well-founded fear of being trafficked again. The government had opposed the asylum claim on the basis that the child, an adolescent and therefore 'not of tender years', had consented to being smuggled in the hope of economic betterment. The court found that the child had only consented to being smuggled in the first place because of the Chinese 'cultural phenomenon of filial piety'. Granting refugee status, the court held that the child was persecuted by virtue of having been 'trafficked', that he had a well-founded fear of future trafficking, and that as a

the grant of asylum to a young Chinese woman whose well-founded fear of persecution was based on her imputed political opinion or her membership in a particular social group 'of women in China who oppose coerced involvement in government sanctioned prostitution'. 20 March 2001 BIA File A74 206 787. The introduction of the US *Trafficking Victims Protection Act 2000* will enable some of applicants who have been 'victims of severe forms of trafficking in persons' to get 'T' visas which can lead to permanent residence in the US.

114 *Moreno v Canada (Minister of Employment and Immigration)* 21 Imm. L.R. (2d) 221, (1993) – case of a sixteen year old child soldier awarded refugee status, without any reference to the applicant's minority. See Wendy Hope Perlmutter, *An Application of Refugee Law to Child Soldiers* December 2000, paper on file with author.

115 Case of *Santos Ramon Zepeda Campos*, 16-year-old Nicaraguan, granted asylum by Arizona IJ on 28 December 2000. On file with the author.

116 *Aguirre-Cervantes v. INS*, No. 99-70861 (9th Cir. 21 March 2001), Mexican girl beaten severely and frequently by father, since the age of 3.

117 Executive Office for Immigration Review, Chicago, Decision by Immigration Judge Zerbe dated 13 March 1998. On file with the author.

minor, following international human rights instruments and irrespective of country customs, he was incapable as a matter of law of 'consenting' to being trafficked.[118]

In some instances, as with gender persecution cases, in order to advance a powerful asylum claim, advocates have tended to juxtapose a western, civilized standard to the 'barbaric' or 'primitive' culture from which the applicant is escaping.[119] Judges have sometimes colluded with this essentializing and reductive approach by denigrating whole cultures. The applicant then is rewarded for seeking out civility. For example, a 12-year-old Jordanian child applied for asylum with his mother on the basis of his acute trauma resulting from the father's long history of severe domestic violence against the mother. According to the judge, the mother was 'targeted for abuse because she is a woman who seeks to have her own identity, who believes in the 'dangerous' Western values of integrity and worth of the individual. ... [She] is not content to live in a harem completely "protected" by her husband, his society, his government'. The judge granted mother and child asylum because they had 'remain[ed] unbowed. They now seek protection in this country for their political belief in the importance of individual freedom. Not just freedom for adult males, but freedom for women and children too'.[120] Some cases where children have received asylum because of the risk of female genital circumcision have also been presented in this way.[121]

Children who can present asylum claims based on their vulnerability and victim-status thus have had some success in securing refugee status. These cases stand in contrast to cases where children's asylum claims are based on their political beliefs, their activist behaviour, their role as decision makers, their conscious choices about their future prospects. In this latter group of cases, minority is not an advantage; indeed it can act as a disqualification. One can identify two different strands to the rejection arguments. On the one hand, the claims of separated child asylum seekers are assimilated to those

118 *Bian v Canada (Minister of Citizenship and Immigration)* Federal Court of Canada-Trial Division, Judgement of Gibson J, 11 December 2000 – IMM-1640-00, IMM-932-00.

119 See In the matter of A and Z [1994] A 72-190-893, A 72-793-219, and discussion of this case in J. Bhabha,'Embodied Rights: Gender Persecution, State Sovereignty and Refugees', 9 *Public Culture* (1996), 3–32, 17.

120 In the matte of A and Z, 14.

121 See for example a decision by the Canadian Immigration and Refugee board awarding asylum to a Somali girl who faced the prospect of female genital circumcision if returned; criticizing this 'archaic tradition', the board ruled that the applicant's status as a 'minor female from Somalia' qualified her for protection under the Refugee Convention. However not all cases where refugee status has been awarded to children fearing FGM have represented the home country in this way. Countries where FGM has been the basis of grants of refugee status to children include Sweden (Migration NewsSheet 17 April 1997), the US (case of Ololuro).

of adults – they are not 'really children', or they are not of tender years,[122] or no special considerations apply. Immigration control considerations, with exclusionary goals, are therefore brought to bear. The case of a 15-year-old Salvadorian who was wounded while fighting with guerilla forces, exemplifies this approach. The child testified that family members had been murdered by both the guerillas and the government army, that he had eventually fled the guerillas and was forced into hiding from both guerillas and government soldiers whom he believed were seeking to arrest or kill him. The US Fourth Circuit rejected his asylum application, despite accepting his credibility and his subjective fear of persecution, because it insisted on holding him to the same objective standard as an adult; it held that the child had failed to show 'that a *reasonable person* in similar circumstances would fear persecution on account . . . [of one of the enumerated grounds in the Refugee Convention].[123] Another example of this line of argument is the Canadian Refugee Determination Division (CRDD) rejection of the asylum claim by a thirteen-year-old Chinese child trafficked along with 8 others into Canada (the decision was overturned on appeal). The CRDD accepted that the claimants 'would be subject to a short period of incarceration upon return, and would be fined varying and negotiable amounts'. However it concluded that 'while their age dictates that their cases be given careful scrutiny and consideration, it does not dictate that they must be viewed necessarily as involuntary participants in an attempt to gain entry'.[124] Courts have tended to discredit testimony that may be more hesitantly put forward, to conclude that children have a less coherent memory. A Canadian federal judge criticized this approach when reversing a decision of the CRDD, regarding two Sri Lankan Tamil children: 'I . . . find that the panel committed a patently unreasonable error of fact that influenced its final conclusions. The panel clearly did not take into consideration the fact that the applicants were ten and twelve years of age when they travelled to Canada and that the two children clearly did not have to keep a log throught their travels. Furthermore, it was quite possible, and perhaps even likely realistic, that both of the applicants could not precisely remember all of the circumstances of the journey, which must certainly have been very stressful in the circumstances'.[125]

The second rejection argument does not assimilate child claimants to adults. Rather it uses their minority as a disqualification. Because they are children, the argument goes, they are not capable of political activism, or

122 See Bian case.

123 *Cruz-Diaz v INS* No. 94-1865 86 Federal Reporter 3d Series, 1996 (4th Cir.).

124 *Bian v Canada*, Para 9–10.

125 *Uthayakumar v Canada (Ministry of Citizenship and Immigration)* IMM 2949–98, Judgment, 18 June 1999.

of being viewed as a political threat or, indeed, of providing reliable testimony about their political experiences. This occurs in several ways: identical political acts carried out by adults and children are discounted in the case of children simply because of their minority – it is suggested that governments would not take actions by children seriously and therefore would not view them as a threat. In several cases such assertions are made despite evidence to the contrary, and are eventually reversed on appeal. In the case of a 16-year-old Salvadorian, the US Board of Immigration Appeals accepted 'the immigration judge's finding that it was unlikely that the National Guard would seek out such a young person'.[126] Ignorance about human rights violations against children fuels this approach. It is also disputed whether children can achieve prominence or leadership positions in political organizations.[127] Second, political acts by children – such as stone throwing, tire burning, street protests, school strikes – are discounted as not being really political, because prevailing judicial conceptions of political activism revolve around an adult norm;[128] there is a direct analogy here to decisions where women's gender-determined political activism – providing shelter for guerillas, cooking, hiding ammunition – is discounted compared to a norm of political activism which is male gendered – leafleting, ambushing, shooting, demonstrating, joining a guerilla army. The concept of a 'political act' in refugee law is insufficiently gender and age inclusive.[129]

126 *Canjura-Flores v INS* 784 F.2d 885 (9th Cir. 1985) 887. The board's position was reversed by the Court of Appeal who accepted the applicant's evidence that young people were likely to be sought out by government forces. See also *Civil v INS* 140 F.3d 52 (1st Circ. 1998) (affirming denial of asylum by immigration judge to a Haitian minor who was overheard by government agents when he publicly supported then opposition leader Aristide; the minor was threatened, his house ransacked, and his pet dog was stoned to death; the IJ concluded 'it is almost inconceivable to believe that the Ton Ton Macoutes could be fearful of the conversations of 15 year old children'. Though the Court affirmed the decision as a whole, it criticized this particular statement, at 56). See also case of Chilean child turned down by Canadian Refugee Status Advisory Committee because decision makers did not consider a 12–13 year old could be perceived as a threat by the Chilean regime, described in G. Sadoway, 'Refugee Children before the Immigration and Refugee Board', 35 *Immigration Law Reporter* 106, at 110.

127 *Rasaq Dipo Salaam v INS* (9th Circ. 18 October 2000) No. 98-71439 (granting petition for review of the BIA's refusal of asylum; BIA had held that it was 'not plausible' that Salaam was a leading member of the Free Nigeria Movement (FNM) at age eighteen. The 9th Circ. found this statement 'based on [the] entirely unsupported assumption [that] ... "important" organizations do not have young leaders').

128 According to a report on decision making on separated child cases in the Netherlands: 'Even where a separated child has been picked up by the police because he accompanied his father to a demonstration, the conclusion is that the arrest is simply the result of being present at a demonstration by chance', Ruxton, Separated Children, 80.

129 See T. Spijkerboer, *Gender and Refugee Status*, 65–74.

8. Conclusion

How does this tension between immigration enforcement and welfare protectionist concerns affect separated child asylum seekers? The enforcement perspective combined with children's handicaps within an adversarial system, would lead one to predict that children fare worse than adults – because they are less able to navigate the system and assemble cogent evidence of persecution, less well represented in the face of a hostile adjudicatory environment, more susceptible to threats of imprisonment or other punishment as incentives to drop asylum claims. The protectionist perspective would lead to the opposite prediction – that the system treats separated children less harshly because they are viewed as being vulnerable victims deserving of social protection.

Both predictions seem to be partly true. My tentative conclusion, based on the sparse evidence available, suggests the following. First, it seems to be the case that a lower proportion of child than adult asylum applicants get refugee status.[130] The main countries from which separated children seeking asylum come parallel those for adults and those where known acute human rights violations and repression take place. There is no evidence, therefore, that separated children's claims are inherently weaker. Indeed given the difficulties of access, the risks of separation and the hurdles separated children face in getting to the point of making asylum applications, one would if anything expect the factors propelling their flight to be stronger. This seems to be the case for women asylum seekers, who appear to have higher recognition rates than men.[131] By contrast minority appears to be a disqualification in getting refugee status. The suggested explanation is that the lower success rate is a reflection of both the procedural and substantive factors examined above: procedurally, the lack of access to adequate legal representation and substantively, the refusal to see children as political agents or targeted subjects of human rights violations. Minority also has other negative consequences for asylum seekers: for example there is evidence that there are longer delays in decision making[132] with a high proportion of separated child asylum seekers spending long periods in limbo, without access to full welfare benefits or

[130] AI, *Most Vulnerable* 49; Ruxton, Separated Children 13 (refugee recognition rates appear to be generally very low (around 1 to 2 per cent) – lower in many cases than those for adults). However the picture is inconsistent; according to one report, Canada recognized 50% of separated children applying for asylum inn 1999, J. Kumin, 'David vs. Goliath', *Refugees* Vol. 1, No. 122 (2001), 13.

[131] Spijkeboer, 17–18.

[132] Separated children fare worse than similarly placed adults in several situations. In the case of the Vietnamese boat people waiting to be resettled from camps in Indochina, 'the special procedures meant that many minors were kept waiting longer than anyone else. By the end of 1993, more than 2,600 minors who had arrived in camps under the age of 16 had

protection.[133] As one separated child, whose asylum application had been pending for 2 years, commented: 'I was happy with my lawyer in the beginning, but now sometimes my lawyer can't find my file and doesn't remember me. I never had much conversation with my lawyer .... Now the lawyer says that my file is lost or transferred. ... Still I am worried, because they can't explain what happened to my file, or what will happen next ...'[134] Other impediments to effective legal representation exist too. In an all-too typical case, a 15-year-old detained child was transferred 1,400 miles from his lawyer of 11 months standing, to a different detention center, without any notice given to either client or advocate.[135] There is also evidence, in some jurisdictions, that a higher proportion of child than adult asylum seekers are detained.

Second, by contrast, separated child asylum seekers appear to have better prospects than adults with respect to remaining in the receiving state. The available evidence is sparse and unsatisfactory, but it suggests that a high proportion of separated children stay on, and that there is a lower rate of removal or deportation than for adults. In some states children have procedural advantages which partly explain this – for example in the US, most separated child asylum seekers are exempt from the expedited removal process;[136] in Sweden asylum cases involving unaccompanied minors are given priority.[137] Some states also appear to be reluctant to return separated children to situations where no protective or supportive family environment exists.[138] As a result in European states most children get some form of humanitarian status, in the US and Canada a high proportion of separated

aged-out, putting them into the normal status determination procedures for adults'. UNHCR, *The State of the World's Refugees 2000* Box 4.4, 94.

133 For several examples of this situation in Europe see Ruxton, *Separated Children*, 84. A particularly disturbing case is that of Luxembourg: 'there are no specific laws and the situation requires clarification; it is possible that children may be left without a status and given the bare minimum for survival until they leave the territory of their own free will or by force'. AI, *Most Vulnerable*, 59.

134 Froehlich interviews.

135 E. Amon, 'Access Denied: Children in INS custody have no right to a lawyer, those who get one risk retaliation', *The National Law Journal*, 9 April 2001.

136 US Children's Guidelines, note 10. Scandinavian states do not refuse children seeking asylum access; Finland and Ireland rarely dismiss children's asylum claims for being 'manifestly unfounded'. Ruxton, Separated Children, 8. 'In the Netherlands there is a special asylum procedure for separated children which recognizes their vulnerability. For example, on arrival separated children are sent to a reception centre to rest'. Ruxton, *Separated Children*, 65.

137 Klingvall in UNCHR and SCF, Documentation, 12.

138 This appears to be the case for many European countries and for Canada; Ruxton, *Separated Children*, 13; Sadoway, Canadian attorney, personal communication, 5 February 2001, on file with author.

children seem to stay on without a regular status, or seem to have unresolved cases which are continued over time.

One can tentatively conclude, then, that minority reduces the chances of obtaining refugee status but that it also reduces the risk of refoulement or return. This is an unsatisfactory compromise between the immigration enforcement and protectionist approaches: it reflects a policy incoherence that urgently needs systematic attention. The result of this state of affairs is that, far from getting preferential treatment as a particularly vulnerable and needy group, separated children are discriminated against with respect to accompanied children or adults who are similarly placed. Significant numbers of separated children are denied the protective status they are entitled to under international human rights and refugee law. They are relegated to a condition of marginality or even illegality, which compounds their fragile often traumatised situation and perpetuates their exclusion from a rights-endowed citizenship.

[17]

Dissident Voices: Refugees, Human Rights and Asylum in Europe

COLIN J. HARVEY
Queen's University of Belfast, Northern Ireland

ABSTRACT

This article examines the law and politics of asylum in Europe. The aim is to explore both the construction of 'Fortress Europe' and the resistance within Europe to the dominant policy response. Human rights law now plays an important part in the struggle to secure decent treatment for asylum seekers in Europe. Its use has exposed serious problems with existing refugee law and policy. In examining the law and politics of human rights this article suggests that dialogic models of law are useful. In particular they bring back into the picture those individuals and groups which make change happen in practice. This allows us to 'ground' the discourses of human rights and refugee law much more securely within concrete political struggles over the terms of asylum policy. At a time when human rights lawyers are becoming part of the international 'mainstream', this article suggests that we must be alive to the importance of dissident voices that remain on the margins.

Introduction

LIBERAL TRIUMPHALISM in the post-Cold War era has coincided with a steady increase in the number of refugees and forcibly displaced persons in the world. In fact the story of the 20th century is one of failure, if judged by the massive human displacement that has followed modernity's path, and the barbarism that often underpins it. The refugee stands as the defining figure of a century that gave displacement an iconic status. Refugees and asylum seekers are faced with increasingly restrictive legal regimes which penalize them for the act of seeking asylum. Northern states, in particular, are now openly hostile to the plight of many of the world's forcibly displaced. A barrage of devices is in operation to ensure that asylum seekers never reach the North. If they do, states have implemented punitive schemes which include detention and the removal or restriction of welfare entitlements. States are currently scrambling to make themselves appear as unattractive as possible to asylum seekers. The situation is rightly characterized as a crisis that is endangering the future of refugee protection. The problem is particularly prominent in Europe. The European Union (EU) is in the process of constructing a more cohesive common asylum and immigration policy which will have implications for the whole region and beyond. The aim in this article is to examine the crisis currently facing the legal regime with a particular emphasis on the EU. In addition, I explore the politics of rights discourse as it impacts on the asylum debate. Although 'Fortress Europe' is a metaphor with substance, rights discourse has been deployed with some success in Europe. To understand and criticize trends in Europe I adopt a dialogic model of legal discourse which I have defended elsewhere. My principal argument is that the institution of asylum is under serious attack from states intent on constructing walls of exclusion around their territories. However, this policy of deterrence and restriction has met with political and legal resistance which has, on occasion, been successful. In any account of EU asylum law and policy it is essential to be able to account for both the transnational political and legal activism that is confronting the dominant narratives in Europe as well as the general restriction evident in state practice. To neglect either element is to undervalue the strength and potential of the resistance to the dominant narratives. The article thus contains a second major pillar. That is a general defence of the relevance of the dialogic approach to understanding the law and politics of human rights.

RECONSTRUCTING REFUGEE LAW

Those working within refugee law are faced with a problem. For a law which on its face claims to offer a humane response to refugee protection in practice operates in exclusionary ways. The legal regime acts as a limiting device which confines the nature and scope of the protection offered by the state to asylum seekers. States are preoccupied not with who is to be included in this legal regime but primarily with those to be screened out. Impressive levels of creativity have been deployed by states in constructing the 'walls of exclusion'. The refugee debate in Europe is trapped within unsophisticated categories which pay little regard to the complexity of refugee movements.

Refugee law consists of the 1951 Convention relating to the Status of Refugees (1951 Convention) and its 1967 Protocol. It contains a definition of 'refugee' which applies to someone who:

> owing to a well-founded fear of being persecuted for reasons of race, religion, nationality, membership of a particular social group or political opinion, is outside the country of his nationality and is unable or, owing to such fear, is unwilling to avail himself of the protection of that country. (Art. 1A(2))

The 1951 Convention contains substantive guarantees for those recognized as refugees. The cornerstone of the legal regime is Article 33(1):

> No Contracting State shall expel or return (*refouler*) a refugee in any manner whatsoever to the frontiers of territory where his life or freedom would be threatened on account of his race, religion, nationality, membership of a particular social group or political opinion.

The United Nations High Commissioner for Refugees (UNHCR) is the intergovernmental organization tasked with refugee protection. In Article 35 of the 1951 Convention states have undertaken to cooperate with the UNHCR in the exercise of its functions. The 1951 Convention is an instrument of its time and the definition, for example, reflects the antidiscrimination concerns that were prevalent in the years that followed 1945. While there are several points to keep in mind, I will mention only two here. First, there is no international monitoring mechanism for refugee law. Unlike other areas of human rights law an individual who is dissatisfied with the result of the national status determination system is unable to challenge this directly at the international level. The concept of responsibility in refugee law is an atomized one which falls onto individual states. Second, there are exceptions to even the most fundamental legal protections. Article 33(2) makes *refoulement* permissible in defined circumstances, even though this norm is described as the cornerstone of the legal regime. Refugee law thus has inherent problems and often stands in sharp contrast to modern trends in human rights law.

Tuitt (1996: 157) has captured the dilemma of the critical scholar approaching refugee law. Serious examination of the issue results in the questioning of the relevancy of refugee law to the refugee. The definition of refugee is far removed from the reality of modern forced migration. The 'gap problem' is particularly severe in this context. The law's image of refugee identity is so narrow that it effectively excludes from its scope the majority of the world's displaced people. Tuitt has argued that as an expression of a specifically 'European' notion of solidarity the 'dimensions of race are endemic in refugee discourse' (pp. 96–106). There is reason to question whether the 1951 Convention reflects an 'essentially European' perspective. It has, for example, proven attractive beyond Europe as a limiting device. It seems odd to question the relevancy of a body of law that is so widely accepted by states. But this is precisely what is happening. As Tuitt recognizes, the fear of the critical scholar is a fear of being without an ideal (p. 157). To expose the severe flaws in this legal regime is to open up the possibility of dismissal and ultimately rejection of a system which does not reflect current realities. The fear of being left without an ideal in refugee legal discourse is well founded. Asylum seekers would be unlikely to benefit from a system where the current norms are dismissed as irrelevant. In this scholars must be careful not to connive with states in a process that will impact negatively on refugees and asylum seekers. For surely it is social movements that tend to *make* law relevant. I suggest in this article that critical scholars must continue to work with a critical conception of refugee law. Refugees and asylum seekers will gain nothing from a process that denies the normativity of existing legal discourses. It is one of the results of stressing the contested nature of legal discourse that it does not necessarily have restrictive implications. Thus I have argued elsewhere for a neorepublican understanding of legality which reconstructs law as a contested conversation (Harvey, 1999a).

Refugee law can, and does, remain a site of interpretative struggle within states. There is evidence from, for example, the UK that struggles over the meaning of refugee law can achieve relatively progressive results. This is evident in some of the more inclusive interpretations of refugee law adopted in cases such as *R* v *Immigration Appeal Tribunal and another, ex parte Shah, Islam and others* v *Secretary of State for the Home Department* [1999] and *R* v *Uxbridge Magistrates' Court, ex parte Adimi* [1999]. While clear limitations remain, it goes some way to suggest that legality can make a difference in the struggle to protect the needs of refugees and asylum seekers. Asylum seekers, and their representatives, are able to make productive use of tensions between the bounded nature of state law and the more open-ended discourse of human rights. This is particularly so if the judiciary in a state views the protection of minorities as a core justification for the judicial role. What has been most intriguing about this issue in the UK, for example, is the willingness of the judiciary to intervene both against government policy and to promote a more expansive conception of the refugee. The asylum debate in the UK coincided with the emergence of a political movement to develop the judicial role into the human rights field. Several members of the judiciary have proven receptive to critical arguments about orthodox constitutionalism. The protection of refugees and asylum seekers provides a suitably noble justification for judicial activism. In national contexts the judiciary have longer-term aims in mind when encouraged to take an expansive view of refugee and asylum law. In judicial training of new refugee law judges, the traditional rule of law narrative is actively 'sold' to the judges. Reconstructing refugee law can have some impact in promoting a critical dialogue about policy direction, and social movements should not be discouraged from engaging with the law's image of the refugee. Refugee law is the exception to the general instrumentalism of policy in this area. For this reason it has been under attack for some time. To fail to recognize its continuing strengths is a mistake (cf. Hathaway, 1997a; Hathaway and Neve, 1997b). But one should not overplay its significance. The majority of those seeking asylum in the EU, for example, are not recognized as 1951 Convention refugees.

The current attack on international refugee law is not framed as a direct assault on the law. In fact one finds states continually referring to the importance of the 1951 Convention. Because of the lack of formal accountability this is a verbal commitment that is easy to make. Careful examination of the area reveals that the justification for restriction is based on the language of human rights. In discourses of justification states have made use of arguments that have general implications for understanding their conceptions of citizenship. In other words, when discussing asylum EU states are giving concrete expression to a general conception of citizenship. The explicit message in EU policy is that the primary aim is rapid restoration of the citizen–state link broken by forced displacement. On this states correctly note that refugee law was only ever intended as a surrogate form of 'international' protection until conditions permitted safe return. The paradigm shift engineered by European states is to a model that places the emphasis on a 'right to remain', with return being the preferred solution to any disruption of this right. While protectionism is extensively derided in economic theory, it underpins the EU's approach to migration management. Refugee lawyers are said to be overly preoccupied with asylum to the detriment of other aspects of forced migration. While asylum is no doubt one aspect of a larger debate about the root causes of oppression, the commitment to prevention is at best half-hearted. There is the additional problem of where a more assertive emphasis on prevention would lead in practice.

The new thinking in refugee law has come from several directions. There is convergence between some strands of critical literature and the policy ambitions of the states of the North. The progressive critique unearths a number of silences in the debate, notably in relation to the structural factors determining who migrates and to where. In this the discourses of containment reflect aspects of, for example, the feminist critique of refugee law (Indra, 1999). Feminist scholars have highlighted the structural factors that often impede women's flight. This literature has focused on the gender dimensions of refugee law and it has helped to draw attention to the plight of the internally displaced. The lesson from this work is that the process of becoming a refugee is gendered (Crawley, 1999: 308–9). As this literature highlights, there is no such thing as the abstract, universal refugee. The point is that criticism of refugee law is not confined to official actors in the EU who are openly dissatisfied with the system. Critical scholars have also developed sophisticated critiques of law and practice. The dilemma is that this work can feed a general climate of dissatisfaction with the institution of asylum. Care must be taken in keeping the different strands of the debate apart. For some states the discourse of prevention, and the notion of a 'right to remain', provided a legitimizing function for existing and new restrictive practices. The constraints of refugee and human rights law do not necessarily make states change their substantive practices. They do, however, alter the way that these practices are justified. Many European states defend their asylum practices with reference to human rights protection and the eventual restoration of the citizen–state link. At its core what this reveals is a commitment to nationally based understandings of rights protection rather than more idealistic universalist models. The subtle message underpinning the response to forced migration is that human rights are primarily citizens' rights.

In assessing this field the differentiated nature of migration must be borne in mind. Much has been written about the pressures and motives that underpin migration (Hammar et al., 1997; Havinga and Böcker, 1999). The legal response to this complexity is to categorize movement into distinct legal fields. External forced displacement is translated, in international refugee law, into refugee movements, with internal displacement also gaining the attention of legal scholars in recent years. A contrast is then made with other forms of migration, such as economic migration. Regulation then takes place within the channels of domestic, and now EU, migration law and policy. Serious concerns have been raised about this exercise in classification. The problem is that it packages what is a much more complex picture into questionable categories. This says as much about the general nature of law as it does about the specifics of the refugee debate. The law's image of the refugee remains, however, a particularly useful example of reductionism and exclusion in practice.

Although asylum and refugee status are frequently treated as if they are synonymous, refugee law contains no reference to asylum. While there exist several ways to challenge return, there is no human right to be granted asylum. In the current international political climate it is difficult to see how it could ever be otherwise. The relevance of this is that it helps in understanding again why international human rights mechanisms have proved so attractive.

So what is to be done with refugee law? A starting point is that despite the fact that a 'universal' regime of protection exists it still matters where protection is sought. The world of refugee protection is a highly differentiated one in which refugee law offers only a false mask of universality. Many states in the north have highly developed status determination systems. This can be contrasted with the struggles of some southern states to cope with massive refugee movements where individualized assessment is impracticable. The sophistication of the bureaucracies do not make them more effective or efficient and most are clearly designed to ensnare the individual in a regime of exclusion. The ritual humiliations of detention, fingerprinting, welfare restriction, backlogs and delays are the reality for asylum seekers within the 'sophisticated' northern systems. The picture is a bleak one and makes talk in the north of the universality of human rights sound very hollow indeed.

A starting point is to recognize what can and cannot be achieved through law in this context. At present an overhaul of the refugee legal system would lead to further restriction. Given this, a feasible response is to struggle within the terms of legal discourse as it currently exists. Refugee law can be reconstructed in a way that at the very least tries to grapple with evident examples of distortion. There are problems and limitations with this reconstructive approach. A criticism of the process of reconstructing meaning, and thus with contesting the process of interpreting refugee law, is that this can downplay the historical conditions that shaped the law. Historicist work stresses the importance of anchoring our interpretation of refugee law solidly in the drafters' intention, because this is the only politically feasible way to discourage erosion of existing standards. Institutional actors, so the argument goes, are much more likely to take this form of reasoning into account. But the security that this model brings is an illusion. This is just as much of a reconstruction of refugee law as any other. The more appropriate response is to recognize the contested nature of the discourse and the perspectives that inform possible reconstructions. Historical context does, however, highlight the tensions that underpinned the drafting process. The 1951 Convention was drafted at a time when the statist paradigm was unquestioned. In this historical context refugee protection was constructed as a compromise between the desire of states to control entry and the continuing existence of mass human displacement. The tensions are an unchanging feature of the asylum debate, whichever state one chooses to examine. The states that drafted this instrument were unwilling to grant a 'blank cheque' for the future. Since then the law's image of the refugee has been a site of struggle from a number of dissenting positions. Advocates continue to struggle within states for more inclusive interpretations of the term that recognize modern realities. They have had some success in this endeavour. Different understandings have also been advanced from other regions which stand in marked contrast to the trends in Europe. The Organization for African Unity (OAU) has adopted a notably expansive understanding of the refugee which goes beyond the 1951 Convention.[1] In Latin America a similar approach has been adopted.[2] Of the main institutional actors in this field perhaps the most revealing development is the operational practice of the UNHCR. It was originally designed as a organization for refugee protection, but in the last decade has seen its role expand into a more broadly humanitarian one. Its largest donors are northern states. Increasingly they are stressing that refugees should remain as close to their states of origin as possible. This 'regionalization', and in some cases 'internalization', of migration has pushed the UNHCR into situations which go beyond its remit, strictly defined. It now works with the internally displaced, and in the 1990s has been involved in consideration, and active promotion, of the 'prevention' of forced displacement. The practical result is that while states in Europe narrow their understanding of responsibility, the UNHCR is being asked to venture far beyond the confines of the legal construction of refugee in other regions. This has caused problems within the organization and dissent has been voiced (Anon, 1997). Both inside and outside the organization there is a belief that it has lost its way. In pursuing a more expansive humanitarian agenda it has moved away from its core function of refugee protection. This is correctly viewed as one part of the law and politics of containment. The UNHCR, as one of the prime sites of knowledge production in refugee law, has been used to legitimize a policy of containment. At its most stark this has involved developed states in financing the UNHCR to keep refugees and asylum seekers out of their territories. In practice the UNHCR has been mandated by the UN to deal with a variety of forms of forced displacement, a practice which stands in sharp contrast to the policies adopted by European states on their own territory. The states that finance refugee protection want results from their investment. At present they are demanding a reduction in the numbers of asylum seekers reaching their territories.

Despite the attempt to 'universalize' the concept of the refugee, by the addition the 1967 Protocol, refugee recognition depends on the context within which it is sought. In other words, while international refugee law offers a legal definition, the refugee emerges in practice from within the institutional and other contexts of states. Insights into the current regime are thus dependent on an understanding of the geopolitics of refugee law and the prevailing conditions within states.

ASYLUM IN THE EUROPEAN UNION

The decision to cooperate on asylum policy in the EU follows from the desire to create free movement within an internal market. The iconic status of the concept of the internal market is the driving force of policy development. EU asylum policy is not the result of a humanitarian imperative of collective action to resolve the problems of the forcibly displaced, but a direct consequence of other policy priorities. The term 'flanking measure' is revealing. EU asylum law and policy is, however, rather more than an afterthought. For supranationalism requires a process of boundary drawing just as much as nationalism (see Fitzpatrick, 1998: 27–45). Membership and belonging in the EU creates exclusion and the fact that distinctions are made is too often neglected in the literature. Inclusivity has it limits within EU constitutional discourse, and exclusion is inscribed in the process. The gaze of policy makers in the EU is now firmly directed at the activities of refugees and asylum seekers. The grand narrative of 'abuse' feeds distrust and helps nurture a culture of hostility towards 'strangers'. National political struggles over the terms of asylum policy are now reflected, and legitimized, at the regional level. This makes transnational political struggle essential.

Given the ambitious aims of the EU, an asylum policy was always going to be on the supranational agenda. It is in the nature of the enterprise that the EU will construct a boundary between 'us' and 'them'. Where this is drawn, and how the mechanism to ensure inclusion is constructed, does not negate the basic fact that these distinctions will be made. This cannot be wished away. The point is that the logic of inclusion/exclusion is inscribed in the move to a supranationalism governed by law. As the EU constructs a self-understanding as a protective supranational entity, which guarantees freedom, security and justice to those who belong, so discourses of exclusion will be deployed against those both inside and outside who do not. Mapping the mechanisms of exclusion is now essential work.

The entry into force of the Treaty of Amsterdam (TOA) should result in a more focused debate on asylum in the coming years. With the amendments to the EC Treaty asylum is now to be found within the EU's 'First Pillar'. States are required to adopt, in the coming years, measures, for example, on minimum standards for granting or withdrawing refugee status. A number of existing problems have not been eradicated and problems of institutional design may well result in further delay. Although expectations have been raised, and some are optimistic, there is little evidence that it will produce a major shift in the basic direction of EU migration policy (Collinson, 1993; Hathaway, 1993; Joly, 1996). The Action Plan on how best to create the area of 'freedom, security and justice' does not appear to herald any major change of basic direction in the field (*Migration News Sheet* January 1999: 1). A Special Council meeting in Tampere in October 1999 did see states commit themselves to a 'full and inclusive' interpretation of refugee law but, as the previous discussion should make clear, such paper commitments are easy to make in this field.

Enlargement will depend on the ability of new member states to follow the EU's lead in immigration and asylum matters. Resources are being targeted at the achievement of this aim. The European Commission, along with a number of other groups, including the German Federal Refugee Office, has announced a new EU project to strengthen the capacity of Central and Eastern European countries to apply EU measures on asylum and immigration (*Migration News Sheet* March 1999: 9). It is clear that the process of enlargement will have a significant impact on the protection of refugees and asylum seekers in Europe. While the extension of the harmonization process will raise standards in some European states, existing weaknesses in the EU regime will be exported.

One of the principal criticisms of EU policy is the resort to informality in areas such as immigration and asylum. As indicated, the measures adopted have largely been of a non-legally binding nature. While this has not prevented an extensive debate and voluminous literature emerging, it has had implications for the accountability of decision making. It offers little scope for a legal challenge to the broad trends in EU policy. In practice, however, the architecture of the EU regime is in place and can be identified. There are problems that will impede its development. It is notable that Article 63 refers to minimum standards only. States may adopt higher standards which diverge. The five-year transitional period is also likely to prove problematic. The requirement of unanimity has slowed things down in the past. There is little reason to believe that this will change over the coming years. The ability of some states to opt in or opt out, while respectful of the idea of flexibility, will exacerbate the lack of uniformity. Given the expansion of the EU, flexibility may become a key term in the years ahead.

The EU is now, post-Amsterdam, defined as an area of freedom, security and justice, in which the free movement of persons is assured in conjunction with appropriate measures with respect to external border controls, immigration, asylum and the prevention and combating of crime. On institutional change the K. 4 Committee has been replaced by the Council Strategic Committee on Immigration, Frontiers and Asylum. The General Affairs Council in December 1998 approved the establishment of the High Level Working Group on Asylum and Immigration. This is a group of high-level civil servants who will be presenting Action Plans to deal with migration from six areas: Morocco; Iraq; Albania/Kosovo; Afghanistan/Pakistan; Sri Lanka; and Somalia. Action Plans have already been produced on, for example, Iraq. This group operates on a cross-pillar basis and formulates what are intended to be comprehensive approaches to migration management.

Measures on asylum are to be adopted in accordance with the 1951 Convention and the 1967 Protocol. There is also a reference to 'other relevant treaties'. The European Convention on Human Rights 1950 (ECHR) is of particular relevance given the EU's expressed commitment to its fundamental human rights guarantees. The adoption of an EU Charter of Rights would internalize, more securely, the productive tensions highlighted in this article. The Action Plan of the Council and the Commission and the

Presidency Conclusions from Tampere provide an insight into thinking about ways forward. There is recognition that immigration law and asylum law are distinct and that the measures adopted suffer from two weaknesses: they are based on 'soft law' and the monitoring arrangements are inadequate. Priority in the area is to be attached to combating illegal immigration and ensuring the integration and rights of those third-country nationals legally present in the EU. As to priorities, the Action Plan lists measures that are to be taken within two years of the entry into force of the TOA. In the asylum field this includes the adoption of minimum standards on procedures for granting or withdrawing refugee status and defining minimum standards on the reception of asylum seekers. Measures to be 'taken as quickly as possible in accordance with the provisions of the Treaty' include minimum standards for giving temporary protection to displaced persons from third countries who cannot return to their country of origin and promoting a balance of effort in receiving and bearing the consequences of receiving displaced persons. Further measures are listed to be adopted within five years.

RESISTANCE WITHIN 'THE FORTRESS'

The dominant logic of EU asylum policy presents significant problems for social movements seeking to resist its consequences. One should not, however, underestimate the opportunities to exploit tensions and promote a more humane response. If there is a problem with the current legal literature in refugee law it is the failure to acknowledge the work and importance of social movements struggling within 'the Fortress'. Resistance to the dominant logic exists.

It should be clear that the asylum debate in the EU is at an important stage. In the transition from 'soft' to 'hard' law a struggle is taking place over the precise shape of EU policy. The law and politics of exclusion will intensify, and serious questions are being raised about the extent to which the logic of exclusion is inscribed in the process. To understand the debate requires knowledge of the institutional dynamics of the EU. But it is also important to note the transnational networks of social movements that already exist. The image of 'Fortress Europe' can downplay the strength of existing migrant networks in Europe. These networks have been engaged in transnational political activism on the asylum issue for some time. The idea of a transnational politics is already a reality. There are a number of important migrant networks in the EU. On refugee and asylum policy there is the European Consultation on Refugees and Exiles (ECRE). ECRE is an umbrella organization of NGOs. It was established in 1974, and it now has over 60 member agencies in 23 countries. The member agencies include all the national refugee councils in Europe. ECRE has an office in Brussels which is headed by a representative whose main functions include lobbying the institutions of the EU on refugee issues. ECRE's objective is:

to promote through joint analysis, research and information exchange, a humane and generous asylum policy in Europe. ECRE is concerned with the needs of individuals who seek asylum in Europe and the development of a comprehensive response to the global refugee problem.

In 1985 ECRE established the European Legal Network on Asylum (ELENA) to serve as a forum for legal practitioners in this field. ELENA has national coordinators who meet annually. Amnesty International (AI) is also active in the EU debate, and has an EU Office that deals with EU refugee and asylum law and policy. As with ECRE the AI EU office is engaged in extensive lobbying on refugee issues in the EU. In this work AI can draw on its extensive network of national activists. Periodic meetings are held in Brussels with the EU representatives from national sections. The representatives from each national section can then lobby government officials at the national level. During the Council meeting in Tampere in October 1999 ECRE held a parallel event in the same location, and its work had an impact on the final text adopted. There are networks in existence that function transnationally and engage with policy formulation and advocacy within the EU. The accountability of actors in these networks is open to debate as is their representativeness. It should not be forgotten that some NGOs are working to their own agendas when engaging in the refugee and asylum debate. In addition, one should not underestimate the structural impediments to transnational political struggle. Technology may assist but does not resolve these basic problems. While the EU may suffer from a democratic deficit there is a general, and more deeply rooted, accountability gap.

Inclusion can raise other problems. With 'mainstreaming' as the new, and rather unfortunate, label for thorough institutional change, there is a problem of co-option. Critical voices may be lost in the general clamour for inclusion. Perhaps it is time to consider the advantages of perpetual critical 'irritants' in law and policy formation. It can be the case that the agendas of social movements are effectively set by the institutions of the EU rather than affected groups. The close relationship between lobbyists and the EU institutions is one feature of this institutional context (Geddes, 1998: 695). If, as I suggest, legal discourse is viewed as contested territory then we should be less uncomfortable with dissident voices that refuse to be co-opted even within the new participatory processes of 'mainstreaming'.

Measuring the impact of this transnational activism on policy formulation is difficult. In the past it is clear from the documentation of, for example, ECRE that they have been disappointed by the process. Questions have been raised about the way that the EU debate is structured. Favell (1998) views the use of the label 'Fortress Europe' as a deliberate political fiction created by actors who can benefit from the image of control it fosters. His argument is that the image of control that this fiction creates is impossible to guarantee. As theorists of the decline of the nation state have reminded us, one of the key themes of the process is the loss of steering capacity. According to Favell, use of the metaphor guarantees an expansion of power and resources to these agents. His suggestion is that the participants are engaged in a discourse that reinforces, rather than undermines, traditional assumptions about notions of European identity. Favell provides an insight into the way that institutional actors perpetuate old metaphors rather than attempt more persuasive redescriptions. This is a warning about where excessive concentration on mapping the priorities of EU institutions can lead. The institutional factors that encourage this are thus brought to the fore. However, Favell's 'realism' is partial and at times wide of the mark. While transnational migrant networks have power, and are making a contribution to the Europeanization of immigration and asylum politics, states retain the dominant voice in this narrative. To concentrate on the instrumental aspects of the work of migrant networks ignores the normative content of this critical activity. This cannot be exclusively defined as manipulation of available resources. There is an abundance of empirical evidence to support the metaphorical use of 'Fortress Europe'. Specifically this is evident in the deployment of visa controls and carrier sanctions. In situations where displacement is likely or ongoing the trend is to impose visa controls on individuals coming from that state. When combined with carrier sanctions this can lead to violations of recognized principles of international law (Nicholson, 1997). The more problematic trend here is the privatization of control evident in such policies. The grand rhetoric surrounding borders collapses when states use the private sector to enforce their immigration control imperatives. Concepts such as 'safe third countries' and 'manifestly unfounded' applications are being deployed to achieve these ends. The preferred option is to link these to accelerated appeals processes. The existing evidence is that these accelerated procedures are not particularly effective in achieving the ends of states. One need only look to the UK's arrangements for evidence of this. Welfare restriction is also a recognizable aspect of the policy response. This raises legitimate concerns about violations of economic and social rights (Cholewinski, 1998). In the governance of asylum states are prepared to be imaginative in the application of their desired policy aims. The failure to achieve policy goals is, however, more instructive and this is where Favell's work is of interest. One could be forgiven, when viewing the array of legal and policy tools applied to control refugee movements, that the idea of a 'Fortress Europe' is far from a political fiction. The 'realist' argument advanced by Favell is not, however, devoid of merit. There is in the 'Fortress Europe' metaphor a substantial overestimation of the regulatory capacities of modern states (and even their success in these practices). This is borne out in the available empirical evidence. Borders are more porous than these images would lead one to believe. Reality is more complex than the images permit. Those who wish to transcend the nation state in one context must be careful not to reify its alleged abilities in others. For fluidity is a two-way street. This image also underplays the extent to which there has been some success in confronting restriction at a number of levels. In other words, social movements and individuals have used human rights discourse, and legal strategies of resistance, with some limited success. Given the existing substance of the EU policy response the metaphor does, however, remain applicable.

The image of 'Fortress Europe' may well operate as a political fiction but there is more to it. There is ample empirical evidence that EU states are attempting to insulate themselves from forced migration. Social movements in the EU are faced with a formidable hegemonic narrative of asylum. The complexity of human migration is reduced to a simple tale of abuse. The realist critique of the metaphorical use of 'Fortress Europe' does raise an important issue. For social movements must be careful not to perpetuate practices by legitimizing distorted stories about asylum in Europe.

There is no single strategy that is appropriate to challenge this dominant logic. What is appropriate is a highly contextualized form of pragmatism that actively seeks to disrupt this logic and offers redescriptions and narratives that unsettle this thinking. This will often involve appeals to values other than human rights. For example, in the refugee debate in Ireland some participants have drawn extensively on international solidarity and thus the past treatment of Irish migrants. The emphasis in this argument is on a global ethic of localized responsibility based upon shared experience. As we see in the next section, rights discourse has, however, proven useful in certain contexts in challenging aspects of asylum policy.

ASYLUM AND THE POLITICS OF HUMAN RIGHTS

As I argue in this article, it is important not to lose sight of the struggles within Europe over asylum policy. This is evident in the law and politics of asylum seekers' rights. Although there is increasing resort to human rights discourse in EU law and policy this has not impacted seriously thus far on refugees and asylum seekers (De Búrca, 1995: 34–5). This may change with the recent alterations to the EC Treaty which make more concrete references to refugee and human rights law in the development of asylum policy. With talk of an EU Charter of Rights the language of rights is likely to figure more prominently in the EU migration debate in the future.

How is the language of human rights used in the asylum context in Europe? In answering this question it is important to remember a point made earlier. Refugee law does not have an international monitoring body that would offer guidance on the consistent application of its norms. There is no mechanism within the legal regime to challenge national restriction. Refugees and asylum seekers must rely on conducive domestic contexts. The struggle over the politics of asylum is largely a national one. However, international human rights mechanisms are becoming more important. The significance of human rights law rests in its multilevel nature. It exists at the national, regional and international levels. At each level institutional mechanisms exist to confront state policy. There are many practical problems involved in making use of these mechanisms. They do, however, open up political spaces by ensuring that state policy remains contested. Because of the focus on 'personhood' rather than nationality, refugees and asylum seekers have been able to make use of these mechanisms.

The aim in this part of the article is to explore how the ECHR is used to challenge national asylum policy. First, I explore the deployment of human rights discourse in the asylum context and, second, in the process begin to think critically about human rights law. This is not to neglect other mechanisms that have been used productively, such as the processes of the UN Committee against Torture and the UN Human Rights Committee (Andryzek, 1997). It is evident that a range of international mechanisms are put to work in political and legal struggles against restriction. In the political struggle against legal restriction social movements have been able, in this sphere, to construct solid strategies of argumentation anchored in human rights discourse.

Refugees and asylum seekers have turned to national protection, regional mechanisms and international human rights law in an attempt to challenge policy developments. In this, social movements are making productive use of the tension inscribed in the process of boundary drawing. For the regulation of membership in political communities is in tension with what I term 'borderless' strains of liberalism and the language of human rights. There is nothing new about this observation. Arendt was fully aware of the tension when she wrote about refugee movements of the 20th century (Arendt, 1973: 267–302). As she noted, abstract commitments to 'human' rights were called into question by state responses to a group which relied exclusively on its 'humanity' as the basis for legal protection. Her argument has a modern resonance:

> The conception of human rights, based upon the assumed existence of a human being as such, broke down at the very moment when those who professed to believe in it were for the first time confronted with people who had indeed lost all other qualities and specific relationships – except that they were still human. *The world found nothing sacred in the abstract nakedness of being human.* (Arendt, 1973: 299, emphasis added)

Arendt is here referring to the fact that refugees rely on the promises held out by internationalism and universalism. In this context the empirical reality did not match the proclaimed 'core values' of states. Rather than accept a purely nationally based model of rights, or an exclusively international model, there is merit in stressing the relational nature of the national/international and local/global. As I suggest, there is a tension between the rights of citizens and the rights of persons which manifests itself in political struggles over the meaning of rights discourse. These concrete political struggles are not, I argue, confined purely to the national level. Refugees and asylum seekers are able to make use of the identified tension by calling into question the scope and substance of constructions of membership. The ideal community of entitlement in human rights discourse is constructed on notions of personhood rather than membership. This exists in a world still solidly divided in law along national lines. At the national level restrictive interpretations of refugee law can be challenged and, as noted above, asylum seekers have had some success in domestic courts. As a group they can also avail themselves of protections afforded by constitutional law. Success has been achieved by trying to detach the refugee debate from immigration control and stressing, to representatives and decision makers, the value of making links to international human rights standards. What are the implications of this form of human rights activism? The increasing proliferation of human rights norms at all levels, and their creative use, has led some to suggest that we are in fact witnessing a move to postnational membership defined with reference not to nationality but to personhood (Soysal, 1994, 1996). This normative framework gains concrete expression, not solely within the formal laws and institutions of democracy, but by its continued deployment in informal arenas. Social movements make persistent use of these instruments to critique flawed practice at the local level. What is also of interest is that the international practice drawn upon does not have to be regarded as international law. Creative use has been made of international guidelines and other non-binding standards to persuade institutional actors, operating in specific national contexts, to pursue changes in direction. A feature of the human rights debate is that standards that would not meet any legal positivist's sources test have an impact beyond their formal legal status. In fact, human rights NGOs often draw on a wide range of 'sources' to construct their argumentation. This process can have a significant political impact. Migrant and representative groups have drawn heavily on *human* rights discourse with some success in Europe. This picture is a complex one, with many overlapping normative orders coexisting. In practice, however, social movements in Europe have used the available avenues of redress in imaginative ways to deploy discourses of personhood against restrictive practice. As I have stressed, this is not a simple story of transcending to a higher plane of internationalism. This a story of the productive deployment of international discourses, drawing upon transnational networks, to exploit tensions within national contexts.

The accountability problems in EU policy formation have impacted on the potential for legal challenges to the processes. Political challenges have occurred, however. While there have been attempts to embed human rights concerns at the political level of policy development, it has been difficult to tackle core elements of the process. This is evident in, for example, the adoption of the safe third country notion. The basic premise in the EU's use of the safe third country notion is that there is sufficient common practice already. This is inaccurate. The English case of *R* v *Secretary of State, ex parte Adan* [1999] is a useful example of the problems that can arise. The appellants were threatened with return to France and Germany on the basis that both these states were safe third countries. The problem was that both France and Germany had a markedly different approach to the interpretation of the 1951 Convention from the UK. While the UK recognizes that asylum seekers who fear persecution by non-state agents are entitled to protection under refugee law, France and Germany do not. The appellants in this case risked ultimate return to their state of origin if the safe third country concept was applied. The Court of Appeal held that France and Germany were not safe third countries within the meaning of UK asylum law. The judgment asserts that international refugee law has a 'true meaning' which was not being applied by France and Germany. What we have in this case is an example of a national court using internationalism against a process of regional integration. This is a form of internationalism adopted, in this case, for 'nationalist' purposes. It permitted the Court of Appeal to indulge in criticism of interpretations of refugee law adopted within France and Germany.

Those seeking to confront state restriction in this area are increasingly drawn to the array of international human rights mechanisms. Again one should try to avoid inflated claims, or generalizations, about the potential of international human rights mechanisms. They have their uses but also their limits. To take one example, the UN Convention Against Torture and Other Cruel, Inhuman or Degrading Treatment or Punishment 1984[3] has been used by those seeking to challenge the asylum and expulsion practices of states in particular to challenge some of the tests that are being applied in the asylum context. For example, in *Haydin* v *Sweden* [1997], the applicant, a Turkish asylum seeker, made a number of unsuccessful asylum requests in Sweden. The Swedish authorities regarded the inconsistencies in his testimony as diminishing his credibility. The Committee in this instance, as in other cases, stressed that complete accuracy is seldom to be expected of torture victims, especially when the victim suffers from post-traumatic stress syndrome. The Committee concluded that substantial grounds had been shown that he would be in danger of being subjected to torture on return. The point is that this international human rights mechanism can be used by individuals to remedy restriction. Many other examples could be provided of the way this international mechanism has been deployed to challenge the treatment of asylum seekers. What is noteworthy, for the purpose of this article, is that in many of the asylum cases that come before the UN Committee Against Torture the individual has been processed by the domestic asylum system and declared not to be a refugee. The Committee's work in the asylum field often highlights the limitations of refugee law.

The ECHR has always been a promising instrument for asserting migrants' rights. This is not least because the Convention specifically provides that states are obliged to 'secure to everyone within their jurisdiction the rights and freedoms defined in Section I of this Convention' (Art. 1). Rights that have proved of particular use in the context under examination in this article include Articles 3, 5, 8, as well as Protocol 4 Articles 3 and 4, and Protocol 7 Article 1 (Mole, 1997). The developing Convention jurisprudence raises a number of issues for refugee protection. At the level of strategy it offers an 'international' avenue of redress, in particular, with regard to the challenge presented to refugee law's limitations and exceptions, even to its most valuable protections.[4] In this it does not stand alone. The European Committee for the Prevention of Torture has commented on the detention of asylum seekers, and immigration detainees generally, in Europe (CPT/Inf (97) 10). The UN Human Rights Committee has followed the approach of the European human rights bodies in its own interpretation of Article 7.[5] This demonstrates that social movements are not the only ones engaged in transnational conversations about the terms of legal discourse.

Article 3 ECHR has proven useful to asylum seekers in Europe. This is because it includes the protection of those threatened with extradition and expulsion even where they have been accused of being involved in activity that would normally warrant deportation (Egan, 1998; Einarsen, 1990). Even though the prohibition on *non-refoulement* in refugee law is frequently described as the cornerstone of the regime, there are exceptions to this norm. For example, Article 33(2) permits *refoulement* where 'there are reasonable grounds for regarding [her] as a danger to the security of the country...' Given the securitization of migration in Europe this presents a significant problem, and is why Article 3 ECHR has become so important. As an absolute prohibition it has closed a gap in refugee law while opening up problems for states wishing to divest themselves of an individual who they believe is a threat to security. This is not to undermine the importance of other Convention rights. Article 8 is relevant to those seeking to challenge deportation on the ground that it will deprive them of their right to family life (Sherlock, 1998). What the Article 3 jurisprudence highlights is the difference between a body of law constructed from contingent historical compromises, with interpretation delegated to individual states (refugee law), and an equally contingent human rights instrument equipped with its own supervisory mechanism (ECHR). The latter creates international institutions with a vested interest in the progressive development of the law and with reconstructions which take the instrument into every sphere of state activity. The contrast between the development of the two international regimes is marked. However, on occasion the judiciary at the national level do find this a useful area to promote their self-understanding as defenders of unpopular minorities. Contrary to what is often stated in general texts on constitutional law, the judiciary have in recent years not been exclusively deferential in this field. While we might accept the practical and immediate result, we also should acknowledge that it is an aspect of what Unger (1996: 72) has described as law's 'dirty little secret'. That is, law's 'discomfort with democracy' (pp. 72–3). One reason for judicial activism in this sphere is that it fits neatly into the institution's dominant self-understanding. The tension identified between national inclusion and human rights discourse maps onto judicial anti-majoritarianism. This institutionalized discomfort with a version of democracy has been exploited by refugee and asylum advocates. Courts are thus given a suitably noble (minority rights protection) justification for their own political activism. This may be cast as excessive cynicism but it appears to be a plausible explanation for judicial activism in this area. It also challenges directly some of the assumptions made in this field. More significantly, it is an explanation that maps developments in legal doctrine onto the changing nature of judicial politics.

TAKING THE STRUGGLE TO 'EUROPE': THE USES AND LIMITATIONS OF THE EUROPEAN CONVENTION ON HUMAN RIGHTS IN THE ASYLUM CONTEXT

One of the most important needs of asylum seekers is a guarantee that they will not be returned to their state of origin. This is reflected in refugee and human rights law in the modern development of the norm of *non-refoulement*. The judicial development of a prohibition on return renders the ECHR highly relevant to the asylum debate in Europe. Whether this makes refugee law peripheral is doubtful, however. For the ECHR is principally concerned with civil and political rights and offers no concrete status to those who are not returned. The difference that continues to matter is that refugee law is a status-granting mechanism which includes guarantees on economic and social rights. This is why states are often so determined to avoid using it. While it is important to probe the use of rights discourse, through an analysis of the ECHR, it is equally essential not to join the general assault on refugee law. It is now the established position under Article 3 ECHR that an individual cannot be extradited or expelled where substantial grounds are shown for believing there would be a real risk to the individual of torture or inhuman or degrading treatment or punishment in the receiving country. Whatever the difficulties involved in bringing a case before the court one practical point must be stressed. In practice states have responded to an application to Strasbourg by reaching a settlement with the applicant.[6] Making use of the ECHR can matter in practice irrespective of whether the case ever reaches the court. This is important for a number of reasons, not least because it encourages us to view the construction of legality beyond the courts. Issues surrounding the practical construction of Convention rights must be located in a context where individuals can use the system pragmatically to achieve their objectives and prevent return in concrete terms. The arguments have a political force in practice that can be neglected in some assessments of the meaning of human rights law.

For the purpose of this article it is necessary to explore the Convention jurisprudence to assess the extent of the impact but also the way rights discourse is used. In extradition cases the principle of non-return was first applied by the court in *Soering* v *UK* [1989], although it had been adopted by the commission before then. In *Cruz Varas* v *Sweden* [1991] the court extended the principle to include the expulsion of asylum seekers. In *Soering* the applicant argued that his extradition to the US would breach Article 3 because of exposure to the death row phenomenon. The court acknowledged the territorial limits of the Convention but stated, in line with its well-established approach, that its provisions had to be interpreted so that they were practical and effective. Special regard had to be had to the character of the ECHR as a human rights instrument and its 'general spirit'. It would not rest easily with the 'spirit' of the Convention if a state was permitted to return an individual to torture elsewhere. The court did not restrict its applicability to torture, stating that it also applied to cases where the fugitive would be subject to inhuman or degrading treatment or punishment. This is where things become more obscure in the judgment and the court refers only to the individual circumstances to determine whether return would he inhuman or degrading. The court held that return would violate Article 3. The extent of Article 3 is uncertain in the case and crucial aspects of the court's reasoning are unclear. The introduction of terms like 'fair balance' is problematic if, as is often stated, Article 3 is an absolute protection. Its use in the case is surprising given the court's consistent emphasis on the fact that no justification exists for its violation. In effect the court was confronted with a problem which could not easily be located within traditional understandings of international legality and responsibility. The ill-treatment would occur in a state that was not a party to the Convention. In strictly contractual terms, the ill-treatment escaped the jurisdiction of the human rights regime. In its desire to make Convention rights both practical and effective the court preferred a more expansive approach to Article 3. The more ethically defensible conception of responsibility that it adopted is a broadly based one. The UK was responsible for the foreseeable consequences upon extradition. The critical reaction to the judgment was inspired by relative unease at the departure from a contractualism that some viewed as underpinning the legitimacy of the Convention system. The court had, through its jurisprudence on Article 3, engineered an expansion of the duties of states at a time when many were actively engaged in building restrictive asylum policies. The construction of Article 3 which it adopted pushed the boundaries of the right outward to achieve the desired result. This highlighted the 'elasticity' of Convention rights and their contested nature, as well as the potential for further expansion. *Soering* is correctly viewed as one of the most important cases the court has decided and it has had important implications for refugees and asylum seekers. The court has spent some time trying to clarify the precise meaning of its original judgment. In making these judgments the court cannot but be aware that it might become a surrogate for national decision making. In setting the standard at a relatively high level the court has attempted to prevent this. While the court broadened the scope of Article 3, it was careful to set the standard of proof at a sufficiently high level. The court is an important institutional actor whose judgments are ineluctably shaped by the institutional and political context within which it functions. Increasingly its judgments must be located within the new political and legal orders of Europe. In this role the court is clearly struggling with the problem of consistency in its interpretation of some key Convention rights.

After *Soering* the need for clarification was apparent. In *Cruz Varas* the applicants were Chilean nationals who had sought and were refused asylum in Sweden. In finding that Article 3 would not be violated the court differed from the commission. In this case the court again clearly signalled an intent not to become a surrogate for national decision making.

Soon after the court was called upon again to rule on similar issues in a case that involved the UK. Again this demonstrated its concern with setting the boundaries of Article 3 at 'acceptable limits'. In *Vilvarajah and Others* v *UK* [1991] the five applicants were Sri Lankan Tamils whose claims for asylum were rejected in the UK. They were subsequently deported to Sri Lanka where three of them were subjected to torture and other ill-treatment while in detention. The court noted that its assessment of the foreseeable consequences of the removal of the applicants at the relevant time had to be a rigorous one. The court took into account that at the relevant time a UNHCR voluntary repatriation programme had begun and stated that the applicant's personal situation was no worse than other members of the Tamil community. The attempt to delimit the scope of protection is evident in this language. Submerged is an understanding of limits and the pragmatics of refugee protection in an 'unjust world'. This is a story of tragic choices. The court is giving voice to a desire to hold disorder at bay by looking to the singular and particular aspects of the case and the factors that single an individual out for ill-treatment. The focus on particularity has rather more general implications and this reconstruction must be seen for what it is: a choice in a context where other reconstructions are possible. The fact that two of the applicants were returned to Sri Lanka without identity cards, because of failures by the UK authorities, again did not give rise to a real risk of Article 3 ill-treatment. As in *Cruz Varas* the court attached significance to the fact that the UK had experience in this area and thus displayed a willingness to defer to its knowledge. The approach is, however, tied to its own legitimacy and place within a European political and legal order. The case was disappointing, as it clearly placed the requirement at a particularly high threshold. The test is an exacting one which stands in sharp contrast to that applied in some jurisdictions on the applicability of refugee law. Here it seems to be the accepted position that a 'reasonable chance' or 'likelihood' of persecution will suffice. This differs from the real risk required under the ECHR.

Should we be surprised at such results? The court, as an institutional actor, was conscious of becoming a 'surrogate' for national protection systems and rapidly moved to establish an 'exceptional standard'. The court sent out a clear message that it is to the asylum systems in states that individuals must look for secure protection. This emphasis on national decision makers is not confined to asylum cases and it rather undercuts some of the arguments examined here about the potential of transnational human rights activism. However, it should be remembered that the court is only one institutional actor among many. Given that Article 3 is so often held out as an example of the principled and absolute nature of some Convention rights, this infusion of pragmatism is instructive. It raises interesting questions about the court's willingness to construct boundaries for itself, thus replicating a core/penumbra division that in its own work it has shown not to exist. In other words, by its actions the court has demonstrated the malleable nature of Convention jurisprudence. Internally, however, the court must construct a form of autolimitation that legitimizes its social practice. It is in this sense a skilled practitioner of reconstruction. This also reflects a fear of politics which suggests there is something above and beyond it. Much of this is familiar. Politics stands, in lawyers' eyes, as the realm of the indeterminate and chaotic. This conception of the political gestures towards a quasi-theological and premodern image of law. A modern understanding would be content with the contested nature of the legal (and thus comfortable with the 'political') and a focus on inclusive dialogue within a deliberative legal community. Formal enactment is not the end of the story but we should observe carefully who is attempting to have the last word. Although some jurists correctly point to the argumentative nature of legal discourse, there is a sense in which orthodox work in the human rights sphere spurns critical dialogue in its search for legitimacy. It would be odd indeed if human rights lawyers were to abandon critical reason in their own search for institutional inclusion and political acceptability.

The securitization of migration is one aspect of the EU's evolution into a protective supranational entity. EU citizens require protection against external and internal threats. Asylum is clearly constructed as a threat to the security of the EU. The link between security and asylum has had serious practical implications as asylum seeking is effectively 'criminalized' in Europe. As suggested earlier in this article, asylum seeking has been problematized to the extent that punitive measures are deemed entirely appropriate. The clearest example of what this can mean in practice is the detention of asylum seekers but it is also evident in policies of welfare restriction (Hughes and Liebaut, 1998). Perhaps the case of most relevance to this issue, and one that demonstrates how human rights law can offer more effective protection than refugee law is *Chahal* v *UK* [1996]. Chahal, a leading figure in the Sikh community in the UK, was a political activist engaged in passive resistance in support of autonomy for Punjab. He was detained pending deportation from the UK for reasons of national security. The court found a violation of Articles 3, 5(4) and 13. The result demonstrates the usefulness of the ECHR, although it is worth noting that Chahal spent a total of six years in detention. Of interest is the strong emphasis on the need for effective domestic remedies in these cases. While the result shows the advantages of the Convention system it confirms that the court is of the view that asylum seekers should look primarily to national protection systems.

The case drew attention to one of the problems with refugee law discussed above. For the regime permits exclusion and return even where the threat of ill-treatment in the state of origin continues. In contrast to human rights law, refugee law contains a distinction between the 'deserving' and the 'undeserving' refugee. This causes discomfort to human rights lawyers in particular. The further problems with gaps in refugee law are evident in the cases that have followed *Chahal*. In *Ahmed* v *Austria* [1996] the applicant was granted refugee status. This was subsequently forfeited after he was sentenced for his involvement in an attempted robbery. The court placed great weight on the fact that he had been granted refugee status in Austria and that this was withdrawn solely because of his criminal activity. The case provides confirmation of the fact that persecution need not come from state agents only. The persecution arose as a consequence of a civil war in which rival clans were vying for power. In addition there was an absence of a public authority which could offer some protection to him.[7] This case confirmed the position adopted in *Chahal* by acknowledging that even where the individual has been engaged in criminal activity in the asylum state this has no bearing on the assessment of risk for Article 3 purposes. The principle clashes markedly with traditional statist views of migration law. In *HLR* v *France* [1997] the applicant was involved in drug smuggling and claimed that his return to Colombia would violate Article 3 because of treatment he expected to receive from other drug traffickers due to his cooperation with the French authorities. In finding that there would be no violation of Article 3 the court did not believe that a real risk had been demonstrated, or that the applicant's situation was any worse than that of other Colombians (cf. Judge Pekkanen, joined by Judges Thor Viljalmsson, Lopes Rocha and Lohmus dissenting). He had, the court stated, also failed to show that the Colombian authorities were incapable of affording him appropriate protection. The case reveals that the standards applicable in these cases are exacting ones and the court is again setting pragmatic limits on the provision. As further evidence of this concern, in *Bahaddar* v *the Netherlands* [1998] the court stated that although Article 3 was absolute the applicant is not thereby dispensed, as a matter of course, from exhausting available and effective domestic remedies and from complying with the formal requirements and time limits laid down in domestic law. The court concluded that the applicant's lawyers had not complied with domestic law time limits and failed to request an extension. Even after the time limit had expired she had not lodged a fresh application even though this was possible in domestic law. The court concluded that domestic remedies had not been exhausted under Article 26.

The principle as applied by the court has implications that go beyond the fact situations discussed thus far. This was demonstrated in *D* v *UK* [1997] when the court held that the removal of a terminally ill individual to St Kitts (his country of origin), where he had no accommodation, family, moral or financial support, or access to adequate medical treatment, would violate Article 3. Again the approach of the court follows a principle already established in the commission's jurisprudence. While in this case it was lack of medical care or facilities which was material, social or environmental factors were also recognized by the commission as possibly giving rise to an issue under Article 3. This opens up a number of themes under this provision. In particular whether, for example, the serious denial of economic and social rights in the state of origin might lead to a violation of Article 3. The incremental approach of the court may not go far beyond the boundaries it has established thus far. By pushing the borders of Article 3 outwards the court is inviting novel argumentation which would nudge it even further in this direction. Why not adopt a more inclusive approach which embraces economic and social rights? Institutional factors, and the wider political and legal context, suggest that the court will continue with the process of autolimitation and the current rational reconstructions of Convention rights. For how could this institutional actor do otherwise? There will be limits to using the established human rights mechanisms. The problems are also structural ones, in the sense that the court is unprepared to challenge the dominant narrative of asylum policy promoted by states. By its past practice, however, it has demonstrated the contested nature of the discourse and thus the potential of continuing engagement.

The examination of some of the case law should indicate how in practice human rights law has been used to give some meaningful expression to the commitment to rights that attach to presence rather than nationality. The focus in these cases is on the risk to the individual upon return rather than her behaviour. If the risk is shown to exist then the individual's activities are not a material factor. One should not, however, overplay the importance of this international protection. The European Convention system remains a long and expensive option and the court is conscious of the number of asylum seekers wishing to challenge state policy. This article presents the court as an institutional actor in the broader European debate on asylum which sets politically pragmatic limits on its own reconstruction of law. The suggestion is that doctrinal development must be contextualized to avoid excessively partial perspectives on human rights law. The point is that the court, as an institutional actor, has implicitly accepted the dominant narrative about the asylum debate in Europe. In recreating a core/penumbra distinction, even where it is so patently lacking, such institutional actors are engaged in a process of self-legitimization. The story accepted within the Convention system is tied ineluctably to narratives of asylum developed at the national level. As I suggest, this is a narrative that is contested. In a strategic move, reminiscent of social scientists who ape the 'scientism' of natural science, the court seeks authority for itself by a process of limitations and boundary drawing. It constructs its legitimacy from the things that it rejects. This approach is also evident in human rights scholarship. Human rights lawyers have adopted an approach that diverges markedly from the totality of legal relations in practice in this area. The dominance of the doctrinal is a partial perspective on the field but one accorded undue scholarly weight in what is regarded as a politically progressive area (see Cotterrell, 1989: 228–31). The result can be human rights law and practice which is strangely unreflective and generally lacking in 'critical bite'.

Focusing squarely on doctrinal work does, however, have its uses and advantages. The jurisprudence of the ECHR does, for example, reveal the weaknesses of refugee law. By using these mechanisms asylum seekers are giving concrete expression to the legal commitment to human rights protection. While this is grounded in the material context of local practices and subject to, often severe, structural constraints, there is a moment of connection in this between the local and, to borrow a phrase from Stychin (1998), the 'relatively universal'. Drawing on a study of rights struggles in Australia he has unearthed the particular problems that arise from the existence of intersecting legal orders. The important point in this is the new avenues that the emergence of rights discourse opens up for international and transnational activism. In other words, rights discourse, in its use by social movements, helps to create the political space for conversations about policy development. It is the disruptive impact of the discourse that is of interest here. For its use ensures that the dialogue about the terms of asylum policy in Europe continues.

Asylum seekers are part of a group for whom rights discourse remains an important site for resistance. There is little doubt that the active social movements operating in this area will continue to make creative use of international mechanisms to achieve their goals. However, human rights scholarship must now begin to move away from inappropriate versions of legal positivism. The complex picture presented by rights discourse deserves a more sophisticated response than most mainstream human rights scholarship seems prepared to offer. Now that human rights has found its place in mainstream legal scholarship it is time for scholars to engage in some critical reflection about the process that brought this about and what the future holds. In practice this is linked with the question of how the human rights movement can retain a critical edge in a world where human rights is becoming a bureaucratized and totally administered system. The recognition given to human rights discourse in its journey from the margins to the mainstream of legal scholarship is important. But the danger is that any critical edge that this discourse has might be lost in a bureaucratized system of monitoring and enforcement that does not deliver on its own promises.

CONCLUSION

The suggestion in this article is that the asylum debate in Europe is best approached through the framework of a dialogic model of law and democracy. This model stresses the disruptive contribution that human rights discourse makes to keeping a critical dialogue going. It promotes 'human rights law without illusions'. Human rights discourse is a malleable tool which does not necessarily have politically progressive consequences. It is, however, in its active use, and thus within political struggles, that human rights law gains its real meaning.

My principal argument in this article is that the dialogic model has both explanatory and critical potential in relation to the uses of human rights discourse in practice. On the explanatory side, it aids in understanding the role of both official and unofficial actors in the human rights sphere. It encourages an interactive understanding of the formation and reconstruction of the meaning of human rights law. The law is thus located in society as a social practice that gains meaning through interpretative struggle. The critical potential springs from the ability to diagnose distorted communication and act upon it. Partial perspectives on human experience can be exposed as such within the context of a continuing conversation about the terms of law and political practice. Too many accounts of human rights law exclude those who make change happen. This can encourage a highly inappropriate form of quietism. The dialogic model brings social movements firmly back into the picture and thus promotes a relational understanding of human rights law and practice.

This article is a modest attempt to examine asylum law within this context. It acknowledges the appalling nature of much of the EU policy response to asylum. The national preoccupation with deterrence and restriction has shifted into the collective logic of the supranational process. But to concentrate exclusively on this is to miss the fact that struggle is ongoing to try to challenge the dominant narratives. This is particularly evident in the politics of rights discourse in Europe. As I argue, rights discourse gains meaning through argumentation and struggle within states and thus is highly contextualized. The use of rights discourse in the asylum debate by states and advocates is instructive. Given the flaws in refugee law it has been put to use in the struggle against restriction in Europe. The picture that emerges from the EU is grim. But it is important not to lose sight of the new political spaces that are emerging within the EU. As suggested, rights discourse can aid in disrupting some of the dominant stories told about asylum seeking in Europe. But it is a discourse that is also used by states to justify restriction and containment. The point is that hard thinking about aims and objectives must precede engagement if the politics of rights is to be successfully negotiated. It is essential that we retain a critical perspective on human rights law and practice that aids progressive political struggle and does not stifle it.

NOTES

This is a revised version of a paper presented at the Rights, Identities and Communities of the European Union workshop held at the University of Leeds in April 1999. I would like to thank Damian Chalmers, Jo Shaw, Carl Stychin and the two anonymous referees for their extremely helpful comments and criticism. I would also like to express my gratitude to John Morison and Kieran McEvoy for their general support and encouragement. I, of course, remain responsible for errors.

1. OAU 1969 Convention on the Specific Aspects of Refugee Protection in Africa 1000 UNTS 46.
2. 1984 Cartagena Declaration on Refugees printed in Goodwin-Gill, (1996: 444–8).
3. See, UNGA 39/46, Article 3. See also UNCAT General Comment on Article 3. See generally: *Haydin* v *Sweden* [1997]; *JUA* v *Switzerland* [1997]; *KN* v *Switzerland* [1997]; *ALN* v *Switzerland* [1997]; *Falalaflaki* v *Sweden* [1997]; *GRB* v *Sweden* [1997]; *IAO* v *Sweden* [1997]; *X, Y, Z* v *Sweden* [1996]; *Abad* v *Spain* [1996]; *HW* v *Switzerland* [1996]; *VV* v *Canada* [1996]; *PQL* v *Canada* [1996]; *R* v *France* [1996]; *D* v *France* [1996]; *RK* v *Canada* [1996]; *EA Switzerland* [1995]; *Mohammed* v *Greece* [1996]; *Tapei Paez* v *Sweden* [1996]; *Tala* v *Sweden* [1996]; *X* v *Switzerland* [1995]; *Aemei* v *Switzerland* [1995]; *X* v *Spain* [1995]; *X* v *Canada* [1995]; *PMPK* v *Sweden* [1995]; *X and Y* v *the Netherlands* [1995]; *ND* v *France* [1995]; *KKH* v *Canada* [1995]; *X* v *the Netherlands* [1995]; *Kisoki* v *Sweden* [1996]; *Mutombo* v *Switzerland* [1993]; *Khan* v *Canada* [1994].
4. Cf. OAU Convention on the Specific Aspects of the Refugee Problem in Africa Article II, there is no exception to the principle of non-return here.
5. See for example *Kindler* v *Canada* [1991] which involved the extradition of an individual; also *Cox* v *Canada* [1993]. See also General Comment 15.
6. For recent examples of this occurring in practice see *El Guarti, Jilali* v *France* [1998]; *Hatami* v *Sweden* [1998]; *Sarialtun, Aziz and Other* v *Germany* [1998].
7. Cf. *Canada (Attorney-General)* v *Ward* [1993] where the Supreme Court of Canada ruled that state complicity was not a prerequisite to a valid refugee claim. The agents of persecution need not be the state. It must, however, be unable to offer protection to its citizens in this context. 'The international community was

meant to be a forum of second resort for the persecuted, a 'surrogate', approachable upon failure of local protection. The rationale upon which international refugee law rests is not simply the need to give shelter to those persecuted by the state but, more widely, to provide refuge to those whose home state cannot or does not afford them protection from persecution. The former is, of course, comprised in the latter, but the drafters of the Convention had the latter, wider purpose in mind. The state's inability to protect the individual from persecution founded on one of the enumerated grounds constitutes failure of local protection' *per* La Forest J. p. 17.

CASES CITED

ALN v *Switzerland* Comm. No. 90/1997
Abad v *Spain* Comm. No. 59/1996
Aemei v *Switzerland* Comm. No. 34/1995
Ahmed v *Austria* [1996] 24 EHRR 278
Bahaddar v *the Netherlands* [1998] 26 EHRR 278
Canada (Attorney-General) v *Ward* 103 DLR 4th 1 [1993]
Chahal v *UK* [1996] 23 EHRR 413
Cox v *Canada* Comm. No. 539/1993
Cruz Varas v *Sweden* [1991] 14 EHRR 24
D v *France* Comm. No. 45/1996
D v *UK* [1997] 24 EHRR 423
EA Switzerland Comm. No. 28/1995
El Guarti, Jilali v *France* Appl. No. 39681/97
Falalaflaki v *Sweden* Comm. No. 89/1997
GRB v *Sweden* Comm. No. 83/1997
Hatami v *Sweden* Appl. No. 32448/96
Haydin v *Sweden* Comm. No. 101/1997
HLR v *France* [1997] 26 EHRR 29
HW v *Switzerland* Comm. No. 48/1996
IAO v *Sweden* Comm. 65/1997
JUA v *Switzerland* Comm. No. 100/1997
KN v *Switzerland* Comm. 94/1997
Khan v *Canada* Comm. No. 15/1994
Kindler v *Canada* Comm. No. 470/1991
Kisoki v *Sweden* Comm. No. 41/1996
KKH v *Canada* Comm. No. 35/1995
Mohammed v *Greece* Comm. No. 40/1996
Mutombo v *Switzerland* Comm. No. 13/1993
ND v *France* Comm. No. 32/1995
PMPK v *Sweden* Comm. No. 30/1995
PQL v *Canada* Comm. No. 57/1996
R v *France* Comm. No. 52/1996
R v *Secretary of State for the Home Department, ex parte Adan The Times* July 28 1999
R v *Immigration Appeal Tribunal and another, ex parte Shah; Islam and others* v *Secretary of State for the Home Department* [1999] 2 All ER 545 (HL)
R v *Uxbridge Magistrates' Court, ex parte Adimi* [1999] 4 All ER 520
RK v *Canada* Comm. No. 42/1996
Sarialtun, Aziz and Other v *Germany* Appl. No. 37534/97

Soering v *UK* [1989] 11 EHRR 439
Tala v *Sweden* Comm. No. 43/1996
Tapei Paez v *Sweden* Comm. No. 39/1996
Vilvarajah and Others v *UK* [1991] 14 EHRR 1
VV v *Canada* Comm. No. 47/1996
X v *Canada* Comm. No. 26/1995
X v *Spain* Comm. No. 23/1995
X v *Switzerland* Comm. No. 27/1995
X v *the Netherlands* Comm. No. 36/1995
X and Y v *the Netherlands* Comm. No. 31/1995
X, Y, Z v *Sweden* Comm. No. 61/1996

REFERENCES

Andryzek, Oldrich (1997) 'Gaps in International Protection and the Potential for Redress through Individual Complaints Procedures', *International Journal of Refugee Law* 9: 392.

Anon (1997) 'The UNHCR Note on International Protection You Won't See', *International Journal of Refugee Law* 9: 267–73.

Arrendt, Hannah (1973) *The Origins of Totalitarianism*. New York and London: Harvest/HBJ.

Bagshaw, Simon (1997) 'Benchmarks or Deutschmarks? Determining the Criteria for the Repatriation of Refugees to Bosnia and Herzegovina', *International Journal of Refugee Law* 10: 566–92.

Beck, Ulrich (1998) 'Democracy Beyond the Nation-State: A Cosmopolitical Manifesto', *Dissent*: 53–5.

Benhabib, Seyla (1992) *Situating the Self: Gender, Community and Postmodernism in Contemporary Ethics*. Cambridge: Polity.

Benhabib, Seyla (1996) 'Toward a Deliberative Model of Democratic Legitimacy', in Seyla Benhabib (ed.) *Democracy and Difference: Contesting the Boundaries of the Political*. Princeton: Princeton University Press.

Bohman, James (1996) *Public Deliberation: Pluralism, Complexity and Democracy*. Cambridge, MA: MIT Press.

Cholewinski, Ryszard (1998) 'Enforced Destitution of Asylum Seekers in the United Kingdom: The Denial of Fundamental Human Rights', *International Journal of Refugee Law* 10: 462–98.

Collinson, Sarah (1993) *Beyond Borders: West European Migration Policy Towards the 21st Century*. London: Royal Institute of International Affairs.

Cotterrell, Roger (1989) *The Politics of Jurisprudence: A Critical Introduction to Legal Philosophy*. London: Butterworth.

Cotterrell, Roger (1995) *Law's Community: Legal Theory in Sociological Perspective*. Oxford: Clarendon.

Crawley, Heaven (1999) 'Women and Refugee Status: Beyond the Public/Private Dichotomy in UK Asylum Policy', in Doreen Indra (ed.) *Engendering Forced Migration: Theory and Practice*. New York: Berghahn Books.

De Búrca, Gráinne (1995) 'The Language of Rights and European Integration', in Jo Shaw and Gillian More (eds) *New Legal Dynamics of European Union*. Oxford: Clarendon.

Dryzek John S. (1990) *Discursive Democracy: Politics, Policy and Political Science*. Cambridge: Cambridge University Press.

Egan, Suzanne (1998) 'Human Rights Considerations in Extradition and Expulsion

Cases: The European Convention on Human Rights Revisited', *Contemporary Issues in Irish Law and Politics* 1: 188–215.

Einarsen, Terje (1990) 'The European Convention on Human Rights and the Notion of an Implied Right to de facto Asylum', *International Journal of Refugee Law* 2: 361.

Elster, Jon (ed.) (1998) *Deliberative Democracy*. Cambridge: Cambridge University Press.

Ewick, Patrick and Susan S. Silbey (1998) *The Common Place of Law: Stories from Everyday Life*. Chicago: University of Chicago Press.

Favell, Adrian (1998) 'The Europeanisation of Immigration Politics', *European Integration Online Papers* 2(10): [http://eiop.or.at/eiop/texte/1998–010a.htm].

Fitzpatrick, Peter (1992) *The Mythology of Modern Law*. London: Routledge.

Fitzpatrick, Peter (1998) 'New Europe and Old Stories: Mythology and Legality in the European Union', pp. 27–45 in Peter Fitzpatrick and James Henry Bergerson (eds) *Europe's Other: European Law Between Modernity and Postmodernity*. Aldershot: Ashgate .

Formet, Carlos A. (1996) 'Peripheral Peoples and Narrative Identities: Arendtian Reflections on Late Modernity', pp. 314–30 in Seyla Benhabib (ed.) *Democracy and Difference: Contesting the Boundaries of the Political* Princeton: Princeton University Press.

Fuller, Lon L. (1969) *The Morality of Law* (rev. edn). New Haven: Yale University Press.

Geddes, Andrew (1998) 'The Representation of "Migrants Interests" in the European Union', *Journal of Ethnic and Migration Studies* 24: 695–713.

Goodrich, Peter (1998) 'Habermas and the Postal Rule', *Cardozo Law Review* 17: 1457–76.

Goodwin-Gill, Guy (1996) *The Refugee in International Law*. Oxford: Clarendon Press.

Habermas, Jürgen (1984) *The Theory of Communicative Action Vol. 1*. Cambridge: Polity.

Habermas, Jürgen (1994) *The Past as Future* (trans., ed. Max Pensky). Cambridge: Polity.

Habermas, Jürgen (1996a) *Between Facts and Norms: Contributions to a Discourse Theory of Law and Democracy*. Cambridge: Polity.

Habermas, Jürgen (1996b) 'Three Models of Democracy', pp. 22–30 in Seyla Benhabib (ed.) *Democracy and Difference: Contesting the Boundaries of the Political*. Princeton: Princeton University Press.

Habermas, Jürgen (1998) *The Inclusion of the Other: Studies in Political Theory*, Ciaran Cronin and Pablo De Greiff (eds). Cambridge, MA: MIT Press.

Habermas, Jürgen (1999) 'The European Nation-State and the Pressures of Globalization', *New Left Review* 235: 46–59.

Hammar, Tomas et al. (eds) (1997) *International Migration, Immobility and Development: Multidisciplinary Perspectives*. London: Berg.

Harvey, C. J. (1996) 'The Right to Seek Asylum in the United Kingdom and "Safe Countries"', *Public Law*: 196–204.

Harvey, C. J. (1997) 'Restructuring Asylum: Recent Trends in United Kingdom Asylum Law and Policy', *International Journal of Refugee Law* 9: 60–73.

Harvey, C. J. (1998a) 'The European Regulation of Asylum: Constructing a Model of Regional Solidarity?', *European Public Law* 4: 561–92.

Harvey, C. J. (1998b) 'Reconstructing Refugee Law', *Journal of Civil Liberties* 4: 159–90.

Harvey, C. J. (1998c) 'Taking Human Rights Seriously in the Asylum Context? A Perspective on the Development of Law and Policy', pp. 213–33 in Patrick

Twomey and Frances Nicholson (eds) *Current Issues of UK Asylum Law and Policy*.

Harvey, C. J. (1999a) 'The Politics of Legality', *Northern Ireland Legal Quarterly* 50: 528–67.

Harvey, C. J. (1999b) 'Strangers at the Gate: Human Rights and Refugee Protection', *Irish Studies in International Affairs* 10: 7–20.

Harvey, C. J. (1999c) 'Refugees and Reform: Between Apologia and Utopia?', *Journal of Civil Liberties* 4: 165–93.

Harvey, C. J. (1999d) 'Talking About Refugee Law', *Journal of Refugee Studies* 10: 101–34.

Harvey, C. J. (1999e) 'Immigration and Asylum Law: New Covenants and Familiar Challenges', *Public Law*: 23–34.

Hathaway, James C. (1993) 'Harmonizing for Whom? The Devaluation of Refugee Protection in the Era of European Economic Integration', *Cornell International Law Journal* 26: 719–35.

Hathaway, James C. (ed.) (1997a) *Reconceiving International Refugee Law*. The Hague: Kluwer Law International.

Hathaway, James C. (1997b) 'The Meaning of Repatriation', *International Journal of Refugee Law* 9: 551–8.

Hathaway, James C. and Alexander Neve (1997) 'Making International Refugee Law Relevant Again: A Proposal for Collectivized and Solution-Oriented Protection', *Harvard Human Rights Journal* 10: 115–211.

Havinga, Tetty and Anita Böcker (1999) 'Country of Asylum by Choice or by Chance: Asylum-Seekers in Belgium, the Netherlands and the UK', *Journal of Ethnic and Migration Studies* 25: 43–61.

Held, David (1995) *Democracy and the Global Order: From the Modern State to Cosmopolitan Governance*. Cambridge: Polity.

Hughes, Jane and Fabrice Liebaut (eds) (1998) *Detention of Asylum Seekers in Europe: Analysis and Perspectives*. The Hague: Kluwer Law International.

Indra, Doreen (ed.) (1999) *Engendering Forced Migration*. Oxford: Berghahn.

Joly, Danièle (1996) *Haven or Hell? Asylum Policies and Refugees in Europe*. Basingstoke: Macmillan.

Kirchheimer, Otto (1961) *Political Justice: The Use of Legal Procedure for Political Ends*. Princeton: Princeton University Press.

Lyons, Carole (1998) 'The Politics of Alterity and Exclusion in the European Union', in Peter Fitzpatrick and James Bergerson (eds) *Europe's Other: European Law Between Modernity and Postmodernity*. Aldershot: Ashgate.

Minow, Martha (1998) *Between Vengeance and Forgiveness: Facing History After Genocide and Mass Violence*. Boston: Beacon.

Mole, Nuala (1997) *Problems Raised by Certain Aspects of the Present Situation of Refugees from the Standpoint of the European Convention on Human Rights*. Strasbourg: Council of Europe Publishing.

Mouffe, Chantal (1992) 'Preface: Democratic Politics Today', pp. 1–14 in Chantal Mouffe (ed.) *Dimensions of Radical Democracy: Pluralism, Citizenship and Community*. London: Verso.

Mouffe, Chantal (1996) 'Democracy, Power and the "Political"', in Seyla Benhabib (ed.) *Democracy and Difference: Contesting the Boundaries of the Political*. Princeton: Princeton University Press.

Mouffe, Chantal (1998) 'Carl Schmitt and the Paradox of Liberal Democracy', in David Dyzenhaus (ed.) *Law as Politics: Carl Schmitt's Critique of Liberalism*. Durham: Duke University Press.

Murphy, Tim (1997) *The Oldest Social Science? Configurations of Law and Modernity*. Oxford: Clarendon.

Nicholson, Frances (1997) 'Implementation of the Immigration (Carrier's Liability) Act 1987: Privatising Immigration Functions at the Expense of International Obligations?', *International and Comparative Law Quarterly* 46: 586–634.

Parekh, Bhikhu (1993) 'The Cultural Particularity of Liberal Democracy', pp. 156–75 in David Held (ed.) *Prospects for Democracy: North, South, East and West*. Cambridge: Polity.

Rosenfeld, Michel (1998) *Just Interpretations: Law Between Ethics and Politics*. Berkeley: University of California Press.

Sherlock, Ann (1998) 'Deportation of Aliens and Article 8 ECHR', *European Law Review* 23: 62–75.

Soysal, Yasemin Nuhoglu (1994) *Limits of Citizenship: Migrants and Postnational Membership in Europe*. Chicago: Chicago University Press.

Soysal, Yasemin Nuhoglu (1996) 'Changing Citizenship in Europe: Remarks on Post-national Membership and the National State', pp. 17–29 in David Cesarani and Mary Fulbrook (eds) *Citizenship, Nationality and Migration in Europe*. London: Routledge.

Stokes, Susan C. (1998) 'Pathologies of Deliberation', in Jon Elster (ed.) *Deliberative Democracy*. Cambridge: Cambridge University Press.

Stychin, C. F. (1998) 'Relatively Universal: Globalisation, Rights Discourse, and the Evolution of Australian Sexual and National Identities', *Legal Studies* 18: 534–57.

Tuitt, Patricia (1996) *False Images: The Law's Construction of the Refugee*. London: Pluto.

Tuitt, Patricia (1997) 'Defining the Refugee by Race: The European Response to "New" Asylum-seekers', in Paddy Ireland and Per Laleng (eds) *The Critical Lawyers' Handbook* 2. London: Pluto.

Tully, James (1995) *Strange Multiplicity: Constitutionalism in an Age of Diversity*. Cambridge: Cambridge University Press.

Unger, Roberto M. (1996) *What Should Legal Analysis Become?* London: Verso.

Van Selm-Thornburn, Joanne (1998) 'Asylum in the Amsterdam Treaty: a harmonious future?', *Journal of Ethnic and Migration Studies* 24: 627–38.

Walzer, Michael (1983) *Spheres of Justice: A Defence of Pluralism and Equality*. London: Blackwell.

Young, Iris Marion (1996) 'Communication and the Other: Beyond Deliberative Democracy', pp. 120–35 in Seyla Benhabib (ed.) *Democracy and Difference: Contesting the Boundaries of the Political*. Princeton: Princeton University Press.

[18]

Reflections on the *Tampa* 'crisis'

ROBERT MANNE

I

Because Australia is a remote island continent it receives fewer applications for asylum from refugees than almost any country in the developed world. And yet, for reasons of some complexity, it has begun, in recent years, to treat those applications with almost unparalleled harshness. In 1994 the federal Labor government decided to detain all asylum seekers, on arrival, in prison-like camps. At this time the number of asylum seekers was small. In October 1999, however, boats from Indonesia bearing refugees, chiefly from Afghanistan and Iraq, began arriving on Australia's north-west coast. Approximately 4,000 boat refugees landed in 2000 and the same number again in the first eight months of 2001. All were sent, at first, to the growing system of detention camps.

In late August 2001, the Howard government, some weeks before a federal election was due, changed the course of refugee policy. A boat bearing mainly Afghan refugees of the persecuted Hazara minority began sinking en route to Australia. With the encouragement of the Australian government, a Norwegian cargo vessel, *MV Tampa*, rescued these refugees. Those on board persuaded the *Tampa* captain to sail towards the Australian territory of Christmas Island. The Howard government, in crisis mode, refused the *Tampa* permission to enter Australian waters. This order was ignored. Eventually the *Tampa* was boarded by Australian troops and the refugees transferred to an Australian frigate. John Howard promised that no asylum seeker arriving by boat would ever again be permitted to land on Australia soil. As Indonesia refused to accept the refugees on board the frigate Australian began now a desperate search for a country willing to take these refugees and also those who arrived subsequently. By the offer of bribes it discovered such a country in the tiny, bankrupt state of Nauru. Soon after Papua-New Guinea offered Manus Island. By such a process Australia began, in late August 2001, to create a new penal-social institution, which I call, (after the man who administered the policy and set it in place, the Minister for Immigration), the Ruddock Archipelago.

There are now several hundred asylum seekers languishing in refugee processing camps on Nauru and Manus Island, new proposals for additional such camps on Fiji, Kiribas and Palau, which seem to be coming to nothing, and 600 or more refugees on Christmas Island, some of whom are cramped together inside a sweltering tin shed. Christmas Island might be Australian territory but it has, at least, in fulfillment of John Howard's pledge that no asylum seeker should ever again set foot on Australian soil, been defined not to be Australia so far as questions of immigration are concerned.

In terms of its purpose, which was to defer refugee boats from Indonesia, the Howard–Ruddock policy is clearly, at least in the short-term, not working. In the two-month period following the *Tampa* crisis — between late August and early November — more boat refugees tried to enter Australia than in any period of Australian history. A refugee deterrent policy, whose immediate impact is an historically unprecedented increase in the number of asylum seekers moving towards Australia, can hardly be described as a success.

The deterrent dimension of the policy has, then, thus far, failed. So in the future will its second dimension — namely the promise to prevent those asylum seekers approaching by boat from ever setting foot on Australian soil. The certain failure of this ambition can be demonstrated in the following way. The agreements between Australia and the Pacific island states of the Ruddock Archipelago must contain sunset clauses, as it were, dates by which the processing of the asylum seekers in the camps must be complete. It is almost inevitable that when the time elapses neither those inmates of the archipelago assessed as genuine refugees nor those not so assessed will have found any country in the world willing to offer them homes.

In the past two years, for example, of the several hundred Middle Eastern asylum seekers in Indonesia assessed by the UNHCR as genuine refugees only a handful have found permanent homes. Since the *Tampa* crisis Australia's name, in Western Europe and North America, so far as refugee questions are concerned, is mud. No western country is likely to be willing to bail us out of our self-inflicted refugee dilemma by taking Ruddock Archipelago refugees off our hands. Nor will western countries provide homes for any of those asylum seekers found by the UN or Australia not to be genuine refugees. There is no way, moreover, that those found not to be genuine refugees can be repatriated to Iraq or to Afghanistan at least in the foreseeable future. Accordingly it is certain that unless the Pacific is to be permanently Middle Easternised by breaches of agreement with Nauru and Papua-New Guinea, in 12 month's time or so most of the Ruddock Archipelago refugees will eventually be brought to Australia as third-class citizens; while the Archipelago non-refugees will also be brought to Australia, most likely to the detention centres, to live under a regime of permanent incarceration. In addition it is also likely that, while present policy persists, new boats of desperate asylum seekers will continue to arrive, with the strong encouragement of Indonesia.

Why with its encouragement? The first and most obvious price of the new Howard–Ruddock refugee policy has been its impact on Australia's relations with Indonesia. The only possible solution to the problem of the Middle Eastern asylum seekers is a return to some version of the late 1970s policy of the Fraser government (1975–83) with regard to the refugees from Indochina, namely to create an agreement with the Indonesian government — for the discouragement of the onward movement of the refugee boats in return for a generous Australia offer to resettle substantial numbers of the Middle Eastern refugees presently on Indonesian soil. The Howard government has not pursued such a policy. It first sought to convince Indonesia to create a refugee detention centre on one of its barren islands, financed by Australia, but without the offer of permanent Australian homes for genuine refugees. Unsurprisingly the Indonesian government turned this suggestion down. More recently we began to try to escort refugee boats back to Indonesia, without bothering to get the agreement of the Indonesian government to what we intended to do. Unconsciously what both these policies suggested was that we thought Indonesia, unlike Australia, was a suitable place for a refugee dumping round. The prickly Indonesians instinctively understood. Indonesia's president, Megawati, refused to talk with the Australian Prime Minister by telephone or at the Shanghai meeting of APEC about refugees. The head of the Indonesian navy openly expressed his government's intention to encourage boats with Middle Eastern asylum seekers on board to make their way to our shores.

It is not only with Indonesia that relations have soured. In Western Europe and North America, Australia's behaviour at the time of the *Tampa* crisis was almost universally condemned. Normally the UNHCR is extremely discreet in its criticisms of supportive nation states. Since the *Tampa*, concerning Australia, its officials have spoken with unusual plainness. The head of the UNHCR, Ruud Lubbers, was recently in Pakistan pleading for an opening of her borders to Afghan refugees. Time and again, he told us, he was asked the following question. If a wealthy, thinly populated, stable country like Australia was unwilling to offer sanctuary to several hundred Afghans how could a poor, overpopulated and politically fragile country like Pakistan, which has two million or more refugees on its soil already, be expected to take hundreds of thousands more? Australian actions, Lubbers made clear, had helped poison the international atmosphere with regard to the offer of sanctuary and the humane treatment of refugees. Recently he claimed that Australia was helping to reintroduce into the treatment of refugees what he called 'the law of the jungle'.

Australia accepts some responsibility for the political and economic stability of the Pacific Island states. To construct on these islands, for our own convenience, refugee processing and internment camps; to inject into their political and social systems dangerous new tension points; to require these states to enforce on their soil a comprehensive media ban within the camps; and to offer, as an inducement for all this, large monetary and diplomatic bribes — was an exceedingly strange way in which to fulfill Australian responsibilities in the Pacific or to demonstrate the value we place on incorruptibility, open government, freedom of speech and human rights.

Nor should we underestimate the impact of the Howard–Ruddock policy on the morale of the Australian sailors involved. Recently it was revealed by a navy psychologist that the work of repelling defenceless, desperate and vulnerable human beings by use of armed naval force had caused almost all those involved in the dirty work serious distress. The reason was simple, he pointed out. Almost all understood that what they were doing was morally wrong. During the election campaign the former chief of the Navy spoke with dismay about the way the service was being politicised.

The oddity of the present situation can be put like this. The Australian government has adopted a deterrent anti-asylum seeker policy that has not deterred. It swears that the refugees we have forced away will never set foot on Australian soil. This mad ambition cannot possibly be achieved, unless the Iraqi and Afghan refugees are to stay on the Pacific Islands permanently. As a result of this policy relations with Indonesia have grown more sour. As a result of this policy Australia's proud reputation as a refugee-friendly nation has been tarnished. As a result of this policy the work of the UNHCR in Pakistan and elsewhere has been made slightly more difficult than it was always certain to be. And as a result of this policy a potentially destabilising new issue has been introduced into the fragile political and ethnic balances of a number of Pacific Island states.

Nor does the oddness of the present situation end here. So popular is this policy in contemporary Australia that during the recent election campaign the Coalition government placed its toughness over border control near the centre of its reelection strategy, obliging the Labor Opposition to agree, in advance, to every nuance of the policy, no matter how damaging to national interest, no matter how indifferent to the requirement of common human decency. How have we arrived at a situation of such peculiarity?

II

In any explanation of our current crisis and of the crisis of the past two years the shadow cast by Australian history must play an important role: the sense of geographic insecurity felt by a thinly spread and newly arrived European people occupying and claiming for itself a vast continent, experiencing deep fears that, unless it was ever vigilant, alien people to the north might take from them what they had so recently acquired. It is hard to know whether it is the arrival of exotic swarthy strangers or the loss of border control which causes contemporary Australians greater alarm.

Yet it is important not to exaggerate this strand in our history. For there are not one but two traditions of relevance to the present crisis. One is the history of White Australia and obsessive border control. The other is the tradition that sees Australia in 1939, albeit somewhat grudgingly, admitting a reasonably large number of Jewish refugees from Germany and Austria; which sees Australia under the Prime Ministerships of Ben Chifley (1945–9) and Robert Menzies (1949–66) play a major role in the acceptance of large numbers of displaced people from the camps of Europe; and which, most importantly for present understandings, sees Australia under the governments of Malcolm Fraser (1975–83) and Bob Hawke (1983–91) accept tens of thousands of refugees and migrants from the countries of Indochina — Vietnam, Cambodia and Laos, the first thousands of whom arrived by boats, spontaneously.

As soon as the boats of the Middle Eastern refugees began arriving in 1999, it was clear that it was the first tradition and not the second that was determining the government's and the public's response. Why was this so?

In part I think it is important to remember that Australia's postwar generosity towards refugees was, peculiarly enough, a benign consequence of the far from benign ideological setting of the Cold War. During this time, refugees from Eastern Europe, from Hungary after 1956, and from communist Indochina, had strong support inside the Australian community, especially from the anti-communist intelligentsia and from the Roman Catholic Church. On the other hand, refugees fleeing right wing regimes, from Chile or Central America or East

Timor under Indonesian rule, had serious support from the left wing intelligentsia and the trade union movement. With the end of the Cold War, the old ideological sympathy for the refugees fleeing from regimes of the left or the right has dissolved. Now the serious friends of the refugees are either isolated individuals, with unusual capacity for empathy, or human rights advocates or their associations, which together, do not have the capacity to withstand the tides of populist opinion.

Yet there is more to be said than this. Over the past five or six years the tide of popular opinion has turned in Australia, during what may be called the Hansonite phase of our history, the period where an anti-immigrant and anti-Aboriginal political party rose in Queensland, managing in 1998 to win more than 20% of the votes in its home state and almost 10% nationwide. Just four years ago its leader, Pauline Hanson, was thought extreme for expressing the view that refugees should only be allowed a temporary stay in Australia, until the situation in their homelands improved. Since that time, the Howard Government, influenced by the Hansonite mood, has overseen the growth of the system of mandatory detention from its modest beginning into a major quasi-punitive regime, under foreign and private control. Since that time Australia has seen the opening or expansion of a number of detention centres in some of the most remote and inhospitable regions of this continent. Since that time, despite overwhelming evidence of terrible breakdown in the detention centres — hunger strikes, riots, self-mutilations, psychiatric illness on a large scale — the Howard Government has stubbornly refused to release asylum seekers from detention until their refugee status has been confirmed, virtually imprisoning in a highly traumatic atmosphere, thousands, not only men but also women and children. Since that time the government has introduced, even for successful refugee applications, a system of temporary visa; blocked access to various social services for refugees; forbidden proven refugees from even applying to have their wives and children reunited with them; and has, with ever increasing determination, taken the Refugee Review Tribunal in hand and radically reduced the capacity of asylum seekers to take their cases for refugee status to the courts.

The astonishing cruelty of these laws was finally understood recently following the incident where 353 asylum seekers on their way to Australia drowned. Three of these were the daughters of an Iraqi man who had been granted refugee status but who was absolutely refused the right, under the new temporary visa regime, even to apply for reunion with his family. As it happens although his daughters died, the man's wife, after two days in the ocean, survived. The man was informed by the Minister that although he was perfectly at liberty to leave Australia to visit his grieving wife in Indonesia if he did so, because of the conditions attaching to his temporary visa, he would, unfortunately, be unable to return.

Not only has the objective situation of the asylum seekers steadily deteriorated over the past five years; so has the climate of opinion concerning the refugees. I noticed when the first boats began arriving almost no interest was taken in the media of the political circumstances from which the people from Afghanistan or Iraq, or from Algeria or Iran, had fled. For all the media cared these people might have been fleeing from Mars. In the absence of interest in the persecution such people faced, the information vacuum was filled by the Minister of Immigration, Mr. Ruddock — with his standard anti-asylum seeker line. Namely that those who arrived in Australia were wealthy and selfish queue jumpers, stealing places from the genuinely needy, frequently terrorists and war criminals in their previous lives, who demanded privileges from Australia with unexampled insolence and who threatened Australia by moral blackmail tactics, using what Ruddock characteristically called 'inappropriate behaviors', such as going on hunger strike or mutilating themselves or slashing their wrists.

It is a genuinely interesting question how far the rapid deterioration in the government and public response to the arrival of the asylum seekers can be explained by the existence of the Hansonite mood; by the existence of an increasingly right wing Howard Government jumping at Hansonite shadows; by a tabloid, talkback radio culture; and by the presence of an undoubtedly competent but equally undoubtedly super-stubborn Minister whose lack of empathy for the suffering of others is so deep as to be difficult to comprehend.

It is also an interesting question as to how far things would have gone differently if Labor had been in government in Australia over the past five and a half years. It was Labor which instigated the current system of mandatory detention for asylum seekers, that is to say the system which incarcerates all those who arrive in Australia without valid papers and which holds them there until they are either found to be refugees or can be repatriated. And it was Labor whose suggestion for a coast guard to chase away the boats of asylum seekers played a role in preparing public opinion for the government refusal to the *Tampa* to anchor in Australian waters. For me one of the most revealing moments in Australian politics was the boast of the leader of the opposition Labor Party, Kim Beazley, during the one and only debate of the recent election campaign, that it was Labor and not the Coalition which had introduced the system of universal mandatory detention for asylum seekers. In contemporary Australia such matters are a cause for pride not shame.

Yet it is important not be too parochial in one's assessment of what is happening in Australia. There is a worldwide preoccupation with the movement of asylum seekers and also with illegal migration from the Third World to the First. In the contemporary Western world the two problems are often, wrongly, thought of as one. Even more importantly, as time passes, Western societies are pulling up their psychological and political drawbridges, interesting themselves almost exclusively in the maintenance of their own living standards, defending themselves from the claims made upon them not only from those seeking a better life, but also from those seeking protection from the most terrible tyrannies. In such an atmosphere, of Western self absorption, the post-World War II legislative framework concerning the rights of asylum seekers and, even more importantly, the postwar ethic about the requirement for the humane treatment of refugees, is increasingly under threat. Something very important appears to be happening to public sensibility in Western societies, including Australia, which of course affects both political parties and governments. Let two examples suffice.

REFLECTIONS ON THE *TAMPA* 'CRISIS'

It is truly astonishing how morally lethargic in recent times Australian opinion has become. In early August 2001 the public television network showed film of a six-year-old boy, limp and lifeless, who had been so stunned by his experience of detention camp that he would no longer eat or drink and could only be kept alive by regular visits to hospital for rehydration. After the screening of this program I assumed that public opinion would erupt in anger and outrage. I was wrong. The story proved to be of no interest to commercial television or the tabloid press. The Minister defended his treatment of Shayan, whom he referred to three times in a single interview as 'it', by hinting that his real problems may have arisen not from detention but from his relations with his stepmother. Soon the Minister was defended by the Sydney tabloid, *Daily Telegraph* columnist, Piers Akerman, by a method unusual for an Australian journalist — namely by the reproduction of the provably false disinformation about Shayan and his parents that was being disseminated by the government-controlled newspaper of the Iranian theological-police state.

Recently a boat of Iraqi asylum seekers was intercepted by *HMAS Adelaide*; warning shots were fired; the boat began to sink. In the confusion a handful of the refugees, wearing life jackets, jumped overboard. It was claimed by the government that there were children among them. A question arose. Did the children jump or were they pushed? As usual the incident's first moral interpreter was the Minister for Immigration, Philip Ruddock. He claimed to know that the children had been thrown overboard by their parents. (The evidence was never produced.) He told us that he had never encountered in his public life a more callous act. The Prime Minister, John Howard from the depths of his understanding of such matters — explained that throwing children into the ocean was not the way 'genuine refugees' behaved. People such as these Iraqis were not welcome in our country. The Liberal Party Senator for Western Australia, Ross Lightfoot, agreed. Such behaviour might be tolerated in a Muslim country; it would not be tolerated here. Decent Australians could not but feel 'disgust' for people so 'repulsive' as these Iraqis. An incident such as this would once have excited astonishment and pity. What desperation must such people feel? In mainstream contemporary Australia it aroused only a barely concealed racist contempt. (After the November 10 election the Australian people belatedly discovered that no children had been thrown overboard at all, and, even more importantly, that naval officers had informed the government of this fact on October 10.)

In Europe the most salient issue fuelling the rise of the extreme right is immigration. Hans-Georg Betz calls this anti-immigrant mood 'exclusionary populism'; the Hungarian social theorist, G.M. Tamas, calls it, partly for provocative effect, 'post-fascism' and, following the work of Seymour Lipset on the sociology of fascism, the new 'extremism of the centre'. In Europe exclusionary populism or post-fascism has influenced the attitudes of the mainstream parties. In Australia, during the *Tampa* crisis, something slightly different occurred. Here the mainstream Liberal Party gazumped the populist right, leaving the extreme right One Nation Party with nothing to do except to accuse the Liberals and their coalition partner, the Nationals, of policy theft, and Labor with little alternative but to agree, in advance, with everything the Coalition now said and did in the refugee area, no matter how unworkable, no matter how cruel. In Australia exclusionary populism has reshaped party politics. More importantly it is the most powerful political passion contemporary Australians appear to feel. In the Coalition's victory of 10 November 2001, its refugee repulsion reelection strategy played a vital part. As a consequence of a victory on such a basis a new chapter in Australian political history — with a different balance between populism and liberalism — has opened.[1]

Note

1 This paper is being concluded on 5 December 2001. It is an updated version of a talk originally given to the Institute of Post Colonial Studies on 29 October 2001.

[19]

The Complexity of Determining Refugeehood: A Multidisciplinary Analysis of the Decision-making Process of the Canadian Immigration and Refugee Board*

CÉCILE ROUSSEAU,[1] FRANÇOIS CRÉPEAU,[2]
PATRICIA FOXEN,[3] FRANCE HOULE[2]

[1]*Department of Psychiatry, McGill University;* [2]*Faculty of Law, University of Montreal;* [3]*Department of Anthropology, McGill University*

Refugee determination is one of the most complex adjudication functions in industrialized societies. In Canada, despite a relatively broad recognition rate and a teleological interpretation of the international refugee definition, dissatisfaction with the decision-making process at the Immigration and Refugee Board (IRB) has been expressed by numerous actors. This paper documents the influence of legal, psychological and cultural factors on the process of refugee determination. Forty problematic cases referred to the research team by professionals were studied using both quantitative and qualitative approaches. The results indicate numerous problems affecting the role and behaviour of all actors: difficulties in evaluating evidence, assessing credibility, and conducting hearings; problems in coping with vicarious traumatization and uncontrolled emotional reactions; poor knowledge of the political context, false representations of war, and cultural misunderstandings or insensitivity. In a majority of cases, these legal, psychological and cultural dimensions interact together, often impacting negatively upon Board Members' ability to evaluate credibility and upon the overall conduct of hearings. These findings suggest that the refugee determination process might benefit from revised selection criteria for Board Members and refugee claim officers, as well as improved training and support for all actors.

Deciding upon refugee claims is a very complex and difficult task. According to Peter Showler, Chair of the Canadian Immigration and Refugee Board (2000), it is the single most complex adjudication function in contemporary Western societies. This complexity stems from the need for the decision-maker to have a sufficient knowledge of the cultural, social and political environment

*A preliminary version of this article appeared, in French, under the title 'Analyse multi-disciplinaire du processus décisionnel de la CISR', in *Refuge, Canada's Periodical on Refugees*, **19**(4): 62–75.

of the country of origin, a capacity to bear the psychological weight of hearings where victims recount horror stories, and of consequent decisions which may prove fatal, and an ability to deal with legal issues such as the subtle international definition of the refugee or the procedures of quasi-judicial hearings involving various pieces of evidence.

Since the mid-1980s, Western States have faced a considerable rise in the number of asylum claims, and the refugee issue has been a recurrent and highly sensitive theme in the media and on the political scene. In order to implement their international obligations under the 1951 Geneva Convention relating to the Status of Refugees and other international human rights instruments, as well as their own constitutional obligations (right to life and security of the person, protection against torture or cruel, inhuman or degrading treatment, right to equality), these States have modified the refugee status determination systems they had adopted for the Eastern European refugees fleeing Cold War communism. They have also set up institutional and procedural arrangements to treat the increased influx of refugee and asylum claims, although such arrangements are often proscribed by the particular interests of nation-states (Loescher 1993; Silk 1986). In many countries, the State institution responsible for the decision, in first instance or on appeal, is an administrative tribunal.

Canada created the Immigration and Refugee Board (IRB) in 1989 by amending the 1985 Immigration Act (c. I-2), after the Supreme Court of Canada (*Singh* v. *Canada*, [1985] 1 S.C.R. 177) had declared the previous procedure unconstitutional due to the absence of a meaningful hearing on the merits. In particular, it introduced an administrative procedure whereby decision-makers have the duty to act in a quasi-judicial manner. Since the latter decide issues of vital importance to claimants for refugee status, the legislator devised a process where claimants would be entitled to a full hearing by the Refugee Determination Division (RDD). Claimants have to prove that they have good grounds to claim refugee status. The standard of proof is somewhat lower than that of the balance of probabilities in that 'there need not be more than a 50 per cent chance (i.e., a probability), and on the other hand that there must be more than a minimal possibility' of persecution (*Adjei* v. *Canada* [1989] 7 Imm. L.R. 169 at 173).

Claimants present their case orally in front of the Refugee Division, which has sole and exclusive jurisdiction to hear and determine all questions of law and fact, including questions of jurisdiction (1985 Immigration Act, art. 67(1)). Two Board Members of the RDD assisted by a Refugee Claim Officer (RCO) hear the claimants. The RCO is not a representative of the Minister, and the latter is not normally represented unless the case involves an exclusion or a cessation of refugee status, or is of particular interest. The proceedings of the RDD are meant to be non-adversarial, another reason why the Minister is not generally represented and a 'contrary case' is not argued. More often than not, the main task of Board Members at the end of the process revolves around assessing the credibility of oral testimonies and of documentary evidence.

The IRB consists of independent members appointed by the Cabinet (1985 Immigration Act, art. 57(2)) after a screening by a committee which makes recommendations to the Cabinet based on very general criteria which are not particularly meaningful: many appointees lack experience in immigration or refugee issues.[1] This absence of specific criteria for the selection of Board Members is a major lacuna in the 1989 system. Despite the important training programme developed by the IRB, many actors in the system (lawyers, NGOs, civil servants, communities, etc.) have signalled, over the past eleven years, numerous instances where the legitimacy of the IRB decision was dubious, for reasons related to the competence of the Board Members and other actors.

Several reports contain recommendations aimed at correcting the difficulties encountered by the IRB in exercising its mandate. The Hathaway Report (Hathaway 1993) dealt with problematic relationships between Board Members, as well as a range of systemic weaknesses. The Crépeau–Houle Report[2] specifically made suggestions concerning the selection and training of Board Members, as well as the independence of the tribunal. The Réseau d'intervention auprès des personnes ayant subi la violence organisée (RIVO), in the name of the Canadian Network for the Health of Survivors of Torture and Organized Violence (CanNet), has prepared a Code of procedure and ethics for the treatment of victims of torture or severely traumatized persons (see http://www.cam.org/~rivo/RIVO99.html), which the IRB is presently helping to review. Some authors, in addition, have pointed to the need for better cultural communication and sensitivity on the part of IRB Members (Barsky 1994, 2000; Pelosi 1996).

Concurrently, international quasi-judicial decisions also point to the difficulty of the refugee determination task. For example, the United Nations Committee against Torture has set stringent criteria that testify to the complexity of such decision-making. Its cases involve the evaluation necessary to decide whether an alien will be deported to his or her country of origin despite a claim that he or she may be at risk of torture, and the Committee has outlined several skills required of decision-makers: very accurate and specific knowledge of the political and social situation in the country of origin (Communication no 120/1998: Australia. 25/05/99. CAT/C/22/D/120/1998) and the ability to understand and evaluate the psychological aspects of the process (Communication no 101/1997: Sweden. 16/12/98. CAT/C/21/D/101/1997).

In addition, the United Nations High Commissioner for Refugees has suggested that similar criteria be used by States when determining refugee status:

> It should be recalled that an applicant for refugee status is normally in a particularly vulnerable situation. He finds himself in an alien environment and may experience serious difficulties, technical and psychological, in submitting his case to the authorities of a foreign country, often in a language not his own. His application should therefore be examined within the framework of specially established procedures by qualified personnel having the necessary knowledge

and experience, and an understanding of an applicant's particular difficulties and needs (UNHCR 1992: par. 190).

These national reports and the international case law and soft law suggest that a thorough examination of the refugee determination process should be undertaken through the lens of various disciplines and should include a multidisciplinary analysis which takes into account the legal, cultural and psychological dimensions of the process. However, there has been no comprehensive multidisciplinary study on the decision-making process to date, and the absence of precedent in the literature highlights the need to devise the appropriate analytical tool for such study.

The general objective of this research project, therefore, was to identify the nature and cause of the discrepancies in appreciation of many cases, between independent decision-makers and impartial specialists (such as the Board Members or the RCO) on the one hand, and professional experts in particular fields (such as lawyers, doctors and psychologists) on the other. More specifically, we wanted to analyse the decision-making process by focusing on the cultural, psychological and legal factors that influence the various actors, and to suggest effective solutions that go beyond the haphazard fixing that is often applied when some embarrassing piece of news finds its way into the media.

This paper describes the methodological approach taken in creating the intellectual tools for the analysis, as well as the results obtained through their use in analysing some forty cases decided by the IRB in Montreal.

Literature Review

Legal Literature

The literature considered here consists essentially of a general review of the case law that emanates from the Federal Court of Canada. This review does not purport to be exhaustive and is limited to the cases that are pertinent to the analysis of the decision-making process.

The Federal Court of Canada has exclusive jurisdiction to review the legality of refugee determinations. Therefore, the function of the Court is to set the legal parameters to be followed by the IRB when it makes decisions. For reasons which are possibly linked to the lack of competence of Board Members, these legal guidelines appear, at times, not to be followed. This results in negative decisions which are often not well-founded and constitute, by this very fact, a breach of the fundamental right to security of the person of the refugee claimants concerned (Article 7, Canadian Charter of Rights and Freedoms).

Board Members can experience difficulties in evaluating evidence, and this often leads to erroneous findings of facts, unreasonable conclusions or a failure to give proper weight to evidence introduced during the course of the proceedings. The Trial Division of the Federal Court can review these errors when judges are of the opinion that the Members did not weigh the evidence properly or mis-stated, misunderstood and misconstrued the evidence presented at the hearing (*Bouguettaya* 2000).

It is entirely open to the IRB to base its decision on documentary evidence rather than testimonial evidence provided it has good reasons to do so after properly weighing the probative value of all the evidence presented at the hearing (*Menaker* 1997). However, when the Board does not have any documentary evidence before it with respect to a central fact of the claim and there is any adverse credibility finding with respect to the applicant, the Board should assess the testimony (*Vidhani* 1995). Normally, the Board should grant the applicant the benefit of the doubt in cases where documentary evidence is lacking (*Chan* 1995). Yet, rejections are often based on the lack of credibility of the claimant on the basis that the story is 'implausible' (*Leung* 1994), but the reasons are unconvincing, if not merely speculative (*Njoko* 1995).

Finally, expert evidence has to be handled carefully by Board Members. They cannot comment negatively on applicants' demeanour, make remarks on their emotional response to their counsel's questioning and determine that they are evasive, incoherent and disjointed in their testimony, if there is a medical report explaining the applicant's behaviour. Specifically, psychiatrists will often conclude that the applicant's 'manner of reporting his history and his emotional reactions while reporting it were consistent with the history which he provided' (*Zapata* 1994). It is not open to the Board to disregard expert evidence without indicating its reasons in the decision, especially when it explains the applicant's demeanour, which led to a finding of lack of credibility (*Sivayoganathan* 1994).

In addition to problems in assessing evidence, Board Members may also demonstrate difficulties in conducting a hearing. The statute imposes a duty on the Board Members to conduct hearings informally and expeditiously. However, in doing so, they have to remain fair towards claimants, especially since procedural safeguards associated with the right to be heard are guaranteed to claimants. With these provisions, it should be clear that considerations of fairness should prevail over those of expeditiousness. In practice, however, this objective is often contradicted by the inquisitorial zeal of RCOs and Board Members.

As a neutral agent, the RCO's role is to bring all the relevant elements of the case to the attention of the Members of the Refugee Division and to communicate the case to the claimants before the hearing so that they will not be taken by surprise. Members can also ask the claimants questions, but they have to be more careful than RCOs in order not to 'cross the line' and appear to be partial. RCOs and Board Members can clarify inconsistencies, falsehoods, confusion or mistakes, but the line of questioning has to end when questions become unfair, harassing or sexist (*Yusuf* 1991). Despite the degree of discretion granted to the Board in assessing credibility, the Board has an obligation to express any negative findings of credibility in clear and unmistakable terms (*Parizi* 1994).

The primary function of the IRB is to weigh and assess the evidence before it. Although there is no obligation of the Board to discuss everv piece of evidence, it is required to address those pieces which contradict the Board's finding on key issues (*Gengeswaran* 1999). Otherwise, the Court may infer that the tribunal made an erroneous finding of fact without regard to the evidence (*Otoo* 1996). What is required is that the Board's reasons demonstrate an understanding of the pertinent issues and of the relevant evidence (*Magana* 1996). The simple statement that the tribunal had reached its decision 'after careful consideration of all the evidence adduced at the hearing' is not sufficient when the decision makes little or no reference to the principal bases of the applicant's claim (*Alfred* 1994).

In addition, Board Members must not give the impression, in their reasons for decision, that they made a painstaking analysis of the transcripts to find contradictions (*Gracielome* 1989). Where the Court feels that the Board has overreached itself in its search for inconsistencies, the Board's decision can be set aside (*Owusu-Ansah* 1989).

Psychological Literature

In terms of the psychological factors, two distinct phenomena deserve particular attention: the influence of traumatic experiences on claimants' testimony and the impact of their stories on the various professionals involved in the legal process.

A very significant number of refugee claimants' accounts include instances of torture, rape, arbitrary detentions, threats, and armed attacks (Fornazzari 1995; Silove *et al.* 2000). These events can engender post-traumatic psychological reactions in the claimants, which often affect both their ability to testify and the content of their testimony. Being forced to recall the traumatic events can trigger powerful avoidance reactions, either conscious or unconscious. These reactions protect the person from retraumatization and the social stigma associated in some cultures with being a victim or with certain specific traumas, sexual violence in particular (Atlani and Rousseau 2000). In some cases, the claimant can be overwhelmed by powerful emotions of anxiety, sadness, and anger leading to temporary loss of control or to dissociation. For people who have suffered torture, the court setting can also evoke interrogation conditions and provoke a panic reaction (Rousseau 2000).

In most cases, however, awareness of the importance of the court decision leads the claimants to mobilize all their resources, so the influence of traumatic experience on their testimony will be more subtle. The literature indicates that trauma can alter the account of an experience in a number of ways. First, it alters perception of time and distorts reports of the time sequence (Terr 1983). Pynoos and Nader (1989) observe that it can also distort spatial perception: people who have had extreme exposure tend to consider retrospectively that they were safer than they were, while more distant observers will describe themselves as directly exposed to the trauma. Memory blocks and a wide range of dissociative phenomena also compromise the coherence of trauma stories (Kirmayer 1996). Finally, difficulty in concentrating is responsible for numerous little mistakes which are easily interpreted as lack of credibility in a legal setting. Because of all these interrelated factors, trauma stories can be very difficult for non-specialists to interpret and psychological or psychiatric expertise may play a key role in trying to disentangle the effects of trauma from credibility issues (Levy *et al.* 1998).

The recounting of traumatic events also indirectly transmits trauma from the claimant to the decision maker or to other professionals involved in the decision-making process. Board Members in particular are subject to major psychological stress due in part to the severity of the traumatic accounts they have to listen to, and in part to the psychological weight of the decisions they must render, some of which can have quite dramatic repercussions on the safety of the refugee claimant. In Canada, most Board Members listen to two claimants' stories each day of the week, for three consecutive weeks, and then have a week without hearings to write their decisions. Studies of war-time trauma in the wake of World War II and the Vietnam War brought to light the fact that war does not only affect those who experience it directly, but also has repercussions on the close social relationships and networks that a person may be involved in (Danieli 1998; Rousseau 1998). The indirect transfer of trauma through verbal accounts has been particularly well documented in therapists who have treated traumatized patients and is known as 'vicarious traumatization' (Watson 1995). In the therapeutic setting, it is the therapists' empathy for the victims that makes them vulnerable, for they cannot use the usual defences of avoidance or denial to protect themselves from the images associated with the story that has been told (Peltzer 1997).

Vicarious traumatization can provoke the development of typical symptoms of post-traumatic stress disorder in exposed individuals (nightmares, flashbacks, startle reactions, avoidance, denial, uncontrolled emotional reactions). Psychodynamic analyses have also demonstrated how traumatic histories can evoke voyeuristic and sadistic impulses in the listener (Vinar and Vinar 1989). Overexposure to these types of accounts often triggers defensive reactions that lead to trivialization of horror, cynicism, and lack of empathy.

Intensive exposure to traumatic stories can also be responsible for more systemic effects, and in particular, for conflicts and disagreements at the institutional level. These confrontations reflect a splitting process where the 'evil' has to be distanced as much as possible from oneself (Jaranson 1995; Moeller and Christiansen 1996). Projection defences involved in the split can result in dismissal or demonization of the 'other', a mechanism which can prove particularly harmful in a court situation. In spite of increasing evidence of the significance of vicarious traumatization phenomena, they have never been studied in the immigration court setting, but it can be hypothesized that they are likely to have a major influence, both at the personal and the institutional level, in the decision-making process.

50 *C. Rousseau, F. Crépeau, P. Foxen, F. Houle*

Cultural Literature

In line with the large numbers of immigrants and refugees arriving in Europe and North America over the past two decades, there is a growing academic and policy literature on cultural processes such as acculturation, adaptation and multiculturalism (and their applications in such fields as health, education, communications and marketing). Many authors have moved beyond traditional unilinear notions of adaptation and acculturation; some, for example, have shown that situations of marginality, alienation and poverty in the host culture impact negatively on refugee well-being more than actual experiences of violence and torture in the home country (Beiser 1993).

Research in the disciplines of anthropology and intercultural communication, in addition, has offered much evidence that communication between people from different cultural backgrounds can lead to radical misunderstandings (Geertz 1973; Knapp *et al.* 1987; Samovar and Porter 1994). Different cultural frameworks—which encompass beliefs, attitudes, motives, practices, world views, as well as notions of time, spatial orientation, causality, truth, social hierarchy and ways of narrating—frame the ways in which people perceive, experience and interpret their social and personal realities, as well as the meanings and significance they assign to everyday occurrences and commonplace understandings. As much research has shown, when people do not share the same cultural references, rules and codes—information that is largely internalized and communicated unconsciously—numerous communication failures occur, ranging from misinterpretations about minute non-verbal cues to different assumptions concerning the essential meaning of concepts (Goffman 1969); moreover, such cultural misunderstandings can lead to feelings of hostility and biased judgements (Aigner 1995).

Much academic attention has also been paid to the institutional processes through which refugee identity is structured and normalized, and to the power relations, discourses and ideologies shaping the experience of refugees worldwide (Zolberg *et al.* 1989; Malkki 1992; Daniel and Knudsen 1995). Some of this scholarship points to the political construction of 'refugee identity', which is framed by international institutions within a discourse emphasizing the victimhood, suffering, and pathology of refugees, and is itself related to the Western discourse on rights and charity (Malkki 1992). In the context of Western host societies in particular, a discourse separating 'deserving' refugees from those deemed to be 'undeserving' or 'false' governs and restricts the acceptance of refugees. Indeed, some authors argue that the juxtaposition of the concept of a 'right' to refuge or asylum with the fear of uncontrolled immigration has led to popular and institutional negative characterizations of refugees as 'queue jumpers', cheats or economic immigrants (Pelosi 1996; Silove *et al.* 2000). Others have argued that within contexts of terror, escape and asylum-seeking, a profound sense of mistrust governs both refugee perceptions of authorities and the way refugees are in turn perceived by authorities and institutional actors in both home and host contexts (Daniel and Knudsen 1995).

Despite the broadening literature on refugees, immigrants, and inter-cultural communication, there exists a relative dearth of information regarding the impact of cultural difference and communication in the refugee determination process itself, or, indeed, within the field of refugee and immigration law in general. Given the critical decisions that are made in refugee hearings, the issue of intercultural misunderstanding is of extreme importance. Such hearings involve the intersection of radically different cultures, assumptions, belief systems and reference points in a highly charged, intense and short-term setting. Refugee claimants are required to prove their claims, which usually involve complex political situations and personal decisions as well as cases of extreme brutality, in a context where they may not be understood, and often with little documentation. As such, small and large cultural misunderstandings can have devastating impacts on hearing outcomes and the lives of those who flee persecution. Kälin (1986) has outlined particular obstacles to the interaction between asylum-seekers and officials, including: a) the manner in which asylum-seekers express themselves; b) the interpreter; c) the cultural relativity of notions and concepts; d) different perceptions of time; and e) the cultural relativity of the concepts of 'lie' and 'truth'. Barsky (1994) has argued that the refugee hearing often becomes a test of the claimant's ability to construct an appropriate image of the 'convention refugee'—that is, to satisfy the expectations of the decision-makers, which themselves are based within particular political, economic, cultural and moral discourses. As a result, claimants who are most able to navigate and understand the expectations of the host country tend to produce a successful 'refugee' image, while others whose narrative style and retelling of events do not fit into such expectations may be misunderstood and rejected.

Two noteworthy studies have examined these processes in refugee hearings at the IRB in Canada, both pointing to some serious difficulties engendered by intercultural miscommunication in this context. Barsky (1994) has looked at how the social discourse surrounding refugees is reproduced and normalized in hearings and throughout the refugee determination process; he illustrates how unstated power differentials and hierarchies interact with cultural assumptions in the production (or rejection) of the refugee 'Other'. Following his lead, Pelosi (1996) points to some common, albeit subtle, pitfalls of intercultural communication and the negative impact of ineffective communication on the outcome of refugee hearings. First, she argues, a claimant's vulnerable state of mind during the hearing may lead to emotional reactions or signs of distress that are misinterpreted by the decision makers. Psychological fragility is often caused or reinforced by the intimidating surroundings of the hearing, by culture shock and bewilderment regarding unfamiliar signs and symbols, by fear of the hearing's outcome or of being misunderstood, or by psychological symptoms caused by trauma, which might range from nervous laughter to a blank and indifferent affect. Such anxiety is often expressed through cultural idioms unfamiliar to the decision-maker, can result in hesitance or contradiction, and may be interpreted as a lack of credibility.

52 *C. Rousseau, F. Crépeau, P. Foxen, F. Houle*

Both Barsky and Pelosi show how the institutional culture of the IRB itself, prescribed within a particular socio-political context and subject to specific world views, codes of behaviour, social standards and professional norms, is limited by its own cultural notions and frameworks for ascribing meaning. As such, the aims of neutrality and objectivity are themselves cultural constructs which, ironically, are severely compromised by the numerous errors of cultural interpretation occurring at various levels within refugee hearings. These misunderstandings—which can determine a person's fate—occur at a subtle, seemingly invisible level, often leaving the actors oblivious to the cultural processes leading to such clashes.

Method

Research Protocol and Sample

The protocol reflects the primary objective, that is, to determine and describe the legal, psychological, and cultural factors associated with lack of consensus on cases of refugee claimants heard by the Immigration and Refugee Board (IRB). It is a cross-sectional retrospective study. The approach is qualitative, with in-depth study of a selected number of cases, definition of appropriate categories in the legal, cultural, and psychological fields, and application of those categories to all the available cases.

The initial sample was to be a selection of cases from three sources: lawyers, health professionals and NGOs, and the IRB. When the IRB refused to take part, the cases were taken from the first two sources using a snowball sampling method. There were three criteria for inclusion: (1) The application for refugee status was refused; (2) There was a major disagreement between at least two of the actors (IRB, lawyers, health professionals and NGO) about the decision; (3) The persons referring the cases had noted major legal, psychological, or cultural problems in the case. Cases handled prior to 1994 and those for which documentation was insufficient for in-depth analysis were excluded.

Eighty-four cases were referred to us by lawyers (60 per cent) and health and community workers (40 per cent). Forty-four cases had to be excluded on the basis of the criteria listed above or because consent could not be obtained from the claimant (impossible to find, deported, etc.). Only four claimants refused their consent; four others never returned our calls, and so we considered them to have refused, which left us with a refusal rate of 17 per cent.

Data were gathered between June 1999 and May 2000. Members of the fieldwork team went all over Montreal to obtain the various documents, which were then sorted and reviewed to ensure the anonymity of those concerned.

Definition of Variables

First, focus groups consisting of researchers and actors from the different settings helped establish the characteristic factors likely to explain divergences in the perceptions and evaluations of the various actors involved in the hearing process. The list was validated and completed when we conducted our qualitative analysis. We divided the factors into three categories, described below.

Legal factors:

—For all actors, problems working within the framework of a procedure that is by its nature inquisitory.
—For Board Members and RCOs, problems assessing the relevance (expert evidence, documentary evidence, etc.) and the weight of the evidence (significance of contradictions between claimant's personal information form (PIF) and oral testimony; use of judicial notice; understanding of the social and political situation in claimant's homeland, etc.).
—For Board Members, problems in conducting a hearing (questioning claimants, respecting code of ethics and legal etiquette, etc.).
—For Board Members, problems in writing the reasons for decision.
—For claimants' lawyers, lack of preparation for the hearing.
—For interpreters, problems in correctly translating claimants' testimony, due to intercultural barriers, such as dialect, verbal and non-verbal behaviour, etc.

Psychological factors:

—For all actors, but especially Board Members and RCOs, problems coping with transmission of trauma, such as:
  —Strong avoidance reactions (direct avoidance, denial, and normalization of extreme situations, sometimes expressed as cynicism, etc.).
  —Uncontrolled emotional reactions in confronting traumatic experiences (anger, victims perceived as aggressors, lack of empathy, reaction formation, etc.).
  —Lack of knowledge of psychological consequences of trauma (symptoms and short-, medium-, and long-term effects, relationship between victim and torturer, etc.).
  —Improper use of expert reports prepared by physicians and psychologists (prejudice or ignorance, status of expert, tendency to take place of expert, etc.).
—For claimants' lawyers, tendency not to protect claimants from being retraumatized.
—For health professionals, lack of clarity of medical and psychological reports presented.

Cultural factors:

—For all actors, but especially Board Members and RCOs:
  —Lack of familiarity with the political and social situation in claimant's homeland.

54 *C. Rousseau, F. Crépeau, P. Foxen, F. Houle*

— Misrepresentations of daily life in a country racked by war or other conflict.
— Simplistic representations of social coherence (stereotypes).
— Cultural misunderstandings, insensitivity and prejudice based on sex, ethnic origin, religion, and sexual orientation.
— Incomprehension of problems with time sequence and narrative coherence in accounts of war and flight.

Analysis

The analysis had three parts:

— Development of a checklist used to classify cases by socio-demographic profile, reasons for and source of referral, and available documents;
— In-depth analysis of ten cases to refine and complement the determination and description of the factors under study;
— Development of an analysis grid based on the factors that could be applied to all the cases to obtain a quantitative picture of the significance of the interrelationships between the factors.

The case files included the IRB decision, the personal information form (PIF) filled in by the claimant on arrival, the documentary evidence, the judicial review application after initial refusal, medical and psychological expert reports, affidavits, identity papers, and various other documents. The complete recordings (on cassettes) of the hearings were obtained for all cases studied in depth and for a number of others, as well.

Most of the cases examined (87.5 per cent) were of claimants who arrived between 1995 and 1998. Hearings lasted anywhere from less than an hour (2.5 per cent) to more than half a day (25 per cent). Seventy per cent of claimants had only one hearing, 20 per cent had two, and 10 per cent had three or four. Compilation of the checklists enabled us to draw up a socio-demographic profile of our sample. Of particular interest is the fact that 75 per cent of claimants were between the ages of 25 and 44 and that men and women were equally represented. Most (57.5 per cent) were from Africa, while 20 per cent were from Latin America, and 20 per cent from Asia.

To select the ten cases for in-depth analysis, we used several criteria to build up a diversified sample in terms of homelands that posed a risk to personal safety (Congo, Cameroon, Burma, India, Mexico, Kazakhstan, Honduras), sex, age, sexual orientation, and family situation.

Each of the selected cases was analysed from three points of view, by legal, cultural, and psychological professionals with extensive knowledge of the issues and experience in content analysis in their respective fields.

Another team of qualified professionals did the quantitative coding of all the cases after the categories were confirmed in each of the three areas.

Findings

Qualitative Findings

Legal Findings: In the last decade, the Federal Court laid down the general principles which must guide the IRB in the decision-making process. However, our research showed that very obvious mistakes in the handling of evidence are still being made and that hearings can still be poorly conducted, both situations often resulting in reasons for decision which are clearly inadequate.

Board Members often conclude that the claimant's story is not credible when they find contradictions between the notes taken by an immigration officer at the point of entry into Canada, the PIF completed by the claimant, and the latter's oral testimony during the hearing. However, in several cases, the 'contradictions' were either minimal, or had been explained at the hearing, or could have been explained had the Board Members asked the appropriate questions. For example, in one case, the claimant explained in oral testimony that the person she was living with was the leader of a cultural group, and that this information was not transcribed in her PIF due either to a confusion on the part of the lawyer or to a bad translation. The panel refused this explanation since, at the beginning of the hearing, she had solemnly affirmed having full knowledge of the contents of her PIF and since the latter had been translated for her.

Evaluation of the evidence from expert witnesses or reports (such as medical or foreign affairs experts) can be capricious. In one case, an expert psychological report provided details of the post-traumatic stress syndrome suffered by the claimant after he was tortured. The report included pictures taken immediately after his arrival in Canada showing his body covered with cigarette burns. A health professional had conducted six consecutive interviews of the claimant, making a thorough assessment of his condition and relating it to the details of his story. Nevertheless, the claim was rejected and the conclusions of the expert report summarily dismissed. One of the Board Members said during the hearing that he always took expert psychological reports 'with a grain of salt'. It was further discovered, during the hearing, that he had not even read the report: after repeated requests from the lawyer, the Chair had to interrupt the hearing so as to allow the Board Member to read it. In addition, the Chair herself made dubious comments about the fact that she herself was a smoker, implying that she did not give much weight to the cigarette burn marks or to the expert report. These actions show a serious lack of appreciation as to the precise reason for having an expert report and what evidentiary weight it carries.

In another case, the RCO acted as an expert on the Thematic Apperception Test (TAT) contained in an expert report. He subsequently made disdainful remarks concerning the subjectivity of psychology, and in particular, of psychoanalysis. Neither the Board Members, nor the RCO took the expert status of the psychologist concerned seriously and they declared that the report and the testimony were not credible overall, without any further explanation.

56 *C. Rousseau, F. Crépeau, P. Foxen, F. Houle*

In a case from Kazakhstan, the claimant had not mentioned in the PIF that her young son had been burned by a Molotov cocktail thrown at their house. During the hearing, she explained that she did not want him to be interrogated, because she wanted to protect him from further suffering. A psychological report presented in evidence revealed the parents' feelings of despair and powerlessness with regard to their son's injuries. The mother also had symptoms of trauma and wanted to protect her son at all costs from being exposed to stimuli capable of triggering additional trauma. The Board Members determined that the claim was not credible based on two omissions, including the fact that the attack on the son was not revealed. This showed a lack of appreciation of the value of the expert report in explaining the avoidance mechanisms seen in a traumatic situation, in the context of a mother's desire to protect her son.

Many cases show little consideration for the documentary evidence provided by the counsel for the claimant, and often this evidence is not even mentioned in the reasoning for rejection of the claim. For example, the members affirmed in one decision that the documentary evidence in no way showed that the claimant's minority group was oppressed, a statement that blatantly and without explanation contradicted documentation provided to the panel.

Board Members also show discomfort in a non-adversarial setting such as the refugee determination process. For example, at the beginning of the hearing of one particular case, the Chair declared from the outset that she did not want to hear the claimant's story as she suspected that he would tell the same story as she had already read in the PIF. She rejected the counsel's request for permission to ask the claimant to clarify various points, and asked the RCO to proceed with her questions. This demonstrates a serious misunderstanding of the role of a hearing in any adjudicative process, which is to allow the matter to be adequately and fully addressed. In several other cases, the Board Members and the RCO argued with the counsel or the claimant, the discussion often becoming heated, an indication of uncontrolled interpersonal conflict. In other cases, Board Members showed outright disbelief of the claimant's story, made inappropriate comments or displayed cynicism. All these patterns of behaviour indicate a lack of appreciation for judicial decorum and etiquette, which should be respected by the members of an administrative tribunal, since these rules exist to ensure that justice is done in a dispassionate manner.

In addition to the conduct of Board Members during hearings, the written decisions often show serious flaws, either by containing only a list of contradictions between the PIF and the oral testimony, or by simply declaring laconically that the claimant is not credible, or by not even mentioning the evidence presented, especially documentary evidence. In one case, the decision starts with a declaration stating that the claimant's testimony was very vague and lacked precision: on the contrary, taped recordings of the hearing show that the testimony was clear, articulate, precise, and that the claimant answered all questions calmly and thoroughly.

In a case from Congo, the hearing focused on events occurring after the rape of the claimant by the military, which was the central event forming the basis of the refugee claim. The question of rape was not addressed during the hearing. The rejection of the claim was based on minor aspects, such as contradictions between the PIF and the oral testimony regarding the question of when exactly the claimant had become conscious of the presence of her brother-in-law in the vehicle that provided her escape. This 'contradiction' was sufficient on its own, in the eyes of the Board Members, not only to reject the claim, but also to conclude that the claim had no credible basis (a finding that prohibits any review of the decision). The Board Members addressed some but not all of the issues arising from the rape, even though they were fundamental elements of the claim. They did not, for example, include the existence of a medical certificate in their deliberation.

In a case from Burma, interrogation of the claimant lasted five hours and was conducted in a disorderly manner. There were constant repetitions of questions to which the claimant had already given satisfactory answers. The repetitions were not justified by the Board Members and were evidence of a confrontational attitude that bordered on harassment. Generally speaking, such repetitions and revisiting of questions creates a tense atmosphere and gives the impression that the Board Members do not believe the claimant. However, it is impossible to identify precisely which facts or events Members find lacking credibility. In fact, this decision demonstrated that the members did not quite know on which grounds to base an appropriate challenge of the claimant. This case revealed a serious lack of preliminary preparation that can be felt throughout the hearing.

In sum, the review of the cases noted above demonstrates that some Board Members fail to carry out their duties effectively. They do not always know how to treat expert evidence, or they use it in ways which are clearly inappropriate. They tend to create an atmosphere in the hearing room that is not conducive to good decision-making. They have also demonstrated difficulty in conducting a hearing correctly. Such basic rules of evidence and procedure are, however, of obvious importance for a tribunal that makes daily decisions concerning people's life, liberty and security.

Psychological Findings: Qualitative data analysis from a psychological perspective suggests major problems in two areas: knowledge, and capacity to transmit knowledge, about the impact of traumatic experiences and the effect of recounting them; and the difficulty of all concerned in coping with vicarious traumatization.

Lack of knowledge of the impact of traumatic experiences is particularly obvious among Board Members and RCOs. Frequently, typical post-traumatic symptoms are misinterpreted as signs that the claimant's story is not credible. Omissions of an event like rape from the PIF are commonly considered to be evidence that it probably did not happen, a judgement that ignores the personal and social consequences of such disclosure. In the case of the young Congolese woman, the Board Members could not understand her non-disclosure of rape

58 *C. Rousseau, F. Crépeau, P. Foxen, F. Houle*

at the border and on the PIF, even though her previous disclosure of this event had had devastating consequences for her: her husband had abandoned her, and her father had been assassinated because he intended to ask for her aggressors, officers of the Kabila regime, to be brought to justice. Dates and time sequences are another major source of misunderstanding. Board Members generally consider that incidents such as detention or events following a major trauma should be reported accurately. In the case of severe trauma, this is often impossible. Classical signs of trauma such as confusion and forgetting details are often met with growing impatience on the part of Board Members and RCOs. In response to this Congolese woman who was raped and could not remember the exact date, nor the date of her conversation with the medical personnel assigned by Immigration, a Board Member said, very sarcastically, 'So you don't remember ...', implying that the claimant was lying.

As previously presented in the legal findings, the Board Members often lack the skills to use medical and psychological expertise to compensate for their own lack of knowledge. On the other hand, these expert opinions can also be misleading. Analysis of the medical and psychological reports shows that therapists have a tendency to predict the claimant's behaviour during the hearing, based on the therapeutic interview. The IRB hearing, however, presents a radically different environment from the secure patient–professional relationship. Although aimed at protecting the claimant, firm statements by a doctor or psychologist can often lead to problems later, because, if the actual testimony contradicts the prediction, the expert's entire report may be called into question, thus damaging the claimant's credibility. The technical jargon used by some experts may also put off some readers, who may overlook important conclusions because they fail to understand them. Some assessments lack clarity, as the appraisal of the capacity to testify is often mingled with an appraisal of the credibility of the patient's story. Finally, sometimes conclusions are too directive and perceived as intrusive by the Board Members.

Vicarious traumatization appears to affect everyone involved in the claimant's case, but it manifests itself differently depending on the actor's role in court. Board Members and RCOs, who are not linked to the claimant (so their reactions are probably more internalized), have the most blatant avoidance reactions. These take numerous forms: direct avoidance, denial, and trivialization of extreme events.

Direct avoidance is manifested by an expressed wish not to hear the traumatic story. In the case of a young claimant from Chiapas, the chairwoman stated repeatedly that she did not want to hear a description of the torture suffered by the claimant, and that reading the PIF was sufficient evidence regarding that issue. She said: 'The details being described, torture and all that, I don't want to hear that'. The lawyer insisted that the claimant recount part of his story and she replied, 'Sir, I personally do not want to hear from him what has happened, what happened to his father or to his two sisters. I find it inhuman to ask him to repeat it [...]. Maybe he experienced it; maybe ... I don't need that'. The claim was rejected for lack of credibility.

Direct avoidance is often presented as a way to protect the claimant, a solicitude which is then contradicted by the fact that accounts of traumatic events are either dismissed or considered not credible. In the case of the young woman from Congo, the RCO insisted: 'I've already told you that I don't want to go into details like that, madam. Especially for you ... this is not necessary. I want to know how you got out [of prison] and what happened before you got out [the rape and mistreatment happened before the claimant escaped]'.

In other cases, avoidance is more indirect and is manifested by totally ignoring traumatic events. A young Latin American homosexual had been assaulted and raped by soldiers. After he filed an official complaint with the police about the attack, he was burgled, threatened over the phone, and attacked again. After his departure for Canada, his partner was killed before he had a chance to join him. The RCO, in her oral summary of all the important facts of the case, failed to mention the murder of the partner, and scarcely a single question was asked about this essential fact. In the hearing of a Burmese woman, the Board Members emphasized factual information that was not always relevant to the case (geographic details, renewal of passports, etc.). The Board Members glossed over the subject of the arrest, rape and abuse of the claimant, her psychological and physical problems (shame, fear, the way she hides the scars), the racist harassment and insults she suffered in her country of origin. They quickly changed the topic, discussing more neutral information, such as the type of building that the claimant was kept in or the existence of a demonstration permit. Besides showing a complete lack of empathy, this treatment of the claimant was a way for the Board Members to avoid or deny her suffering and dismiss its importance.

Trivializing horrific events is another form of avoidance that often manifests itself as cynicism. As demonstrated in the case of the Mexican mentioned earlier, confronted with the claimant's multiple cigarette burns, a Board Member said, 'You know, I smoke ...'. This apparent cynicism is indicative of a traumatic situation being treated as normal. Establishing a parallel between an everyday occurrence like smoking, and torture, renders the torture innocuous.

Very commonly, confronting the claimant's traumatic experiences provokes uncontrolled emotional reactions in the other people present. Although most hearings begin on a courteous note, this often turns to anger or hostile exchanges. In the case of a claimant from Central America, soldiers assaulted him and another man, leaving the latter in what appeared to be a state of shock or a coma. The claimant asked the soldiers (who were the only ones around) for help for his companion and was brutally told to leave, which he eventually did. The dead body of the other man was discovered a few days later. In the course of the hearing, a Board Member, showing clearly that he did not believe the story, angrily asked the claimant how he could have asked for help from their torturers; five minutes later, and still angry, he asked how the claimant could have left his companion in the hands of their torturers. These responses show a very strong emotional reaction, a lack of empathy, and an association of the victim with the aggressor, all symptoms of an inability to cope with the emotional stress created by the hearing.

In the case of the young woman from Burma, the general tone, which was courteous at the beginning of the hearing, became progressively more charged. The Board Members even became provocative at times, repeating the claimant's words and being sarcastic. For example, a Board Member asked the claimant if she was in the habit of disobeying her parents. The members also laughed among themselves. They seemed to be creating a psychological distance from the emotional intensity of the problems experienced by the claimant, to the point where they were no longer able to listen with empathy. As a consequence of their own psychological self-protection, they first took an adversarial stance, then showed scorn for the claimant. These attitudes in turn influenced the claimant's reactions, which ranged from anxiety, demonstrated in the tone of voice and rhythm of speech, to impatience, manifested as disrespect for the rules of the hearing, and finally to total helplessness (crying).

Sarcasm can also provoke rebound anger in the claimant. In a Honduran claimant's hearing, the following dialogue occurred:

> Board Member: 'Were they shooting at you because they wanted to kill you or were they shooting at you because you were trying to run away?'
>
> Claimant: 'I was just in the middle of the plantation and I heard some shooting and I thought, that's what I think, that they try to kill us.'
>
> Board Member (sarcastically): 'So you're not sure?'
>
> Claimant (becoming angry): 'Do you think that they were shooting at ... at ... the plants ... at the corn plants?'

Lawyers, while often forming close alliances with their clients, can also react inappropriately to the tense atmosphere of the hearing, for example laughing about an obviously sad situation. They also have a tendency to expose their clients to retraumatization, so as to present more convincing testimony. In one case, a lawyer accepted the chairperson's suggestion that an eleven-year-old child's torso be stripped during the hearing in order to show his scars, which was totally unnecessary, since there was already a thorough medical report and pictures of the child's body in the file. The child was severely retraumatized by the event, and the actors even noticed it during the hearing. One Board Member, caught off guard, reacted by stating: 'He can just think of me as his grandmother.'

Finally, the difficult emotional climate also has repercussions on relations among the parties. Sometimes interpersonal conflicts between the actors (often between the lawyer and either the Board Members or the RCO) turn into an open fight for control and power over the hearing, to the detriment of the decision, which is put at stake by the fight.

Cultural Findings: Numerous types of cultural misunderstanding or miscommunication can be found in the cases examined. In several of these, Board

Members and RCOs demonstrate a very poor understanding of the political complexities of violence, and of the nature of persecution where ethnic, religious, cultural and political antagonisms interact. Simplistic assumptions regarding political violence are evident in each case; the Board Members often seem to posit war as a Manichaean situation where clearly-defined groups function in opposition to or in alliance with one another, and where an individual, if truly persecuted, will immediately flee. This lack of basic knowledge concerning the political and social situation in the country of origin often contributes to their final decision.

In a case involving a Tutsi claimant from Rwanda, for example, the Board Members demonstrated a highly simplistic assessment of the genocide/post-genocide situation, and the changes wrought by ethnic violence over time. They argued that Tutsis should be safe in Rwanda since the government is Tutsi, and that the government is democratic since it released Hutu prisoners; they rejected the expert witness's testimony which outlined a more complex political situation, stating that the latter was biased. In a case from Chiapas, Mexico, a Board Member described the conflict as a clear-cut situation where landless indigenous peasants were fighting a repressive army; in consequence, he argued that the claimant's uncle, an army official, could not possibly have been able to buy land in Chiapas in 1995, saying that 'this seems to me completely out of context and unimaginable' (translated from French). In fact, much of Chiapas has been heavily militarized, with pockets of Zapatista support existing in some areas while others side with the army; that an army member would have been able to buy property at this time is perfectly plausible.

In several cases, the Board Members' concept of daily life in a country at war, in low-intensity conflict, or in situations of persecution, was simplistic or false. They seemed unable to envisage situations where localized violence reigns as conflicting groups struggle for power, or where the military or police are involved in corruption, intimidation and abuse of power. In a Kazakh case, the Board Members' lack of comprehension regarding local ethnic persecution (of the Dungan population) was clear. As one of their main arguments for rejecting the claim, the Board Members stated that, rather than being persecuted by nationalist Kazakhs due to their ethnic status, the claimants were in fact afraid of a particular Kazakh individual. In most situations of ethnic violence, however, pre-existing local disputes and power struggles (between individuals, families or groups) become drawn into the dynamics of violence; often, ethnic difference is utilized by particular community members as a justification for persecution, oppression or revenge.

Board Members also often seem incredulous at the arbitrary behaviour of the authorities (police, army, government) as recounted by claimants. The notion that terror and persecution are implemented precisely through arbitrariness, chaos and impunity seems difficult for them to grasp, and the inability of claimants to provide a rational reason for such abusive behaviour leads them to further doubt their story. In a case from Burma, for example, the Board Members found it contradictory that although the claimant's military persecutors covered her eyes when kidnapping her, they failed to do so again upon her release. They are unable to enter the 'illogical' atmosphere of terror and impunity, where uncontrolled military or police often commit human rights abuses without fear or precaution.

Simplistic representations of war and persecution lead some Board Members to assume that all 'normality' or daily life is altered or comes to a standstill in situations of violence. Clearly, however, the attempt to maintain one's sustenance, home, family and social relations is a survival mechanism for those caught in situations of turmoil, and most do not choose to leave until they have truly abandoned hope. In the Kazakh case, for example, the Board Members questioned how the family could have continued living within a certain margin of normality—that is, by continuing to operate their business and moving only when necessary—despite being targeted. Reasoning the other way, some Board Members question the credibility of claimants who are unable to maintain normal social relations under extreme conditions. In a case from Mexico, they seemed incredulous that the claimant's uncle 'deserted' his family after being targeted by the army, and that the 18-year-old claimant himself did not return home after being tortured to find out about his sisters. Here the notion that maintaining contact with family members, especially if one has been branded subversive, could endanger the entire family—particularly in places where army strategies are to attack families rather than individuals, and where the only option then is to 'disappear'—was not entertained by the Board Members.

Finally, in two cases, the Board Members were highly insensitive to the use of rape as a political weapon. They showed little empathy for claimants who stated that they were raped by authorities during detention, and rejected such claims due to the women's lack of evidence. In many cultures, however, rape results in a loss of honour for the woman and her family, who, as a consequence will not request documentation from a medical authority. In both of these cases, despite the claimants' clear trauma and shame, the Board Members were abrupt, dismissive and showed discomfort about the rape testimony.

The inability to fathom life in other cultures and situations, or even the plight of refugees in Canada, also creates false expectations of cultural coherence at a more general level, often reinforcing an atmosphere of suspicion and leading to the assumption of contradiction and non-credibility. Misinterpretations of other cultural norms are based, on the one hand, on assumptions of a universal Canadian cultural 'logic', and on the other on simplistic notions or stereotypes regarding other cultures. In a Mexican case, for example, a Board Member could not believe that a middle class family in Chiapas would not have a telephone, though this is not uncommon in the region. In a case from Cameroon, the Board Members were incredulous that a female claimant could at once work in her parents' business, care for her children and participate in political activities; as they stated in their written decision, 'a mother of five has no time for political involvement'. Their assessment of this woman's capacity for political work, which was one of the main reasons for rejecting her claim, was culturally misinformed and inappropriate, since in many cultures it is common for children to be raised by the extended family.

Board Members sometimes show an inability to appreciate cultural norms surrounding family relations and values in other cultures. In an Indian case, for example, the Board Members constantly questioned the behaviour of the claimant's father, in particular his calm attitude upon being told that his daughter was missing. As the claimant stated, her father was trying to maintain her reputation since her absence from home might have been interpreted as improper. The Members did not seem to understand, in this cultural context, how important it is for a father to protect his daughter's (and family's) reputation, and the strength of character required to hide one's emotions from strangers.

Cultural misunderstandings may also affect the ability to appreciate styles of narration, expression and emotion by cultural 'others', which in turn leads to erroneous interpretations of crucial elements of the claimant's testimony. In many cultures, a strong identification with a collective identity—whether based on family, lineage, clan, language group or a broader sense of ethnicity—often blurs the boundaries between individual and community. Descriptions of traumatic events are then narrated in the context of one's broader community or ethnic loyalties. This blurring of the 'I' and the 'we'—absent in a Western style of discourse which stresses the boundaries of individualism—reflects not only a cultural narrative style but also the manner in which many persecuted people experience and interpret the violence against them. In the Kazakh case, the commissioners interpreted this style as an attempt to conceal the 'personal' nature of the claimants' persecution. In addition, different cultures have varying codes regarding the contextual appropriateness and expression of emotions. In the context of IRB hearings, where claimants are recounting painful stories of trauma to strangers, the expression of emotions (by claimants) and the interpretation of emotional styles (by Board Members) are culture-specific and can be puzzling to both parties. For example, the strong public emotional reserve characterizing some groups (often those with a history of marginality or persecution) can lead claimants to downplay certain elements of their story or to choose answers which, to Western ears, may seem incomplete, elusive or lacking in credible detail.

Cultural misunderstandings can lead to frustration, impatience and sometimes subsequent aggression on the part of Board Members, who may then fail to listen properly to the testimony presented, dismiss information, and reject or distort the evidence provided by expert witnesses or lawyers. In several cases, this lack of cultural comprehension leads Board Members to demonstrate a profound insensitivity and lack of respect, compassion and objectivity toward the claimants, or to deflect hostility onto the lawyer, the expert witness or even the interpreter. Through such hostile projections, victims (i.e. claimants) are sometimes portrayed by the Board Members as aggressors or as deserving of the abuse they have received. In one case, for example, the claimant was implicitly associated with 'known war criminals' who have been able to obtain refugee status with the help of expert medical testimony, which was denounced as generally unreliable. And in several cases, this frustration leads Board Members to constantly interrupt the claimants' answers; as such, they shift rapidly from requiring detailed explanations to silencing the claimant who tries to provide them, leaving the latter perplexed and unable to know whether or not, and how, to answer.

Finally, lack of cultural understanding or receptivity often translates into suspicion and cynicism with respect to the testimonies presented. As a result of these misunderstandings, Board Members often perceive 'contradictions' where there are none, attempt to 'poke holes' in stories, and refuse to take into account the claimants' clarifications. As we have seen, the assumption of contradiction runs from minor details of the accounts to the broader political contexts of the stories, leads to unfounded assumptions and shifts in argument, and ultimately impacts on the overall assessment and prevents a fair or objective decision; indeed, smaller 'contradictions' are often generalized to a 'lack of credibility' regarding the whole story.

Quantitative Findings

The quantitative analysis of the 40 cases revealed that 20 per cent of the files present only one type of problem (juridical, cultural, or psychological), while 27.5 per cent show problems in two of the areas, and 52.5 per cent present problems in all three fields. This indicates an important overlap between the factors identified and may allow us to understand why purely legal and administrative efforts to improve the system might have failed to address the inherent problems.

At the legal level, the most prevalent problems concern the administration of evidence (87.5 per cent) and the social and political conditions of the country of origin (62.5 per cent). Problems in interpreting administrative and international law are also frequent (40 per cent). Finally, in more than a quarter of the cases (27.5 per cent), the rules of conduct and politeness were breached.

At the psychological level, we encounter problems of massive avoidance of traumatic content, which is a typical manifestation of vicarious traumatization (75 per cent), and lack of empathy (75 per cent). The expression of prejudice (67.5 per cent) and behaviour that denotes a certain cynicism (50 per cent) were also very prevalent. Finally, in more than a third of cases (35 per cent), it is possible to detect signs of emotional distress related to secondary trauma that is transferred to a number of different actors.

In the cultural field, lack of understanding of the refugee's cultural, social and political context of origin is a principal factor (72.5 per cent). Difficulty in properly assessing the social relations of the claimant is also important (52.5 per cent). Within the context of both the hearing and the decision, prejudices, stereotypes and difficulties in communicating play a role in 42.5 per cent of the files.

Denial was considered to be a problem by the coders in more than 90 per cent of the files. This phenomenon is partly due to the selection criteria: all the files had a negative decision that was based on non-credibility of the claimant.

The results do not permit a clear distinction between psychological and cultural denial of reality in addition to ideological disagreements between the parties. As a rigorous, all-inclusive definition of denial was difficult to put into practice, we considered it best to omit it from the conclusions.

Systemic Findings

Even though the objective of our research was not of a systemic nature, we discovered and documented certain elements that, in addition to the characteristics of individual actors, appeared to have an important influence on the process.

The non-adversarial process seems to create much confusion as to the respective roles of the actors. The interventionist attitude of many Board Members often leads to a tense atmosphere including emotional reactions and, at times, aggressive behaviour by all actors. This has a very negative impact on the civility of the judicial debate, and adds to the confusion of many claimants who no longer know who they have to convince and against whom they have to defend themselves. As there is no 'official adversary', the lawyer often does not know what attitude to take toward the Board Members, who often present themselves as protective of refugees while simultaneously adopting aggressive attitudes towards the claimants. If the lawyer tries a conciliatory approach, he runs the risk of appearing unconvincing or of approving unacceptable demands, such as the stripping of the little boy's torso to show the scars. If he tries an aggressive approach, he risks antagonizing the Board Members. Depending on the Board Members' attitude in the case, the RCOs are often cautious, asking general questions, drawing unhelpful conclusions: in one case, the RCO simply concluded that the Board Members would have to determine whether the claimant was credible. At other times, especially when the Board Members do not intervene much, the RCO acts as a public prosecutor, cross-examining the claimant on each and every detail that could point to a 'contradiction'. In many cases, the RCO is the person most ill at ease in the system: it might be advisable to rethink their role, whatever other solutions may be adopted. The interpreters may also be affected by the unacknowledged interpersonal conflicts between the actors, and have a tendency to side, for emotional reasons, with one or other of the actors, which might show in their attitudes.

The general climate of tension is either concretized in direct conflicts, or displaced against one of the other actors. All this confusion results in much uneasiness in the way the actors interact. Not only is there a confusion in the legal role of each actor, but this confusion has a tremendous impact on the psychological and cultural dimensions, which as seen above already reinforce the general sense of uncertainty.

Discussion

Our results suggest a wide overlap among legal, psychological and cultural factors which appear problematic in the IRB decision-making process. The majority of cases not only present problems in more than one domain, but the meanings of specific events vary in these domains in a complex way. For example, breaking the rules of politeness in a hearing is a legal error and can have catastrophic consequences psychologically if the frightened claimant becomes increasingly confused. In the same way, the lack of contextual and cultural understanding or sensitivity often leads the Board Members or RCO to focus on insignificant details, which elicits rejection feelings in the claimant and leads to very poor administration of the evidence in the decision.

This interlocking of different domains becomes further complicated by institutional and systemic issues. The double bind in which the non-adversarial process places the claimant, from the explicit discourse 'we are here to protect you' to the implied construing of the refugee as a liar, if not a criminal, is structured, on the one hand, around societal representations of the refugee and of the 'pure' victim, and, on the other, around political and public opinion pressure to align Canada's rates of acceptance of refugees with those of most other Western countries. Indeed, our data suggest that there exists a 'culture of disbelief' within the structure of the IRB; however, given our restricted sample and methodology, such a claim would require further research.

Taken one by one, the legal, cultural and psychological aspects of the workings of the IRB Members are not sufficient, on their own, for us to call into question the decision-making process. Each of these aspects can be used in isolation to make particular decisions appear well-founded. However, the convergence of the political dimensions to a case (and any lack of understanding thereof), the unspoken personal processes at work, the social representations of each actor and the emotional burden of the hearing on the decision-makers, makes their task difficult, and causes analysts, such as the authors of this article, to have difficulty in finding solutions to this problem.

Our results suggest possible avenues to increase the capacities of the Board Members to fulfil their roles. Board Members should be selected, and should be known to be selected, according to their abilities and experience. These abilities and experience should cover three areas:

— Legal knowledge: refugee law, immigration law, human rights law, conduct of judicial hearings, how to interact with counsels and claimants, how to assess the evidence, how to write decisions; etc.
— Experience in the field: work in countries torn by war or internal strife; work with refugees or displaced persons; sensitivity to the dynamics involved in working with people from other cultures, in terms of communication and understanding; etc.
— Psychological abilities: capacity to bear the suffering of all actors, including themselves; experience in dealing with traumatized persons; etc.

It is unrealistic to expect each Board Member to be excellent in all three areas, but it would be important for candidates to show experience and skills in all three, with some degree of excellence in one or two. Only then would they be confident enough and command enough respect to use the position of authority that they hold in order to impose standards of quality on the behaviour of all other actors.

The training of all actors must be improved. A continuing and well-designed training programme oriented towards cultural and psychological sensitivity as well as a basic social science framework concerning issues of war, poverty and the refugee process should be offered to all actors. This training should avoid being just a check-list of the basic 'differences' of other cultural norms, modes of communication, psychological reactions to trauma and various political upheavals throughout the world. Rather, it would propose a broader discussion concerning 1) the construction, perception and experience of cultural difference; 2) the complexities and nuances of situations of political violence, low-intensity conflict, ethnic strife, illiteracy, rural culture, etc.; 3) the refugee experience; 4) the diversity of responses to trauma and their influence on the hearing.

The limitations of this pilot project should be borne in mind when interpreting the results presented here. These include: the local character of the cases examined, the lack of estimation of inter-rater agreement between coders, the paucity of data on Board Members' backgrounds, as well as the small sample involved. These limitations signal a need for caution with regard to the possibility of generalizing the results, and suggest the need for further studies. Subsequent research should ideally be conducted in various sites, and should complement the qualitative perspective by using an epidemiological approach that would highlight the prevalence of the problems detected. The participation of the IRB in the conceptualization and implementation of such a research project would be highly valuable.

However, taking into account these limitations, our results suggest that in order to understand and resolve the problems faced by the IRB, a radically different approach is needed. On the one hand, this study confirms empirical knowledge from refugee advocacy groups and refugee studies scholars on the inadequacies within the system. Research data can strengthen this position, often dismissed as mainly ideological, and fuel the fight to improve the system at the supranational level, pressuring States on the basis of their international image. On the other hand, the complexity of the dynamic observed points to the fact that an administrative tribunal like the IRB cannot be transformed without an internal realization that work is needed; and that, even if this internal realization is triggered by external pressure, it should rely on partnership, negotiation and building a certain level of trust among all concerned. Modifying the administrative parameters without addressing the underlying representations will probably just replicate the multiple unsuccessful attempts to transform the system. A multidisciplinary perspective is essential to understanding both the personal and systemic factors that appear to be problematic in the refugee determination process. The gaps or deficiencies identified here demonstrate that the integration of legal, cultural and psychological dimensions should not only inform future research, but should also be reflected in the selection and training of the various actors. The Board Members, the RCOs and the other professionals involved have a heavy responsibility to guarantee the right of asylum and the protection of refugees. Only a critical vision that encourages a creative role for each actor in the system as a whole can help fulfil this mandate.

1. Biographical information on the latest appointees may be found on the website of Citizenship and Immigration Canada, at: www.cic.gc.ca, under 'What's new?'
2. Crépeau, F. and Houle, F., 'Compétence et indépendance: Clefs de la crédibilité de tout processus de reconnaissance du statut de réfugié', Mémoire déposé auprès de la Ministre de la Citoyenneté et de l'Immigration lors des consultations sur le Rapport Trempe-Davis-Kunin, 6 March 1998, 32 pp. A more recent version of the same, adapted to Bill C-31 that was studied by Parliament between March and October 2000 (though never adopted) and C-11 (essentially identical to C-31) which was tabled in the House on 21 February 2001, can be found under the citation: Crépeau, F. and Houle, F., 'La sécurité des réfugiés et la compétence des commissaires de la CISR: les silences inopportuns du projet de loi C-11'/'The Security of Refugees and the Abilities of IRB Members: the Inappropriate Silence of Bill C-11', 12 March 2001. It can be found at: http://www.juris.uqam.ca/cedim/indexfr.html _ Recherches.

AIGNER, U. M. (1995) *Intercultural Communication: Considerations and Limitations as Reflected in Translation, with Practical Applications for Canadian Refugee Claimants.* Montreal: Communications, McGill University.

ATLANI, L. and **ROUSSEAU, C.** (2000) 'The Politics of Culture in Humanitarian Aid to Refugees having Experienced Sexual Violence', *Transcultural Psychiatry* **37**(3): 435–465.

BARSKY, R. F. (1994) *Constructing a Productive Other: Discourse Theory and the Convention Refugee Hearing.* Amsterdam/Philadelphia: John Benjamins Publishing Company.

—— (2000) *Arguing and Justifying: Assessing the Convention Refugees' Choice of Moment, Motive and Host Country.* Aldershot: Ashgate.

BEISER, M. (1993) 'After the Door has been Opened: The Mental Health of Immigrants and Refugees in Canada', in V. Robinson (ed.), *The International Refugee Crisis: British and Canadian Responses.* London: Macmillan, p. 213–227.

DANIEL, E. V. and **KNUDSEN, J. C.** (1995) *Mistrusting Refugees.* Berkeley: University of California Press.

DANIELI, Y. (1998) *International Handbook of Multigenerational Legacies of Trauma.* New York: Plenum Press.

FORNAZZARI, X. (1995) 'The Trauma of Exile and Resettlement', in K. Price (ed.), *Community Support for Survivors of Torture: A Manual.* Toronto: Canadian Centre for Victims of Torture, pp. 14–22.

GEERTZ, C. (1973) *The Interpretation of Cultures: Selected Essays.* New York: Basic Books.

GOFFMAN, I. (1969) *Social Interaction.* Chicago: University of Chicago Press.

HATHAWAY, J. C. (1993) *Rebuilding Trust: Report of the Review of Fundamental Justice in Information Gathering and Dissemination at the Immigration and Refugee Board of Canada,* Ottawa.

JARANSON, J. M. (1995) 'Government Sanctioned Torture: Status of the Rehabilitation Movement', *Transcultural Psychiatric Research Review* **32**: 253–286.

KÄLIN, W. (1986) 'Troubled Communication: Cross-Cultural Misunderstandings in the Asylum Hearing', *International Migration Review* **2**(2): 230–241.

KIRMAYER, L. J. (1996) 'Landscapes of Memory: Trauma, Narrative, and Dissociation', in P. A. M. Lambek (ed.), *Tense Past: Cultural Essays in Trauma and Memory.* New York: Routledge, pp. 173–198.

KNAPP, K., ENNINGER, W. and **KNAPP-POTTHOFF, A.** (1987) *Analysing Intercultural Communication.* Berlin: Mouton de Gruyter.

LEVY, V., DONGIER, P., LILLO, C., HÉBERT, D. and **CÔTÉ, M.-L.** (1998) *Personne ayant subi la violence organisée. L'évaluation psychologique et médicale dans le processus de revendication du statut de réfugié.* Réseau canadien pour la santé des victimes de la torture et de la violence organisée (RIVO), Montreal, pp. 18.

LOESCHER, G. (1993) *Beyond Charity: International Cooperation and the Global Refugee Problem.* New York/Oxford: Oxford University Press.
MALKKI, L. (1992) 'National Geographic: The Rooting of Peoples and the Territorialization of National Identity among Scholars and Refugees', *Cultural Anthropology* **7**(1): 24–44.
MOELLER, S. and **CHRISTIANSEN, L. K.** (1996) 'How Dealing with Traumatized Refugees Affects the Therapist and the Institution Concerned', in K. Pelzer (ed.) *Counselling and Psychotherapy of Victims of Organised Violence in Sociocultural Context.* Frankfurt: IKO—Verlag für Interkulturelle Kommunikation, pp. 240–243.
PELOSI, A. M. (1996) *Intercultural Communication in the Refugee Determination Hearing.* Montreal: School of Social Work, McGill University.
PELTZER, K. (1997) 'Counselling and Rehabilitation of Victims of Human Rights Violations in Africa', *Psychopathologie africaine* **28**(1): 55–87.
PYNOOS, R. S. and **NADER, K.** (1989) 'Case Study: Children's Memory and Proximity to Violence', *Journal of American Academy of Child and Adolescent Psychiatry* **28**(2): 236–241.
ROUSSEAU, C. (1998) 'Familial History of War Trauma in Refugee Adolescents: A Longitudinal Study', in D. I. Hassall (ed.), *Protecting Children: Innovation and Inspiration—Te Hui Taumata monga Tamariki '98.* Auckland, New Zealand: International Society for Prevention of Child Abuse and Neglect (ISPCAN), pp. 15–16.
—— (2000) 'Les réfugiés à notre porte: violence organisée et souffrance sociale', *Criminologie* **33**(1): 185–201.
SAMOVAR, L. and **PORTER, R.** (1994) *Intercultural Communication: A Reader.* Belmont, CA: Wadsworth.
SHOWLER, P. (2000) Oral statement at the Spring meeting of the Canadian Council for Refugees, Vancouver, June.
SILK, J. (1986) *Despite a Generous Spirit: Denying Asylum in the United States.* Washington: United States for Refugees.
SILOVE, D., STEEL, Z. and **WATTERS, C.** (2000) 'Policies of Deterrence and the Mental Health of Asylum Seekers', *Journal of the American Medical Association* **284**(5): 604–611.
TERR, L. (1983) 'Time Sense Following Psychic Trauma: A Clinical Study of Ten Adults and Twenty Children', *American Journal of Orthopsychiatry* **54**: 244–262.
UNHCR (1992) *Handbook on Procedures and Criteria for Determining Refugee Status.* Geneva: UNHCR.
VINAR, M. and **VINAR, M.** (1989) *Exil et torture.* Paris: Éditions Denoël.
WATSON, S. (1995) 'Preparing Caregivers to Work with Survivors of Torture: The Importance of Self-awareness and Self-care', in K. Price (ed.), *Community Support for Survivors of Torture: A Manual.* Toronto: Canadian Centre for Victims of Torture, pp. 111–119.
ZOLBERG, A. R., SUHRKE, A. and **AGUAYO, S.** (1989) *Escape from Violence: Conflict and the Refugee Crisis in the Developing World.* Oxford: Oxford University Press.

Reported Cases

Adjei v. *Canada (Minister of Employment and Immigration)*, (1989) 7 Imm. L.R. 169 at 173 (F.C.A.).
Alfred v. *Canada (Minister of Employment and Immigration)*, (1994) 76 FTR 231.
Bouguettaya v. *Canada (Minister of Citizenship and Immigration)*, [2000] A.C.F. no 992 (j. Lemieux).
Chan v. *Canada (Minister of Employment and Immigration)*, [1995] 3 S.C.R. 593 (S.C.C.).
Gengeswaran v. *Canada (Minister of Citizenship and Immigration)*, (May 19, 1999), Doc. IMM-4318-98 (FTD).
Gracielome v. *Canada (Minister of Employment and Immigration)*, (1989) 9 Imm. L.R. (2d) 237 (FCA).
Leung v. *Canada (Minister of Employment and Immigration)*, (1994) 81 FTR 303.
Magana v. *Canada (Minister of Citizenship and Immigration)*, (May 8, 1996), Doc. IMM-1608-95 (FTD).
Menaker v. *Canada (Minister of Citizenship and Immigration)*, (Oct. 27, 1997), Doc. Imm-3837-96 (FTD).
Njoko v. *Canada (Minister of Employment and Immigration)*, (January 25, 1995), Doc. A-1698-92 (FTD).
Otoo v. *Canada (Minister of Citizenship and Immigration)*, (February 9, 1996), Doc. IMM-5056 (FTD).

Owusu-Ansah v. *Canada (Minister of Employment and Immgration)* (1989) 8 Imm. L.R. (2d) 106 (FCA).
Parizi v. *Canada (Minister of Citizenship and Immigration)*, (1994) 90 FTR 189.
Singh v. *Canada (Minister of Employment and Immigration)* [1985] 1 S.C.R. 177.
Sivayoganathan v. *Canada (Minister of Citizenship and Immigration)*, (1994) 86 FTR 152.
Vidhani v. *Canada (Minister of Citizenship and Immigration)*, [1995] 3 F.C. 60.
Yusuf v. *Canada (Minister of Employment and Immigration)*, (October 24, 1991) A-1116-90 (F.C.A.).
Zapata v. *Canada (Solicitor General)*, (1994) 82 FTR 34 (FTD).

MS received May 2001; revised MS received February 2002

[20]

The Dublin Convention and its Effects on Asylum Seekers in Europe

Nicola Scuteri

The Dublin Convention and its Effects on Asylum Seekers in Europe

The paper I will be presenting is part of a research project carried out during the year 2000 under the "Odysseus" program of the European Commission regarding the implementation of the Dublin Convention in Europe. Although I will attempt to provide a picture of the situation in Europe as a whole, it is the German case which will be presented in greater detail.

The basis of the Dublin Convention was provided by a mutual recognition of responsibility for asylum seekers between EU member states. In attempting to "harmonize" European asylum policy, it did not unilaterally restrict refugees' options regarding applying for official status on European soil; it also established certain procedural guarantees for refugees throughout the EU, aiming to further reduce the need for continued intra-European migration on the one hand as well as the danger of being sent from country to country without possibility of being granted recognition, and eventually expunged (the so-called "chain deportation"). Nevertheless, the provisions of the Convention do leave refugees in a virtually powerless situation vis-a-vis the member state deemed responsible for deciding their fate. This circumstance is particularly lamentable in view of the fact that whereas the EU has thus attempted to reorganize the "distribution" of refugees, standards for their recognition continue to vary, for instance with Germany still refusing to recognize non-governmental persecution as a grounds for granting asylum.

Overall, it can be said that the Dublin Convention has been incapable of producing the desired results. Its effectiveness has been hampered by the large amount of bureaucracy and the costs associated with its operation, as well as by the stringent criteria for proof regarding the migration route of the refugees under consideration. The circumstances under which many of them are forced to enter a member state often result in either the loss or deprivation of papers altogether, or in an incomplete administrative record about their travel route. This fact was bemoaned by many of the official interviewees, who pleaded for a loosening of proof requirements in order to be able to utilize the Convention to a greater extent. It also has to be noted that, because the ultimate goal is referral to another country, the consideration of applicants under the Convention often leads them to disappear and hide from the authorities, as they fear deportation.

The interviews with affected asylum seekers showed that the administrative desire to "distribute" applicants more evenly often ignores their needs and misinterprets their reasons for choosing a particular country of destination. The vast majority of asylum seekers cited the presence of friends, relatives, or acquaintances as the governing factor in their decision for a specific destination country. Hence, it is networks more than any other factors which have been shown to influence migratory movements within EU territory – an aspect obliquely ignored by legal proposals governing asylum policy, which continue to concentrate on procedural matters.

Die Dublin-Konvention und ihre Auswirkungen auf Asylsuchende in Europa

Der hier vorgelegte Aufsatz ist Teil eines Forschungsprojekts, das im Jahr 2000 im Rahmen des "Odysseus"-Programms der Kommission der Europäischen Union durchgeführt wurde und das sich mit der politischen Umsetzung der Dublin-Konvention befasste. Obwohl die Situation in Europa insgesamt dargestellt wird, soll hier das deutsche Beispiel detailliert präsentiert werden.

Die Grundlage der Dublin-Konvention bildete die gegenseitige Anerkennung der Verantwortung für Asylsuchende zwischen den EU-Mitgliedsstaaten. Im Bemühen um eine "Harmonisierung" der europäischen Asylpolitik schränkte die Konventi-

on nicht einfach einseitig die Optionen von Flüchtlingen hinsichtlich der Erlangung eines offiziellen Status auf europäischem Boden ein; sondern sie richtete durchaus gewisse Verfahrensgarantieren für Flüchtlinge innerhalb der EU ein, welche den Zwang zu einer fortgesetzten innereuropäischen Weiterwanderung reduzieren als auch die Gefahr mindern sollte, von Land zu Land ohne die Möglichkeit einer Anerkennung weitergereicht und schließlich möglicherweise abgewiesen zu werden (so genannte Kettendeportation). Dennoch halten die Klauseln der Konvention Flüchtlinge in einer offenbar machtlosen Position gegenüber dem Mitgliedsstaat, dem die Verantwortung zufällt, über ihr Schicksal zu entscheiden. Besonders beklagenswert ist dieser Umstand angesichts der Tatsache, dass obwohl die EU den Versuch unternommen hat, die "Flüchtlingsverteilung" zu reorganisieren, die Standards für die Flüchtlingsanerkennung weiterhin variieren: Beispielsweise weigert sich Deutschland immer noch, Verfolgung durch Nicht-Regierungsinstanzen als Grund für die Asylgewährung anzuerkennen.

Insgesamt hat die Dublin-Konvention nicht die erwünschten Resultate erbracht. Ihre Effektivität wird einerseits durch den enormen bürokratischen Aufwand und die damit verbundenen Verfahrenskosten und andererseits durch die vorgeschriebenen stringenten Beweiskriterien hinsichtlich der Migrationsroute von Flüchtlingen eingeschränkt. Die Umstände, unter denen viele Flüchtlinge zur Einreise in ein Mitgliedsland gezwungen werden, beinhalten häufig den Verlust persönlicher Dokumente oder ermöglichen nur einen lückenhaften Bericht über die Reiseroute. Diese Tatsache wurde von vielen der befragten Fachleute bemängelt; hier wurde für eine Lockerung der Beweiszwänge plädiert, die es ermöglichen soll, die Konvention in einem größeren Umfang anzuwenden. Zudem führt das Bestreben, Flüchtlinge in das zuletzt passierte Land abzuschieben, häufig dazu, dass Asylbewerber nach der Dublin-Konvention es vorziehen unterzutauchen, da sie die Abschiebung befürchten.

Die Interviews mit betroffenen Asylbewerbern haben gezeigt, dass die administrativen Bemühungen um eine "Umverteilung" von Bewerbern häufig deren Bedürfnisse übergeht und die häufig angeführte Anwesenheit von Freunden, Verwandten und Bekannten als vorherrschendes Kriterium für die Wahl des Zufluchtslandes fehlinterpretiert. Mehr als alle anderen Faktoren sind es jedoch bestehende Netzwerke, die ganz offensichtlich den größten Einfluss auf Wanderungsbewegungen innerhalb der EU zeitigen – ein Aspekt, der von der herrschenden Asylpolitik ignoriert wird, die sich weiterhin auf Verfahrensangelegenheiten konzentriert.

****

The legal status of refugees in Europe

Post-War Europe has traditionally been a centre for immigration from around the world. Given its relative political stability and progressively solidifying democratic structures, it has also assumed the role of a safe haven for many refugees seeking asylum because they were being persecuted in their respective countries of origin.

This factor came to assume greater importance over traditional forms of immigration in the period following the 1973 oil crisis, when European labour markets had largely been saturated and entry into the EU began to be facilitated mainly by way of either family reunion or the granting of official refugee status. Concerns about the economic consequences of immigration have since led to its being conceptualized, in the political sphere, mainly as a "burden" upon the host countries affected by the phenomenon. This apprehension in turn evoked appeals for a more "just" distribution of that burden among EU member states. To the extent that Europe began to act more and more like a homogenous state entity, its self-definition vis-a-vis the outside has gained increased significance. The continued efforts at European unification have come to be characterized by the enhancement of freedom of movement within the EU, accompanied by an almost simultaneous restriction of the freedom of entry into that Union, a development directly affecting refugees as part of the immigrant population.

The basis for this two-fold development can be seen in the 1957 Treaty of Rome and its affirmation of the principle of free movement of people within Europe, originally related primarily to the economic sphere. In subsequent years, however, the scope of this agreement has been expanded to address the wider social and political ramifications of the term "movement". With regard to immigration control, the first substantial evolution of this idea was the 1985 Schengen agreement bewteen France, Germany, and the Benelux countries, inaugurating the gradual abolition of internal border controls and a simultaneously strengthening the common external borders. Thus, the ideal of freedom of movement *within* the common territory was to be furthered. Significantly, however, this freedom has always been tailored to benefit EU citizens and their dependents, whereas its adverse effects have been experienced most noticeably by immigrants.

The specific treatment of asylum seekers, however, was not addressed until 1990, when the Dublin Convention came to replace the relevant sections of Schengen. This agreement was designed to counteract the tendency of many asylum seekers to cross intra-European borders on their way to their final destination, the place where they would eventually apply for asylum, a trend that, in the public perception, had disadvantaged countries located at the centre of Europe. Instead, the EU being conceived of as a legal entity with equivalent protective guarantees for refugees in each member state, asylum seekers were to be delegated back to the country where they first entered EU territory and lodge their applications there. In this context it is worth mentioning that there has been a distinct change in the prevalence of asylum seekers' travel routes following the collapse of the Iron Curtain. Whereas Germany, one of the instigators of the agreement, had originally hoped to benefit from its provisions, as most of its immigrants were travelling via Southern Europe in the 1980s, the new era has shown a different picture, characterized by a new immigration into Europe from the East, mainly via Germany, and in many cases with Germany as the final destination. In this respect, the main goal of the agreement, reducing the "burden" of asylum seekers, was seriously undercut by these unforeseen political developments.

The basis of the Dublin Convention was provided by a mutual recognition of responsibility for asylum seekers between the member states. Thus, in attempting to "harmonize" European asylum policy, it did not unilaterally restrict refugees' options regarding applying for official status on European soil; it also established certain procedural guarantees for refugees throughout the EU, aiming to further reduce the need for continued intra-European migration on the one hand as well as the danger of being sent from country to country without certainty of being granted recognition, and eventually expunged (the so-called "chain deportation"). Nevertheless, the provisions of the Convention do leave refugees in a virtually powerless situation vis-a-vis the member state deemed responsible fro deciding their fate. This circumstance is particularly lamentable in view of the fact that whereas the EU has thus attempted to reorganize the "distribution" of refugees, standards for their recognition continue to vary, for instance with Germany still refusing to recognize non-governmental persecution as a grounds for granting asylum. In addition, the plight of many applicants is worsened by additional laws affecting the exchange of refugees between countries. These Safe Third Country Laws and bilateral agreements enable a deportation to a state which may have entirely different standards for judging the justification of any given application and preclude recognition, for instance on the grounds of a preemptive denial of the existence of reasons of flight in the refugees' country of origin. Ironically, these agreements also further undermine uniformity of procedure – an explicit aim of the Dublin Convention.

The project

The ODISSEA project attempted to assess the success of the Dublin Convention in reaching its objectives. This entailed a structural analysis of application procedures and administrative responsibilities in each of the member states. In addition, statistics on the number of asylum cases treated under the rules of the Dublin Convention were assembled. But ODISSEA was also designed to go beyond that, examining the experiences of affected parties on both sides. Hence, officials as well as asylum seekers in Italy, Germany, Spain, France, and Austria were interviewed about their experiences with the new legal framework. In the case of the refugees, particular emphasis was placed on assessing their reasons for migrating to specific European countries, crossing intra-European borders in defiance of the aims of the Convention. It was hoped that such an assessment would facilitate better insights into factors that had been neglected by lawmakers in drafting the document.

The *Berliner Institut für Vergleichende Sozialforschung* conducted interviews with representatives of government and non-government organizations as well as with refugees and asylum seekers residing in Germany, who were however about to be relocated to Italy or Spain because of the Dublin Convention. Central questions of the interview focused on their itinerary, their reasons for continuing the journey, why they elected a particular country and whether this phenomenon was confined to particular groups. Besides information concerning individual or collective aims and reasons for the continuation of their migratory journey, these interviews also provided an overview of their knowledge about asylum procedures and the restrictions imposed by the Dublin Convention.

Legal background of asylum policy in Germany

Agreements and Main Laws

- The Geneva Convention of 1951 and the New York Protocol of 1967
- The German Constitution of 1949 ("Grundgesetz"), Section 16a (1)
- The Law Amending Asylum Procedure Aliens and Nationality Provisions – Asylum Procedure Act ("Asylverfahrensgesetz") of 1 July 1993
- The Aliens Act of 9. July 1990 ("Ausländergesetz")
- The Schengen Agreement and the Dublin Convention

"Victims of political persecution" benefit from the right to asylum in the Federal Republic of Germany under Article 16a, paragraph 1 of the Basic Law provided they are not EU citizens and have not entered the country from so-called "safe third countries". This constitutional article, amended in 1993, continues to be the basis for granting asylum. The asylum procedure, from application to recognition or termination of the stay of the applicant, is regulated by the Asylum Procedure Act of 1993.

Civil war refugees are exempted from these rules. There are specific provisions in the Aliens Act that apply to them. For instance, Section 32 of the Aliens Act (AuslG) defines their status, which, among other things, derives from a corresponding declaration of willingness to accept them from the Federal and state governments. Their presence in Germany is tolerated; a long-term residence permit can be issued only under very limited conditions.

Section 54 of the AuslG permits suspending the deportation of aliens on "international law and humanitarian grounds", including threats arising from civil wars. Such protection from deportation is granted by the Conference of State Ministers of the Interior. Only threats to personal safety from civil wars are recognized as obstacles to deportation, however, although recognized refugees enjoy unlimited protection from expulsion (Section 51 of the AuslG).

The legal situation of recognized refugees is relatively secure. Unlike civil war refugees and asylum applicants, they receive unlimited residence permits, the right to be joined by their families (spouses and children), and work permits. Asylum applicants whose reception procedure, which usually takes three months, has been completed and who have been granted exception permission to stay are given a so-called general and limited permit to work if the job they have found cannot be filled by a German applicant or an alien with a better residence status. Civil war refugees generally receive this limited work permit as well. Since this work permit depends on the specifics of local and regional labour markets, the employment offices have a great deal of latitude and make use of it to varying degrees.

Social and economic background

The residence of the asylum applicant is prescribed when the application is made. The applicant is obliged to reside there. Until a decision is adopted on acceptance of the application he is accommodated in an initial reception facility, which is generally a central facility of the state. A change of residence, for instance when family members are resident in Germany, requires authorisation. If after initial examination the application is accepted for further processing, the applicant is 'distributed' in accordance with the existing quotas for the various states and is usually housed in group accommodation. It is possible to move into a flat of one's own under certain conditions, but permission is required.

In 1997 social assistance was curtailed for asylum applications without long-term authorisation to stay. The legal foundation for this is the Asylum Applicant Benefit Bill of 1993. As a matter of principle, social assistance is meant to cover only basic needs. In recent years, more and more asylum applicant groups as well as the civil war refugees have been made subject to these limited benefits. The principle applied is that wherever possible the benefits should take the form of non-cash resources. This is supplemented by a small amount of pocket money. The details, however, are arranged by various measures of the federal states. Recognized refugees receive the same social assistance as German citizens.

Unlike asylum applicants, they are also entitled to a six-month language course (although subject to special preconditions). This also applies to the "quota refugees" recognized by the FRG since the end of the seventies (mostly boat people from Vietnam), but not to civil war refugees.

As a rule, education and training opportunities are not available to asylum applicants. In most of the federal states there is no compulsory schooling, although the right of their children to attend school is generally conceded to asylum applicants. An asylum applicant can only be given a traineeship if there is no other applicant with precedence. In principle asylum applicants also have the possibility of attending university, but this possibility is limited by capacity problems and the residence requirement. There is no financial assistance for such training, and authorisation to stay cannot be extended because of studies or training. These limitations do not apply to recognized refugees.

There are no figures on the unemployment rate among recognized refugees or asylum seekers. It can be assumed, however, that many of them have found employment outside the first labour market (subject to compulsory social insurance), to some extent in the illegal sphere. For some years, the demand for special grounds for asylum for women has been raised outside parliament, but so far they have not been satisfied.

The integration of refugees depends for the most part on their residence status. For all groups other than the recognized refugees, the so-called quota refugees and the non-deportable "de facto" refugees with long-term authorisation to stay, integration into German society is not desired by the state. Accordingly, their integration into current promotion programmes of all kinds is authorized only in exceptional cases.

Family reunion

Recognized refugees have the right to be joined by their family members (spouses and children under the age of 18). Permission for family reunification with other family members may be granted without the obligation of being able to support and accommodate them. Persons with other status principally have no right to family reunion, only in exceptional cases may it be granted on humanitarian grounds.

Political framework

The political foundations of refugee reception follow from this intention. There is a basic political consensus in Germany about an exclusively temporary tolerance of asylum applicants, which has to be ended as promptly as possible after their application has been turned down. Contrasting with this political intention, however, the number of deportations is stagnating. Since the increase in numbers of refugees at the end of the Seventies, therefore, all the measures taken, including the 1993 amendment of the Constitution, have been directed towards dissuasion of further refugee migration. These measures extend from curtailment of proceedings, central accommodation, restrictions on employment and social assistance to the establishment of detention centres to ensure deportation. Germany is also one of the programmatically leading countries of the European Union with regard to non-repressive strategies, such as the promotion of voluntary return, the use of development policy measures to prevent flight, etc. Germany still retains this especially active role today, for instance in the case of demands for implementation of the programmes for the return of Yugoslav civil war refugees.

The asylum procedure in practice

Any person whishing to apply for asylum in the Federal Republic of Germany needs to first submit an application to the local *Federal Office for the Recognition of Foreign Refugees* (Bundesamt für die Anerkennung ausländischer Flüchtlinge/BAFI). The headquarters of the Federal Office for the Recognition of Foreign Refugees is located in Nuremberg, while there are 32 branches all over Germany. However, asylum can also be applied for with border officials at Germany's external borders and at all international airports. The border officials will then forward the application to the relevant BAFI office. There, the personal details of the asylum seeker in question will be secured (photograph, fingerprints, examination of passport or other documents, etc.), and this information is entered into the *Central Register for Aliens* (Ausländerzentralregister/AZR). In order to ensure that all possible proof regarding the asylum seekers' identity, travel route, etc. will be collected, the applicant is obliged to undergo a body search carried out by the relevant officials. Thereafter asylum seekers are given a hearing during which they have to present their case.

Concerning an asylum procedure, German Law prescribes that asylum seekers receive a *Residency Allowance* (Aufenthaltsgestattung) for the duration of their asylum procedure. The Residency Allowance is issued for a period of three to six months and can be extended if required. This residency status, however, is restricted to the district of the relevant Aliens' office, which means that asylum seekers are only entitled to freedom of movement within the area of responsibility covered by the local Alien's Office. Asylum seekers are generally obliged to live in a reception centre for a minimum period of three months, after which they can be compelled to move to a particular community or other accommodation facility. Thus asylum seekers can be distributed to other German states, even if they have family relations residing in the particular community where they first lodged their application. Furthermore people seeking asylum on German territory are generally not issued a work permit and are therefore dependent upon welfare handouts.

Applicants are generally assisted through the *Asylum Applicant Benefit Bill* (Asylbewerberleistungsgesetz), which came into effect on 1 November, 1993. This law secures minimum benefits covering the necessary provisions of food, accommodation and clothes, and in some states pocket money amounting to around 80.00 DM per month, while in other states only vouchers are issued. Basic medical insurance is also provided. Higher benefits according to the federal law for public welfare are only possible if the asylum seeker has received the lower benefits for a minimum period of three years and officials have checked that the possibility of departure or deportation is inconceivable because of humanitarian, legal or personal reasons.

The implementation of the Dublin Convention

As in other member states, the Dublin Convention came into effect in Germany on 1 September, 1997. Since then no separate Dublin Convention asylum procedure has been developed. Rather all asylum seekers need to undergo the standard German asylum procedure, and it is generally after the hearing that the suspected Dublin cases are selected out of the whole bulk of asylum applications. The guidelines by which individual cases are accorded to the Dublin Convention Procedure correspond to general EU ones without any German peculiarities. Those who go through the Dublin Convention Procedure receive the same treatment as other asylum seekers.

It is during the hearing, which needs to take place at the latest three days after the asylum application has been lodged, that the responsible officials must establish whether there are any grounds on which another member state might be responsible for the processing of the asylum application in question. If a particular case is considered to fall under the Dublin Convention Procedure it no longer continues to be administered by the local section of the *Federal Office for the Recognition of Foreign Refugees* (BAFI) but is passed over to the *Coordination Centre Schengen/Dublin, International Tasks* (KSD/IA) located at the headquarters of the *Federal Office for the Recognition of Foreign Refugees* (BAFL) in Nuremberg.

The *Coordination Centre Schengen/Dublin, International Tasks* (KSD/IA) is divided into three departments: 1) Dublin Convention Procedure; 2) International Tasks; 3) Statistics. The department Dublin Convention Procedure is responsible for the implementation of the agreement in Germany and centrally administers all Dublin cases in the country. It seeks to establish which signatory states could be responsible for the processing of the numerous asylum applications and is therefore involved in constant dealings and exchanges of information with those countries in an effort to settle the various cases. If the KSD/IA decides that according to Art. 4 of the Dublin Convention no member state can be found responsible for the examination of an asylum application, then the case will be finalized according to national asylum policy.

When instead the KSD/IA comes to the conclusion that another signatory state might be responsible for the processing of an asylum application, then the "Standard Form for the Requirement of the Examination of an Asylum Application's Responsible State" will be completed. In addition, a written statement – in an agreed language with the signatory state and underlining the reasons for this decision – will be submitted to the relevant authorities of that state. If the given state rejects responsibility for this case within three months, then Germany has the right to appeal the decision. If the given state once more rejects the claim, then the KSD/IA hands the case back to the responsible local BAFI section, where the asylum procedure will be brought to an end according to standard German asylum policy. In a case where an asylum seeker withdraws his or her application during the procedure, the Dublin Convention is no longer applicable.

If on the other hand, an asylum seeker did not withdraw his or her application and the given signatory state agrees to take over the case, then he or she will be deported to that state and the asylum seeker will receive an "expulsion warning" from Germany. The asylum seeker is entitled to appeal against this decision within two weeks, but the appeal has no delaying effect on the deportation, which should be carried out within one month. Because carrying out the deportation largely depends on the confirmation by the member state which has accepted the take over, it can sometimes take longer than a month, particularly in the case of Italy this deadline is often not kept (according to KSD/IA, the average time for a confirmation from Italy is 4-6 weeks).

The hand-over formalities are organized by the KSD/IA in cooperation with the responsible local Alien's office (Ausländerbehörde), the receiving institution and the border police. Leaving Germany can take place voluntarily within a stipulated time, but generally occurs in the company of an official. Finally the asylum seeker is given a "Laissez-Passer" in all languages of the signatory states which substitutes the often missing passport. Once the asylum seeker has reached her or his destination she or he will not be allowed to re-enter Germany for as long as his or her legal status remains that of an asylum seeker. Entry into Germany is only possible for a recognized refugee who has obtained a permanent residency status in the respective country of asylum.

Should there be a case in which it is discovered that the asylum seeker had not travelled through the signatory state which accepted the take over, then the asylum application is rejected and the asylum seeker requested to leave Germany within a week.

Germany has been instrumental in developing the Dublin Convention Procedure, a process which began in the mid-Eighties. In those days the Iron Curtain still provided Germany with an almost impenetrable frontier to the East and the focus tended to be on refugee movements using routes through southern and western Europe. When the Dublin Convention was finally drafted in 1990 this situation began to change quite rapidly as a result of the collapse of Communist regimes in eastern Europe. By the time the Convention came into force on September the first 1997, Germany had long since become the prime destination for refugees and asylum seekers coming from or travelling through Eastern Europe, thus refugee movements from Southern and Western Europe towards Germany had dwindled into relative insignificance by comparison.

The Dublin Convention proposes that at least one state be made responsible for the examination and processing of an asylum application in territory of the European Union. In Germany however it is mostly Art. 16a Abs. 5 GG of the German constitution, also known as the *Safe Third Country Law*, which mandates the return of asylum seekers to so-called "safe third countries". This law applies in most cases to asylum seekers who have travelled through one of Germany's bordering countries to the East, namely Poland and the Czech Republic. When the *Safe Third Country Law* was introduced in 1993, agreements were concluded with all of Germany's neighbouring countries, and it proved to be an effective means of reducing the number of people seeking asylum on German territory. For those EU countries which had previously been part of the *Safe Third Country Agreement*, namely France, Netherlands and Austria, the Dublin Convention now takes priority over it.

Apart from being characterized by a large amount of bureaucracy, the Dublin Convention has revealed itself as costly, time consuming and ultimately incapable of producing satisfactory results for Germany. In fact, Germany receives almost twice as many asylum applications than those it hands over to other EU countries. During 1999, Germany handed 1,720 asylum seekers over to signatory states, while receiving 3,403 form other countries. Additionally, of all Take-Over Requests from Germany to other signatory states, only about half meet with approval, while only about half of these were actually handed over. In 1999, Germany filed 5,690 Take-Over Requests, of which only 2,819 received a positive reply from signatory states, out of which the above mentioned 1,720 cases were actually handed over. Thus, out of all Take-Over Requests to member countries only about a quarter are successful. This is partly due to the fact that numerous asylum seekers simply go underground and disappear if engaged in the Dublin Convention Procedure. What the statistics do not reveal, is that many of those asylum seekers who are eventually returned, are handed over with several months of delay because they disappeared during the Dublin Convention Procedure and do not reemerge until later.

Furthermore Take-Over Requests to signatory states are comparatively low in numbers mainly because the Dublin Convention is only applied when it is believed, on the basis of some indicative and concrete proof (eg. documents, cash, receipts, etc.) that the asylum seeker has actually travelled through a member state. Asylum seekers who have entered Germany through an EU country mostly do so illegally across an open border, and are therefore rarely body-searched immediately upon their arrival. By the time asylum seekers get around to lodging their application and are subjected to the hearing (during which a body search is compulsory), they have usually liberated themselves of all documents and possible indications which could irrefutably prove that they travelled through a third country. When asylum seekers are questioned about which countries they travelled through in order to reach Germany, they usually reply that their trip took place at night, generally in an enclosed environment, and that consequently they were unaware of their whereabouts.

So far only the border police and customs officials have access to the Schengen Information System (SIS), where data about lodged and already processed asylum applications is made available. The BAFI sections however are not yet equipped to make use of the SIS for themselves, although they can obtain this information from the border authorities. Nevertheless, in order to render the implementation of the Dublin Convention more efficient, the *Federal Office for the Recognition of Foreign Refugees* is currently working towards securing their own access to the SIS.

Litigation

On the practice of litigation regarding the Dublin Convention, it must first of all be mentioned that hardly any research has been carried out on the subject in Germany. This is possibly due to the fact that the Dublin Convention is scarcely implemented in Germany and remains largely obscure, even for those dealing with it.

Generally speaking, if a given signatory state has accepted the take-over of an asylum seeker then she or he is entitled to appeal against this decision within two weeks. The appeal, however, has no delaying effect on the deportation, which should be carried out within one month after the signatory state in question has confirmed the case. We can therefore assume that once it is clear that a case falls under the Dublin Convention and the given signatory state agrees to assume responsibility for the asylum seeker, possibilities of halting a deportation from Germany are rather scarce, unless one chooses to disappear and stay on illegally. There are nevertheless exceptions.

According to a former Judge, Mr *Michael Meier-Borstel*, now member of staff at the Federal Commissioner for Foreigners' Affairs, there has been a case of a family residing in Tübingen who was to be returned to Italy within the framework of the Dublin Convention. This family appealed against this decision on the grounds that in Italy their youngest child, who was suffering from serious health hazards, would not receive the necessary health care. On these grounds the family in question was permitted to remain in Germany.

Legal as well as general refugee consultation centres, which were contacted throughout the research project, also drew attention to the fact that asylum seekers affected by the Dublin Convention or other bilateral agreements, stood a better chance of avoiding a return to another country if they were seriously traumatized or acutely ill and consequently considered unable to travel.

At the stage where asylum seekers are still only suspected of falling under the Dublin Convention, there are of course possibilities of appeal aimed at excluding a case from this procedure. An example for this is offered by the following case which involved a married Roma couple from Kosova with three children, who in February 2000 had come to Germany from Italy:

The flight of this family from Kosova had already begun in 1999. The reason for their flight was the fact that members of the Roma minority were in serious fear for their lives, due to attacks by part of the Serbs as well as the Kosova Albanians. On their way to Germany the husband was separated from his wife and children, who thereafter spent around 6-7 months in Italy with a regular permit. The husband, who had entered Germany illegally and was staying there with his brother, eventually found out that his wife and children were residing in a refugee camp in the town of Bari. He consequently decided to travel to Italy in order to pick up his family and bring them to Germany. When he joined his family in October 1999, they were soon transferred to a reception centre for refugees in Naples. There they had to share their accommodation with predominantly Kosova Albanians. The family was now once again the subject of serious threats by part of the Albanians. Numerous requests to the relevant Neapolitan authorities to accommodate the family in another reception centre were ignored. Furthermore, due to the lack of financial assistance, they had to beg in the streets in order to support themselves. At this point the family saw no other solution but to escape this situation and try to continue their flight to Germany, which had been their original destination.

Once in Germany they all found accommodation with the husband's brother, already residing there. Thereafter the family decided to apply for a toleration status of residence at the relevant Aliens' Office. They did not apply for asylum, but only wanted temporary protection. Once the Aliens' Office woke up to the fact that the Family had previously been in Italy, the family was ordered to appear and was questioned in detail about their travel route. Consequently their toleration status was cancelled and they were issued with transit visas valid until the 24th of

April 2000. The possibility of returning the applicants to Italy in line with the Dublin Convention was being investigated, if the latter state would accept the take-over.

The applicants were so afraid of being sent back to Italy that they contacted various consultation centres. There their fears were re-enforced by being told that they would probably have to return to Italy due to the Dublin Convention, and that in Italy there had recently been numerous cases of asylum seekers being forcibly returned to former Yugoslavia. For fear of being returned to Italy and then deported to former Yugoslavia, the applicants did not even contact the relevant Aliens' Office in order to extend their transit visa.

However, there was no reply from Italy regarding the case in question. Furthermore the family's lawyer appealed against the decision of returning the applicants to Italy within the framework of the Dublin Convention, because they had not applied for political asylum, but only for temporary protection. They did not intend to remain in Germany permanently, but merely until the situation in their home country had improved and they could return without fear for their lives. Because the Dublin Convention is only applicable to asylum seekers, it was considered illicit to implement it in this case.

Summary of interviews conducted with representatives of government and non-government organizations concerning the Dublin Convention in Germany

These expert-interviews with representatives of government and non-governmental organizations were conducted in order to assess the implementation of the Dublin Convention in Germany from the point of view of people who are involved in its practice. Furthermore we believed these interviews to be necessary when it became clear that it would be very unlikely to reach the target of interviewing 35 asylum seekers awaiting to be sent back to Italy or Spain under the Dublin Convention Procedure.

The following summaries do not represent the official position of the organization in question, but are merely the personal opinions and assessments of the persons interviewed.

16.02.2000
Commissioner of Foreigners' Affairs of the Berlin Senat
Interview conducted with Mr Robin Schneider and Ms Blümel

According to Mr Schneider and Ms Blümel of the Commissioner of Foreigners Affairs of the Berlin Senat (ASB), the Dublin Convention is generally scarcely applied in Germany. One practical indicator regarding this statement is the fact that since the Dublin Convention became law in Germany, not a single asylum seeker who was affected by it has searched advice at the consultation centre of the ASB. Another indicator is that since Otto Schily became Germany's Minister of the Interior, the ASB has not received any information or other material concerning the Dublin Convention.

One reason why the Dublin Convention is applied only in exceptional cases in Germany is the fact that the individual *Länder* (federal states) are responsible for receiving, integrating, as well as expelling refugees and asylum seekers. The Dublin Convention procedure however, if applied, is being dealt with centrally by the KSD/IA. Basically this means that awareness about the Dublin Convention is, as a whole, rather low at a local level.

On the question of why asylum seekers continue their journey and often choose Germany as a destination, better welfare provisions and the flourishing black labour market in Berlin were mentioned as major pull factors. Asylum seekers are provided with food, accommodation, clothes, basic medical insurance and 80.00 DM pocket money a month. Also, many asylum seekers are able to find illegal employment in construction and catering.

Additionally, in contrast to other EU countries, in Germany it is the *Safe Third Country Law* which represents the major agreement regulating the return of asylum seekers to third countries, rather than the Dublin Convention.

25.02.2000
Labour Welfare Association
Central Consultation Centre for Non-European Refugees
Interview conducted with Ms Katharina Vogt

Since the Dublin convention came into effect no major changes have occurred regarding the work at the Central Consultation Centre for Non-European Refugees. Asylum seekers are advised of the possibility of being returned to the first safe country of arrival, but generally nothing happens because they have entered Germany illegally and liberated themselves of all their documents, making it impossible to pin down indicative proof of their travel route. Most asylum seekers who informally confessed to staff of the consultation centre of having come to Germany via Italy were Kurds from Irak, who had good possibilities of being recognized as refugees in Germany regardless. In the experience of the centre, asylum seekers are generally not aware of the Dublin Convention. Also, in the last year or so there have been no cases of asylum seekers who mentioned to have come to Germany via Italy or Spain, rather they travelled through a non EU country.

It was suggested that the main reason for which asylum seekers decide to continue their journey and come to Germany, was the presence of friends and family already living in Germany, particularly with regard to some nationalities and ethnic groups such as the Kurds. Furthermore many asylum seekers seem to believe that conditions in Germany are better than in other countries regarding social welfare and jobs.

It was pointed out that the Dublin Convention was not being applied as much as had been expected, mainly because it is generally considered as being too complicated when put into practice.

06.03.2000

Commissioner for Foreigners' Affairs of the Federal Republic of Germany

Interview conducted with Mr Michael Meier-Borstel

According to Mr Meier-Borstel the main problem regarding the Dublin Convention in Germany is that it does not live up to its aims. Refugees coming to Germany from Italy generally travel through Switzerland or Austria. In the case where Germany has been entered through Switzerland, Poland and Czech Republic the *Safe Third Country Law* applies, while the Dublin Convention applies to EU countries only.

The Dublin Convention was initiated around the mid-1980s parallel to the Schengen Agreement. In those days the Dublin Convention still made a lot of sense for Germany. With the fall of the iron curtain, however, the situation changed quite dramatically and consequently the Dublin Convention lost most of its potential effectiveness, because the vast majority of asylum seekers and refugees now enter Germany through eastern Europe. To date, Germany in particular is discontent with the implementation of the Dublin Convention and is one of the main forces behind the re-assessment of the agreement at the European level.

In cases where asylum seekers come to Germany through Poland and then continue their journey to the Netherlands, they can be returned to Germany in accordance with the Dublin Convention. Theoretically it would be possible for Germany to return these asylum seekers to Poland outside the framework of the Dublin Convention, however this has so far never been the case.

Because national policy continues to be applicable, it is often not clear whether asylum seekers should be returned according to the Dublin Convention or other bilateral agreements. To date, Germany implements the Dublin Convention less than most of its European counterparts. In fact, within the framework of the Dublin Convention, twice as many asylum seekers are sent to Germany as are handed over to other signatory states.

10.03.2000
Federal Ministry of Justice
Interview conducted with Mr Rothfuß

The Federal Ministry of Justice participates on various Working Groups of the European Council, for example on migration and family reunion. Other government institutions such as the Ministry of the Interior and the Ministry of Foreign Affairs also actively participate within these Working Groups.

The Ministry of Justice is normally not involved with the implementation of the Dublin Convention. Exceptions exist in cases where problems arise with a signatory state. For example when many refugees from Irak to suddenly came to Germany and the Netherlands, these two signatory states complained to a Working Group of the European Council about the lack of proof regarding the asylum seekers' travel route. In such cases the Ministry of Justice is invited to participate in debates and can suggest possible amendments.

As far as the Schengen Information System (SIS) and Eurodac (the European system for collection, storage, exchange and comparison of fingerprints) are concerned, even though they are not being fully implemented as yet due to unresolved administrative barriers, from a legal point of view Germany clearly takes part in them.

17.03.2000
Federal Office for the Recognition of Foreign Refugees
Coordination Centre Schengen-Dublin/International Tasks
Interview conducted with Ms Bartels and Mr Lindemann

Because of very few bilateral agreements with countries such as Italy and Spain, the Dublin Convention represents an asset for Germany, as it facilitates the return of asylum seekers who have travelled through those countries.

The central agency and local branches of the Federal Office for the Recognition of Foreign Refugees (BAFI) are not yet connected to the SIS, only border police and customs officials along Germany's external borders have access. However the BAFI is able to obtain necessary information through those border officials. however, This situation is expected to change in the not too distant future.

Within six months after the asylum application has been lodged, the Dublin cases are "offered" by the BAFI sections to the Coordination Centre Schengen-Dublin. The signatory state which is supposed to take the asylum seeker has three months to reply. If there is no reply within those three months, then Germany is obliged to process the asylum application as normal. There are no sanctions if a signatory state fails to reply within the prescribed time-frame.

The time which passes between a positive reply from a signatory state and the actual handover of the relevant asylum seeker varies depending on the country in question, the average time in the case of Italy ranges from around four to six weeks.

A major problem concerning the implementation of the Dublin Convention is the overall delay in the processing of asylum applications. Of all Take-Over Requests, less than 60% receive a positive reply, yet in only 20-25% of cases is the asylum seeker actually handed over to the given signatory state. The majority of asylum seekers involved in the Dublin Convention procedure either simply disappear or even withdraw their asylum application altogether. The fact that the Dublin Convention is no longer applicable once an asylum seeker has withdrawn its application was judged as one of the main gaps regarding its proper implementation.

Another problem is that many of those 20-25% of asylum seekers who are eventually returned, very often are handed over with several months of delay because they disappeared during the Dublin Convention Procedure and only re-emerged at a later stage.

According to the Centre the main reasons for asylum seekers to continue their journey from southern European countries to Germany were, in order of priority:
1) Family reunion
2) The right to join family members
3) Higher social benefits
4) Better possibilities of using litigation

17.03.2000
UNHCR Germany
Interview conducted with Ms Züffle

The UNHCR Germany generally supports the Dublin Convention, mainly because it offers more protection to asylum seekers than other bilateral agreements. Particularly important is the fact that the Dublin Convention minimizes the possibilities of chain-deportations. The fact that there is no material harmonization of refugee aid at a European level was considered as a major drawback and as one relevant reason for the onward migration of asylum seekers. It was feared, however, that standards of refugee aid would deteriorate in Germany through such material harmonization.

On the other hand a European harmonization of asylum procedures could on some fronts also improve German standards, because Germany is the only country in the EU which does not recognize non-government persecution.

A further problem for the implementation of the Dublin Convention is the fact that not all nationalities enjoy the same rights across all signatory states – an asylum seeker from Afghanistan for example would be recognized as a refugee in the United Kingdom but not in Germany.

Problematic is also the fact that asylum seekers and refugees have almost no voice and are merely objects of the procedure. Relevant information for asylum seekers and refugees continues to be insufficient. Despite the numerous refugee advice centres, the Dublin Convention remains largely unintelligible for those afflected by it.

Once the Federal Office for the Recognition of Foreign Refugees has secured its access to the SIS it will hopefully contribute to an acceleration of the process, which currently tends to be overly time-consuming.

As far as asylum seekers' motives for their onward migration to Germany is concerned, Ms Züffle also emphasized the presence of a large exile-community in the Federal Republic, particularly with regards to some ethnic groups such as Kurds, Arabic-speaking people and Roma, as well as Southeastern Europeans generally. Furthermore, the idea that asylum seekers and refugees are well provided for in Germany seems to be widespread. In Italy, for example, asylum seekers receive money only for the first 45 days; there are also few and generally low-standard accommodation facilities, while in Austria asylum seekers are at first put into a detention centre.

The countries of origin for refugees and asylum seekers who come to Germany via Italy are predominantly: former Yugoslavia, Iraq, Albania, Algeria, Morocco, and Tunisia. Through the Dublin Convention, asylum seekers are subjected to a kind of double uprootedness; instead of finding peace, they are once more removed, often unwillingly, from their environment. In addition, the asylum seekers are clearly lacking information on what awaits them in the country to which they are being handed over.

29.03.2000
Ministry of the Interior
Interview conducted with Mr Kloth

One of the main problems according to Mr Kloth is the criteria of Article 6 of the Dublin Convention concerning the proof of asylum seekers' travel route. To prove that an asylum seeker has been to Italy is quite possible, but there is often no chance of proving that the person in question did not also travel through Greece before reaching Italy. The same problem applies to Austria. Article 8 of the Dublin Convention is instead often applied.

To further the implementation of the Dublin Convention it would be necessary to minimize the amount of proof needed for a successful Take-Over Request to a signatory state. Criteria could be established to consider as the first transit state the one in which political asylum was applied for earliest.

Another drawback of the Dublin Convention is the long precessing time until the hand over. Three months was considered as being too long because many asylum seekers tend to disappear during this time. The deadlines are in part too generous and there are no effective sanctions in place if those deadlines are not respected. In unequivocal cases it has occurred that border officials implemented the Dublin Convention immediately.

Assessment of expert interviews

Generally speaking all institutions in question more or less agreed that the Dublin Convention Procedure has so far had a restricted impact on the overall asylum policy as it is practized in Germany. They all displayed a general lack of confidence regarding the way the Dublin Convention is put into practice. The reason for this can perhaps be traced down to the fact that its implementation has proved to be an expensive, overly bureaucratic and particularly time consuming undertaking with scarce results.

Most interviewees agreed that aspects of the Dublin Convention were indeed positive in principle, such as guaranteeing asylum seekers an asylum procedure within the European Union. Although the need for an increased harmonization of asylum procedures within the European Union was stressed as being necessary to better implement the Dublin Convention, most interviewees expressed concerns regarding the possibility of a deterioration of refugee aid and protection to the lowest common denominator. In connection with the European harmonization of asylum procedures, the majority of interviewees also referred to the recent Amsterdam Treaty which aims at such harmonization within the next five years and also foresees a review of the Dublin Convention.

Those organizations which through their work were more directly involved with asylum seekers and refugees drew attention to the fact that information on the Dublin Convention was generally scarce. The majority of asylum seekers and refugees seem unaware of the Dublin Convention and it remains largely unintelligible even for those who are affected by it. Furthermore there is a lack of information for asylum seekers on what actually awaits them in the country they are being handed over to.

The majority of interviewees also agreed that the main cause for which asylum seekers continue their journey to Germany from countries such as Spain and Italy is largely connected to family reunion or the presents of relatives and friends in Germany. In addition, the better social benefits in comparison to Italy and Spain were also mentioned by all interviewees as reasons for asylum seekers to choose Germany as their destination.

Finally, there seems to be general agreement amongst experts working in the field that the Dublin Convention will only make sense and thus start being applied as it should be, if:

- The time schedules of the administrative procedure are shortened considerably and appropriate sanctions put in place for not respecting deadlines.
- The amount of proof necessary for a successful Take-Over Request to a member state is minimized.
- A way is found of applying the Dublin Convention also to those asylum seekers who withdraw their application.
- There is more transparency and information on the Dublin Convention, and asylum seekers can be provided with reliable information on what awaits them in the country they are being returned to.
- Further uniformity of asylum procedures and welfare provisions have been achieved among all signatory states.

Assessment of asylum seekers' interviews

Unfortunately, but as nevertheless expected, the target of 35 interviews with asylum seekers waiting to be returned to Italy or Spain under the Dublin Convention Procedure was not met. Only 11 interviews with asylum seekers in Germany, whose first country of arrival in the EU was Italy, have been completed. The reasons for the difficulties we faced regarding the completion of those interviews are manifold and will be explained briefly.

First of all it needs to be stressed that the Dublin Convention in Germany is only implemented in exceptional cases and that therefore the number of Dublin cases is relatively low in comparison to the total number of asylum seekers. In 1999 a total of 95,113 people applied for asylum in Germany out of which 5,690 were suspected Dublin cases. Out of the total of suspected Dublin cases, 3,053 were Take-Over Requests to Italy and only 18 to Spain. The number of Take-Over Requests, however, is not indicative of the situation, because out of those 3,053 Take-Over Requests to Italy, only 1,035 met with approval, 618 were refused, and the remaining 1,400 were missing a reply, while in the end only 561 were handed over. Out of the 18 Take Over Requests for Spain, 12 were approved of and the rest received a negative reply; finally only 8 were handed over.

The real problem is that the majority of asylum seekers who are believed to fall under the Dublin Convention and are therefore at risk of being deported to another country, quickly disappear or withdraw their asylum application altogether, and are consequently not to be found anywhere. In addition, according to the Coordination Centre Schengen/Dublin, even those 561 asylum seekers who were returned to Italy in 1999 were not all to be found, because many of them were actually older Dublin cases who had disappeared and were traced, largely accidentally, some time later and then immediately returned. Furthermore, because of very strict German Privacy Laws government authorities such as for example the *Ministry of the Interior*, the *Coordination Centre Schengen/Dublin*, the *Federal Office for the Recognition of Refugees* or the *Refugee Reception Centres* will not allow any access to personal data concerning asylum seekers or refugees, including information on in which part or city of Germany Dublin cases are to be found or in which reception centres they are housed.

The only possibility to reach these asylum seekers would have been through NGO's or lawyers which offer consultation to them. All major Refugee Consultation Centres in Berlin-Brandenburg have been contacted, but unfortunately none had contact with Dublin Cases, only few of them recalled some isolated cases in the past. We also contacted all headquarters of welfare organizations in Germany and various lawyers who work with refugees, but even there they were mostly not aware of any Dublin Cases at present, having dealt with more of them in the past when the Kosova crisis was at its height. Those organizations which were possibly aware of mostly suspected Dublin cases generally refused to cooperate, explaining that they did not want to destroy the relationship of trust they had build up with their clients by letting unknown strangers interview them regarding their travel route.

Finally, a very cooperative consultation centre for refugees in Münster helped us to interview 11 asylum seekers who were to be returned to Italy, the majority of them not on the basis of the Dublin Convention, however, but through the general bilateral agreement between Italy and Germany. The fact that only 11 interviews were completed and the difficulties we faced are nevertheless indicative of the peculiar situation which exists in Germany regarding the implementation of the Dublin Convention.

In addition, it needs to be stressed that these interviews may not be truly representative, not only due to their low number but also because all interviewees were Yugoslav nationals from Kosova and members of either the Roma/Ashkali minority. Nevertheless, it can be said that the results of the interviews do in broad strokes correspond with what had been stated during the phase of the expert-interviews as well as with the interviews which had been conducted with asylum seekers in the other countries.

For all of them Italy was their first safe country of arrival in the EU, and all of them entered illegally by sea, arriving predominantly on the coast around Bari. The vast majority of interviewees, with the exception of one, had chosen Germany as their original destination before departure. Thus Italy was considered merely as a stopover on the way to Germany, possibly because it was the easiest EU country to be reached from where they departed.

In order to reach Germany it can be assumed that all of them travelled through Austria; only three interviewees did not make a reference to Austria regarding their travel route, but this is probably because, as one interviewee himself admitted, that they made no distinction between Germany and Austria and thus did not realize that they had travelled through another country between Italy and Germany.

As far as their motives for choosing Germany as the original destination is concerned, it can be said that the results of the interviews correspond with what had been suggested through the expert interviews with representatives of government and non- governmental institutions. The majority of interviewees had family members already living in Germany who offered them help and support, one had friends and acquaintances here, and only two had no relations or acquaintances in Germany.

Good conditions and benefits for asylum seekers as well as work opportunities were also mentioned by many as reasons for coming to Germany. For those who had relatives or acquaintances in Germany, it was through them that they were informed about the good conditions for asylum seekers and the work opportunities which existed. Of the two cases lacking relations or acquaintances, one was motivated to come to Germany due to the good conditions and benefits for asylum seekers as well as the work opportunities. His aim was to live peacefully in Germany until the situation in Kosova had stabilizsed and meanwhile to work in order to support his family which was left behind. The other case did not give any detailed specification with regard to his reasons for having come to Germany, rather, it was the bad conditions in Italy which had motivated him to move on to another country. Germany was possibly chosen because he heard of the better conditions and benefits for asylum seekers there from other refugees in Italy.

Two interviewees reported on the bad conditions in Italy. One emphasized the lack of financial assistance and proper accommodation and the fact that they depended for help upon the church community. The second case lamented the fact that there were too many Albanians in Bari and that they were routinely threatened by them.

None of the interviewees had applied for asylum in Italy, which can first of all be traced to the fact that most of them did not want to remain there in the first place. In addition, however, it needs to be mentioned that references were made to the lack of information regarding the very possibility of applying for asylum in Italy.

On the reason why the asylum seekers were not able to reach the country of final destination once arrived in Europe, the most common answer was that they were accommodated in a refugee camp upon their arrival in Italy, from which they were temporarily not permitted to leave. The lack of financial resources was also mentioned as one of the barriers deterring the continuation of their journey. In some cases their family relations had come from Germany in order to pick them up in Italy.

As far as information on the Dublin Convention and transfer procedure is concerned, the results of the interviews confirm the assumption made earlier in the report that for most asylum seekers such information remains scarce. Only in two cases the interviewees claimed to have been informed about it, while the other nine were either not informed at all or incompletely.

Concerning their situation in Germany, it corresponds to the general situation of asylum seekers in the country. They are or were housed in reception centres, although some stayed with relatives after a period in a reception centre, mainly due to their fear of being deported. Most interviewees received the basic benefits according to the *Asylum Applicant Benefits Bill* of 1993, three of them received the higher benefits of *Social Assistance* (Sozialhilfe), and only one interviewee claimed to be supported by relatives and was not receiving any benefits at all.

On the basis of those 11 interviews, it can be concluded that the main reasons for asylum seekers' onward migration from Italy to Germany are, in order of priority:
1) The presence of relatives in Germany
2) Better conditions and benefits for asylum seekers
3) Work opportunities

Conclusion and results

By 1997, the Dublin Convention had been implemented in all EU countries. The Dublin Convention procedure generally becomes relevant at the next stage after the refugee's application has been lodged. In most cases an interview, apart from evaluating the factual grounds for the asylum request, attempts to establish the immigration route that brought the applicant to the respective country. If a different member state is believed to have been the original reception country, Dublin procedures are set into operation. This process is then administered by a central agency which makes the appropriate requests to the member country presumably affected. Although deadlines and the jurisdiction of specific authorities may vary from country to country, the procedure provides for a possibility of appeal, both on the part of the refugee and the state, and if no satisfactory solution is found, applicants remain within the country where they lodged their application, where the case will then be administered by the local authorities.

Overall, it can be said that the Dublin Convention has been incapable of producing the desired results. Its effectiveness has been hampered by the large amount of bureaucracy and the costs associated with its operation, as well as by the stringent criteria for proof regarding the migration route of the refugees under consideration. The circumstances under which many of them are forced to enter a member state often result in either the loss or deprivation of papers altogether, or in an incomplete administrative record about their travel route. This fact was bemoaned by many of the official interviewees, who pleaded for a loosening of proof requirements in order to be able to utilize the Convention to a greater extent. It also has to be noted that, because the ultimate goal is referral to another country, the consideration of applicants under the Convention often leads them to disappear and hide from the authorities, as they fear deportation.

On the side of the officials, there were also frequent complaints about incongruous deadlines for responding to takeover requests between member states. Likewise, the absence of sanctions to respond to cases of neglecetd deadlines was criticized. As a result of this state of affairs, statistical figures showed that the number of cases actually picked out for treatment under the Dublin Convention is very small, and that, of those cases actually considered under the applicable rules, only a small fraction (in the case of Germany, about 20-25%) are concluded to the satisfaction of the requesting member state.

The interviews with affected refugees showed that the administrative desire to "distribute" applicants more evenly often ignores their needs and misinterprets their reasons for choosing a certain country as their destination. Rather than vying for superior social benefits (even though social provisions by the state and expected work opportunitieses did prove to be a factor in some applicants' decision), the overwhelming majority cited the presence of friends, relatives, or acquaintances as the governing factor in their decision for a specific destination country. Hence, it is networks more than any other factors which have been shown to influence migratory movements within EU territory – an aspect obliquely ignored by legal proposals governing asylum policy, which continue to concentrate on procedural matters. This focus, however, obfuscates the pressing need for the establishment of common European standards for the recognition of refugees, without which there can be no just handling of the issue, neither with regard to the refugees nor the member states' shared responsibilities.

References

Ackermann, A.: 1990, Das Erstasylabkommen von Dublin, in: Asyl, 90/4, pp. 12-19.

Angenendt, Steffen: 1997, Perspektiven einer deutschen Migrationspolitik, in: Angenendt, Steffen (ed.), Migration und Flucht. Aufgaben und Strategien für Deutschland, Europa und die internationale Gemeinschaft. Bonn, pp. 275-293.

Anthias, Flora/Lazaridis, Gabriella (eds.): 1999, Into the margins. Migration and exclusion in Southern Europe. Aldershot.

Barwig, Klaus/Brinkmann, Gisbert/Huber, Bertold/Lörcher, Klaus/Schumacher, Christoph (eds.), 1994, Asyl nach der Änderung des Grundgesetzes. Entwicklungen in Deutschland und Europa. Hohenheimer Tage zum Ausländerrecht. Baden-Baden.

Basso-Sekretariat Berlin: 1995, Europäische Asylpolitik: zwischenstaatliche Vereinbarungen und Asylrechtsstandards der EU- und EFTA-Staaten im Überblick, in: Basso-Sekretariat Berlin (ed.), Festung Europa auf der Anklagebank. Dokumentation des Basso-Tribunals zum Asylrecht in Europa. Münster, pp. 244-288.

Basso-Sekretariat Berlin (ed.), 1995, Festung Europa auf der Anklagebank. Dokumentation des Basso-Tribunals zum Asylrecht in Europa. Münster.

Bierwirth, Christoph; Forschungsstelle Dritte Welt: 1991, Europäische Aspekte des Asylrechts. (Arbeitspapiere zu Problemen der Internationalen Politik und der Entwicklungsländerforschung, 6). München.

Bleckmann, Albert: 1992, Verfassungsrechtliche Probleme einer Beschränkung des Asylrechts. Zur Notwendigkeit der Harmonisierung des Asylrechts im Zuge des Europäischen Einigungsprozesses. Köln/Berlin/Bonn/München.

Blumenthal, U. von: 1990, Dublin, Schengen and the harmonization of asylum in Europe. Genf.

Bolten, J.: 1991, From Schengen to Dublin: The new frontiers of refugee law, in: Meijers, H. et al. (ed.), Schengen. Interantionalisation of central chapters of the law on aliens, refugees, security and the police. Dodrecht.

Bolten, J.J.: 1991, From Schengen to Dublin: The new frontiers of refugee law, in: Nederlands Juristenblad, no. 5, pp. 165-178.

Boulanger, Pierre-Pascal: 1990, La libre circulation des personnes dans la Communauté Européenne. Analyse des textes et projets: du Traité de Rome aux Accords de Dublin de juin 1990. Paris.

Bundesminister des Innern (ed.): 1992, Bericht über den Stand der Harmonisierung des Asylrechts in Europa. Bonn.

Bundesrat/Bundesregierung: 1992, Entwurf eines Gesetzes zu dem Schengener Übereinkommen vom 19. Juni 1990 betreffend den schrittweisen Abbau der Grenzkontrollen an den gemeinsamen Grenzen. Drucksache 121/92. Bonn.

Bunyan, Tony: 1991, Towards an authoritarian European state, in: Race & Class, 32/3, pp. 19-27.

Comite European pour la Defense des Refugies et Immigres (C.E.D.R.I.): 1990, Schengen: Documents collected by CEDRI relating to the Schengen agreements. Basel.

Conference of the Representatives of the Governments of the Member States (ed.): 1997, Addendum to the Dublin 2. General outline for a draft revision of the treaties. Brussels.

Costanzo, Simona: 1999, Migration aus dem Maghreb nach Italien. Soziale und räumliche Aspekte der Handlungsstrategien maghrebinischer Migranten und Migrantinnen in Kampanien, Süditalien. Passau.

Drüke, Luise; Weigelt, Klaus (ed.): 1993, Fluchtziel Europa. Strategien für eine neue Flüchtlingspolitik. München.

Europäische Union/Der Rat (eds.): 1995, Aufzeichnung des französischen Vorsitzes für die Gruppe Asyl. Mindestgarantien für Asylverfahren gemäß dem Dubliner Übereinkommen. Brüssel.

Fabbricotti, Alberta: 1991, La politica dell'immigrazione nell'accordo di Schengen, in: AWR-Bulletin, 29(38)/1, pp. 16-21.

Gamrasni-Ahlen, N.: 1992, Recent European development regarding refugees: the Dublin Convention and the French perspective, in: Asylum Law and Practice in Europe and North America, pp.109-123.

Geißler, Heiner: 1993, Deutschland – ein Einwanderungsland?, in: Cohn-Bendit, Daniel/Funcke, Liselotte/Geißler, Heiner/Sölle, Dorothee/Wahdatehagh, Wahid/Iranbomy, S. Shahram (eds.), Einwanderbares Deutschland oder Vertreibung aus dem Wohlstands-Paradies? Frankfurt/M., pp. 9-23.

Gerlach, Alex: 1991, Asylanträge in der Europäischen Gemeinschaft. Die asylrechtlichen Regelungen des Dubliner und des Zweiten Schengener Übereinkommens, in: AWR-Bulletin, 29/1, pp. 34-41.

Gerlach, Axel: 1993, Dubliner Asylrechtskonvention und Schengener Abkommen: Lohnt sich die Ratifikation?, in: Zeitschrift für Rechtspolitik, pp. 164-166.

Gerster, Johannes: 1993, Das neue Asylrecht – Auswirkungen in Deutschland und auf Europa, in: Drüke, Luise/Weigelt, Klaus (eds.), Fluchtziel Europa. Strategien für eine neue Flüchtlingspolitik. Bonn, pp. 159-172.

Gesellschaft zur Unterstützung Asylsuchender (GGUA)/Löhlein, Harald: 1990, Europa grenzenlos – grenzenlos asylfeindlich? Materialien zur europäischen Asylpolitik. Münster.

Goppel, Thomas: 1994, Weltweite Migration als Problem europäischer Flüchtlings- und Ausländerpolitik, in: Ockenfels, Wolfgang (ed.), Problemfall Völkerwanderung. Migration – Asyl – Integration. Trier, pp. 15-36.

Graßhoff, Roland: 1993, Die Entwicklung des Asylrechts in der Bundesrepublik und europaweite Bestrebungen in der Asylpolitik, in: Gorzini, Mehdi Jafari/Müller, Heinz (eds.), Handbuch zur interkulturellen Arbeit. Wiesbaden, pp. 202-215.

Grosch, Klaus: 1995, Festung oder offene Grenzen. Entwicklung des Einwanderungs- und Asylrechts in Deutschland und Europa. O.O.

Hailbronner, K.: 1990, The right to asylum and the future of asylum procedures in the European Community, in: International Journal of Refugee Law, 2/3, pp. 341-360.

Hailbronner, Kay/Thiery, Claus: 1997, Schengen II und Dublin – Der zuständige Asylstaat in Europa, in: ZAR – Zeitschrift für Ausländerrecht und Ausländerpolitik, 17/2, pp. 55-66.

Hailbronner, Kay: 1995, New techniques for rendering asylum manageable. Konstanz.

Hailbronner, Kay: 1993, Die Asylrechtsreform im Grundgesetz, in: Zeitschrift für Ausländerrecht und Ausländerpolitik – ZAR, 13/3, pp. 107-117.
Heinelt, Hubert (ed.): 1994, Zuwanderungspolitik in Europa. Nationale Politiken – Gemeinsamkeiten und Unterschiede. Opladen.
Huber, Berthold: 1994, Voraussetzeungen der Anerkennungsfähigkeit einer Asylentscheidung eines anderen EG-Mitgliedstaates, in: Barwig, K./Brinkmann, G./Huber, B. /Lörscher, K./Schumacher, C. (eds.), Asyl nach der Änderung des Grundgesetzes. Enwicklungen in Deutschaland und Europa. Hohenheimer Tage zum Ausländerrecht. Baden-Baden, pp. 123-134.
Knösel, Peter: 1997, Asylrecht in Deutschland und Europa – sind Flüchtlinge per se ungleich?, in: Büro gegen ethnische Diskriminierungen in Berlin und Brandenburg; Friedrich-Ebert-Stiftung (ed.), Migration und Antidiskriminierungspolitik in Europa. Berlin, pp. 34-39.
Koch, Gustav: 1994, Das neue Asylrecht in Deutschland, insbesondere die Regelungen über die "sicheren Drittstaaten" und die Rücknahmevereinbarungen, in: AWR-Bulletin. Vierteljahresschrift für Flüchtlingsfragen, 32/4, pp. 208-216.
Köppinger, Peter: 1993, Einwanderung nach Deutschland und in die EG: Entwicklungen, Zahlen, Begriffe, Perspektiven, in: Akademie der Diözese Rottenburg-Stuttgart (ed.), Flüchtlinge und Asylsuchende in Deutschland. Einführende Texte. Stuttgart, pp. 29-44.
Kugelmann, Dieter: 1998, Spielräume und Chancen einer europäischen Einwanderungspolitik, in: ZAR – Zeitschrift für Ausländerrecht und Ausländerpolitik, 18/6, pp. 243-249.
Kumin, Judith: 1995, Asylum in Europe: sharing or shifting the burden?, in: U.S. Committee for Refugees (ed.), World refugee survey 1995. Washington, pp. 28-33.
Leuninger, Herbert: 1997, Die Festungsmentalität. Anforderungen an ein neues Asylrecht und eine neue Asylpolitik in Europa, in: Migration und soziale Arbeit. Junge Einwanderer in Deutschland, 3-4/ 97, pp. 124-125.
Löper, Friedrich: 2000, Das Dubliner Übereinkommen über die Zuständigkeit für Asylverfahren, in: ZAR – Zeitschrift für Ausländerrecht und Ausländerpolitik, 20/1, pp. 16-24.
Lützel, Christof: 1997, Die Migration in Deutschland, Frankreich und in der Europäischen Union, in: Bizeul, Yves/Bliesener, Ulrich/Prawda, Marek (eds.), Vom Umgang mit dem Fremden. Hintergrund – Definionen – Vorschläge. Weinheim/Basel, pp. 20-59.
Malgesini, Graciella: 1993, Torwächter im Süden Europas. Migrationspolitik in Spanien, in: Arbeitsgruppe 501 (ed.), Heute hier – morgen fort. Migration, Rassismus und die (Un)Ordnung des Weltmarkts. Freiburg, pp. 113-119.
Marshall, Barbara: 1996, Refugee Policy in Germany and the EU. RIIA Discussion Paper, No. 63. O.O.
Miller, Judith: 1991, Strangers at the gate, in: New York Times Magazine, 15 September, pp. 33-35, 81, 86.

Monar, J.: 1994, Comprehensive migration policy: elements and options. Leicester.

Muus, Philip/European Research Centre on Migration and Ethnic Relations/ERCOMER (eds.): 1997, Exclusion and inclusion of refugees in contemporary Europe. Comparative Studies in Migration and Ethnic Relations, 3. Utrecht.

Nascimbene, Bruno: 1992, Le tendenze comunitarie. La definizione di una politica delle Comunità europee in materia di migrazioni, in: Sergi, Nino/Carchedi, Francesco, L'immigrazione straniera in Italia. Il tempo dell'integrazione. Rome, pp. 249-270.

Neusel, Hans: 1993, Anmerkungen zur europäischen Asyl- und Zuwanderungspolitik aus deutscher Sicht, in: Drüke, Luise/Weigelt, Klaus (eds.), Fluchtziel Europa. Strategien für eine neue Flüchtlingspolitik. Bonn, pp. 153-159.

N.N.: 1999, Langer Weg zum "harten EU-Recht" Die Amsterdamer Beschlüsse und die Drittstaaten-Angehörigen, in: DAMID. Development and Migration in International Dialogue, 9/6-7, p. 5.

N.N.: 1999, Schotten dicht. Zur Asylpolitik der europäischen Union, in: HUch! Humboldt Universität collected highlights. Zeitung der studentischen Selbstverwaltung, 23, p. 8.

Nuscheler, Franz: 1995, Internationale Migration – Flucht und Asyl. Opladen.

Ooyen, Monika van/Schubert, Katina: 1992, Repression im Europa der Freizügigkeiten. Die BRD als fast flüchtlingsfreie Zone, in: Vorgänge. Zeitschrift für Bürgerrechte und Gesellschaftspolitik, 31/4, pp. 17-25

Pfahlert, Susanne/Sextro, Uli/Thimmel, Andreas: 1994, Asyl in Deutschland und Europa (2. akt. Aufl.). Mainz.

Renner, Günter: 1996, Was bleibt vom deutschen Asylrecht?, in: ZAR – Zeitschrift für Ausländerrecht und Ausländerpolitik, 3, pp. 103-109.

Rohrböck, Josef: 1996, Das Übereinkommen von Dublin und das österreichische Asylrecht, in: Wiederin, Ewald (ed.), Neue Perspektiven im Ausländerrecht. Wien, pp. 45-110.

Sanderson, Nick: 1993, Kriterien für Asylverfahren, in: Drüke, Luise/Weigelt, Klaus (eds.), Fluchtziel Europa. Strategien für eine neue Flüchtlingspolitik. Bonn, pp. 134-140.

Scheffer, Thomas: 1994, Was kommt nach der Festung? Zuwanderungspolitiken in der Europäischen Union, in: Die Brücke e.V., 78/4. Saarbrücken, pp. 18-23.

Schilling, Roland S.: 1995, Refugees and immigration in Europe and the Third World, in: Heckmann, Friedrich/Bosswick, Wolfgang (eds.), Migration policies: a comparative perspective. Forum Migration. Bamberg, pp. 263-266.

Schindler, Thomas/Widermann, Peter/Wimmer-Heller, Ulrike/Körner, Berndt: 1997, Fremdenrecht. Praxiskommentar mit allen einschlägigen Gesetzen (samt ausführlichen Erläuterungen), Verordnungen und internationalen Abkommen. Loseblattausgabe.

Sieveking, Klaus: 1999, Security of residence and expulsion. The German experience. Nijmegen.

Spijkerboer, Thomas: 1993, A bird's eye view of Asylum law in eight European countries. Amsterdam.
Standing Committee of Experts on International Immigration, Refugee and Criminal Law (ed.): 1991, Schengen: opinions, recommendations and proposals concerning the international implications on ratification of the Implementing Agreement for the Schengen Agreement, as recently modified by the agreement of March 29, 1991, between the Schengen Countries and the Republic of Poland, with accompanying Protocol. Utrecht.
Storey, Andy: 1994, The asylum policies of the European Union: a developing problem. Dublin.
Taschner, Hans-Claudius: 1993, Plädoyer für eine europäische Asylpolitik aus der Sicht der EG-Kommission, in: Drüke, Luise/Weigelt, Klaus (eds.), Fluchtziel Europa. Strategien für eine neue Flüchtlingspolitik. Bonn, pp. 140-146.
Terre des Femmes e.V./Hübel, Susanne (eds.): 1994, Frauen auf der Flucht. Geschlechtsspezifische Fluchtursachen und europäische Flüchtlingspolitik. Tübingen.
Tomasi, Lydio F./Miller, Mark J.: 1993, Post-cold war international migration to Western Europe: neither fortress nor invasion, in: Rocha-Trindade, Maria Beatriz (ed.), Recent migration trends in Europe. Europe's new architecture. Lissabon, pp. 15-31.
Trócaire. The Catholic Agency for World Development (ed.): 1992, Third World migrants and refugees in the "common European home". Trócaire North South Issues, 18. Dublin.
Turner, Amedee: 1993, Initiativen des Europäischen Parlaments auf dem Gebiet der Innen- und Justizpolitik der Europäischen Union, in: Drüke, Luise/Weigelt, Klaus (eds.), Fluchtziel Europa. Strategien für eine neue Flüchtlingspolitik. Bonn, pp. 146-149.
Ulmer, Mathias: 1996, Asylrecht und Menschenwürde. Zur Problematik der "Sicheren Drittstaaten" nach Art. 16 a Abs. 2 und 5 GG und die Harmonisierung des Asylrechts in Europa. Frankfurt/M./ Berlin/ Bern/ New York/ Paris/Wien.
Velling, Johannes: 1993, Schengen, Dublin und Maastricht – Etappen auf dem Weg zu einer europäichen Immigrationspolitik. ZEW Discussion Paper. Mannheim.
Webber, Frances: 1995, Die europäische Asylpolitik verletzt Menschenrechte, in: Basso-Sekretariat Berlin (ed.), Festung Europa auf der Anklagebank. Dokumentation des Basso-Tribunals zum Asylrecht in Europa. Münster, pp. 32-49.
Weick, Günter (ed.): 1993, National and European law on the threshold to the single market. Frankfurt/M./Berlin/Bern/New York/Paris/Wien.
Westphal, Volker: 1998, Die Berücksichtigung der Schengener Durchführungsübereinkommens bei aufenthaltsrechtlichen Maßnahmen, in: ZAR – Zeitschrift für Ausländerrecht und Ausländerpolitik, 18/4, pp. 175-180.
Wihtol de Wenden, Catherine: 1993, Immigration policies in European countries

facing the double pressure coming from the East and the South, in: Rocha-Trindade, Maria Beatriz (ed.), Recent migration trends in Europe. Europe's new architecture. Lissabon, pp. 49-62.

Wollenschläger, Michael/Becker, Ulrich: 1990, Harmonisierung des Asylrechts in der EG und Art. 16 Abs. 2 S. 2 GG. Rechtsvergleichende Bestandsaufnahme und Reformperspektiven in den zwölf EG-Staaten, in: Europäische Grundrechtezeitschrift, 17/1-2, pp. 1-10.

Zimmermann, A.: 1993, Asylum law in the Federal Republic of Germany in the context of international law, in: Zeitschrift für Ausländisches öffentliches Recht und Völkerrecht, 53/1, p. 87.

Nicola Scuteri
Berliner Institut für Vergleichende Sozialforschung
Schliemannstr. 23
10437 Berlin

Name Index